P9-ARZ-648

NINTH EDITION

Social Welfare

A History of the American Response to Need

Mark J. Stern
University of Pennsylvania

June Axinn
Late of University of Pennsylvania

 Pearson

330 Hudson Street, NY, NY 10013

Director, Teacher Education & the Helping Professions: Kevin M. Davis
Portfolio Manager: Rebecca Fox-Gieg
Content Project Manager: Pamela D. Bennett
Media Project Manager: Lauren Carlson
Portfolio Management Assistant: Anne McAlpine
Executive Field Marketing Manager: Krista Clark
Executive Product Marketing Manager: Christopher Barry
Procurement Specialist: Deidra Smith
Cover Designer: Melissa Welch
Cover Photo: Getty Images/eliskapodzimkova
Full-Service Project Management: Udhaya Harisudan, Lumina Datamatics, Ltd.
Composition: Lumina Datamatics, Ltd.
Printer/Binder: LSC Communications
Cover Printer: LSC Communications
Text Font: 10.5/12 pt Dante MT Pro

Library of Congress Cataloging-in-Publication Data

Names: Stern, Mark J., author. | Axinn, June, author.
Title: Social welfare : a history of the American response to need / Mark J.
    Stern, University of Pennsylvania, June Axinn.
Description: New York : Pearson, [2018] | Revised edition of Social welfare,
    c2012. | Includes bibliographical references and index.
Identifiers: LCCN 2016049784| ISBN 9780134449913
Subjects: LCSH: Public welfare—United States—History—Sources. | Social
    service—United States—History—Sources. | Child welfare—United
    States—History—Sources.
Classification: LCC HV91 .S6235 2018 | DDC 361.60973—dc23 LC record available at https://lccn.loc.gov/2016049784

3 2019

ISBN-10:   0-13-444991-6
ISBN-13: 978-0-13-444991-3

Preface

This book has gone through many stages. Initially, the volume was planned as a collection of historical documents with brief introductory statements. The documents were to be materials pertinent to an understanding of the development of social welfare policies and programs in the United States. As work progressed, it became clear that the documents did not always support long-established interpretations found in popular secondary sources. The introductory statements became longer and longer as what we found became more intriguing. The core of the book is now the historical narrative. The documents included have been chosen to illuminate the history.

The ninth edition of *Social Welfare: A History of the American Response to Need* examines the most current social welfare issues in historical perspective. Chapter 9 has been revised to cover the period from 1992 to 2016. It examines how the administrations of Bill Clinton, George W. Bush, and Barack Obama have influenced social welfare policy. Earlier editions analyzed the beginnings of the "turn to the right" of the 1980s. This edition explores the effects of the drive to reduce federal spending for public programs further and to turn control and responsibility for social welfare over to the states and the private sector.

As in every period treated in the book, from the Colonial era to the present, social welfare policy is put into economic, demographic, and political contexts. The accelerating shift to a postindustrial economy, with its accompanying loss of manufacturing jobs, and the increasing bifurcation of income and wealth set the background for the weakening safety net.

New to This Edition

For this edition, the structure of chapters has been thoroughly revised. Each chapter is organized around three elements: changes in the social and economic conditions of the period, innovations in social welfare, and the role of social movements.

The introduction and the historical chapters have been revised and expanded to include new sections on:

- The history of relationships between American Indians and Europeans during the Colonial era and the treatment and status of Native Americans.
- The impact of immigration on the nation's demography and the debate over immigration policy.
- Expanded discussions of social movements throughout American history and their impact of social welfare.
- An analysis of the impact of the recession of 2007–2009—the worst in the past 60 years.
- The implementation of the Affordable Care Act passed by Congress in 2010.

In addition, new to this edition is the format of the text.

- Each chapter features Learning Outcomes to give you an idea of what will be covered in the chapter. These correspond to the sections that are within the chapters.
- At the end of each section, a quiz is available through clicking the question mark icon. This will help you to assess your knowledge of the information in that section.
- Periodically, you will see video ▶ icons that will lead you to short videos to enhance the information you have received in the text.
- At the end of each chapter after the Documents, you can check your understanding of the chapter content by clicking on the question mark icon and taking a short assessment.

Acknowledgments

Graduate students in the social work program of the University of Pennsylvania have used successive editions of this book. Thanks go to all of them for their thoughtful contributions.

Many colleagues, both in social work and in related fields, have been particularly helpful. It is especially pleasant to acknowledge June's niece, Amy Hirsch, of Community Legal Services of Philadelphia, and June's son, David Axinn, formerly director of Blair County Legal Services of Altoona, Pennsylvania, and now a partner in the firm of Cohen and Axinn, Hollidaysburg, Pennsylvania. They have each made insightful comments and suggestions from their frontline positions. We thank June's daughter, Constance Johnson, who as legal research analyst at the Law Library of Congress provided invaluable bibliographic aid. In addition, I want to acknowledge the following reviewers, who provided suggestions for enhancements for this new edition: David Fauri, Virginia Commonwealth University; Robert Hawkins, New York University; Carol L. Langer, Colorado State University–Pueblo; and William Rowe, Southern Connecticut State University.

Hal Levin, one of our most treasured colleagues, coauthored the first two editions of *Social Welfare*. Although Hal died in 1983, his name appeared as a coauthor of the book for the next 16 years. His contribution to the book—especially its attention to the historical development of social administration—remains considerable. June Axinn, whose name still appears as an author, died in 2006. However, her scholarship remains the foundation, and her incisive approach to social welfare continues to animate this edition.

During the last years of Hal's life, I joined the faculty of the University of Pennsylvania School of Social Work. For a short period, the three of us enjoyed our collaboration, which included developing an understanding of the impact of the rise of conservatism on social welfare, as well as more mundane pursuits like agreeing on a place to eat lunch. After Hal's death, June and I continued this work that appeared in *Dependency and Poverty: Old Problems in a New World* (Lexington Books, 1988) and regular discussions of history and contemporary social welfare.

Sidney Axinn and Susan Seifert, our spouses, made important contributions to this volume. Their wit, humor, and support make all things possible.

Mark Stern

Brief Contents

1. Introduction: How to Think About Social Welfare's Past
   (and Present)   1

2. The Colonial Period: 1647–1776   15

3. The Pre–Civil War Period: 1777–1860   34

4. The Civil War and After: 1860–1900   77

5. Progress and Reform: 1900–1930   115

6. The Depression and the New Deal: 1930–1940   156

7. War and Prosperity: 1940–1968   205

8. Conservative Resurgence and Social Change: 1968–1992   251

9. Social Welfare and the Information Society: 1992–2016   285

Contents

1 **Introduction: How to Think About Social Welfare's Past (and Present)**   1

    DOCUMENT: Introduction   10

        An Act for the Relief of the Poor, 43 Elizabeth, 1601   11

2 **The Colonial Period: 1647–1776**   15

    The Poor Laws in the Colonies   17

    Conquest, Expansion, and Population Growth: Native Americans, Immigration, and Slavery   23

    Social Change and the Challenge to the Poor Laws   26

    Veterans: A Special Class   29

    DOCUMENTS: The Colonial Period   31

        An Act of Supplement to the Acts Referring to the Poor, Massachusetts Bay, 1692   31

        The Binding of Moses Love, 1747   33

3 **The Pre–Civil War Period: 1777–1860**   34

    Social and Economic Conditions   36

        Population Growth and Migration   36

        Slavery and Free Labor   38

    Reform and Social Change   42

        Labor Unrest   42

        Religious and Political Reform   43

        The Expansion of Public Education   44

        The Expansion of Suffrage   44

        Moral Reform   45

    Social Welfare Programs and Services   47

        Institutionalization   47

        Child Saving   53

        Retreat from the Almshouse   56

    DOCUMENTS: The Pre–Civil War Period   59

        The First Annual Report of the Managers of the Society for the Prevention of Pauperism in the City of New York, 1818   60

Constitution, By-Laws, & c., of the Female Orphan Asylum of Portland, Maine, 1828   67
President Franklin Pierce: Veto Message—An Act Making a Grant of Public Lands to the Several States for the Benefit of Indigent Insane Persons, 1854   73

4   The Civil War and After: 1860–1900   77

Changing Economic and Demographic Realities   77
Population Changes   79
Naturalization and Citizenship   79
Regional Shifts   81
The Aging: The Group That Was Left Behind   83

Innovations in Social Welfare Services   83
The Welfare of Soldiers and Veterans   84
Social Welfare: Reconstruction and the Freedmen's Bureau   86
Social Welfare and Urban Expansion   89
The Charity Organization Movement   90
The Settlement House Movement   95
A New View of Child Welfare   97

Social Movements During the Late 19th Century: The Reform Impulse   100
The Social Welfare of Women   100
The Labor Movement   102
The Agrarian Movement   103

Conclusion   105

DOCUMENTS: The Civil War and After   106
An Act to Provide for the Relief of Indigent Soldiers, Sailors and Marines, and the Families of Those Deceased, 1887   107
The Economic and Moral Effects of Public Outdoor Relief, 1890   108
An Act to Prohibit the Coming of Chinese Laborers to the United States, September 1888, and Supplement, October 1888   111

5   Progress and Reform: 1900–1930   115

Changing Economic and Demographic Realities   116
An Urban and Industrial Society   116
Poverty and the Working Class   118
African Americans, Native Americans, and Immigrants   119

Innovations in Social Welfare   122
Regulating Working Conditions   124
Expanding Public Welfare   126
Protecting Vulnerable Families   128
Social Work and the Black Population   132
The Social Welfare of Veterans   133
Professionalizing Social Work   134

Social Movements in the Early 20th Century   136
Coalitions for Reform   136
Regulating Business   138

Organized Labor   *138*
Women, Work, and Suffrage   *139*
The End of Reform   *141*

DOCUMENTS: Progress and Reform   143
The Family and the Woman's Wage, 1909   *144*
Funds to Parents Act, Illinois, 1911   *146*
Public Pensions to Widows, 1912   *147*

6 The Depression and the New Deal: 1930–1940   156

Changing Economic and Demographic Realities   156
The Economic Collapse   *156*
Agricultural Crisis   *158*
Family Life   *162*

Innovations in Social Welfare   163
The Hoover Response to Crisis   *163*
FDR and the First New Deal   *164*
Public Money for Relief   *166*
Federal Emergency Relief Administration (FERA)   *167*
The Second New Deal   *168*
The Social Security Act   *170*
Expanding Social Security: The 1939 Amendments   *172*
Public Assistance   *173*
The Changing Role of the Social Work Profession   *176*
New Alignments in Social Welfare   *178*

Mass Movements During the 1930s   180
Veterans and the Bonus   *181*
Older Americans   *182*
Labor and Social Welfare   *182*
Setbacks for Women   *185*
The Eclipse of Reform   *185*

Conclusion   186

DOCUMENTS: The Depression and the New Deal   188
Monthly Reports of the Federal Emergency Relief Administration, 1933   *189*
Social Security Act, 1935   *195*

7 War and Prosperity: 1940–1968   205

Changing Economic and Demographic Realities   207
Population Shifts   *207*
Technology, Productivity, and Economic Insecurity   *210*
World War II   *212*
Wartime Economic and Social Advances   *214*
Postwar Optimism   *215*

Innovations in Social Welfare   218
    Veterans and the GI Bill   218
    The Attack on Public Welfare   219
    Poverty and the Reform of Welfare   220
    The War on Poverty   225
    Expanded Benefits for the Aging   230
    Controlling Public Assistance   230

Social Movements and Reform After World War II   232
    Expanding the Civil Rights of African Americans   232
    A Renewed Feminist Movement   234
    Civil Rights and Juvenile Justice   235

DOCUMENTS: War and Prosperity   236
    Message on the Public Welfare Program, 1962   237
    Economic Opportunity Act, 1964   243
    In re Gault, 1967   246

8 Conservative Resurgence and Social Change: 1968–1992   251

Economic and Social Trends   252
    A Struggling Economy   252
    Changing Employment Patterns   253
    The Changing Family   254
    Poverty and Income Distribution   256

Innovations in Social Welfare   258
    Expenditures for Social Welfare   258
    Challenging the Welfare State: Welfare Reform   260
    Child Welfare and the Aging   263
    The Unemployed   266
    Veterans   268
    Personal Social Services   268

Social Movements   269
    The New Right   269
    The Expansion of Civil Rights   270
    Women   274

Conclusion   275

DOCUMENTS: Conservative Resurgence and Social Change   276
    Message on Reform in Welfare, 1969   277
    Standard of Review for Termination of Disability Benefits, 1984   283

9 Social Welfare and the Information Society: 1992–2016   285

Social and Economic Change   287
    The Economy: Productivity, Growth, and Employment   287
    Poverty   290

Changes in Family Composition 292
America's Changing Demography 293

Innovations in Social Welfare 293
The Fall and Rise of Health Care Reform 293
The Failure of Comprehensive Reform in the 1990s 294
Achieving Comprehensive Reform in 2010 296
Addressing Poverty and Dependency: The Scope of Welfare Reform 298
The Changing Dynamics of the Welfare Debate 298
The New Consensus over Welfare Reform 300
The Impact of Welfare Reform 301

Social Movements and Grassroots Change 302
Welfare Reform and "Immigration Control" 302
The Return to Voluntarism and the Rise of Privatization 303
The Continuing Battle for Social Justice 306
Education 306
Affirmative Action in the Labor Market 307
Abortion and the Right to Privacy 308
The Great Lockup 310

Conclusion 311

DOCUMENTS: Social Welfare and the Information Society 313
Personal Responsibility and Work Opportunity Reconciliation Act, 1996 314
State of California, Proposition 187, Illegal Aliens—Public Services, Verification, and Reporting, 1994 317
U.S. Supreme Court Lawrence v. Texas, 2003 321

Notes 329

Credits 344

Index 349

1

Introduction:
How to Think About
Social Welfare's
Past (and Present)

LEARNING OUTCOMES

• Summarize the major factors that
  influence changes in social welfare
  during a particular historical era.

• Assess the impact of welfare reform
  and health care reform on the well-
  being of Americans.

• Summarize the role of social
  movements in contemporary
  American social controversies.

DOCUMENT: Introduction   10
*An Act for the Relief of the Poor,
    43 Elizabeth, 1601   11*

Those who cannot remember the past are condemned to repeat it.

—George Santayana

*History is more or less bunk. It's tradition. We don't want tradi-
tion. We want to live in the present, and the only history that is
worth a tinker's damn is the history that we make today*

—Henry Ford

How important is the history of social welfare and social work? The
answer lies somewhere between these two quotations. As Santayana
asserts, many of the challenges we face today echo the problems that
others have faced in the past. The limitations of resources, the hostility
to the poor and dependent, and the ethical issues involved in intervening in the private lives of clients are issues social workers and policy
makers have faced in the past. Yet, at the same time that the past can be
a guide, it can also be a straitjacket, constraining our actions and preventing us from understanding what is novel about our times.

Here's the thing. History can be useful in both of these situations. At the same time, it allows us to understand how current public assistance and child welfare policies echo the misconceptions of past generations, it can allow us to understand the novelty of current patterns of family life. It can't help a practitioner decide on a particular strategy for engaging a client, but it can help the practitioner understand the set of social forces that put them in a room together.

American history is more than the chronology of elections and wars often covered by textbooks. Although often ignored, our history includes the struggles of many individuals and groups to improve the opportunities of ordinary people and to reduce the role of discrimination and exclusion in our society. This book tells this story, the history of American social welfare. It explores the political and economic forces, values and ideas, and social institutions that have influenced the development and reform of social welfare policies and programs over the course of American history.

Although often ignored, our history includes the struggles of many individuals and groups to improve the opportunities of ordinary people and to reduce the role of discrimination and exclusion in our society.

The goals of social welfare programs derive from the goals of the larger society for itself and from the dominant ways that people make sense of the world around them. In turn, decisions about who is needy and how they are to be helped bear upon economic development, political organization, social stability, and family integrity. Social welfare programs involve a redistribution of resources from one group to another. Our political culture has often resisted using government to redistribute resources, relying instead on the market to carry out this function. Through much of our history, Americans have valued private assets over public goods and individual autonomy over collective choices.

Decisions about who should benefit from public policies often polarize Americans. Should we be more generous with programs for older Americans or children? Does providing aid to a group discourage independence or allow it to flourish? These issues were debated 200 years ago, just as they are today.

Yet, despite these value conflicts, social realities—economic crises, wars, and civil disorder—have led us to embrace many active social policies. Although it sounds like a contradiction, very often Americans are ideological conservatives and pragmatic liberals.

Decisions about benefit levels and eligibility often communicate whether a program is intended to invite or discourage participation. The extent to which needy individuals are viewed as beneficiaries, recipients, clients, or consumers suggests the intent of the program. Welfare *recipients*, for example, are subject to behavioral requirements that would be unthinkable for Social Security *beneficiaries*.

The geographical and demographic scope of the United States—the size and diversity of its population—as well as legal and social traditions related to volunteerism, to separation of church and state, to states' rights, and to local responsibility—all complicate legislative and administrative decisions in social welfare matters. Throughout American history we have debated the proper role of the federal, state, and local governments in funding and administering programs. Some have argued that federal programs can assure equal treatment across the country, while others have argued the local governments are more likely to understand the needs of their residents. Although private nonprofit organizations have often played an important role in *administering* social programs, government has more often than not provided the funding. Since the 1990s, for-profit corporations and professionals in private practice have assumed a more central role in providing services, but again, government has usually provided the funding. The number and complexity of these decisions result in bills—like the 2010 health care reform law—that are thousands of pages long.

The history of social welfare is also a story of the growing professionalism of those who administer social services—that is, with the history of the social work profession.

The early development of the public and voluntary sectors of social welfare was accompanied by the development of service providers appropriate to their purposes: both the overseer of the poor and the lady bountiful. Yet, as social welfare programs and services have become more institutionalized, service providers have been required to acquire and demonstrate their skills and capacities. Social workers originally drew their inspiration from the struggle against poverty and want, but as they became more professional, they often sought to define their unique skills as associated with psychology and individual adjustment. The tension between social work as a *social change* profession and social work as an *individual adjustment* profession has gone on for a century and will likely continue in the future. At the end of the day, however, social work practitioners have no choice but to address both social injustice and the immediate needs of their clients. Thus, the philosophical tension between individual and social change surfaces in one's professional practice as one decides how *both* to address the everyday problems faced by one's clients and to assess one's professional responsibility to pursue social justice in imperfect systems.

When this book was originally conceived four decades ago, it argued that social welfare policy and pro-family policy were essentially the same. Yet, as the authors made this claim, the politics of domestic life were in the process of exploding. The gender question—whether men and women should be treated the same—had been simmering in politics since at least the years before the Civil War, when many questioned the propriety of female abolitionists addressing "mixed" crowds of men and women. However, during the 1970s, the legalization of abortion and the failed attempt to add the Equal Rights Amendment to the Constitution provoked schisms that have yet to be overcome. If anything, the battle over gender has become more contested in recent years as struggles over marriage equality and questions (often raised by transgender commentators) about whether using the categories *male* and *female* themselves as exhaustive categories has reinforced the divide.

From the beginning, a separate channeling of family welfare and child welfare, originating with English Poor Laws, and, therefore, at one with the fabric of an English colonial milieu, divided social welfare responses for the worthy poor—the disabled and children—from those for the unworthy—the able-bodied poor. The incorporation of the English Poor Laws into the legislative framework of American colonial governments differentiated those who were unable to work from those who were potentially employable. Poor Law programs were vitally concerned with those who were employed and who might be in danger of falling into pauperism. The family was effective to the degree that it maintained the social order and the economic viability of its individual members. To a considerable extent, social welfare programs for poor people in the 20th century retain this orientation.

The essential worthiness of children and the importance of nurturing their potential for social and economic contribution led to stated, public concern for their well-being as members of families and eventually to grudging recognition of the needs of families. The 20th century was proclaimed the Century of the Child, and pressures to make the label stick resulted in the calling of the first White House Conference on Children in 1909 and to a positive statement of public policy in regard to child care. Home and family life were declared to be society's goal for children, an enunciation of the rights of children. Economic necessity, many felt, should not require that a mother leave her child care responsibilities for work outside the home. Time and reality have demonstrated more and more ambivalence of policy and practice in child welfare. The 21st century began with one-fifth of U.S. children living in poverty.

The changing status of women was a pivotal event in social welfare history. Until the middle of the 20th century, married women rarely worked in the formal economy, yet they provided the vast majority of care, typically to members of their family. By the 1970s, a majority of married women were working for wages or salaries. Although women's entry into the labor force allowed many of them to take advantage of their skills and education and helped many family budgets that were strained by inflation and economic stagnation, it created a "caring gap" because women had less time to care for sick or dependent members of society. Today, much of this work is still done by women, but now they are more often poorly paid aides rather than family members.

Government financial capacity often has more influence than the needs of clients on social welfare policy. During the 18th and 19th centuries, state and local governments collected few taxes and provided few services, whereas the federal government's role in social welfare was usually limited to the well-being of veterans. The entry of the federal government into social welfare policy greatly expanded the social welfare budget (Figure 1.1). However, attacks on "tax-and-spend" policies during the late 20th century reversed the growth of direct public spending on social welfare. The economic crisis that began in 2007 challenged policy makers, regardless of their political ideology. Should the government increase spending to stimulate the economy and increase the budget deficit, or should the government cut spending to balance government budgets even if it served to prolong and deepen the crisis?

The needs of the aging now receive great attention in the United States. But concern for the welfare of our older citizens was not consistent before the Great Depression. In the late 19th century, special attention was paid to the needs of older white men who were veterans, but by the time of the Great Depression, the aging were one of the poorest groups in American society. The chapters that follow will trace the evolution of the policy that has given older Americans some relative advantage within the social welfare system.

The chapters that follow will also give the social welfare needs of two groups, veterans and blacks, special attention to demonstrate two extremes in social policy in the United States. Veterans have usually enjoyed better social welfare benefits than the rest of the population because of their service in the armed forces. They have played an important role in the expansion of public welfare programs because veterans' programs have often set precedents for benefits later extended to others. For example, in recent years, the federal government has committed increased funding to reduce homelessness among veterans, which has inspired homelessness advocates to call for an expanded effort to end homelessness generally.

For people of color—blacks, Hispanics, Native Americans, Asian Americans, and those who identify as multiracial—a very different picture emerges. From the beginning of European colonization, white invaders oppressed Native Americans. Genocide remains an essential part of American history. Although all people of color have faced discrimination and marginalization, African Americans' historical experience—slavery, segregation, and disenfranchisement—merits particular attention. Black Americans, the largest of these groups until the early 21st century, suffered the dual oppressions of color and class, of racial discrimination and poverty. Like other people of color, they have been relegated to a social and economic role that has left them more vulnerable to the risks of the market economy. Simultaneously, whites have often seen black Americans' economic marginalization not as a product of racism, but as proof of their genetic inferiority and cultural deficiencies. Even when the government adopted policies to address past discrimination—as it did after the Civil War and again during the 1960s—it has typically lacked the political will and financial resources to accomplish their goals.

Figure 1.1　The expansion of government responsibility for the economic welfare of older Americans represented a break with past approaches to social welfare.

America—it is often said—is a nation of immigrants. As the number of immigrants has surged during periods of economic prosperity, anti-immigrant sentiment has often led to efforts to restrict their flow, setting off some of the nastiest episodes in the history of American racism. The expansion of the foreign-born population has had a complicated relationship to overall race relations. Within a few decades, America may well become a *minority majority* nation in which nonwhites make up a majority. At the same time, the expansion of immigration sometimes has diverted the nation's attention from the long-term marginalization of African Americans.

Anti-immigrant attitudes or nativism existed in the United States from the very first days. The treatment of Native Americans is one example. In the Colonial period,

Benjamin Franklin expressed concern about the German language and culture spreading in Pennsylvania, and the Federalists worried about the Irish and French. In the years before the Civil War, fears about immigrants gave rise to a short-lived political party, the Know-Nothings, while during the depression of the 1870s, anti-Chinese agitation—often tied to labor unions—led to the exclusion of the Chinese from entering the United States, legislation that was not repealed until the Second World War. Nativism triumphed in the 20th century, as Congress passed laws in 1921 and 1924 that virtually cut off European immigration for four decades. The entry of millions of new immigrants since the 1970s has again provoked two persistent reactions: a cosmopolitan belief that immigrants enrich American society and a defensive fear that they will steal jobs and dilute the "national character" (itself a product of generations of immigration).

Economic growth is intimately connected to trends in social welfare. As the country became richer, social welfare programs usually expanded, regardless of which political party was in power. The disparate treatment of different groups persisted, but policies became more generous for all.

For those living today, it is hard to imagine the plight of 18th-century Americans who barely produced enough to survive. The well-being, the very existence, of the colonies depended upon the maximum contribution of each of the colonists. The dominant ideologies of the Colonial period focused on human's "original sin" and the necessity of stern treatment for the unproductive. These beliefs, in turn, justified coercive alternatives to relief—the workhouse, indenture, apprenticeship, contracting out, and so on.

In contrast, the contemporary economy has an unprecedented capacity to produce consumer goods. Where a majority of Americans needed to work in agriculture to feed the nation, now 3 per cent of the labor force can produce enough food to feed all Americans and a large share of the rest of the world. As a result, as a society we have more flexibility in allocating resources to different social groups. The growth of social welfare expenditures in the 20th century reflected, in part, the increased ability of society to meet the social welfare needs created by industrial society and its impact on family structure. Yet, this development was hardly linear. The decline of manufacturing after the 1970s undermined many of the social arrangements that supported an ever-expanding welfare system.

An examination of the history of the American response to dependency gives evidence that ideology often followed from the dynamics of the economy. The colonial perception of work as moral and idleness as immoral makes little sense, in an affluent society, in which individual well-being is so dependent on social conditions. Ironically, the unrivaled expansion of America's productive capacity has occurred as older ideas of personal responsibility and punitive work-oriented policies have gained new legitimacy. The renewed war on dependency and idleness comes at a time when low-paying, unstable service jobs have replaced the more permanent manufacturing employment of a previous era.

For several decades, many Americans were able to maintain their standard of living in the face of stagnant wages by increasing their use of credit. During the recession of 2007–09, we discovered that this consumer debt, including college loans and risky mortgages, had created an illusion, a bubble that suddenly burst. In the wake of the recession, we've witnessed renewed demands for a living wage, including universal affordable health care and an increased minimum wage.

History is no elegant machine that turns out the same results over and over again. But it makes sense to pay attention to these four factors to try to make sense of the past:

- Economic productivity
- Perceptions of social institution's effectiveness

- Views of human nature
- Past decisions about social welfare

The society's level of productivity at a particular historical moment places obvious constraints on how generous social welfare programs can be. High levels of output and affluence increase the possibilities for choice; and the degree of equality in a society can, and indeed often does, increase as national income rises. At the same time that wealth makes some redistribution possible, it also makes redistribution psychologically necessary; our concept of what might be a tolerable level of poverty varies with gross domestic product. American history, however, suggests that affluence does not automatically translate into generosity.

Perceptions of social institution's effectiveness strongly influence the initiation and development of social welfare programs. We often draw a distinction between a *residual* and an *institutional* philosophy of social welfare. The residual approach assumes that the array of other social institutions, including the market economy, families, and other social organizations, are capable of meeting the needs of most people. Social welfare should be seen as a stopgap system that is relevant only when the other institutions fail.

Watch this video on "Who Sees Poverty"

What connections can we draw between the global poverty debate and US social welfare policy?

https://www.youtube.com/watch?v=Xg0MgrF_DLs

In contrast, institutional approaches to social welfare are premised on the belief that we live in an interdependent society. We are all subject to the risks of modern life—aging, illness, unemployment, and disability, to name some of the most important. Therefore, it makes sense—in the name of social solidarity—for us to make provisions for those of us who will fall victim to these risks.

Ironically, when a society is functioning well, it's easy to see the consumers of social welfare benefits and services as individual failures, while when the economy fails or social order is disrupted, we're likely to look for collective solutions to life's problems. In a way, this turns reality on its head, because it is precisely the provision of collective solutions that allows society to function most effectively.

Views of human nature unquestionably influence the response to human need. A belief in the superiority of any group in the population—indeed, any racial, ethnic, religious, or sexual elite—becomes a basis for discrimination and exploitation. Our original creed was that "all men are created equal," but we've often acted as if some Americans are "more equal" than others. From the earliest interactions between Europeans and American Indians through the welfare reform debates of the 1990s, people have used nonhuman metaphors—wolves, dogs, and alligators—to justify the exclusion of some people from the dignity and support they deserved.

If people are seen as basically lazy, social welfare programs are devised to deter their use. A 19th-century listing of the causes of dependency highlighted individual character flaws and argued that the help given to the poor aggravated the problem. The dominant 19th-century response to dependency was the organization of "friendly visitors" to uncover the dishonesty and deviant behaviors of the poor. Alternatively, if people are considered essentially good, the response to need is more likely to be guided by the offer of incentives and the development of programs that provide opportunity for self-advancement.

Watch "Are We Becoming More Unequal?"

What assumptions about human nature are behind the different speakers' answer to the question?

https://www.youtube.com/watch?v=371ySKWZ9mU

Throughout American history, the poor have been considered both blessed and condemned by God, both virtuous and sinful, and both lazy and ambitious. And these contrasting views have often been held simultaneously. In connection with the family, for example, the prevailing 19th-century view of Charity Organization Society leaders that family members had to be deterred from a base, inherited instinct for pauperism was countered by

Settlement House movement leaders' conviction about the constructive force of human aspiration. To the former, pauperism—its effects upon the individual, the family, and society—was a disease to be eradicated. Settlement house workers' belief that poverty resulted from the denial of opportunity led them to advocate for legislative reform designed to affirm and expand human dignity.

The trajectory of welfare reform from the 1960s to the 1990s underlines the value conflicts that run through social welfare policy. The rejection of work-based welfare reform proposals in the 1970s was significant. Although the proposals were steeped in the work ethic, this did not dispel opponents' fears that adding the working poor to the welfare rolls would lead to widespread moral decline and increased costs. The link between work and the receipt of income security benefits was not strong enough to dispel the threat to our economic system that Congress saw in a guaranteed annual income—no matter how low that income was. The success of conservative welfare reform during the 1980s and 1990s ended efforts to balance support for the work ethic and a decent standard of living to even our poorest citizens. Rather, by 1996, government used punitive regulations to prevent millions of eligible families from even applying for aid.

The impact of cultural bias is clear throughout our history. The Poor Laws, as they developed in England during the shift from agriculture to factory production, were an effort to deal with disjuncture and the conflict in that society between feudal lords and emerging industrialists. The adoption of the Poor Laws by the American colonies represented the imposition of laws that were inappropriate to American realities. The renewed vigor with which the Poor Laws were administered during the post–Civil War period demonstrated again the significance of historical heritage. The reliance upon family responsibility and local settlement as requirements for financial relief was detrimental not only to industrial expansion, but also to family welfare. The importance of mobility and of the nuclear family to successful urbanization and industrialization went unheeded. The racially discriminatory application of the Poor Law principles to the freed slaves, its advocates claims, would help African Americans achieve the independent status of other American citizens.

Previous policy decisions cast a long shadow on contemporary social welfare policy debates. The creation of the Social Security system during the 1930s influenced almost all decisions about policy for the aged that followed. By the same token, the failure to include health care in the original Social Security system allowed the health care field to be dominated by private, often for-profit hospitals, insurance companies, and providers. By the time Congress passed comprehensive health care legislation in 2010, past decisions assured that public policy would have to accommodate these private interests. A public option became the flashpoint for debate and was ultimately abandoned in favor of subsidies for private insurance.

In summary, the congruence of technology and the level of output, the view of society, the view of human nature, and the historical heritage will influence policy choices. This does not mean that these four factors contribute equally at any given moment. The very fact that the family, from the point of view of public policy, has been considered primarily an economic unit suggests that the degree to which each factor will exert influence on policy will depend upon existing economic conditions. The response to human need during the 1930s was remarkably different from that during the high-employment era of the 1970s. Yet both were periods during which need *per se* was widely recognized and civil disorder was threatened.

This volume is organized around historical eras and gives a description of the economic, political, and cultural context for each. The chapters are organized around three sections: changing social conditions, innovations in social welfare, and the emergence of social movements. Underlying this organization is a theory of policy change. At any given time, the existing social welfare system is confronted by two challenges. On the one hand, the foundations of the social order change as the population grows and its composition changes, different sectors of the economy grow or shrink, and people experience the traumas of war, drought, or dislocation. On the other hand, people join together in social movements that propose different ways of making sense of the changes around them and of influencing them. Sometimes these movements are reactive—harkening back to "the ways things used to be." At other times, they seek new untried ways of coping with new difficulties. In time, some movements often succeed and become the new conventional wisdom, while others drop by the wayside.

One way to make history real is to examine the actual documents that changed policy. This book examines social welfare programs and institutions through the use of legislative documents, judicial decisions, administrative rulings, and statements of public and voluntary social welfare leaders. These documents give the reader the opportunity to put himself/herself back into history and consider the past not as a given, but rather as a set of choices made by earlier generations of Americans. We, like they, make history and live with the consequences of their and our choices.

DOCUMENT

Introduction

The document that accompanies this chapter is an Act for the Relief of the Poor, better known as the Poor Laws of 1601, passed by the English Parliament during the 43rd year of the reign of Queen Elizabeth. It is the only document in this book not derived from the American experience. Its inclusion is based on the tremendous and lasting influence that the British Poor Law tradition has had on American social welfare policy and programs.

Underlying the provisions of the Act for the Relief of the Poor are those features that have been identified as Poor Law principles. The overriding importance of work and workforce participation was primary. In providing support for the needy, individual and family responsibility came first. The act sets forth the qualifications for the selection of overseers of the poor, their duties, and accountability. In addition, the act details the provisions to be made for various categories of poor persons and the ways in which benefits are to be funded and administered.

The Poor Laws of England and Western Europe were a reaction against economic dependency and a statement that those who could earn a living were expected to do so. Those who were incapable of working were to be provided for, either by relatives if possible, or by the local community. But those who were able to work should. A primary concern with the work effort has dominated U.S. social policy throughout the years.

At the end of the 20th century, the influence of the Poor Law tradition on the American response to need has become stronger than at any time since the late 19th century. The legislation originally devised to deal with the upheavals of the shift from feudalism to an industrial society has provided a foundation for social welfare policy as we move from an industrial to a service economy.

THE

STATUTES AT LARGE,

From The

Thirty-ninth Year of Q. Elizabeth,

TO THE

Twelfth Year of K. Charles II. inclusive.

To which is prefixed,

TABLE containing the TITLES of all the STATUTES during that Period.

VOL. VII.

DANBY PICKERING, of Gray's Inn, Esq;

Reader of the Law Lecture to that Honourable Society.

Edited by Joseph Bentham, CAMBRIDGE, Printer to the University;

Charles Bathurst, at the

Cross-Keys, opposite St. Dunstan's Church in Fleet-Street, London 1763.

CUM PRIVILEGIO.

An Act for the Relief of the Poor, 43 Elizabeth, 1601

Be it enacted by the authority of this present parliament, That the church-wardens of every parish, and four, three or two substantial householders there, as shall be thought meet, having respect to the proportion and greatness of the same parish and parishes, to be nominated yearly in *Easter* Week, or within one month after *Easter*, under the hand and seal of two or more justices of the peace in the same county, whereof one to be of the *quorum*, dwelling in or near the same parish or division where the same parish doth lie, shall be called overseers of the poor of the same parish: and they, or the greater part of them, shall take order from time to time, by and with the consent of two or more such justices of peace as is aforesaid, for setting to work the children of all such whose parents shall not by the said church-wardens and overseers, or the greater part of them, be thought able to keep and maintain their children; and also for setting to work all such persons, married or unmarried, having no means to maintain them, and use no ordinary and daily trade of life to get their living by: and also to raise weekly or otherwise (by taxation of every inhabitant, parson, vicar and other, and of every occupier of lands, houses, tithes impropriate, propriations of tithes, coal-mines, or saleable underwoods in the said parish, in such competent sum and sums of money as they shall think fit) a convenient stock of flax, hemp, wool, thread, iron and other necessary ware and stuff, to set the poor on work: and also competent sums of money for and towards the necessary relief of the lame, impotent, old, blind, and such other among them, being poor and not able to work, and also for the putting out of such children to be apprentices . . . .

* * *

III. And be it also enacted, That if the said justices of peace do perceive, that the inhabitants of any parish are not able to levy among themselves sufficient sums of money for the purposes aforesaid; That then the said two justices shall and may tax, rate and assess as aforesaid, any other of other parishes, or out of any parish, within the hundred where the said parish is, to pay such sum and sums of money to the church-wardens and overseers of the said poor parish for the said purposes, as the said justices shall think fit, according to the intent of this law: (2) and if the said hundred shall not be thought to the said justices able and fit to relieve the said several parishes not able to provide for themselves as aforesaid; Then the justices of peace at their general quarter-sessions, or the greater number of them, shall rate and assess as aforesaid, any other of other parishes, or out of any parish, within the said county for the purposes aforesaid, as in their discretion shall seem fit.

* * *

IV. And that it shall be lawful, as well for the present as subsequent church-wardens and overseers, or any of them by warrant from any two such justices of peace, as is aforesaid, to levy as well the said sums of money, and all arrearages, of every one that shall refuse to contribute according as they shall be assessed, by distress and sale of the offender's goods, as the sums of money or stock shall be behind upon any account to be made as aforesaid, rendering to the parties the overplus; (2) and in defect of such distress, it shall be lawful for any such two justices of the peace to commit him or them to the common goal of

11

the county, there to remain without bail or mainprize until payment of the said sum, arrearages and stock: (3) and the said justices of peace, or any one of them, to send to the house of correction or common goal, such as shall not employ themselves to work, being appointed thereunto, as aforesaid: (4) and also any such two justices of peace to commit to the said prison every one of the said church-wardens and overseers which shall refuse to account, there to remain without bail or mainprize until he have made a true account, and satisfied and paid so much as upon the said account shall be remaining in his hands.

* * *

V. And be it further enacted, That it shall be lawful for the said church-wardens and overseers, or the greater part of them, by the assent of any two justices of the peace aforesaid, to bind any such children, as aforesaid, to be apprentices, where they shall see convenient, till such man-child shall come to the age of four and twenty years, and such woman-child to the age of one and twenty years, or the time of her marriage; the same to be as effectual to all purposes, as if such child were of full age, and by indenture of convenant bound him or her self. (2) And to the intent that necessary places of habitation may more conveniently be provided for such poor impotent people; (3) be it enacted by the authority aforesaid, That it shall and may be lawful for the said church-wardens and overseers, or the greater part of them by the leave of the lord or lords of the manor, whereof any waste or common within their parish is or shall be parcel, and upon agreement before with him or them made in writing, under the hands and seals of the said lord or lords, or otherwise, according to any order to be set down by the justices of peace of the said county at their general quarter-sessions, or the greater part of them, by like leave and agreement of the said lord or lords in writing under his or their hands and seals, to erect, build, and set up in fit and convenient places of habitation in such waste or common, at the general charges of the parish, or otherwise of the hundred or county, as aforesaid, to be taxed, rated and gathered in manner before expressed, convenient houses of dwelling for the said impotent poor; (4) and also to place inmates, or more families than one in one cottage or house; one act made in the one and thirtieth year of her Majesty's reign, intituled, *an act against the erecting and maintaining of cottages*, or anything therein contained to the contrary notwithstanding: (5) which cottages and places for inmates shall not at any time after be used or employed to or for any other habitation, but only for impotent and poor of the same parish, that shall be there placed from time to time by the church-wardens and overseers of the poor of the same parish, or the most part of them, upon the pains and forfeitures contained in the said former act made in the said one and thirtieth year of her Majesty's reign.

* * *

VII. And be it further enacted, That the father and grandfather, and the mother and grandmother, and the children of very poor, old, blind, lame and impotent person, or other poor person not able to work, being of a sufficient ability, shall, at their own charges, relieve and maintain every such poor person in that manner, and according to that rate, as by the justices of peace of that county where such sufficient persons dwell, or the greater number of them, at their general quarter-sessions shall be assessed; (2) upon pain that every one of them shall forfeit twenty shillings for every month which they shall fail therein.

* * *

VIII. And be it further enacted, That the mayors, bailiffs, or other head officers of every town and place corporate and city within this realm, being justice or justices of peace, shall have the same authority by virtue of this act, within the limits and precincts of their jurisdictions, as well out of sessions, as at their sessions, if they hold any, as is herein limited, prescribed and appointed to justices to the peace of the county, or any two or more of them, or to the justices of peace in their quarter-sessions, to do and execute for all the uses and purposes in this act prescribed, and no other justices of peace to enter or meddle there: (2) and that every alderman of the city of *London* within his ward, shall and may do and execute in every respect so much as is appointed and allowed by this act to be done and executed by one or two justices of peace of any county within this realm.

★ ★ ★

X. And further be it enacted by the authority aforesaid, That if in any place within this realm there happen to be hereafter no such nomination of overseers yearly, as if before appointed, That then every justice of peace of the county, dwelling within the division where such default of nomination shall happen, and every mayor, alderman and head officer of city, town or place corporate where such default shall happen, shall lose and forfeit for every such default five pounds, to be employed towards the relief of the poor of the said parish or place corporate, and to be levied, as aforesaid, of their goods, by warrant from the general sessions of the peace of the said county, or of the same city, town or place corporate, if they keep sessions.

★ ★ ★

XI. And be it also enacted by the authority aforesaid, That all penalties and forfeitures beforementioned in this act to be forfeited by any person or persons, shall go and be employed to the use of the poor of the same parish, and towards a stock and habitation for them, and other necessary uses and relief, as before in this act are mentioned and expressed; (2) and shall be levied by the said church-wardens and overseers, or one of them, by warrant from any two such justices of peace, or mayor, alderman, or head officer of city, town or place corporate respectively within their several limits, by distress and sale thereof, as aforesaid; (3) or in defect thereof, it shall be lawful for any two such justices of peace, and the said alderman and head officers within their several limits, to commit the offender to the said prison, there to remain without bail or mainprize till the said forfeitures shall be satisfied and paid.

★ ★ ★

XII. And be it further enacted by the authority aforesaid, That the justices of peace of every county or place corporate, or the more part of them, in their general sessions to be holden next after the feast of *Easter* next, and so yearly as often as they shall think meet, shall rate every parish to such a weekly sum of money as they shall think convenient; (2) so as no parish be rated above the sum of six-pence, nor under the sum of a half-penny, weekly to be paid, and so as the total sum of such taxation of the parishes in every county amount not above the rate of two-pence for every parish within the said county; (3) which sums so taxed shall be yearly assessed by the agreement of the parishioners within themselves, or in default thereof, by the church-wardens and petty constables of the same parish, or the more part of them: or in default of their agreement, by the order of such justice or justices of peace as shall dwell in the same parish or (if none be there dwelling) in the parts next adjoining.

* * *

XV. And be it further enacted, That all the surplusage of money which shall be remaining in the said stock of any county, shall by discretion of the more part of the justices of peace in their quarter-sessions, be ordered, distributed and bestowed for the relief of the poor hospitals of that county, and of those that shall sustain losses by fire, water, the sea or other casualties, and to such other charitable purposes, for the relief of the poor, as to the more part of the said justices of peace shall seem convenient.

* * *

XVI. And be it further enacted, That if any treasurer elected shall willfully refuse to take upon him the said office of treasureship, or refuse to distribute and give relief, or to account, according to such form as shall be appointed by the more part of the said justices of peace; That then it shall be lawful for the justices of peace in their quarter-sessions, or in their default, for the justices of assize at their assizes to be holden in the same county, to fine the same treasurer by their discretion; (2) the same fine not to be under three pounds, and to be levied by sale of his goods, and to be prosecuted by any two of the said justices of peace whom they shall authorize. (3) Provided always, That this act shall not take effect until the feast of *Easter* next.

* * *

XVII. And be it enacted, That the statute made in the nine and thirtieth year of her Majesty's reign, intituled, *An act for the relief of the poor*, shall continue and stand in force until the feast of *Easter* next; (2) and that all taxations heretofore imposed and not paid, nor that shall be paid before the said feast of *Easter* next, and that all taxes hereafter before the said feast to be taxed by virtue of the said former act, which shall not be paid before the said feast of *Easter*, shall and may after the said feast of *Easter* be levied by the overseers and other persons in this act respectively appointed to levy taxations, by distress, and by such warrant in every respect, as if they had been taxed and imposed by virtue of this act, and were not paid.

 Recall what you learned in this chapter by completing the Chapter Review.

2

The Colonial Period: 1647–1776

LEARNING OUTCOMES

- Compare the Poor Laws to public assistance policies in the United States since 1996.

- Summarize the major population and economic changes of the Colonial period.

- Explain how the expansion of democratic values during the American Revolution was accompanied by increasing criticism of the Poor Laws.

- Compare social provision for veterans with that for other social groups.

CHAPTER OUTLINE

The Poor Laws in the Colonies   17

Conquest, Expansion, and Population Growth: Native Americans, Immigration, and Slavery   23

Social Change and the Challenge to the Poor Laws   26

Veterans: A Special Class   29

DOCUMENTS: The Colonial Period   31

   An Act of Supplement to the Acts Referring to the Poor, Massachusetts Bay, 1692   31

   The Binding of Moses Love, 1747   33

The earliest white settlers of New England came to North America to establish the ideal religious community, "a city upon a hill" that would provide an example for European reform. Yet, as soon as they arrived, they were confronted with a set of realities that forced them to adapt their ways. A radically different ecology, complex relationships with Native Americans, and different economic and demographic realities forced them to tailor the institutions they had brought from England—including the Poor Laws—to these new realities.

Although the early Puritans thought of their migration as an "errand in the wilderness," North America had been the home of indigenous peoples for millennia. Although never rivaling the civilizations of Central and South America, the Southwest and Midwest had been the center for cultures that supported large cities and significant religious institutions, thanks in part to the expropriation of the resources of ordinary residents; but those civilizations had collapsed long before the arrival of Europeans. Furthermore, climate change in the 16th and 17th centuries—what environmental historians call the "little Ice Age"—reduced the growing season across much of North America, putting more pressure on scarce resources. Still, at the beginning of the 17th century, somewhere between 2 million and 8 million indigenous people lived north of the Rio Grande.[1]

As early as 1647, at the first session of its colonial legislature, Rhode Island announced the Elizabethan Poor Law principles that stressed, most importantly, public responsibility for relief of the poor who could not work, and work for the able-bodied:

> It is agreed and ordered by this present Assembly, that each towne shall provide carefully for the relief of the poor, to maintain the impotent, and to employ the able, and shall appoint an overseer for the same purpose. Sec. 43 Eliz.[2]

Needy widows and their children would receive aid but were expected to help with their own support by working. Those judged able to work and those who had worked in the past were expected to support themselves through work. They were not generally eligible for public aid even though they might be poor, despite working.

Considering the severe economic and physical privations of the early European settlers, it is not surprising that public responsibility for relief should have been buttressed by the principles of English Poor Law: local responsibility, family responsibility, and the residency requirement of legal settlement. These principles had been evolving in England and Western Europe for some 200 years and had been codified in 1601 in the Poor Law.

The principle of local responsibility made public aid the domain of towns and cities. Family responsibility originally denoted the legal obligation of support that adults had for their minor children and grandchildren and for their aged parents. Settlement, added in 1662, made a designated period of residence a requirement for the receipt of assistance. Settlement—the fact that only residents of a particular community were entitled to aid—was a response to the new economic realities of early modern Britain. Population growth had combined with new commercial opportunities to push a large share of the rural population off the land. Although the emergence of textile and mining industries offered new opportunities, the supply of labor outstripped the new demand. The ultimate effect was the creation of a large class of mobile labor—vagabonds, beggars, and tramps—that were no longer tied to a particular locality. In a society dominated by parishes and communities, this floating labor supply challenged conventional ideas about both economy and social order. They were people in need, and the Poor Laws, in providing public relief, were designed to meet—and control—their needs.

The terms upon which relief was offered reflected much more than the interests of the poor. Parliament was subject to conflicting pressures. The owners of large farms wanted to ensure the availability of local, low-cost, seasonal workers; the emerging industrialists needed to encourage the migration of factory labor; and the town officials wanted to minimize the need to levy taxes to support the homeless. The decision of Parliament to make local settlement an eligibility condition for relief reflected the power of the landed gentry. In supporting this interest, the government provided an incentive for labor to remain on the farms—the risk of leaving was clear. At the same time, they were able to satisfy the towns' concern for minimizing local costs. Furthermore, by limiting the mobility of the poor, government could respond to the interest of landowners and of industrialists in maintaining law and order.

In accordance with the Act of Settlement of 1662, newcomers could be returned to their place of legal residence even though there was no actual application for assistance.

That it shall and may be lawful upon complaint made by the churchwardens or overseers of the Poor of any Parish . . . for any two Justices of the Peace . . . where any Person or Persons are likely to be chargeable to the Parish shall come to inhabit . . . to remove and convey such Person or Persons to such Parish where he or they were last legally settled.[3]

The policy objectives of the Poor Laws, however, could be shifted to respond to changing conditions. By 1795, as urban centers grew and immigration increased, the Poor Laws were amended to control relief costs. Behavioral restrictions on relief recipients increased, and punishment, including whipping for not working, became more widespread. Residency requirements were made stiffer, but the penalties for vagrancy eased. A passport system was introduced, permitting increased mobility of labor between communities.

THE POOR LAWS IN THE COLONIES

Although the long evolution of the Poor Laws in England served both as a hindrance and as an aid to the process of commercial development, that evolution was always contingent on the availability of surplus labor. The climate of the American colonies was strikingly different. There was no persistent unemployment problem; no mass of employables had been pushed off the land; no industries existed to pull workers into towns; and no pool of workers awaited hiring. Initially there was neither an economic reason nor a law-and-order reason to reduce mobility. The rationale for the adoption of the Poor Laws rested on other grounds.

In the main, those colonists who were potential recipients of relief were the poor who were largely incapable of self-support: the ill, the disabled, the elderly, orphans, and widows with young children. Widows and their children made up a large percentage of the poor—as high as half in some towns.[4]

Frequent wars, in part a response by Native Americans to the invasion of their land by the settlers; recurring epidemics of smallpox, dysentery, measles, and yellow fever; major uncontrollable fires; high child mortality rates; and the hazards of fishing and the consequent loss of life at sea—all gave rise to economic need. These risks to which the colonists were subject were ones for which all held common concern. The colonists were small bands of individuals joined together in enterprises whose success depended upon the contribution and well-being of each. The smallness of their numbers made it possible to keep friendly, public watch over individual misfortunes. Their isolation made this public oversight of community affairs a matter of individual self-interest. The Poor Laws ensured individual and public protection. Those settled colonists known to be in need through no fault of their own could be helped with cash relief in their own homes or in the homes of neighbors. Relief for people in home—that is, family—settings was well regarded because of the order and stability such settings promised for the community as a whole.

In 17th-century New England, the modern boundaries between public and private and church and state would have made little sense. Community leaders sought to ensure that sinful behavior was suppressed, including idleness, which in an agricultural society could threaten everyone's well-being. At first, there was no voluntary sector to respond to people's troubles. The Scots Charitable Society was established in Boston in 1657.[5] In 1713, the Friends Almshouse was established in Philadelphia to provide relief for poor

Watch this video on King Philip's War.

How can the Native American perspective on British colonists change our understanding of early American history?

https://www.youtube.com/watch?v=jxVvD-0Jwjs

Quakers.[6] In 1724, the Boston Episcopal Society was formed, and in 1767, the Society of House Carpenters was organized in New York.[7]

Voluntary responses to need remain an enduring feature of American social welfare. Yet, like later efforts, the resources of colonial charitable societies and churches fell far short of the need they sought to address. As a result, the Poor Laws remained the primary "safety net" of Colonial society. The laws offered some support to the disabled and served as a deterrent to the able-bodied who might consider not working. The specific provisions regarding settlement and family responsibility limited the number of inhabitants for whose relief the town might be called upon to accept responsibility.

The family (and its structure) was a central force for maintaining economic, social, and political stability. The vast majority of the colonists were farmers, and their farms were isolated, small, and poorly equipped. For the most part, these farming families had to supply their own food, clothing, and equipment as well as their own education, entertainment, and health care. Family governance was hierarchical—generally with the husband in command. Women were not entitled to vote, had little part in governance, and lived in patriarchal families. Indeed, even their clothing was designed to show their sexual subordination.[8] Within this structure, all persons made valued contributions. Men and boys cleared fields, farmed, cut wood, and trapped. Women and girls spun thread, engaged in weaving, turned cloth into clothes, and took responsibility for myriad internal household chores. Men and women together worked to produce and to improve whatever implements, utensils, furniture, and weapons the household needed.

Childbearing was viewed as a productive contribution to the family economy, because young children often took on important chores and older children served as a form of social security for their aging parents. If the husband was killed or disabled, the wife moved naturally into the family and economic role he had held. In English colonies, more than in Spanish or Portuguese colonies, women in the Colonial period could—and did—hold property, run small businesses, and work for wages.[9]

During the 18th century, even as the colonies became more firmly established and the colonists benefited from improved technology, expanding commercial activities and shipbuilding, and increased trade with the native population, home manufactures flourished as a supplementary source of income. Improvements in the spinning wheel—particularly after 1765, when the invention of the spinning jenny made it possible for a person to spin 8 to 10 yarns simultaneously—made possible some home production for market sale. With men continuing to concentrate on farming, the newly oriented home manufacturing fell largely to women. In effect, women—and children—began to expand a function that had long been theirs, and did so in their own homes so that their work was easily integrated into family life.

The increasing centrality of women's work to the colonial economy drove a number of changes. In 1750, Boston opened a group of spinning schools for female children. In 1751, the Society for Encouraging Industry and Employing the Poor was founded to promote the manufacture of woolen cloth and to employ "our own women and children who are now in great measure idle."[10] The Massachusetts Province Laws of 1753–54 supported the manufacturing of linen, again with the employment of women and children in mind:

> The number of poor is greatly increased . . . and many persons, especially women and children, are destitute of employment and in danger of becoming a public charge.[11]

The colonies welcomed home manufacturing and the employment it provided. Cities and towns could cut the taxes that supported dependents and, instead, offer employment to women and children who might otherwise be "useless, if not burdensome, to society."[12]

The dire language of the Poor Laws and subsequent legislation designed to ensure their rigorous administration rested on cultural as well as economic factors. The popularity of spinning schools and the enthusiastic attendance at and participation in spinning bees sponsored by New England townships in the years preceding the Revolutionary War suggest the extent to which the essential isolation of the colonists had "produced a home-bred, home-living, and a home-loving people—a people who found both their employment and their pleasure in their own and their near neighbor's home."[13]

The importance of home and family was balanced against a commitment to worldly engagement that would later be labeled the "Protestant work ethic." A fuller explanation of the meaning and operation of the Poor Laws must take account of the moral underpinnings provided by Puritan Calvinism.

Many New England colonists had emigrated to escape religious persecution and to seek freedom to worship in accordance with their own religious beliefs. The result was a unity of church and government peculiarly suited to New World conditions. With individual status and economic reward a manifestation of predestined grace, the Puritan work ethic allowed the Puritan elite to reconcile their commitment to the collective with an interest in private gain. Although poverty could not be equated with unworthiness, it could suggest—especially if public relief was necessary—a character and moral flaw. Philanthropy was encouraged, but charity reflected a concern for the salvation of the rich—the stewards of God's wealth—more than a concern for the poor. Despite the family's usefulness, the impetus to maximize individual and family well-being did not center on the individual as a family member or on the individual family as a unit. When a family was in trouble, the concern was to save its potentially productive members. Hence, there developed social welfare measures such as farming out, indenture, and apprenticeship, which provided a family structure for governance and a means for productivity.

Poor Law provisions for public aid were inconsistent in their treatment of the family as a social entity to be helped. Indeed, the provisions for relief established categories of individuals—the young, the old, the disabled, and the able-bodied. By implication, the family consisted of a number of individuals living together for the purpose of ensuring self-support and, by extension, avoiding the necessity for support by taxpayers. At the same time, the Poor Laws were quite expansive in their definition of family responsibility for supporting dependents. Not only parents and children but also grandparents and grandchildren could be tapped for support. This expansive definition of family responsibility, which would survive in some place until the 20th century, articulates a residual definition of social welfare, in which the public sector was only responsible after individual and family resources failed to address the problem. In this context, the family that could not maintain financial independence was not simply unsuccessful but actually dangerous, both economically and morally. Such families could not by example, precept, or education be expected to prepare the young for adult, independent living. The colonists, therefore, provided for the binding out of children as apprentices for "better educateing of youth in honest and profitable trades and manufactures, as also to avoyd sloath and idleness wherewith such young children are easily corrupted"[14] and required that in addition to a trade, children learn to "read and understand the principles of religion & the capital laws of this country."[15] These were preventive measures designed to protect children from the contagion of parental failures.

Unattached, neglected, or dependent children could be placed with persons willing to take responsibility for their care and who would educate and train them for a useful calling. Persons assuming such a responsibility for children were expected to recoup their expenses from the child's work. Thus, indenture and apprenticeship were designed to protect against the danger of pauperism and to ensure that children were immediately profitable to themselves and to the community.

Apprenticeship reflected colonial society's concern with the home life, the work life, and the spiritual life of the child. Ideally, each child would grow up "under some orderly family government"[16] that would provide support and an opportunity for learning both for economic and for religious salvation. When the natural family did not provide these essentials, apprenticeship to a contracted family was an alternative that often eased the burden on the public treasury.

> If after warning and admonition given by any of the Deputies; or Select-men, unto such Parents or Masters, they shall still remain negligent in their duty, in any the particulars aforementioned, whereby Children or Servants may be in danger to grow Barberous, Rude or Stubborn, and so prove Pests instead of Blessings to the Country; That then a fine of ten shillings shall be levied on the Goods of such negligent Parent or Master, to the Towns use, except extreme poverty call for mitigation of the said fine.
>
> And if in three months after that, there be no due care taken . . . then a fine of twenty shillings to be levied. . . .
>
> And Lastly, if in three months after that, there be no due Reformation of the said neglect, then the said Selectmen with the help of two Magistrates, shall take such children and servants from them, and place them with some Masters for years (boyes till they come to twenty-one, and girls eighteen years of age) which will more strictly educate and govern them according to the rules of this Order.[17]

Apprenticeship was used for economy and for control. New England colonies varied in practice, but all reacted to the economic hardships of the wars with the native population and the increase in the number of poor families by looking toward an expansion in indenture and apprenticeship for job training, religious training, and education. The emphasis for Native American children, apprenticed to the English, was particularly on Christian education and the imposition of European religious beliefs on the native population.[18]

The practice of indenturing the children of the poor did not always occur without protest. When the British government sent a large group of Palatine German refugees to Manhattan in 1710, Governor Robert Hunter issued an order to apprentice the children to families in faraway Westchester, Long Island, and Rhode Island, to keep them off public support. The parents, despite illness and destitution, protested the separation and loss.[19]

Children of poor parents—both in and out of the almshouse—were subject to bonding and indenture. Complaints about cruel treatment and lack of appropriate education and job training increased as the 18th century progressed.[20]

The counterparts of the systems of indenture and apprenticeship for children were the systems of indenture contracting or farming out for adults. In accordance with colonial welfare legislation, overseers of the poor were empowered "to take effectual care that . . . persons of able body living within the same town or precincts thereof (not having estates otherwise to maintain themselves) do not live idly or misspend their time loitering, but that they be brought up or employed in some honest calling, which may be profitable unto themselves and the public."[21]

To the end that individuals be profitable to themselves and to the commonwealth, indenture contracts enforced labor by sentencing potential paupers to servitude, sometimes to a master of their own choosing and sometimes to an assigned master. Under farming out, the adult poor could be turned over to the bidder willing to contract, at the lowest charge to the community, to take on the care of paupers and to put them to work. Such a care might permit the individual to remain home. Assistance to the elderly, under this formulation, was quite flexible. It ranged from care in a private home for those who were feeble all the way to assistance in finding employment if the older person was capable of working.[22]

By the middle of the 18th century, cities began to build institutions like jails and almshouses to replace individual homes for criminals and those poor who were very old, disabled, or seriously ill. Yet, these institutions remained small and less separated from the community than later institutions would be. As demand for help rose, cash relief and noninstitutional help became harder to obtain. Urban poverty and unemployment increasingly meant commitment to a privately owned workhouse, a publicly owned house of correction, a poor farm, or an almshouse where care or proper punishment and hard labor could more easily be administered. The first almshouse was established in Rensselaerswyck, New York, in 1657. Plymouth ordered the construction of an almshouse in 1658, and Boston did the same 2 years later.

The early development of workhouses and almshouses—welfare mechanisms that were both sophisticated and expensive—was a response to the rapid population growth experienced by the colonies and of the increased fiscal capacity of some colonies. Occasionally, where towns could not afford such institutions, private philanthropists made contributions to the public effort.[23]

The popularity of indenture as a means of dealing with dependency was indicative of the transition to a "free" labor system in which employers were free to hire and fire as they saw fit and workers had to find a buyer for their labor. The new mobility of the population in the late 17th and early 18th centuries placed strains on all forms of established authority. Community leaders could not regulate people as they moved in and out of town. Even colonial authorities were challenged to cope with a hard-to-follow population of floating laborers. The binding of labor to a particular authority was one means of slowing this mobility and the social disorder it might breed.

Colonial welfare legislation stressed the provision of indoor reliefs; that is, care offered in homes other than one's own or in institutions. Nevertheless, the seasonally unemployed might benefit from tax remissions, and the overseers of the poor could legally provide outdoor relief—money payments to persons permitted to remain in their own homes because their poverty resulted from physical disability, widowhood, or old age. Taxes were collected for the latter purpose. Frequent wars coupled with postwar recessions created increased demands for help. In crises, private philanthropy supported the practice of outdoor relief by the provision of items such as blankets and stockings. During the severe winter of 1761–62, the Quakers in Philadelphia distributed fuel stamps—"tickets of recommendation"—to be redeemed for wood.[24]

Even worthiness had its limits. The stigma of poverty was not reserved for the undeserving. In 1718, a statute of the Province of Pennsylvania made it obligatory that every person receiving public relief "upon the shoulder of the right sleeve . . . in open and visible manner, wear . . . a large Roman P. together with the first letter of the name of the county, city or place whereof such poor person is an inhabitant, cut either in red or blue cloth, as by the overseers of the poor, it shall be directed and appointed."[25] In New York, relief recipients were required to wear badges inscribed with the large letters "N.Y."[26]

The coercive work features of the Poor Laws and the meagerness of relief provisions deterred many of the eligible from seeking aid. Not only did the laws spell out the kinds of care that might be made available to those who applied, but they also directed the overseers to seek out those whose situations or ways of living portended financial burden for the community. Direct deterrence was enhanced by the Poor Law principle of family responsibility, requiring that "the father and grandfather and the mother and grandmother and the children of every poor, old, blind, lame, and impotent person, or

The stigma of poverty was not reserved for the undeserving. In 1718, a statute of the Province of Pennsylvania made it obligatory that every person receiving public relief "upon the shoulder of the right sleeve . . . in open and visible manner, wear . . . a large Roman P."

other poor person not able to work . . . shall at their own charges relieve and maintain every such poor person as the justices of the peace . . . shall order and direct."[27] The overt demand that relatives support each other in time of need was covertly strengthened by the stigma of resorting to public aid.

It's striking to a contemporary observer how many features of contemporary welfare policy can find their origins in the colonial Poor Laws. The residual character of the Poor Laws—that is, the fact that public responsibility was simply a "safety net" to be used after private or voluntary efforts failed—continues to guide contemporary relief policy. In addition, features such as the large variation in policy between different localities and states, the use of work requirements to "divert" potential recipients, the removal of children from "unfit" parents, and, of course, the stigmatization of the poor are as much a part of social welfare policy today as they were in the 17th century.

The Poor Laws were designed to protect those who held legal claim to settlement in particular localities. They offered protection against strangers who threatened the stability—namely, the morality and physical safety—of a society concerned with order and wary of new ways and different cultures. In regard to strangers, the Poor Laws demonstrated most clearly their law-and-order nature. The requirement of settlement for public assistance—for example, 40 days in New York, 3 months in Massachusetts, a year in North Carolina—underlined the absence of local responsibility for outsiders.

By the end of the 18th century, residency requirements had become even stricter. In New York, for example, the time needed to establish settlement rose to a year and the annual rental value required more than doubled, increasing from 5 pounds to 12 pounds a year.[28] Beyond that, "warning out" the practice of expelling strangers became more common. Strangers were carefully screened. In the 1690s, the newcomer was suspect, and major efforts were made to reduce the potential costs of support for migrants. Those few who could ensure their financial independence and future contribution to the community were permitted to remain and to acquire settlement. More frequently, they were escorted to the town limits.

The low numbers of the reported poor in the early years of the 18th century are deceptive. They did not usually include people receiving temporary relief, for example, during the severe winter months. Nor did they include the "near poor" and those needy but ineligible people, displaced Native Americans, and nonresidents who were poor but excluded from aid. Even with the small number who received help, the cost of aid made up a large part of the total budget and sometimes even exceeded total tax receipts.[29] The colonists were concerned with the threat to economic survival posed by possible drains on the public treasury resulting from the potentially poor and sick outsider. This fear often outweighed the value of labor skills the stranger might bring.

Additional evidence that the protection of society, rather than the care of the poor, dictated the writing of the colonial Poor Laws is offered by the fact that the laws contain no expression of concern for the poor beyond the concise statements of provision for their care. The laws do, however, make explicit the rights and duties of the overseers of the poor and spell out in detail methods for selecting and appointing overseers, their taxing powers, their responsibilities, and their accountability—as well as the penalties to which they were subject if they performed improperly. The laws indicate that the tasks of the overseers were considered onerous. In Pennsylvania, for example, the overseers were appointed to a one-year term of office but, on penalty of having to serve a second year or pay a heavy fine, were required to set forth the names of their successors.[30]

(?) Assess your comprehension of "The Poor Laws in the Colonies" by completing this quiz.

CONQUEST, EXPANSION, AND POPULATION GROWTH: NATIVE AMERICANS, IMMIGRATION, AND SLAVERY

In New England, the township became the unit of colonial Poor Law administration, and, as might be expected, the major foci of administrative practice implementing welfare legislation were work and religion. Although they were adapted to local conditions and to variations of religious tenets, colonies outside of New England also adopted the poor-relief system of England.

The colonists, whether Anglican as in Virginia, Puritan as in Massachusetts Bay, or Catholic as in Maryland, were English in their political and social heritage. The English character of these colonial enterprises was enhanced by the fact that they were essentially private enterprises. All were financed through private capital raised by investment organizations such as the London and Massachusetts Bay companies or, as in the case of Maryland, by individual landowners ready to risk their own fortunes. In either instance, royal support was given in the form of charters or land grants. Colonization was an element of the global competition of European powers for supremacy of the new global economy. In the Southern colonies, the usual motivation of colonization—the search for gold and other precious substances—failed but was replaced by America's first cash crop—tobacco. Thanks to the *Doctrine of Discovery*, Europeans could claim sovereignty over land not occupied by Christians and consider indigenous peoples as uncivilized, barbarous, and consequently without rights to their land. The colonists' success derived from a combination of patriotism, profit seeking, religious fervor, and belief in the superiority of English culture.

The newcomers to America were not just settlers; they were conquerors as well. The English and the Europeans attacked and conquered the resident population in many ways, both direct and indirect. The first impact of Europeans often arrived before the settlers themselves. With no immunity to a variety of pathogens including smallpox, measles, mumps, and influenza, epidemics started with the first contact and then spread inland as infected Indians came into contact with more distant tribes. It's likely that, within a century of first exposure, 95 percent of the indigenous population of eastern North America perished. Although there were instances of deliberate exposure of Native Americans to infected blankets (for example, near Fort Pitt during the middle of the 18th century), most of the death toll of disease was the result of normal interactions with Europeans.

The newcomers to America were not just settlers; they were conquerors as well.

And there was a lot of interaction between the people. Particularly during the early 18th century, American Indians became an important part of the expanding global market of the era. A bovine epidemic in Europe created a shortage of leather, which Native Americans filled by hunting millions of white-tailed deer. Most American Indian cultures valued trade not only as an economic transaction but also as a symbol of the reciprocal relationships between different people. To fill this demand, Europeans produced a variety of goods for the American Indian market, including brass kettles, tools, woolen textiles, and jewelry as well as the better-known weapons and liquor.

However, the integration of American Indians into the global economy was short-lived. The wars of the mid-18th century, which forced the French and Spanish out of eastern North America, undermined a balance of power diplomacy on which peaceful relations were based. By the end of the century, the pattern of broken treaties, violence, and displacement that would characterize European-indigenous relations for the next century and a half was firmly set.[31]

The process of establishing colonies was not, however, an easy task for the newcomers. The colonists shared a common experience of hardship and scarcity in America. The severity of the New England winter, the "horrid snow" described by Cotton Mather,[32] was counterpart to the unexpected, unbearable heat that brought death to one-half of the Virginia settlers during their first summer in America. Captain John Smith, a leader of the Virginia Company, wrote, "Nothing can be expected thence, but by labor."[33] In the South, as in the North, the Poor Laws constituted a reasonable response to a situation in which financial disaster and death seemed imminent and which, in fact, did produce social and physical disabilities.

The intent of the original colonists to settle permanently in the New World was strengthened by the rapid addition of new settlers and new settlements. The English revolution that led to the overthrow of King Charles I in 1649, the establishment of the Puritan Commonwealth, and the restoration of the monarchy in 1660 spurred emigration, especially of those who were seeking freedom and purity of religion. The emigrants to New England were of all classes of English society and consisted of whole families and individuals ready to establish homes and families in the new country.

The Restoration of the British monarchy sparked an increased emigration of Puritans to New England and reinforced the dominance of Puritanism in colonial America. Later, French Huguenots and Scottish Calvinists emigrated to Carolina as a result of religious persecution and trade restrictions. The possibilities for religious and political freedom and for economic stability brought additional settlers—Welsh, Jews, and Swiss—and the colonial population soared. By 1640, more than 27,000 Englishmen were scattered through Massachusetts, Connecticut, Rhode Island, New Hampshire, Maine, Maryland, and Virginia. In 1690, there were 200,000 inhabitants; by 1710, there were 350,000; and in 1760, 1.5 million people lived in the 13 colonies, representing many parts of Europe and Africa. The numbers of Africans grew from the original 20 brought in 1619 to 16,700 in 1690; 44,900 in 1710; and 325,000—22 percent of the population—in 1760.[34]

European population growth in the New England colonies was controlled by the factors that led to their founding. The colonists were bound by a common set of religious and ethical motivations and, for the most part, had underwritten the expenses of their passage and of supplies through the purchase of shares in a joint enterprise. The New England colonies, despite official ties to England, were essentially independent and used their independence to accept and reject immigrants on the basis of religious beliefs and potential for economic self-sufficiency. Although slavery persisted in the North through most of the 18th century, African American slavery was not central to the Northern economy.

A different pattern evolved in the South, reflecting the different base for settlement and the economic base that developed. Virginia was settled solely as a commercial enterprise. A large number of its settlers were working-class Englishmen who paid for their passage through indenture contracts, a 4- to 7-year commitment to work. In 1625, documents show that 487 people—almost 40 percent of Virginia's population—were indentured servants.[35] The South grew as it developed tobacco and prospered with the establishment of plantations. Some Native Americans were enslaved for service in Florida and Georgia; some were traded in the Caribbean islands. The first blacks to come to Virginia came as indentured workers. As servants and as freemen, they had much in common with their white counterparts in terms of status and problems. However, the chasms of skin color and culture quickly differentiated white servants from black chattel. By the middle of the 17th century, much of the Southern economy was based on the use of slave labor to produce crops for export—indigo, low-land cotton, but especially tobacco.

Watch this video on slavery and the Atlantic economy.

How were the histories of indigenous peoples of North America and African Americans connected?

However, the chasms of skin color and culture quickly differentiated white servants from black chattel. By the middle of the 17th century, much of the Southern economy was based on the use of slave labor to produce crops for export—indigo, low-land cotton, but especially tobacco.

With New England practicing selectivity in the acceptance of immigrants and the South relying increasingly upon the use of slave labor, immigrants were funneled into the Middle Atlantic colonies. Large numbers were unable to pay for their passage and came under contracts of indenture. It is estimated that two-thirds of the settlers in Pennsylvania came under such provisions of servitude. German and Scotch-Irish families who arrived during the 18th century came as "redemptioners," people who had made a down payment on passage and who used the promise of work as collateral for the balance. Indentured servitude resulted for those who defaulted.

By the close of the Colonial period, British North America had prospered. When Georgia was declared a crown colony in 1752, all 13 American colonies were formal geographic and political entities. Between 1700 and 1776, a great deal of cultural, social, political, and economic change occurred. Population growth had occurred not only by natural increase but also by way of immigration. The resulting intermingling of various religious, ethnic, and racial groups lent a cosmopolitan air to the busy ports of trade and entry—Boston, New York, Philadelphia, and Baltimore. The regular plying of sailing vessels between North America and the European continent brought not only economic returns to all but also, to the upper classes, the latest turns of fashion in dress, *belles lettres*, and social amenities. The establishment of active legal and political ties between the separate colonies and London and the frequent exchange of representatives required lent additional encouragement to the maintenance of continental social graces, at the same time that the separation of the American and European continents presented the colonies with opportunity for self-government.

The colonies took an early interest in expanding schooling because their leaders believed that the population should be able to read the Bible. A college—soon to be called Harvard—was established at Cambridge in the Massachusetts Bay Colony as early as 1636. By the mid-18th century, William and Mary, Yale, the University of Pennsylvania, Princeton, Brown, Rutgers, and Dartmouth were all established. The ties of communication among the colonies were fostered by a flood of printed materials and broadsides and the practice of letter writing. Newspapers proliferated, and the instituting of a mail service, carried regularly by 1732 between Massachusetts and Virginia, was additionally encouraging to writings of all kinds.

The many changes that marked colonial life sharpened class differences. By the time of the American Revolution, many residents were already third- and fourth-generation Americans. By the middle of the 18th century, a new elite, based on commercial success, had come to dominate both Northern and Southern societies. Beneath this class existed a middle stratum, again largely Protestant, of farmers, artisans, and small tradesmen. Alongside and below this group existed another large group—often neither English nor Protestant, sometimes nonwhite, and almost always without property.

Different bases for prosperity for the North and South resulted in different views of people and of their need for social welfare programs. New England and the Middle Atlantic colonies shifted from sole dependence upon farming and fishing to home manufacturing, shipbuilding, and trading. These colonies were sufficiently urbanized to add the risks of a market economy to those of colonial frontier life. Problems of dependency increased with the influx of poorly paid immigrants and with the growing numbers of disabled men resulting from the wars of European powers in America and wars with Indians. Particularly stark were the needs of elderly and disabled blacks, who had been freed as a way of avoiding their care in old age.[36] These factors, combined with an economy of scarcity and with a growing population, made the enforcement of the Poor Laws attractive to town governments.

In the South, the introduction of slavery and the continued reliance on an agricultural economy prevented the development of a large, free, laboring class. If the large plantation holdings of Virginia contrasted sharply with small tenant farmer holdings of Carolina, the two were, nevertheless, joined in a feudal system that created a degree of economic stability. The milder climate, the availability of fertile land, and the mixture of less austere religious sects fostered a warmer, more favorable view of the free men. As early as 1728, William Byrd, a prosperous and educated gentleman who served on a commission set up to run the dividing line between Virginia and North Carolina, may have exaggerated when he observed the way of life in North Carolina:

> Surely there is no place in the World where the inhabitants live with less labour . . . by the great felicity of the Climate, the easiness of raising Provisions. . . . Indian Corn is of so great increase, that a little Pains will Subsist a very large Family with Bread, and then they may have meat without any pains at all, by the Help of the Low Grounds, and the great Variety of Mast that grows on the Highland.[37]

While such ease of living might have led to laziness and an "Aversion to Labor," as Byrd feared, the fact was that it also led to greater tolerance of human misfortune—again for free men. By the middle of the 17th century, Virginia had adopted both the Poor Laws and apprenticeship to provide for poor free men: white and black, orphans, illegitimate children, and mulatto children of white women. Native Americans were excluded from these arrangements. There was no recognition of any social welfare needs that Native Americans, slaves, or indentured servants might have, and it was left to these groups to rely on their own informal self-help mechanisms.

> **?** Assess your comprehension of "Conquest, Expansion, and Population Growth" by completing this quiz.

SOCIAL CHANGE AND THE CHALLENGE TO THE POOR LAWS

Although many features of the Poor Laws anticipated modern welfare arrangements, they were driven by efforts to maintain a hierarchical, stable social order. The Poor Laws were a product of a society that used the legal system to constrain a dynamic population during a time of social change. In America, as in England, efforts at control increasingly were at odds with the fluidity of the emerging social order.

We've already encountered many of the social forces that were propelling social change during the 18th century. High fertility and lower mortality led to a natural increase in colonial populations far greater than that in Europe at the same time. As cities grew, the social bonds that reinforced a sense of community became weaker. Rich and poor urbanites were less likely to see a sense of reciprocal obligation; indeed, they might see their natural state as one of conflict.

> **▶ Watch this video on Jonathan Edwards's most famous sermon.**
>
> How was Edwards's evocative language associated with the expansion of individualism in the colonies?
>
> https://www.youtube.com/watch?v=TtHijgqceXo

These economic and social changes were accompanied by a shift from a communal to an individualistic cultural perspective. Nowhere was this more evident than in religion. During the earlier Colonial era, religion reinforced the belief that the individual was subservient to the community. But beginning in the 1740s, evangelical Protestantism swept the colonies in the form of the Great Awakening, beginning with the preaching of Jonathan Edwards in Northampton, Massachusetts. In place of the calm exegesis of earlier sermons, Edwards used vivid imagery to push his listeners to an altered emotional state. Parishioners would interrupt his sermons with moaning and cries.

Other ministers, many itinerants who would move from community to community, soon picked up Edwards's approach. Religion became less about people's relationship to their community and more about their individual connection to God.

The sense of *Americans* as a separate people was reinforced during the Seven Years' War (often called the French and Indian War) during which Americans bore much of the fighting in North America. After the war, British efforts to reassert its control of the colonies led to confrontations and ultimately open conflict (Figure 2.1). Ultimately, the

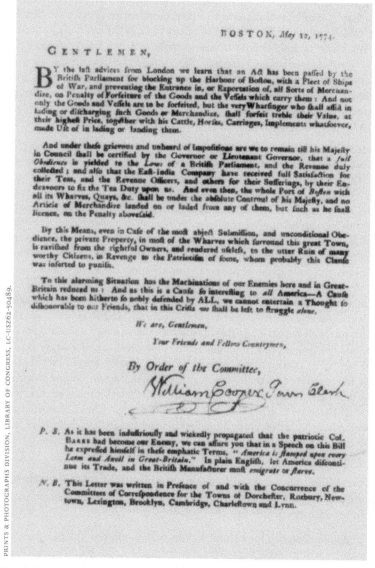

Figure 2.1 Revolutionary War Broadside, May 12, 1774. The British attempted to reinforce their control of the colonies after the Seven Years' War. However, American resistance to these efforts, including the Boston Port Bill, pushed some Americans to move toward independence.

North American colonies declared independence and fought what became a civil war between the advocates of independence and residents who remained loyal to Britain.

In the years following the Revolution, the United States was governed by its first constitution, the Articles of Confederation. However, after a period of democratic expansion during the war, political elites reasserted their control during the 1780s and called for a stronger national government that could assert its superiority over the individual states. In 1787, representatives convened in Philadelphia and produced the current U.S. Constitution, which, along with a Bill of Rights, was ratified in 1789.

If society was essentially a group of individuals, the traditional bonds of reciprocity that undergird the Poor Laws lost their effectiveness. For many in authority, the response to the Poor Laws' ineffectiveness was to make them more restrictive. Yet, for others, the alternative conclusion was that the entire effort to help the poor was counterproductive. For them, the effort to help the poor would make poverty more attractive. Anticipating later generations of "welfare reformers," Benjamin Franklin argued for the abolition of the Poor Laws. As Franklin saw it, the causes of poverty were of the individual's own making; the social system worked well, the growing wealth of the upper classes was justified, and an assumption of social responsibility would inevitably aggravate the problem by fostering further dependency.

> I have sometimes doubted whether the laws peculiar to England, which *compel the rich to maintain the poor*, have not given the latter a dependence, that very much lessens the care of providing against the wants of old age.
>
> I have heard it remarked that the *poor* in *Protestant* countries, on the continent of Europe, are generally more industrious than those of *Popish* countries. May not the more numerous foundations in the latter for relief of the poor have some effect toward rendering them less provident? To relieve the misfortunes of our fellow creatures is concurring with the Deity; it is godlike; but, if we provide encouragement for laziness, and supports for folly, may we not be fighting against the order of God and Nature, which perhaps has appointed want and misery as the proper punishments for, and cautions against, as well as necessary consequences of, idleness and extravagance? . . .
>
> However, as matters now stand with us, care and industry seem absolutely necessary to our well-being. They should therefore have every encouragement we can invent, and not one motive to diligence be subtracted; and the support of the poor should not be by maintaining them in idleness, but by employing them in some kind of labour suited to their abilities of body, as I am informed begins to be of late the practice in many parts of England, where workhouses are erected for that purpose. If these were general, I should think the poor would be more careful, and work voluntarily to lay up something for themselves against a rainy day, rather than run the risk of being obliged to work at the pleasure of others for a bare subsistence, and that too under confinement.[38] [Italics in original]

Franklin's view highlights a belief in the responsibility of people for their own welfare in an ordered society that rewards industry and thrift. Franklin rationalized poverty and inequality in income distribution:

> Much malignant censure have some writers bestowed upon the rich for their luxury and expensive living, while the poor are starving, & c.; not considering that what the rich expend, the labouring poor receive in payment for their labour. It may seem a paradox if I should assert, that our labouring poor do in every year receive *the whole revenue of the nation*; I mean not only the public revenue, but also the revenue or clear income of all private estates, or a sum equivalent to the whole . . . .

> In support of this position I reason thus. The rich do not work for one another. Their habitations, furniture, cloathing, carriages, food, ornaments, and everything in short, that they or their families use and consume, is the work or produce of the labouring poor, who are, and must be continually, paid for their labour in producing the same.[39]

Some went so far as to argue that, for the market economy to function, individual earned income should never be supplemented. This would compel labor force participation and ensure a supply of workers willing to perform menial, difficult, and unpleasant tasks.

> It seems to be a law of nature, that the poor should be to a certain degree improvident, that there may always be some to fulfil the most servile, the most sordid, and the most ignoble offices in the community. The stock of human happiness is thereby much increased, whilst the more delicate are not only relieved from drudgery, and freed from those occasional employments which would make them miserable, but are left at liberty, without interruption, to pursue those callings which are suited to their various dispositions, and most useful to the state. As for the lowest of the poor, by custom they are reconciled to the meanest occupations, to the most laborious works, and to the most hazardous pursuits; whilst the hope of their reward makes them cheerful in the midst of all their dangers and their toils.[40]

By the end of the Colonial era, the poor and unfortunate were no longer seen as an organic part of the social order. Often they were literally outsiders; addressing their problems was no longer the responsibility of respectable citizens. As Americans began to consider the meaning of "liberty" and "equality" in their political thought, these words meant little for the poor—free and enslaved—whose well-being was increasingly marginalized.

> **?** Assess your comprehension of "Social Change and the Challenge to the Poor Laws" by completing this quiz.

VETERANS: A SPECIAL CLASS

Welfare measures for veterans, however, differed from those applied to the general population. The English "Acte for Reliefes of Souldiours" of 1593 set the tone for colonial legislation. It had recognized both the special services and the special needs of disabled soldiers and sailors and provided relief for this group *as a right* on the basis of disability, with payments scaled to military pay. As early as 1624, the colony of Virginia passed similar legislation. In 1636, Plymouth Colony declared that any soldier injured in defense of the colony was entitled to support.

> That in case necessity require to send forces abroad, and there be not volunteers sufficient offered for the service, then it be lawfull for the Governor and [his] assistants to presse [men into service] in his Majesties name . . . provided that if any that shall goe returne mamed & hurt, he shall be mayntayned completely by the Colony duringe his life.[41]

Other colonies followed the precedent, and by 1777, all but Connecticut had made special provisions for veterans. The entitlement to these provisions did not carry the onus of pauperism and, equally important for the future, carried no requirement of local settlement. Colonies, not towns, were responsible for financing and administration. The pattern was so well accepted that the Continental Congress in 1776 adopted a report of the Committee on Disabled Soldiers and Sailors recommending to the states pensions for invalid and disabled veterans.[42] This special attention to veterans, and in some instances to other persons identified as the "unsettled poor," broke ground for eventual contributions by the states and by the federal government to social welfare.

Of more immediate interest, however, is the logic by which the colonies selected veterans for preferential treatment—domiciliary care, pensions for elderly and disabled veterans, and outdoor relief for widows and children of veterans. This selection for special treatment was, after all, consistent with the colonial view of humanity. Veterans had participated in an unusual kind of work. In doing so, they had made an extraordinary contribution to the commonwealth at the same time that they had made visible their own individual worth. Certainly such work and such worthiness were not to be deterred in a society where their special services were so badly needed.

DOCUMENTS

The Colonial Period

The two documents selected to illustrate the thrust of social welfare during the colonial era are *An Act of Supplement to the Acts Referring to the Poor* (Massachusetts Bay, 1692) and the contract of indenture entitled *The Binding of Moses Love* (1747). The documents illustrate legislative and judicial actions taken to achieve societal stability and individual well-being. For society and the individual, the actions were protective and preventive and called upon a family unit to perform the functions of a social welfare institution. Where no natural family existed to support members in need, a substitute family was found. The number of colonists was very small, and the community itself functioned in part as an extended family.

An Act of Supplement expresses governmental concern for all the inhabitants of Massachusetts Bay. The act explicitly states that its provisions extend beyond those who receive public alms; its intent is to ensure that all single persons under the age of 21 years live "under some orderly family government." The significance of such an assurance stems from the nature of a society in which government and family mirrored one another in their responsibility to fulfill God's plan that people work and produce. Both were organized in a fixed hierarchical structure in which each individual had been called to an assigned place. Fulfilling one's responsibility within the structure was a duty to oneself, to the community, to God. Family government was protective of the individual who might be tempted to fall away from that responsibility and protective of the community that would bear the cost of such a fall. The family model reinforced the Puritan values of work and frugality as religious observances. In a society of scarcity, such a joining of religious and secular concerns was particularly felicitous.

The Binding of Moses Love demonstrates that the colonists observed the human condition with a certain solicitousness. Moses Love was bound out when only 2 years and 8 months of age. The indenture contract is concerned with avoiding future dependency of the children of the poor. Support, education, and employability are the long-term goals. All in all, the rights and responsibilities bestowed on Moses Love's master are those of a parent. As indicated in *An Act of Supplement*, this discharge of governmental and familial responsibilities toward children generally endeavored "to defend them from any wrongs or injuries" and to prepare them for economic self-sufficiency in adulthood.

The family model reinforced the Puritan values of work and frugality as religious observances. In a society of scarcity, such a joining of religious and secular concerns was particularly felicitous.

The ACTS AND RESOLVES, Public and Private

of the

PROVINCE OF THE MASSACHUSETTS BAY:

CHAPTER 14.

AN ACT OF SUPPLEMENT TO THE ACTS REFERRING TO THE

POOR,

&c.

Whereas the law for the binding out poor children apprentice is misconstrued by some to extend only to such children whose parents receive almes; for explanation whereof—

1692–3, ch. 28, & 7

Be it declared and enacted by His Excellency the Governour, Council and Representatives in General Court assembled, and by the authority of the same,

Selectmen or overseers of the poor to bind out poor children, &c.;

[Sect. 1.] That the selectmen or overseers of the poor in any town or district within this province, or the greater part of them, shall take, order and are hereby impowred from time to time, by and with the assent of two justices of the peace, to set to work, or bind out apprentice, as they shall think convenient, all such children whose parents shall, by the selectmen or overseers of the poor, or the greater part of them, be thought unable to maintain them, (whither they receive almes or are chargeable to the place or not), so as that they be not sessed to publick taxes or assessments, for the province or town charges; male children till they come to the age of twenty-one years, and females till they come to the age of eighteen years, or time of marriage: which shall be as good and effectual in law, to all intents and purposes, as if any such child were of full age, and by indenture of covenant had bound him or herself, or that their parents were consenting there [un] to: provision therein to be made for the instructing of children so bound out, to read and write, as they may be capable.

—to inquire into the usage of such as they bind out.

And the selectmen or overseers of the poor shall inquire into the usage of children bound out by themselves or their predecessors, and endeavour to defend them from any wrongs or injuries.

And, for the better preventing of idleness, and loose or disorderly living,—

Be it further declared and enacted by the authority aforesaid,

Selectmen or overseers of the poor to set to

[Sect. 2.] That the selectmen or overseers of the poor, or the greater part of them, be and are further impowred, by and with the assent of two justices of the peace, to set to work all such persons, married or unmarried, able of body, having no means to maintain them, that live idlely and use or exercise no ordinary and daily lawful trade or business to get their living by. And no single person of either sex, under the age of twenty-one years, shall be suffered to live at their own hand, but under some orderly family government; nor shall any woman of ill fame, married or unmarried, be suffered to receive or entertain lodgers in her house. And the selectmen or overseers of the poor, constables and tythingmen, are hereby ordered to see to the due observance of this act, and to complain and inform against any transgressions thereof to one or more justices of the peace, or the court of general sessions of the peace, who are hereby respectively required and impowred, upon due conviction of the offender or offenders for living idely or disorderly, contrary to the true intent of this act, to commit or send such offenders to the house of correction or work-house, there to remain and be kept to labour, until they be discharged by order of the court of general sessions of the peace, unless such person or persons so complained of shall give reasonable caution or assurance, to the satisfaction of the justice or court, that they will reform: provided, this act shall not be construed to extend to hinder any single woman of good repute from the exercise of any lawful trade or imployment, for a livelihood, whereto she shall have the allowance and approbation of the selectmen or overseers of the poor, or the greater part of them, any law, usage or custom to the contrary notwithstanding: provided,—

No single person under twenty-one years old to live out of family government.

[Sect. 3.] This act shall continue in force for the space of three years next coming, and to the end of the session of the general assembly next after. *[Passed November 27; published December 3.]*

Volume I. Boston: Wright & Potter, Printers to the State, 1869.

★ ★ ★ ★

THE BINDING OF MOSES LOVE, 1747

This Indenture made the fourteenth day of September Anno domini 1747 by and between Luke Lincoln, Benja Tuckor, Nathall Goodspeed and John Whittemor all of Leicester in the Covnty of Worcester selectmen of sd Leicester on the one part, Matthew Scott of Leicester aforesaid yeoman on the other part Wittnesseth that the above sd selectmen by virtue of the Law of this province them Impowering & with the assent of two of the Majesties Justices of the Peace for sd Covnty hereto annexed to put and bind out to the sd Matthew Scott & to his heirs Execvtors & Adminrs as an Apprentice Moses Love a Minor aged two years and Eeight Months with him & them to Live and dwell with as an apprentice dureing the term of Eighteen years and fovr months (viz) untill he shall arrive to the age of twenty-one years—he being a poor Child & his parants not being well able to support it. Dureing all which the sd apprentice his sd Master his heirs Execvtors & Adminrs shall faithfully serve at such Lawfull imployment & labovr as he shall from time to time Dureing sd term be Capable of doing and performing & not absent himself from his or their service without Leave & In all things behave himself as a good & faithful apprentice ought to do and the sd Matthew Scott for himself his heirs Execvtors & Adminrs do Couenant promise and grant to & with the above sd selectmen of Leicester aforsaid & with their successors in the office or trust of selectmen of Leicester aforsaid & Inbehalf of sd apprentice that he the sd Matthew Scott his heirs Execvtors & Adminrss shall & will Dureing the term aforsd find and provide for the sd apprentice sufficient Cloathing meet drink Warshing and Lodging both in Sickness & in health & that he will teach him or cavse him to be tavght to read & write & siffer fiting his degree if he be Capable of Learning and at the Expiration of the term to Dismiss him with two suits of apparril one to be fitt for Lords days In Wittness where of the partyes to these present Indentvrs haue Interchangably set their hands & seals the day and year first written. Signed sealed & Delivered in presence of

    Steward Southgate
    John Brown

                Luke Lincoln (seal)
                Benja Tucker (seal)
                John Whittemor (seal)

New England Historical and Genealogical Register, Boston, 1880, Vol. XXXIV, p. 311.

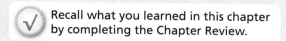

Recall what you learned in this chapter by completing the Chapter Review.

The Pre–Civil War Period: 1777–1860

LEARNING OUTCOMES

- Describe the major social and economic changes of the pre–Civil War years.
- Contrast the goals of the different social reform movements of the pre–Civil War years.
- Assess the effectiveness of innovation in social welfare programs and services during the early 19th century.

CHAPTER OUTLINE

Social and Economic Conditions 36
  Population Growth and
    Migration 36
  Slavery and Free Labor 38

Reform and Social Change 42
  Labor Unrest 42
  Religious and Political
    Reform 43
  The Expansion of Public
    Education 44
  The Expansion of Suffrage 44
  Moral Reform 45

Social Welfare Programs and
Services 47

Institutionalization 47

Child Saving 53

Retreat from the Almshouse 56

DOCUMENTS: The Pre–Civil War
Period 59
  *The First Annual Report of the
    Managers of the Society for the
    Prevention of Pauperism in the
    City of New York, 1818* 60
  *Constitution, By-Laws, &c., of
    the Female Orphan Asylum of
    Portland, Maine, 1828* 67

1946- CAROL M. HIGHSMITH ARCHIVE, PRINTS & PHOTOGRAPHS DIVISION, LIBRARY OF CONGRESS, LC-DIG-HIGHSM-13382.

The American Revolution was a political watershed for the United States. American society was in the middle of a social and economic transition that had begun by the end of the 17th century and would not be completed until the Civil War. The result of this process— the emergence of a liberal, capitalist society—would touch every part of American culture, from the work people did to the beliefs they held to the institutions they developed. It held particular significance for the poor and needy. Whereas in the 18th century, the poor had been seen as an organic part of society, by the 19th century, they were increasingly cast as *deviants*—outside the normal social order and in need of reform.

During the years from the Revolution to the Civil War, well-off Americans alternated between an optimistic hope that they could improve the poor by changing their environment, and fear that only by containing the poor could they prevent them from threatening the entire society. Whether in hope or fear, the actions of the powerful during these years defined the problems of the poor in a way that did little to address their fundamental life challenges. Instead, the powerful constructed a variety of new institutions to contain deviant populations. Although they often used utopian language focused on perfecting the functioning of society, a more coercive reality lay underneath the appealing language.

The emergence of a liberal, capitalist society, however, was not complete. Although most of the nation expanded democratic institutions and the operation of economic markets during these years, the states of the American South moved in the opposite direction. The cotton economy, which hardly existed at the time of the Revolution, became the region's dominant industry. The world that cotton planters constructed to support that crop led them to revive slavery and contain democratic forces.

CHAPTER OUTLINE *(Continued)*

President Franklin Pierce: Veto Message—An Act Making a Grant of Public Lands to the Several States for the Benefit of Indigent Insane Persons, 1854   73

Still, one piece of unfinished business left over from the Revolution could not be avoided. The issue of slavery and race—the foundation of American prosperity and the greatest challenge to its political creed—slowly but inexorably overshadowed all other issues. Ultimately, the nation was forced to endure its greatest tragedy so that the "peculiar institution" of American slavery could be eliminated.

With their declaration of independence from England and the beginning of the Revolutionary War, the now-independent states established a loose confederation for governance. But the Articles of Confederation—The United States' first constitution—gave the central government few powers during its first decade. James Madison, predicting its failure, cited the confederation as "nothing more than a treaty of amity of commerce and of alliance between ... independent and Sovereign States."[1]

Not everyone agreed with Madison. Many democrats had fought Britain to reduce centralized authority. The Articles retained broad support as part of the Revolutionary legacy, but more conservative members of the political elite saw them as fundamentally flawed. They engineered a constitutional convention in 1787—ostensibly to revise the Articles—that proposed an entirely new and more centralized form of government. Its proponents accepted a set of compromises with skeptics to protect individual liberties—the Bill of Rights—to gain their support, and then fought a two-year battle at the state level to ratify the proposal. What we now know is the U.S. Constitution established a new government, which began to function on March 4, 1789, when George Washington took the oath of office in New York as president.

The Declaration of Independence, the Articles of Confederation, and the Constitution were based on limited democratic ideals. In the colonies, only adult, white men of property were eligible to vote. During the first three decades of the century, the property requirements were eliminated. Most white men could vote, but women, blacks, and Native Americans could not. Tribes were ruled to be "domestic dependent nations," and Native Americans were thus considered aliens, not citizens. As the Constitution had specified, the census—the official enumeration of the population of the United States, which was the basis for the number of representatives of each state in Congress—counted slaves as three-fifths of a person. As a result, Southern states were allotted Congressmen and electoral votes based on their enslaved population. Native Americans did not count at all.[2]

The Preamble of the Constitution of the United States cited the promotion of the general welfare as one of the reasons for forming the new government. Nevertheless, there was no mention of social welfare concerns among the carefully enumerated powers of the government's legislative body, the Congress. Since the Constitution specifically reserved to the states such powers as had not been delegated to the central government, providing for the social welfare needs of families and individuals remained the responsibility of the separate states, much as it had been the responsibility of the separate colonies. A public-private partnership of local government and charities was the typical means of addressing want and deprivation.

The years between the ratification of the Constitution of the United States and the outbreak of the Civil War were years of major political, economic, and social changes. These changes were accompanied by, and in turn furthered, rapid population growth, enormous geographical expansion, productivity increases on the farm and in the workshops and factories, and heated political and ideological struggles. In 1800, the United States still sought to shake off its identity as former colonies; by 1860, the country could be considered a world power. The pre–Civil War period was one of excitement and turmoil, expansion and recession, opportunity and frustration, and exhilaration and discontent. It was a period of rapid change necessarily affecting the welfare of individuals and families.

SOCIAL AND ECONOMIC CONDITIONS

Population Growth and Migration

Population growth, composition, and migration make up one aspect of the pre–Civil War transformation.[3] In 1790, families had many children, and the ordinary life span was quite short. One result was that less than 2 percent of the population was 65 years or older and the median age was only 16. Those who survived until old age were revered by the colonists. At public meetings, the best seats were assigned to the oldest men, then to the oldest women. Wealth, race, and gender counted, but age remained an important mark of status.

By 1860, despite continued immigration, the population had aged. Old age was more common, and the median age of the population rose to about 20 years. Seniority, for example, was no longer the basis for preferential seating in the town's meetinghouse. Increasingly, wealth, income, and property became the essential measures of social status. Clothing styles for men reflected the shift in generational power. Wigs were replaced by hairpieces to make men look younger; jackets were cut to be narrow at the waist and broad at the shoulders, with straight backs. In contrast, throughout the 19th century, the desire to hide women's bodies and demonstrate their sexual subordination prevailed over the glorification of youthful styles.[4]

By 1860, the African American population stood at 4.5 million, of whom 4 million were slaves. As early as 1774, the Continental Congress had prohibited further importation of slaves into the colonies after December 1, 1775. This prohibition was not entirely successful, and the question was again debated at the Federal Convention of 1787, where it was agreed that the further importation of slaves would cease after January 1, 1808.

The end of the slave trade as mandated in the Constitution restricted the growth of the African American population to the difference between births and deaths, while white immigration continued. Still, compared to most slave populations in the Western Hemisphere, the African American population continued to grow. As white immigration continued, however, African Americans' share of the population fell from 19 percent in 1800 to 14 percent in 1860. In 1860, the census enumerated 4,521,000 persons, of whom 3,954,000 were slaves. And the country had become more urban. In 1800, only 6 percent of the population lived in urban areas; by 1860, almost 20 percent did so.

The total population of the country (excluding Native Americans, who were not counted) numbered 3,929,000 in 1790, the year of the first U.S. census. By 1800, the population had risen by 34 percent to about 5,297,000, of whom 1,002,000—19 percent—were nonwhite and 322,000—6 percent—lived in urban areas. By 1830, on the eve of massive migrations, especially from Ireland and Germany, the total population stood at 12,901,000. By 1840, it reached 17,120,000; in 1850, it was 23,261,000; and in 1860, it was 31,513,000.

▶ **Watch this video on the slave trade.**

Why did the United States end the international slave trade peaceably in 1808, but had to fight a Civil War to end slavery?

Population growth had been the result of several factors, including resident births and the purchase, annexation, and cession of populated territories. The most important cause of the population explosion, however, was the extraordinary wave of immigration beginning during the 1830s, when 538,381 immigrants arrived in the United States. Immigration rose to 1,427,337 during the 1840s and peaked during the 1850s with the arrival of 2,814,554 individuals. Even the Civil War did not deter migrants; 2 million immigrants arrived during the 1860s.

Of the total of 1,427,337 immigrants to the United States during the 1840s, nearly 900,000 arrived from Ireland and 400,000 from Germany. Spurred by famine in the former and political repression in the latter, immigration from these two countries continued at extremely high levels during the 1850s, when together they accounted for 87 percent of immigrants. Almost all the immigrants landed at entry points between Baltimore and Boston, and most remained in the Northern region of the country, where they congregated in cities. The Irish, coming primarily from a background of peasant farming, with little education, moved into canal and railroad construction, domestic service, and the developing textile industry. The Germans were more likely to be farmers or skilled artisans and moved more quickly into steadier and better-paying jobs.

Whether from Ireland or Germany, the immigrants were often perceived as a threat to resident Americans. The Irish were predominantly Catholic and the Germans were often Catholic or Jewish in an overwhelmingly Protestant country. Moreover, they came at a time of initial industrial conflict. The sudden availability of workers ready to take employment at lower than generally accepted wages and the introduction, by German immigrants especially, of radical political philosophies upset American labor and industry alike. Further, many of the immigrants arrived in need of immediate employment or emergency financial aid. The addition of newcomers to the rolls of public charges provoked opposition and agitation against them.

Whether from Ireland or Germany, the immigrants were often perceived as a threat to resident Americans.

Xenophobia—the fear of foreigners—has a long history in the United States. Fear of the influence of the French Revolution led the Federalist Party to pass the Naturalization Act of 1795, which increased the residence requirement for naturalization for free, white persons to 5 years from the 2 previously specified. Three years later, the Alien and Sedition Acts legislated 14 years for residency, required registration of all aliens, and gave the president the power to expel any alien deemed dangerous. Although most of this legislation was repealed and residence requirements returned to the 5-year level, the early years of the republic showed deep distrust of foreigners. The immigrant wave of the 1840s and 1850s gave impetus to the American Party—called "Know Nothings" because of its origins in secret fraternal orders—built on anti-immigrant, anti-Catholic, and antiblack feelings.

As in the present day, however, nativist sentiment was balanced by the embrace of cosmopolitanism by many Americans. The immigrant restrictions of the 1790s were quickly repealed after the fall of the Federalist Party in 1800. Although many "Know Nothing" voters moved into the nascent Republican Party in 1856, the new party firmly rejected anti-immigrant rhetoric.[5]

Although population growth between 1790 and 1860 was most spectacular in the Northern areas of the country, growth occurred in the South as well. In 1850, the population of the 15 Southern states (Delaware, Maryland, Virginia, North Carolina, South Carolina, Georgia, Florida, Alabama, Mississippi, Louisiana, Tennessee, Kentucky, Missouri, Arkansas, and Texas) was about 10 million, of whom 3 million were slaves. This slave population was an increase from the 1.5 million counted in 1820. Between 1820 and 1850, the number of free blacks had increased from 234,000 to 434,000. Although the slave population was ignored in public and involuntary social welfare measures, its effect upon the well-being of the country, as reflected in economic and social reform activity, was enormous.

As the black and white population grew, the Native American population was devastated. Wars, diseases, broken treaties, the loss of homeland, and the destruction of the game upon which many Native people depended upon for food and clothing all took their tolls. The Creeks, Seminoles, Cherokees, and countless other tribes were in dire trouble. Many were pushed out of the East and beyond the Mississippi to live. The reservation replaced the range, at an enormous cost in population, lifestyle, and culture for the native population. The federal government—through the Removal Act of 1830—forced the removal of the Choctaw, Cherokee, and several other tribes to territories west of the Mississippi in what came to be known as the "Trail of Tears."

Population growth prior to the Civil War was matched by territorial expansion. Territorial additions included the Northwest Territory, secured by treaty with Great Britain in 1783; the Louisiana Purchase from France in 1803; the Florida Purchase from Spain in 1819; the Texas annexation in 1845; the Oregon and Mexican territories secured by treaties with Great Britain and Mexico in 1846 and 1848, respectively; and the Gadsden Purchase from Mexico in 1853. Thus, by 1860, the country's land area reached to the Pacific Ocean, and its Northern and Southern borders were fixed. The 13 original states had increased to 33. In 1790, the original 13 states contained 94 percent of the total population. Only 250,000 of a total population of 4 million persons lived in the land west of the boundaries of these states. In 1860, half the population lived in trans-Appalachian regions despite the heavy European immigration into the Northeast.[6]

Slavery and Free Labor

The territorial expansion of the United States stoked regional tensions. Beginning with the Missouri Compromise of 1820, which allowed Missouri to enter as a slave state while Maine became a free state, the expansion of territory and admission of states pitted the North and South against one another. Many Northerners opposed the Mexican-American War of 1846–48 because it expanded opportunities for slavery's expansion.

Although western expansion and development was encouraged on ideological grounds, economic realities drove political decisions. The invention of the cotton gin in 1793 had made cotton production a base of the Southern economy and slavery the most profitable form of labor. The economy of New England was shaped by the introduction of the spinning jenny and the power loom, which brought together the processes of spinning and weaving in a single establishment. In contrast, the Southern planter class controlled the most fertile land and the enslaved labor force to work it. The textile factories of the North were smaller operations; their need for labor was fluctuating by season and by the business cycle. As a group, these industrialists required the availability of a large but free labor force, a group for which they need feel no responsibility during economic slowdowns.

The New England and Southern states quite naturally moved to opposing sides on questions related to territorial expansion and to the acceptance of new states into the Union. The cultivation of cotton lent itself not only to the use of slave labor but also to the creation of large plantations. What is more, the agricultural system used to produce cotton accelerated soil depletion, so the Southern planter class saw territorial expansion as a necessity. New England, with its concern for a large, readily available supply of free labor, was initially opposed to territorial expansion because of the threat such an expansion represented to the retention of an adequate labor pool on the Eastern Seaboard.

Although industry expanded before the Civil War, the United States remained a rural and agricultural nation. As a result, government land policy remained an arena for political dispute. The federal government's policy on selling public lands became increasingly flexible and generous during the pre–Civil War period. Originally, the government's policy was to sell only large tracts of land, a policy that favored large landholders. In 1800, and again in 1820, the government reduced the minimum number of acres required for purchase. This policy, which encouraged small landholders, was further liberalized in 1832 when the government recognized the right of preemption that permitted squatters to take possession of land without a cash-down payment and to pay for it later.

Today, it is hard to imagine that controversies over tariffs—the taxes levied against imported goods—could provoke widespread political upheaval. Yet, even before the antislavery campaign increased regional tensions, tariffs almost tore the country apart. Northern manufacturing states were in severe competition with Great Britain to buy their raw material—cotton—and to sell their products—textiles. The North sought high-tariff protections against the importation of foreign-made goods. The South, on the other hand, seeking high prices for raw cotton and low prices for finished products, favored low tariffs and competition among industries, domestic and foreign.

The issue came to a head in 1832 when South Carolina declared that the tariff laws of 1828 and 1832 were unconstitutional and would not be enforced in the state. President Andrew Jackson took a strong stand against the idea that individual states could nullify federal laws and succeeded in gaining congressional support for a Force Bill that authorized him to use federal troops to enforce the law (Figure 3.1). This strong stance—plus the passage of a less severe compromise tariff law in 1833—resolved the crisis. Yet, the nullification crisis became the template for the regional struggle over the balance of federal and states' rights that would continue until the Civil War.

Figure 3.1 Although Andrew Jackson was associated with a widening of democratic values for white men, he also developed a reputation for his crimes against Native Americans both before and during his presidency.

The expansion of cotton production in the South and its use in the textile industries of Great Britain and the North were the key economic drivers of the period. In 1792, the year before the invention of the cotton gin, the annual production of cotton was about 6,000 bales. In 1794, the year after the cotton gin's invention, production rose to 17,000 bales. By 1800, 73,000 bales were being produced, and by 1860, 3,841,000 bales.[7] Just as the South's production of raw cotton outstripped the country's production of all other agricultural products, New England's production of finished cotton goods outstripped the country's manufacture of all other goods. The value of cotton products, which stood at $46 million in 1840, rose to $116 million in 1860.[8] The needs of these two areas spurred the development of the Middle Atlantic states, which produced farm commodities, meat and dairy products, lumber, and other necessities. In addition, the Middle Atlantic states became the shipping and banking centers for the country. Truly, the South, New England, and the Middle Atlantic states were closely joined, and the tie that bound was made of cotton. The digging of canals and building of railroads opened the West, an important factor in its own right, but additionally so in view of the way in which its resources served to strengthen the dependence of the other areas, one upon the other.

The rise of King Cotton extinguished the hope that African American slavery would die a natural death.

The rise of King Cotton extinguished the hope that African American slavery would have a natural death. At the end of the Revolution, Northern whites that objected to slavery could tell themselves that it was an archaic institution that could not survive long in an independent nation. With the rise of cotton, slavery became the bedrock of the entire American economy. It would take a bloody social conflict to bring it to an end.

The economic realities that led the South and New England to different solutions to the questions of labor supply had inevitable consequences for the social well-being of their workers. The dominance of slave labor in the South slowed the growth of public welfare institutions. Slaves were considered chattel or property, the protection or exploitation of which was totally the responsibility of the slave master. Free blacks were left to help themselves. Self-help among the slaves was common, but the very fact of being owned left with the owner the responsibility for maintaining his property in working order. An apologist for slavery defined it as a "system of labor which exchanges subsistence for work."

> Slavery makes all work, and it insures homes, food and clothing for all. It permits no idleness, and it provides for sickness, infancy, and old age. It allows no tramping or skulking, and it knows no pauperism.[9]

Outside the plantation, there were stretches of territory cultivated by small farmers without slave labor. These "hardy yeomen" occupied areas generally not suitable for growing cotton, but quite suitable for raising cattle and for cultivating corn and wheat. As a class, they were prosperous and independent. There remained only the poor whites, also farmers, but because they were landless or owned the most worthless, worn-out land, their subsistence was most precarious. Nevertheless, they were not directly subjected to the economic fluctuations created by the commercialization of agriculture.

Despite the overall picture of self-sufficiency, there were Southerners who found themselves in need. The poor whites, although generally capable of independence, were one such group. But in developing Southern towns, there were others—abandoned and orphaned children, mulattoes, freed slaves. The dominance of slavery, however, blocked the development of public welfare institutions in the South.

Destitution in the North during the pre–Civil War period was more directly related to urbanization, industrialization, and the development of the factory system. In 1791, the year of Hamilton's *Report of Manufacture*, household manufacture of wool and cotton cloth was occurring in all of the states and could still be characterized as "a vast scene."[10] The first successful cotton mill, using the principle of the spinning jenny, had already been put into operation in Pawtucket, Rhode Island, and by 1809, 62 mills were operating in New England, with 25 more in the process of construction.[11] New England had thus become the textile manufacturing center of the country. The introduction of the power loom in the factory at Waltham, Massachusetts, was the impetus for further development.

The large-scale production of cotton textiles required, first of all, the construction of factories so expensive that their costs had to be borne by absentee owner-investors. Operation of the factories required the recruitment of large numbers of workers to towns. In New England, the workers recruited during the early years of industrialization were young women from farm families living in surrounding areas. To attract these young women, the factory owners erected dormitories or saw to the development of boarding homes, where social, religious, and educational activities for workers could be planned and supervised.[12]

The labor force of young women expanded as a result of difficulties in the New England agricultural economy. The growing ease with which young women were recruited for factory work paralleled the rise of commercial farming, the decline of the household manufacturing of cloth, and the transfer to the market of services formerly performed at home. The reality of large families as a liability could, for the moment, be mitigated by the fact that girls could earn wages for use in an increasingly commercial society. Harriet Martineau, a traveler to the United States in 1835, reported her visit to "the corporate factory-establishment at Waltham":

> Most of the girls live in houses provided by the corporation, which accommodate from six to eight each. When sisters come to the mill, it is a common practice for them to bring their mother to keep house for them and some of their companions, in a dwelling built by their own earnings. In this case, they save enough out of their board to clothe themselves, and have their two or three dollars a week to spare. Some have thus cleared off mortgages from their fathers' farms; others have educated the hope of the family at college; and many are rapidly accumulating an independence.[13]

Young, native-born women took factory jobs for only a few years. Soon, immigrants from French, Canada, and other nations replaced them. Often, parents and children worked in the same factories, representing the first permanent factory labor force. At that point, native-born women moved into occupations such as teaching. If financially able, they moved into a new genteel ethos of homemaking.

America's first industrial workers were not a social class; the young women who worked in factories eventually left to marry or pursue other work. By the 1830s, however, they had been replaced by a more permanent group of workers—often immigrants—whose prospects for advancement were limited. The risks that we associate with industrialization—unemployment, disability, and displacement—became a new reality on the social landscape.[14]

The success of the textile factories fostered the development of other manufactures required for the maintenance of that industry and that industry's employees. The "factory system" was applied to other industries and spread rapidly throughout the New England and Middle Atlantic states, with the result that centers of considerable size, offering employment to males as well as females, to skilled as well as unskilled laborers, developed. Whereas 202,000 persons lived in urban centers in 1790, 6.2 million were living in cities in 1860. The growth of older cities demonstrates what was happening.[15] New York City's population grew from 123,000 in 1820 to 805,000 in 1860; Philadelphia's jumped from 112,000 in 1820 to 562,000 in 1860; Boston's went from 43,000 to 177,000;

and Baltimore's from 62,000 to 212,000, during the same years. In addition, many new cities sprang up not only in New England and the Middle Atlantic states but in the West and the South as well.

Industrialization and urbanization led to many problems for which social welfare measures—particularly financial aid—were necessary. The expansion of wage labor was associated with increased mobility of the labor force. With extended kinship ties frequently broken by distance and with adults away from home at work, families were more and more subject to forces beyond their control and dependent upon services supplied from outside the family unit. The hazards of the developing market economy in which families depended on wages and in which industrial competition kept wages low and employment uncertain were aggravated by a series of economic depressions—one, 1815–21; another, 1837–43; still another, 1857–59. Only the years 1850–56 showed vigorous, sustained recovery. The long stretch between 1815 and 1859 was a difficult time for individuals and families who were not physically or psychologically free to move to the open lands and opportunities of the West. These people included many immigrant families; disabled veterans of the War of 1812, the Mexican War, and the Indian Wars; the ill and disabled; children who had been orphaned or abandoned; and older people who had no children or spouses to support them and who found themselves forced into involuntary retirement because of ill health or unemployment.

> ? Assess your comprehension of "Social and Economic Conditions" by completing this quiz.

REFORM AND SOCIAL CHANGE

The emergence of large reform movements during the antebellum period represented a split vision of American society. On the one hand, many movements associated with the middle class saw their society as fundamentally sound but in need of some improvement around the margins. On the other hand, other movements raised the fear that America was corrupt at its core. With the rise of evangelical Protestantism after the second Great Awakening of the 1820s, the conviction that Americans needed to attack sin propelled a variety of movements against alcohol, prostitution, and other forms of vice. Ultimately, this same sensibility would drive the movement to abolish slavery.

Labor Unrest

Much of the response to unemployment and inequality of income distribution took the path of reform activities. Such activities supported a view of the basic soundness of the economic order at the same time that they demonstrated new convictions about the potential for change of individuals and of aspects of the social structure. As early as 1827, with the formation of the Mechanics' Union Trade Association in Philadelphia, an effort was made to organize all skilled artisans. Although attempts at a combined national association failed, labor entered the depression starting in 1837 with at least five national trade unions: cordwainers, comb makers, carpenters, weavers, and printers.[16] These unions, and the workers' political parties that developed during the 1830s, demanded action in regard to a number of reform and protection issues:

1. Equal and universal free education
2. The availability of public lands for settlement
3. The depreciation of child labor and apprenticeship abuses

4. Restrictions on competitive prison labor

5. Better working conditions for women

6. Establishment of a 10-hour workday without any decreases in wages

7. Governmental control of currency

8. The right to organize

9. Provision of jobs for the unemployed in public works programs[17]

They did not demand a change in basic property relationships, but they did demand a larger share of the product of the existing economic system. What they objected to was not private property, but the loss of independence that wage labor entailed. Indeed, for many male trade unionists, the new manufacturing systems were a core challenge to their manhood.[18]

Whatever hardships labor suffered, the promise of a new world for common people seemed real enough. Small establishments—manufacturers, tradesmen, and entrepreneurs—dominated the economy. Similarly, westward migration had produced large numbers of small, independent landowners. It appeared to resident Americans and immigrants alike that the country's economic growth and geographic expansion were of their own making and that their own toil had produced a situation in which dreams could come true.

Religious and Political Reform

The generation of the American Revolution was typically motivated by secular beliefs, but in the early decades of the 19th century, American Protestantism made a comeback. Yet, as it returned, Protestants embraced a more optimistic and humanistic set of beliefs. The colonial view of humanity as predestined to damnation gave way to a view of people as having the power to change, if properly led. The new age of reason meant that individuals could respond to the godliness of their own nature and could control their own destinies, including economic and social welfare.

The major religious movement of the early 19th century was the "Second Great Awakening." During the 1820s and 1830s, a wave of religious fervor swept the country, leading to mass revival meetings and conversions. Upstate New York experienced these so frequently that it became known as the "burnt-over district." Women took a leading role in the Second Great Awakening, although often barred from becoming ministers. The impulse to cleanse society of sin encouraged women to pursue campaigns against a variety of evils, which led to many of the reform movements discussed below.

During the 1820s and 1830s, a wave of religious fervor swept the country, leading to mass revival meetings and conversions. Upstate New York experienced these so frequently that it became known as the "burnt-over district."

With the election of Andrew Jackson to the presidency in 1828, Jacksonian democracy symbolized the possibility of egalitarianism and a spur to its further achievement. Elections became more frequent, with many state and local offices changing hands every year. After a period of political disorganization—symbolized by the 1824 presidential election in which no candidate won a majority of the Electoral College—the Jackson campaign organized the Democratic Party with party operatives in every state united around an ideology that stressed limited government and a suspicion of special interests that sought to benefit from government action. Legislatures reduced or eliminated restrictions of the enfranchisement of white men—especially property requirements—although women would have to wait nearly a century to secure the right to vote.

Areas of reform activity included the extension of suffrage, temperance, more effective poor relief, humane treatment for the insane, rehabilitation of criminals, child saving, and, of course, the drive for the abolition of slavery.

The Expansion of Public Education

A large part of the reform effort centered on free public education, which for some was seen as a weapon in the battle for egalitarianism, for democracy. Horace Mann labeled education "the great equalizer of the conditions of men—the balance-wheel of the social machinery."[19] For Native Americans, "education and conversion usually went hand in hand," with religious conversion the dominant force.[20] Only through education could the rich and poor be brought together.

> Now surely nothing but universal education can counterwork this tendency to the domination of capital and the servility of labor . . . But, if education be equably diffused, it will draw property after it by the strongest of all attractions: for such a thing never did happen, and never can happen, as that an intelligent and practical body of men should be permanently poor. Property and labor in different classes are essentially antagonistic; but property and labor in the same class are essentially fraternal.[21]

There was a widespread agreement that "universal and complete" education "would do more than all things else to obliterate factitious distinctions in society." Democracy could be real if the poor could be made the equal of the rich. Education could instill the means and will to make it so.

Yet, educational expansion could also serve non-egalitarian purposes. In addition to expanding literacy, public education taught regularity and the importance of following instructions, important skills for an emerging working class. The establishment of public high schools in large cities by midcentury provided public resources for the training of an occupational elite. It would not be until the 20th century that high schools served a majority of the population.

This drive for education was left to the states for development and moved from New England to the West, where Jacksonian political democracy was most advanced. The Middle Atlantic states—New York, Pennsylvania, New Jersey, and Delaware—experienced more difficulty, but by midcentury, these states had permissive statutes allowing for the establishment of schools by localities. In the South, no statewide systems of public education were in operation before the Civil War.

The Expansion of Suffrage

The opening of the West must be credited with the rapid advance of white male suffrage.

> As people went westward and formed new states, they made new constitutions. In the western country there were few great differences in wealth . . . much the same state of poverty and hope. Naturally, under such conditions . . . all were equally capable of bearing the responsibility of voting or governing. The new states of the days after the War of 1812, Indiana, Illinois, Alabama, and Missouri, provided white manhood suffrage though Mississippi clung to a tax provision.[22]

Connecticut liberalized its suffrage qualifications in 1818. Massachusetts followed in 1820. In 1821, New York legislated universal male suffrage, even for free blacks if they owned property. Other states followed and male political democracy became a reality.

Women did not achieve legal and political equality with men, but the reform period was the beginning of a long campaign for women's rights. In 1848, the first Women's Rights Convention was held in Seneca Falls, New York. A "Declaration of Sentiments," modeled after the Declaration of Independence, was adopted. Women demanded equal civil and political rights and began the long struggle for suffrage.

Not so clearly recognized was the effect of industrialization and urbanization upon the economic structure of the family. The technological revolution, which gained such momentum during the pre–Civil War period, spelled the beginning of a decline in farming as a chief means of support and the virtual end of the family system of manufacturing. Not only had wages, *per se*, become a basic means of family support, but these wages were being earned away from home. From this economic reality evolved separate worlds for men and women. All that went on outside the home—particularly in the areas of work and politics—was the world of men. For the middle class, the world of women centered in the home, the family, and the church. The pastoral letter read on July 28, 1837, from the pulpit of all Congregational churches in New England described a proper woman operating in her "proper sphere."

Watch this video on the Seneca Falls convention of 1948.

Why was the right to vote a controversial topic for a women's rights meeting?

> The appropriate duties and influence of women . . . are unobtrusive and private . . . . When the mild, dependent, softening influence of women upon the sternness of man's opinion is fully exercised, society feels the effects of it in a thousand forms. The power of woman is in her dependence, flowing from . . . that weakness which God has given her for her protection, and which keeps her in those departments of life that form the character of individuals and of the nation.[23]

Moral Reform

Although barred from formal politics, women often led reform movements, including temperance, suffrage, and the abolition of slavery. They moved from a concern for the rooting out of individual imperfections that would lead to unhappy family living to a demand for explicit political recognition and power, and then to larger social issues. Often, their reform efforts were tied to an implicit critique of male-dominated social habits, as was the case with the Temperance Movement.

Spurred by the growth in corn production by the pioneer farmers of the Ohio River Valley and the burgeoning distilling industry of the East, whiskey became abundant and cheap—and drinking whiskey is something of a national pastime for men, women, and children.[24] During the first three decades of the 19th century, annual per capita consumption increased to more than five gallons. After 1830, as a result of the Temperance Movement and of stiff federal taxation, it dropped to less than two gallons per capita.[25] Before that, however, the proliferation of unregulated taverns that encouraged drinking, particularly on the part of male laborers, aggravated perceptions of social chaos and disorder in the lower class, especially immigrants. The loss of time from work because of drunkenness on the part of the male breadwinner and the habit of spending time at the saloon on payday were real threats to family well-being. The unavailability of adequate jobs for women made them dependent upon men for the family's support. The physical abuse that often accompanied the drinking added to the urgency of temperance as "a matter of women's rights as well as a religious and humanitarian reform."[26]

The American Society for the Promotion of Temperance was founded in 1826 and engaged in widespread propaganda against intemperance. The Temperance Movement involved itself in social and political activities, and by 1860, it boasted a membership of a number of formal social groups and more than a million individuals. One state (Maine) had voted for prohibition. The Temperance Movement would become more vocal and politically stronger after the Civil War—eventually evolving into a demand for Prohibition—but the attention given to the problem during the antebellum period was an evidence of a growing concern about the relation of drinking to unemployment and to pauperism.

During the 1830s and 1840s, thousands of local and state temperance societies were formed with the intention of regulating or prohibiting the sale of liquor. While these societies generally had women's auxiliaries appended, an independent women's gesture was made when Amelia Bloomer founded the newspaper *The Lily*. In her first editorial, Bloomer wrote:

> It is WOMAN that speaks through the LILY. It is upon an important subject, too, that she comes before the public to be heard. Intemperance is the great foe to her peace and happiness.[27]

Tales of victimized women, of victimized families, led Bloomer and *The Lily* to an alliance with those more specifically focused on women's rights.

The efforts of *The Lily* were not isolated. Middle- and upper-class women, spurred by evangelical fervor and optimism, turned to a variety of moral reform movements— like the crusade against prostitution. It was not difficult to see these moral reform efforts as a thinly veiled criticism of dominant male culture. Although only a small minority of women would move from this criticism to overt feminism, the moral reform efforts of the antebellum era are a critical stage in the emergence of a distinctive women's perspective in social welfare.

The Temperance Movement addressed itself to the economic costs of drinking and also served as a reflection of the crusading, religious spirit of the era, an era of striving for perfection and beauty as a response to the reality and harshness of a changing society. The democratic, educated, temperate, spiritual individual was the ideal, and reform activity was an acknowledgment of human perfectibility as well as a spur to the accomplishment of aspirations. For some, the larger world seemed too oppressive, and they withdrew to utopias such as Brook Farm or Walden Pond or to the intellectual and metaphysical world of transcendentalism. For others, the reform of people and of institutions that stifled progress was cause enough for the good fight.

The assurance of opportunity and liberation underlay the zeal of adherents to particular causes and provided the moral force that brought Quakers, Transcendentalists, free blacks, activist women, and reformers of all types together in the abolitionist cause. The new religious humanitarianism, the growing democratic thrust, and the moral force surrounding black uprisings on behalf of freedom made abolition the central and urgent core of the Northern reform movement. At the same time, in the South, the principles of Jeffersonian democracy and its apologetic approach to slavery lost out to an aggressive ideological defense. The egalitarian leadership of the Revolutionary generation passed from the moderate Virginians to the extremists of South Carolina, and eventually the aristocratic worldview that represented the interests of a small group of planters prevailed. The white South united in an effort to maintain and extend slavery.

Abolitionism pulled together many strands of the reform era. An optimistic view of human nature—perfectionism—made the existence of human bondage that much more obnoxious. If the solution to the labor problem of the North was expanded opportunity for free labor, then the expansion of slavery into the West was intolerable. Although Southerners often chided the North for its treatment of the poor, Northerners continued to see the extension of a liberal, capitalist social order as the solution to most of the nation's ills. Ultimately, this vision could not be reconciled with the enslavement of 4 million human beings.

The Temperance Movement addressed itself to the economic costs of drinking and also served as a reflection of the crusading, religious spirit of the era, an era of striving for perfection and beauty as a response to the reality and harshness of a changing society.

? Assess your comprehension of "Reform and Social Change" by completing this quiz.

SOCIAL WELFARE PROGRAMS AND SERVICES

For the most part, reform during the pre–Civil War period was geared to the reform of individuals—not to reform of systems—and the effort was to find an environment in which individual changes might be encouraged. Increasingly, reformers turned to formal institutions as a means to address a variety of social problems, including crime, mental illness, and poverty.

Institutionalization

The rise of formal institutions as the primary response to social problems had complex origins. Certainly, the religious fervor of the Second Great Awakening and the optimism of Jacksonian democracy played a role. At the same time, as society became more mobile, traditional, informal social control became less effective. Finally, the idea to simply lock up difficult and frightening individuals had appeal, whether or not it helped the incarcerated.

During the 18th century, criminals were often dealt with through the infliction of physical pain or social disgrace. Increasingly in the early 19th century, writers came to believe that criminality was a product of a bad environment, which led the perpetrators to their actions. It was reasoned, then, that removing criminals from these bad influences would bring about a change in their character. The penitentiary was born as a means to use social isolation as a means of reforming prisoners. The New York penitentiary in Auburn and Eastern State Penitentiary in Philadelphia became the models for this approach. At Eastern State, prisoners were intended to remain in solitary confinement during their entire stay, although problems with overcrowding undermined the intent of its designers.

> This rare 1929 film gives you a feel for what life in Eastern State Penitentiary was like in the early 20th century.
>
> How do these conditions compare to the ideals of penitentiary life when Eastern State was first established?
>
> https://www.youtube.com/watch?v=jcN0lhDiw-U

The "insane asylum" also sprung from some advocates' belief in the effectiveness of institutionalization. The memorials written by pioneer reformer Dorothea L. Dix to encourage provisions for the construction of hospitals for the insane exemplified contemporary efforts to help people fulfill their potential through the use of specialized facilities. Institutions for the insane, children, the disabled, and the poor were particularly important in this regard, since they offered attention to classified needs and surcease from worldly instability. Dix wrote about "the mischiefs which result alike from religious, social, civil, and revolutionary excitements,"[28] excitements that characterized the pre–Civil War period and that were deemed responsible for the increase in mental illness. In the same vein, society was held responsible for an increase in crime and pauperism. The economic growth, geographic expansion, and extension of political democracy that had created a world of opportunity had also created a world of change, insecurity, and temptation. A society laying claim to a belief in human perfectibility but given to the creation of environmental and human disorders must provide order—and cure—for both. Institutions were thought to do just that.

During the pre–Civil War period, 32 hospitals were built for the insane. Their advocates believed they and other specialized institutions would, or could, cure both human and societal ills. Speaking particularly of the insane, Dix said:

> To confine the insane to persons whose education and habits do not qualify them for this charge, is to condemn them to mental death. . . .
>
> Under well-directed hospital care, *recovery is the rule—incurable* [italics in original] permanent insanity the exception. . . .

> But cure alone . . . is not the sole object of hospital care. . . . Of vast importance is the secure and comfortable provision for . . . the incurable insane. Their condition . . . is susceptible of amelioration, and of elevation to a state of comparative comfort and usefulness.[29]

Professional and humane treatment could cure, especially if that treatment was offered in an ordered, stable milieu that provided the sick individual with relief from excitement and with a sense of dignity. At the least, it would ameliorate symptoms. In either case, the conviction that individuals were capable of self-perfection required that they be treated as though they might perfect themselves. The institution became the answer to the individual's ailment and, simultaneously, in its exemplification of needed reform, the answer for society's ills.

The development of specialized institutions for dependent populations often began in the private sector, but its advocates ultimately looked to government for financial support. Dorothea Dix's Memorial to Congress in 1848 asking that 5 million acres of public land be given to the building of institutions for the insane was a challenge to the federal government to support reform. In time, Congress passed a bill allocating 10 million acres, taking cognizance of the needs not only of the insane but also of the blind and the deaf. President Pierce's veto in 1854 denied the federal government's responsibility for the social welfare of the country. In so doing, however, the veto upheld the historic responsibility of the states in matters of social welfare, when people could not sustain their own social well-being through self-endeavor or private charity.

[handwritten margin note: welfare responsibility of state]

> I readily and, I trust, feelingly acknowledge the duty incumbent on us all as men and citizens, and as among the highest and holiest of our duties, to provide for those who, in the mysterious order of Providence, are subject to want and to disuse of body or mind; but I can not find any authority in the Constitution for making the Federal Government the great almoner of public charity throughout the United States. . . . And if it were admissible . . . I can not avoid the belief that it would in the end be prejudicial . . . to the noble offices of charity. . . .
>
> If the several States, many of which have already laid the foundation of munificent establishments of local beneficence, and nearly all of which are proceeding to establish them, shall be led to suppose . . . that congress is to make provision for such objects, the fountains of charity will be dried up at home.[30]

The Pierce veto reinforced the pattern of state responsibility and of private charity dominance in social welfare.

The Pierce veto reinforced the pattern of state responsibility and of private charity dominance in social welfare. Veterans were the only group for which the federal government maintained direct responsibility. By 1790, Congress had taken over financial support for disabled veterans, veterans' widows, and orphans of veterans. Pensions were established for those groups during the Revolutionary War and were extended without serious questioning to participants of the War of 1812, the Seminole Indian Wars, and the Mexican War of 1846–48. The federal government eventually granted benefits to able-bodied veterans of each war. The pensions were small and the numbers of veterans covered were few because of the time that had elapsed between each war's end and congressional action. Nevertheless, at a time when the federal government was not involved in other social welfare activities, the veteran pensions established precedent that would expand with the increase in the number of veterans after the Civil War.

The view of poverty and of the plight of families in need changed very little from that of the Colonial period. Welfare legislation passed by the founding states had represented the continuation of colonial and provincial law. As new states entered the

Union, their public welfare provisions tended to copy those of established states. Unemployment and sharp increases in relief roles reconfirmed the ultimate responsibility of government for the relief of individual suffering but, at the same time, fostered an expanded definition of the responsibility of relatives. In most Northern states, grandchildren were legally responsible for the financial support of their grandparents; in many states, brothers and sisters were responsible for one another. The humane conviction that the poor were an inescapable obligation meant the provision of minimal, survival relief. But, more than ever, the view was that relief should be unnecessary and that government was obligated to minimize the cost to the taxpayer for the care of the poor. Only the legislation of the Southern and Western states tempered this view with any concern for the "comfort of the poor" or with legislation less restrictive than that of New England.

welfare not taxpayer rece

The more restrictive approach of the Northeastern and North Central states often was a response to the higher demands placed on the states by unemployment and destitution in more economically developed regions. In his 1824 report on the relief and settlement of the poor, John V. N. Yates, secretary for New York State, wrote that "populous places have at all times, been burdened with a larger proportion of paupers, than places where a thin or scattered population is found."[31] At the time of the report, well over half the population of the country was still living on the Atlantic Coast. The beginning influx of immigrants, who tended to remain in Eastern cities, aggravated the reaction to public outdoor relief giving, since they frequently were among the unemployed. Indeed, what appears to be an overreaction to public outdoor relief giving—New York City, for example, with a population of 203,000, had expended only $16,000 in 1830[32]— might have been a veiled stance against immigrants. Similarly, the influx of foreigners strengthened the argument that relief giving be left to benevolent societies and to the rich. The uncertainty of private charity was in itself considered a virtue, for it instilled in the newcomer that most American of all values, independence. Furthermore, private charity reinforced the old belief that the rich should expect deference from those of more modest means.

The belief that individuals were responsible for their poverty did not go completely unchallenged. Thomas Paine as early as 1792 and Mathew Carey in 1833 both saw poverty as related to the failure of the economic system. Paine urged the abolition of the Poor Laws and the establishment of a system of pensions, family allowances, subsidized education, and guaranteed employment.

> By the operation of this plan, the poor laws, those instruments of civil torture, will be superseded, and wasteful expense of litigation prevented. The hearts of the humane will not be shocked by ragged and hungry children, and the persons of seventy or eighty years of age, begging for bread. The dying poor will not be dragged from place to place to breathe their last, as a reprisal of parish upon parish. Widows will have a maintenance for their children, and not be carted away, on the death of their husbands, like culprits and criminals; and children will no longer be considered as increasing the distresses of their parents. The haunts of the wretched will be known, because it will be to their advantage, and the number of petty crimes, the offspring of distress and poverty, will be lessened. *The poor, as well as the rich, will then be interested in the support of government, and the cause and apprehension of riots and tumults will cease* [italics in original].[33]

Mathew Carey, a renowned pamphleteer on political and economic matters, responded to the charge that the poor rates and the aid of private philanthropy demoralize the poor and lead to corruption of pride in independence. His "appeal to the wealthy of the land" was written to refute "certain pernicious errors" that prevailed respecting the situation of the poor:

1. That every man, woman, and grown child, able and willing to work, may find employment.

2. That the poor, by industry, prudence, and economy, may at all times support themselves comfortably, without depending on eleemosynary aid. . . .

3. That their sufferings and distresses chiefly, if not wholly, arise from their idleness, their dissipation, and their extravagance.

4. That taxes for the support of the poor, and aid . . . by charitable individuals . . . are pernicious, as . . . they foster their idleness and improvidence, and thus produce, or at least increase the poverty and distress they are intended to relieve.[34]

Through comparisons of average annual wages and subsistence expenses for workers in selected occupations, Carey demonstrated the inevitable gaps between income and need—the necessity for financial supplementation. He demonstrated further that only 549 paupers had been supported with outdoor relief—that most suspected form of relief—in Philadelphia in 1830 and that the aid granted had averaged 46¼ cents per week—less than 7 cents per day. Pointing up how many of those supported were families with children, the disabled, or the aged, Carey argued that the poor rates and the aid of benevolent societies "far from producing the pernicious effects ascribed to them are imperiously necessary." Rather than look to the poor as the cause for the rise in poor rates, he concluded that one must look to the workings of a market economy in a society becoming increasingly dependent upon machines "for the low rate of wages is the root of mischief."

> A cause has been steadily and powerfully operating to increase the poor rates. . . .
> I mean the rapid and oppressive reduction of wages, consequent on the wonderful improvements in machinery. Manual labour succumbs in the conflict with steam and water power; and everything that supersedes the demand for that labour must increase competition, lower wages; produce distress and . . . increase the poor rates.[35]

The arguments of Paine and Carey looked both forward and backward. Like the Colonial Poor Laws, they retained an idea of community responsibility for needy residents. At the same time, they foreshadowed the idea that in a complex market society, wage-earners could not realistically prepare for the risks associated with accidents, disability, or old age. They helped to prevent the abolition of public relief in most localities despite the powerful forces aligned against it. So distinguished a leader as Josiah Quincy—congressman, mayor of Boston, and chairman of a state committee to study the pauper laws—considered the Poor Laws "too deeply riveted in the affections, or the moral sentiment of our people to be loosened by theories, however plausible."[36]

The physically disabled aside, public and private sources generally agreed that the causes of poverty were to be found in individual character flaws and in organizations that encouraged and promoted dependency. The New York Society for the Prevention of Pauperism was founded "to investigate and as far as possible to remove the causes of mendicity, to devise plans for ameliorating the condition of the poor and wretched, and to secure their successful operation."[37] The society successfully petitioned the Corporation of the City to appoint five members of that body to the Board of Managers of the society, thus encouraging the board "to calculate upon municipal countenance and aid." The first annual report (1818) of the society listed the causes of poverty as ignorance, idleness, intemperance, and imprudence (especially to marry). The report listed the following as tending to aggravate the causes of poverty: lotteries, pawnbrokers, houses of ill fame, and the numerous charitable institutions. Although public relief and private benevolence did admittedly relieve some misery and suffering, the long view of the society, as expressed by its president and its chairman of the Committee to Prepare a Report on the Subject of Pauperism, was that charity encouraged idleness and extravagance on the part of the poor, relaxed their need for industry, and eventually diminished that "wholesome anxiety to provide for the wants of a distant day, which alone can save . . . from a state of absolute dependence, and from becoming a burden to the community."[38]

New York City had already erected "buildings for eleemosynary purposes, at an expense of half a million dollars, and. . . . [was being called upon] for the annual distribution of 90,000 dollars more."[39] Failure to find a solution to the burgeoning expense of supporting an increasing number of paupers was frightening:

> Without a radical change in the principles upon which public alms have been usually distributed, helplessness and poverty would continue to multiply—demands for relief would become more and more importunate, the numerical difference between those who are able to bestow charity and those who sue for it, would gradually diminish, until the present system must fall under its own irresistible pressure, prostrating, perhaps, in its ruin, some of the pillars of the social order.[40]

The agreement that pauperism could be prevented and cured only by erecting "barriers against the encroachments of moral degeneracy" fostered a review of contemporary relief practices and a search for barriers that could, at one and the same time, save the poor from pauperism and the rich from taxation. Voluntary organizations, such as the New York Society for the Prevention of Pauperism and the Associations for Improving the Condition of the Poor that developed later in several large cities, sought "to remove the various causes of mendicity" primarily through friendly advice. The Association for Improving the Conditions of the Poor and its successors during the 19th century did little to reduce want. Indeed, they were often formed on the belief that treacherous paupers were taking advantage of less hard-hearted philanthropists. They did, however, support the view that the pauper should properly be excluded from the social order. If outdoor relief were abolished, they hoped, the pauper would have no alternative but to seek aid within the almshouse.

> The New York Society's Sub-Committee on Ignorance was charged as follows: "This Committee shall report the number of children who do not attend any school; the number of adults who cannot read; the number of families and individuals who do not attend public worship; and the causes which prevent."[41]

Ignorance and the lack of religious fervor—in the eyes of the Association—reinforced pauperism.

Dissatisfaction with public outdoor relief, especially of the able-bodied, focused on its effectiveness in relieving or preventing poverty. Many believed that cash assistance promoted the very opposite of its intended purpose. So strongly was this view held that the state of Delaware prohibited local outdoor relief. Philadelphia abolished it from 1827 to 1839 and Chicago from 1848 to 1858. Debates over the proper role of public relief were most intense where the problem was most serious, in the East. Many states, including Massachusetts, New York, New Hampshire, and Pennsylvania, formed commissions to study the problem. In their anxiety to ensure an appropriate work-spirit for the transient poor who might be employable, the reports tended to ignore the bulk of those receiving relief, the permanent poverty of children and the elderly.

In 1821 in Massachusetts, Josiah Quincy's "Report of the Committee to whom was Referred the Consideration of the Pauper Laws of this Commonwealth" placed in "strong light the objections to the entire principle of our existing pauper laws" but despaired of the laws being abolished. Among the committee's recommended principles for the operation of a relief system, two were particularly important:

1. That of all modes of providing for the poor, the most wasteful, the most expensive, and the most injurious to their morals and destructive of their industrious habits is that of supply in their own families.

2. That the most economical mode is that of Alms Houses; having the character of Work Houses, or Houses of Industry, in which work is provided for every degree of ability in the pauper; and thus the able poor made to provide, partially at least for their own support, and also to the support, or at least the comfort of the impotent poor.[42]

In summary, the report stressed the responsibility of society to diminish pauperism and recommended the use of a single administrative mechanism, the almshouse, for doing so—"denying for the most part all supply from public provision, except on condition of admission into the public institution."[43]

In 1823, in response to rising costs of relief, the Senate and Assembly of the State of New York resolved that the secretary of state study and report on the expenses and operation of the Poor Laws in New York, as well as in other states, for the purpose of suggesting improvements in the New York welfare system. Secretary Yates's report, submitted in February 1824, divided the poor of the state into *the permanent poor*, that is, those who received support regularly during the year studied, and *the occasional poor*, that is, those who received help during part of the year (perhaps briefly during the autumn and winter months). He found 6,896 of the first group, and 15,215 of the second. Of the total of 6,896 permanent poor, only 1,789, "though not in the vigor of life," could be considered capable of earning their subsistence. Among the permanent poor not capable of earning their subsistence were 2,604 children under 14 years of age. Yates did not specify the number of families represented by the 6,896 individuals classified as permanent poor, but he did assert that 1,585 of the total were men who had been reduced to that state by drinking and "of consequence, that their families . . . were reduced to the same penury and want."[44]

Yates reported four major findings: (1) the poor, when farmed out, were frequently treated with barbarity and neglect, (2) the education and morals of the children of paupers were almost wholly neglected, (3) there was no adequate provision for the employment of the poor for the inculcation of industrious habits, and (4) there was little attention being given to the disbursement of public funds appropriated for the support of the poor. As a single, total remedy for all these evils, Yates recommended the adoption of the "poorhouse plan" for every county of the state. In accordance with the plan, the poorhouses to be erected in each county would be houses of employment where paupers might be "maintained and employed . . . in some healthful labor, chiefly agricultural, their children to be carefully instructed, and at suitable age, to be put out to some useful business or trade." As for sturdy beggars or vagrants—most likely the occasional poor—they were to be confined to penitentiaries connected to the poorhouses and subjected to a regimen of discipline consisting of "a rigid diet, hard labor, employment at the stepping mill, or some treatment equally efficacious in restraining their vicious appetites and pursuits."

The recommendations of the Yates report called for a separation of the worthy and unworthy poor: long-term care in houses of employment for the former and short-term penitentiary or workhouse confinement for the latter. The two types of houses were to be physically joined to form a system of almshouse care for the poor.

> Until a system . . . can be devised, which with economy and humanity, will administer relief to the indigent and infirm, incapable of labor, provide employment for the idle, and impart instruction to the young and ignorant, little hope can be entertained of meliorating the condition of our poor or relieving the community from the growing evils of pauperism.[45]

Thus the almshouse would be that particular institution given to the creation of an environment in which concern for the worthy poor and attention to their needs would contrast with the punitive conditions for those capable of work. Yet, few counties ever committed the resources necessary to enforce this split.

Historically, the Yates report is significant, since it gained widespread attention and established indoor almshouse care as the major approach to the relief of the poor in the United States. In 1857, a state Select Senate Committee to Visit Charitable and Penal Institutions reported the existence of 55 almshouses, exclusive of the almshouses and poorhouses in New York and Kings counties.[46] Massachusetts listed 83 almshouses in 1824; there were 219 in 1860. By 1860, Pennsylvania had 31 county institutions, in addition to local almshouses. By 1860, Maryland had almshouses in all but one county, and that county was permitted the use of the facility in Baltimore.[47]

As the Civil War approached, almshouse care was being used extensively throughout the United States. As with other institutions—asylums, houses of refuge, reformatories—the reform impulse quickly gave way to custodial realities. Grand plans to classify the poor and operate two institutions in one gave way to fiscal austerity and Spartan conditions. In 1824, however, the almshouse seemed the obvious answer for all who deviated (or might deviate) from self-reliance—the impotent elderly or disabled, the potent able-bodied, and the eventually potent child. The emphasis in the Yates report upon saving the poor from pauperism and upon deterring the able-bodied from accepting relief showed how strongly held belief could render the widespread poverty of the era invisible. Nowhere is this more evident than in the child-saving activities of the era.

Child Saving

Stirrings of dissatisfaction with almshouse care, especially for children, developed soon after the Yates report appeared. This dissatisfaction was based in part on the reform, crusading interests of the era. The period was one of growth of democratic concepts and of increased concern for individual self-realization. In child welfare, this meant a new awareness of children as children—young people who must grow into adults were able to participate in a democratic government. It seemed to the reformers that neither the undifferentiated almshouse nor the environment provided by the family—particularly the poor family—would provide the requisite discipline and education for children.

The mischief and excitements attributable to urbanization have led to social change and unrest. Self-realization and individual freedom were not to be confused with license and self-indulgence. Democracy was not to be extended to family life and the relaxation of parental authority. Fear of permissiveness in the care of children was aggravated by the growing presence of immigrants, who, it was thought, were unaware of traditional American child-rearing practices. The goal for a reformed American society was the return to the well-ordered institutions of the Colonial era. If children were to save the country for democracy, they must first be saved themselves.

Again, the institution—this time with specialized concern for dependent, neglected, and delinquent children—offered an approach that appeared to be both humane and comforting for the individual, a substitute for the supposedly poorly functioning families of workers and immigrants.

Institutions for children had appeared early on the American scene but were few in number until the 19th century. The first American institution for children, founded in 1729, was a private institution for girls established in New Orleans by the Ursuline Sisters. The Bethesda House for Boys, founded in 1740 near Savannah, Georgia, was also privately supported. The first government-supported institution was established in 1790 in Charleston, South Carolina, and remained the only publicly funded institution for children until the turn of the century. The Charleston Orphan House was founded for the "Purpose of Supporting and Educating Poor Orphan Children, and Those of Poor, Distressed and Disabled Parents, Who Are Unable to Support and Maintain Them."[48]

During the first half of the 19th century, the number of children's institutions increased rapidly so that by 1851, there were 77, with an additional 47 built over the next decade.[49] Most of these institutions were orphan asylums or simply asylums for dependent children; some were houses of refuge, reformatories for delinquent children. Most were privately controlled by religious, social, or foreign-born national groups, although many received government subsidies. The first private institution to receive a state subsidy was the Orphan Asylum of New York, which was granted a subsidy by an act of the state legislature in 1811. Similar grants were made in other states. The New York (City) House of Refuge and the Philadelphia House of Refuge were opened in 1825 and 1828, respectively. Both were supported by a combination of city appropriations, state subsidies, and voluntary contributions. By 1860, the state subsidies became the norm.

Institutions wholly supported by public funds were also developed, generally to meet the needs of special classes of children. The Boston House of Reformation, established in 1826, was the first reformatory for juveniles funded by a municipality. The first state reform school, the House of Refuge for Delinquent Boys, was established in Massachusetts in 1847. A "School for Idiots," under the superintendency of Dr. Samuel Gridley Howe, was opened in 1848, also in Massachusetts. Similar publicly funded schools were opened in the next decade in Albany, New York; Columbus, Ohio; and Lakeville, Connecticut.

Because so many reformers saw working-class and poor families as the source of social problems, they constructed institutions that isolated their inmates from these influences. Starting with distrust for the competence of poor parents, superintendents of children's institutions discouraged contact with parents. As for the actual care provided, in both orphan asylums and institutions for delinquents, the goal was submission and obedience on the part of the child. The Charleston orphan asylum saw itself as educating boys to become disciplined workers and citizens. The construction of houses of refuge for delinquent children spoke most pointedly to pre–Civil War concerns about the care of children. The delinquent child highlighted the "vicious tempers and habits" that could develop in an environment where authority and governance did not exact obedience and submission.[50] How easily the willful, offending child could become the adult criminal, the contributor to societal breakdown! The movement for institutions devoted to delinquent children began with the establishment of the New York Society for the Prevention of Pauperism in 1819 and the New York House of Refuge in 1826. By 1857, the number of such institutions had grown sufficiently to warrant a national convention of refuge superintendents.

Houses of refuge, like institutions for dependent, homeless children, offered a model for family home care, a combination of shelter, routine, and discipline. Isolated and shielded from outside, particularly from own-family influences, delinquent children were subjected to a "vigorous course of moral and corporal discipline" with the intent that they "be made tractable and obedient"[51] and, ultimately, good citizens. As indicated by the report of the investigation of the Philadelphia House of Refuge in 1835, the success of such an institution was thought to be measured by the extent to which its practices were a demonstration of parenting and parental responsibilities fulfilled.

> The inmates present a healthy appearance; their clothing is comfortable, and their fare is abundant and wholesome. Their labour is suited to their age and capacity—regular, but not severe. Their government . . . is parental. . . . They have their regular hours of labour, and instruction; while every attention is paid to induce habits of industry, the greatest possible care is had for their intellectual improvement. . . .
>
> To this unfortunate class, the advantages of this institution are peculiarly adopted. Here then vicious tempers and habits are restrained—their minds improved—principles of virtue inculcated; and not a few, who were on the broad road to ruin, have been rescued from destruction and prepared for usefulness.[52]

The model of "home life" offered by the house of refuge and by other child-caring institutions was semimilitary, characterized by discipline, training, and rehabilitation. The design of the institution and the imposition of a controlled, regulated environment were meant to hasten the reform of the inmates. Thus, the realization of the goal of child saving through institutionalization did little to tailor care to the needs of the child.

The advocates of child institutionalization did not go unchallenged. Charles Loring Brace, the founder of the Children's Aid Society of New York, was an early, vocal critic of institutionalization. Despite the increase in special institutions for children, the unquestioned acceptance of institutional child care declined during the 1850s. This decline resulted partly from an inability to build specialized institutions in sufficient numbers to absorb the growing number of dependent, homeless, orphaned, and delinquent children. Economic uncertainty was increasing, and for widows and other adults without economic resources, surrendering their children to institutions was not rare. In New York City alone, according to a police report in 1852, "there were an estimated 10,000 abandoned, orphaned, runaway children roaming the streets."[53] The catchall almshouse, rather than the specialized institution, remained the most available form of care for children.

Other factors contributed to a less positive view of institutional child care, including the rise of public education and the decline of opportunities for legal indenture and apprenticeship. The pattern of child-caring institutions had included a relatively short period of institutional housing during which education and re-education for orderly living were provided. Having satisfactorily completed this period of rehabilitation, the institution placed out boys as apprentices and girls as domestic servants. The spread of public, compulsory education made the educational efforts of child-caring institutions appear inadequate and unnecessary and, moreover, took the child back into the very community from which he or she was to have been "saved." Similarly, the gradual disappearance of cottage industries meant not only the disappearance of work opportunities that could be selected and put under surveillance by the institution but also the disappearance of family care as an aspect of indentured apprenticeship. Simultaneously, increasingly heavy migrations from Europe, combined with stretches of economic recession to make for a surplus of adult workers, rendered child labor less profitable.

As the apprenticeship system declined, the indenturing of children changed for the worse. The value of the instruction received from the "masters" became less, and the value of the services rendered by the children increased.[54]

Brace founded the Children's Aid Society of New York in 1853 to advance a new approach to child care. The circular announcing the formation of the society expressed the urgency of the task ahead.

But a small part of the vagrant population can be shut up in our asylums. . . . The class increases. Immigration is pouring its multitudes of poor foreigners, who ... leave young outcasts everywhere abandoned in our midst. For the most part ... [they] grow up utterly by themselves. No one cares for them, and they care for no one. . . . Every cunning faculty is intensely stimulated. They are shrewd and old in vice when other children are in leading-strings.[55]

Conceptually, Brace was bent on saving children through the provision of education and shelter and, ideally, through separation of children from parents.

Efforts to secure adequate and proper shelter for dependent children led Brace to the notion of foster home care:

The workers . . . in this movement [foster home placement] felt from the beginning that "asylum-life" is not the best training for outcast children in preparing them for practical life. In large buildings, where a multitude of children are gathered together, the bad corrupt the good, and the good are not educated in the virtues of real life. The machinery, too, which is so necessary in such large institutions, unfits a poor boy or girl for practical handwork.[56]

Brace became convinced that foster home placement outside of New York City was the best possible solution. So he chose the farms and ranches of the West, where "the best of all Asylums for the outcast child . . . [would be] the farmer's home."[57] The fact that farm labor was in demand in the West and, therefore, that large numbers of children could be absorbed fit neatly with a romantic conception of country life. During the 12-year period, 1853–1864, the Children's Aid Society of New York placed 4,614 children with Western farmers. The Society's efforts to place children in the West continued until after World War I. In the end, over 120,000 children had ridden the "orphan trains."[58]

The experience of Brace's foster children fits no neat generalization. After spending days on the trains, the children would arrive at a destination where they would be "viewed" in a public place. Local residents interested in obtaining a child would select a child, and in a matter of minutes, a bargain was struck. Certainly, many of the children felt exploited by their new guardians and ran away, often finding their way back to New York City. At the same time, many of the children became integral parts of their foster families and benefited from the move. What is certain is that the Children's Aid Society's policy was to block communication between the children and their living relatives.

Brace's advocacy of Western foster care inspired other child-saving agencies to use similar placement methods, removing dependent children from city environs, either to the West or to the rural environs of the city. The Church Home Society was founded in Boston in 1855, the Henry Watson Children's Aid Society in Baltimore in 1860, and the Home for Little Wanderers also in New York in 1861. With their emphasis upon child saving, these organizations, like institutions and almshouses, offered programs that did not individualize the child.

Retreat from the Almshouse

The Children's Aid Society advocacy of sending children to the West was only one part of a broader critique of institutional care during the years before the Civil War. Increasing state subsidy led to broader oversight of institutions. Ultimately, the gap between the promises of the moral entrepreneurs who created institutions and their reality led political and civic leaders to wonder if this was the best solution to the problems of a new democracy. In New York, the state Select Senate Committee to Visit Charitable and Penal Institutions made its report in 1857. The committee had been appointed

> . . . to visit . . . all charitable institutions supported or assisted by the State, and all city and country poor and work houses and jails . . . to examine into the conditions of the said establishments, their . . . government, treatment, and management of the inmates, the conduct of the trustees, directors, and other officers . . . and all other matters whatever pertaining to their usefulness and good government.[59]

The committee made its visits during the summer and autumn months when the "average number in the poor house is twenty-five percent less than in the winter" and made the following overall statement about what was found:

> The poor houses throughout the State may be generally described as badly constructed, ill-arranged, ill-warmed, and ill-ventilated. The rooms are crowded with inmates; and the air, particularly in the sleeping apartments, is very noxious, and to casual visitors, almost insufferable.[60]

Still further:

> The evidence taken by the committee exhibits such a filth, nakedness, licentiousness, general bad morals, and disregard of religion and the most common religious observances, as well as of gross neglect of the most ordinary comforts and decencies of life, as if published in detail would disgrace the State and shock humanity.[61]

The committee recalled that almshouses had been originally designed to be "comfortable asylums for worthy indigence" and gave examples of how they had been permitted to become "unsuitable refuge for the virtuous poor, and mainly places of confinement for the degraded."[62]

The care of old people, of worthy adults who were suffering temporary reversals, of the insane, and of children was found to be especially outrageous. The committee recommended outdoor relief for worthy adults and specialized institutional care for children and the insane, the object being the removal of these classes from the almshouses.

> A . . . more efficient and economic auxiliary in supporting the poor, and the prevention of absolute pauperism, consists . . . in the proper and systematic distribution of *outdoor* [italics in original] relief. Worthy indigent persons should . . . be kept from the degradation of the poor house, by reasonable supplies of provisions . . . at their own homes.[63]

It was recommended that the insane be removed to state asylums.

In Massachusetts, too, almshouse care was found wanting. A special committee was appointed in 1858 to "investigate the whole system of public charitable institutions of the Commonwealth." The committee found the system of state almshouses to have "grave disadvantages."

> For example: (1) partisan administration, (2) tendency of breaking up families to perpetuate dependency, (3) greater difficulty in placing children, (4) or finding work, (5) increased costs of transportation, (a) involved extra school and church facilities, (b) increased risks from fire and from moral and social contamination.[64]

The committee recommended that the almshouse system be abandoned at the earliest convenience.

The impetus for the attack on the Poor Law practice of outdoor relief and the subsequent rise in the use of almshouses and specialized institutional care was attributed to external factors and to individual behavior flaws.

The rise in immigration and the growth and increased crowding of cities created what was considered an unstable atmosphere, not conductive to mental health or stable labor-force behavior. The increased availability of alcohol and other forms of entertainment was a further factor believed to contribute to irresponsible behavior and poverty. In addition, the Poor Laws themselves, which provided a safety net for families in need, were judged to be part of the problem of rising incidence of need.

The response was the construction of many specialized institutions aimed at providing a stable environment for the poor and the mentally ill. The regularity of institutional life was to be a force for "cure" of those in need; the unpleasantness of life in the almshouse was to discourage the requests for assistance.[65]

Neither direct criticism of almshouse care, as in the New York and Massachusetts reports, nor indirect criticism, as implied in efforts to remove special classes of indigents, produced an immediate retreat from such care. The eruption of the Civil War was, certainly, a prime factor for the hiatus. Perhaps, the nature of the population of inmates is even more telling. Although estimates vary widely, there is general agreement that more than half the inmates were foreign-born.[66] The probability is that most people agreed with Brace that these were "dangerous classes" and that fear rather than concern was the mark of public opinion. Almshouse care remained the dominant form of care for the poor until the Progressive Era of the late 19th century.

? Assess your comprehension of "Social Welfare Programs and Services" by completing this quiz.

DOCUMENTS

The Pre–Civil War Period

Three documents have been selected to illustrate the tenor of social welfare during the pre–Civil War period: *The First Annual Report of the Managers of the Society for the Prevention of Pauperism in the City of New York (1818); Constitution, By-Laws, &c., of the Female Orphan Asylum of Portland, Maine (1828);* and *President Franklin Pierce: Veto Message—An Act Making a Grant of Public Lands to the Several States for the Benefit of Indigent Insane Persons*, the act granting public lands to the various states for the benefit of indigent persons (1854). The documents demonstrate several major themes:

1. That the causes of poverty are outside the economic system and that poverty can be abolished through the reform of individuals

2. That institutions can serve as mechanisms for the rehabilitation of individuals and of the social order

3. That the development and administration of social welfare programs are local public and voluntary social welfare concerns, rather than a responsibility of the federal government

The managers of the Society for the Prevention of Pauperism in their First Annual Report give evidence of the change that had occurred in society's view of people. The Puritan doctrine of a fixed social structure gave way to one in which achievement was limited only by failure to fulfill individual potential. It was the Age of Reason, and the will of God yielded to free will. The rational man could reach perfectibility, if he willed to do so. The problem for social welfare then, as for all institutions, was to create an environment in which individual reform and perfectibility were encouraged and could take place. The managers of the society were particularly frightened by the growth of pauperism, which they believed was fostered in a rapidly changing society. The report of the managers demonstrates the extent to which rational human beings, freed of heavenly strictures, could rationalize the harsh treatment of the poor.

During the pre–Civil War era, institutions were founded to provide and demonstrate the well-ordered environmental setting in which human perfectibility could flourish. Children's institutions were particularly important in this regard, since the future of the country quite literally depended upon the kind of adults that children became. The Female Orphan Asylum of Portland, Maine, was established to "carry into effect, *means* for the support, instruction and employment of female children, from three to ten years of age." The bylaws of the asylum demonstrate the premium placed upon stability and regularity in the daily lives of children. Their clothing, their fare, their instruction, and their activities are proscribed in rules and regulations so as to inculcate "habits of *order, neatness,* and *industry.*" Of equal importance was the prevention of parental interference "in the management of the children." Indeed, parents could not visit except in the presence of the asylum's governess. To be preferred was the parent's relinquishing all claim to the child, thus freeing the institution for its work. At the age of 11, the children were generally "placed out" with virtuous families, and the asylum followed their conduct and circumstances until they had reached age 18.

President Pierce vetoed "the ten-million acre bill" in the belief that the bill would eventuate in the "transfer to the Federal Government the charge of all the poor in all the States." His decision to veto was based on the constitutional guarantee that those powers not specifically delegated to the United States by the Constitution were reserved for the states. Since he could find no specific delegation of authority for social welfare, the president interpreted the Constitution to mean that social welfare matters involved issues of states' rights and, therefore, required the exercise by each state of its own police power to provide for the welfare of its inhabitants. In addition to the constitutional question of states' rights, the president's decision was steeped in historical precedent by which programs to meet social welfare needs had long been the province of local and voluntary organizations. The veto was to sustain the tradition until the depression of the 1930s.

The First Annual Report of the Managers of the Society
for the Prevention of Pauperism in the City of New York

Read and Accepted October 26, 1818

To which is added:

A REPORT ON THE SUBJECT OF PAUPERISM,

dated February 4, 1818

The Managers of the Society for the Prevention of Pauperism
in the City of New York, REPORT

That their anticipation of the importance and difficulty of their duties has been fully realized. Their first efforts were necessarily directed to the development of the objects which they were appointed to consider. Though these objects were specified as far as practicable; though the nature of the duty allotted to the Board was pointed out, as well as the general aspect of the plan, such as the Managers should have in view, yet the basis only was laid, and it was their work to erect the superstructure. They were not at a loss for materials. These were more and more exhibited to them in the multifarious ramifications of their labours. But it was not an easy task to arrange them in proper order, and to dispose of them to advantage; it therefore required time, deliberation, and assiduity, to digest an effectual plan, and to take measures for rendering it subservient to the momentous purposes of the Society.

In order to investigate, and as far as possible to remove the various causes of mendicity; to devise plans for meliorating the condition of the poor and wretched, and to secure their successful operation, the Managers, immediately after their appointment, respectfully solicited the Corporation of this city to appoint five Managers from that body, agreeably to the 6th article of the constitution. The favourable result of this application warrants the Board to calculate upon municipal countenance and aid.

The 3rd article of the By-laws declares that "each attending Committee shall consist of as many members of the Society as the Board may think necessary. They shall make rules, or by-laws, to govern themselves; keep a book, wherein they shall enter their proceedings, and report to the Board at every stated meeting, a summary of their proceedings, with their opinions on the most adviseable course for the Board to pursue relative thereto."

Nine Standing Committees were accordingly appointed, to carry into effect the views of the Managers, as stated in the following extract from the minutes:—

DISTRICTING COMMITTEE

This Committee shall consist of as many members of this Board as there are wards in the city, who shall form a general plan of operations;—and as soon after as possible each person shall, in his respective ward, associate with as many members of the Society as may be thought adviseable, who shall divide the ward into as many districts as they may think proper. These sub-committees shall embrace in their operations the duties specified on the 12th and 13th pages of the printed Report on the subject of Pauperism.

IDLENESS AND SOURCES OF EMPLOYMENT

The object of this Committee shall be to devise means for the employment of the poor.

INTEMPERANCE

This Committee shall inform the Board as to the number of places where ardent spirits are retailed in small quantities;—what quantity is drunk, with an estimate of its cost, and the class of citizens most subject to the vice of intemperance.

The Committee shall give opinions at large on every thing connected with this subject, including the law, police regulations, officers, & c. & c.

LOTTERIES

This Committee shall report the number of lottery offices in the city; the amount of money annually expended; the probable waste of time occasioned by lotteries; the usual percent advance on tickets; the extent of the evil arising from the insuring of tickets, how far the restraining laws are enforced, & c. & c.

HOUSES OF ILL FAME

This Committee shall report the probable number of houses of this description; families that live by prostitution; and in what particular the police regulations on the subject may be amended.

PAWN-BROKERS

This Committee shall report the number of pawn-brokers, their manner of doing business, and the best mode of correcting the evils arising therefrom.

CHARITABLE INSTITUTIONS

This Committee shall inform the Board as to the number in the city; the gross and annual amount of their funds, and the mode respectively adopted by them, in the distribution of charity to the poor.

GAMBLING

This Committee shall report the number and kinds of gambling houses, and their opinion as to the best mode of diminishing or suppressing them.

This Committee shall report the number of children who do not attend any school; the number of adults who cannot read; the number of families and individuals who do not attend public worship; and the causes which prevent. . . .

In the years 1788–1789, there were under the old system,

Paupers	7391
In the Hospital	894
—Penitentiary	446
—Orphan House	1000
Total	9731

In the years 1798–1799, when the new system was in operation, there were

Paupers	3090
In the Hospital	894
—Penitentiary	147
—Orphan House	600
Total	4731

Exhibiting a decrease in *one city* of 5026.

It is evident, therefore, that the object of the New York Society for Preventing Pauperism is such as cannot, in the nature of things, be speedily accomplished. Habits and vices, which take their rise from the worst passions and propensities of men, however deplorable in their effects upon individuals and society, will yield to no sudden remedies. They must be supplanted gradually by the influence of appropriate agencies, by the assiduities of patient and persevering labour, by the constant and meliorating operations of benevolence. The measures pointed out in the document appended to this Report, are adapted ultimately to remove those evils which so much afflict society, and which the severest enactments of civil authority have been found unable to repress. Let the moral sense be awakened, and a moral influence be established in the minds of the improvident, the unfortunate, and the depraved; let them be approached with kindness and an ingenuous concern for their welfare; inspire them with self-respect, and encourage their industry and economy: in short, enlighten their minds, and teach them to care for themselves. These are the methods of doing them real and permanent good, and relieving the community from the pecuniary exactions, the multiplied embarrassments, and threatening dangers of which they are the authors. Happily, the object proposed by this institution is one which may be aided by every individual, whatever be his circumstances; though it prospectively demands the concurrence and patronage of all. The public is called upon not so much for pecuniary subscriptions and benefactions, as for friendly advice, for vigilant attention to the common good, for the adoption of wholesome opinions, and the exertion of a salutary influence. They who experience the ill effects of pauperism and its attendant evils, are urged, not to make fresh sacrifices and incur additional embarrassments, but to act upon the defensive, to employ the means of prevention, to check an inundation which threatens to overwhelm them. They are invited to adopt measures which cannot possibly be hurtful in any instance; which seem alone adapted to the end in view, which are required by the necessity of the case, and sanctioned by the results of experience.

The Managers consider the information which they have thus laid before the Society, of sufficient moment to encourage every member, and to stimulate the citizens generally, to give their utmost sanction and support to this truly benevolent institution, whose aim is to improve the temporal and moral condition of a considerable portion of this community.

Conscientiously engaged in so good a cause, let *all* rely on the blessing of that Almighty Father who "maketh his sun to rise on the evil and the good, and sendeth rain on the just and on the unjust."

MATTHEW CLARKSON, President

Joseph Curtis, *Sec'y, pro tem.*
   New-York, Oct. 26, 1818.

New York: Printed by J. Seymour, 49 John-Street, 1818.

★ ★ ★

REPORT
ON THE
SUBJECT OF PAUPERISM.

To the "New-York Society for the Prevention of Pauperism."

The Committee appointed to prepare a Constitution for the government of the Society, and a statement of the prevailing causes of pauperism, with suggestions relative to the most suitable and efficient remedies, Report,

That we entered upon the duties assigned us, under a strong conviction of the great importance of the subject of Pauperism. We were persuaded that on the judicious management of this subject depend, in a high degree, the comfort, the tranquility, and the freedom of communities.

We were not insensible of the serious and alarming evils that have resulted, in various places, from misguided benevolence, and imprudent systems of relief. We knew that in Europe and America, where the greatest efforts have been made to provide for the sufferings of the poor, by high and even enormous taxation, those sufferings were increasing in a ratio much greater than the population, and were evidently augmented by the very means taken to subdue them.

We were fully prepared to believe, that without a radical change in the principles upon which public alms have been usually distributed, helplessness and poverty would continue to multiply—demands for relief would become more and more importunate, the numerical difference between those who are able to bestow charity and those who sue for it, would gradually diminish, until the present system must fall under its own irresistible pressure, prostrating perhaps, in its ruin, some of the pillars of social order.

It might be long indeed before such a catastrophe would be extensively felt in this free and happy country. Yet it is really to be feared, as we apprehend, that it would not be long before some of the proximate evils of such a state of things would be perceived in our public cities, and in none, perhaps, sooner than in New-York. Although these consequences are but too apparent from the numerous facts which recent investigations have brought to light, particularly in Great Britain, and in some parts of the United States, yet we are very sensible of the difficulties attendant upon every attempt to provide an adequate remedy for poverty, and its concomitant wretchedness.

The evil lies deep in the foundation of our social and moral institutions; and we cannot but consider it as one of the most obscure and perplexing, and at the same time, interesting and imposing departments of political economy.

While there exists so great a disparity in the physical and intellectual capacities of men, there must be, in every government, where a division of property is recognized by law and usage, a wide difference in the means of support. Such, too, is the complication of human affairs, the numerous connexions, and close dependencies of one part upon another, it is scarcely to be presumed, and it would be extravagant to expect, that under the most moral, and the wisest civil regulation to which human society is susceptible of attaining, partial indigence and distress will not be experienced to an amount that will ever demand the exercise of Christian benevolence.

The great and leading principles, therefore, of every system of charity, ought to be, *First*, amply to relieve the unavoidable necessities of the poor; and, *Secondly*, to lay the powerful hand of moral and legal restriction upon every thing that contributes, directly and necessarily, to introduce an artificial extent of suffering; and to diminish, in any class of the community, a reliance upon its own powers of body and mind for an independent and virtuous support. That to the influence of those extraneous, debilitating causes, may be ascribed nine tenths of the poverty which actually prevails, we trust none will doubt, who are extensively acquainted with facts in relation to this subject.

The indirect causes of poverty are as numerous as the frailties and vices of men. They vary with constitution, with character, and with national and local habits. Some of them lie so deeply entrenched in the weakness and depravity of human nature, as to be altogether unassailable by mere political regulation. They can be reached in no other way, than by awakening the dormant and secret energies of moral feeling.

But with a view to bring the subject committed to our charge more definitely before the Society, we have thought it right, distinctly to enumerate the more prominent of those causes of poverty which prevail within this city; subjoining such remarks as may appear needful.

1st. IGNORANCE. Arising either from inherent dullness, or from want of opportunities for improvement. This operates as a restraint upon the physical powers, preventing that exercise and cultivation of the bodily faculties by which skill is obtained, and the means of support increased. The influence of this cause, it is believed, is particularly great among the foreign poor that annually accumulate in this city.

2d. IDLENESS. A tendency to this evil may be more or less inherent. It is greatly increased by other causes, and when it becomes habitual, it is the occasion of much suffering in families, and augments to a great amount the burden of the industrious portions of society.

3d. INTEMPERANCE IN DRINKING. This most prolific source of mischief and misery drags in its train almost every species of suffering which afflicts the poor. This evil, in relation to poverty and vice, may be emphatically styled the *Cause of Causes*. The box of Pandora is realized in each of the kegs of ardent spirits that stand upon the counters of the 1600* licensed grocers of this city. At a moderate computation, the money spent in the purchase of spirituous liquors would be more than sufficient to keep the whole city constantly supplied with bread. Viewing the enormous devastations of this evil upon the minds and morals of the people, we cannot but regard it as the crying and increasing sin of the nation, and as loudly demanding the solemn deliberation of our legislative assemblies.

4th. WANT OF ECONOMY. Prodigality is comparative. Among the poor it prevails to a great extent, in an inattention to those small but frequent savings when labour is plentiful, which may go to meet the privations of unfavourable seasons.

5th. IMPRUDENT AND HASTY MARRIAGES. This, it is believed, is a fertile source of trial and poverty.

---

*Since this Report was written, the number of licenses has been very considerably reduced by the present chief magistrate of the city.

6th. LOTTERIES. The depraving nature and tendency of these allurements to hazard money, is generally admitted by those who have been most attentive to their effects. The time spent in inquiries relative to lotteries, in frequent attendance on lottery offices, the feverish anxiety which prevails relative to the success of tickets, the associations to which it leads, all contribute to divert the labourer from his employment, to weaken the tone of his morals, to consume his earnings, and consequently to increase his poverty. But objectionable and injurious to society as we believe lotteries to be, we regard as more destructive to morals, and ruinous to all character and comfort, the numerous self-erected lottery insurances, at which the young and the old are invited to spend their money in such small pittances, as the poorest labourer is frequently able to command, under the delusive expectation of a gain, the chance of which is as low, perhaps, as it is possible to conceive. The poor are thus cheated out of their money and their time, and too often left a prey to the feelings of desperation: or, they are impelled by those feelings to seek a refuge in the temporary, but fatal oblivion of intoxication.

7th. PAWNBROKERS. The establishment of these offices is considered as very unfavourable to the independence and welfare of the middling and inferior classes. The artifices which are often practised to deceive the expectation of those who are induced, through actual distress, or by positive allurement, to trust their goods at these places, not to mention the facilities which they afford to the commission of theft, and the encouragement they give to a dependence on stratagem and cunning, rather than on the profits of honest industry, fairly entitle them, in the opinion of the Committee, to a place among the *causes of Poverty*.

8th. HOUSES OF ILL FAME. The direful effects of those sinks of iniquity upon the habits and morals of a numerous class of young men, especially of sailors and apprentices, are visible throughout the city. Open abandonment of character, vulgarity, profanity, &c. are among the inevitable consequences, as it respects our own sex, of those places of infamous resort. The effects upon the several thousands of females within this city, who are ingulphed in those abodes of all that is vile, and all that is shocking to virtuous thought, upon the miserable victims, many of them of decent families, who are here subjected to the most cruel tyranny of their inhuman masters—upon the females, who, hardened in crime, are nightly sent from those dens of corruption to roam through the city "seeking whom they may devour," we have not the inclination, nor is it our duty, to describe. Among "the causes of poverty," those houses, where all the base-born passions are engendered—where the vilest profligacy receives a forced culture, must hold an eminent rank.

9th. THE NUMEROUS CHARITABLE INSTITUTIONS OF THE CITY. The Committee by no means intends to cast an indiscriminate censure upon these institutions, nor to implicate the motives, nor even to deny the usefulness, in a certain degree, of any of them. They have unquestionably had their foundation in motives of true philanthropy; they have contributed to cultivate the feelings of Christian charity, and to keep alive its salutary influence upon the minds of our fellow-citizens; and they have doubtless relieved thousands from the pressure of the most pinching want, from cold, from hunger, and probably, in many cases, from untimely death.

But, in relation to these societies, a question of no ordinary moment presents itself to the considerate and real philanthropist. Is not the partial and temporary good which they accomplish, how acute soever the miseries they relieve, and whatever the number they may rescue from sufferings or death, more than counterbalanced, by the evils that flow from the expectations they necessarily excite; by the relaxation of industry, which such a display of benevolence tends to produce; by that reliance upon charitable aid, in case of unfavourable times, which must unavoidably tend to diminish, in the minds of the labouring classes, that wholesome anxiety to provide for the wants of a distant day, which alone can save them from a state of absolute dependence, and from becoming a burden to the community?

In the opinion of your Committee, and in the opinion, we believe, of the greater number of the best writers, of the wisest economists, and of the most experienced philanthropists, which the interesting subject of Pauperism has recently called into action; the balance of good and evil is unfavourable to the existence of societies for gratuitous relief:—that efforts of this nature, with whatever zeal they may be conducted, never can effect the removal of poverty, nor lessen its general amount; but that indigence and helplessness will multiply nearly in the ratio of those measures which are ostensibly taken to prevent them.

Such are the consequences of every avowal on the part of the public of a determination to support the indigent by the administration of alms. And in no cases are measures of this kind more prolific in evil, than where they are accompanied by the display of large funds for the purposes of charity; or where the poor are conscious of the existence of such funds, raised by taxation, and of course, as they will allege, drawn chiefly from the coffers of the rich.

How far these evils are remediable, without an entire dereliction of the great Christian duty of charity, is a problem of difficult solution. The principle of taxation is so interwoven with our habits and customs, it would, perhaps, in the present state of things, be impossible to dispense with it. But while our poor continue to be thus supported, to prevent the misapplication and abuse of the public charity, demands the utmost vigilance, the wisest precaution, and the most elaborate system of inspection and oversight.

To what extent abuses upon our present system of alms are practised, and how far the evils which accompany it are susceptible of remedy, we should not at present feel warranted in attempting to state. The pauperism of the city is under the management of five Commissioners, who, we doubt not, are well qualified to fulfil the trust reposed in them, and altogether disposed to discharge it with fidelity. But we cannot withhold the opinion, that without a far more extended, minute, and energetic scheme of management than it is possible for any five men to keep in constant operation, abuses will be practised, and to a great extent, upon the public bounty; taxes must be increased, and vice and suffering perpetuated.

Lastly. Your Committee would mention WAR, during its prevalence, as one of the most abundant sources of poverty and vice, which the list of human corruptions comprehends. But as this evil lies out of the immediate reach of local regulation, and as we are now happily blessed with a peace which we hope will be durable, it is deemed unnecessary further to notice it.

Such are the causes which are considered as the more prominent and operative in producing that amount of indigence and suffering, which awakens the charity of this city, and which has occasioned the erection of buildings for eleemosynary purposes, at an expense of half a million of dollars, and which calls for the annual distribution of 90,000 dollars more. But, if the payment of this sum were the only inconvenience to be endured—trifling, indeed, in comparison would be the evils which claim our attention. Of the mass of affliction and wretchedness actually sustained, how small a portion is thus relieved! Of the quantity of misery and vice, which the causes we have enumerated, with others we have not named, bring upon the city, how trifling the portion actually removed, by public or by private benevolence! Nor do we conceive it possible to remove this load of distress, by all the alms-doing of which the city is capable, while the causes remain in full and active operation.

Effectually to relieve the poor, is therefore a task far more comprehensive in its nature, than simply to clothe the naked and to feed the hungry. It is, to erect barriers against the encroachments of moral degeneracy;—it is to heal the diseases of the mind;—it is to furnish that ailment to the intellectual system which will tend to preserve it in healthful operation.

But can a task of this nature come within the reach of any public or any social regulation? We answer, that to a certain, and to a very valuable extent, we believe it can. When any measure for the promotion of public good, or the prevention of public evil, founded upon equitable principles, is supported by a sufficient weight of social authority, it may gradually pass into full and complete operation, and become established upon a basis as firm as a law of legislative enactment. And in matters of private practice, reformation which positive statute could never accomplish, social and moral influence may thoroughly effect. . . .

To conclude, the committee has by no means intended, in the freedom with which it has thus examined the causes of pauperism, and suggested remedies, to encourage the expectation that the whole of these remedies can be speedily brought within the power and control of the society. A work of so much importance to the public welfare cannot be the business of a day; but we nevertheless entertain the hope, that if the principles and design of this Society shall, upon mature examination and reflection, receive the approbation of the great body of our intelligent fellow-citizens, and the number of its members be augmented accordingly, it will be able gradually to bring within its operation all the important measures suggested in this report. By what particular mode these measures shall be encountered, whether through the agency of large and efficient Committees of this Society, or by auxiliary societies, each established, for a specific purpose, under the patronage of the parent institution, and subordinate to its general principles, we leave to the wisdom and future decision of the Society.

On behalf of the Committee,
JOHN GRISCOM, *Chairman.*

New-York, Second month 4, 1818.

* * *

CONSTITUTION, BY-Laws, & c., of the

Female Orphan Asylum of Portland, Maine

Act incorporating the Female Orphan Asylum

of Portland

STATE OF MAINE

In the year of our Lord one thousand eight hundred and twenty-eight.

AN ACT to incorporate the Female Orphan Asylum of Portland.

SECTION 1. *Be it enacted by the Senate and House of Representatives, in Legislature assembled,* That Sally M. Smith, Thankful Hussey, Mary B. Storer, Charlotte Andrews, Mary Radford, Mary B. Merrill, Elizabeth L. Fox, Elizabeth G. Atwood, Susan Richardson, Nancy Cushman, Marcia Hill, Alice Ilsley, Lois W. Dana, Susan E. Wood, and Eliza L. Goddard, their associates and successors be, and they hereby are, constituted a body politic and corporate by the name of the Female Orphan Asylum of Portland, with power to prosecute and defend suits at law; to have and use a common seal, to make and establish any by-laws for the management of their affairs, not repugnant to the laws of the State; to take and hold any estate, real or personal, for the purpose of supporting, instructing and employing female children, the first attention to be given to orphans; and to give, grant, bargain or sell the same; and with all the powers and privileges usually granted to other societies instituted for purposes of charity and beneficence.—*Provided,* that the value of the real estate of said corporation, shall never exceed forty thousand dollars, and the annual income of the whole estate of said corporation shall not exceed twenty thousand dollars.

SECTION 2. *Be it further enacted,* That the first meeting of said corporation shall be holden at such time and place, and be notified in such manner, as a majority of the persons named in this act shall direct.

SECTION 3. *Be it further enacted*, That the powers granted by this Act, may be enlarged, restricted, or annulled at the pleasure of the Legislature.

In the House of Representatives, February 16, 1828. This Bill, having had three several readings, passed to be enacted.

JOHN RUGGLES, *Speaker.*

In Senate, February 18, 1828. This Bill, having had two several readings, passed to be enacted.

ROBERT P. DUNLAP, *President.*

February 18, 1828, Approved.

ENOCH LINCOLN.

STATE OF MAINE
Secretary of State's Office,
Portland, February 20, 1828.

I hereby certify, that the foregoing is a true copy of the original, deposited in this Office.
ATTEST, A. NICHOLS, *Secy. of State.*

Shirley and Hyde, Printers

★ ★ ★

CONSTITUTION

OF THE

Female orphan asylum

OF PORTLAND

ARTICLE 1. This Society shall be called The Female Orphan Asylum of Portland, and being strictly a charitable Institution, no article shall be admitted into this Constitution, which shall recognize the peculiar sentiments of any particular denomination of Christians, but all shall be considered as enjoying equal rights and privileges.

ART. 2. The *object* of this Institution shall be to provide and carry into effect, *means* for the support, instruction and employment of female children, from three to ten years of age: the first attention to be paid to Orphans.

ART. 3. Any lady who shall subscribe and pay a sum not less than *two* dollars annually, shall become a member of said Society; her membership however to cease, whenever she shall refuse or neglect to pay said annual subscription.

ART. 4. The Society shall meet on the second Tuesday in September annually, for the purpose of electing by *ballot* a Treasurer, and a board to consist of fifteen managers: which board shall choose from among themselves a first and second Directress, a Secretary, and an Assistant Secretary if necessary: and they shall have power to fill their own vacancies.—Not *less* than *five* shall constitute a quorum for transacting business.

ART. 5. The Managers shall superintend the concerns of the Society, enact their own rules and by-laws; shall have the entire direction of the children committed to them; shall provide for them a suitable Governess; shall see that they are properly clothed, fed and instructed; shall determine where they shall be placed when their age and acquirements are such, as to render it proper for them to leave the Asylum; and in all respects exercise over them a *maternal care*.

ART. 6. The first Directress shall preside at all meetings, and in case of equal division give the casting vote. Upon any urgent occasion the first or second Directress, or in their absence the Secretary, or when requested in writing by twenty members of the Society, *any five* of the Managers shall call a special meeting of the Society, which shall be duly notified.

ART. 7. The Secretary shall register the names of the members; shall notify the meetings of the Society, by causing to be published in one or more of our newspapers the time and place of said meeting, at least seven days previous thereto; and shall record their transactions. She shall also meet with and record the proceedings of the Board. She shall receive all the *dues* of the Society, pay them over to the Treasurer, and at each stated meeting of the board, render an account of the sums thus received and paid over, and of such as still remain due.

ART. 8. The Treasurer shall always be a single woman of the age of twenty-one years or upwards; and shall give a bond with sufficient sureties. She shall meet with the Managers when necessary, and shall render to them and to the Society, a statement of its property, with her receipts and payments whenever requested.

ART. 9. All donations shall be reserved as a fund for *building*, and after that object is accomplished, shall go to the establishment of a *permanent fund*.

All subscriptions and the interest on donations, shall be appropriated to defray the annual expenses of the Society.

ART. 10. The Governess shall board the children committed to her care by the Managers, and instruct them in Reading, Writing, and Sewing, with the various branches of domestic employment, and shall make report of their conduct and improvement to the Managers, whenever requested.

ART. 11. The children shall be dressed in a plain manner and treated with kindness. If sick, they shall be visited by a regular physician, whose services shall be paid by the Society, when not rendered gratuitously.

ART. 12. The yearly *tax* shall be accounted *due* at the annual meetings of the Society.

ART. 13. Any alteration of this *Constitution*, not subversive of the *original object* of the Institution, may be made at any special meeting of the Society, called by the Managers for that purpose, by a vote of *two thirds* of the members present.

OFFICERS AND BOARD OF MANAGERS

For the Year Ending Sept. 1828

Mrs. Sally M. Smith, *First Directress*,
Mrs. Thankful Hussey, *Second Do*.
Mrs. Mary B. Storer, *Sec'ry*.
Mrs. Elizabeth L. Fox,
Mrs. Alice Ilsley,
Mrs. Eliza L. Goddard,
Mrs. Lois W. Dana,
Mrs. Susan Wood, *Managers*.
Mrs. Charlotte Andrews,
Mrs. Marcia Hill,
Mrs. Elizabeth G. Atwood,
Mrs. Mary S. B. Merrill,
Mrs. Mary Radford,
Mrs. Susan Richardson,
Mrs. Nancy Cushman,
Miss Lucretia Frothingham, *Treasurer*.

} *Managers*.

BY-LAWS

April 1828

1. Regular Meetings of the Board of Managers shall be held on the first Tuesday in every month, for the purpose of attending to the concerns of the Society. These meetings shall be opened with prayer.

2. The first Directress shall preside at all meetings of the Board; and in case of equal division give the casting vote. In her absence the second Directress shall preside; and in the absence of both, a Moderator shall be chosen for the meeting.

The first Directress shall have power to call special meetings of the Board whenever necessary; and in her absence, the second Directress; and in the absence of both, the Secretary shall call a special meeting whenever requested by *three* Managers.

The special meetings of the Board shall be notified by the Secretary.

3. A collecting Committee shall be appointed annually by the Board of Managers, whose duty shall be to collect all the annual subscriptions to the Society, and pay them over to the Secretary.

This Committee shall consist of such a number as the Board shall from time to time think necessary.

4. When the Treasurer is required to attend any meeting of the Board, she shall be notified by the Secretary, four days previous thereto; and at every such meeting, she shall render an account of monies received, and paid out, and remaining in her hands. And at the end of every six months, she shall settle her accounts with a Committee to be appointed for that purpose by the Board.

5. All accounts against the Society, shall be laid before the Board of Managers, and if allowed, an order shall be drawn by the Secretary on the Treasurer for payment of the same; and no monies shall be paid without such an order, drawn in pursuance of a vote of the Board.

6. A Committee consisting of three Managers shall be chosen every quarter, whose duty it shall be, to examine into the circumstances of children proposed for admission into the Asylum; and also to inquire respecting those persons who may apply to take a child out of the Asylum; and they shall make report to the Board of Managers.

7. It shall be the duty of the Secretary, to place in the Managers' Room in the Asylum, the names of this Committee, with their places of residence.

8. A list of such children as are approved by the Board for admission into the Asylum, shall be kept by the Secretary; priority of application shall give right to admission, unless in the opinion of a majority of the managers at a regular meeting, the circumstances of a child shall require immediate relief.

9. No child shall be received into, or dismissed from the Asylum, or placed in any family, without a vote of the Board at a regular meeting.

10. No child shall be received into the Asylum, until its parents or relatives have relinquished all claim to it. Should, however, any child under the protection of the Society, be claimed by her connexions, she shall be returned to them, whenever all expenses incurred on her account are reimbursed.

11. No relative or friend shall interfere in the management of the children in the Asylum; or visit them except in the presence of the Governess; nor at any time, when their visits are disapproved by the Board.

12. At a suitable age, the children shall be placed in virtuous families, until the age of Eighteen, or marriage within that age; unless some other way for their gaining a livelihood should offer, which the Managers shall deem more eligible.

No child shall be placed out of the Asylum before she has attained to the age of *eleven* years, unless some special circumstance shall render it expedient.

13. In putting out the children, subscribers shall always have the preference. Every child on her leaving the Asylum, shall be supplied by the Society, with one suit of every day wearing apparel. And any person on taking a child, must provide all other clothing necessary for her.

14. A Committee shall be chosen from time to time, whose duty shall be, to make inquiry respecting the conduct and circumstances of the children placed out by the Managers; particularly to ascertain whether they are properly instructed, and treated with kindness; and report to the Board.

15. A Committee of two Ladies shall be chosen every month to provide for the house; to procure and attend to the clothes of the children, and to examine into their improvement; inquire respecting their treatment, and report at every meeting of the Board.

16. A sample of the Bread, meat, and other provisions used in the Asylum, shall be produced to the Board or monthly Committee, whenever required.

17. In case of sickness, the children shall be committed to the care of such Physicians as the Board shall direct.

18. Twenty-five subscribers in any town adjacent to Portland, shall be entitled to place a child in the Asylum, for so long a time as they pay their annual subscription.

19. The Governess shall always be a woman of piety. She shall be chosen by ballot; and a majority of the whole Board shall be necessary to constitute a choice.

20. No alteration in, or addition to, these By-Laws shall be made, unless two thirds of the whole Board of Managers shall concur, at a special meeting notified for that purpose four days previous thereto.

RULES AND REGULATIONS

FOR THE GOVERNMENT OF CHILDREN IN THE ASYLUM

1. All the children on the Sabbath, shall, if the weather permit, regularly attend public worship with the Governess, at such place as the Board shall direct; and during the intervals of worship, they shall read in the Bible and other religious books. They shall also attend the Sabbath School attached to the Society with which they worship.

It shall be the duty of the Governess to pay particular attention to their observance of the Sabbath, teaching them by precept and example, to reverence and keep it holy.

2. The Governess shall read a chapter in the Bible, and pray with the children every morning. She shall attend them at their meals, see that proper order is observed, and that grace is said before and after. She shall teach them to pay a sacred regard to truth, and to the performance of every moral duty; and shall give them such religious instruction as is suited to their age and capacity.

3. The Governess shall instruct the children in reading, writing, arithmetic, plain needle work and knitting.

Those who are old enough, shall mend their own clothes, and assist by weekly rotation, in the domestic business of the family. The Governess shall be particularly careful to educate them in habits of *order, neatness,* and *industry.*

4. The Governess shall not be absent a night from the Asylum, without permission from one of the Board.

She shall visit the children's rooms every night before going to bed. She shall not suffer any of the children to be absent from the Asylum, without special permission in writing from one of the Managers.

GENERAL DIRECTIONS

From the first of April to the first of October, the Children shall rise at six o'clock, say their Prayers, wash themselves, comb their hair, make their beds, and clean their chambers; breakfast at seven; play or work in the garden until nine, when the governess shall read a chapter in the Bible and pray with them; attend school until twelve, dine at one, play until two, attend school until five, after which, play one hour. In the evening say their Prayers, go to bed at eight, wash their feet every night.

From the first of October to the first of April, the Children shall rise at seven o'clock, say their Prayers, wash themselves, comb their hair, make their beds and clean their chambers;—breakfast at eight, attend prayers; school and play hours as before. In the evening, say their Prayers; go to bed at Seven; and wash their feet once a week.

BILL OF FARE

BREAKFAST

Sunday and Thursday mornings, tea, coffee, chocolate or shells, with bread. All other mornings, milk or milk-porridge and bread.

SUPPERS

Sunday nights, tea with bread and butter. All other nights bread, hastypudding, or rice with milk.

DINNERS

Fresh meat, salt beef and pork, salt fish, fresh fish, dried beans and peas, vegetables, and puddings.

CLOTHING

Factory Gingham or Calico for Summer, Bombazette for Winter.

The Society commenced their operations the first of April.

Their House is situated on the corner of Free and South Streets.

Mrs. ABIGAIL RICH, *Governess*.

Miss SARAH RICH, *Assistant*.

The present number of Children belonging to the Asylum, is ten.

At a late meeting of the Board of Managers it was *voted*, "that it is expected, no person will visit the Asylum except in company with one of the Managers, or without a written permission from one of them."

The necessity of such a regulation it is presumed, will be obvious to all; and the Managers take this opportunity to inform all interested in the Institution, that the House is open to inspection, and they will be happy to wait on those who wish to visit it.

FORM OF OBLIGATION

To be signed by a Parent or Guardian on surrendering a child or ward to the protection of the Female Orphan Asylum of Portland.

I, the Subscriber, do hereby surrender my daughter (or Ward) to the Managers of the Female Orphan Asylum of Portland, and to their successors in Office, and to their sole and exclusive care, guardianship and direction, to be by them exercised according to the Rules and Regulations of the Society aforesaid, until my said daughter (or Ward) shall have arrived at the age of eighteen years.

In witness, whereof, I have hereunto set my hand and seal, this   day of   in the year of our Lord, one thousand eight hundred and

SIGNED, SEALED AND DELIVERED IN
PRESENCE OF US,

★ ★ ★

PRESIDENT FRANKLIN PIERCE: VETO MESSAGE

An Act Making A Grant of Public Lands
to the Several States
for the Benefit of Indigent Insane Persons

Washington, *May 3, 1854*

To the Senate of the United States:

The bill entitled "An act making a grant of public lands to the several States for the benefit of indigent insane persons," which was presented to the Senate, the House in which it originated, with a statement of the objections which have required me to withhold from it my approval.

In the performance of this duty, prescribed by the Constitution, I have been compelled to resist the deep sympathies of my own heart in favor of the humane purpose sought to be accomplished and to overcome the reluctance with which I dissent from the conclusions of the two Houses of Congress, and present my own opinions in opposition to the action of a coordinate branch of the Government which possesses so fully my confidence and respect.

If in presenting my objections to this bill I should say more than strictly belongs to the measure or is required for the discharge of my official obligation, let it be attributed to a sincere desire to justify my act before those whose good opinion I so highly value and to that earnestness which springs from my deliberate conviction that a strict adherence to the terms and purposes of the federal compact offers the best, if not the only, security for the preservation of our blessed inheritance of representative liberty.

The bill provides in substance:

First. That 10,000,000 acres of land be granted to the several States, to be apportioned among them in the compound ratio of the geographical area and representation of said States in the House of Representatives.

Second. That wherever there are public lands in a State subject to sale at the regular price of private entry, the proportion of said 10,000,000 acres falling to such State shall be selected from such lands within it, and that to the States in which there are no such public lands land scrip shall be issued to the amount of their distributive shares, respectively, said scrip not to be entered by said States, but to be sold by them and subject to entry by their assignees: *Provided*. That none of it shall be sold at less than $1 per acre, under penalty of forfeiture of the same to the United States.

Third. That the expenses of the management and superintendence of said lands and of the moneys received therefrom shall be paid by the States to which they may belong out of the treasury of said States.

Fourth. That the gross proceeds of the sales of such lands or land scrip so granted shall be invested by the several States in safe stocks, to constitute a perpetual fund, the principal of which shall remain forever undiminished, and the interest to be appropriated to the maintenance of the indigent insane within the several States.

Fifth. That annual returns of lands or scrip sold shall be made by the States to the Secretary of the Interior, and the whole grant be subject to certain conditions and limitations prescribed in the bill, to be assented to by legislative acts of said States.

This bill therefore proposes that the Federal Government shall make provision to the amount of the value of 10,000,000 acres of land for an eleemosynary object within the several States, to be administered by the political authority of the same; and it presents at the threshold the question whether any such act on the part of the Federal Government is warranted and sanctioned by the Constitution, the provisions and principles of which are to be protected and sustained as a first and paramount duty.

It can not be questioned that if Congress has power to make provision for the indigent insane without the limits of this District it has the same power to provide for the indigent who are not insane, and thus to transfer to the Federal Government the charge of all the poor in all the States. It has the same power to provide hospitals and other local establishments for the care and cure of every species of human infirmity, and thus to assume all that duty of either public philanthropy or public necessity to the dependent, the orphan, the sick, or the needy which is now discharged by the States themselves or by corporate institutions or private endowments existing under the legislation of the States. The whole field of public beneficence is thrown open to the care and culture of the Federal Government. Generous impulses no longer encounter the limitations and control of our imperious fundamental law; for however worthy may be the present object in itself, it is only one of a class. It is not exclusively worthy of benevolent regard. Whatever considerations dictate sympathy for this particular object apply in like manner, if not in the same degree, to idiocy, to physical disease, to extreme destitution. If Congress may and ought to provide for any one of these objects, it may and ought to provide for them all. And if it be done in this case, what answer shall be given when Congress shall be called upon, as it doubtless will be, to pursue a similar course of legislation in the others? It will obviously be vain to reply that the object is worthy, but that the application has taken a wrong direction. The power will have been deliberately assumed, the general obligation will by this act have been acknowledged, and the question of means and expediency will alone be left for consideration. The decision upon the principle in any one case determines it for the whole class. The question presented, therefore, clearly is upon the constitutionality and propriety of the Federal Government assuming to enter into a novel and vast field of legislation, namely, that of providing for the care and support of all those among the people of the United States who by any form of calamity become fit objects of public philanthropy.

I readily and, I trust, feelingly acknowledge the duty incumbent on us all as men and citizens, and as among the highest and holiest of our duties, to provide for those who, in the mysterious order of Providence, are subject to want and to disease of body or mind; but I can not find any authority in the Constitution for making the Federal Government the great almoner of public charity throughout the United States. To do so would, in my judgment, be contrary to the letter and spirit of the Constitution and subversive of the whole theory upon which the Union of these States is founded. And if it were admissible to contemplate the exercise of this power for any object whatever, I can not avoid the belief that it would in the end be prejudicial rather than beneficial in the noble office of charity to have the charge of them transferred from the States to the Federal Government. Are we not too prone to forget that the Federal Union is the creature of the States, not they of the Federal Union? We were the inhabitants of colonies distinct in local government one from the other before the Revolution. By that Revolution the colonies each became an independent State. They achieved that independence and secured its recognition by the agency of a consulting body, which, from being an assembly of the ministers of distinct sovereignties instructed to agree to no form of government which did not leave the domestic concerns of each State to itself, was appropriately denominated a Congress. When, having tried the experiment of the Confederation, they resolved to change that for the present Federal Union, and thus to confer on the Federal Government more ample authority, they scrupulously measured such of the functions of their cherished sovereignty as they chose to delegate to the General Government. With this aim and to this end the fathers of the Republic framed the Constitution, in and by which the independent and sovereign States united themselves for certain specified objects and purposes, and for those only, leaving all powers not therein set forth as conferred on one or another of the three great departments—the legislative, the executive, and the judicial—indubitably with the States. And when the people of the several States had in their State conventions, and thus alone, given effect and force to the Constitution, not content that any doubt should in future arise as to the scope and character of this act, they ingrafted thereon the explicit declaration that "the powers not delegated to the United States by the Constitution nor prohibited by it to the States are reserved to the States respectively or to the people." Can it be controverted that the great mass of the business of Government—that involved in the social relations, the internal arrangements of the body politic, the mental and moral culture of men, the development of local resources of wealth, the punishment of crimes in general, the preservation of order, the relief of the needy or otherwise unfortunate members of society—did in practice remain with the States; that none of these objects of local concern are by the Constitution expressly or impliedly prohibited to the States, and that none of them are by any express language of the Constitution transferred to the United States? Can it be claimed that any of these functions of local administration and legislation are vested in the Federal Government by any implication? I have never found anything in the Constitution which is susceptible of such a construction. No one of the enumerated powers touches the subject or has even a remote analogy to it. The powers conferred upon the United States have reference to federal relations, or to the means of accomplishing or executing things of federal relation. So also of the same character are the powers taken away from the States by enumeration. In either case the powers granted and the powers restricted were so granted or so restricted only where it was requisite for the maintenance of peace and harmony between the States or for the purpose of protecting their common interests and defending their common sovereignty against aggression from abroad or insurrection at home.

I shall not discuss at length the question of power sometimes claimed for the General Government under the clause of the eighth section of the Constitution, which gives Congress the power "to lay and collect taxes, duties, imposts, and excises, to pay debts and provide for the common defense and general welfare of the United States," because if it has not already been settled upon sound reason and authority it never will be. I take the received and just construction of that article, as if written to lay and collect taxes, duties, imposts, and excises *in order* to pay the debts and *in order* to provide for the common defense and general welfare. It is not a substantive general power to provide for the welfare of the United States, but is a limitation on the grant of power to raise money by taxes, duties, and imposts. If it were otherwise, all the rest of the Constitution, consisting of carefully enumerated and cautiously guarded grants of specific powers, would have been useless, if not delusive. It would be impossible in that view to escape from the conclusion that these were inserted only to mislead for the present, and, instead of enlightening and defining the pathway of the future, to involve its action in the mazes of doubtful construction. Such a conclusion the character of the men who framed that sacred instrument will never permit us to form. Indeed, to suppose it susceptible of any other construction would be to consign all the rights of the States and of the people of the States to the mere discretion of Congress, and thus to clothe the Federal Government with authority to control the sovereign States, by which they would have been dwarfed into provinces or departments and all sovereignty vested in an absolute consolidated central power, against which the spirit of liberty has so often and in so many countries struggled in vain. In my judgment you can not by tributes to humanity make any adequate compensation for the wrong you would inflict by removing the sources of power and political action from those who are to be thereby affected. If the time shall ever arrive when, for an object appealing, however strongly, to our sympathies, the dignity of the States shall bow to the dictation of Congress by conforming their legislation thereto, when the power and majesty and honor of those who created shall become subordinate to the thing of their creation, I but feebly utter my apprehensions when I express my firm conviction that we shall see "the beginning of the end."

It is a marked point of the history of the Constitution that when it was proposed to empower Congress to establish a university the proposition was confined to the District intended for the future seat of Government of the United States, and that even that proposed clause was omitted in consideration of the exclusive powers conferred on Congress to legislate for that District. Could a more decisive indication of the true construction and the spirit of the Constitution in regard to all matters of this nature have been given? It proves that such objects were considered by the Convention as appertaining to local legislation only; that they were not comprehended, either expressly or by implication, in the grant of general power to Congress, and that consequently they remained with the several States.

The general result at which I have arrived is the necessary consequence of those views of the relative rights, powers, and duties of the States and of the Federal Government which I have long entertained and often expressed and in reference to which my convictions do but increase in force with time and experience.

I have thus discharged the unwelcome duty of respectfully stating my objections to this bill, with which I cheerfully submit the whole subject to the wisdom of Congress.

FRANKLIN PIERCE

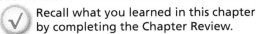 Recall what you learned in this chapter by completing the Chapter Review.

4

The Civil War and After: 1860–1900

NATIONAL ARCHIVES AND RECORDS ADMINISTRATION.

CHANGING ECONOMIC AND DEMOGRAPHIC REALITIES

The Civil War and its aftermath were defining years in the history of social welfare and social work. At the end of the war, the nation undertook its most far-reaching effort at social reform as it attempted to *reconstruct the South* as a liberal, democratic society. Yet, the combination of Southern resistance and white racism defeated the experiment in a few years. In the wake of Reconstruction's failure, social activism was channeled into narrower and more limited endeavors. The Charity Organization and Settlement House movements grew out of this cautious approach to reform. Social work, which had its origins in these two movements, continued to share this caution. A focus on individual change over social reform, a distrust of the competence of the poor, and a preference for voluntary over government action would characterize social work over much of its first century.

Science and invention progressed rapidly and propelled growth in all sectors of the economy—transportation, communication, agriculture, mining, and manufacturing. A second Industrial Revolution—tied to electricity, steel, and chemistry—began to remake

LEARNING OUTCOMES

- Identify the ways that the Civil War influenced the development of the American economy and politics.
- Explain the origins of the social work profession during the late 19th century and its impact on its development later.
- Specify the major social movements of the late 19th century and the social problems they addressed.

CHAPTER OUTLINE

Changing Economic and Demographic Realities   77
  Population Changes   79
  Naturalization and Citizenship   79
  Regional Shifts   81
  The Aging: The Group That Was Left Behind   83

Innovations in Social Welfare Services   83
  The Welfare of Soldiers and Veterans   84
  Social Welfare: Reconstruction and the Freedmen's Bureau   86
  Social Welfare and Urban Expansion   89
  The Charity Organization Movement   90
  The Settlement House Movement   95
  A New View of Child Welfare   97

Social Movements During the Late 19th Century: The Reform Impulse   100
  The Social Welfare of Women   100
  The Labor Movement   102
  The Agrarian Movement   103

Conclusion   105

CHAPTER OUTLINE *(Continued)*

DOCUMENTS: The Civil War and After   106

An Act to Provide for the Relief of Indigent Soldiers, Sailors and Marines, and the Families of Those Deceased, 1887   107

The Economic and Moral Effects of Public Outdoor Relief, 1890   108

An Act to Prohibit the Coming of Chinese Laborers to the United States, September 1888, and Supplement, October 1888   111

▶ **Watch this video on the depression of 1873.**

In what ways did this depression have a different impact that our more recent economic slowdowns?

https://www.youtube.com/watch?v=D57dgatuPPg

manufacturing, while the extension of railroad lines—the first transcontinental railroad was completed in 1869—created a truly national transportation network. The railroad spurred changes in business organization as well. Its national sweep required railroad companies to raise capital, create facilities, and manage workers on a national and international scale. These challenges laid the foundation for the modern corporation that would come to dominate the economy by the early 20th century.

Population doubled during the last 30 years of the century, fueled to a great extent by a new wave of European immigration at the close of the Civil War. Gross national product rose from about $6.7 billion to an estimated $16.8 billion, which led to a substantial increase in per capita income.[1] The increase in national income improved the lives of most Americans, although African Americans, Latinos, and Native Americans were more often excluded from the full benefits of this growth.

The war and the industrial development it hastened laid the foundation for the acquisition of huge fortunes, and the postwar railroad boom fostered the accumulation of individual wealth. Soon the formation of industrial corporations and trusts and the expansion of the stock market made it possible to extend and exploit the technological innovations of the period. The accumulation of economic and political power by an urban elite, however, contrasted with the continued misery of the urban working class and rural poor. Moreover, cyclical fluctuations brought panic, depression, and severe unemployment during 1873–1878 and 1893–1898. Population growth, the normal hazards of an increasingly industrial and urban society, and the recurring periods of economic depression forced American cities to confront mass unemployment.

For the North, the war brought prosperity. The increased output of war goods and rising prices of food and clothing stimulated the process of industrialization. Demand for labor was high, and the need for workers to fill newly created jobs, as well as the old ones left vacant by men away at war, encouraged immigration and the growth of cities. The end of the Civil War and the return to civilian production furthered the process of industrialization and economic growth.

The war was a catalyst for Northern growth, but for the South it meant the devastation of land, property, transportation facilities, and credit institutions. While the Northeast and Midwest saw increasing concentration of property and wealth, the decline of the plantation system in the South led to a decentralization of land ownership. While jobs were plentiful in the North, workers in the South—white and black—struggled to find employment and a means of self-support. The process of Southern reconstruction eventually led to the beginnings of industrialization and, of even more significance for the eventual shape of the Southern economy, to the rise of tenant farming. Although the Southern economy grew, the gap between the industrial North and the agricultural South widened through the remainder of the 19th century.

The last great frontier of the West was settled during these years, as immigrants and migrants from the East relocated to land that had previously belonged to Native Americans. A fashion for buffalo hides nearly eliminated the herds that had dominated the Great Plains, and with them, a major food supply for the Plains' tribes. The railroads created towns that became the centers for agricultural development. In 1860, the five states immediately west of the Mississippi—Texas, Arkansas, Missouri, Iowa, and Minnesota—had only 15.3 million acres in improved farmlands. These same five states had increased improved farmlands to 50 million acres in 1880 and 87 million acres in 1910. An era ended in 1890 when the superintendent of the census wrote, "Up to and including 1880 the country had a frontier settlement but at present the unsettled area has been so broken into isolated bodies of settlement that there can hardly be said to be a frontier line."[2] In 1860, the area west of the Mississippi River included only 7 states; by 1900, there were 18. By the turn of the 20th century, the continental United States included 45 states and only three territories.

The last decades of the 19th century are remembered as a "gilded age" because economic growth benefited elites more than ordinary people. Yet, these increases in inequality fueled a variety of social movements that would influence social politics over the next century. Women who mobilized in the battle against slavery played a central role during Reconstruction and then fought for equal rights. New labor movements and an agrarian revolt were ultimately unsuccessful but raised issues and solutions that continued to resonate in American policy debates.

Population Changes

Territorial expansion and industrial and agricultural growth went hand in hand with growth and shifts in population. The country's overall population grew from 36 million in 1865 to 76 million in 1900—an increase of 40 million, or 111 percent.[3] The proportion of blacks in the total population remained comparatively stable—13 percent in 1865 and 12 percent in 1900. White males' life expectancy at birth in 1860 was 38 years and that of females was 40.5 years. By 1900, these figures had increased to 48 years for males and 48 years for females. Although life expectancy increased—largely as a result of declines in infant and child mortality—the share of the population over the age of 65 remained low—only 4 percent in 1900.

Naturalization and Citizenship

The Homestead Act of 1862, the end of the Civil War, the opening of the Oregon territories, the development of new agricultural machinery to farm the prairies, and the gold rush all contributed to the westward movement. The Oklahoma land rush and the finishing of the transcontinental railroad to the Pacific coast accelerated the process.

The years after the Civil War were devastating for the Native American nations. The Western expansion of white settlers disrupted the economic, demographic, and social organization of Native American life. The Northern Civil War army was deployed against indigenous people with the close of the war. The federal government used almost any pretext to displace Native Americans from their land and destroy their capacity for an independent life. Civil War generals like Philip Sheridan earned new reputations leading a genocidal battle against the Western tribes.

By the 1890s, nearly all Native American nations were conquered and located on reservations. Chief Joseph of the Nez Perce had declared, "I will fight no more forever," and Geronimo of the Apache nation was imprisoned. In the course of three centuries, the Native American population had been reduced by 90 percent. On reservations, Native Americans were subjects, not citizens. The Dawes Act of 1887 permitted naturalization for Native Americans not living on reservations. Those on reservations were considered members of another, dependent nation.[4]

The years after the Civil War were devastating for the Native American nations. The Western expansion of white settlers disrupted the economic, demographic, and social organization of Native American life.

In exchange for their land, tribal nations were at first settled on fertile ground. They were promised annual cash stipends and were to be taught how to live self-sufficiently as farmers on reservations. But the tribal nations were moved again and again to more barren areas. Most reservations had too little grazing land for buffalo, and the land was too unproductive to grow sufficient food. Added to this were the plagues, whiskey, and corrupt agents on both sides who stole supplies and sources of support. The result for most tribes was widespread poverty. In the words of President Rutherford B. Hayes in 1877:

> The Indians . . . have been driven from place to place. The purchase money paid . . . has still left them poor. In many instances, when they had settled down upon land assigned to them by compact and begun to support themselves by their own labor, they were rudely jostled off and thrust into the wilderness again. Many, if not most, of our Indian wars have had their origin in broken promises and acts of injustice on our part.[5]

Lip service, however, did not change whites' behavior. Even sympathetic whites saw assimilation and the elimination of Native America's folkways as the only alternative to annihilation. Because reformers devalued tribal traditions, culture, and languages, they sought to bring Native Americans into the mainstream. Children were taken from their parents and reservations and sent to military-style boarding schools, where they were forced to give up their traditions. Their hairstyles, dress, languages, food, and religions were westernized. After school, they returned to their reservations, prepared for life neither on nor off the reservation.

Thirteen million immigrants arrived in the United States between 1865 and 1900, accounting for 32 percent of the increase in population.[6] In the 1870s and early 1880s, they came largely from Great Britain, Scandinavia, and Germany. Toward the end of the 19th century, a new wave of immigration came from Russia, Austria–Hungary, Poland, and other parts of eastern Europe. The new immigrants went to the mines, steel mills, textile factories, and other manufacturing establishments of the Eastern Seaboard and the farms of the Midwest. Businessmen welcomed them as cheap labor, but labor unions resented them as competition.[7]

The issue of immigration presented a complex dilemma for many Americans. On the one hand, since its founding as a "city upon a hill," Americans had seen their country as a beacon to the rest of the world. The United States was a nation of immigrants. How could it turn its back on that legacy? At the same time, the increase in southern and eastern European immigration added a racial element to the debate. Not only were immigrants poor and competing for jobs but also they did not share the cultural background of earlier generations. Anti-immigrant fervor fueled a wave of scientific racism in which scientists and pseudoscientists claimed to have discovered several European races, each with different qualities and capacities. Darwin's theory of natural selection provided another pretext for differentiating groups. *Social Darwinism*, a philosophy developed by Herbert Spencer and others, saw social development as similar to Darwin's evolutionary principles. Rather than adding to America's diversity, the new immigrants entered a battle of "survival of the fittest."[8]

The Asian population, which had come to the United States in large numbers first during the California gold rush of 1848 and later as laborers recruited for the building of the railroads of the West, met with even more discrimination and more barriers. Immigration of Chinese, largely Cantonese and male, rose sharply during the period. With the completion of the rail system to the Pacific coast and the end of the need for a large supply of cheap laborers, economics and racism led to the expulsion of many Asians from Pacific coast cities. A series of legislative acts at the end of the 19th century first restricted immigration and finally excluded the Chinese population in the United States.

In 1868, Congress adopted the 14th Amendment to the Constitution, which was designed to protect the rights of the newly freed slaves. It declared that anyone born in this country was automatically a citizen. But Chinese, indeed all Asians, born abroad had no rights to citizenship at any time. Two years later, Congress passed the Naturalization Act of 1870, which limited naturalization to "white persons and persons of African descent."

Arguing that the Chinese were basically inassimilable, the Chinese Exclusion Act of 1882 reflected the interests of organized labor and its fear of cheap labor. It built on a heavy layer of racial prejudice. The act excluded Chinese immigration of laborers (although not manufacturers), at first for 10 years and then permanently. Originally, the act provided for Chinese workers going back to China to get readmission certificates. But in 1888, President Grover Cleveland canceled all certificates and prevented the readmission of many.

Regional Shifts

Internal migration and immigration combined to change the social profile of the United States during the four decades of the 19th century. Although cities grew, the majority of the population remained rural. In the countryside, the West and South diverged after the Civil War as tenancy and sharecropping ensnared the South in a cycle of underdevelopment that had profound implications for poor whites and African Americans.[9]

By the end of the century, large cities were no longer confined to the Atlantic coast. In 1860, there had been eight cities with populations over 100,000—four in the East, three in the Midwest, and one in the South. By 1900, there were 36 cities with populations over 100,000—17 in the East, 13 in the Midwest, 3 in the South, and 3 in the Far West.[10] Unquestionably, the process of urbanization had made great strides. In 1860, 20 percent of the country's population lived in cities; by 1900, 40 percent did. Yet, even that figure is misleading, because the definition of a "city" in 1900 was a place with at least 2,500 residents.[11]

The economic crises of the late 19th century—1873, 1885, and 1892—also forced cities to confront a new social phenomenon—mass unemployment. Orthodox economic theory, which believed that "supply creates its own demand," held that widespread unemployment was impossible, while political ideas about independence and manhood challenged the new reality of millions of workers who were dependent on large employers and distant markets. While local political leaders scrambled to respond to the needs of the unemployed, often by creating public employment projects, social welfare leaders continued to hold to the belief that the labor market, not relief, was the solution to the problem.[12]

In addition to machines that revolutionized industrial and agricultural activities, achievements in the realm of applied science opened new fields of communications (the telegraph and telephone), transportation (air brakes, automobiles), and business machines (typewriters, for example). In contrast to the first Industrial Revolution, industrial growth during the late 19th century was driven by scientific research. No wonder, then, that leaders in voluntary and public social welfare should look to science and to the organization of scientific knowledge for new approaches to the alleviation of poverty.

The structure of rural life in the post–Civil War period changed in response to shifts in the organization of agriculture. The major crop of the prewar South was cotton, with some land devoted to tobacco and sugar. The plantation system, based on African American slave labor, was the dominant way in which land and labor were organized. With the end of slavery, many plantations were divided into smaller plots that were farmed by tenants who either paid rent or were sharecroppers, who provided a share of each year's crop as payment to the landlord. The average size of a farm in the South Atlantic states dropped from 353 acres in 1860 to 108 acres in 1900. Almost half the farms were tenant operated. The high rate of tenancy prevented small farmers from improving their individual well-being. Most tenants found themselves heavily in debt and dependent upon a rich landowner for credit and provisions.[13]

The postwar South saw some diversification of products, especially the development of corn as a cash crop and of fruit orchards. But this was small and largely confined to independent white farmers. Cotton remained king. Familiarity, ready marketability, and, most critically, the dependence for capital on conservative credit sources prevented further diversification. By 1877, cotton output surpassed the prewar level of 4.5 million bales.[14] Recovery in cotton production both fueled and limited the postwar recovery of the Southern economy.

Farmers in the Midwest and West, too, experienced major structural shifts. As in the South, the average size of a farm decreased; unlike the South, this was a response to a major change in output. The vast Western lands provided an opportunity for raising cattle and sheep and for growing wheat and corn. The availability of land resources for exploitation and for settling was particularly opportune at the close of the Civil War when millions of demobilized veterans sought to realize their dream of independent landownership. Congress eased the path to ownership by passing the Homestead Act in 1862, which allowed farmers to claim land and then gain ownership after working it for five years.

After 1869, several other rail lines crossed the continent. Through land grants, Congress chartered the construction of the Northern Pacific to connect the Great Lakes with Puget Sound, the Southern Pacific and Santa Fe to tie the Mississippi Valley with the Pacific coast, and the Denver and Rio Grande to slice through the mountains of Colorado to Salt Lake City. The building of state-supported rival lines and of branch lines served to connect the states of the West with each other and the West with the East. In addition to being direct transportation links with Eastern markets, the railroads stimulated trade carried on ships operating from the Great Lakes and connecting with ports in New York State and in foreign countries. The invention of the refrigerated railroad car in the 1870s allowed meat packers to slaughter cattle in the Midwest and ship the meat to Eastern markets. Soon, Chicago emerged as the center of the industry.

Western crop acreage increased and, with the introduction of fertilizers, productivity rose. As a result, the country's production of wheat had jumped from 173 million bushels in 1859 to 600 million bushels in 1900; the production of corn rose from 839 million bushels in 1859 to 2.7 billion bushels in 1900.[15] With the value of wheat and corn exports up to $73 million and $85 million, respectively, by 1900, the farm belt was feeding the world as well as the nation.[16]

The opening of the West was speeded, too, by the discovery of precious metals—gold, silver, and zinc—and soon by the realization of the existence of vast supplies of copper, coal, iron ore, and petroleum. The rise in the value of mining from 1 percent of the nation's total output on the eve of the Civil War to 5 percent in the last year of the century was a mark of advancing Western enterprise as well as a base for Eastern industrialization.[17]

The expansion of manufacturing and cities fueled the recovery of the South and the settling and development of the West. In the country as a whole, the number of manufacturing establishments grew from 140,000 in 1860 to 208,000 in 1900. Between these years, the number of employees grew from 1 million to 4.7 million—a 370 percent increase; the value of manufactured products rose from $1.8 billion to $11 billion—a 505 percent increase. Capitalization grew by 789 percent during these years. Manufacturing had become more capital-intensive, necessitating the eventual move toward larger units of manufacturing and decreased competition.[18] The value of manufacturing output rose by 515 percent from the period immediately preceding the Civil War to the end of the century. The value of agricultural output rose by 127 percent during the same period. Although both had increased in value, they had reversed positions in relative importance.[19] In 1900, the industrial heartland of the nation was still bounded by a parallelogram anchored by Boston and Baltimore to the east and Chicago and St. Louis to the west.

The dominance of the East in manufacturing is demonstrated by the fact that 67.3 percent of the country's manufacturing establishments were located in New England and the Middle Atlantic states in 1859. Although manufacturing grew in the Western states, the New England and Middle Atlantic states continued to account for 52.4 percent of all manufacturing enterprises at the end of the century.[20]

The Aging: The Group That Was Left Behind

Most older Americans in the last half of the 19th century were not destitute. Many of the men worked. Voluntary retirement was almost unknown. Illness or disability might keep one out of the labor force, recurring economic crises might make jobs very difficult to find, but, overall, labor-force participation rates were high for older men.[21] Many older men supported themselves and their spouses. In other cases, an older person often lived with an adult child. For most of the aged, most of the time, the family, be it small or extended, was the chief source of support.

It was the older person without familial aid, who could no longer work, and who had never earned enough to be able to put away a nest egg, who was most at risk of becoming a resident of the poorhouse. Women had lower incomes and fewer marketable skills, were less likely to be covered by Civil War pensions, and outlived their spouses, all factors increasing the chances of their spending their last days in an almshouse. But mothers, more than fathers, were apt to receive familial support and to live with their children. Additionally, more women than men received outdoor relief, and women were more likely than men to be placed in specialized institutions rather than in a general almshouse. Women, when they did enter the poorhouse, tended to enter at a younger age and be dependent longer than men, since they had so little means of support, but the proportion of men was considerably higher than that of women.[22]

As the almshouse went out of fashion in the last years of the 19th century, other groups of dependents were removed to specialized institutions. Increasingly, almshouses were transformed into "old folks homes." The deaf and dumb, the mentally ill, and children were all defined as worthy of special treatment. But the aged, especially aged men, tended to be left in poorhouses out of proportion to their presence in the poverty population. In 1855, 15 percent of the people in almshouses were aged; by 1886, that figure had reached 37 percent.[23]

? Assess your comprehension of "Changing Economic and Demographic Realities" by completing this quiz.

INNOVATIONS IN SOCIAL WELFARE SERVICES

War is the business of government. Four years of the bloodiest conflict in American history caused an expansion of the size and scope of the U.S. government without precedent. Government spending in the North rose from less than 2 percent of gross domestic product in 1860 to over 13 percent in 1865. Ironically, the Confederacy, which was founded on the doctrine of states' rights, also had to expand the functions of the central government in order to field armies and marshal its scarce economic resources in the battle with the Union.

The expansion of government's role did not end with the cessation of fighting. The demands of the postwar world—displaced populations, orphaned and widowed families, and the changing legal, social, and economic status of four million African Americans—demanded an expanded government in the late 1860s and 1870s.

By the mid-1870s, however, the cycle of activist government was waning. The challenge of reconstructing the South as a biracial democracy foundered in the face of white resistance and the continuing economic power of the planter class. The Union hero, Ulysses S. Grant, gained the presidency in 1868 but then oversaw an increasingly corrupt administration. Radical Republicans—who had championed efforts to recreate Southern society—lost influence to a Democratic Party anchored by Southern elites and a more business-friendly and cautious Republican Party.

Thus, from the 1870s until the 1890s, older American influences—voluntary action and limited government—reasserted themselves. For social welfare, this translated in a set of innovations focused on voluntary agencies operating at the state and local levels. The two great movements of the period—the Charity Organization and the Settlement House movements—differed on their strategies, but shared a commitment to white Protestant values and the importance of nongovernmental organization taking the lead in social welfare.

Yet, this cycle, too, ran its course. The deep depression of the 1890s overwhelmed the capacity of voluntary agencies and raised questions about whether individual moral or genetic failings were the root causes of poverty. By the 1890s, challenged by a variety of newer social movements, social welfare thought and action began to change again.

The Welfare of Soldiers and Veterans

During and immediately after the Civil War, the social welfare needs of soldiers and their families demanded attention in all sections of the country. During the war years, 2.3 million served in the Union forces, of whom 719,000 died and 280,000 were wounded—a casualty rate of 43 percent. Participants in the Confederate forces totaled 781,000, of whom 307,000 died and 100,000 were wounded—a casualty rate of 52 percent.[24] Whether for medical care, domiciliary care, or financial support, the needs of veterans were considered apart from the needs of the civilian population and as deserving of state and federal governmental support.

Federal legislation affording benefits to soldiers and veterans was passed first by Congress for the Union forces and, later, was confined to veterans of the Union. In July 1862, Congress enacted a pension system covering individuals disabled in the line of duty, as well as widows, children, and dependent relations of those who were killed. Efforts to encourage enlistment, such as the Enrollment Act of 1863, stated each citizen's obligation to defend the country and the right of the federal government to impose that obligation.[25] But the enactment of additional legislation in the veterans' behalf clarified the reciprocal nature of the obligation—the necessity for taking care of "our battered heroes . . . in such a way as to maintain the military spirit and the national pride . . . and to keep in the eye of the Nation the price of its liberties."[26]

The U.S. Sanitary Commission was established in 1861 by the secretary of war in response to a recommendation by the Women's Central Relief Association of New York. The association represented the joined forces of the women comprising the Women's Central Association of Relief for the Sick and Wounded of the Army, the Advisory Committee of the Boards of Physicians and Surgeons of the Hospitals of New York, and the New York Medical Association for furnishing hospital supplies in aid of the army.

Pointing to "the spontaneous and earnest efforts" of women in many parts of the Union to perform volunteer service on behalf of an essentially volunteer army, the relief association called for a governmental body responsible "to keep the women of the loyal states everywhere informed how their efforts may be most wisely and economically employed."[27]

The New York association, like its counterparts in many other localities, was aware of the recent experience with sanitary science in the Crimean War, particularly as publicized through the testimony of Florence Nightingale in parliamentary hearings in Britain. The Sanitary Commission, as set forth in an address to the secretary of war on May 18, 1861, focused on prevention, such as the supervision of the diet and hygiene of the troops, as well as on providing medical and nursing services.

The acting surgeon general of the United States acquiesced, and, on June 13, 1861, President Abraham Lincoln approved the appointment of a Commission of Inquiry and Advice in respect of the Sanitary Interests of the U.S. Forces.

The voluntary nature of the commission—its dependence upon contributions of money and labor—is reflected in its original and popular title, the People's Commission of Sanitary Inquiry and Advice.[28] Once appointed, the commission "prepared to go to work without a dollar in its treasury." Subsequently, "the irrepressible determination of the American people to manifest . . . their direct personal interest in the soldier" led to "countless forms of popular sympathy" demonstrated in "clamorous and persistent . . . offers of relief as the war went on."[29] The commission became the channel for directing this national outpouring of contributions toward the relief and comfort of the Union forces.

The nine officially appointed members of the commission were men, despite the fact that women's groups funded and implemented its programs. The work of overseeing the welfare of the military was performed with the belief that the country could "never half repay them for the sacrifices they have made or half balance our debt of gratitude."[30] From the start, these groups supported the commission's promotion of national concern for the care veterans would receive once the war was over.

On March 3, 1865, Lincoln signed an act to incorporate a national military and naval asylum for the relief of totally disabled officers and men of the voluntary forces of the United States. Subsequently, this enabling legislation was strengthened by the provision of funds to make possible the building and operation of a group of national homes, first for Union veterans suffering economic distress due to wartime disabilities and, later, for economically distressed veterans whose disabilities were not service connected. The country's view of the needy Union veteran as worthy was illustrated in an 1871 report of a congressional committee that had investigated the conditions of the early national homes:

> Liberal expenditures have been made to provide . . . facilities for recreation and for intellectual and moral culture, as well as . . . good quarters, food, clothing, and hospital attendance. The constant and proper aim of the management is . . . that the asylums were in no sense almshouses . . . but homes which the disabled soldiers have earned for themselves.[31]

During the Civil War and for the 25 years following it, the federal government liberalized the terms of entitlement to pensions and raised the level of benefits. The founding of the Grand Army of the Republic (GAR), a veterans' organization, in 1866 formed an organized constituency able to push for progressive liberalization of benefits. That year, annual federal expenditures for Union veterans' pensions totaled $15 million; by 1882, this doubled; and by 1889, it reached $86 million.[32] In 1890, pushed by pension claims agents and the GAR, and responding to the large number of disabled and destitute veterans, Congress acted to keep veterans from dependency on "the frigid bosom of public charity." The Dependent Pension Act of 1890 dropped the requirement that disability be service connected and instead provided pensions for veterans (and their wives) who had served at least 90 days and who were unable to earn a living by physical labor. By 1898, expenditures tripled and the number of veterans covered jumped from less than 420,000 to more than 745,000.[33]

By 1900, federal and state responsibility for the care of needy and disabled veterans and their dependents was well established. Cash payments, medical services, and domiciliary care were all parts of a system that viewed the social welfare of veterans and their families as a special obligation of the society as a whole. The obligation was being met through legislative provisions that, for their time, were generous and couched in language meant to protect the beneficiary's right to help and to avoid a pauper's label. New York State, for example, in 1887 went so far as to prohibit "sending indigent soldiers, sailors, and marines (or their families, or the families of those deceased), to any almshouse (or orphan asylum) without the full concurrence and consent of the commander and relief committees of the post of the Grand Army of the Republic."[34]

The successful efforts to expand Civil War pensions ultimately provoked a backlash. Pensions became entwined with electoral politics as the two political parties competed with each another to determine which was more supportive of veterans. During election season, congressmen and federal officials would often travel through crucial states signing veterans up for pensions and assuring voters that their party could be counted on to keep expanding the program.[35]

Late in the century, reform leaders often pointed to the "prostituting and degrading" of the pension system as a lesson in the evil associated with "big government." At a time when other nations' reformers were looking to government to improve the social conditions of ordinary people, American Progressives stood out for their suspicion of government programs and their advocacy of voluntary action.

Federal largesse did not extend to Confederate veterans. In national homes established at Kecoughtan, Virginia, and Johnson City, Tennessee, only those Southerners who had served on the Union side were welcome. Some Southern states created pension programs for Confederate veterans, but like much Southern social welfare, it did not match the generosity of federal pensions. As with Northern veterans, aid for Southern soldiers and their families was outside the stigma of poor-relief laws. Southern localities enacted special legislation, including special taxes, to provide emergency assistance to Confederate veterans and their dependents. As the war progressed, responsibility shifted from voluntary agencies to local government, and then to state governments and the Confederate Congress. The Confederate veteran was considered by his government and his neighbors to be as worthy as his Northern counterpart, although actual benefits in the South lagged behind those in the North.

Social Welfare: Reconstruction and the Freedmen's Bureau

During the war, the Southern states had experienced widespread destruction as well as severe declines of agricultural output. With the end of the war, wounded veterans and their families, widows and orphans of slain soldiers, large numbers of freed and homeless blacks, and a civilian population were all made needy by the war itself. Near famine resulted from drought and widespread dislocation of the labor force. The situation was worse for lack of an extensive prewar public or private welfare system to draw upon.

> By 1900, federal and state responsibility for the care of needy and disabled veterans and their dependents was well established. Cash payments, medical services, and domiciliary care were all parts of a system that viewed the social welfare of veterans and their families as a special obligation of the society as a whole.

In the immediate postwar period, the individual states gave first attention to the needs of veterans and their dependents for artificial limbs and cash pensions. Concern for the orphans of Confederate soldiers led to the establishment of orphanages and of apprenticeship procedures. As for the general white population, most Southern states set up central public welfare stations for the distribution of food and clothing.

The *Black Codes*, which every Southern state except Tennessee enacted, epitomized Presidential Reconstruction. The former Confederate states attempted to reinstitute a system of control of black labor. Encouraged by the conciliatory policies of Andrew Johnson, a Southerner who became president when Lincoln was assassinated in April 1865, Southern legislatures passed laws to deny African Americans rights and to compel them to work for their former masters.

The *Black Codes* limited property rights, forbade working as artisans and mechanics, and otherwise specified the kinds of economic activities in which freed blacks could engage. The codes of Georgia, for example, stated that "all persons strolling about in idleness would be put in chain gangs and contracted out to employers."[36] In effect, the codes used the old Poor Law provisions in regard to vagrancy to secure state revenues while simultaneously organizing workers to be used in reconstruction and industrial pursuits. Vagrants were rounded up, labeled criminal, and subjected to leases as long as 20 years.[37]

Black children were also pushed into dependency. In 1865, for example, Mississippi declared all blacks younger than 18 years old who were orphans, or whose parents could not support them, available for apprenticing. Former masters were given preference. Black children were not afforded such guarantees in regard to food, clothing, and education as were written into indentureship agreements for white children.

The problems of Presidential Reconstruction led Congress in March 1867 to take charge of policy toward former Confederate states. In order to assure that African Americans were not denied basic rights, Congress, led by the "radical" wing of the Republican Party, required the Confederate states to call state conventions to create more representative state governments and ratify the 14th Amendment to the Constitution—assuring the citizenship rights of newly freed slaves—as a prerequisite for readmission into the Union. By 1870, all the Southern states had complied.

Congressional Reconstruction ushered in a brief era in which activist state governments, supported by multiracial political coalition, enacted legislation to improve the status and welfare of poor people, whether black or white. Through the 15th Amendment to the Constitution, African American men gained the vote and, with it, seats in the federal and state legislatures. In South Carolina, where African Americans controlled state government for several years, the legislature moved to provide access to land for freed blacks. Across the South, states moved to expand access to schooling for poor blacks and whites.

Although a majority of white Southerners remained hostile to policies that expanded the rights of African Americans, the federal government—supported by occupying armies—underwrote these fledgling democracies through the activities of the Freedmen's Bureau.[38] Even before the close of the war, it was evident that Northern effort would be required to bring the South relief from destitution. The Port Royal Experiment of 1862 represented one such effort and became the model for the Freedmen's Bureau. When, in the face of the Union army's advance into South Carolina, whites abandoned the plantations of the Port Royal area, 10,000 slaves were left to fend for themselves. Their distress led the president to authorize (but not fund) an experimental relief and rehabilitation program. Two volunteer organizations, the National Freedmen's Relief Association of New York and the Boston Education Commission, supplied most of the funding and labor. Several hundred volunteers saw to the distribution of food and clothing and the rehabilitation of abandoned and pillaged homes. In addition, they established schools for black children and attempted to use free labor in large-scale cotton cultivation.

For all the experiment's success, the needs of the South were beyond the resources of volunteer organizations. Congress established the Bureau of Refugees, Freedmen, and Abandoned Lands—more familiarly known as the Freedmen's Bureau—in March 1865, two months before the end of the war. The bureau was placed in the War Department; however, since no appropriations for relief purposes or salaries were made, the bureau was dependent upon the military for whatever aid was distributed in the way of food, clothing, and medical supplies. In 1866, President Johnson vetoed an extension of the life of the Bureau, objecting, as had President Pierce before him, to the federal government's assumption of responsibility for social welfare. "A system for the support of indigent persons in the United States," he wrote, "was never contemplated by the authors of the Constitution."[39] In reasoning typical of the era, he placed responsibility for recovery from slavery on its victims. Legislation that delayed "a self-sustaining condition must have a tendency injurious alike to their character and their prospects." Yet, the realities of total war and its repercussions undermined the conventional wisdom of the era, a pattern that would repeat itself in subsequent wars. The veto was overridden and the life of the bureau was extended by two years.

Watch this video on the Freedmen's Bureau.

Would African American history have been different if the Bureau had been able to continue its work?

https://www.youtube.com/watch?v=rRf2sYOF8oQ

The extension was fostered by the fact that the bureau, faced with the extreme hunger and poverty of whites as well as blacks, had helped both; both protested the threatened withdrawal of relief. The 1866 act provided the first direct appropriation—$6.9 million—for the bureau's work, and in 1867, in response to the threat of famine, Congress authorized the use of funds for all destitute and helpless Southerners regardless of wartime loyalties. It set a precedent for federal participation in social welfare during emergencies.

Originally, the Freedmen's Bureau had been established to deal with transient, homeless blacks and with the management of abandoned and confiscated property. In time the bureau took on the task of organizing freed blacks into a labor force. Bureau agents not only sought jobs and organized work opportunities for freed men, but they also drew up and supervised labor contracts for blacks in their relation with whites. General Oliver O. Howard, who carried responsibility for the operations of the bureau, saw to the adjudication of labor disputes and to the prevention of re-enslavement. Yet, neither the bureau nor Congress ever implemented land redistribution as a way of increasing blacks' economic power.

The Freedmen's Bureau was the first federal welfare agency and, between 1865 and 1869, the major source of public welfare in the South. During its existence, the bureau engaged in numerous social welfare activities. It provided transportation home for refugees and aided in reuniting families. In its first three years, it distributed 18.3 million rations, about 5.2 million of which went to whites. By the end of its fourth year of existence, it had distributed 21 million rations, about 6 million having gone to whites. In addition to distributing medical supplies, the bureau established 46 hospitals. It set up orphan asylums for children and participated in the establishment and running of 4,329 schools for black children. Among institutions of higher learning, it helped found or support Howard, Atlanta, and Fisk universities, Hampton Institute, and Talladega College.

The bureau was subject to a good deal of criticism. There was, of course, the basic concern about large-scale federal aid to the needy. Southern planters and townspeople correctly saw the Freedmen's Bureau as improving the bargaining position of black labor and accused the bureau of fostering idleness and pauperism. Indeed, these concerns led General Howard to retrench on direct relief giving and to break up camps that had been organized to provide government-created jobs. Southern opposition and the political reverses of "radical Republicans" in the North led to the demise of the Freedmen's Bureau in 1872.

The South's experiment in racial democracy could not withstand Southern whites' willingness to resort to violence. The Ku Klux Klan and other "night riders" terrorized African Americans who were active in politics, as well as their white supporters. Northern Republicans who had originally supported Reconstruction grew more wary of supporting African Americans in the face of white resistance and electoral setbacks. In 1875, violence organized by white "redeemers" allowed conservatives to take back control of several state governments through force. The following year, a deadlocked presidential election provided an opportunity for Southern states to demand the withdrawal of federal troops as the price for supporting the election of Rutherford B. Hayes. The experiment in biracial democracy came to an end.[40]

The return of white rule reversed most of the gains of Reconstruction. Although retaining the right to vote, blacks rarely won elections, and when they did, the results were often reversed through violence. Economically, the planter class regained its dominance of Southern agriculture, forcing poor whites and blacks into overwhelming debt and peonage. African Americans turned to building community-based institutions in the face of political defeat and white hostility.

Reconstruction led to some expansion of state governments' expenditures for social welfare and education for blacks and whites. However, by the end of the century, "Jim Crow" laws segregated the races at school and public accommodations and disenfranchised most African Americans, in spite of the guarantee of the 15th Amendment. Eventually, Southern states adopted a pattern of separate welfare institutions—orphanages, mental hospitals, and almshouses—for blacks and whites.

Social Welfare and Urban Expansion

With the demise of federal responsibility, the domination of social welfare returned to private groups in the Northeast, where urban problems were multiplying. Since the war had been fought in the South, the North was not faced with the necessity of rebuilding. Industrialization to meet the needs of the war provided it with the organization and experience for further expansion at the war's close, when the needs of the South and of the rapidly developing West for manufactured items and for markets were pressing. A high protective tariff served to prevent domestic buyers from buying foreign-made goods. Not surprisingly, the East, as the industrial center of the country, became the center for credit, the center for economic and political power, and the center of labor unrest.

The recession of 1873–1878 was a period of serious unemployment. Concern with poverty and with pauperism led to different organizational responses from labor and from philanthropic groups. During the Civil War, the labor movement began to regain its strength as workers found that the wartime labor shortage gave them greater bargaining power. Craft unions were organized in sufficient numbers to warrant the calling of the first National Labor Congress in 1866.

The power of railroads and business increased during the postwar era as corporate forms appeared and as the development of pools, legal trusts, holding companies, and consolidations was accompanied by a decline in free market competition. Numerous corporate attempts to regulate production and prices within industries, quantity discounting and rebating, wild speculation—all occurred as struggles for monopoly and control took place between larger and larger units of operation.

The ability of industrial giants to manipulate labor was enhanced by the presence of a large reserve labor force willing to work for lower wages. In 1886, many unions joined a movement to demand the eight-hour day, but the Haymarket riot—which was provoked by the Chicago police and private security agents—undermined the movement.

During the late 19th century, labor unions organized to demand an eight-hour day. However, lack of unity among workers, court injunctions, and private security forces undermined their effectiveness

The financial problems of working people were aggravated by the conviction among leaders of organized charities that the purpose of modern philanthropy was to suppress pauperism rather than to aid the needy. In 1895, in the midst of widespread unemployment, the New York Association for the Improvement of Conditions among the Poor railed against longshoremen striking to prevent a cut in wages:

> Every man has a right to work or not . . . but no man has a right to refuse to support his family and himself when he is able to do it; and no one has a right to prevent others from working, as these strikers persistently attempted to do, while they are themselves idling about the streets and wharves and corner liquor shops.[41]

It came as no surprise, then, that union members viewed supporters of benevolent societies as antilabor.

The emergence of powerful big businesses led to some federal and state efforts to regulate interstate and intrastate commerce and to a resurgence of union activity. The Interstate Commerce Act of 1887 was an effort to limit the ability of railroads to play one section of the country against another, to their own advantage. By 1890, 14 states and territories had antimonopoly provisions in their constitutions, and 13 states had antitrust laws.[42] Demands for some forms of federal regulation led to the passage of the Sherman Antitrust Act. Although efforts to limit the growth of big business remained politically popular for several generations, they were largely ineffective.

The Charity Organization Movement

The failure of Reconstruction led many middle-class social activists to see government programs as inevitably flawed. During the late 19th century, these reformers led a concerted effort to wrest control of social welfare from the public sector and to establish a system that was organized and efficient. The Charity Organization Movement (the first Charity Organization Society was founded in Buffalo in 1877) was modern in methods and outlook, but its view of the poor as slothful, mendacious, and treacherous looked back to an earlier era. Although the Charity Organization Movement would initiate many of the practices of modern social work, including casework, educational and training programs, and the individualization of services, its ideological blinders prevented it from significantly changing the plight of the urban poor.

In a large measure, the strength of the Charity Organization Movement was derived from its promise of a scientific approach to poverty and pauperism. The frequent communications between American and European scientists had led to widespread knowledge of Darwinian theory and of Herbert Spencer's application of that work to social theory. The new religion preached the need for a laissez-faire economy in which the fittest would become the richest. It feared that social welfare measures that supported dependency and misfits would end in racial decline. The belief in the possibility of an evolution toward a more affluent society, combined with belief in the openness of that society to individual achievement, made the acquisition of personal wealth not only a sign of fitness, but a condition of moral superiority as well. Andrew Carnegie, the capitalist, and Amos G. Warner, the economist and social welfare leader, could agree with Russell Conwell, the educator and minister, who said:

> You ought to be rich. . . . When a man could have been rich just as well, and he is now weak because he is poor, he has done some great wrong; he has been untruthful to himself; he has been unkind to his fellowmen. We ought to get rich if we can by honorable and Christian methods, and these are the only methods that sweep us quickly toward the goal of riches.[43]

The Charity Organization Movement accepted social Darwinism as its theoretical underpinning for helping—or not helping—the poor and called this process *scientific charity*. Thus, the belief that the times required a new orientation to social welfare matters resulted in the application of science to the development of a delivery system that continued to focus on individual pathology rather than the failures of social organization.

The report to the first Conference of Charities and Corrections by its Department (Committee) of Social Economy set the stage for voluntary domination of social welfare. This report of pauperism in the city of New York, written in 1874 at a time of economic depression, condemned the giving of outdoor relief, whether in the form of public funds or publicly displayed soup kitchens, as inducing many to become paupers. The report contrasted the benevolence of the business community (in spite of its own temporarily embarrassing impoverishment) with the unwillingness of the poor (having become accustomed to depending upon the bounty of others) to accept work at markedly lower wages. The fact of the depression itself, the reality of need, was all the more reason for rigidly limiting—after careful house visitation—relief and connecting it to work. Available statistics of pauperism showed "a condition of things . . . less alarming than had been supposed." This did not, however, mitigate the fear of the transmittability of pauperism from adult to child and from relief recipient to worker. Concern persisted that pauperism might degenerate the individual's physical and mental powers to final extinction.[44]

The growth in numbers and power of the Charity Organization Societies in major cities continued the focus on voluntary, rather than government, efforts to address need. In 1890, at the 17th annual meeting of the National Conference of Charities and Corrections, Josephine Shaw Lowell, perhaps the leading advocate for the private sector, declared that public relief should be given only in cases of extreme distress, "when starvation is imminent." Since it is difficult to prove the imminence of starvation, conditions of deterrence must be maintained. The refuge from pauperism, according to Lowell, was self-support or help provided by private sources presumably after investigation and determination of worthiness.[45] Even then, when contributors to the New York Charity Organization Society asked Lowell, its president, how much of their contribution would go to the poor, she responded hopefully, "Not one cent."[46] Her conservatism about assistance, however, did not prevent Lowell from founding the National Consumer League in 1890.

The harshness expressed by Lowell must be seen in the context of contemporary beliefs about the corruptibility of human nature and suspicions about the capacity of government to respond effectively to social problems. The widespread corruption associated with local and national politics led many middle- and upper-class reformers to see government as part of the problem, not part of the solution.

The sequence of events that led to the widespread institutionalization of private charity simultaneously justified the emergence of a leisure class. In a world in which the individual was seen as captain of his or her own fate, poverty and wealth were viewed as equally natural, if not equally desirable. Denying the rich the full enjoyment of their wealth or preventing the poor from suffering from deprivation violated their view of social justice. The optimism of the American people in accepting the economic system as structurally viable, as offering endless potential for every individual willing to work and the "rags-to-riches" myth popularized by the juvenile novels of Horatio Alger Jr., was rooted in some reality. Despite recessions and bitter labor disputes, the view held that, for the most part, the economy *was* working successfully. Its moments of faltering were not equated with failure, especially on the Eastern Seaboard where millions of immigrants could realistically compare present living conditions with those from which they had fled. The thousands of Irish who had escaped the famine and great hunger resulting from the potato crop failures of 1845–1848 could give witness by their own changed circumstances. Immigrants from all over Europe—whose coming was slowed somewhat during the Civil War but resumed with the onset of peace—could point to their own comparative success. Their perception was supported by a rapidly rising gross national product, by the existence of national boundaries that quite literally provided lands for cultivation, and by an element of truth in the Horatio Alger myth. The steady movement of immigrants into commercially successful ventures and into politically powerful positions confirmed the view of class mobility. And, there was always the example of a Carnegie or a Rockefeller to demonstrate how far a poor boy could go if he would take advantage of the opportunities the country offered.

The complement of the American gospel of success was the belief that failure was attributable to individual weakness. Although poor people's failings were usually defined in moral terms, increasingly as the 19th century came to an end, the language of race and genetics was used to support the argument. As the century drew to a close, the fear of feeblemindedness led to the creation of a new class of institutions and fueled an interest in forced sterilization.[47]

Empirical evidence was sought to sustain this position. The Reverend Oscar C. McCulloch's Report to the 15th Annual Conference of Charities and Corrections on the Tribe of Ishmael, a study of 250 related families, was viewed as a frightening example of social degradation brought on by the degeneracy of the inherited influences of pauperism.[48]

No less an authority than Amos G. Warner, the general agent for the Charity Organization Society of Baltimore, stressed deterioration of character as an immediate cause of poverty. He emphasized this despite his equal awareness of the relationship of the less immediate but perhaps more important contribution of objective environmental factors to poverty. Although in his famous work of 1894, *American Charities*, Warner found unemployment and illness to be the causes of almost half of the poverty cases, he included the following in his listing of objective causes of poverty: "evil associations" and "unwise philanthropy." The latter apparently fostered subjective causes such as "indolence," "lubricity," and a variety of "unhealthy appetites."[49]

In such an atmosphere, public welfare seemed not only unnecessary, but counterproductive. The ideal of charity was service on the part of the well-to-do, service whereby the poor could learn self-respect and resolution, which would build character. This ideal was carried out by an army of "friendly visitors" recruited by the Charity Organization Societies and trained for the service. The appeal of friendly visiting, balanced by the promise of scientific methodology in investigating the need for relief, led in some cities

CHARLES F. BRETZMAN COLLECTION, PRINTS & PHOTOGRAPHS DIVISION, LIBRARY OF CONGRESS, LC-USZ62-83407.

Figure 4.1   Friendly visitor. Fearing a widening gap between the rich and poor in the late 19th and early 20th centuries, charity organization societies relied on "friendly visitors" to engage, instruct, and sanction working-class families.

to turning over the responsibility for investigating applications for relief to the local Charity Organization Society (Figure 4.1).

The overall purpose of the societies was the maintenance of virtuous families. Guidelines for establishing eligibility for relief often showed the virtue of a family to be derived from the virtue of the breadwinner. Thus, if the breadwinner was disabled or had died, then the widow and her children might be found eligible. Where poverty resulted from the breadwinner's drinking or from his having deserted his family, the removal of the children for placement among more wholesome associates might be considered best.

Charity Organization leaders were not alone in their beliefs about inherited tendencies toward pauperism. Nor is it fair, with the wisdom of hindsight, to picture them as totally destructive in their work with families. Warner's statistically based delineation of objective environmental causes of poverty and the social fact finding of other welfare leaders helped foster social legislation. Such a legislation brought about reform in housing, working conditions for women, child labor practices, and sanitation—all of which were to improve the individual's and the family's opportunity for self-betterment and success. An awakening interest in eugenics and social Darwinism provided a framework for some support of social legislation, but it carried with it the position that there was no major defect in society itself. Quite simply, the inability to take advantage of enhanced opportunity was further evidence of individual weakness.

The leaders of voluntary charity were not content with simply improving their "scientific charity"; they sought to eliminate the competition posed by public sources of welfare as well. Beginning with the efforts of Brooklyn in 1879, a number of cities moved to eliminate outdoor relief so that the needy would be forced to rely on voluntary charities. Although the outdoor relief cutoff fit well into the philosophical position of the Charity Organization Movement, it flowed from practical considerations as well. Democratic politicians had successfully used outdoor relief and public employment as means of assuring the loyalty of voters.[50]

In the end, friendly visiting had an unexpected impact. Initially, charity leaders had imagined that the relationship of the visitor and the client would be one-directional; the poor family would learn lessons of thrift and efficiency from the worker. Yet, over the last decades of the 19th century, the relationships became more complex than anticipated. In the end, the generation of middle-class women and men who were involved in charity work came away from the experience with a new appreciation of the difficulties faced by poor families. As the 19th century came to a close, old beliefs about the moral foundation of poverty were eclipsed.

Among public welfare leaders, especially, there were those ready to point out social causes of poverty and to assert society's responsibility for helping meet individual and familial needs. At the 13th Conference of Charities and Corrections in 1886, Fred H. Wines questioned the use of statistics for the pseudoscientific purpose of proving individuals to be the cause of poverty and crime. He urged the conference to look at the "three or four great facts" that characterized modern social life: the invention of labor-saving machinery, the aggregation of capital in the hands of large and wealthy corporations, the aggregation of population in great centers, and the emancipation of women. Taken together, he felt these characteristics had changed the relation of people to one another and might "account in some degree for the present measure and manifestations of pauperism" and other social ills.[51]

At the 17th Conference of Charities and Corrections in 1890, Franklin B. Sanborn spoke more specifically about family welfare and made a strong plea for outdoor relief, which he defined as "family aid." In analyzing the purposes for which family aid was expended in Massachusetts, he pointed out that reports of outlays for aid to the poor in their own families often overstated the sum actually expended by including payments for the sick in hospitals, burials, and so on. As for the able-bodied poor in almshouses, Sanborn said, "that mythical class . . . are scarcely found in this country in public establishments, except for a few months in the cold season, when the number of employments . . . is considerably reduced by Nature herself." The statement is reminiscent of the Yates report of 1824, but unlike Yates, Sanborn concluded in favor of cash payments to families in their own homes. Asking that the poor be classified according to their real character and needs and not herded together in a common "receptacle" for all forms of poverty, Sanborn pointed out that "there are persons, be the number greater or less, who need public relief ᵢ their own homes, and who can receive it there with greater advantage both to themselve and to the public than anywhere else." In a telling argument—probably embarrassing foɪ his listeners—he pointed out that outdoor relief must continue not only because it is less costly than indoor relief, but also because there would never be "almshouses, workhouses, hospitals, and other places of indoor relief in sufficient number to contain all the poor at any season, or half of them in seasons of special destitution." In a final burst, Sanborn said that one reason cash relief had been distributed, even to the point of abuse, was "the desire to prevent the breaking up of families, the corruption of the young, and the unspeakable distress of the old and the virtuous, by throwing them into forced association with the dregs of mankind, in what was ironically termed a charitable establishment."[52] It was in response to and in disagreement with Sanborn that Josephine Shaw Lowell addressed the conference on the demoralizing effects of public outdoor relief.

In time, hostility to the philosophy and methodology of Charity Organization became openly vocal and widespread. Charles D. Kellogg, chairman of the National Conference of Charities and Corrections' Committee on History of Charity Organization, reported in 1893:

> The very name of Charity Organization indicates a paramount purpose to bring about cooperation of those engaged in ministering to the poor . . . Yet cooperation is one of the most difficult of attainments . . . In some cities there exists a distinct hostility in the older charitable societies to Charity Organization. They resent the implication that their work may need amending.[53]

These "older charitable societies" were understandably suspicious of Charity Organization's assumed authority for standard setting in a field in which they had long been functioning. They were particularly aroused by the threat to their autonomy in being asked to "sustain [through cooperation] a society that is purely administrative,"[54] that is, a society to whom they would be accountable for their relief activities.

Charity Organization's emphasis on reducing fraud was taken to be the sole purpose of registering and investigating applicants for relief. Thus, charity organizers were accused of lumping the honest with the dishonest poor to the detriment of the former and the inhumane neglect of the latter.[55] In the words of a popular poem:

> The organized charity scrimped and iced
> In the name of a cautious, statistical Christ.[56]

Trade unions were particularly incensed by scientific charity during periods of recession and unemployment. They interpreted Charity Organization's investigation methods and its stress upon the debilitating effects of relief as creating unnecessary suffering and as prolonging an "unfair social system as a result of which workers find themselves unemployed."[57]

Finally, the motives of the influential and wealthy leadership were suspect. Hostility toward Charity Organization Societies grew out of the view that the societies might just be "devices for saving the taxpayer, and secured for them the title 'Society for the Suppression of Benevolence.'"[58]

The Settlement House Movement

At the end of the 19th century, a second major movement developed in the voluntary sector of social welfare: the Settlement House Movement. Inspired by the efforts of Canon Samuel Barnett's Toynbee Hall in London to bring the privileged and underprivileged together to overcome the effects of spiritual and social disintegration, Stanton Coit and Charles B. Stover founded the Neighborhood Guild of New York City in 1887. Their hope in opening this first American settlement house, where educated persons might live among the poor newcomers to the United States, was to bring about a sense of neighborliness that could lead to the making of good citizens. In 1889, Jane Addams established Hull House in Chicago and Vida Scudder founded the College Settlement in New York. Located in large cities, these settlement houses emphasized neighborhood services and community development.

Settlement houses and Charity Organization shared many characteristics. They were both dominated by upper- and middle-class white Protestants who viewed the expanding and diverse working-class population of the city with trepidation. Members of both movements believed that these populations could be "improved" if they adopted the family norms and values of their benefactors. Finally, they both were suspicious of public welfare and believed voluntary action was the key to addressing the problems of urban residents. The groups differed, however, in their views of families, in their views of society, and, ultimately, in their views of social welfare as a helping mechanism.

Charity Organization Societies had come into being for the express purpose of organizing voluntary and public charities to direct toward worthy families the relief-giving services of others.[59] Their particular concern was with the poor, and especially with those individuals whose flawed character permitted them to sup at the public trough while contributing nothing to the public larder. Their investigations of applicants for relief—investigations that led eventually to the development of casework methodology and to the emergence of a social work profession—were meant to individualize each poor family so that particular flaws could be detected and overcome and independence could be regained. The Charity Organization Societies did make an effort to separate the "worthy" poor from the "unworthy" poor to help the former adequately, but the fear of encouraging pauperism led for the most part to a basic philosophy that deterred all from asking for help. In essence, the orientation of the Charity Organization toward relief was in line with the Poor Law tradition and led to competition with public officials for supremacy in handling relief matters. In many localities, Charity Organization Societies took on the job of investigating relief applicants for public agencies, a job they had assumed very early for private relief societies.[60]

Settlement house workers were more likely to see social conditions as an important cause of poverty and dependency. Much of the clientele served by settlement houses consisted of migrants and immigrants whose problems quite clearly were associated with making the transition from rural to urban living and from a known to an unknown culture. Whatever their problems with the culture or the language, clients of settlement houses were less likely to be viewed as pathological by workers. When such families could not cope, settlement leaders believed that social conditions shared part of the blame. As a result, social reform was more central to settlement work than to the operation of charity organization societies.[61]

The Charity Organization and Settlement House movements in the early years were quite different in goals, in techniques, and in service programs. The Charity Organization was bent upon preventing pauperism. To aid in this process of reformation, Charity Organization Societies engaged heavily in the detection of fraud and the establishment or promotion of "various well-proved schemes for the encouragement of thrift and self-help."[62] Settlement houses, on the other hand, from their inception moved toward the socialization of the normal, adequately functioning family, and their goal was reflected in the three strands of their program activities: neighborhood clubs providing recreational and educational opportunities, social research in regard to family and community needs, and, especially, social action leading to legislative and political change.

Much of the clientele served by settlement houses consisted of migrants and immigrants whose problems quite clearly were associated with making the transition from rural to urban living and from a known to an unknown culture.

Jane Addams, the founder of Chicago's Hull House and the preeminent leader of the Settlement House movement in the United States, stated the difference between the Charity Organization Society and the settlement:

> The settlement does stand for something unlike that which the charity visitor stands for. You are bound, when you are doing charitable work, to lay stress upon the industrial virtues. . . . Now the settlement . . . does not lay perpetual and continual stress upon them. It sees that a man may, perhaps, be a bit lazy, and still be a good man and an interesting person. . . . It does not lay so much stress upon one set of virtues, but views the man in his social aspects. . . . To adjust an individual to civilization as he finds it round him, to get him to the pitch which shall induce him to push up that civilization a little higher . . . is perhaps the chief function of a settlement.[63]

As the century drew to a close, the differences between Charity Organization and Social Settlements (COS) became less sharp. COS leaders such as Mary Richmond, who outlined the basis for casework in *Social Diagnosis*, grounded their work increasingly in observation and practice, not in sweeping moral judgments. Meanwhile, settlement house workers soon found that good intentions and sympathy were not enough; they, too, needed to provide practical services to community residents if they were to maintain their credibility. Most importantly, workers in both areas began to see the virtue of individualization; care needed to be tailored to the specific needs of the client. By the turn of the century, the milieu that would create the social work profession was in place.

A New View of Child Welfare

By the turn of the century, the lines of disagreement between private and public welfare leaders were drawn. The private sector, despite contributions to social legislation, had opted for a professional service approach to people in need. Many in the public sector had moved away from the use of almshouses toward an income approach based upon the social necessity of giving and receiving cash relief.

The prominence of Northern social welfare leaders tended to obscure emerging efforts to meet needs in the South and West. As urban population centers grew in these areas, officials tended to follow the path of institutionalization developed 50 years earlier in the East. While the North argued the pros and cons of outdoor relief, the South and West started to build and expand almshouses, mental hospitals, orphan asylums, and correctional institutions. By then, however, their goal was custodial, not remedial; for by 1880, it was clear that institutions throughout the United States were not succeeding in providing an environment for the rehabilitation of the lives of the inmates, but were offering protection for the larger society against criminals, paupers, and the insane.

Dependent children did not generate the same fears as poor and dependent adults. Rather, the public good required that children be rescued from a life of dependency or criminality and helped to become productive citizens. A new view of child welfare developed; child care was to be separate and special.

The legal implications of this new approach were reflected in the enactment of the first juvenile court act in 1899, An Act to Regulate the Treatment and Control of Dependent, Neglected, and Delinquent Children.[64] This act, which established separate treatment and control for children, was of major significance because it had common-law derivations. Thus, the newly established juvenile court moved child welfare away from an orientation of statutory criminal law, which had previously governed child welfare cases.

As the world of childhood diverged from that of adults, welfare leaders came to see the mixing of dependent children and poor adults as a moral evil. New York State was the first to remove children to foster family homes and to specialized institutions, and other states followed suit.

The eighth annual report of the New York State Board of Charities (submitted January 15, 1875) contained Commissioner William F. Letchworth's study of pauper and destitute children in the state's almshouses.[65] Despite a strenuous effort at removal, in 1874, 593 children remained in almshouses (9 percent of all inmates), nearly 300 of whom were described as intelligent children, over two years of age, who needed proper training and care to fit them for useful stations in life. The slow pace of removing children from almshouses led to the board's recommendation that "the commitment of children of intelligence over two years of age, to county poor-houses, be prohibited by statute"; and on April 24, 1875, an Act to Provide for the Better Care of Pauper and Destitute Children was passed by the senate and assembly of the state of New York. It became unlawful for any child over 3 and under 16 years of age to be committed to a county poorhouse "unless such child be an unteachable idiot, an epileptic or paralytic, or . . . otherwise defective, diseased or deformed, so as to render it unfit for family care."[66]

The removal of dependent children from almshouses was driven in part by the idea that poverty could be self-perpetuating, a notion that later generations would call the "vicious cycle" of poverty. Institutional care as devised during the pre–Civil War period was intended to provide for the child a model of disciplined, organized, productive life as a substitute for disorganized family living. Instead, almshouse care was found to expose children to adult paupers, frequently the child's own parents, so that the model supported the very pattern it was intended to supplant. The removal of children would break up these families, by placing the children in good, humble foster homes. In these homes, according to Anne B. Richardson, reporting to the 13th annual Conference of Charities and Corrections (1886) on the care of dependent and delinquent children in Massachusetts, the children are restored to conditions of family life where strains produce character.[67]

Amos G. Warner of Charity Organization reiterated the point in 1894:

> The child who is born in an almshouse and grows up there is almost always a pauper, because his bad heredity is reinforced by such an environment. . . . The child that grows up in an infant asylum or orphans' home has at most an imperfect opportunity for right development, and the original possibilities of its nature are but faintly reflected by its career. With a child boarded out in a private family, or given to foster parents while still an infant, the conditions are better and more might be inferred if we could compare its characteristics with those of its parents.[68]

In Pennsylvania, as in New York and Massachusetts, anxiety existed about the retention of children in almshouses. The *Report of the Commissioners of Public Charities for the Year 1882* expressed the dangers of permitting children to be in constant association with "these imbecile and debased paupers":

> It must be kept in view that they are one and all *involuntary* and *helpless* prisoners, not from any fault of their own, but too often inheriting the worst traits of a degraded parentage; and, if to this inborn nature is added the results of the society and example of the most degraded of our race, are we to expect anything better from them than their training will promise?[69]

The commissioners recommended to the state legislature an act to prevent and forbid the detention of children between the ages of 2 and 16 years in poorhouses or almshouses. The act was passed in 1883.[70]

Reports from New York, Massachusetts, and Pennsylvania showed that the removal of children already resident in almshouses was slow. Charles S. Hoyt, secretary of the New York State Board of Charities, reporting on "The Causes of Pauperism" (1877), was shrill in denouncing "the practice of receiving parents and children into poorhouses together" and of retaining them there as families. His contention that heredity entered so largely in the problem of pauperism led him to assert unequivocally that it was against sound policy to keep pauper families, whether in or out of the almshouse, together; "in fact the sooner they can be broken up the better."[71] Certainly the fear of hereditary influences would lead to anxiety in regard to the slowness of the process of removal. At the same time, the threatened removal of children had an equally important if less publicized effect—that of deterring families from entering the poorhouse. Thus, poor families who required public help were doubly deterred, for if they entered almshouses, they would face deplorable living conditions as well as the possibility of family breakup.

A number of reasons underlay the slowness of reducing the number of children in almshouses. Oddly enough, one reason was simply that the laws against accepting children were not always known or understood by almshouse superintendents. During the next decade, the movement to deinstitutionalize children lost ground, and a concern for keeping families intact emerged. The 1883 report of the Pennsylvania Board of Commissioners of Public Charities, for example, mentioned the acceptance of families in almshouses, especially bereaved and immigrant families who must have temporary help but for whom outdoor relief was not available because of "mistaken notions of economy."[72] Such a temporary use of the almshouses made it possible for families to stay together. The report urged the wider use of outdoor relief as even more efficacious in preventing the breaking up of homes.

Eventually, the momentum for removing children from almshouses accelerated. Child welfare leaders began to state a rationale for individualizing the needs of children—a parallel reaction, perhaps, to the Charity Organization emphasis upon individualizing families. In his report for 1888, Charles W. Birtwell, general agent of Boston's Children's Aid Society, described the agency's changing practices:

> The aim will be in each instance to suit action to the real need—heeding the teachings of experience, still to study the conditions with a freedom from assumptions . . . as complete as though the case in hand stood absolutely alone.[73]

In his report for 1893, Birtwell made the logical connection between the individualized child and the individualized family.

> These children cannot be divorced from the natural relations of family life without loss . . . and therefore we must humbly set ourselves to learn the ways in which family ties may be strengthened and parental responsibilities maintained.[74]

The census of 1890 showed that the number of children in the country's almshouses had decreased by 36 percent, from 7,770 in 1880 to 4,987 in 1890.[75] In part this was a result of the continuing work of the Children's Aid Society of New York. Part of the decrease could be attributed to a combination of positive concern for families and for individual character leading to the removal from almshouses of entire, intact families who were then sent to the West, where both employment and a "proper" moral climate were generously available. The philosophy of Charles Loring Brace was now serving a larger purpose.

? Assess your comprehension of "Innovations in Social Welfare Services" by completing this quiz.

SOCIAL MOVEMENTS DURING THE LATE 19TH CENTURY: THE REFORM IMPULSE

Although government led the effort to reconstruct Southern society after the Civil War, by the 1870s both government and the economy were back in the hands of traditional social elites. Women, workers, poor farmers, and African Americans were effectively marginalized as state governments and the federal government used their economic and military power to reinforce the status quo. Women who had been central to prewar social reform were shocked to find their demand for the vote ridiculed. Workers mobilized and organized, but their demands were met by injunctions, strikebreakers, and armed troops. Farmers—South and West, black and white—struggled against drought, debt, and the power of the railroads. Although white resistance closed off the prospect of interracial cooperation at the end of Reconstruction, at the end of the century, an agrarian movement that culminated in Populism tried again to unite farmers from different regions and different races into a coherent social movement.

The Social Welfare of Women

Women leaders' prominence in the Charity Organization Movement, and in social welfare generally, reflects the extent to which women entered public life during and after the Civil War. The period held enormous consequences for women—particularly middle-class women. Expanded affluence offered independence and leisure, and women sought to establish for themselves a proper place more nearly equivalent in significance and power to that of men.

During the war, women had participated in the abolition movement, but the drive for women's rights had ceased as they became engaged in wartime tasks. As they did in the Sanitary Commission, women—in the South as well as in the North—took on war-related services for which the government had been unprepared. Women took jobs vacated by men going off to battle. They worked in industries and businesses, on farms and plantations, and in the professions. They worked "at the bench" and loom; they taught and nursed; they organized and managed.

Yet, the increased public role of women in the economy and society did not translate easily into political power. The 14th and 15th Amendments to the Constitution—designed to expand the citizenship and voting rights of African Americans—also made voting an explicitly male activity. It would be more than a half century until American women gained the right to vote.

In 1869, women in the suffrage movement split over support of the 15th Amendment. The American Equal Rights Association, which had carried on the fight for women's rights since 1866, was replaced by two contesting groups: the National Woman Suffrage Association, led by Susan B. Anthony and Elizabeth Cady Stanton; and the American Woman Suffrage Association, the group that had supported the 15th Amendment. In 1890, they reunited as the National American Women's Suffrage Association. Yet, the women's movement purchased consensus by waffling on racism. The new association asserted that women could increase the size of the educated voting population and reduce the influence of the ignorant populace. In the South, this argument for women's suffrage was coupled with efforts to curtail the political and civil rights of African Americans.[76]

For all the publicity they engendered, the number of women formally associated with the national suffrage movement was small, probably never more than 10,000.

Nevertheless, large numbers of women did join organizations that represented more widespread and acceptable interests. The women's auxiliaries of the Patrons of Husbandry (the Grange), the General Federation of Women's Clubs, and especially the Women's Christian Temperance Union (WCTU), for example, were organizations in which women found companionship as well as outlets for interests and energies in a limiting world.

The technological revolutions that changed the world of work changed women's domestic labor as well. Indoor plumbing, electric lighting, and household labor-saving devices, and the spread of commercial canning and baking, were examples of technological innovations that reduced the hours of labor for housekeeping. The falling birthrate among middle-class families[77] as well as the availability of inexpensive immigrant and black domestic help furthered the process by which native-born, middle-class white women were released from work at home. The founding of women's colleges offered additional opportunities. Vassar was founded in 1865, Smith in 1871, and Bryn Mawr in 1885. Finally, in an era whose purported ideal was the married woman in the home, there was an excess of females in most of the Northeastern states, where women provided leadership for the feminist movement.[78] Women's organizations and organizational activities were the result.

The national WCTU was formed in 1874 and constituted a nationalization of earlier local efforts to contain the manufacture and sale of alcoholic beverages. In the postwar era, the intent of the movement was abstinence and prohibition. Within 20 years, the union's membership totaled more than 200,000 women, representing "the most influential women's organization in the country."[79] Unlike the derision to which suffragists were subjected, members of the WCTU were recognized as active in a legitimate cause. Their concern about observed deleterious effects of alcoholism on the family and about the possible further deterioration of family life was considered well within the bounds of women's concerns, particularly because women were considered to possess moral superiority. The work of the WCTU was labeled *home protection*; the union's first president, Frances E. Willard, called upon all Christian women to join the crusade.[80]

Women's attraction to the Temperance Movement had complex social and psychological roots. On the one hand, it represented a middle-class reaction to the disorder of the early industrial city. The middle class had not yet been able to separate itself physically from other social classes. The perceived disorder and moral corruption of the working class was constantly on display. At the same time, it represented a *gendered* response to the realities of marriage in the late 19th century. Alcohol was at the center of the male world of leisure—dominated by taverns, clubs, and brothels—a world from which respectable women were excluded. In addition, the connection between drink and domestic violence could hardly have eluded women's sensibilities. Finally, the temperance campaign represented a cultural response of native-born Protestants to cities increasingly dominated by Catholic and Jewish ethnic groups.[81]

With moral superiority the foundation for a proper women's sphere and the home and family the appropriate locale of the operation, conflicts inevitably marked the wider women's movement. Why should women venture into the public sphere? The answer to this question was relatively easy in the matter of temperance. Even college education could be justified as "education for motherhood."[82] Friendly visiting for the Charity Organization Societies could be seen as instilling the virtues of independent American family life in the poor. But the right to vote, as demanded by suffragists, was another matter. The right to vote was a call for political power, and those few women who demanded it were suspect. Even when Willard determined that the purpose of the WCTU could be achieved only by way of women's votes, her call was cloaked in the mantle of "home protection."[83] And, even then, the union's resolution, passed at its national convention in 1877, called for women's voting only in local elections and only on the question of prohibition.

For the middle class, the idea of working women represented a thorny issue. The ideal woman of the postwar era might work before marriage, but not after. Thus, despite an expansion in the kinds of jobs women held,[84] many women found themselves increasingly "dependent on the money wages of their husbands or fathers, wages that they themselves did not earn."[85] The era's concept of "true womanhood" helped limit opportunities for economic and social independence.

Nevertheless, women did work. In 1890, 4 million women, 14 years and older, were employed—18 percent of the female population, 17 percent of the civilian labor force. By 1900, 5 million women—many of them married—were working outside the home.[86] Edith Abbott, in her study of women in industry, attributed the presence of married women and of older women in the job market largely to the employment of immigrants, children of immigrants, and blacks.[87]

Whatever the middle-class ideal, foreign-born and black women, along with many American-born white women, had to work to support the family economy, which was dependent on the wages of children and sometimes wives as well as those of their husbands. The double bind of lower-class women did not go unnoticed by Josephine Shaw Lowell:

> Of course there are women who can attend to home duties and also do outside work; but the average woman cannot do it; and the division of work between man and woman is discriminated by their natures . . . he to do the outside work, the woman to do the inside work. . . . I think one of the causes of poverty is that we have adopted the theory for poor people—not for ourselves—that it is the business of women to help support the family. . . . When the husband dies, the double work that ought to be done by both father and mother, come to the widow.[88]

The Labor Movement

The potential of large-scale associations of laborers to counter the power of industry and to protect workers against the risks of industrial society had led in 1878 to the organization of the International Labor Union (ILU) and to the initial attempts of the Knights of Labor to consolidate many trade unions and grades of workers. With the demise of the ILU in 1882, the Knights began to grow. In 1883, membership stood at 50,000; in 1886, the membership skyrocketed to 700,000.[89]

Despite its phenomenal growth, the Knights of Labor was torn by internal dissension. There was a fundamental difference between the leadership, which persisted in the repudiation of the strike except as a weapon of last resort, and the membership, which found that strikes and boycotts could secure important gains. The leadership was convinced that strikes were futile, since "a strike cannot regulate the laws of supply and demand, for if it cuts off the supply, it also cuts off the demand by throwing consumers out of work, thereby curtailing their purchasing power."[90] The decline of the Knights of Labor came swiftly.

Nineteenth-century unions' concern with social welfare went beyond issues of wages and control. Many unions—like the Knights of Labor and those in the

> ▶ **Watch this video on the Knights of Labor.**
>
> What lessons can we take from its history for the relationship of social welfare to organized labor?
>
> https://www.youtube.com/watch?v=SteWSnKVhOE

railroad industry—connected to an older tradition of fraternal organization. These organizations often sponsored insurance and other forms of economic security for their members, a function that laid the foundation for the expansion of employee benefits during the 20th century.

Leadership in the labor movement shifted to the American Federation of Labor, a federation of craft unions, which saw labor's advance not in the abandonment of a capitalist mode of organization, but in increasing workers' wages. By 1900, labor became increasingly militant in achieving its ends. The battle of labor was for job protection and for a fair share in the nation's economic growth. It was also a battle against poverty and against the country's view of the poor. The white, male, skilled workers who made up a majority of unionized workers went to pains to differentiate working men like themselves from those who were dependent on relief. As long as unions discriminated against immigrants, African Americans, and women, they were vulnerable. The exclusion of African Americans from unions, for example, explains why black workers were often used as strikebreakers during this era.

The depression of the 1890s rekindled labor militancy. Coxey's Army attempted to organized thousands of unemployed workers to march on Washington demanding relief. The American Railway Union—led by Eugene V. Debs—pioneered the idea of an industrial union to replace the narrow craft unions (conductors, engineers, firemen) that had dominated railroads before then. Yet, the success of the union in shutting down much of the nation's system during its 1894 Pullman strike was met with injunctions against the union, the jailing of its leaders, and the use of troops to run the trains (Figure 4.2).[91]

The Agrarian Movement

The problems of farmers in interstate commerce were recognized in 1889, when the Department of Agriculture was raised to the rank of an executive department and its head made a secretary with cabinet status. Federal recognition of the challenge of labor led, in 1884, to the creation of the Bureau of Labor Statistics, with authority "to collect information upon the subject of labor, its relation to capital, the hours of labor, and the earnings of laboring men and women, and the means of promoting their material, social, intellectual, and moral prosperity."[92]

In the face of new economic realities, both farmers and workers sought to organize to protect their interests. By 1875, some 30,000 local granges, with a combined membership of 2.5 million, organized farmers and farm laborers.[93] Concerned originally with securing legal protections against railroads, the granges increasingly engaged in a broad range of political activities designed to strengthen farmers in their relation to corporate enterprise. In addition, Southern and Western farming communities experimented with new financial institutions and political movements to combat the dominance of the East.

In the face of new economic realities, both farmers and workers sought to organize to protect their interests. By 1875, some 30,000 local granges, with a combined membership of 2.5 million, organized farmers and farm laborers.

The depression of the 1890s had sparked a widespread rural rebellion of smaller farmers—the Populist movement. Populism started as a variety of local efforts to address the problems of debt faced by farmers in the West and South. An age-old problem of farmers was the reality that their crops tended to be harvested at the same time. As a result, they were forced to sell their product when the supply was largest and, as a result, prices were lowest. The Populists proposed a system of government-run storage facilities, which would allow farmers to wait until prices were more favorable before selling their products. The movement sought the support of the Knights of Labor to bridge the urban-rural divide.[94]

The Populists discovered that their proposals were generally ignored by the two major parties. As a result, as the depression of the 1890s worsened, they mobilized

Figure 4.2 The vanguard of anarchy. In the wake of layoffs and wage reductions, the American Railway Union struck the nation's railroads in 1894. Elite publications like *Harper's Review* saw the strike as a threat to civilization and labeled its leaders as anarchists and revolutionaries.

around the idea of a third party that would unite farmers and other laboring classes across regions and races. The new party enjoyed success in the elections of 1892 and 1894, sometimes on its own and in other states by "fusing" with the minority party. Yet, "fusion" became the party's undoing. First, its success in unseating Democrats in the South and Republicans in the West supported accusations that political intrigue—not reform—was the party's real purpose. Finally, in 1896, pressure to fuse with the Democrats in supporting William Jennings Bryan for the presidency led the party to lose its independent identity.

Although they failed as a political party, Populism put forward a number of reform ideas that were picked up by later reform movements. A graduated income tax, railroad regulation, and the direct election of senators were among many proposals that came to fruition during the 20th century.

> **?** Assess your comprehension of "Social Movements During the Late 19th Century: The Reform Impulse" by completing this quiz.

CONCLUSION

If Rip Van Winkle had fallen asleep during the Civil War and awakened at the end of the 19th century, he could hardly have been more astounded. A rural society of isolated communities had given way to a dynamic, industrial society increasingly dominated by cities.

The social welfare realities at the turn of the 20th century, too, would have seemed new and strange. The hope in institutionalization that had animated reform before the Civil War was nearly spent by the turn of the century, even though the institutions remained, now generally warehouses for unwanted and feared populations. The dynamic public sector of the Civil War years also had generally disappeared. The most visible federal role in welfare at the turn of the century was the Civil War pension system, which would continue to support large numbers of older Americans for decades to come. Instead, the social welfare scene of the 1890s was dominated by voluntary social welfare organizations, often staffed and led by middle-class women.

Yet, change was in the air. The depression of the 1890s had sparked a widespread rural rebellion of smaller farmers—the Populist movement. Although Populism had fallen apart after its electoral defeat in 1896, its core message—that democracy had a role in improving the lives of ordinary citizens—was not totally lost. As the new century began, new social movements would influence the course of American history and the efforts of government and professionals to address the problems of poverty, exclusion, and disaffiliation.

The Civil War and After

Three documents are used to highlight the direction of social welfare developments from the close of the Civil War to the turn of the century. The documents include the State of New York's *An Act to Provide for the Relief of Indigent Soldiers, Sailors and Marines, and the Families of Those Deceased* (1887); an excerpt from Josephine Shaw Lowell's address, *The Economic and Moral Effects of Public Outdoor Relief*, delivered at the National Conference of Charities and Corrections (1890); and *An Act to Prohibit the Coming of Chinese Laborers to the United States*, September 1888, along with its October 1888 amendment. They were a follow-up to the *Chinese Exclusion Act of 1882*. The immigration legislation represents a markedly different response to perceived social problems in the post–Civil War era.

New York's legislation to provide relief for indigent servicemen and their families is an example of one state's special attention and positive response to the claims of veterans. The legislation provides state funding for relief, a shift from strict adherence to local responsibility for relief giving and from the requirement of local residence. Need was to be determined and relief was to be administered by designated relief committees in each post of the GAR, a veterans' organization. Placement of indigent servicemen or their families in an almshouse without the consent of the GAR was prohibited. By definition, veterans were not paupers and not subject to the ordinary conditions prescribed for handling the needs of the poor.

However, other Americans in need were viewed with more caution, their worthiness not above suspicion. The excerpt from Lowell's address is significant for its demonstration of the current view of mankind and the poor. During the postwar era, an earlier view of man's perfectibility gave way to a view of the corruptibility of the individual. Social Darwinism supported a theory of social evolution that permitted the abandonment of those who could not sustain themselves or add to the resources of society. Lowell fell short of arguing for complete abandonment, admitting that some persons do "need relief (that is, *help*) in their own homes." What she could not accept was the use of public funds for relief giving, seeing no good in such giving for the community at large. In fact, she saw an "inverse ratio between the welfare of the mass of people and the distribution of [public] relief." The moral weakening of the individual who received public relief led to a weakening of people in the larger society.

Lowell was a leader among those who sought to apply scientific methodology to philanthropy. She was a major supporter of a new delivery system, the Charity Organization Society, whose original intent was to use volunteer counseling services in an attempt to avoid the necessity for cash relief.

While veterans were thought to have made their contribution to society and be entitled to aid and cash assistance when in need, and other needy Americans were perhaps potentially productive and therefore to be encouraged with services and advice, Chinese workers were regarded very differently. No longer needed as workers on the railroads, they were deemed a threat to other laborers. Since they were distrusted because of their different race, religion, culture, and language, the solution was seen as avoidance. In 1882, legislation was passed that permitted no further immigration of workers from China. The legislation of 1888 went further and moved to reduce the number of Chinese in the United States.

During the 18th century and the first half of the 19th century, immigration and suffrage were largely uncontrolled by federal activity, and in practice states had considerable freedom to regulate the right to vote as well as the right to hold office. This changed after the Civil War. The federal government moved to define its control over who came to this country and who became a citizen. In this process, it established legal rights for African Americans, but it continued to deny them to Native Americans and introduced new restrictions against immigrants. The most severe immigration and naturalization discrimination was practiced against those from Asia. The Chinese exclusion acts wanted to accomplish exactly that. Legislation was passed in 1882 and amended several times after that. The September 1888 legislation barred new laborers from arriving, although it permitted "Chinese officials, teachers, students, merchants, or travelers for pleasure or curiosity" to enter. Additionally, it prohibited any Chinese laborer in the United States from returning once having left "unless he has a lawful wife, child, or parent in the United States, or property therein of the value of one thousand dollars." One month later, it became illegal for "any Chinese laborer . . . who shall depart . . . to return."

In terms of social welfare, veterans were thought to be very worthy; they had done valued work. The American poor were somewhat worthy; they might be helped to become independent members of society. But Chinese workers were feared; they were to be excluded not only from social welfare, but also from any participation in the life of the country.

LAWS OF THE STATE OF NEW YORK
ONE HUNDRED AND TENTH SESSION
January 4–May 26, 1887
Chap. 706

AN ACT to provide for the relief of indigent soldiers, sailors and marines, and the families of those deceased.

PASSED June 25, 1887; three-fifths being present.

The People of the State of New York, represented in Senate and Assembly, do enact as follows:

SECTION 1. For the relief of indigent and suffering soldiers, sailors and marines, who served in the war of the rebellion, and their families, or the families of those deceased, who need assistance in any town or city in this State, the proper auditing board of such city or town may provide such sum or sums of money as may be necessary, to be drawn upon by the commander and quartermaster of any post of the Grand Army of the Republic in said city or town, upon the recommendation of the relief committee of said post, in the same manner as is now provided by law for the relief of the poor, provided said soldier, sailor and marine, or the families of those deceased, are and have been resident of the State for one year or more, and the orders of said commander and quartermaster shall be the proper vouchers for the expenditure of said sum or sums of money. *[Town or city auditing boards may grant relief to indigent soldiers, etc. Expenditure, how supervised. To whom, relief may be granted.]*

§ 2. In case there be no post of the Grand Army of the Republic in any town in which it is necessary that such relief, as provided for in section one, should be granted, the town board of said town shall accept and pay the orders drawn as hereinbefore provided, by the commander and quartermaster of any post of the Grand Army of the Republic, located in the nearest city or town, upon the recommendation of a relief committee, who shall be residents of the said town in which the relief may be furnished. *[Relief committee in certain towns.]*

§ 3. Upon the passage of this act the commander of any post of the Grand Army of the Republic, which shall undertake the relief of indigent veterans and their families, as hereinbefore provided, before the acts of said commander and quartermaster may become operative in any city or town, shall file with the city clerk of such city, or town clerk of such town, a notice that said post intends to undertake such relief as is provided by this act. Such notice shall contain the names of the relief committee of said post in such city or town, and of the commander and other officers of said post. And the commander of said post shall annually thereafter, during the month of October, file a similar notice with said city and town clerks, and also a detailed statement of the amount of relief furnished during the preceding year, with the names of all persons to whom such relief shall have been furnished, together with a brief statement in each case, from the relief committee upon whose recommendation the orders were drawn.

[margin note: Notice to city or town clerk, of taking charge of relief.]

[margin note: Annual statement as to relief, etc., how filed.]

§ 4. The said auditing board of any city or town may require of the said commander and quartermaster of any post of the Grand Army of the Republic, undertaking such relief in said city or town, a bond with sufficient and satisfactory sureties for the faithful and honest discharge of their duties under this act.

[margin note: Bond of relief committee.]

§ 5. Superintendents and overseers of the poor are hereby prohibited from sending indigent soldiers, sailors, and marines, (or their families, or the families of those deceased), to any alms-house (or orphan asylum) without the full concurrence and consent of the commander and relief committee of the post of the Grand Army of the Republic, having jurisdiction as provided in sections one and two. Indigent veterans with families, and the families of deceased veterans, shall, whenever practicable, be provided for and relieved at their homes in such city or town in which they shall have a residence, in the manner provided in sections one and two of this act. Indigent or disabled veterans of the classes specified in section one, who are not insane, and who have no families or friends with whom they may be domiciled, may be sent to any soldiers' home. Any indigent veteran of either of the classes specified in section one, or any member of the family of any living or deceased veteran of said classes, who may be insane, shall, upon recommendation of the commander and relief committee of such post of the Grand Army of the Republic, within the jurisdiction of which the case may occur, be sent to any insane asylum, and cared for as provided for indigent insane in section twenty-six of chapter one hundred and thirty-five of the laws of eighteen hundred and forty-two.

[margin note: Duties of overseers and superintendents of poor, as to committals to alms-house, etc.]

[margin note: Outdoor or home relief, to be given when possible.]

[margin note: Soldiers' Home, relief at.]

[margin note: Care of indigent insane veterans.]

§ 6. This act shall take effect immediately.

* * *

PROCEEDINGS OF THE NATIONAL CONFERENCE OF CHARITIES AND CORRECTIONS

1890

THE ECONOMIC AND MORAL EFFECTS OF PUBLIC OUTDOOR RELIEF.

BY MRS. CHARLES RUSSELL LOWELL, OF NEW YORK.

I have not been able to assent to the report of the Chairman of the Committee on Indoor and Outdoor Relief, only because, as it seems to me, he does not draw the distinction which is necessary between public and private relief.

I admit, of course, that there are persons who need relief (that is, *help*) in their own homes, and that both Pitt's argument and Mr. Sanborn's argument apply to such: "Great care should be taken, in relieving their distresses, not to throw them into the great class of vagrant and homeless poor." Such people, however, are, to my mind, not proper subjects for public relief at all; for what is public relief, and upon what grounds is it to be justified? Public relief is money paid by the bulk of the community (every community is of course composed mainly of those who are working hard to obtain a livelihood) to certain members of the community, not, however, paid voluntarily or spontaneously by those interested in the individuals receiving it, but paid by public officers from money raised by taxation. The only justification for the expenditure of public money (money raised by taxation) is that it is necessary for the public good. That certain persons need certain things is no reason for supplying them with those things from the public funds. Before this can be rightly done, it is necessary to prove that it is good for the community at large that it should be done. . . .

The practice of any community in this particular is a matter of great importance, for there can be no question that there is an inverse ratio between the welfare of the mass of the people and the distribution of relief. What some one has called "the fatal ease of living without work and the terrible difficulty of living by work" are closely interrelated as cause and effect; and, if you will permit me, I will try to show by a short allegory what this relation is.

Once upon a time there lived in a valley, called the Valley of Industry, a people who were happy and industrious. All the goods of this life were supplied to them by exhaustless subterranean springs of water, which they pumped up into a great reservoir on the top of a neighboring hill, the Hill of Prosperity, from which it flowed down, each man receiving what he himself pumped up, by a small pipe which led into his own house, a moderate amount of pumping on the part of every one keeping the reservoir well filled.

Finally, a few of the inhabitants of the Valley, more keen than the rest, reflected that it was unnecessary to weary themselves with pumping, so long as every one else kept at work. The Hill of Prosperity looked very attractive; and they therefore mounted to a convenient point, and put a large pipe into the reservoir, through which they drew off copious supplies of water without further trouble. The number of those who gave up pumping and withdrew to the Hill was at first so small that the loss did not add very much to the work of the mass of the people, who still kept to their pumping, and it did not occur to them to complain; but those who could followed the others up the Hill until it was all occupied, and by this time, although those who remained in the Valley did find their pumping a good deal harder than it was when all who used the water joined in the work, yet every one had become so accustomed to some people using the reservoir water without doing any pumping that it had come to be considered all right, and still there were no complaints. Meanwhile, the people on the Hill of Prosperity having nothing to do but enjoy the prospect, some of them began to explore the neighboring country, and soon discovered another valley at the foot of the Hill, running parallel with the Valley of Industry, and called the Valley of Idleness, and in it were a few people who had wandered from the former Valley (for the two were connected at the farther end), and who were living in abject misery, with no water, and apparently no means of getting any, so long as they stayed where they were. The people from the Hill of Prosperity were very much shocked at the suffering they found. "What a shame!" they cried. "The poor things have no water! We have plenty and to spare, so let us lead a pipe from the reservoir down into their Valley." No sooner said than done: the pipe was carried into the Valley of Idleness, and the people were made more comfortable. But as soon as the news was brought into the Valley of Industry, some of the pumpers who were tired or weak, and some who were only lazy, left their pumping, and hastened into the neighboring Valley, to enjoy the "free" water; but the pipe was not very large, and soon there was want and suffering again, and the people from Prosperity Hill were much disturbed, and decided to lay down another small pipe, which they did. But the result was the same, for the new supply of water attracted more people from the Valley of Industry. And so it went on, new pipe, more people, new pipe, more people, until the inhabitants of Prosperity Hill were full of distress about it, and exclaimed, "It seems a hopeless task to try to make these people happy and comfortable!" And they would have given up in despair, but a new idea occurred to them; and they said, "They do not seem to know how to take very good care of their children, and we will therefore take their children from them, and teach them to be comfortable and happy." So they built large, fine houses for the children, and they carried water in large pipes into the houses. And some of them said, "Let us put faucets, so as to teach them to turn on the water when they need it." But others said: "Oh, no! How troublesome it is to have to turn a faucet when you need water! Let them have it as we do, free." And sometimes one or other would suggest that, perhaps, after all, it was not quite right to waste so much of the water from the reservoir, and that the large pipe itself, which supplied the Hill of Prosperity, ought to have some means of checking the flow; but the answer was, "It is necessary and right that the water should be wasted; for otherwise the people in the Valley of Industry would have nothing to do, and they would starve." Usually, however, the Prosperity Hill people were too much engaged in taking care of the inhabitants of the Valley of Idleness to give much thought to those of the Valley of Industry; and their anxiety was quite justified, for they had to keep up a perpetual watchfulness, the people increasing so fast that it was necessary constantly to lay more pipe to keep them from the most abject suffering, and even this device never succeeded for very long, as I have said.

In fact, no one thought much about the Valley of Industry or its people. Those in the Valley of Idleness only thought of them long enough to reflect how silly they were to keep on pumping all the time and making their backs and arms ache, when they might have water without any exertion, by simply moving into their Valley. The children born in the Valley of Idleness did not even know there was a Valley of Industry, or any pumps, or any pumpers, or any reservoir: they thought the water grew in pipes, and ran out because it was its nature to. As for the people on the Hill of Prosperity, they were, as we have seen, rather confused in their views in this particular; and, besides thinking that their waste of the water from the reservoir was what kept the people in the Valley of Industry from starving, they used also to say sometimes: "How good it is for those people to have such nice, steady work to do! how strong it makes their backs and arms! how it hardens their muscles! What a nice, independent set of people they are! and *what* a splendid quantity of pure, life-giving water they get out of our reservoir!"

Meanwhile, you can imagine, though they could not, that it was rather hard on the men in the Valley of Industry, not only to have the water they pumped up drawn off at the top to supply two other communities, but also to have their own ranks thinned and their work increased by the loss of those who were tempted into the Valley of Idleness, to live on what the Prosperity Hill people and the Valley of Idleness people like to call euphemistically "free water," because they got it free, though actually it was not free at all; for the Valley of Industry people paid for it with their blood and muscle.

I might go on to tell you how the situation was still further complicated and made harder for them, and indeed for almost everyone, when a few of them obtained control of the inexhaustible subterranean springs; but here, I think, the allegory may end for the purposes of this Conference, and it seems to me to teach a lesson which we may well heed.

★ ★ ★

An Act to Prohibit the Coming of Chinese Laborers to the United States
September 13, 1888
Fiftieth Congress, Session 1

Be it enacted by the Senate and House of Representatives of the United States of America in Congress assembled, That from and after the date of the exchange of ratifications of the pending treaty between the United States of America and His Imperial Majesty the Emperor of China, signed on the twelfth day of March, anno Domini eighteen hundred and eighty-eight, it shall be unlawful for any Chinese person, whether a subject of China or of any other power, to enter the United States, except as hereinafter provided.

Chinese laborers. Immigration prohibited. Post, p. 504.

SEC. 2. That Chinese officials, teachers, students, merchants, or travelers for pleasure or curiosity, shall be permitted to enter the United States, but in order to entitle themselves to do so, they shall first obtain the permission of the Chinese Government, or other Government of which they may at the time be citizens or subjects. Such permission and also their personal identity shall in such case be evidenced by a certificate to be made out by the diplomatic representative of the United States in the country, or of the consular representative of the United States at the port or place from which the person named therein comes. The certificate shall contain a full description of such person, of his age, height, and general physical features, and shall state his former and present occupation or profession and place of residence, and shall be made out in duplicate. One copy shall be delivered open to the person named and described, and the other copy shall be sealed up and delivered by the diplomatic or consular officer as aforesaid to the captain of the vessel on which the person named in the certificate sets sail for the United States, together with the sealed certificate, which shall be addressed to the collector of customs at the port where such person is to land. There shall be delivered to the aforesaid captain a letter from the consular officer addressed to the collector of customs aforesaid, and stating that said consular officer has on a certain day delivered to the said captain a certificate of the right of the person named therein to enter the United States as a Chinese official, or other exempted person, as the case may be. And any captain who lands or attempts to land a Chinese person in the United States, without having in his possession a sealed certificate, as required in this section, shall be liable to the penalties prescribed in section nine of this act.

Classes permitted to enter.

Certificates to be obtained.

Penalty for violation.

SEC. 3. That the provisions of this act shall apply to all persons of the Chinese race, whether subjects of China or other foreign power, excepting Chinese diplomatic or consular officers and their attendants; and the words "Chinese laborers," whenever used in this act, shall be construed to mean both skilled and unskilled laborers and Chinese employed in mining.

Scope of act.

SEC. 4. That the master of any vessel arriving in the United States from any foreign port or place with any Chinese passengers on board shall, when he delivers his manifest of cargo, and if there be no cargo, when he makes legal entry of his vessel, and before landing or permitting to land any Chinese person (unless a diplomatic or consular officer, or attendant of such officer), deliver to the collector of customs of the district in which the vessel shall have arrived the sealed certificates and letters as aforesaid, and a separate list of all Chinese persons taken on board of his vessel at any foreign port or place, and of all such persons on board at the time of arrival as aforesaid. Such list shall show the names of such persons and other particulars as shown by their open certificates, or other evidences required by this act, and such list shall be sworn to by the master in the manner required by law in relation to the manifest of the cargo.

Master to deliver certificates, etc., on arrival in United States.

List to be delivered.

Contents of list.

Diplomatic and consular officers.

Penalty.

Return of laborers prohibited.

Conditions for permission to return.

Property requisites.

Identification of Chinese wishing to return.

Certificate.

Transfer void.

Extension of period.

No entry without certificate.

Chinese permitted to land only at certain ports.

The master of any vessel as aforesaid shall not permit any Chinese diplomatic or consular officer or attendant of such officer to land without having first been informed by the collector of customs of the official character of such officer or attendant. Any refusal or willful neglect of the master of any vessel to comply with the provisions of this section shall incur the same penalties and forfeitures as are provided for a refusal or neglect to report and deliver a manifest of the cargo.

SEC. 5. That from and after the passage of this act, no Chinese laborer in the United States shall be permitted, after having left, to return thereto, except under the conditions stated in the following sections.

SEC. 6. That no Chinese laborer within the purview of the preceding section shall be permitted to return to the United States unless he has a lawful wife, child, or parent in the United States, or property therein of the value of one thousand dollars, or debts of like amount due him and pending settlement. The marriage to such wife must have taken place at least a year prior to the application of the laborer for a permit to return to the United States, and must have been followed by the continuous cohabitation of the parties as man and wife.

If the right to return be claimed on the ground of property or of debts, it must appear that the property is bona fide and not colorably acquired for the purpose of evading this act, or that the debts are unascertained and unsettled, and not promissory notes or other similar acknowledgments of ascertained liability.

SEC. 7. That a Chinese person claiming the right to be permitted to leave the United States and return thereto on any of the grounds stated in the foregoing section, shall apply to the collector of customs of the district from which he wishes to depart at least a month prior to the time of his departure, and shall make on oath before the said collector a full statement descriptive of his family, or property, or debts, as the case may be, and shall furnish to said collector such proofs of the facts entitling him to return as shall be required by the rules and regulations prescribed from time to time by the Secretary of the Treasury, and for any false swearing in relation thereto he shall incur the penalties of perjury. He shall also permit the collector to take a full description of his person, which description the collector shall retain and mark with a number. And if the collector, after hearing the proofs and investigating all the circumstances of the case, shall decide to issue a certificate of return, he shall at such time and place as he may designate, sign and give to the person applying a certificate containing the number of the description last aforesaid, which shall be the sole evidence given to such person of his right to return. If this last named certificate be transferred, it shall become void, and the person to whom it was given shall forfeit his right to return to the United States. The right to return under the said certificate shall be limited to one year; but it may be extended for an additional period, not to exceed a year, in cases where, by reason of sickness or other cause of disability beyond his control, the holder thereof shall be rendered unable sooner to return, which facts shall be fully reported to and investigated by the consular representative of the United States at the port or place from which such laborer departs for the United States, and certified by such representative of the United States to the satisfaction of the collector of customs at the port where such Chinese person shall seek to land in the United States, such certificate to be delivered by said representative to the master of the vessel on which he departs for the United States. And no Chinese laborer shall be permitted to re-enter the United States without producing to the proper officer of the customs at the port of such entry the return certificate herein required. A Chinese laborer possessing a certificate under this section shall be admitted to the United States only at the port from which he departed therefrom, and no Chinese person, except Chinese diplomatic or consular officers, and their attendants, shall be permitted to enter the United States except at the ports of San

Francisco, Portland, Oregon, Boston, New York, New Orleans, Port Townsend, or such other ports as may be designated by the Secretary of the Treasury.

SEC. 8. That the Secretary of the Treasury shall be, and he hereby is, authorized and empowered to make and prescribe, and from time to time to change and amend such rules and regulations, not in conflict with this act, as he may deem necessary and proper to conveniently secure to such Chinese persons as are provided for in articles second and third of the said treaty between the United States and the Empire of China, the rights therein mentioned, and such as shall also protect the United States against the coming and transit of persons not entitled to the benefit of the provisions of said articles. And he is hereby further authorized and empowered to prescribe the form and substance of certificates to be issued to Chinese laborers under and in pursuance of the provisions of said articles, and prescribe the form of the record of such certificate and of the proceedings for issuing the same, and he may require the deposit, as a part of such record, of the photograph of the party to whom any such certificate shall be issued.

Secretary of the Treasury to prescribe regulations, etc.

Form of certificate, etc.

SEC. 9. That the master of any vessel who shall knowingly bring within the United States on such vessel, and land, or attempt to land, or permit to be landed any Chinese laborer or other Chinese person, in contravention of the provisions of this act, shall be deemed guilty of a misdemeanor and, on conviction thereof, shall be punished with a fine of not less than five hundred dollars nor more than one thousand dollars, in the discretion of the court, for every Chinese laborer or other Chinese person so brought, and may also be imprisoned for a term of not less than one year, nor more than five years, in the discretion of the court.

Punishment to master of vessel unlawfully bringing Chinamen.

SEC. 10. That the foregoing section shall not apply to the case of any master whose vessel shall come within the jurisdiction of the United States in distress or under stress of weather, or touching at any port of the United States on its voyage to any foreign port or place. But Chinese laborers or persons on such vessel shall not be permitted to land, except in case of necessity, and must depart with the vessel on leaving port.

Vessels in distress.

SEC. 11. That any person who shall knowingly and falsely alter or substitute any name for the name written in any certificate herein required, or forge such certificate, or knowingly utter any forged or fraudulent certificate, or falsely personate any person named in any such certificate, and any person other than the one to whom a certificate was issued who shall falsely present any such certificate, shall be deemed guilty of a misdemeanor, and upon conviction thereof shall be fined in a sum not exceeding one thousand dollars, and imprisoned in a penitentiary for a term of not more than five years.

Punishment for counterfeiting certificate, etc.

SEC. 12. That before any Chinese passengers are landed from any such vessel, the collector, or his deputy, shall proceed to examine such passengers, comparing the certificates with the list and with the passengers; and no passenger shall be allowed to land in the United States from such vessel in violation of law; and the collector shall in person decide all questions in dispute with regard to the right of any Chinese passenger to enter the United States, and his decision shall be subject to review by the Secretary of the Treasury, and not otherwise.

Landing passengers.

Sec. 13. That any Chinese person, or person of Chinese descent, found unlawfully in the United States, or its Territories, may be arrested upon a warrant issued upon a complaint, under oath, filed by any party on behalf of the United States, by any justice, judge, or commissioner of any United States court, returnable before any justice, judge, or commissioner of a United States court, or before any United States court, and when convicted, upon a hearing, and found and adjudged to be one not lawfully entitled to be or remain in the United States, such person shall be removed from the United States to the country whence he came. But any such Chinese person convicted before a commissioner of a United States court may, within ten days from such conviction, appeal to the

Arrest of Chinese unlawfully in the United States.

judge of the district court for the district. A certified copy of the judgment shall be the process upon which said removal shall be made, and it may be executed by the marshal of the district, or any officer having authority of a marshal under the provisions of this section. And in all such cases the person who brought or aided in bringing such person into the United States shall be liable to the Government of the United States for all necessary expenses incurred in such investigation and removal: and all peace officers of the several States and Territories of the United States are hereby invested with the same authority in reference to carrying out the provisions of this act, as a marshal or deputy marshal of the United States, and shall be entitled to like compensation, to be audited and paid by the same officers.

Sec. 14. That the preceding sections shall not apply to Chinese diplomatic or consular officers or their attendants, who shall be admitted to the United States under special instructions of the Treasury Department, without production of other evidence than that of personal identity.

Sec. 15. That the act entitled "An act to execute certain treaty stipulations relating to Chinese," approved May sixth, eighteen hundred and eighty-two, and an act to amend said act approved July fifth, eighteen hundred and eighty-four, are hereby repealed to take effect upon the ratification of the pending treaty as provided in section one of this act.

Approved, September 13, 1888.

★ ★ ★

An Act, a Supplement . . .

October 1, 1888

Fiftieth Congress, Session 1

Chap. 1064.—An act, a supplement to an act entitled "An act to execute certain treaty stipulations relating to Chinese," approved the sixth day of May eighteen hundred and eighty-two.

Be it enacted by the Senate and House of Representatives of the United States of America in Congress assembled, That from and after the passage of this act, it shall be unlawful for any Chinese laborer who shall at any time heretofore have been, or who may now or hereafter be, a resident within the United States, and who shall have departed, or shall depart, therefrom, and shall not have returned before the passage of this act, to return to, or remain in, the United States.

Sec. 2. That no certificates of identity provided for in the fourth and fifth sections of the act to which this is a supplement shall hereafter be issued; and every certificate heretofore issued in pursuance thereof, is hereby declared void and of no effect, and the Chinese laborer claiming admission by virtue thereof shall not be permitted to enter the United States.

Sec. 3. That all the duties prescribed, liabilities penalties and forfeitures imposed, and the powers conferred by the second, tenth, eleventh, and twelfth, sections of the act to which this is a supplement are hereby extended and made applicable to the provisions of this act.

Sec. 4. That all such part or parts of the act to which this is a supplement as are inconsistent herewith are hereby repealed.

Approved, October 1, 1888.

 Recall what you learned in this chapter by completing the Chapter Review.

Appeal.

Punishment of person aiding.

Diplomatic and consular officers.

Prior acts to be repealed.

Vol. 22, p. 58.

Vol. 23, p. 115.

October 1, 1888.

Exclusion of Chinese laborers. Vol. 22, p. 59. *Ante,* p. 476.

No certificates for return to be issued.

Penalties.

Repeal provisions.

5

Progress and Reform: 1900–1930

LEWIS WICKES HINE, PRINTS & PHOTOGRAPHS DIVISION, LIBRARY OF CONGRESS, LC-DIG-NCLC-01131.

The rapid social and economic changes of the late 19th century had caught many Americans by surprise. As the new century dawned, they felt like strangers in their own land. In the countryside, the creation of a global market for agricultural goods meant that the price of wheat in Kansas was tied to not only the success of the year's harvest, but how well farmers in Canada and Australia did as well. In the cities, a predominantly native-born, white middle class, and a foreign-born working class studied one another across barriers of social class, language, and culture. But the striking economic reality of the era was the emergence of economic giants: trusts, monopolies, and corporations.

Over the first 30 years of the 20th century, Americans from all walks of life tried to come to terms with these changes and their implications for their welfare. It was an era of experimentation and innovation, but ultimately, most of the reform efforts of the era fell short of their goals. Although the motivation for reform was in abundant supply, Progressive reforms lacked two critical ingredients for success: ideas and institutions.

Intellectually, Americans lacked a set of coherent ideas for changing the economic and social structure. Many of their ideas

LEARNING OUTCOMES

- Summarize the major shifts in America's economic and social structure during the early 20th century.
- Explain how *maternalism* was a successful strategy for expanding social welfare during the Progressive Era.
- Compare the success of reform movements before World War I with their decline during and after the war.

CHAPTER OUTLINE

Changing Economic and Demographic Realities   116
An Urban and Industrial Society   116
Poverty and the Working Class   118
African Americans, Native
   Americans, and Immigrants   119

Innovations in Social Welfare   122
Regulating Working Conditions   124
Expanding Public Welfare   126
Protecting Vulnerable Families   128
Social Work and the Black
   Population   132
The Social Welfare of Veterans   133
Professionalizing Social Work   134

Social Movements in the Early 20th Century   136
Coalitions for Reform   136
Regulating Business   138
Organized Labor   138
Women, Work, and Suffrage   139
The End of Reform   141

DOCUMENTS: Progress and Reform   143
The Family and the Woman's Wage,
   1909   144
Funds to Parents Act, Illinois,
   1911   146
Public Pensions to Widows, 1912   147

looked to the past, to returning to a society dominated by small-town values. Others, like the creation of a socialist commonwealth that would eliminate capitalism, never received serious consideration by most Americans.

The institutional realities of the early 20th century, too, could not support serious reform. The forces that were reshaping economic and social life were national and international in scope. Yet, most Americans owed their allegiance to social institutions that were local or sectarian. Fraternal organizations, political parties, and labor unions—even if they were affiliated with national federations—were effective only in addressing local issues.

If reform were to succeed, it would need to reach across the rigid cultural barriers that dominated American society in the early 20th century: the lines between the countryside and the city, between workers and the middle class, between foreigners and native born, and between men and women.

The Progressives made a start at building the ideas and institutions that could ultimately reform American society, but it was only a start. Ironically, many of its gains occurred after the end of the Progressive Era with America's entry into World War I. After the war, the dominant political climate turned more conservative as the culture sought "100 percent Americanism" and "normalcy."[1] Below the surface, many reform movements would continue to grow, although their eventual success was years away.

CHANGING ECONOMIC AND DEMOGRAPHIC REALITIES

By the 1920s, the United States had become the richest country on earth—a world leader in farm and manufacturing output. By 1925, it was producing 55 percent of the world's iron ore, 66 percent of the steel, 62 percent of the petroleum, 52 percent of the timber, 60 percent of the cotton, 80 percent of the sulfur, and 95 percent of the automobiles.[2]

An Urban and Industrial Society

Revolutions in technology and communication began to knit America into a single country. The American frontier had disappeared only in the last decade of the 19th century. By the turn of the 20th century, train lines connected cities and regions. During the 19th century, most workers walked to work, which meant they needed to live near their jobs. By the early 20th century, trolley lines and commuter trains made it possible for people to live in one section of town and work or shop in another. Before the 1920s had ended, the automobile had become an increasingly common form of transportation, often accounting for half of a city's commutes to work.

The telephone had an equally dramatic impact on communications. In 1890, only about 2 percent of American homes had a telephone. By 1930, 40 percent did. No longer did it take days or hours to get word across town or across the nation. During the first three decades of the 20th century, motion pictures and radio improved people's access to information and culture from across the world.

Twentieth-century inventions and innovative managerial skills revolutionized industry and agriculture. Between 1899 and 1929, the total output of manufacturing increased by 273 percent.[3] Growth occurred throughout the period but was particularly stimulated by the war, when new industries were developed to replace the previously imported German dyes, chemicals, and optical instruments. When European industries were left devastated by World War I, the United States became the leading world supplier of both manufactured and agricultural products.

The period from the turn of the century to the depression of the 1930s saw the development of new power supplies, greater mechanization, and the spread of "scientific management." Whereas in 1913, it had taken 14 hours to assemble a car, in 1914, the job was done in 93 minutes. By 1925, Henry Ford was able to produce an automobile every 10 seconds.

In agriculture, too, mechanization and new sources of power joined with improved transportation to increase productivity. The value of agricultural output rose steadily, due almost entirely to the increase in crop yields per acre. As farming became mechanized, labor was freed to move into manufacturing. By the end of the period, although the United States had only 4 percent of the world's farmers and farm laborers, it was producing nearly 70 percent of the world's tobacco, 25 percent of the oats and hay, 20 percent of the wheat, 13 percent of the barley, and 7 percent of the potatoes.[4]

Technological progress and relatively steady employment levels resulted in a climbing gross domestic product (GDP), despite brief recessions. GDP stood at about $17 billion in 1900 and $104 billion in 1929. Per capita GDP rose by 73 percent in the first 30 years of the century.[5]

The increase in GDP was based on the ability of the agricultural sector to support a growing urban, industrial population. Between 1900 and 1930, the population of the United States increased by 47 million to reach 123 million. During these years, the total number of persons living in urban areas increased by 38 million to a total of 69 million. Forty percent of the population lived in urban areas in 1900; this rose to 51 percent in 1920 and to 56 percent in 1930.[6] The "push" of agricultural mechanization and the "pull" of manufacturing growth affected both black and white workers. For the United States as a whole, 27 percent of the black population and 49 percent of the white population lived in urban areas in 1910; in 1930, 44 percent of the black population and 58 percent of the white population lived in urban areas.[7] Although the Southern African American population remained predominantly rural, in the Northern and Western parts of the country, blacks concentrated in urban areas. The expanding demand for labor and cut-off of European immigration during World War I accelerated these population shifts.

Between 1920 and 1930, some 6 million people moved from farms to cities, resulting for the first time in a net loss—of 1.2 million—in farm population. As cities grew, they became commercial and industrial in character. The number of cities with populations of at least 100,000 grew from 38 in 1900 to 83 in 1930.[8] The growth was haphazard, causing crowded, unsanitary, tenement living. Families, both from abroad and from rural areas, were unfamiliar with urban living. Their social and economic vulnerability provided opportunities for political leaders—often organized into citywide "machines"—to gain their allegiance. Although city governments succeeded in addressing many social problems, especially where building infrastructure could also provide jobs, contracts, and kickbacks, the social and cultural needs of the urban working class were often ignored.

Growth and change occurred in the organization of industry as well as in its output. In 1897, about a dozen corporations other than railroads were capitalized at $10 million. By 1903, the number had risen to 300, of which about 50 were capitalized at more than $50 million; 17 were capitalized at more than $100 million; and one, U.S. Steel, became the first billion-dollar corporation. These were the years in which some of the largest trusts in America were formed: Standard Oil, Consolidated Tobacco, and American Smelting, in addition to U.S. Steel. At the same time, many corporations became "vertically integrated," controlling their supply of raw materials as well as networks for distributing and selling their goods. The efforts of the federal government to regulate big business were largely ineffective. By 1914, large corporations dominated anthracite coal, agricultural machinery, sugar, telephone and telegraph, and public utilities in addition to iron and steel, railroads, oil, tobacco, and copper. Control of American industry had shifted from individual owners to a professional managerial class responsible to a board of directors often controlled by a small and powerful group of investment bankers.[9]

Paralleling the concentration of corporate power was a concentration of wealth and income. As the nation prospered, the income and asset growth at the top far exceeded that of either the middle class or the working class. Andrew Carnegie, for example, was said to have had an average annual income of more than $10 million—not subject to any income tax—at the turn of the century. In 1899, the richest 1.6 percent of the population had received 10.8 percent of national income. By 1910, this had jumped to 19 percent. The percentage of national income that went to the top 10 percent of the population increased from 40 to 50 percent between 1910 and 1930.

Rising wages and relatively steady employment meant that working-class incomes rose, too, but at a much slower rate. A 1915 report by the Commission on Industrial Relations took the critical question of the era to be, "Have workers received a fair share of the enormous increase in wealth which has taken place in this country during the period, as a result largely of their labor?" Its response: "The answer is emphatically—No!"[10]

Poverty and the Working Class

The commission's report pointed out that during 1890–1912, personal wealth had increased 188 percent, but the aggregate income of wage earners in manufacturing, mining, and transportation had risen only 95 percent. The wage earner's share of the net product in manufacturing had actually declined. The commission estimated that to achieve a minimum decency level, an average family of 5.6 members required an annual income of $700. Because 79 percent of the country's fathers earned less than $700 a year, earnings from other family members were necessary to sustain a family. Although reformers railed against child labor, many low-income parents were moved more by economic necessity than by moral injunctions. The Census Bureau reported that 1,750,000 children between 10 and 15 years of age were gainfully employed in 1900; by 1910, this number had dropped to 1,600,000. In 1930, however, the figure still stood at 667,000.[11]

The report of the Commission on Industrial Relations concluded that, despite the labor of wives and children, and the widespread practice of taking in boarders and lodgers, 50 to 66 percent of working-class families were poor and that a third lived in "abject poverty." Other estimates confirmed the judgment of poverty and risk. Robert Hunter, a social worker writing in 1904, estimated the poverty population at 10 million. Father John A. Ryan, an ethical theorist and economist writing in 1906, found that the average family needed an annual income of at least $600 and that 60 percent of all wage earners received less.[12] Within the ranks of the working class, as the American Federation of Labor (AFL) succeeded in unionizing some crafts, dissatisfaction was further aggravated by the notable difference in payments to skilled and unskilled workers. Each recession (1910–1911, 1914–1915, 1920–1921) meant increased unemployment and wage cuts, especially for unskilled workers—largely ex-farmhands, African Americans, and immigrants. Indeed, by 1928–1929, social welfare agencies were reporting increased caseloads.

From 1919 to 1929, manufacturing output increased by 53 percent, while the number of wage earners in manufacturing remained stable.[13] Annual real earnings rose and the length of the workweek fell, so that for the employed it was a prosperous period. A significant share of families crossed a watershed. During the late 19th century, a majority of families experienced poverty at some point during its life cycle. As a result, parents formulated strategies—like sending children to work or taking in boarders—as hedges against an economic emergency. By the early 20th century, the threat of extreme poverty subsided for two groups—more skilled workers in expanding industries like automobile making, and white-collar workers in service industries. As a result, many of these families shifted to new family strategies—including prolonging children's education and practicing contraception.

The pre–World War I period was one of prosperity marked by rising farm income. The closing of the frontier, however, meant rising land prices. This, combined with rising costs of mechanization, made easy access to low-cost credit to buy land and machinery a major issue for most farmers. For the marginal farmer, land became more and more difficult to acquire. As the average size of farms started to grow, farm tenancy, already prevalent in the South, began to spread to the Midwest. In 1900, 35 percent of the nation's farms were tenant operated; by 1930, this had risen to 42 percent. For black farmers in the South, the figure reached 79 percent in 1930. The demands of World War I had led to an overextension of agriculture. The debt burden, cutthroat competition, and declining profits pushed the farm sector into depression before the slowdown hit industry. Between 1919 and 1929, the number of farms actually declined.[14]

African Americans, Native Americans, and Immigrants

The well-being of African Americans in the early 20th century was worse than at any time since the end of slavery. With the end of Reconstruction, African Americans had lost any real political power; they had been abandoned to the "oppression of those who had formerly exercised unlimited domination" over them. They still retained some of the political and civil rights they had won after the Civil War.[15]

The Populist revolt of the 1890s created fear among the white elite, however, that an alliance of poor whites and blacks might challenge their power. In the early years of the 20th century, Southern states moved to pass Jim Crow laws that excluded African Americans from voting or serving on juries, segregated schools and public accommodations, and provided economic elites with even more power with which to control black workers.[16]

The segregation and suppression of Jim Crow was given judicial respectability by the Supreme Court's approval in 1896 of the "separate but equal" doctrine in the *Plessy v. Ferguson* case.[17] Rationalization of the necessity for segregation was epitomized by the widespread acceptance of D. W. Griffith's 1915 film *The Birth of a Nation*, in which freed blacks were stereotyped as cruel, vengeful rulers over starving, helpless whites and as "racially incapable of understanding, sharing, or contributing to Americanism."[18] In this atmosphere, Booker T. Washington's belief that African Americans should focus on acquiring skills and better work habits found support among whites, who gained comfort and conviction from the seeming acquiescence of the country's outstanding Negro leader—the founder of Tuskegee Institute—in policies of social segregation and political cooperation. Washington wrote:

> The wisest among my race understand that the agitation of questions of social equality is the extremest folly, and that progress in the enjoyment of all the privileges that will come to us must be the result of severe and constant struggle rather than of artificial forcing. No race that has anything to contribute to the markets of the world is long in any degree ostracized. It is important and right that all privileges of the law be ours, but it is vastly more important that we be prepared for the exercise of these privileges.[19]

▶ **Watch this video on the Great Migration.**

How did the movement of African Americans to the North and West before 1930 influence social welfare policy during the 1930s and after?

Progressivism—especially in the South—was tied to efforts to restrict the rights of African Americans. Halting efforts by Populists to forge a biracial alliance were countered by moves toward "honest government" that included restrictions on the franchise.[20] Sunk in the tenancy-mortgage morass of the sharecropper and crop-lien systems that kept them in perpetual debt and subjected to lynching and harassment, the black population began to migrate to urban areas. In 1900, there were only 2 million blacks living in cities. The largest single group was in Washington, DC, Baltimore, New Orleans, Philadelphia, and New York each had more than 60,000 black residents.[21] Spurred by the labor demands of World War I, the net migration of blacks to Northern states amounted to 426,000 between 1910 and 1920 and jumped to 713,000 during the next decade.[22]

The beginning of the flight from the South coincided with a period of dramatically increased labor productivity, as mass production techniques and assembly lines were introduced. But for blacks forced off the farms and trying to gain entry into the labor market, times were always hard. Although there were not enough black migrants in the cities for them to have political or economic clout, their numbers were sufficient to foster white hostility, both because of competition with whites for jobs and because of their use, along with immigrants, as strikebreakers in labor disputes. Discrimination dominated white–black relations, and blacks were successfully excluded from the ranks of organized labor. Indeed, African Americans were even excluded from unskilled factory jobs in most cities, even though these jobs were near the bottom of the occupational ladder (see Figure 5.1).

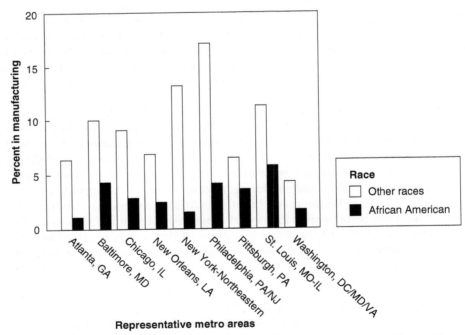

Figure 5.1 Racial discrimination in manufacturing jobs. African Americans migrated from rural to urban areas during the early years of the 20th century; yet, they continued to face severe discrimination. In most cities, even factory employment was closed to them.
Source: U.S. Census 1910, author's calculation

A new feature of African American life in Northern cities was residential segregation. In the South, African Americans typically lived in small towns on isolated farms. In the North, white residents and landlords conspired to push most black residents into small, overcrowded enclaves. Yet, the growth of the black population in many cities pushed black families to seek housing outside their neighborhoods. In response to the expanding black sections of Baltimore, the city council passed the nation's first residential segregation plan in 1910. Clashes between whites and blacks over maintaining the color line resulted in frequent riots, the most notorious of which took place in Chicago in 1919.

The black population was generally unaffected by reform activities and the social welfare benefits that resulted from them. In an era marked by economic progress and social mobility, this group remained poor and powerless. More social legislation aiding and protecting the working class was passed during the Progressive Era than had been passed in any previous century. For the most part, however, legislation affecting the labor of women and children, workmen's compensation, regulation of hours and wages, and industrial safety all applied to industries in which black participation was minimal. This fact eluded social welfare reformers who tended to view the problems of all minorities as coextensive with the problems of immigrants. Despite periodic race riots, the relatively small number of blacks in the cities of the North (where most agitation for social reform was concentrated) and their segregation from the mainstream of economic, political, and social life made it possible to ignore their special problems. When reformers did focus on the needs of African Americans, they often provided help on a segregated basis. For example, in Chicago, philanthropists funded social services in the black ghetto, so African Americans would not create white reprisals by seeking help at settlement houses in white neighborhoods.[23]

For Native Americans, too, conditions improved very slowly. They were poor, largely uneducated, and deprived of citizenship and suffrage. Of those living on reservations, almost three-quarters of the children received no schooling. Much of the education that occurred was in boarding schools, which alienated the children and left them prepared for very little. Not until 1928 were federal funds increased, and not until the mid-1930s did states receive special funds to provide public education for Native Americans.[24] Only in 1924 were Native Americans recognized as citizens of the United States of America.[25]

The first three decades of the 20th century marked a high-water mark for the flow of European immigrants to the United States and the imposition of rigid controls on that flow. During the depression of the 1890s, less than half a million immigrants entered the United States each year, but with the return of prosperity, their numbers swelled to a peak of 1.2 million in 1907, a number that was not surpassed until the 1990s.

Not only did the number of immigrants increase, but their composition changed as well. Between 1820 and 1899, 18.7 million immigrants entered the United States, a bit more than 233,000 per year. In the next 15 years, 13.4 million came, nearly 900,000 per year. Three countries had accounted for a majority of immigrants during the 19th century—Britain, Ireland, and Germany—but during the early years of the 20th century, national backgrounds that had been largely absent entered the United States in increasing numbers. More than 3 million Italians, 2.6 million Russians (a majority of whom were Russian Jews), and 1.3 million Hungarians entered the United States. The number of Poles was large as well, although because they were divided between the German, Austro-Hungarian, and Russian empires, we do not have official figures on their numbers.[26]

Anti-immigrant sentiment had been present in the United States since the early Republic, but the new composition of immigrant flows and the fears and disillusionment of the white Protestant population after World War I propelled a major change in

In the North, white residents and landlords conspired to push most black residents into small, overcrowded enclaves. Yet, the growth of the black population in many cities pushed black families to seek housing outside their neighborhoods. In response to the expanding black sections of Baltimore, the city council passed the nation's first residential segregation plan in 1910.

policy. Eventually, nativist sentiment prevailed, and the nation's immigration laws grew more restrictive between 1917 and 1924. The 1921 immigration act imposed national quotas on European immigration that favored Northern and Western Europeans and those quotas were tightened by the 1924 law. Reflecting anti-Catholic and anti-Jewish sentiments of the era, the quotas were intended to slow the immigration rates of southern and eastern Europeans and to limit the total number of foreigners admitted.[27]

However, despite the constraints of World War I and the legislative restrictions of the 1920s, the number of foreign born as a percentage of the total population stayed at 13 to 14 percent—one of seven people were immigrants. An even larger number of people had at least one foreign-born parent. Immigrants and their children accounted for more than one-third of the population. Most—about 75 percent—lived in cities, where rapid population growth meant a period of booming construction.[28]

> **?** Assess your comprehension of "Changing Economic and Demographic Realities" by completing this quiz.

INNOVATIONS IN SOCIAL WELFARE

Middle- and upper-class white women, including the founders of social work, exercised unprecedented political influence during these years. Although the search for gender equality motivated many of them, their broadest influence was tied to their traditional roles as mothers and wives. Maternalism—an ideology based on the moral authority associated with women's traditional role—provided a means of uniting women whatever their position on equality. A variety of reforms, including mother's pensions, the creation of the Children's Bureau, child and women labor legislation, and efforts to improve maternal and child health, were tied to the rise of maternalism.[29]

On the federal level, Congress, in 1907, banned political contributions by corporations. In 1913, the 17th Amendment to the Constitution provided for direct election of senators. In 1919, the 19th Amendment, providing for women's suffrage, was passed. It was ratified by the required 36 states just one year later, bringing victory to this cause after almost 75 years of campaigning.

On a state and local level, 20 states introduced the initiative (making it possible for the citizenry to propose legislation) and the referendum (making it possible for voters to pass on measures introduced in legislative bodies). By 1915, direct primary and presidential preference laws were on the books of two-thirds of the states, challenging the power of political bosses.

Efforts to reform local politics highlighted a value conflict among Progressives between efficiency and democratic control. Although local governments and political machines were often corrupt, they also were responsive to lower-middle- and working-class voters. In many cases, upper-class professionals led efforts to reduce the power of these voters by increasing the role of professionals and experts in running city government. The drive for efficiency, economy, and honesty in the administration of local governments began in Galveston, Texas, in 1900, when the entire political machinery of mayor, council, and bureaus was abolished and replaced by a board of commissioners. Thereafter, the commission form of government spread rapidly, especially in smaller cities, where its structure—generally five commissioners elected at large and each responsible for a particular department—was most appropriate. Starting with Dayton, Ohio, in 1914, many cities embraced the city manager type of government—a government run by an appointed expert in city administration. Efforts to reform local politics highlighted a value conflict among Progressives between efficiency and democratic control.

In public welfare administration, change resulted in an initial shift of responsibility from local overseers of the poor to local or county departments of welfare. Kansas City, Missouri, established a city department of welfare in 1910, with authority to provide for the relief of the poor and the care of delinquents, the unemployed, and other needy groups. St. Joseph, Missouri, established a county–city department of public welfare, and Chicago set up the Cook County Bureau of Public Welfare, both in 1913.

The rise of public welfare marked a dramatic break with late 19th-century thought about poverty. In place of a voluntary movement to limit "indiscriminate almsgiving," philanthropic leaders called for government action to reduce the distress of the poor. Increasingly, Progressives came to see that poverty was primarily an economic, not a moral, condition.

Nor did the country's entry into World War I completely stop local governmental restructuring. Westchester County, New York, established a department of welfare in 1916. In 1917, an important reorganization of the Illinois state government occurred with the passage of the Civil Administrative Code, which provided for the grouping of all state functions and activities into nine departments, each with its own director. Among the nine was a Department of Welfare with its director of public welfare responsible for administering the state's assistance, services, and institutional programs. The Illinois code was emulated by other states and was the start of a new era in public administration. In many states, for example, public welfare services were consolidated into statewide systems administered by appointed heads of state departments of welfare. Both in the statewide scope of the organizations and in the removal of department executives "from current political responsibility, except through [the ultimate political responsibility of] the governor,"[30] the trend foreshadowed the requirements of the Social Security Act of 1935.

No reform activities were more representative of the Progressive Era than those that occurred in the arena of social welfare. The reform movement responded to and fostered the new profession of social work. Individual social workers, through research, persistence, and expertise, moved to the forefront of advocacy for social legislation. Theodore Roosevelt himself, acting on the commonly held conviction that all were personally responsible for the current state of affairs depicted so graphically in muckraking literature, called upon each citizen to contribute to "reform through social work."[31] Social work, acting on society's will for social change, carried that projection in two sometimes converging but basically different operations—the Charity Organization and Settlement House movements.

The reform movement responded to and fostered the new profession of social work. Individual social workers, through research, persistence, and expertise, moved to the forefront of advocacy for social legislation.

Those who labored for social reform were primarily concerned, as a matter of social justice, "to bring the power of the state and national governments into the economic struggle on the side of women, children, and other unprotected groups."[32] Whether prompted by the Charity Organization hope to sustain and strengthen individuals in their own efforts to cope or by the Settlement House conviction that any intervention short of intrinsic societal restructuring must be considered only "a down payment toward justice,"[33] social workers could find common ground for the work that needed doing.

At the height of the reform movement, between 1905 and the beginning of World War I, leaders of the Charity Organization and Settlement House movements came together on behalf of social reform activity. Changing views of the family prompted the participation of organized charity in reform. In 1900, Charles Faulkner's presidential address at the National Conference of Charities and Corrections had labeled the family "the unit of social order" and laid out a program of education in the home and in the school for the moral improvement of individuals. His Darwinian bent took him from a concern for the maintenance of "the blessings and protection of society through its family life" to call for avoiding "unrestrained comingling of . . . defectives with the people."[34] By 1908, however, Mary Richmond was arguing for the protection of family life against the onslaughts of a hostile environment.

Richmond, whose *Social Diagnosis* was an important milestone in the evolution of casework, referred to the family as "the great social unit, the fundamental social fact." She demanded changes in agency practices, action in regard to child labor laws, industrial safety regulations, and protection of working women, as well as administrative changes in industrial operations to strengthen family life. She challenged the members of her social work audience to ask themselves, "Have we at least set plans in motion that will make the children better heads of families than their parents have been?"[35] Richmond's challenge was based on a new recognition of "the overwhelming force of heredity plus the environment that we inherit." Social workers and their allies advocated for legislation to regulate tenement and factory construction; to prevent and compensate for industrial accidents and diseases; to prohibit child labor and provide for compulsory education; to improve sanitary and health conditions; to provide social insurance as security against unemployment, retirement, or death of the breadwinner; and to protect workers—especially women—in regard to minimum wages and working hours.

Improvement in housing conditions had been a concern of social workers at least since 1882, when the Boston Associated Charities appointed a Committee on Dwellings of the Poor. In the same year, the New York and Buffalo Charity Organization Societies combined to get a tenement housing bill through the state legislature. During the next decade, they allied themselves with settlement residents and others to investigate and publicize the housing conditions of the poor. The New York City Tenement House Law was passed in 1901. Aimed at preventing the construction of lightless, airless tenements, the law became a model to follow. Similar legislation was passed for Chicago in 1902; by 1910, most large cities had inaugurated some housing reform.

Regulating Working Conditions

No reform crusade better illustrates Progressives' belief in maternalism than their advocacy of child and women's labor legislation. In 1900, nearly 2 million children aged 10 to 15 and almost 5 million women over 15 were in a labor force totaling about 29 million.[36] Twenty-eight states had already adopted some legal protections for children. By 1914, as a result of the continued assault by the National Child Labor Committee, the National Consumer's League, the General Federation of Women's Clubs, and others, almost all the states had laws covering hours and conditions of child labor in factories, mills, and workshops and setting minimum ages for leaving school.[37]

But the laws were weak and inadequate. Owen R. Lovejoy, secretary of the National Child Labor Committee and chairman of the Committee on Standards of Living and Labor of the National Conference of Charities and Corrections, reported the following:

> No state has made any adequate plan to protect its children to sixteen years from bare-handed contact with the red hot tools of our industrial competition. Nearly half the states have no effective way of protecting children even to the fourteenth birthday. Several permit their employment at twelve or even younger.[38]

The first unsuccessful attempts to bring child labor under federal control were made in 1906, when bills were introduced in Congress to prohibit the interstate shipment of articles produced in factories or mines employing children. In 1912, the Children's Bureau was created to report, among other things, on "dangerous occupations, accidents and diseases of children, employment legislation affecting children."[39] The bureau's

investigations bolstered the report of the secretary of labor as to the need for child protections, and further efforts to obtain federal regulation of child welfare followed. The
Keating-Owen bill was passed by Congress in 1916, but it was found unconstitutional
two years later on the grounds that it transcended "the authority delegated to Congress over commerce."[40] Subsequent improvements in child labor legislation remained
with the states; by 1930, all of the states and the District of Columbia had taken legal
measures to safeguard the employment and working conditions of children. In many
instances, old provisions had been strengthened.[41]

In the country as a whole, child labor had steadily declined so that by 1930, less than
5 percent of the children between 10 and 15 years of age were employed, compared
to 18 percent in 1900. Even in the South, which had lagged in regulatory legislation,
the ratio of children employed in its newly developing textile industry was no higher
than that in its Northern counterpart. These advances were chronicled in the census of
1930. Despite within-industry equivalency, however, there were large industrial and geographic differences. For example, only 3 percent of children between 10 and 15 years
were at work in industrial Rhode Island, whereas 24 percent were at work in Mississippi,
a state in which child welfare laws were loosely enforced and the all-white legislature
cared little about the well-being of black children. Nor did the census takers secure information concerning the paid employment of children under 10.[42]

Women, who constituted a fifth of the labor force in the early 20th century, were
also the focus of protective legislation. Maternalists argued that, like children, women
needed to be protected from the physical harm of long work hours.

The National Consumer's League, under the leadership of its executive, Florence
Kelley, was particularly active in regard to legal protections for working women. Under
the aegis of the league, Kelley and Josephine Goldmark, a social worker, completed
research that was successfully used by Louis Brandeis in arguing the constitutionality of
Oregon's law limiting working hours for women to 10 hours per day. Brandeis marshaled
data from around the world to support his case, that women's physical well-being—and
ability to give birth and rear children—was threatened by an excessively long workday.
Ironically, when the Supreme Court sided with Brandeis in upholding the Oregon law in
1908, a Progressive victory was built on the assumption of women's inherent weakness.

By 1912, the year in which the Committee on Standards of Living and Labor of the
National Conference of Charities and Corrections made its report, the battle had shifted
to the eight-hour day and the six-day workweek. The committee predicted, "The day will
come—come tripping on the heels of social regulation—when our manufacturers and
merchants will be able to distribute . . . [their products] without compelling the sacrifice
of the health of our mothers or burning out the eyes of our little children who now bend
over their work . . . at all hours of the night."[43]

Progressive women, many of them social workers, were able to use women's traditional roles as wife and mother to win successes in regulating women's and children's
labor. However, by basing their arguments on the special vulnerability of women and
children, they faced difficulties in extending labor law to the adult male population.
It also prevented women's groups from finding common cause with organized labor.

The average workday at the close of the Civil War remained at 11 hours.[44] A movement to limit the workday to eight hours collapsed in 1886, when the violence and aftermath of Chicago's Haymarket Square riot proved disastrous to the Knights of Labor.
In 1900, according to an estimate based on information of the Bureau of Labor Statistics,
the average standard workweek was still more than 57 hours, having declined very little
during the previous decade.[45] For industry as a whole, there was wide variation so that
unorganized workers, such as those in the blast furnaces of steel mills, ordinarily worked

a 12-hour day and 84-hour week, whereas organized workers in the building trades had achieved a 48-hour week, working 8 hours a day, six days a week.[46]

During the early years of the 20th century, workers struggled to develop responses to the threat of unemployment. Workers viewed the eight-hour movement as a way to increase the number of jobs by reducing the hours worked by each worker. Unionized workers, who remained a small share of the total workforce, also experimented with work-sharing systems, in which workers would reduce their weekly hours of work so that fewer workers would be laid off, and voluntary unemployment funds, in which union members would make weekly contributions and then draw benefits if they were laid off. However, these efforts rarely were sufficient to cope with sharp increases in joblessness during depressions.

Differentials in work hours between unionized and nonunionized industries indicate the significance of unionization for reduced work hours. Average weekly hours in 1900 for unionized manufacturing industries were 53, compared to 62 for nonunion manufacturing. By 1920, unionized manufacturing hours had declined to 46 per week and nonunion manufacturing to 54. Unionized manufacturing had achieved the eight-hour day and nonunion manufacturing had made significant gains. The gap between organized and unorganized labor narrowed.[47]

In response to the increased militancy of labor following World War I, major corporations pursued the "American plan" during the 1920s. This combined "welfare capitalism"—the expansion of programs to employees, including unemployment and pension benefits—with an aggressive antiunion campaign. Companies like the Ford Motor Company employed "social secretaries" to provide social services to workers. Yet, without a fully developed set of professional ethics, these social workers often reported "undesirable" behavior to employers, including labor union membership and drinking. Although welfare capitalism died during the Great Depression, the idea that employers would provide significant social welfare benefits to their employees became one of the defining features of American social welfare.

Expanding Public Welfare

Progressive reformers struggled to find strategies to address the major hazards of an industrial society—accident, illness, death of the breadwinner, old age and retirement, and unemployment. Industrialization and urbanization required enormous change on the part of the family. Economic survival required mobility, freedom to move from farms to industrial sites where jobs existed. The mobile family was almost by definition a small family. Having moved to the cities, the families were then trapped by low wages and a lack of resources and industrial skills. Most family members had to stand ready to work to meet the costs of urban living. The family became increasingly dependent for income on factory owners, who themselves felt no responsibility for their workers' welfare, and on nonfamily members for services previously performed internally—child care for working mothers, for example. The family of the Progressive Era was a unit caught in the stress of a period of social change, a unit socially and economically insecure in its day-to-day living and vulnerable to anxieties about an unknown future.

Reformers proposed two strategies to cope with families' increased economic vulnerability. Some suggested that social insurance—contributory plans that would provide aid to workers—was the best model, while others focused on modernizing public assistance programs—targeted to low-income families. During the Progressive Era, each won a victory with the adoption of workmen's compensation and mother's pensions.

During the 19th century, legal precedent largely absolved employers from responsibility for workers' injuries. Workers were deemed to have assumed risk by accepting employment. The "fellow servant" principle—that employers were not liable if another worker contributed to the injury—ballasted this position. Yet, by the early 20th century, local and state courts frequently found reasons to support lawsuits brought by injured workers and encouraged employers to find ways of avoiding expensive litigation.

Workmen's compensation for injuries resulting from industrial accidents was first discussed at the American Sociological Conference of 1902. During this same year, when the National Conference of Charities and Corrections appointed a committee to investigate the topic, Maryland's Workmen's Compensation Act was declared illegal. The fact that no one could be found to appeal this decision of the lower court did not impede growing national enthusiasm for such a measure. Action was spurred by the realization that "the industries of our country every year claim an army of 15,000 men killed, and some half a million injured."[48] President Theodore Roosevelt's enthusiastic support of Senate action resulted in the Federal Employee's Act of 1906.

Commissions in Massachusetts and Illinois recommended industrial insurance in 1904 and 1907, respectively, but failed to lead to legislative action. Discussion of workmen's compensation occurred again at the annual meetings of the National Conference of Charities and Corrections in 1905 and 1906; a National Conference on Workmen's Compensation was held in 1909. By 1910, the year of the second National Conference on Workmen's Compensation, a groundswell of support had developed. Many industrial employers were attracted to workmen's compensation as a means of reducing lawsuits and bringing predictability to the cost of industrial accidents. In 1911, the year regarded "as the beginning of an intelligent grappling with the problem," 10 states enacted workmen's compensation laws.

Yet, other efforts to enact social insurance were less successful. The issue of old age security was raised for discussion in the United States in the decade before World War I. The number of older people in the population had risen as birthrates fell, and, at the same time, industrialization increased the likelihood of dependency in old age. The more advanced European industrial nations, France, Germany, and England, had already instituted old age support systems. Both the National Conference of Charities and Corrections and the Progressive Party endorsed the principles of social insurance as a response to economic need from unemployment, illness, and old age in 1912. Case studies documented the inability of individuals to save for their own old age, the inadequacy of private charity, and the inability or unwillingness of industry to provide private pensions. Nonetheless, attempts to provide income in old age either through public or through private pensions failed. At the outbreak of World War I, only Arizona and Alaska had even limited pension plans, and less than 1 percent of American workers were covered by private insurance. The economic status of the elderly declined and their dependence on public welfare rose steadily.

In the years immediately following World War I, reform groups, especially the National Consumer's League, the American Association for Labor Legislation, and the National Women's Trade Union League, gave health insurance their first priority, and the impetus toward old age pensions came to a standstill.

Only with the coming of the Great Depression at the end of the 1920s did the old age pension movement begin to gather support. Then the research and leadership of social reformers, economists, and social scientists had a new grassroots base of support. The Fraternal Order of Eagles, a broad-based popular group, began to organize community pension clubs and lobby for state pension bills. Three states—Montana, Nevada, and Pennsylvania—passed voluntary, limited pension bills in 1923. Most other states followed suit in the next few years. By 1927, the American Association for Old Age Security, headed by Abraham Epstein, was created to work for an income support program for the elderly. Together with the American Association for Labor Legislation, they lobbied for old age assistance pensions and laid the groundwork for the enactment of social security.[49]

By 1929, however, they had achieved little success. In all, 11 states had pensions for the aging that reached only 1,000 beneficiaries with total benefits of $222,000. The first mandatory system was legislated in California, where the percentage of people over 65 was twice the national average and unemployment among the aged was high. In every state that had pensions, the payments were far too low and the coverage was woefully inadequate.[50]

Protecting Vulnerable Families

Although the drive for social insurance stalled during the 1920s, maternalist efforts to link reform to the protection of women and children succeeded. Legislation to regulate the working conditions of women and children and to insure against loss of income due to industrially caused illness and accident was one part of a package that might loosely be identified with family welfare. The development of juvenile courts and federal efforts to improve maternal and child health and widows' pensions completed this agenda. Social workers and other women professionals worked as researchers and advocates in moving these proposals forward.

As professional services developed, social research became a tool for advancing social legislation. Social work's contribution to social reform during the Progressive Era was in large measure derived from its introduction of systematic surveys to the study of social problems. This was best illustrated by the Pittsburgh Survey of 1907–1908, directed by Paul Kellogg, a social worker and assistant editor of *Charities and the Commons*, the national journal published under the auspices of the New York Charity Organization Society. An article in the March 1906 issue of *Charities and the Commons*, "Neglected Neighborhoods in the Alleys, Shacks and Tenements of the National Capitol," led to the suggestion by the chief probation officer of the Allegheny County (Pennsylvania) Juvenile Court that a similar investigation be made in the Pittsburgh area. The suggestion was favorably received by the Publications Committee of the Charity Organization Society and an advisory committee was formed. Among the members of the committee, in addition to Kellogg, were William H. Matthews, head worker at Kingsley House in Pittsburgh; Robert A. Woods, another leading settlement house worker and former Pittsburgh resident; Florence Kelley, director of the National Consumer's League; and John R. Commons, a well-known economist. Funding was secured from a number of sources but primarily from the Russell Sage Foundation, which used the survey as its initial large investment in social research.

The Pittsburgh Survey was "the first major attempt to survey in depth the entire life of a single community," and for this purpose, Kellogg pulled together a study team of workers and students of social welfare and the social sciences. The findings, published serially in *Charities and the Commons* and later in book form, covered "wages, hours, conditions of labor, housing, schooling, health, taxation, fire and police protection, recreation [and] land values." They became widely known not only through their publication in professional literature but also through their being brought to the public's attention in popular periodicals such as *Collier's Weekly*.[51]

Similarly, social research was a major weapon of the National Child Labor Committee, whose primary interest was child labor legislation. The officers of the National Child Labor Committee included persons who were active on the many fronts of the social reform movement. Edgar Gardner Murphy had seen to the formation of the committee. Also on the committee were Jane Addams, founder of Hull House; Florence Kelley; Felix Adler of Columbia University and longtime crusader for tenement housing reform; Lillian Wald, founder of the Henry Street Settlement House; and Edward T. Devine and Robert W. DeForest, executive and president, respectively, of the New York Charity Organization Society. An awareness of the value of coalitions for achieving social welfare goals was demonstrated when the committee set up headquarters in Chicago's United Charities Building, which also sheltered the Association for the Improvement of the Conditions of the Poor, the Charity Organization Society, the Children's Aid Society, and the National Consumer's League.

As early as 1906, the National Child Labor Committee was able to have introduced in Congress a bill for the establishment of a children's bureau. As part of a campaign to have the bill passed, the committee was successful in influencing President Roosevelt to call the 1909 White House Conference on Child Dependency. The president established the theme of the conference by extolling the virtues of home life and by urging that children "not be deprived of it except for urgent and compelling reasons."[52] The conference went on record as favoring home care for children—care in their own home as well as foster home care—and recommended the creation of a publicly financed bureau to collect and disseminate information affecting the welfare of children and a national voluntary organization to establish and publicize standards of child care. The first, the Children's Bureau, was created in 1912; the Child Welfare League of America followed in 1921.

The juvenile court movement was an expression of a growing consensus as to the importance of differentiating the needs of children. The first juvenile court law, An Act to Regulate the Treatment and Control of Dependent, Neglected, and Delinquent Children, had been enacted in 1899 by Illinois, where the Illinois State Conference of Charities had taken responsibility for having the act drafted. The law applied to children under 16 years of age and provided for a special juvenile courtroom and record-keeping system and for probation officers "to take charge of any child before and after trial as may be directed by the court." Within 10 years, similar laws had been passed in 22 states. By 1919, all the states except Connecticut, Maine, and Wyoming had enacted juvenile court laws emphasizing the "principle of separate treatment of juvenile delinquents and . . . cure rather than punishment."[53] Once again, Illinois set the character of juvenile probation services, when several agencies assigned social workers to the court in the hope of making the state's new juvenile court law operate effectively by providing casework services.

A group of social workers associated with Hull House and Chicago's School of Social Service Administration, including Edith and Grace Abbott and Julia Lathrop, were instrumental in the establishment of the Children's Bureau in 1912, and Lathrop became its first director. The Children's Bureau documented the threats to maternal and child health that was crucial to the passage of the Act for the Promotion of the Welfare and Hygiene of Maternity and Infancy, better known as the Sheppard–Towner Act, in 1921.

The Sheppard–Towner Act approved appropriations for five years to states designating a child hygiene or child welfare division to carry responsibility for the local administration of the act's provisions. The general purpose of the act was educational. Instruction in maternal and infant care was offered by nurses and physicians through itinerant conferences held either in homes or at established health centers. Instruction in maternal and infant care was also offered to professionals involved in teaching or caring for mothers and young children. The life of the Sheppard–Towner Act was extended for two years in 1927, with the understanding that the act would lapse after June 30, 1929. At the time of its expiration, 45 states and Hawaii were cooperating. Although organized opposition by physicians led to the demise of the Sheppard–Towner Act, the programs it established were ultimately incorporated into the Social Security Act in 1935.[54]

The recommendation of the White House conference that children not be deprived of home care except for "urgent and compelling reasons" stimulated controversy. On one side were those social workers who supported the conference's position that private—not public—funds be used to prevent the removal of children from their own homes. On the other were prominent juvenile court judges such as Ben Lindsey and Merritt Pinckney, whose daily practice required the institutionalization of children of poor (though competent) mothers. There was an underlying conflict, too, posed by the question of whether mothers should work at all. Before the enactment of the first mother's pension in 1911, while the possibility of such pensions was still being explored, the question of balance between pension and earnings was major. A speaker at the National Conference of Charities and Corrections in 1910 stated the problem:

> The first question to consider, after regular relief on a pension basis has been decided upon, is whether it should be a full pension or whether the widow should be encouraged to earn. At a recent meeting of the Secretaries of the Boston Associated Charities . . . most . . . felt that a day or two of work a week outside was really better for the mother than to keep her always at home, for life can be too dull some times.[55]

The emergence of mother's pensions represented changes in the ideas and institutions that guided social welfare in the early 20th century. Although leaders in the Charity Organization Movement still held to their belief in strict investigation and limited aid, frontline social workers had come to learn that the inadequacy of aid to widows with children had caused irreversible harm to these families. The old tenets of voluntary charity were supplanted by a maternalist belief that women's role as mothers provided the surest compass to guide social welfare policy. Although often advocated by women who had chosen to remain unmarried and childless, maternalism provided a means for broadening public support for reform, because it did not threaten traditional ideas about a woman's sphere. As a result, mother's pensions were embraced by the General Federation of Women's Clubs and the National Congress of Mothers (predecessor to the Parent–Teachers Associations), support that was critical to their passage.[56]

The first mother's pension law was passed by Missouri in April 1911. The law had been enacted at the behest of a single county and its provisions left the decision to provide assistance to the individual counties. The first statewide mandatory law, the Funds to Parents Act, was passed by the General Assembly of Illinois in June 1911. Many social work leaders were shocked by the sudden adoption of laws providing public funds for the aid of dependent children in their own homes. Richmond's objection that the Funds to Parents Act had been "drafted and passed without consulting a single social worker" expressed the view of an older generation of charity workers for which the expansion of public welfare was anathema. Yet, a younger generation of social workers—the first products of professional social work schools and training programs—embraced the idea that public welfare was critical to improving the condition of the poor.[57]

After the passage of the act, social workers did rally to help establish the program and to survey its operation. But Richmond, for all her concern with the burdens that society placed on family life, maintained that the supervision of social workers was necessary to ensure that "the children of the widow are in school, that they are morally protected, that their health is safeguarded, that they have a good chance to grow up right."[58] Frederic Almy, secretary of the Buffalo Charity Organization Society, was more willing to permit experiments in public relief giving. Nevertheless, he viewed private charity as safer. He warned that "to the imagination of the poor the public treasury is inexhaustible and their right, and that they drop upon it without thrift, as they dare not do on private charity." Almy stressed the importance of professional casework in investigating the need for relief and for redeeming recipient families. And, since such a help was not characteristic of public relief giving, he favored having public relief funds administered by voluntary agencies. He objected to relief being dispensed without professional help, for "like undoctored drugs, untrained relief is poisonous to the poor. . . . Poor charity is worse than none."[59]

The number of states with Mother's Assistance programs increased rapidly. Within two years of the passage of the Illinois Funds to Parents Act, 20 states had provided cash relief programs for widows with children, and within 10 years, 40 states had done the same.[60] The Children's Bureau's study of Mother's Assistance, conducted in 10 representative localities during October 1923 to April 1924, reported that "the principle of home care for dependent children as a public function is generally accepted in this country." The bureau also reported generally good relationships between the voluntary agencies and the public agencies studied and, of most importance, that families were functioning with the help of Mother's Assistance "on a par with . . . self-supporting families."[61] By the 1920s, then, both the ideas and institutions of "scientific philanthropy" had come to a dead end. Even before the Great Depression caused political upheaval, the public sector had established itself as the innovator in addressing poverty and need.

Widows' pensions were intended to provide sufficient income so mothers would not have to enter the paid labor force, but state legislatures failed to match this intention with sufficient funding. Emma O. Lundberg, director of the Children's Bureau, and C. C. Carstens, executive of the Child Welfare League of America, made this clear when they addressed the national conference in 1921. Carstens noted:

> The granting of this aid [mother's pensions] was intended to meet the needs of the budget. . . . In theory this was a clearly established policy . . . but in practice . . . in many of the states the mother is expected to earn a very large share of the budget and much more than it is best that she should earn in view of her own needs and those of her children.[62]

A Children's Bureau report of a study of the administration of mother's pensions suggests the latent intent of inadequate budgets.

> It was the testimony of the workers in the field and of the executives that the aid did not tend to develop a spirit of dependency but on the contrary developed self-confidence, initiative, and generally a desire for economic independence as at early a date as possible.[63]

The example of someone in the family working was important. To be expected then was the failure of another intent of the various state mother's and widow's pensions—that is, the education of women, particularly immigrant women, for American motherhood:

> The degree to which mothers receiving aid were encouraged to join clubs and classes of an educational character varied greatly. . . . In some communities the grants were too small to permit the mothers to give their time to anything more than housekeeping and gainful employment.[64]

 Watch this video on the arrival of immigrants at Ellis Island in 1908.

What issues might an early 20th-century settlement house worker want to raise with them?

Although states' responsibility for social welfare expanded during these years, federal programs were restricted to insuring federal employees against a loss of income due to retirement or disability and to insuring the families of veterans against the loss of the breadwinner's life. Insurance programs operated or required by the states were few, scattered, and inadequate. In the private sector—notably in the railroad industry—pension systems were started and then collapsed. For the most part, then, the responsibility for resolving family economic problems continued to fall on local public welfare departments or on private agencies. The sparseness of the public effort is shown in the data on public welfare expenditures at federal, state, and local levels. In 1913, they totaled only $57 million—1 percent of total government expenditures and only 0.1 percent of the GNP.[65]

Social Work and the Black Population

Neither the public nor the private sector was responsive to the needs of black families. In 1905, the year in which W. E. B. Du Bois and his followers met at Niagara Falls to consider legal solutions to Negro problems, an entire issue of *Charities and the Commons* was devoted to "The Negroes in the Cities of the North."[66] In 1909 and 1910, *The Survey* gave the news of the first and second national Negro conferences, respectively, at which the National Association for the Advancement of Colored People was organized.[67] In 1913, *The Survey*, in recognition of the 50th anniversary of the Emancipation Proclamation, carried a special collection of articles on the status of Negroes.[68]

The primary interest of Charity Organization Societies, however, was not in African Americans, nor in their deprivation or segregation as factors requiring broad social reform. Nonetheless, their emphasis on character reform might have helped fuel public discussions of blacks' ability to function in a civilized society. In the 1905 examination of blacks in the cities of the North, for example, the famous anthropologist Franz Boas said:

> There is every reason to believe that the Negro when given facility and opportunity will be perfectly able to fill the duties of citizenship as well as his white neighbor. It may be that he will not produce as many great men as the white race and that his average achievement will not quite reach the level of the average achievement of the white race, but there will be endless numbers who will be able to outrun their white competitors, and who will do better than the defectives whom we permit to drag down and to retard the healthy children of our public schools.[69]

Many agencies enforced a color line and refused to serve African Americans, a reflection of discrimination and the small number of African Americans living in cities.

Such an interest in the plight of blacks as might have developed from direct contact was constrained by the relatively few blacks in the caseloads of Charity Organization Societies. Many agencies enforced a color line and refused to serve African Americans, a reflection of discrimination and the small number of African Americans living in cities. In Chicago in 1900, for example, blacks numbered 108,000 in a total population of 1,698,000. They ranked 10th among the city's ethnic groups.[70] Following Booker T. Washington's call for self-reliance, the National Urban League was established in 1910 to address the economic struggles of urban African Americans and to promote interracial cooperation.

Settlement houses in Americans' expanding cities continued to accept segregated services. Among the leaders and allies of the Settlement House Movement, however, many gave greater prominence to the race problem. Louise de Koven Bowen, Sophonisba Breckenridge, and others spoke out in opposition to discrimination and prejudice that held minorities responsible for the economic and social condition to which they had been condemned. Kelley and Wald were among those who gathered for the first meeting of the National Committee on the Negro held in New York on May 31, 1909. Addams was among a group of distinguished white reformers who joined Du Bois and the Niagara group in founding the National Association for the Advancement of Colored People. When antiblack discrimination surfaced at the Progressive Party's presidential convention of 1912, Addams debated leaving. Her decision to remain suggests again the tenor of the times. The party's nominee, Theodore Roosevelt, eventually lost the election, partly because his having entertained Booker T. Washington at the White House dashed any hope of gaining votes in the solid South.

Despite the many new ideas influencing social welfare and reform in these years, many 19th-century beliefs about poverty and dependency still retained their power. Family problems were indicative of the deviant family, the family that was unable and unwilling to make use of its own potential and the abundant opportunities provided by American society. Unquestionably, a great deal had been accomplished as America's attention shifted to the war in Europe.

The Social Welfare of Veterans

Throughout American history, veterans have received special treatment in the social welfare system. During the early 20th century, two groups of veterans—those from the Civil War and those from World War I—commanded the most attention. Most men who had fought in the Civil War had reached retirement age by the early years of the century, and their economic needs were a major domestic policy issue during these years. As the Civil War generation aged, America's entry into World War I created a new generation of veterans. The entitlements of World War I veterans influenced politics during the 1920s and dramatized the nation's problems during the early years of the Great Depression.

In the late 19th century, the federal government had enacted generous pensions for Union veterans with disabilities and the dependents of soldiers who died in the Civil War. These pensions had become important in competition between Republicans and Democrats during many elections. Yet, in the first decade of the 20th century, a much larger number of veterans reached old age. As their ability to support themselves declined, they too turned to the federal government for support.

As in other periods of American history, poor veterans avoided the strict use of eligibility rules used to deny aid to the needy. Indeed, in the early years of the century, eligibility for pensions was liberalized by classifying old age alone as qualifying a veteran for pension and by easing the length of service and the supporting documentation that were necessary to qualify for a pension.

As a result, the number of veterans receiving pensions and their cost increased during the first 20 years of the 20th century. By some estimates, nearly half of all native-born elderly men living in the North at the turn of the century received pensions. The number of pensioners peaked at around a million in the first decade of the century, but disbursements for pensions increased until 1912, when it reached $170 million. Armed forces participants in World War I numbered 4,744,000.[71] The war brought about an enormous expansion of benefits and services, first to attract enlistees, and later to compensate veterans and their families for services rendered.

On September 2, 1914, only one month after the declaration of war in Europe, Congress passed the War Risk Insurance Act, insuring enlistees in the merchant marines against the hazards of submarine warfare. In 1917, President Wilson appointed the Council of National Defense to review and make recommendations in regard to veterans' benefits. The Council's report, incorporated shortly after into law, introduced a new concept: the offer of readjustment and rehabilitation services, along with monetary benefits. The new package of benefits and services included the following:

1. Compulsory allotments and allowances to families of soldiers, paid for by the soldiers themselves and by the government
2. A system of voluntary insurance against death and total disability
3. Medical and surgical hospital treatment, as well as prosthetic appliances for those injured in the line of duty
4. Vocational rehabilitation services for injured veterans who could not resume prewar occupations

At the close of the war on November 11, 1918, Congress again addressed veterans' benefits. Not only had an enormous number of Americans served in the armed forces, but a large number—116,000—had died, and an even greater number—204,000—had been wounded. By mid-1920, the Public Health Service had increased its total available beds to 11,639 in 52 hospitals. A year later, Congress authorized the use of available beds in army and navy hospitals and in National Homes for Disabled Volunteer Soldiers. The necessarily rapid expansion of in-hospital services to meet the needs of wounded veterans helped clarify the returning veterans' need for outpatient and nonmedical services. By 1920, a haphazard system spread responsibility for veterans across a variety of agencies—the Bureau of War Risk Insurance, the Rehabilitation Division of the Federal Board for Vocational Education, the Public Health Service, and the armed services themselves.

Early in 1921, President Warren G. Harding appointed the Dawes Commission to devise a program for the immediate and future needs of ex-servicemen "to the end that the intention of Congress to give the full measure of justice to ex-servicemen may be adequately, promptly, and generously met." The commission's report concluded that "no emergency of war itself is greater than is the emergency which confronts the Nation in its duty to care for those disabled in its service and now neglected."

Congress took up consideration of the commission's report and incorporated most of its recommendations in Public Law 67–47, passed on August 9, 1921. The commission's most important recommendation, the creation of a single entity to administer veterans' affairs, resulted in the establishment of the Veterans' Bureau. The bureau brought together most veterans' benefits, including medical care, insurance payments, and vocational rehabilitation services.[72]

Congress, responding to pressure from veterans' groups, expanded services in 1924, adding hospital services for honorably discharged veterans with nonservice-connected disabilities. The enactment of this law highlighted the strength of the constituencies organized to advance and to protect the social welfare rights of this particularly "worthy" group of Americans.

Professionalizing Social Work

The professionalization of social work had begun with the formation of voluntary charitable associations after the Civil War. It expanded with the growth of reform organizations. For a time during the Progressive Era, charity organizations and settlements worked together for social reform, but eventually their different ideologies drove them away from each other and toward professionalization as an alternative to advocating reform.

No such constituencies as supported veterans' rights—neither the Charity Organization nor the Settlement House Movement—stood ready to support public relief giving as a major requirement for the maintenance of family welfare. In voluntary social welfare as well as in corporate management, the 1920s were years of bureaucratization and professionalization. For Charity Organization Societies and for settlements, scientific philanthropy had led to internal organizational changes paralleling the managerial changes of corporate enterprise. The developing of supervision, of supervisors accountable for the successful operation of professional workers, was a further example of internal adherence to structural authority. Beyond that, Charity Organization Societies were largely responsible for the formation of Councils of Social Agencies accountable for social welfare planning and of Federated Funds that undertook "effective economy" in funding the social welfare establishment.[73]

The definition of scientific philanthropy was broadened to encompass developments in helping methodology. The failure of friendly visiting, the hiring of paid agents, and, finally, the emergence of social workers were sequential steps in the search for techniques to deal in an individualized manner with the challenges faced by poor families. The body of techniques that were codified in Richmond's *Social Diagnosis* (1917) and *What Is Social Casework?* (1922) established casework as a major methodology of social work. As codified by Richmond, casework was based on the thorough gathering of data about a family. Only later did social workers incorporate the theories of Sigmund Freud and others into the method. In addition, the development of casework from friendly visiting, at a time when these Charity Organization Societies were relinquishing responsibility for social reform, not only reawakened an old image of the rich helping the poor, but also strengthened the view of individual and family responsibility for social and economic problems.

The overriding interest of Charity Organization Societies in relief, their longtime charity organizing purposes, and their slowness in moving toward a focus on family welfare are reflected in the successive names given to the societies' national association. Not until 1919, when the era of professionalization had begun to take hold, did the association's name include the word family: American Association for Organizing Family Social Work. Not until 1930, with the adoption of Family Welfare Association of America as its name, did the title suggest an aggressive force for the welfare of families. This slow evolution of purpose from charity organization to social work organization to family welfare can be traced through a review of the *Proceedings of the National Conference of Charities and Corrections* (1880–1929). Particularly striking is the extreme fragmentation of topics discussed at the conference and the limited focus on the family as a unit or with the interaction between family life and social institutions.[74]

The settlement movement moved toward its own brand of professionalism. Social reform activity diminished as an area of functional responsibility, and "social group work," a methodological approach to helping through recreational and educational activities, became the core of Settlement House programming. The extent of the shift was indicated by George Bellamy of Cleveland's Hiram House in 1914, when he addressed the National Conference on the use of recreational programs by neighborhood centers to help neighborhood residents maintain community control and strengthen family life. "It is far better," he said, "for the city to throw the responsibility of self-support and self-improvement upon the people themselves than to hire at great expense . . . others to entertain the community. We need a recreation by the people, not for the people."[75] In 1926, Mary K. Simkhovitch addressed the National Federation of Settlements on settlement goals for the "next third of a century." She argued that settlements had "turned the social welfare corner" and were "launched on the larger task of social education" in an effort to democratize and civilize industrial society by popularizing art and developing the creative instinct.[76]

The definitive statement on the professionalization of social work was made by Porter R. Lee in his presidential address at the National Conference in 1929, which argued that the profession should abandon social reform and assume an institutionalized role in the community. Lee traced the development of social work as "a movement directed toward the elimination of an entrenched evil" and its culmination as a profession with a professional responsibility for operating "a methodical, organized effort . . . to make enduring the achievement of the cause."

> In the last analysis I am not sure that the greatest service of social work as a cause is contributed through those whose genius it is to light and hand on the torch. I am inclined to think that in the capacity of the social worker, whatever his rank, to administer a routine functional responsibility in the spirit of the servant in a cause is the explanation of the great service of social work.[77]

? Assess your comprehension of "Innovations in Social Welfare" by completing this quiz.

Amazingly rapid development occurred in social work during 1900–1929. The Charity Organization and Settlement House movements claimed a concern with the family as the core unit of society, and each, to its own lights, developed its program so as to try to bring stability and fulfillment to family living. While the economy appeared to prosper, social work turned to family dynamics and individual personality development.[78]

SOCIAL MOVEMENTS IN THE EARLY 20TH CENTURY

Coalitions for Reform

Progressivism grew out of middle-class concerns that the battle between big business and labor would engulf American society. It was the first attempt to fashion a political ideology between unregulated capitalism and a more radical alternative.

Progressivism grew out of middle-class concerns that the battle between big business and labor would engulf American society. It was the first attempt to fashion a political ideology between unregulated capitalism and a more radical alternative. Reformers, however, found themselves pulled in two directions. Culturally, they had much in common with the social and economic elite whose actions they feared. Although many reformers had sympathy for the plight of workers, they were suspicious of the political and labor leaders who were their representatives. Although many Progressives worked hard to forge new coalitions for reform, their contradictory impulses often undermined their effectiveness.

The industrial collapse of 1893 produced hardships for 4 million unemployed and for small businessmen, farmers, and investors. Many demanded a change in power relationships and the development of a more equitable system of distribution of wealth and income. The march of "General" Jacob Coxey's army of the unemployed on Washington, DC, in 1894, the increased prevalence of strikes and industrial violence, the growth of union membership (particularly in the Western Federation of Miners and the United Mine Workers), and the strength of the Populist movement were part of an agrarian/working-class coalition for reform.

In the early years of the 20th century, the reform movement shifted toward the center. The AFL, representing more highly paid craft workers than the older, industrial unions, became the dominant force in the labor movement. Writers and educators undertook an exposé of big business; new political leadership took on the task of city and state reforms; and social workers worked on behalf of the poor segregated into urban slums. Social protest became the property of intellectuals and professionals.

It became clear to more and more Americans that laissez-faire and small business no longer characterized their economy. The era of small business firms engaged in competition had supported a model of individual achievement, but the emergence of large corporations or trusts engaged in monopolistic market control made this model appear irrelevant. In a competitive, individualistic society, the dominant social theorists had argued for social reform based on individual change; the corporate universe of the 20th century seemed to require a reform of institutions.

During most of the 19th century, it had been liberal dogma that the limited government action was good for the economy and society. In the early 20th century, more Americans were willing to ask if government had a role in creating a more just social order. A "new liberalism" based on a belief in positive government action and the critical role of professional expertise provided the ideological basis for many Progressives. Research would provide knowledge of social and political problems, and the extension of democratic institutions in government would lead to enactment of the appropriate legislation. In retrospect, it was a romantic and an optimistic belief in rational, peaceful, and democratic social change.

Progressives wanted to maintain the cultural values of an earlier time—individuals, opportunity, "lifting one's self by one's bootstraps"—even as the social order that supported those values disappeared. This contradiction limited the effectiveness of many reform efforts. No issue better illustrates the contradictory stance of Progressives than their belief that immigrants would eventually adopt the language, tastes, and culture of white Protestants. In settlement houses, southern and eastern Europeans were encouraged to eschew olive oil and garlic in their cooking in favor of butter and bland ingredients.[79] Efforts to Americanize immigrants extended to the growing Latino population of the Southwest, where children were encouraged to abandon their native language and culture (Figure 5.2).[80]

In the early 20th century, more Americans were willing to ask if government had a role in creating a more just social order. A "new lib-eralism" based on a belief in positive government action and the critical role of professional expertise provided the ideological basis for many Progressives.

LEWIS WICKES HINE, PRINTS & PHOTOGRAPHS DIVISION, LIBRARY OF CONGRESS, LC-DIG-NCLC-05087.

Figure 5.2 Scenes from "The Twig of Thorn" given by a club of working girls in King Philip Settlement, Fall River, Massachusetts, 1916. Settlement houses worked to improve living conditions, inter-group relations, and the cultural lives of the residents of working-class neighborhoods.
Source: Library of Congress.

The reform activities of the Progressive Era were spearheaded by many groups, some working independently, some working cooperatively as particular issues warranted cooperation, some working for individual aggrandizement, and some working altruistically for the larger society. One group was composed of small businessmen who were anxious to control and stop the domination of trusts and banking establishments. They were joined by writers, social workers, lawyers, and clergymen, as well as other professionals who were suspicious of big business. Farmers, in search of easy credit, also became a part of the struggle against the domination of "organized money."

The growth of the Socialist Party in the early years of the century strengthened the hand of reformers by raising the specter of more radical alternatives to Progressive reform. Starting with a membership of less than 5,000 in 1900, it enrolled 118,000 members by 1912, including many of the nation's leading intellectuals—John Dewey, Stuart Chase, Paul Douglas, Jack London, Walter Lippmann, and Alexander Meikeljohn. Eugene Debs, leader of the 1894 railroad strike, ran for president as the Socialist candidate in 1912 and polled 6 percent of the popular vote. More important, perhaps, was the Socialists' success that same year in electing more than 1,000 members to various public offices. Socialist doctrines were widely reviewed, discussed, and quoted. Socialists were sometimes allied in specific causes with other reform groups. The growth of the Socialist Party and its increased visibility served as a threat and a catalyst for more moderate reform groups seeking regulation of industry. The Socialist Party's opposition to American entry into World War I in 1917 led to government suppression and the jailing of many leaders, including Debs.[81]

Regulating Business

During the Progressive Era, the federal government took some halting steps to regulate business in the public interest. In 1902, President Theodore Roosevelt instructed the attorney general to bring suit under the Sherman Antitrust Act against the Northern Securities Company, a consolidation of railways including the Northern Pacific, the Great Northern, and the Chicago, Burlington, and Quincy systems. The Supreme Court sustained the government's appeal and effectively frustrated the plan of E. H. Harriman to bring all the important railways in the country under his control. In 1906, Congress passed the Hepburn Act, which permitted the Interstate Commerce Commission (ICC) to fix the rates of railroads; of storage, refrigeration, and terminal facilities; and of sleeping car, express, and pipeline companies. In 1910, authority was extended to the ICC to regulate telephone and telegraph companies.

Economic and regulatory reforms took various shapes. As a result of Upton Sinclair's *The Jungle* and of other exposés of the food and pharmaceutical industries, editors of popular journals and the American Medical Association, among others, formed a coalition to secure passage of the Food and Drug Act in 1906. In 1909, the 16th Amendment, which established a federal income tax, was introduced in Congress by Cordell Hull. By 1913, it had been ratified by the states and became law. During this same year, Congress created the Federal Reserve System, a first step by the federal government to regulate banking.

Organized Labor

Through much of the 19th century, federal and state courts had restricted the ability of workers to organize unions. A new wave of organizing gained greater public attention during these years. The passage of the Clayton Antitrust Act in 1914 represented the success of small business and labor unions to unite behind efforts to control the power of big business. The act also provided some safeguards for organizers, by restricting the use of injunctions against unions. Although these provisions were ultimately watered down by the Supreme Court, the Clayton Act represented an important step in acknowledging working people's right to organize. The Federal Trade Commission Act established a commission whose purpose was to bring to bear the knowledge and advice of a group of economic experts on "unfair" methods of competition and infractions of antitrust laws.

The democratic thrust of the Progressive Era made political reform a partner of economic reform. Just as muckraking publications had reported lurid instances of fraud and graft and of monopolistic control in industry, in railroading, and in public utilities, they detailed corruption in state and local governments, in the courts, and in the U.S. Senate.[82] A veritable avalanche of widely read, eagerly awaited exposés of *The Shame of the Cities* or "The Treason of the Senate" led the way to political change. The effort was twofold: to expand citizen participation in political affairs and to increase governmental responsiveness and honesty. Progressives worked for women's suffrage, the secret ballot, direct primaries, direct election of senators, initiative, referendum, recall, and municipal home rule. In addition, they demanded civil service reform, the short ballot, the regulation of campaign expenditures, accountability and leadership on the part of elected officials, and the commission and city manager plans of municipal government.

Women, Work, and Suffrage

In 1900, the National American Women's Suffrage Association (NAWSA), representing the joining of the two earlier rivals in the women's suffrage movement, was still unclear as to directions for achieving votes for women. The association's flirtation with "educated suffrage," offering to counter the votes of lower-class blacks and immigrants with those of middle-class women, contributed to conflict between black and white women, middle-class women from lower-class women, nonworking women from working women, and native-born women from immigrant women. At the same time reform organizations, including the NAWSA, discovered that sewing these divisions could ultimately prevent success. In addition, the limitations of a single-issue organization became apparent as other women's groups moved to the fore. These new organizations—for example, the National Consumer's League, the National Women's Trade Union League, and the Young Women's Christian Association—were concerned both with matters affecting women and social injustice issues that affected both women and others. For example, the NAWSA publication, *The Woman's Journal*, supported the garment workers' strike of 1909 and 1910 and reported the tragic Triangle Shirt-Waist Company fire of 1911, which led to the death of 146 workers, as demonstrating the need for women's votes to ensure "more effective factory legislation and a larger number of [factory] inspectors."[83] This broadened view resulted in increased membership. By 1910, the official numbers in NAWSA had risen to 100,000; in 1917, the membership stood at 2 million.

Part of the reality of the Progressive Era was the increasing participation of women in the labor force. In 1900, there were more than 5 million gainfully employed female workers. Most worked as unskilled factory hands or as domestics; most were foreign born or black; some were married. The number of female workers increased rapidly to meet the demands of this generally prosperous era—later, the added demands of Europe at war, and finally, in 1917, the demands of the United States itself as its own male workers, drafted for wartime service, had to be replaced. By 1910, the number of gainfully employed women had risen to 8 million. Although the end of World War I brought a return to traditional gender roles for many men and women, by 1920, the number of

 Watch this video on women's suffrage.
Compare the treatment of women's rights protestors to African American or labor activists.

https://www.youtube.com/watch?v=SeOHPfsCtFo

women in the paid labor force had risen to more than 8.5 million.[84] The formation of the National Women's Trade Union League and its activities in supporting existing unions of women wage earners testifies to the increase in the numbers of women workers, their beginning entrance in skilled positions, and their increasing political consciousness.

Progress toward the unionization of women—like among men—was nevertheless slow and difficult. Much of the history was characterized by spontaneous work stoppage and strikes against low wages and torturous working conditions. These strikes resulted in efforts to organize, but even when success in gaining demands followed, unionization tended to fall apart. In skilled industry, the responsibility for this can be traced to the overall antagonism of male workers, who accused women of scabbing during strike actions on the part of male-dominated unions, of taking men's jobs, and of lowering wage rates. These antagonisms carried over in the halfhearted attempts by the AFL, an organization of craft unions made up of skilled workers, to organize women's unions or to admit women into existing organizations. The AFL, like its constituents, was suspicious of women's commitment to work, of their staying power during strikes, and of their effect upon wages. The AFL's lack of interest was encouraged by the fact that by far the largest number of women continued to work in unskilled jobs—in textiles, shirt and waist making, laundries, and domestic service. Among these unskilled workers, foreign-born and black women predominated. Black women particularly suffered exclusion from unionizing efforts, even from the efforts of other unskilled workers.

The task of bringing together the work-related and suffrage-related concerns of women was not easy. Concern for their physical, moral, and emotional well-being sprang from the conviction that "the prime function of woman must ever be the perpetuating of the race. . . . The woman is worth more to society . . . as the mother of healthy children than as the swiftest labeler of cans."[85] The result was a great deal of effort to estimate "a living wage" for women and to clarify the special needs of women in regard to working hours and working conditions. Although similar concerns were being explored in connection with all workers, very special legislative protection was sought for the unique circumstances of women. The culmination of these concerns for women, reflecting the additional burdens they had assumed during World War I, came with the establishment by Congress in 1920 of the Women's Bureau within the Department of Labor.

By the time of the armistice in 1918, women's groups had become accustomed to cooperation. This unity of action comprised a powerful political force. Under the direction of Carrie Chapman Catt, who had been reelected its president in 1915, the NAWSA was revitalized and led the final march toward victory. Catt was able to gain President Wilson's support. Not the least of that support derived from the contribution of women and of women's organizations to the war effort. The 19th Amendment to the Constitution was approved by Congress on June 4, 1919, and ratified by the required number of states on August 26, 1920. The NAWSA went out of existence but was revived as the League of Women Voters.

The end of World War I also brought success to another women-led movement, the drive for Prohibition. The battle against alcoholic beverages was long and complicated. It combined a Progressive concern for the workers' health and family stability with a reaction by Protestant and rural people against the diversity and growth of urban populations. In fact, the strength of the National Women's Christian Temperance Union combined with the government's wartime conservation efforts—that is, the need to limit the use of grain for the production of liquors—to win congressional approval for Prohibition sooner than women's suffrage. The 18th Amendment to the Constitution prohibiting the manufacture, sale, and import or export of liquor was ratified in 1919.

The success of Prohibition was short-lived. Its political success was derived from the conservative shift in politics during and after World War I. The suppression of socialists and other antiwar groups and increasing antipathy toward immigrants buoyed the movement. Once enacted, however, the practical difficulties of enforcing Prohibition were reinforced by the hostility of an increasingly urban population. Al Smith, governor of New York and the Democratic nominee for president in 1928, was only the most celebrated of political leaders who openly flaunted the law. Rather than moralizing urban populations, Prohibition turned "bootlegging" into a major industry that many law-abiding Americans patronized. Urban resistance to Prohibition ultimately led to its repeal by the 21st Amendment to the Constitution in 1933.

Organized women were successful on a host of issues during the Progressive Era. Certainly, achieving suffrage and passing Prohibition were two significant victories. Women would go on to serve important roles in other reform movements over the next half century, but political feminism would not revive as a separate movement until the late 1960s.

The End of Reform

The end of World War I did not see a return to reform activity. The years between the close of the war and the Depression of the 1930s were a time of peace during which many Americans achieved individual prosperity. They found it through credit and installment buying and through participation in the glittering promises of speculation. They did not concern themselves with the problems of those left behind by economic growth or with the obvious abuse of power and influence by those who led the way in speculative activity. Despite the recession of 1921, urban standards of living improved. Booming profits, high levels of employment, and rising real wages meant that Americans felt able to purchase and enjoy a flood of new products—cars, radios, home electricity, motion pictures, and silk stockings. There was new life in the doctrine of laissez-faire and a renewed belief that what was good for business was good for the nation. The solution to poverty did not lie in corporate regulation, minimum wages, social insurance, or public welfare, but rather in providing an atmosphere that was encouraging to business.

Americans were determined to believe assurances offered by President Herbert Hoover in his inaugural address:

> We in America today are nearer to the final triumph over poverty than ever before in the history of any land. The poorhouse is vanishing among us. We have not yet reached the goal, but given a chance . . . we shall soon with the help of God be in sight of the day when poverty will be banished from this nation.[86]

At the close of the war, the era of the reform coalition had come to an end, and a new era of professionalization of social work had begun. The change seems attributable to a number of factors. The war itself had wrought havoc among social work leaders who, prior to the events leading to the country's involvement, had in the main counted themselves pacifists. Addams was a leader in pacifist causes. Her membership on the Platform Committee of the Progressive Party in 1912 was an effort to further specific social goals despite her disagreement with the party's stand in regard to war and defense.[87] World War I split those who could not abandon a lifetime's philosophical stance from those who supported the war and saw this support as serving their country in a time of crisis. The Russian Revolution and the common misperception that the triumphant Bolsheviks were German allies further split the reform spirit of social workers.

Government suppression played a role in quieting voices of dissent. During World War I, antiwar activists were accused of disloyalty. The post office banned their literature and the most vocal leaders were jailed. The Russian Revolution and labor unrest after the war sparked a "Red Scare" orchestrated by U.S. Attorney General Mitchell Palmer. The wartime and postwar fear of subversive activity, sparking a demand for law and order, led to severe political repression, to expulsion of radical aliens, and, in turn, to hostility toward expressions of need for political change or political redress. Even modest efforts at community revitalization, like the pioneering Social Unit Plan in Cincinnati, were labeled "socialistic" and saw their funding cut off.[88] Emphasis shifted to personality reform, as psychoanalysis—the work of Sigmund Freud—offered a new professional direction for social workers and social work education.

The push for social reform was further dissipated by the stemming of the flow of immigrants. The increase in immigration during the early years of the 20th century, with masses of immigrants coming from eastern Europe at a time of anarchy and revolution there and of labor unrest and wartime preparation here, had stimulated efforts for social reform and socialization. Severe legal restrictions caused the numbers to drop dramatically and almost disappear during the late 1920s. As immigration declined, ethnic communities were increasingly dominated by a second generation more oriented to life in the United States.

While the impetus toward social reform had waned, the Progressive Era was one of major if limited importance. The first Mother's Pension law was enacted in 1911 and established the principle that single mothers of young children should receive support to stay at home as parents. It was the beginning of a safety net that was to prevail for 85 years.

The prosperity of the 1920s—with its surge of economic growth and affluence accompanied by the hope for the imminent disappearance of poverty—came on top of the seeming achievement of many of the goals of the reform movement and decreased the pressure for further social legislation. In actuality, the reform spirit of the agencies regulating business was often reversed by administrative practices; new political bosses arose to negotiate the ballot reforms, and much of the social legislation passed by the states was thrown out by the courts. The moral fervor that pervaded the Progressive movement shifted to the drive against alcoholic beverages. The success of Prohibition became a crowning moral victory.

With social reform abandoned, character reform was revived as an orientation toward people in need. Emil Frankel's *Poor Relief in Pennsylvania*, a statewide survey published in 1925, demonstrated the persistent suspicion of public relief and of relief recipients. In a report that generally attacked historic fears of public welfare, Frankel supported the significance of professional social work service, if only to allay the fear that public aid would be considered a right. Frankel wrote:

> Outdoor relief without constructive service can lead only to increasing dependency because while a certain portion of the families receiving relief may pull themselves out of a rut with the aid of the grants, a good many will not. . . .
>
> A good many have the feeling that inasmuch as the poor fund is raised through public taxation they have a right to demand relief and are entitled to it as a matter of course. And a good many families feel that although they may not be in need of relief they can see no reason why they should not get it when other families do.[89]

Public and voluntary orientations toward relief giving—especially toward public relief—seemed to have changed little since the inception of the Charity Organization in 1877. The views and foreboding of Frankel, a public official, were not unlike those of Lowell, who had argued in 1890 that public relief should be given only in cases of extreme distress, "when starvation is imminent." The refuge from pauperism, according to Lowell, was self-support or help provided by private sources. The similarity in their views is probably not surprising when one considers the 1918 appeal of Francis McLean, director of the American Association for Organizing Charities, that member agencies aid "in the socialization [i.e., professionalization] of both staff and methods of work of . . . public family social work agencies."[90] Not until 1921 was membership in the association extended to public agencies.

? Assess your comprehension of "Social Movements in the Early 20th Century" by completing this quiz.

DOCUMENTS

Progress and Reform

The three documents that follow, Florence Kelley's statement on *The Family and the Woman's Wage* (1909), the text of the first *Funds to Parents Act* (1911), and the National Conference of Charities and Corrections discussions of *Public Pensions to Widows* (1912), highlight major tensions in social welfare during the Progressive Era and the role of maternalism in driving change.

Kelley, both as an individual and as secretary of the National Consumer's League, was in the forefront of social welfare reform activity during the Progressive Era. Her close personal connections with leaders in the Settlement House Movement and the coalitions they formed with other groups on behalf of an array of social welfare measures make her utterances a reflection of the settlement view. She pictured the family and family members as needing economic and legal protections against industrial and political hindrances that prevented their full democratic participation in society. Kelley's special interest was in wages and working hours and their meaning for family welfare. In *The Family and the Woman's Wage*, she challenges the depth of the value placed on the home as "the fundamental thing in our national life." Her point is that truly valuing the home and the family would require legislation to regulate the conditions and places of employment of children, in this instance, girls—and the working hours and wages of women. She is convinced of the importance of home life for children and, therefore, of the necessity for making it financially possible for mothers and children to remain in the home. Her outcry against the economic exploitation of women and children is, therefore, not only a demand for higher wages, but also a condemnation of conditions that make it necessary for them to work at all. The necessity to work, she believed, distracted the mother from the care of children: "if one really thought about the family and the home . . . one should have none of that work today."

Kelley's argument can seem confusing to modern ears. Her assertion of women's and girls' unique vulnerability seems to harken back to older ideas of separate spheres for men and women, but she marshals these ideas to support the expansion of government oversight of industry and to challenge society to bring its values and behavior into alignment. By doing so, Kelley and other maternalists hoped to enlist more conservative and conventional women in the struggle for social reform.

One result of the kind of agitation for reform encouraged by Kelley was the Funds to Parents Act, passed by the state of Illinois in June 1911. The act provided public funds for the care of dependent and neglected children, making it unnecessary to remove them from their own homes when parents were otherwise adequate. The significance of the act resides in its being the first demonstration of public responsibility for supporting the care of children at home. The act is, therefore, the predecessor of the Aid to Dependent Children program included in the Social Security Act in 1935.

The discussions of Frederic Almy, Mary Richmond, Homer Folks, and Merritt Pinckney of "public pensions to widows" indicate the controversy resulting from the passage of the Funds to Parents Act. Supporting widows and dependent children in their own homes was still a controversial issue for workers in charities and corrections, despite the recommendation of the first White House Conference on Children. By 1912, however, the discussants of public pensions no longer addressed themselves to this particular question. Their arguments centered on the use of public, rather than private, funds and on the necessity for social work professionals to oversee the use of funds.

Almy, secretary of the Buffalo Charity Organization Society, wavers in his opinion. He is not entirely afraid of public funds—"neglect is the great pauperizer, not relief"— but he is afraid of relief that is not professionally dispensed: "untrained relief is poisonous to the poor." Richmond, a most eminent figure in social work, is also fearful of the possible lack of supervision over the use of funds by recipients. For her, the question is twofold. First, there is the issue of money versus service as a key to helping. Second, there is the fear that increases in public funding will dry up sources of private funding— that bad money will drive out good money—and that private agencies might themselves become pauperized through dependence on government grants. Folks, secretary of New York's State Charities Aid Association, also argues for private funds and private agency control. He concludes, however, "If we do not secure from private sources sufficient funds, then, without hesitation we ought to have a system of public relief for widows." As might be expected, Judge Pinckney, who spearheaded the drive to make public funds available for the care of dependent children, disagrees with opponents of public funding. Speaking from experience, he insists that his court is "doing something toward administering this law efficiently, intelligently, and honestly, too, and through public channels."

PROCEEDINGS OF THE
NATIONAL CONFERENCE OF CHARITIES
AND CORRECTIONS

1909

THE FAMILY AND THE WOMAN'S WAGE
BY MRS. FLORENCE KELLEY, SECRETARY OF THE NATIONAL
CONSUMER'S LEAGUE

There is no subject concerning which we more persistently live in a fool's paradise than this of woman's wage. We say on all occasions that we consider the home the fundamental thing in our national life. If we really valued the home, such things could not happen as I saw last Thursday in the night court in the city of New York. A girl, seventeen years of age, was taken away by a policeman from her two-year-old, fatherless boy to spend three years in a prison which, with the bitterest irony, we call a house of mercy. No charge has been proved against her. As a little cash girl, at fourteen years, in the enlightened city of New York, she went out from her home and worked under the temptations of a great department store. Before her fifteenth birthday her little fatherless boy was born, because of the conditions under which our laws allowed her to work. Her mother thought that the home needed the little girl's wages more than the little girl needed protection. When she was seventeen years old she had been working nearly a year, every night, in a telephone exchange, and she could bear it no longer. She was so weary that she could not even endure being with her little boy during the day. Finally she left her work, which meant taking six dollars a week out of her mother's family budget. She took her child and went away to look for other work, for her mother refused to keep the child unless the six dollars a week were paid. After a week she confessed herself beaten and sent the little boy back through a neighbor to his grandmother, with word that she believed she would have work in a few days and could take care of him. This mother sent her daughter to prison for three years under no other charge than that, for less than a week, the girl had not been able to maintain herself and her little boy and was therefore "a wayward girl."

That girl, after she comes out of prison, will never make a home for her little boy. Her heart is effectively broken; three years hence it will be effectively hardened. There are thousands of little cash girls working in our stores, and thousands of young girls never before did in the history of the world, because there never were telephone exchanges to be served in the dead of night.

If we valued home life as we hypocritically say that we do, there would not be one of these young girls away from the family home in the dead of night serving the public, not because they serve it better than men would do, but because they are cheaper and because the interest of the stockholders and the bondholders of the corporation is of greater importance than the sacrifice of these young girls. Now every man and woman of us who passively consent, as we do, to be served by telephone exchanges which employ these young victims in the night, everyone of us who is not striving to get legislation, and protesting as only subscribers can protest, is *particeps criminis* with these employers and stockholders. If there be a telephone exchange in this country which is served at night exclusively by men over twenty-one years of age, I beg that its patrons stand up now. I have never been able to hear of one in any city.

Lest anyone should believe that the young girls in New York City are less cherished in this service than those of other cities, I know of a city not far from Buffalo, where, within a month, a factory inspector took out of a leading hotel a girl under sixteen years of age who worked regularly until three o'clock in the morning serving a telephone exchange in that lobby, subject to the insults of passing travelers. But on her sixteenth birthday there will be no legal offense if her cruel father sends her back insisting, like the mother of the telephone girl, upon having six dollars a week.

The telephone exchange commands girls chiefly because there they are paid fifty-two weeks in the year, while the rest of our industries are so ill-organized that very few of them offer steady work throughout the year.

It may be said that I have spoken unjustly of the store where the first little girl was working. It is true that many young girls go as cash girls into stores and advance until they become clerks, and come out unhurt, so far as one can see, from that experience. It is also true that some of our boys came home sound in mind and limb from the Cuban war. Some children do not take scarlet fever, although exposed to it. Some unvaccinated people never take smallpox. But the risk is not greater which the families took who sent their sons to the Cuban war, than the risk these parents take who send their little girls into department stores. The protest cannot be made too strong, to those who believe that they value the home, against sending future mothers and makers of homes out of the schools knowing nothing of that which they should know when they shall have homes of their own, into institutions, commercial and otherwise, which, as Mr. Lee has said, "diseducate" the children and unfit them for life in the home.

It is not only the earnings which the future mothers bring into the homes that are earned at a frightful social price. The widows of working men, cleaning the filthy floors of railway stations, and hotels, and stores, and offices on their knees, after inhaling first the dust from the dry broom—is there any greater exposure to tuberculosis conceivable than that of the weary mother of little children doing such work at night? A friend of mine has conceived the monstrous idea of having a night nursery to which women so employed might send their children. And this idea was seriously described in so modern a publication as Charities and the Commons "before it changed its name" without a word of editorial denunciation. The mothers of young children cannot be sent away from their homes to do such work without the gravest social injury, any more than daughters can be sent away so young and untrained as they are sent in this country today. The proper place for a workingman's widow who has young children is in her home taking care of those children, unless she is a bad woman or a drunkard, or so ill that her proximity is a menace to the health of her children. But assuming that the mother is bad or ill, there is nothing gained by sending the children away for a few hours a day to a nursery. If she is infectious she would infect the children in their close sleeping quarters.

There is no subject concerning which we are more foolish than this of the wages of women in their homes, this idea of establishing institutions to take little children away from good mothers during their working hours, insisting that widowed mothers shall perform the tasks of fathers while some hired person pretends to be mother to their little ones.

There are conditions under which the day nursery is acceptable. For instance, where the mother is temporarily in the hospital for treatment from which her convalescence may be reasonably prompt; or, if there is illness in a home and the mother ought to be relieved temporarily of the care of the children. But when Americans boast of a national, or state, or city society of day nurseries (instead of humbly apologizing that we need more than one in Greater New York) we show how little we value the presence of the mother in her home. The day nursery which encourages the mother to go out to work, leaving the larger children to spend their day on the street and to buy penny lunches, is an argument for school luncheons for the larger children. No money earned in the United States costs so dear, dollar for dollar, as the money earned by the mothers of young children.

When we permit mothers to work in the homes industrially, on a large scale, as is the case in New York, we have the degradation of the home by industry, and the mother distracted from the care of the children through the invasion of the home. If we really thought about the family and the home as we say we do, we should have none of that work today.

***

LAWS
of the
STATE of ILLINOIS

Enacted by the
FORTY-SEVENTH GENERAL ASSEMBLY
at the
REGULAR BIENNIAL SESSION

BEGUN AND HELD AT THE CAPITOL, IN THE CITY OF
SPRINGFIELD, ON THE FOURTH DAY OF JANUARY
A.D. 1911, AND ADJOURNED SINE DIE ON THE
FIRST DAY OF JUNE, A.D. 1911.

Printed by authority of the General Assembly
of the State of Illinois.

Juvenile Courts—Funds to Parents

1. Amends section 7, Act of 1907. 7. As amended, provides for
funds to parent or parents.

(Senate Bill No. 403. Approved June 5, 1911.)

AN Act to amend an Act entitled, "An Act relating to children who are now or may hereafter become dependent, neglected or delinquent, to define these terms, and to provide for the treatment, control, maintenance, adoption and guardianship of the person of such children," approved June 4, 1907.

SECTION 1. Be it enacted by the People of the State of Illinois, represented in the General Assembly: That section 7 of the Act entitled "An Act relating to children who are now or may hereafter become dependent, neglected or delinquent, to define these terms and to provide for the treatment, control, maintenance, adoption and guardianship of the person of such children," approved June 4, 1907, be and the same is hereby amended so as to read as follows:

7. If the court shall find any male child under the age of seventeen years or any female child under the age of eighteen years to be dependent or neglected within the meaning of this Act, the court may allow such child to remain at its own home subject to the friendly visitation of a probation officer, and if the parent, parents, guardian or custodian consent thereto, or if the court shall further find that the parent, parents, guardian or custodian of such child are unfit or improper guardians or are unable or unwilling to care for, protect, train, educate or discipline such child, and that it is for the interest of such child and the people of this State that such child be taken from the custody of its parents, custodian or guardian, the court may make an order appointing as guardian of the person of such child, some reputable citizen of good moral character and order such guardian to place such child in some suitable family home or other suitable place, which such guardian may provide for such child or the court may enter an order committing such child to some suitable State institution, organized for the care of dependent or neglected children, or to some training school or industrial school or to some association embracing in its objects the purpose of caring for or obtaining homes for neglected or dependent children, which association shall have been accredited as hereinafter provided.

If the parent or parents of such dependent or neglected child are poor and unable to properly care for the said child, but are otherwise proper guardians and it is for the welfare of such child to remain at home, the court may enter an order finding such facts and fixing the amount of money necessary to enable the parent or parents to properly care for such child, and thereupon it shall be the duty of the county board, through its county agent or otherwise, to pay to such parent or parents, at such times as said order may designate the amount so specified for the care of such dependent or neglected child until the further order of the court.

APPROVED June 5, 1911.

★★★

PROCEEDINGS OF THE
NATIONAL CONFERENCE OF CHARITIES
AND CORRECTIONS

1912

PUBLIC PENSIONS TO WIDOWS
EXPERIENCES AND OBSERVATIONS WHICH LEAD ME
TO OPPOSE SUCH A LAW.

By Frederic Almy, Secretary Buffalo Charity Organization Society.

This paper will not discuss the recent laws giving pensions to widows in Illinois, Missouri, California, Michigan and Oklahoma, or the bills now pending in New York and Ohio, or the State Commission studying this subject in Massachusetts, or the efforts in

Colorado, but will discuss general principles. I find I am scheduled to oppose such laws, though for over a year in the SURVEY and elsewhere I am on record as well disposed towards them, though of the opinion that private charity is, for the present, safer.

Widowhood is a most innocent cause of poverty, especially pitiful because of its pain and waste, and very costly to society because the poverty is apt to increase in geometrical progression, two-fold, four-fold, or even more in each generation, as the neglected children mature. Sickness is also usually an innocent cause of poverty, though there are sexual diseases of appetite. The poverty of a family is still greater when the husband is not dead but is a living cost and danger. In such cases, the children have a father's counsel but less food than if they had none.

Neglected childhood is, in all the world, the very most innocent, appealing and frequent cause of poverty and crime. Poverty is often chosen, but the pauper child never chooses his poverty and his curses punish the society which has so foolishly neglected him. The cry of the children has been heard; street children are gone, factory children are going and the institution child must go. Home made children give the best results and even the foster home must go, unless the parents of the child are unfit.

A stupid fear of spending on the part of the Philistines of charity, who do not comprehend it, and a fear of pauperizing on the part of the Pharisees of charity, who have made a creed of it has made us penny wise and pound foolish. Neglect is the great pauperizer, not relief. The devil of pauperizing has been made a bogy of. That devil has his claws cut long ago by organized charity; but organized charity hates to give, and in some cities gives only in secret. When organized charity learns to be generous, without blushing, it will come into its own, and the widowhood of poverty will then get as liberal indemnity as the widowhood of industrial disaster. Such widowhood is just as innocent; and it is just as dangerous to society if not relieved.

I should like to see in every city a survey of all the children who are in institutions and in foster homes, and then a statement of the cost of maintenance of those children among them whose own homes are more fit except for poverty. I have always favored private out-door relief, but it is inadequate, and to-day all over the country, except in a few cities, families of widows are being ruthlessly scattered for lack of charity. Will public out-door relief be more adequate or better? Students of public out-door relief know well how it increases pauperism, but does not neglected childhood increase pauperism even more?

For nearly twenty years I have been a charity organization secretary and a special student and opponent of public out-door relief. In Charities for 1899, I had elaborate articles on the public and private out-door relief of forty cities. I know the dangers of relief, but last year at Boston I said, with Devine, "Our resources for relief are woefully inadequate. Our use of relief has been most sparing and timid. I am inclined to believe that we have caused more pauperism by our failure to provide for the necessities of life, for the education and training of children, and for the care and convalescence of the sick, than we have by excessive relief, even if we include indiscriminate alms." Can we harness public relief as we have harnessed steam and electricity through skillful engineers, so that we can have its power without its danger?

Why am I opposed to this plan of public pensions for widows? My opposition is not academic. I do not care whether the relief is a public or a private function, or whether it is given by the poor master, or by the Juvenile Court as in Chicago, or by children's guardians, or by a board of home assistance as proposed in New York. I think much, very much, of Thomas Mackay's classic argument that to the imagination of the poor the public treasury is inexhaustible and their right, and that they drop upon it without thrift, as they dare not do on private charity, and this argument is one that cannot be met by any excellence of administration; but I remember too that pauperizing by alms is no worse than pauperizing by neglect. Moreover, Mackay's argument applies mainly to indolence and improvidence, which are voluntary. The poverty of widowhood is not usually due to lack of thrift, and what widow ever became a widow because aid was public rather than private?

The crux of my opposition to public pensions today is that the public does not stand for fit salaries for relief. I am an advocate of more adequate relief, but I am an advocate first of more adequate brains and work for the poor. Relief without brains is as bad as medicine without doctors. I would much rather see doctors without medicine, or salaries without relief, as is the practice of some of the best of our charity organization societies. Like undoctored drugs, untrained relief is poisonous to the poor. Good charity is expensive, and poor charity is worse than none, yet what city would support adequate case work for its public aid?

In Buffalo where we have had organized charity for thirty-five years and for five years much talk and less practice of adequate relief, public opinion supports adequate salaries for a large staff in the charity organization society. Nevertheless, the city poor office has but five investigators, while we have fourteen, of better ability. Moreover, the city investigators merely investigate, while we make plans, find friends and find money from natural sources. Last month the money found by our paid visitors from relatives, employers and friends nearly equalled the total of their salaries, and if we add the wages for work found by them it would have exceeded their salaries. Of course these visitors gave the poor also a service which is worth ten times more than the money they get for them; but I find that the monthly statement of this money got by them for their poor, does much to justify the salaries in the eyes of the public.

Will the voters stand in any city for the salaries without which charity is a pest and curse? Even in Chicago where a bad law in a good cause is redeemed by a good judge, I do not find any indication of adequate case work. Judge Pinckney has voluntarily associated with himself a salaries case committee, paid for by private charities and not from the public treasury; but the record stories, which I have glanced at in the few days since I undertook this paper, would not pass muster for case work in some cities. They show good diagnosis and study of temperament, but I have not noticed in them search for relatives who can give, or attempts to find work or to find better paid work, or official records of the school attendance of children as a condition of aid, or constructive plans for removing poverty. A pension committee needs all of these things for its action. Even under Judge Pinckney, the Chicago relief looks like mere relief, which keeps the family from deteriorating after the bread-winner has gone. Indemnity relief may have no higher function than to prevent deterioration, but charity relief aims to redeem the family. It is not too much to ask that the tax payers' money should be educational and constructive.

How does the adequacy of Judge Pinckney's relief compare with private charity relief? I have only Buffalo to compare with. Judge Pinckney has pretty nearly carte blanche; his work has been splendidly guarded and intelligent and is the high-water mark of what can be expected today of public charity. In eleven months (to June 1, 1912) 316 families had an average of $262.00 each per year. In Buffalo, which is above the average in private relief, 707 widows applied last year, of whom 230 had money aid, averaging $35.00 a year each. This means nothing, however, for the figures include old widows without children, widows who had one month's casual aid, etc., twenty-four widows, who had our aid for twelve consecutive months, averaged $152.00 per annum from us or with city aid included, $180.00 per annum, which is 70 per cent of the Chicago aid. The Buffalo families have earnings, however, and aid from relatives, as the Chicago families must have had also. The only fair comparison would be the budgets rather than the pensions, and these I have not on tap for Buffalo, though I have been given the Chicago figures. The maximum C. O. S. pensions in Buffalo were $301.00 and $307.00 per year. An adequate family budget for the poor is not less than $700.00 a year.

A fact of the very first importance in this connection was stated last year in my Boston paper at this Conference that out of 2,240 families treated in that year by the Buffalo Society only seven were found to be absolutely dependent for as much as even six months with no income at all from earnings, relatives, lodgers, or any source except charity. This shows clearly both the danger of exaggeration and the need of investigation.

Salaries are usually far more adequate with private charity than with public. Money relief is inadequate with either, but bad, very bad, as the relief given by private charity has been in many cities it has not been so bad or so niggardly with individual families as public outdoor relief. We still find doles with either public or private charity, though $2.00 a week orders to widows every one, two, or three weeks (with $2.00 weekly or $104.00 a year as a maximum for the family) is still typical with public charity, but the rare exception with private. The private charity which has not the energy to find adequate relief will not be likely to have the wisdom to use it wisely when found. The valuable pension system of private charity is not half developed as a money raiser. It is my belief that modern organized charity is the most liberal as well as the most tender, personal and effective charity that the world has ever known. Politics exist with either public or private charity, but more with public charity. Fit men are more often found by private charity than by public where the tail of a long ticket is often designated by party managers with little public attention. The valuable co-operation of volunteers through case committees is a splendid part of the Chicago plan and exists with Boston out-door relief but is as exceptional with public charity as it is universal with private charity.

Will public relief check the giving of private relief as suggested in Chalmers "seven fountains" so that nothing will be gained because private givers will leave it all to the public treasury? My elaborate study in Charities, in 1899 seemed to show that just this happened, and that private giving was trifling in cities where public aid was given. Dr. Devine thinks this and said at the last New York State Conference of Charities at Watertown that public out-door relief would require at least a million dollars a year in New York City and that he firmly believed from ample experience in Berlin, Paris, and this country, that with it there would be more neglected poverty and distress than without it. Dr. Devine thinks private relief most inadequate, however, and so do Alexander Johnson, Folks, Hebberd, Tucker, Kingsley and many others who differ as to public pensions.

The question is active in New York State where the report of the congestion commission February 28, 1911, which was reviewed at length in the Survey for March 11, 18, and 25, 1911, was followed by the report to the New York City Conference of Charities and Correction rendered last May after a year's consideration. This report advocated public pensions to widows. Both this report and the New York bill recognize the danger of public administration as inadequate and provide that the public money shall go through private charities. If this is a return to public subsidies to private charities it seems to me indescribably bad, for such subsidies lead to sectarian appeals, to lobbying and to a scrambling at the public trough for patronage.

I have the detail of many of the state bills and laws, but they cannot be described in a paper so short as this must be if there is to be time for discussion.

It is no light thing to reverse a policy of many years in regard to public out-door relief. It was abolished in New York and Brooklyn thirty years ago, and in many of our chief cities and it was thought to be a dead issue in this Conference. Times change, however, and I am not willing to believe that in this day public out-door relief cannot be successful. It weighs with me that the equally delicate work of child placing is successfully done by public charity, though the arguments against it would be similar. Over and over private charity has blazed the way for what became public safety after standards had been developed and established, and this process I believe in. The curse of the old name of city out-door relief is something and the new and better associations will make it easier to keep up the new and better standards.

I am myself still opposed to public pensions, though with their aims I am so much in sympathy that I shall welcome experiments, in states not my own which may demonstrate whether they will succeed. Even if in the beginning such public relief does not reach the best standards of private relief I shall be willing to wait before judging if it improves steadily. Universal suffrage does not give immediate good government.

This paper has been prepared under extreme pressure as a basis for discussion. It is not a straddle, but voices the doubts which I have been expressing publicly for some time. I am here to learn.

DISCUSSION

MR. HOMER FOLKS—It seemed to me I could best make my thoughts on this matter clear by asking a few questions in serial order and then answering them as best I could. So far as I deal with facts I have in mind entirely the facts in New York City.

The first question is this: Is it desirable that children of widows of good character and efficiency be kept with their mothers? Is poverty alone a sufficient cause for breaking up families?

I think that all of us here probably without exception would answer this first question in the affirmative. There are those who would answer it in the negative, but they don't come to conferences, and we have to deal with them when we get home. I think we can assume that substantially all those present would agree with the conclusion of the White House Conference in that regard. I, at least, stand without qualification on the answer as stated in those conclusions.

Again, if such families should be kept together, should the relief come preferably from private sources?

I take it that there is difference of opinion. A very considerable, and perhaps an increasing number, probably, would say that they would have no special preference, or even prefer public relief. Personally, I take the other side. Under present circumstances I decidedly prefer the relief of such families from private sources for these three reasons:

First, it is desirable to develop and maintain private relief giving, and that this offers a clear and easy division of the field—the public authorities to maintain the public institutions and the private societies to give the family relief.

Second, the administration of public family relief is perhaps admitted by all to be decidedly difficult. I do not agree with Mr. Almy that the difficulty lies in getting adequate salaries for relief officers. I think it is the rule that public work pays better salaries than private work. Charity may be the one exception, but if it is, I believe we can change that particular exception, and that adequate money for adequate salaries for an adequate number of officers, could be had.

But the more difficult point is the clumsiness of the machinery by which public employees are selected. It is still difficult, to be sure, by any process that we now know of to get competent people at a given time for a given job in the public service.

But the most serious objection of the three is, that I think there is a subtle psychological, but very important difference between the feeling of reliance upon private relief and the feeling of reliance upon public charity claimed as a matter of right. I am not so sure, in the case of widows, that it is not a matter of right. A feeling of reliance upon a steady and regular income wisely adapted to the family needs and the family budget, ought to be a good thing. I am not so sure that it is not a desirable thing in the home of the widow or where the totally disabled wage earner is concerned, but certainly it is a very dangerous thing in other households where there is a wage earner, able-bodied, but disposed to shirk his responsibility.

If it is preferable that relief come from private sources, is sufficient relief now given from private sources to such families? Speaking as to New York: I doubt if any person would have the hardihood to say that such is the case at the present time and for one, I have to state most emphatically, that it is not sufficient, and that families of that character are not kept together and that considerable numbers of children of widows who should be kept at home are committed, and that the process which Judge Pinckney described of the tearing apart of children from their mothers for poverty alone, occurs from time to time in every borough of the City of New York.

Third. If it is desirable that such families should be kept together and if the relief should come preferably from private sources, and if sufficient relief does not come now, is it, after all, a very serious thing to break up such families and send the children to institutions? I doubt whether any person present would answer that question thus put, in the negative, and yet some of our best friends do by their actions, answer it in the negative, because, while this breaking up of families goes on admittedly and openly, they do not actually do anything in a large way to stop it.

It is suggested sometimes that the proper course is to relieve in the best and finest and most constructive and up-to-date method such families as can be aided by existing resources. As to what is to happen to the other families not so aided, no particular reply is made.

What should we think of a city which had a thousand destitute aged persons and which was about to construct a new almshouse, and which proposed plans for an entirely modern building to accommodate two hundred persons, and pointed with pride to its sanitary arrangements, its bath rooms and cottage plan, and spoke of this as a model provision for the aged poor, but refused to answer the question as to what is to happen to the other eight hundred? What would the people of the city think of that sort of a municipal policy? But in my judgment that would be far more defensive, far less serious than to provide adequately for a few families leaving others to the tender resources of nothing.

Now, if it is desirable that these families be kept together, and if the relief should come preferably from private sources, and if it is really a very serious matter, is it possible to find from private sources sufficient relief? Some say yes and some say no, and I say that I do not think any of us know, for the reason that in New York it has never been intelligently tried.

We have possibly between six and seven thousand children of widows in institutions in New York City. Not all of them should be at home. Is it possible to secure from private sources sufficient additional funds to provide for them? I am not sure, and I hope the relief societies will make one more combined serious, final effort to secure such funds. But I think they should distinctly realize that this is the last call for dinner, and if they don't get together and secure such funds they will be provided from some other source in some other way.

Now, just one question more: If it develops that sufficient private resources are not to be had, is the evil of breaking up families as we are now doing, a lesser evil than public relief to widows? A good many say yes. My opinion is distinctly not; and that if we do not secure from private sources sufficient funds, then, without hesitation we ought to have a system of public relief for widows.

HON. MERRITT W. PINCKNEY—I am not convinced, notwithstanding what I have heard, against the "Funds to Parents" law—no, I am not convinced. I have listened with great interest to a very able and intelligent paper read by Mr. Almy. Anybody who knows him, knows of his ability to grasp this subject, must treat what he says with the highest consideration, and I do. If I had known him as well and liked him as well as I do now, before I came to Cleveland, I don't know whether I would have taken the opposite side of any question that he was to discuss. He certainly looks to me as though he was by experience authorized to speak, and I want to thank him personally, too, for the way he treated the subject. He didn't shut the door in our faces and say, "Stay outside." He didn't say to us, "The honest and judicious administration of the law of the Funds to Parents Act is impossible, go away and don't bother me." He left the door open, as I always believe he has left his mind open, for honest, intelligent thought, regardless of what his years of experience have been, and regardless of what his thought was on any particular subject, and I want to thank him for that consideration.

It comes to me now that someone of the speakers said it will cost a million dollars to try this out in the City of New York. I have read with interest the report of the State Board of Charities for the State of New York for the year 1911, and I recognize Mr. Hebberd as the Secretary of that Board. I assume that those gentlemen in their experience and grasp of this subject, and in their study of it, in their service to the State of New York, have made investigation and inquiry and have consulted with the various organizations, private and otherwise, through the State of New York, and therefore, when I read in their report that it is confessedly admitted by the private charities in the City of New York that they have not the adequate means to meet the needs of the dependents in that city, that it stands for something; and when I see in that report that thirty-four thousand five hundred and thirty children were in dependent institutions at the close of the fiscal year ending September 30, 1910, that it must take three hundred and fifty thousand dollars of New York's money to take care of those children for one month and that it must take for the year something over four million of dollars. I say, when these gentlemen, after their investigation, tell us these things and report that many of the children could have been taken care of at home in the normal condition of family life, that it means something, and I say it would pay the City of New York, as an experiment, to keep some of those children at home with their mothers instead of sending them away to institutions, even if it did cost one million dollars.

I want to say to Judge Baker from Boston, when you say that the administration of this relief ought not to be left to the Juvenile Court of Chicago, or to any Juvenile Court, I say, Amen! but I do say it is possible to so frame a law that public officials will be able to administer this relief.

Now, Mr. Persons, I want to say to you that it is probably due to the short time allowed me that I did not explain about these eight hundred and fifty families who were refused relief. I have the figures here on those families and I think there must be three hundred and fifty of them who were, through undisclosed property interests, money or funds of some kind, amply able to take care of themselves. That shows, if it shows anything, that we have a committee that is doing its work of investigation and inquiry well.

So, out of eight hundred and fifty families, three hundred and fifty were able to take care of themselves, and naturally, under the law, we couldn't give them relief. And of the other five hundred there are various reasons set down for refusing them relief. They were turned over to other agencies to be taken care of. Under the law, we say that these families, for reasons set down by the conference group after consultation with the Court, are not entitled to relief, but they are taken care of wherever it is necessary to take care of them.

Now, with reference to supervision, I wish to say to Miss Richmond that she is mistaken when she says that there is no supervision in Chicago. I will admit, ladies and gentlemen, after eleven months, under a law that is too brief, and into which we have had to read certain essentials before we undertook to administer it—I will admit that the law is not complete. I will admit that we are in the beginning of the dawn, but I say we are doing something toward administering this law efficiently, intelligently and honestly, too, and through public channels.

Don't let us be satisfied with what is partial, but let us ask for all. Why, we have been working for years now, for what? For compulsory insurance against accident, sickness, old age and invalidity.

Let us nail our colors to the mast and insist on what we have been asking for these many years, the full program; insurance against industrial accident, insurance against sickness, insurance against old age, insurance against invalidity, and compulsory insurance against all these four items in every State of the Union.

MISS M. E. RICHMOND—Mr. Senior has struck the keynote, I think. We must not attempt to meet our present difficulties, serious though they be, in such a bungling way as to put up permanent barriers against their solution. So far from being a forward step, "funds to parents" is a backward one—public funds not to widows only, mark you, but to private families, funds to the families of those who have deserted and are going to desert!

The breaking up of homes through poverty alone is, as I have said, a serious evil, but its prevention demands elements that this Chicago experiment, so carefully watched and safeguarded by some of the best known social workers in the country, conspicuously lacks. Even here, with their hearty good will and earnest co-operation, and with a judge willing to aid them, there has been practically no competent supervision of the pensioned families; there has been, in some cases, less adequate relief than private charity was giving, and far less supervision. If this has been the case in Chicago, what may we expect, at this stage of social service development, from experiments less co-operative and under administrations less able to withstand undue influence?

Another point in my too brief four minutes: This Illinois bill was drafted and passed without consulting a single social worker, and then they had to ask the social workers to come to their rescue in order that the worst might not happen. Watch your Legislatures carefully, when you go back to your several states, and see that the social workers are consulted in time.

Miss Lathrop has said that the private charities have been "pauperized" in Chicago by the new law, and are turning their cases over to the court. There is another aspect of that. No private fund for relief can successfully compete very long with a public fund, whether the latter is adequate or not. Inevitably the sources of private charitable relief dry up. A greater danger threatens in the state of New York, where it is actually proposed publicly to pay private charities for the relief of widows one hundred cents for every fifty that they spend in relief from their own funds—a two for a cent plan that will be an admirable way of hammering down our standards of adequate treatment in such cases. If we spend any of the fifty cents in seeing that the children of the widow are in school, that they are morally protected, that their health is safeguarded, that they have a good chance to grow up right, we are to get less than a dollar for the family; but if we, or our colleagues, spend all of the fifty cents on material relief, we get a dollar. The methods of public pensioning so far proposed are full of such incongruities as I have pointed out.

When a widow is granted relief under the law, the last thing that is said to her in court by myself, is to explain to her the necessity of accounting to a regular probation officer as to how she spends her money. And she is cautioned to keep her receipts, and that probation officer's duty is to visit that family regularly, and report on that family, giving it such supervision as it is possible for him or her to give. I don't say that this is enough, but I say that somewhere along the line, when we have had the experience and we get right down to what is possible to do under public administration, that we can rightly supervise and investigate and control this situation.

Now, I noticed in Mr. Almy's paper, the argument which he read, that to the imagination of the poor the public treasury is inexhaustible, and they drop on it without thrift—that is a forceful statement, that is true, but which is the worse, the pauperizing by alms or by neglect? For my part, I would rather have a pauper with a well-filled stomach than a pauper who is starving to death.

 Recall what you learned in this chapter by completing the Chapter Review.

The Depression and the New Deal: 1930–1940

NATIONAL ARCHIVES AND RECORDS ADMINISTRATION.

LEARNING OUTCOMES

- Compare the impact of the Great Depression to that of the recession of 2007–2009.

- Summarize the major program innovations of the New Deal.

- Explain how the social movements of the 1930s had lasting impacts on social welfare.

CHAPTER OUTLINE

Changing Economic and Demographic Realities   156
    The Economic Collapse   156
    Agricultural Crisis   158
    Family Life   162

Innovations in Social Welfare   163
    The Hoover Response to Crisis   163
    FDR and the First New Deal   164
    The Second New Deal   168
    The Changing Role of the Social
        Work Profession   176
    New Alignments in Social
        Welfare   178

Mass Movements during the 1930s   180
    Veterans and the Bonus   181
    Older Americans   182
    Labor and Social Welfare   182
    Setbacks for Women   185
    The Eclipse of Reform   185

Conclusion   186

DOCUMENTS: The Depression and the New Deal   188
    *Monthly Report of the Federal
        Emergency Relief Administration,
        1933*   189
    Social Security Act, 1935   195

The economic prosperity of the 1920s was both real and imaginary. Factory workers and second-generation ethnics experienced better economic times than during any previous era of American history. Like the subprime mortgage "bubble" of the early 2000s, however, much of the economic growth of the 1920s was fueled by speculation and plain fraud. Thanks to the availability of consumer credit, working families no longer had to save patiently for years to purchase an icebox or a radio; for a few dollars down and a few more every month, they could bring these new consumer products home. Like the 1990s, some economists and politicians believed that depression was a thing of the past.

CHANGING ECONOMIC AND DEMOGRAPHIC REALITIES

The Economic Collapse

The crisis that descended upon the country had not come without forewarning. In addition to the large-scale stock speculation, several other factors indicated the precariousness of the prosperity of the 1920s. A study by the Brookings Institution analyzed the income and savings of families in the richest pre-Depression year, 1929, and found that almost 6 million families, 21 percent of the population, had annual incomes of less than $1,000. These families of necessity spent $2.1 billion more than they earned. The next income group, the 5.8 million families with incomes between $1,000 and $1,500, had very slight savings—less than $200 million. Thus, 40 percent of the population had no reserves to fall back on when the Depression set in. The fact was that 30 percent of American families had incomes under $3,100 and saved little during 1929.

The Brookings study had declared that $2,000 in 1929 prices was sufficient to supply a family with only basic necessities. An annual income of $2,500 was a very moderate one. Nevertheless, 60 percent of all families had incomes below $2,000, and 71 percent of all families had incomes below $2,500.[1] Despite the talk of prosperity, low incomes were the reality for the vast majority of American families even before the Depression hit.

Equally clear is the reason for the collapse of consumption once the unsoundness of the economic situation became evident and the fear of its consequences took hold. Families reduced their consumption, provoking a new second round of increased unemployment, from "overproduction of capital; overambitious expansion of business concerns; overproduction of commodities . . . the maintenance of an artificial price level for many commodities."[2] The gross national product (GNP) dropped yearly from an all-time high of $103.1 billion in 1929 to reach $55.6 billion in 1933. GNP started upward in 1934, reached $90.4 billion in 1937, but fell back to $84.7 billion the following year. Not until 1941 did national income reach pre-crisis levels.[3]

The crash of 1929 was the start of a 12-year period of deprivation. Other economic indicators followed the same pattern. Unemployment, which had averaged about 4 percent of the civilian labor force in the 1920s, rose by 4 million during 1930. In 1933, the year that marked the depth of the Depression, an average of 13 million persons, some 25 percent of the civilian labor force, were unemployed, and many more could find only part-time employment. Despite recovery programs, 14 percent of the American workforce was still jobless in 1937, and by 1938, that figure had risen again to 19 percent.[4]

In a situation in which earnings for most workers were near poverty level, security was necessarily measured in terms of steady employment. Unemployment of a breadwinner was disastrous for a family. The finding of the Relief Census conducted by the Federal Emergency Relief Administration (FERA) during October 1933 that 3 million families, consisting of more than 12.5 million persons (about 10 percent of the population), were dependent upon unemployment relief suggests the scope of the disaster that had befallen the country.

The clear barrier between the deserving and undeserving poor that had guided social welfare policy for a century weakened as a result of mass unemployment. Through earlier economic crises, Americans had retained their faith that the United States was the land of opportunity and that anyone who really wanted to work could find a job. But Progressivism had increased understanding of how structural forces could limit opportunity and increase unemployment. In 1924, a century after the Yates report had provided a rationale for using the almshouse to motivate the poor to find work, the venerable New York Association for Improving the Conditions of the Poor released a study that argued that assistance levels were too low and that raising them might enable recipients to break the "vicious circle of poverty."[5] The Depression demonstrated that one could be poor and unemployed because of social—not individual—dysfunction. Both the temporary relief programs developed to meet the exigencies of the Depression and later permanent programs of the Social Security Act underlined the risks of a complex economy and the vulnerability produced by economic breakdown.

The emergence of a distinctive subculture among professional social workers was one contributor to this new understanding of need and deprivation.

The emergence of a distinctive subculture among professional social workers was one contributor to this new understanding of need and deprivation. Illustrative and factual support for such dissent began to appear in the publications of the Family Welfare Association of America (FWAA) and of the National Federation of Settlements. The FWAA journal, *The Family*, reported a study of breakdown in family income during 1928. One thousand cases, including 3,996 individuals known to three Boston family-relief agencies, were analyzed for factors associated with dependency. Of the total 1,000 cases, 41 percent showed that "some form of physical incapacity made charitable aid necessary," while 30 percent of the families were dependent as a result of joblessness.[6]

Still, this new recognition that unemployment was a structural risk of an industrial society sat uncomfortably with older characterizations of the poor. Thus, the Boston agencies still concluded that 7 percent of their clients were dependent because they had "bad character." This was in sharp contrast with the results of Amos Warner's classic study, *American Charities*, of 1892, which found intemperance to be the cause of dependency in one-fifth of the cases studied. The principal researcher of the later study hoped that the analysis would contribute to an understanding of "the inevitable economic maladjustments in a society which distributes its wealth to individuals capable of earning it . . . and assumes that the family system of consumption surviving from an earlier economic organization will have its needs supplied."[7]

In 1931, the Unemployment Committee of the National Federation of Settlements sponsored *Case Studies of Unemployment*, an account of 150 cases offering "cross-sections of human experience where unemployment is due to industrial rather than individual causes."[8] Looking beyond the immediate crisis, the National Federation declared:

> Experience has taught us to recognize broken work not merely as a symptom of financial crises, but as a recurring fault of modern production. We are confronted by unemployment, not as a single episode in the history of a household, but as something that may come again and again, impeding and stopping the normal development of the family.[9]

Agricultural Crisis

For farmers, generally, the Depression of the 1930s seemed an extension and deepening of a crisis that had descended during the 1920s with the collapse of domestic and European demand for farm commodities. At first, the problem seemed part of the general economic recession that plagued the country during 1920 and 1921; but subsequent improvements, during the 1920s, in the overall situation did not bring full recovery to farmers. Thus, whereas the share of agriculture in the national product had been 13 percent in 1919, its share was only 10 percent in 1929.[10] The situation became desperate during the 1930s. The ratio of prices for commodities sold by farmers to prices paid for purchases—using 1909–1914 as the base period—fell from 92 percent in 1929 to 58 percent in 1932.[11] Total farm income dropped to $2.5 billion in 1932, less than one-half of total farm income in 1919. Individual farm income dropped from $945 per farm in 1929 to $379 per farm in 1933.[12] Ironically, farm production fell by less than 5 percent, dashing hopes for an increase in prices of farm commodities. Farm debt soared as the value of farm property declined sharply. Farmers organized, demonstrated, and threatened a nationwide strike.

Despite agricultural difficulties, the Depression brought about a brief reversal of the long-term trend in the decline in the farm population. In 1929, 30.6 million persons—25 percent of the total population—lived on farms; by 1933, the farm population had risen to 32.4 million—26 percent of the total population. After 1933, the number of persons living on farms resumed its downward trend.[13] Disenchantment with the realities of farm living had set in, industrial production had started a slow recovery, and, perhaps most important, relief, when needed, was more readily available in the cities. As with farm population, the number of farms rose during the early Depression years and then began to fall.

The human crisis of the Great Depression was exacerbated by ecological disaster. After decades of plowing the semiarid land of the Great Plains and destroying the grasses that held topsoil intact, drought hit the region in three waves—1934, 1936, and 1939—which led to a series of catastrophic dust storms. The worst of the storms, in May 1934, blew millions of pounds of Great Plains soil to Chicago and, a few days later, to Eastern cities. Farmers who had held on through the agricultural depression of the 1920s and 1930s were finally defeated as their farms literally blew away.

The Dust Bowl, in turn, provoked a humanitarian crisis as millions of families from Kansas, Arkansas, and Oklahoma—generically called "Okies"—headed west in search of work and new homes. The population of California that was born in Oklahoma, for example, increased by 118,000 between 1930 and 1940. John Steinbeck's *The Grapes of Wrath* and Dorothea Lange's photographs for the Farm Security Administration preserved their jarring experience of economic deprivation, exploitation, and personal trauma (Figures 6.1 and 6.2).[14]

Watch this video on the Dust Bowl.

Compare the causes and responses to this ecological disaster with the current debate over global warming.

https://www.youtube.com/watch?v=PGUyJe5rlcw

The Roosevelt administration's New Deal package responded to the farmers' plight and unrest with legislation and administrative regulations designed to ease credit and to raise commodity prices through restricting output. In particular, the Agricultural Adjustment Act (AAA), approved by Congress on May 10, 1933, authorized the imposition of production controls to achieve a balance between production and consumption of farm commodities at the index parity level of farm income enjoyed during 1909–1914.

The restriction of output contributed to a decline in the number of farms during the Depression years. By 1940, the number of farms stood at 6,097,000, representing a 10-year loss of almost 200,000 farms.[15] Since the number of farms owned or operated by whites remained essentially unchanged, the loss was almost entirely among black farms—down from 15 percent of the total number of farms in 1930 to 12 percent in 1940. This rapid decline testifies to the precarious position of black farmers in the Southern agricultural economy. As farm prices fell, black tenant farmers were more likely to face eviction. At the same time, many African Americans were evicted because of their involvement with the Southern Tenant Farm Union that attempted to negotiate fairer conditions for poor black and white farms. These efforts to push poor African Americans off rural farms contributed to the rapid black migration to Northern cities over the next three decades.

Growth in farm ownership and in the average size of farms was stimulated directly and indirectly by New Deal policies. As tenants were forced off the land, the percentage of fully owned farms increased as the total number of farms fell. The percentage of fully owned farms rose from 46 in 1930 to 51 in 1940; the percentage of black farms that were fully owned rose from 17 to 23 in the same period.[16] Farm ownership was accompanied by a steady increase in farm size—from an average of 150.7 acres in 1930 to an average of 167.1 acres in 1940.[17]

Following his inauguration, President Roosevelt consolidated all federal agricultural credit agencies into the Farm Credit Administration. Congress authorized loans to save farmers from the immediate danger of foreclosures, to underwrite production costs, and to regain lost property on easy credit terms. The result of this package of New Deal

Application for funds for Rural Rehabilitation camps for migratory laborers in California.

Introduction

"...we found filth, squalor, an entire absence of sanitation, and a crowding of human beings into totally inadequate tents or crude structures built of boards, weeds, and anything that was found at hand to give a pitiful semblance of a home at its worst. Words cannot describe some of the conditions we saw." (Federal report on Imperial Valley, California).

. . . . .

"No provision is made for sanitation, water supply, or even general camp cleanliness... A sorry picture is presented of a condition that threatens to be a serious menace to those communities where squatter camps exist. Moving the occupants away simply spreads the condition..." (California Department of Industrial Relations report on squatters camps).

. . . . .

It may be true that alien Mexicans... live better in Imperial Valley than they do in their own country, but this cannot constitute an excuse for countenancing poverty and squalor in the United States." (General Pelham D. Glassford, Federal Conciliator in Imperial Valley, California).

Decent camp facilities for seasonal workers in agriculture are an urgent need in California. Every month more thousands of migratory families are being set in motion to serve the 1935 harvests which are already under way. Camp conditions remain about as they were in 1933 and 1934. The incessant labor strife which marked those years is not stilled; 1935, too, is already building its own strike record. Living conditions remain a basic aggravating factor in these disturbances.

The present application is the first request by the California Division of Rural Rehabilitation for FERA funds in the name of elevation of the living standards of depressed laborers. Therefore, a somewhat fuller presentation is made of the unique role of labor in agricultural California than might otherwise seem necessary to a simple proposal for decent camps. But California labor deviates from the national rural labor pattern in many essential respects. Inevitably, the problem of its rehabilitation is so uniquely affected thereby that the more salient features of its background have been set forth in the following outline.

PRINTS & PHOTOGRAPHS DIVISION, LIBRARY OF CONGRESS, LC-DIG-PPMSCA-19155.

Figure 6.1 Application for federal emergency funding to construct migrant worker housing in California, 1935

farm legislation, including the AAA, was to raise net farm income from $2.5 billion in 1932 to more than $5.9 billion in 1935. Additionally, the $9.6 billion farm mortgage debt load of 1930 was reduced to $7.6 billion in 1935 and to $6.6 billion in 1940.[18]

New Deal legislation, designed to help farmers through easy credit, supported not only farm ownership but also the introduction of farm machinery, which, in turn, encouraged the development of larger farms. The Farm Security Administration had authority to lend money to make it possible, among other things, for farmers to become landowners and to refinance and rehabilitate their lands.

PRINTS & PHOTOGRAPHS DIVISION, LIBRARY OF CONGRESS, LC-DIG-PPMSCA-19156.

Figure 6.2   The application for migrant worker housing funds was accompanied by photographs by Dorothea Lange of existing conditions. Kern County, California, February 1935

In its early years, New Deal legislation spelled disaster for the most marginal group of farmers—tenants. In general, government support was for large farmers, with little assistance going to the small farmer. Not until 1935 was a tenant clause added to the AAA requiring farmers to keep the same number of tenants they had when they joined the program.[19] As the most marginal part of the farm population, tenant farmers and sharecroppers bore the heaviest burden of the agricultural depression. Homeless, they joined the other jobless and dispossessed who wandered the country.

The reduction in farm tenancy sparked two important migrations. Many African American and white Southerners found their way to the industrial centers of the Midwest and the East, where they played an important role in the social and political crises of those cities during the postwar years. More immediately, tens of thousands of dispossessed farmers streamed westward, where they joined Mexican Americans and Asian Americans in the labor force for California's expanding agricultural region. The Roosevelt administration stepped in both to improve conditions in California and, through the Civilian Conservation Corps (CCC), to reduce wind erosion on the Great Plains.

The conflicting thrusts of New Deal policies were particularly dramatic in the development of agricultural and land policy. Native Americans saw some relief from their difficulties in land ownership during the period. The Dawes Act of 1887 had divided their land. But, in too many cases, Native American land was allotted to white people. In 1934, the Indian Reorganization Act helped end this practice. Additionally, Congress gave the tribes more than a million acres of new land, permitted greater autonomy in local government, improved health services and education, and supplied credit for agricultural development and industrial projects. Native Americans were given preferential hiring in the Bureau of Indian Affairs, and the development of native crafts was encouraged. The secretary of the interior still exercised political control, regulated land management, and supervised expenditures. Nevertheless, New Deal policy provided a new beginning for the relationship of the federal government and Native Americans, one that acknowledged the government's past mistakes and the importance of indigenous culture and autonomy.[20]

Family Life

A summary of staff reports prepared in 1935 for the Committee on Economic Security declared "the chief aim of social security is protection of the family life of wage earners, and the prime factor in family life is the protection and development of children."[21] As the Depression deepened, social workers insisted that the economic base of the family be strengthened and that the federal government share in the cost.

The relative prosperity of the 1910s and 1920s had made working-class families more vulnerable to economic hard times. The "breadwinner" family with a father working, a full-time female homemaker, and children in school became more common during these years, replacing the multi-earner family strategies of the 19th century. When the Depression hit, male unemployment left the family without any income on which to fall back.

In the mid-1930s, E. Wight Bakke's studies of family life and unemployment documented the painful process of readjustment that loss of work initiated. In some cases, unemployment led to strengthen family ties as members worked together to get through the crisis, whereas in other cases, it led to a disintegration of both family relations and connections to neighbors and kin.[22]

Changes in the family were particularly evident in the move of women working outside the home. The number of wage-earning women 16 years of age and over increased from 1,701,000 in 1870, when the Bureau of the Census first collected such data, to 10,546,000 in 1930.[23] During the 1920s, the increase in female employment was 29 percent, while the increase in the female population was 22 percent. The number of employed married women had reached 3,071,000 in 1930, a nearly 300 percent increase over the 769,000 employed at the beginning of the century. Were it not "for the retardation of business activity which was well under way at the time of the 1930 census, probably even more women would have reported themselves as occupied." As it was, 33 percent of those who worked were in domestic and personal services, 18 percent were in manufacturing and mechanical industries, 19 percent were in clerical occupations, and 12 percent were in trade and transportation.

The unemployment crisis of the 1930s delayed the formation of new families—getting married and having children. The marriage rate per 1,000 unmarried women declined from 92 percent in 1920 to 68 percent in 1930.[24] In 1933, the birthrate was 18.4 per 1,000 of population, down from 27.7 per 1,000 of population in 1920 and from 21.3 in 1930.[25]

Unemployment struck women as well as men, with discrimination falling heavily upon the former as jobs became scarcer and men displaced women. At the same time, the well-paid industrial and construction work performed by most men was more liable to layoffs than the lower-paid, unskilled work performed by most women. One result was role reversal, wherein wives worked and supported families, while husbands were confined to the home. Although the divorce rate showed no appreciable change between 1920 and 1940, family instability was evidenced by a sharp increase in suicide and desertions.[26]

> **?** Assess your comprehension of "Changing Economic and Demographic Realities" by completing this quiz.

INNOVATIONS IN SOCIAL WELFARE

The economic crisis that began in 1929 pushed political leaders to scramble for solutions. During the Hoover administration (1929–1933) and the first years of the Roosevelt administration, these solutions very often looked backward to older economic orthodoxies. Only with the failure of those ideas, and with a push from social movements, did the Roosevelt administration finally embrace newer ideas, including moving social welfare from an afterthought to a central tenet of social and economic policy.

The Hoover Response to Crisis

President Herbert Hoover had been seen as a Progressive during the 1920s because of his leadership of the effort to feed a hungry Europe after World War I, but he had retreated to an advocacy of "rugged individualism" during his 1928 campaign. He believed that government's proper role was to encourage voluntary action, a conviction that failed to match the magnitude of the economic dislocation of the Great Depression. In 1930, President Hoover engaged in a major campaign of optimistic rhetoric and a minor campaign of public works that failed to stop the precipitous economic decline. This refusal to depart from traditional ideas and policies imposed serious limitations on the administration's response to the crisis. Trapped by the hope of his own prediction of an early return to economic normalcy and by his belief in balanced budgets, laissez-faire, and states' rights, Hoover was reluctant to have the federal government assume new responsibilities and powers.[27] This was especially true in matters of social welfare, long considered a province for state and local activities as well as the special domain of private voluntary activity. Not until 1932 did Congress charter the Reconstruction Finance Corporation (RFC) "to provide emergency financing facilities for financial institutions to aid in financing agriculture, commerce and industry, and for other purposes."[28]

Hoover, like much of the country, was out of touch in two respects. First, the magnitude of the economic crisis was hard to comprehend for those who had three meals a day and no specter of foreclosure or joblessness haunting them. Just as importantly, the demographic profile of the nation had changed. The children of the immigrant wave of the early 20th century were the first generation in American history that was predominantly industrial and urban. The older bromides of rugged individualism held little meaning for them. In contrast, the expansion of urban liberalism at the local level underscored the importance of government action in providing security and improving the life circumstances of ordinary citizens.

In effect, the RFC became federally mandated aid for businessmen, while individuals and families were left to the mercy of inadequate state and local treasuries. Later, in 1932, the powers of the RFC were extended to permit federal loans to states "for relief and work relief to needy and distressed people and in relieving the hardship resulting from unemployment."[29] But even then the need for direct relief, as indicated by the findings of the National Federation of Settlements' case studies of unemployed families, generally went unheeded:

> Neither savings in cash, nor in homes, furniture, or personal keepsakes, neither charity nor getting into debt to butcher and baker, neither moving to cheaper quarters nor scrimping on food, nor the enforced labor of mothers and children gave adequate assurance of livelihood.... All combined, these makeshifts did not offer a reasonable solution of their predicament nor one which we should tolerate as part of our going life.[30]

The platform statements of the Republican and Democratic Parties demonstrated the essential conservatism of both parties in 1932. Ironically, the Republican platform gave more explicit recognition to the human suffering occasioned by the Depression and to the need "to bring encouragement and relief to the thousands of American families that are sorely afflicted."[31] The Democratic platform did not use the word *depression* at all, and although it did mention the "unprecedented economic and social distress of the times," it did not refer to the personal consequences of this distress. Nevertheless, the Democratic platform called for public works and unemployment and old age insurance. The Republican platform "true to American traditions and principles of government . . . [confirmed] the relief problem as one of State and local responsibility"—and voluntary action.

FDR and the First New Deal

During the 1932 presidential campaign, the Democratic nominee, Franklin D. Roosevelt, moved slowly toward a more innovative position as he pledged a New Deal for the American people. On the one hand, he advocated increased spending for the unemployed and more public works; on the other hand, he advocated a 25 percent cut in federal expenditures.[32] Roosevelt's original program did not see social welfare programs as central to economic recovery. He hoped that restricting competition through programs like the National Industrial Recovery Act and the Agricultural Adjustment Act would increase corporate profits and revive the economy. Welfare payments were a short-term emergency measure that Roosevelt hoped to end as soon as possible. During his first term, however, political and economic dynamics served to make social welfare measures more central to New Deal economic policy. It slowly dawned on government officials that increasing the purchasing power of ordinary people was more important than business profits in stimulating economic growth.

Roosevelt was no radical. In his 1932 speech accepting the presidential nomination, Roosevelt had stated:

> The great social phenomenon of this depression, unlike others before it, is that it has produced but a few of the disorderly manifestations that too often attend upon such times.
>
> Wild radicalism has made few converts, and the greatest tribute that I can pay to my countrymen is that in these days of crushing want there persists an orderly and hopeful spirit on the part of the millions of our people who have suffered so much.[33]

The eloquence of the speech could not mask the traditionalism of the proposed program for recovery: economy in government, shorter working hours, public works financed and self-sustained by the issuance of government bonds, protective tariffs for industry and agriculture, and increased prices for industrial and farm products. The pledge of assistance with "distress relief" seemed almost an afterthought.

Between Roosevelt's victory in November 1932 and his inauguration in March 1933, the Depression deepened and spread globally. The effects of the crisis were visible for all to see. In addition to the inability of the stock market to sustain a rally, banks were closing, industries were failing, and farms were going into bankruptcy. Corporate profits, farm income, and wage earnings all fell, and the need for money brought the meaning of economic collapse into every home. By the time that Roosevelt came into office, governmental intervention in social and economic affairs was expected and accepted—particularly on the federal level.[34]

New Deal policy contained a combination of three contradictory strategies in economic policy. First, there was a basic belief in the efficacy of the market system as a tool of economic control, if only prices could be pushed upward. Second, there was the traditional view of the importance of a balanced budget; whenever possible, the Roosevelt administration moved to cut expenditures and reduce deficits. Finally, and often in conflict with what was seen as sound fiscal policy, there was the Keynesian theory of "effective demand," which saw the key to recovery in increased spending—government programs to increase purchasing power and direct spending for public works to increase employment. The regulated economy and the free market economy, compensatory finance and debt reduction, all played their parts in New Deal programs.

The early responses of the New Deal were, despite the rhetoric of change, conservative. Roosevelt's initial emphasis was to try to instill confidence and specifically to induce inflation in the expectation that a price rise would increase profits and thus stimulate output.

The banking crisis required immediate attention. There were 4,400 bank failures between 1930 and 1932, and by January 1933, panic was widespread. Runs and heavy withdrawals led one state after another to declare "bank holidays." When Roosevelt took office on March 4, 1933, banks were either closed or severely curtailed in 47 states. Within two days, on March 6, FDR had declared a national bank holiday, forbidden all gold payments and exports, and instituted new penalties for hoarding gold. Three days later, Congress met in special session, the start of the "Congress of the Hundred Days," and passed an emergency Banking Bill. The emergency legislation that supervised the reopening of the banks and the more permanent banking reforms instituted within the next few years demonstrated the determination of the Roosevelt administration to maintain and restore the free enterprise system. Banking was not nationalized. Instead, the federal government, through the Federal Reserve banks, the RFC, and the Treasury Department, was to aid and regulate the banking industry to strengthen private financial institutions. In order to extend the system of control and to offer increased security to investors as well as to depositors, the Glass–Steagall Act regulated stock exchanges and the financial operations of holding companies.

In housing, too, the New Deal moved to preserve the concept of private property. The thousand homeowners threatened with foreclosure each month in 1933 were helped to refinance their mortgages through the Home Owners Loan Corporation, established in June 1933. The home construction industry, almost at a standstill in 1933, was revived through the National Housing Act of 1934, which insured loans for home repairs and mortgages for new houses.

Roosevelt hoped to induce inflation through experimental monetary policy measures. There was a retreat from the gold standard, a forced devaluation of the dollar, and a program of gold and silver purchases. He expected currency manipulation, support, and regulation of credit institutions, along with rising prices, to increase business investment.

Despite the talk and promise of inflation, prices did not rise. In part this was due to the reluctance of the Federal Reserve to expand the money supply and in part due to the deflationary impact of fiscal policy. The Economy Act of March 11, 1933, called for major cuts in government spending in an effort to balance the budget. Although Congress restored the cuts, political leaders were slow to understand that government spending was the key to stimulating the economy. Budget deficits were kept small, seen as a problem more than a solution; and, in fact, when production started to show real signs of recovery in 1937, government spending was cut and taxes increased. As a result, production, which in 1937 finally reached 1929 levels for the first time since the stock market crash, dropped precipitously in 1938, and unemployment rose again.[35]

In industry, as in agriculture, New Deal policy sought to regulate prices and output. The National Industrial Recovery Act of 1933 (NIRA) was based on the belief that the economy suffered from overproduction and called on industries to fix prices and limit output. It was designed to meet labor's demand for limited hours of work in order to spread employment and business's demand for the relaxation of antitrust laws in order to stabilize output and raise prices and profits.

Title I of the NIRA established a set of industry codes that would end cutthroat competition, raise prices, limit output, and provide for workers a shorter workweek at a stable wage. Each industry was, in theory, to be regulated by a tripartite committee representing management, labor, and the public. An interim, blanket code was established with the Blue Eagle, as posted by business, as its symbol of acceptance. Within a few weeks, almost 2.5 million employers, with 16 million workers, had signed codes. By September, within three months of the inception of the codes, the ten largest industries were brought under the National Recovery Administration (NRA). All the codes contained minimum wage and maximum hour scales; all contained provisions for collective bargaining. In practice, however, the industry codes reflected the price and output policies of the dominant firms in each industry, and competition restraint operated to the serious disadvantage of small businessmen. When the Supreme Court declared the NRA unconstitutional in May 1935, it was already under severe attack.

Although the economy revived a bit as a result of the NIRA, in 1935, 20 percent of the labor force was still unemployed, industrial output was still far below its 1929 level, and GNP was still far below the level of prosperity. Paralleling the irony of the AAA's curtailment of food production and destruction of livestock when people were starving, the NRA limited competition and output, while much of the public faced daily deprivation.

Watch this video on Roosevelt's advocacy for the National Industrial Recovery Act.

Did Roosevelt pioneer the use of advertising methods to "sell" his program?

https://www.youtube.com/watch?v=Ddti62eYw3U

Title II of the NIRA allocated $3.3 billion for a Public Works Administration (PWA) program. Had this money been used speedily to increase employment and purchasing power, it might have been an extremely helpful stimulant. PWA was intended, however, for capital investment and pump priming. Under the cautious direction of Harold Ickes, its immediate expansionary potential was never realized.

Public Money for Relief

One of the most urgent and immediate problems of Roosevelt's first year in office was the problem of relief. In response, he proposed three types of remedial legislation: (1) grants to states for direct relief, (2) public works programs to stimulate investment, and (3) immediate public employment programs.

Even before the Depression, a large share of relief was paid with public funds, although it was generally administered by voluntary family agencies directly or by family agency workers. This realization stimulated a reconsideration of alignments between voluntary family and public welfare agencies. In effect, the Depression had created a functional crisis for family agencies. These agencies had historically opposed the giving of public relief and the development of public welfare agencies, arguing that they were best equipped to handle relief problems. Now, with the coming of the Depression, they could not meet the financial demands regardless of how much they wanted to help. Furthermore, mushrooming caseloads of newly poor families whose only need was money distracted attention from families requiring professional case-work services.

Noting that the four large family agencies of Manhattan had received, during November 1930, 5,739 applications for "material need" and only 669 other types of applications, social worker Gordon Hamilton admitted that voluntary agencies had "attempted to carry . . . many types of problems which should be carried under public auspices." She suggested the appropriateness of a public family agency geared primarily to offering financial help but also offering casework help when requested by the family. In such a realignment of public–private welfare relationships, "the contribution of private social work to welfare administration is chiefly through urging a professional rather than political considerations in the selection of personnel, the idea of budgeted rather than fixed relief, and the attempt to offer trained casework service to those who desired it."[36]

Even before the Great Depression, relief efforts were dominated by public funds. A compilation of the Department of Statistics of the Russell Sage Foundation of relief expenditures of 81 American cities showed that 74 percent of such expenditures ($31 million) had come from public funds during the last year before the Depression, 1929. Expenditures in 1930 for relief were about double those of in 1929. Seventy-five percent of relief expenditures ($51 million) had come from public funds. An emergency appeal for private funds reduced the share of public relief expenditures to 66 percent during 1931, but public relief expenditures had, nevertheless, increased to $54 million.[37]

By 1931, it was clear, too, that local units of government could not keep pace with the need for public funding. Municipal welfare payments, where they existed, were painfully small. As the Depression deepened, the need for relief increased, and the local relief resources were exhausted in more and more cities and counties.

As governor, Roosevelt had advocated for New York's Temporary Relief Administration in 1931, the first state program to appropriate funds to be disbursed to cities and counties for home-relief and work-relief programs. Other states followed suit so that by the close of 1931, New Jersey, Rhode Island, Illinois, Wisconsin, Ohio, and Pennsylvania had joined New York in making relief funds available to localities. Efforts to obtain federal participation in relief funding also occurred during 1931, but were defeated by presidential veto. These state efforts, and particularly New York's, provided the model for the federal program.

Federal Emergency Relief Administration (FERA)

On May 12, 1933, acting on the overwhelming need of states for money for relief, Congress established FERA to channel a half-billion dollars in relief money through state and local welfare agencies. That same month, the PWA was established as a stimulant to business investment. In November 1933, recognizing the urgent need for jobs, and interpreting flexibly the provisions of the NIRA, President Roosevelt established the Civil Works Administration (CWA) and made $400 million of PWA money available to finance programs of "civil works." Both FERA and CWA came under the direction of Harry Hopkins. When CWA proved too expensive a means of job creation, the Emergency Work Relief Program was established within FERA. Subsequent temporary measures to deal directly with unemployment and the needs of the unemployed led to the creation of the Federal Surplus Commodities Corporation, and the CCC. From the beginning of the New Deal, a three-fold approach to income maintenance was envisioned: cash relief, short-term work relief, and the expansion of employment through the pump-priming effects of public works.

FERA remained the major relief program of the New Deal during its first 2 years. In authorizing direct grants to states for relief, the legislation established a new relationship between the federal government and the states and overturned earlier definitions of federal responsibility (according to the Constitution) to "provide for the general welfare." It was established "to provide for cooperation by the Federal government with the several States and Territories and the District of Columbia in relieving the hardship and suffering caused by unemployment and for other purposes." Half of the appropriation was to be made available to the states on a matching basis—$1 of federal money for every $3 of state and local expenditures; the other $250 million was to be distributed to the states on the basis of need without matching funds.[38]

Of more immediate importance, however, was the speedy flow of cash to the needy. Grants for seven states were approved one day after Hopkins took office in May 1933, and by the end of the following month, $51 million had been paid out to 45 states, the District of Columbia, and the territory of Hawaii. During the last half of 1933, about 3.5 million people were supported, and by the end of December 1933, $324.5 million had been distributed—with all states and territories participating. In the 3 years of its existence, FERA spent more than $3 billion. The states also increased their relief expenditures during this period. In all, something over $4 billion was distributed in cash and work relief by federal and state governments.[39]

Relief money was not always distributed fairly. Racial discrimination in the administration of funds was a major problem. As with other New Deal programs, particularly in Southern rural areas, the black population found it difficult to get on relief rolls. For example, the CCC had racial quotas, the AAA distributed funds based in part on race, and the codes for pay rates of the National Labor Administration discriminated against people of color. Blacks were more apt to receive relief in Northern cities. Overall, they suffered much higher rates of unemployment and poverty, and this was reflected in the relief rolls. In 1933, nearly 18 percent of all black family heads were certified for relief—about twice the rate for white breadwinners.[40]

In part, the shortfalls of the relief effort reflect the speed with which the federal government tried to establish a federal–state public welfare program. The need was widespread and immediate, and the administrators of FERA tried to provide cash to meet that need as quickly as possible. Difficulties arose, too, from a conflict between ideology and necessity. The philosophy of the New Deal was relief for the unemployed through the provision of jobs. Direct relief was to be a temporary, necessary expedient until those who were employable could be employed. For the moment, in the emergency, "employables" and "unemployables" were brought together in one program, but direct relief for the able-bodied was only a stopgap measure.

Hopkins, the president's mentor on welfare matters, had indicated as much in his clarification of the purpose of the Federal Emergency Relief Act. Addressing the National Conference of Social Workers, Hopkins had said:

> The intent of this act is that relief should be given to the heads of families who are out of work and whose dependency arises from the fact that they are out of work, and to transient families, as well as the transient men and women roaming about the country. . . .
>
> Our job is to see that the unemployed get relief, not to develop a great social work organization throughout the United States.[41]

The Second New Deal

The president didn't fully share Hopkins's commitment to relief. As he formulated a second round of social legislation—the Second New Deal—in 1935, cash relief again took a back seat to social insurance and work relief. In proposing a large work relief program, FDR's distaste for relief was evident:

> The Federal Government must and shall quit this business of relief.
> I am not willing that the vitality of our people be further sapped. . . . We must preserve not only the bodies of the unemployed from destitution but also their self-respect, their self-reliance and courage and determination.[42]

However, Roosevelt's condemnation of relief as the "subtle destroyer of the human spirit" did not lead him to ignore government's important role in social welfare.[43] To the contrary, he contrasted cash relief with the positive role that work relief and social insurance should play for Americans. Roosevelt established the Committee on Economic Security to develop a permanent plan of income security for individuals and families. The committee's recommendations were to echo the president's belief that promoting the economic security of the public did not conflict with the preservation of a market economy.

In his congressional message of January 4, 1935, President Roosevelt had separated the productive from the nonproductive poor, accepting primary responsibility for the former, the group that was "the victim of a nation-wide depression caused by conditions which were not local but national."[44] Approximately 5 million families and single people were then on the relief rolls. FERA estimated that 3.5 million of these recipients were employable, and FDR was determined to give them employment "pending their absorption in a rising tide of private employment." Although not abandoning the additional 1.5 million people remaining on the relief rolls, he nevertheless stated his intention that those who in the past had been "dependent upon local efforts" be maintained again "by State, by counties, by towns, by cities, by churches, and by private welfare agencies."

The New Deal sought to use social insurance—unemployment compensation—as a substitute for cash relief for the unemployed. As the Committee on Economic Security was developing such a plan, the president's interim solution was the establishment of the Works Progress Administration (WPA) to "supersede the Federal Emergency Relief Administration with a coordinated authority . . . charged with the orderly liquidation of our present relief activities and the substitution of a national chart for the giving of work." As for those who could not work, said the president, "I stand ready through my personal efforts, and through the public influence of the office that I hold, to help these local agencies to get the means necessary to assume this burden."[45]

The WPA, funded in 1935 at $4.9 billion, actually spent more than twice that amount in its lifetime. Eventually, it provided jobs for 8 million Americans in a wide range of activities, from heavy construction to the painting of murals in local libraries and orchestral performances in schools. For those for whom jobs were provided, life was much improved. Wages were higher than relief payments, and there was no deterrent income eligibility test. But work projects got underway slowly, and many employables never found work at all.

The federal government did not immediately substitute work relief for all cash relief. Congress did not pass the Emergency Appropriation Act until April 1935, and the act included requested funds to cover a period of transition from cash relief to work relief. The work was constituted by executive order in May, and Hopkins was appointed its administrator. Actual liquidation of FERA did not begin until the closing months of the year, and the final emergency relief grants went out to the states in December 1935.

By the end of 1935, with the phasing out of federal participation in direct relief underway, with the inability or unwillingness of many states to replace the lost funds, and with the transfer of employables to WPA projects slower than had been contemplated, the transition period became a "bitter one for families on relief in many parts of the country."[46] The problem was exacerbated by the slowness with which the public assistance programs of the Social Security Act—programs designed to help some categories of unemployables—were implemented by the states.

Social workers were wary of the phasing out of federal funding for direct relief. Some had been catalysts for the organization of client groups of which they were themselves members. Many had a personal and professional intimacy with problems resulting from unemployment and a new understanding of poverty and the poor.[47]

Private agencies were not able to pick up the slack even as much as they had prior to 1933 because the events of the Depression had begun to define a new role for them. Hopkins's administration of FERA had formalized the changed relationship between public and voluntary family agencies. Regulation No. 1 of the *Rules and Regulations* promulgated by FERA required that public relief funds be administered by public agencies. Recognition was given to the thousands of private family and child welfare agency workers who had helped with the administration of public funds, but Regulation No. 1 required that they be designated as public officials working under the control of public authority.[48] The process by which private family agencies had already begun to delineate the uniqueness of their service was now accelerated and suddenly required consideration of alignments not only with public agencies, but also with private child welfare agencies.

FERA's Regulation No. 3 clarified further the separation of public and private agencies in regard to administering public relief funds. At the same time, the regulation revealed the extent to which public officials were influenced by private agency experience. Regulation No. 3 required the investigation and the demonstration of need on the part of the individual family. Means testing and budgeting to ensure that "no relief is given to persons unless they are actually in need and that such relief . . . is adjusted to . . . actual needs"[49] was the outcome. The use of trained and experienced investigators, at least in supervisory positions, regular home visiting, and attention to state relative responsibility laws, were required.

FERA's *Rules and Regulations* represented an advance in standard-setting over pre-Depression approaches to public giving. They also established certain operating principles that would have negative consequences in later years: administrative discretion, rather than legal definitions, for establishing eligibility for aid; a professional casework service orientation toward relief giving; and a subtly pervading, if unnoted, reservation that relief was somehow a necessary evil. For the moment, however, people were helped, and their need was of primary importance. Hopkins stated:

> We are now dealing with people of all classes. It is no longer a matter of unemployables and chronic dependents, but of your friends and mine who are involved in this. Everyone of us knows some family of our friends which is or should be getting relief.[50]

Hopkins's statement, his administration of FERA, and his realization that "however well this thing is administered, this enormous relief business can never be anything more than a makeshift"[51] set the stage for a major shift in the federal approach to income maintenance. The change had several facets. For the short run, there had been a switch in the allocation of federal funds to employment—work relief—programs and a return to the states of responsibility for the direct relief of unemployables. For the long run, there were to be permanent social security programs.

The Social Security Act

The Social Security Act, signed into law by President Roosevelt on August 15, 1935, was the major legislative achievement of the New Deal. It was a landmark in American political and social history, reflecting a public commitment to the economic rights of people and, consequently, extending federal responsibility for social welfare. The act, from the point of view of program provisions, administrative structuring, and federal–state fiscal arrangements, represented a watershed for the mingling of old and new orientations toward people as social and economic beings.

During the early decades of the 20th century, Congress considered, but did not accept, plans to provide old age and unemployment insurance. By 1935, however, demographic, economic, and political pressures for federal action were overwhelming.

The aged as a percentage of the population were increasing at twice the rate of general population growth as life expectancy rose and birthrates fell. They suffered severe unemployment and for the most part had little in the way of savings to fall back upon. Existing state pensions reached only 5 percent of the aged and, in any case, were unable to provide anywhere near adequate support. Private pensions were virtually nonexistent. The elderly and their adult children were faced with an unbearable burden. Roosevelt's Advisory Council on Economic Security noted that:

> Many children who previously supported their parents have been compelled to cease doing so, and the great majority will probably never resume this load. . . . The Depression has deprived millions of workers past middle life of their jobs. . . . Regardless of what may be done to improve their condition, this cost of supporting the aged will continue to increase. In another generation it will be at least double the present total.[52]

The Social Security Act evolved from the work of the Committee on Economic Security, which submitted its report to the president on January 15, 1935. The report was accompanied by drafts of bills representing an expedient "piecemeal approach" whose primary aim was "the assurance of an adequate income to each human being in childhood, youth, middle age, or old age in sickness or in health."[53] Within an overall recommendation that the federal government assume responsibility for employment assurance, the committee made specific recommendations in regard to security against the risks of unemployment, retirement in old age, and ill health. Additional recommendations provided for the current security of old people and children through the provision of federally aided, state-administered pensions. Finally, the committee recommended an array of employment, health, educational, and rehabilitative services. Many of these were to be administered by the states, with standard setting to be stimulated by the federal government through the offer of financial and other types of assistance.

Having made sweeping recommendations in regard to federal involvement in a program of assurances against the hazards of life, the committee recognized the need for residual relief for "genuine unemployables—or near unemployables." The committee commended the care and guidance of this group to the states—and to social workers:

> With the Federal Government carrying so much burden for pure unemployment, the State and local governments . . . should resume responsibility for relief. The families that have always been partially or wholly dependent on others for support can best be assisted through the tried procedures of social casework, with its individualized treatment.[54]

President Roosevelt recommended the committee's report to Congress as the basis for legislation. His message emphasized the soundness of the committee's proposals and the caution with which they should be considered.

> The detailed report of the Committee sets forth a series of proposals that will appeal to the sound sense of the American people. It has not attempted the impossible nor

has it failed to exercise sound caution and consideration of all the factors concerned: the national credit, the rights and responsibilities of States, the capacity of industry to assume financial responsibilities and the fundamental necessity of proceeding in a manner that will merit enthusiastic support of citizens of all sorts.[55]

The president's sense of fiscal and political realities led him to specify legislative principles that necessarily emphasized a modest beginning program of social insurance: no health insurance, no federal administration of relief programs, state leadership in unemployment compensation and public assistance, and no use of the general revenues for old age insurance. Not unexpectedly, then, the Social Security laws, when enacted, were more conservative than the recommendations of the Committee on Economic Security.

The policy of the United States in regard to permanent programs of income maintenance was stated in the preamble to the Social Security Act of 1935:

> An Act to provide for the general welfare by establishing a system of Federal old-age benefits, and by enabling the several States to make more adequate provision for aged persons, blind persons, dependent and crippled children, maternal and child welfare, public health, and the administration of their unemployment compensation laws.[56]

The law's program provisions covered loss of income due to unemployment (Unemployment Compensation), inability to participate in the labor force due to age or disability (Federal Old Age Insurance, Old Age Assistance, Aid to the Blind, Aid to Dependent Children [ADC]), the promotion of the welfare of mothers and children (Maternal and Child Health Services, Services for Crippled Children, Child Welfare Services), and the encouragement of adequate state and local public health services. Provisions for the extension and improvement of maternal and child health services offered by local health authorities restored programs that had languished or collapsed when the Sheppard–Towner Act had been permitted to expire in 1929.

Coverage for health care remained Social Security's unfinished business for the next 75 years. Successive administrations and Congresses entertained proposals for closing the gap, which ultimately led to the enactment of Medicare and Medicaid in 1965 and the Affordable Care Act in 2010. In future years, as the economics and politics of health care became more complex, the failure to include health insurance in the 1935 act closed off possibilities for the emergence of a rational and comprehensive approach to health care.

Expanding Social Security: The 1939 Amendments

The enactment of Federal Old Age Insurance and Grants to States for Unemployment Compensation in 1935 recognized flaws in the country's private enterprise market system and the need for institutional change to mitigate unavoidable economic and social distress. Insurance against the hazards of unemployment and of retirement in old age bolstered the security of beneficiaries and of the private enterprise system itself because these institutional reforms, aimed at meeting universal needs, guaranteed permanent economic stabilizers for both.

The structure of Social Security was meant to fit the demographic and market structure of most families: one wage earner, working full time for a full year with just a few employers during a working life. It was a model for an industrial economy. In future years, changes in family life—increasing divorce rates, declining widowhood, and the expansion of married women's labor force participation—exposed flaws in the program's structure. They also revealed the difficulties in reforming a program that influenced the expectations of a large share of the adult population. Liberals were frustrated by the constraints on program expansion, and conservatives discovered roadblocks in their efforts to privatize the program.

Social insurance started out closely modeled on private insurance, with benefits tightly tied to contributions. Although the 1935 law was conservative, the 1939 amendments added benefits for the spouses and children of deceased workers and expanded the number of workers covered by old age insurance. The formula for calculating benefits was adjusted to become more redistributive in its structure.

The desire to model social insurance after private insurance programs was reflected in the concept of a reserve fund to hold the assets of the program. A trust fund is essentially a bookkeeping mechanism for specifying that particular revenues be related to specific programs. The original concept in 1935 was to establish a fund in accordance with accepted actuarial principles; at any time, the fund should be large enough to pay off all future obligations. But by 1939, Congress began to worry that the assets might grow too large. The law required Social Security assets to be invested exclusively in special issues of U.S. government bonds. The fear was that there would not be enough government debt for appropriate investment. After 1939, the trustees abandoned a full actuarial reserve to a partial or contingency reserve fund that would build assets to meet needs for a limited period of time.

The 1935 Social Security Act and its 1939 amendments had many flaws. Many workers, including domestic workers and farm laborers, were excluded from coverage (a problem that was addressed only in 1950). In addition, other common sources of poverty, including disability and the desertion of one's spouse, were ignored by its insurance provisions.

Although it was hard to see at the time, the greatest flaw of the Social Security Act was its construction of a two-class social welfare system. Workers who were regularly employed in established industries were protected against the major risks of an industrial society—old age, unemployment, and (eventually) disability. Workers with less stable industries would continue to rely on the old poor law system for aid. The decisions of Congress to exclude the major industries that employed African Americans—domestic and farm labor—quickly imposed a racial division on this class structure.[57]

Although it was hard to see at the time, the greatest flaw of the Social Security Act was its construction of a two-class social welfare system.

Public Assistance

Although the Depression had obscured the line between the worthy and unworthy poor, the New Deal often revived this division. The Social Security Act established a dual system for federally supported income maintenance. The result for the country was a three-part approach to public relief. The act provided for federally administered insurance programs and federally aided, state-administered assistance programs for selected groups. The grant-in-aid, state-administered financial assistance programs served to separate again the old poor from the new. The new poor, the unemployed, were covered by social insurance and the old "worthy" poor by categorical public assistance. Left to the states was the third group, the "unworthy" poor, for whom states and localities were to develop programs without federal aid.

The creation of federally aided categories of assistance evolved from longtime state efforts to help certain classes of the poor whose circumstances could not readily be attributed to personal inadequacy and who, therefore, were not to be stigmatized as recipients of the dole. State provisions of aid for the aged, the blind, and the widowed were generally viewed as pensions without stigma. By 1935, aid to the blind was available in 24 states; aid to the aged in 34 states; and aid to mothers in all states and jurisdictions except Alabama, Georgia, and South Carolina. The decision of Congress to lend federal support for the beneficiaries of these programs acknowledged the legitimacy of their claim. Besides, many policy makers believed that public assistance would eventually wither away as federal measures for social insurance, maternal and child welfare, and public health work took hold.[58]

The contrast between the act's social insurance and public assistance programs was striking. While old age insurance became a federal responsibility, Congress chose to allow states to continue to define their own welfare policies, albeit with increased federal funding and oversight. By focusing federal aid on specific categories of the needy—the elderly, the blind, and dependent children—the Social Security Act reinforced earlier policy decisions for differentiating these groups from the able-bodied poor. Indeed, until 1950, mothers of dependent children did not qualify for their own grant.

Still, the public assistance titles of the Social Security Act were not simply a return to older policy traditions. The federal public assistance categories were community-oriented, in that they required that recipients be living in their own homes. Furthermore, the Social Security Act defined assistance as "money payments," requiring that grants be made in cash. Finally, the act mandated the opportunity for a fair hearing for any individual whose claim for assistance was denied. In future years, Supreme Court decisions would use this mandate to broaden residents' welfare rights.

Federal oversight of public assistance pushed recalcitrant states—especially in the South—to bring greater transparency and professionalism to their assistance programs. The act required states to submit plans making assistance programs mandatory in all political subdivisions, appointing a single state agency responsible for administering or supervising the state's assistance program, ensuring the efficiency of state program administration, and guaranteeing compliance with the Social Security Board's regulations and reporting requirements. Of equal significance was that the federal government pushed states to reduce or eliminate burdensome residency requirements, a break with public assistance's Poor Law legacy. For all the differences still possible under its essentially permissive requirements, the act did succeed in bringing the federally funded public assistance programs to all the states and in giving the various programs an identifiable common base.

The Social Security Act had profound significance for family welfare generally, and for the roles of family members in particular. For women, the addition to Old Age Insurance of dependents' benefits in 1939 reinforced their roles as wives and homemakers. Despite the increase in the labor-force participation of women, the act did not cover many traditionally female jobs. It penalized heavily for interrupted employment and compensated inadequately for pay discrimination. Thus, over the years, many women workers discovered that their contributions to Social Security counted for nothing, because their spousal benefits were higher than those they had earned through work.

For the larger society, Old Age Insurance and Old Age Assistance meant that a major portion of the financial burden of caring for aged parents was lifted from adult children. The money thus freed could be shifted to the care of minor children. The adequacy of ADC benefits was questionable from the start.

The Committee on Economic Security had described mothers' pensions as "defensive measures for children."

> They are designed to release from the wage-earning role the person whose natural function is to give her children the physical and affectionate guardianship necessary not alone to keep them from falling into social misfortune, but more affirmatively to rear them into citizens capable of contributing to society.[59]

Despite the committee's encouragement and the seeming popularity of Mothers' Aid among the states, the social work profession gave limited attention to ADC during congressional hearings. Katherine Lenroot, chief of the Children's Bureau,[60] and Jacob Kepecs, president of the Child Welfare League (CWL) of America,[61] were the only social workers to testify in favor the new program.[62] Edwin Witte, executive for the committee, stated after the passage of the Social Security Act that the poor outcome of provisions for dependent children, as compared to provisions for other needy groups, was mainly due to this lack of interest.[63]

The inattention to provisions for dependent children resulted, first, in the administration of ADC along with the adult categories of assistance, instead of the Children's Bureau as originally intended. Second, as the title "aid to dependent children" suggested, caretakers did not receive their own grant until 1950. Third, the grant-in-aid formula limited federal payments to one-third of a total of $18 per month per family provided for one dependent and to one-third of $12 per month provided for additional dependent children. The formula contrasted sharply with that used for Old Age Assistance. In the latter instance, the federal government offered payment monthly of one-half of $30 for each eligible person. The contrast between the provisions for dependent children and for the aged and the blind foreshadowed future development of the programs. Aid for the elderly and blind (later expanded to include people with disabilities) would eventually become full federal programs with more generous benefits, while ADC—equated with welfare—experienced repeated attacks at the federal and state levels for the next six decades and was eventually scrapped.

ADC retained mother's pensions' bias toward divorced or unmarried women. The older, states' Mothers' Aid programs, for the most part, did not provide for payments for children born out of wedlock. Many social workers felt unprepared either to accept these clients or to fight for them. By June 1938, 604,142 children in 40 states were being helped by ADC. It is estimated that less than 4 percent of these children lived with unmarried mothers. Sixteen percent of the reporting states had not accepted any children of unwed mothers.

The low coverage rate reflects the unwillingness to move from the old Mothers' Aid to the less restrictive coverage. While neither the Social Security Act nor the Social Security Board regulations restrict coverage to children of unmarried mothers, the decision to give localities administrative authority for ADC assured that older, moralistic interpretation of "immoral" women would influence who received benefits. In a 1939 article, Mary S. Labaree noted the variation in local policies:

> There is surprising little of a censorious attitude towards girls with limited opportunities in our mountain counties. . . . Give aid to dependent children . . . to an unmarried mother from an undesirable home but . . . consider . . . the unmarried from a good family with good background has committed an inexcusable act.
>
> Any mother is considered fit to care for her child unless she is so unfit that a petition for neglect should be filed.
>
> If all the children in a family were illegitimate the commission would decide this was not a fit mother. If only one or two were illegitimate it might be overlooked or forgiven.
>
> It is a matter of state policy that the parent must not have had an out-of-wedlock child within a year.[64]

Local administration also assured racial discrimination in the public assistance. As with other New Deal programs, Southern senators and congressmen provided decisive votes for many pieces of New Deal legislation, but the price of their support was to allow their states to discriminate against African Americans. Local control became the most convenient mechanism for allowing discrimination without violating the Constitution. With congressional authority, local welfare administrators denied benefits to most eligible African Americans. In some rural counties, ADC was used to support families when plantation owners didn't need workers and then cut off during planting and harvesting seasons. As one field supervisor put it, "Communities . . . see no reason why the employable Negro mother should not continue her usually sketchy seasonal labor or indefinite domestic service rather than receive a public-assistance grant."[65] From its start, the economics of the marketplace, concepts of morality and appropriate sexual behavior, and racism combined to limit the scope and the effectiveness of this program.

The Social Security Act of 1935 put federal social welfare policy on its trajectory for the remainder of the 20th century. The division between insurance programs that were "earned" and assistance programs that were not grew stronger during the next 50 years. The groups that received insurance coverage, including people with disabilities who were added to the program in 1956, saw their poverty rates decline steadily between 1940 and 2000. Over the same years, poor mothers and their children were left behind; their proportion of all poor people increased steadily in subsequent decades.

The Changing Role of the Social Work Profession

Thus the attitude of the social work and social welfare community toward the Social Security Act as a family welfare measure is noteworthy. The act itself had been approved on August 15, 1935, but federal funds did not become available until February 1936. Beyond that, the process of having states submit plans for the administration of public assistance and of having those plans approved by the newly created Public Assistance Board proved slow. By mid-November 1936, 42 states had finally received grants for Old Age Assistance. Only 26 states had received grants for ADC, bearing out the lack of concern for this group of recipients. The states, in their reluctance to move into this category of assistance, reflected the attitude of the federal government in its differential treatment of children.

All in all, social workers were alarmed by the course of events, and the delegate conference of the American Association of Social Workers, held in Washington, D.C., February 14–16, 1936, considered carefully "this business of relief." The delegates gave public hearing to a number of convictions and concerns.[66]

1. That the factors that made relief necessary were demoralizing, not the act of receiving relief itself
2. That the work provided by WPA should be productive in itself and not just a technique for avoiding idleness
3. That need should be the criterion for federal assistance and that separating employables from unemployables left the matter to the uncertain mercies of states and localities
4. That there was a residual relief problem caused by the fact that WPA work relief payments were inadequate to cover the needs of large families and by the fact that some groups were not covered by the federally aided public assistance categories at all
5. That permissive requirements for state participation in federally aided public assistance programs threatened irresponsibility

The dissatisfaction expressed at the delegate conference did not alter the course of events. The collapse of social work's pressure for a return to a federal program geared primarily to direct relief seems first of all due to the political odds against such a return but also to a conflict among social workers as to their professional view of the poor and of the needs of the poor.

Aubrey Williams, deputy administrator for the WPA, expressed his bewilderment and concern at the "growing disposition on the part of social workers to advocate the return of the federal government to direct relief." He implied that this pressure resulted from the tendency on their part to see caseworkers as necessary to the poor and casework as a necessary adjunct to poor relief. "To put caseworkers into the old poor relief system," Williams argued, "is to put new wine into old bottles that will crack." He warned that the demolition of the WPA would give social workers "3.5 million people on direct relief and nothing else" and, in a final thrust, said that "the sooner social work as a profession can turn its back on direct relief as a valid form of social treatment, the better off will be the nation and the higher the standing of social work."[67] Like Hopkins back in 1933, Williams seemed to be saying that federal programs should not be used "to develop a great social work organization throughout the United States." Those who led the attack against the WPA could not easily dismiss the accusation.

Having been admonished by Williams to think of new approaches to unemployment and income security, the delegates were also treated to Ewan Clague's description of the potentialities of the provisions of the Social Security Act.[68] Perhaps because it did join, no matter how uneasily, new social insurance and old public relief measures, the act offered some satisfaction to those social workers who had urged social reform through social insurance and to those who urged reform through the professionalization of relief giving.

During the early years of the Depression, social workers clarified their own views about relief and about people who needed financial help. The professional literature between 1930 and 1935 abounds with discussion and controversy. One issue, federal versus state and local responsibility for relief, was settled quite easily. State and local coffers were empty. The issue of public versus private responsibility for relief was similarly resolved. A third issue was that of cash versus in kind. In 1933, Dorothy Kahn, director of the Philadelphia County Relief Board and soon to become chairman of the American Association of Social Workers, made "an ardent appeal for one form [of relief giving], namely, cash."[69] As demonstrated by the categorical programs of the Social Security Act, the proponents of cash payments won the day. The literature would suggest that social workers believed the issue of right versus privilege as a basis for financial aid to have been settled in favor of the right to assistance. Certainly, this was true for the social insurances whose benefits were related to worker contributions. As for the categorical programs, the Social Security Act's use of the word *claim* in connection with the receipt of benefits distributed in cash and the right to a fair hearing both indicated an entitlement to public assistance, no matter how conditioned that entitlement might be. Hopkins thought the federal administering agency, along with state and local boards, would pass benefits on "as a pension without stigma."[70]

Perhaps most important to an understanding of the fate of ADC was the issue of social insurance versus public assistance. Although both types of programs were included in the Social Security Act, the reality was that the social insurance mechanism was favored as an approach to income security. The strengthening of the work ethic by relating premiums and benefits to earnings and the attempted simulation of actuarial, private insurance soundness (with almost no contribution from the general revenue) was designed to ensure the political attractiveness of social insurance.

Of course, the current unemployment crisis required public relief programs, but whatever fears remained about supporting public, non-work-related programs could be allayed with the belief that such programs would wither away. The need for Old Age Assistance would disappear as Old Age Insurance matured and covered an increasing number of workers. Of importance, too, was the fact that survivors of workers, although not sufficiently provided for, had not been entirely forgotten. The Committee on Economic Security had recommended that a death benefit be paid to a worker's surviving dependents should the worker die before the age of 65 or before the amount of his own contributions had been paid to him as an annuity.[71] The committee had also given consideration to the future when "families and widows would be given primary consideration in broad plans for survivors' insurance or insurance for widows and orphans."[72] The Social Security Act did in fact provide for a lump sum benefit to survivors as recommended by the Committee on Economic Security. There was reason to believe that insurance coverage eventually would be extended to widows and orphans and that ADC, like Old Age Assistance, would fade in significance. Perhaps that is one reason why the Senate and House committees heard only perfunctory social work support for ADC and little social work criticism of its deficiencies as a program.

New Alignments in Social Welfare

An exploration of social work's attitude toward ADC must take into account that the Depression required social workers to clarify not only their views about relief and relief recipients but also alignments between public and private social welfare. Inevitably, this meant a reconsideration of the functions of professional social work. Regulation No. 1 had begun the reversal of a tradition whereby voluntary agencies shaped the contribution of public agencies to social welfare. The enactment of the Social Security Act furthered the process and established the dominance of public welfare. The impact on voluntary agencies—on voluntary family agencies, in particular—was enormous. Voluntary family agencies and family agency personnel had impeded the development of public welfare prior to the Depression. And, despite their beginning development of casework as a professional methodology and of family counseling as a professional function, they had remained absorbed with problems of relief giving. With the onset of the Depression, they became involved in cooperative efforts to help families needing relief because of the unemployment crisis, and their day-to-day practice consisted chiefly of relief-related activities. The FWAA described the extent of its member agencies' involvement:

> Every good public program owes something to the pioneer work of private agencies. . . . Private agencies have readily loaned or released trained persons for service in public agencies, often at a great cost to their own programs. Supervisory and advisory aid have been accorded continuously by many private agencies to public agencies. In addition . . . private agencies have also engaged actively in obtaining general support of public welfare programs.[73]

Now, with the passage of the Social Security Act, family agencies seemed devoid of a viable social welfare function. Family agency workers, who in large measure carried the professional status for social work, seemed similarly affected. Both agencies and workers needed to find a raison d'être, and perhaps the knowledge of this, as much as anything else, underlay the heated discussions of public welfare at the February 1936 delegate conference of the American Association of Social Workers. The apparent collapse of organized social work support for unemployment relief suggests a perception that professional social work practice and relief giving were separate entities, however overlapping their concerns.

This recognition was confirmed in March 1936, when the FWAA published a report of responses by member agencies to questions related to "the crisis in community programs." Of the 93 agencies responding, agreed that "it would be folly for private agencies . . . to attempt to meet any appreciable part of the unemployment relief burden . . . being abandoned by the Federal Government." They agreed that it was essential "to hold firmly to the principle that intensive casework treatment is the primary function of a family service organization." Nevertheless, when asked to list developments of new or more clearly defined channels of services to the community, the agencies gave "a great variety of answers which constitute[d] a confusing picture." Many listed their emphasis on "intensive casework" as a new development.[74]

The extent to which voluntary agencies were threatened by the Social Security Act's establishment of a permanent public welfare structure and by the vacuum created by the loss of a primary relief-giving responsibility can also be discerned from FWAA's report of responses to its questionnaire. When asked what they were doing to rally community support for public welfare, one-third of the respondents expressed interest in helping but were inactive; another one-third were indifferent. Perhaps they felt all the more upset by the fact that the problem was again largely of their own making. If earlier they had impeded the development of an adequate public sector of social welfare, now they must share responsibility for the existence of a permanent, powerful establishment they could not control. Furthermore, the existence of such an establishment required change at the core of the voluntary agency.

Despite the frequent reference in the social work literature to a "right to assistance," this view was inconsistent with the philosophy that guided the development of voluntary social welfare. The latter had begun with an assumption of a character flaw for which— as with man's original fall—man was himself responsible. This view of human nature as essentially evil and of society as the blameless victim of human frailty led to religious, eventually voluntary, social welfare efforts to change the human being. The Protestant ethic was particularly concerned with work, thrift, and financial independence. When voluntary social welfare secularized this ethic, the family agency tied social work practice and relief giving into a single package. Public welfare was to be avoided at all costs.

The Depression of the 1930s revolutionized conventional thinking about social need. The discovery that people could be unemployed and in need through no fault of their own led, first, to an admission of fault in the economic and social system and, second, to a conception of the individual-at-risk in the system. Society, therefore, had an obligation to help. In such a circumstance, financial need was truly secularized—one might say publicized—and the need for public welfare was inherent. Furthermore, the acceptance of social responsibility for financial need led quite naturally to the depersonalization of relief giving. Relief recipients needed money, not service. They did not require the skill of professional service and could best be helped by government aid administered objectively. Federal and state aid represented a decision to separate financial assistance and service provision.

Voluntary social agencies renewed efforts to define a unique professional service function. The widespread dissemination of Freudian theory demonstrating the significance of parent–child relationships brought home the psychological underpinnings of family survival. Having moved away from providing relief for families, voluntary family agencies moved to the further development of highly skilled "casework treatment to assist individuals in removing their own handicaps." The Freudian symbiotic tie of parent to child suggested family, rather than individual, treatment, and attention was focused on the relationship between voluntary family and children's agencies and on the possibility of their merging.

In November 1937, the FWAA distributed an outline of points discussed in meetings of its Committee on Relationship between Family and Children's Work in a meeting of that committee with a similar committee of the CWL of America.

In considering the relationship between family and children's case work . . . it is evident that they have the same roots in social case work, as far as the basic knowledge and equipment of the case worker are concerned. . . .

Any family case work agency is also a children's case work agency, in the sense that it has the same obligation for skilled treatment of the problems of children in families as it does for meeting the needs of adults. Any children's case work agency, dealing with children in their own homes or in foster homes, is or should be a family case work agency, in so far as it attempts to treat children's needs in relation to the family setting, or to deal with those difficulties in family relationships that affect the child.[75]

Relationships between voluntary family and children's agencies would be the subject of controversy throughout the 1940s and 1950s; but already in 1937, mergers between family and children's agencies were considered because of similarities in method and overlaps in their clients. As casework with individuals eclipsed social work with groups and communities, differences between family and children's agencies seemed less important. In the *Social Work Year Book, 1951*, Frank J. Hertel reported:

> Figures available to FSAA [Family Service Association of America] over the past eight years show that the number of its member agencies engaging in this multiple service [family and child welfare services] increased from 46 in 1942 to 82 (33 percent of the member agencies) by the close of 1949. Of these, 42 had expanded their services to include child placement, whereas 40 represented the merging of two or more agencies . . . to provide the services formerly considered special to each.[76]

By 1960, the number of merged family and children's agencies holding common membership in FSAA and CWL had risen to 60. In 1974, FSAA and CWL were themselves considering a merger, which they finally rejected.

At the same time that there was a strong trend toward the merging of concerns of family and child welfare agencies, specialized services for each appeared in response to the strains the Depression put on family life. Marital counseling emerged as a particular concern, and the first marriage clinic opened in 1930. A variety of family support programs—visiting housekeepers and parent education programs, to name just two—developed and the number of child guidance clinics increased.

> **?** Assess your comprehension of "Innovations in Social Welfare" by completing this quiz.

MASS MOVEMENTS DURING THE 1930S

Through most of American history, social movements served as a bellwether of future developments in social welfare and social justice concerns. Often, decades would pass between the emergence of a social movement and the realization of its objectives. Indeed, many social movements of the Progressive Era saw their ambitions fulfilled during the New Deal.

The 1930s were unique, however, in that a number of social movements enjoyed a more direct impact on social legislation. Two factors contributed to this success. First, the scope of the economic and social emergency served both to dramatize the problems and broaden the appeal of social movements. Second, the economic emergency provoked an institutional crisis that allowed ideas that would typically have been excluded from "respectable" consideration to receive a hearing. The role of social movements in the New Deal was particularly significant in its early years, when (what one historian called) "thunder on the left" drove the New Deal agenda to a more radical policy agenda than it had previously considered.

The immediate institutional impact of the "thunder" was a massive shift in the composition of Congress. After the 1930 elections, Republicans still controlled both houses of Congress; but 4 years later, Democrats held a 69–25 majority in the Senate and a 322–117 majority in the House of Representatives. Many Democrats were newly elected members who were committed to taking stronger steps to address the emergency.

The major social movements of the period focused on the distress experienced by veterans, older Americans, and the labor movement. Less successful efforts included the organization of unemployment councils in many American cities and the Communist Party.

Veterans and the Bonus

The Depression years were years of distress for veterans as for others, but the difference was that their visibility as veterans and as a strongly organized constituency meant a continuing ability to elicit special consideration. Almost immediately after World War I, veterans began pushing for a bonus that would provide an economic redress to balance the wartime earnings of workers in industry. A bill making such provisions in the form of "adjustment compensation certificates" was passed over President Calvin Coolidge's veto in 1924. Payments were to come due in 1945. By 1930, with unemployment mounting, demands for immediate payment began to be made. The demand culminated in June 1932 in the "bonus march" on Washington, DC, of some 15,000 to 20,000 veterans, many accompanied by their families. The march ended a month later when, on the order of President Hoover, army troops were dispatched to clear the veterans from their Washington campsites. However, despite Hoover's objections and over his veto, Congress passed a bill allowing veterans to obtain, in cash, half the value of the certificates.

Smaller bonus marches were attempted in 1933 and 1934, but with little immediate success. Payment of the bonus was made in 1937, the year of a disastrous reversal of the long climb out of the Depression. The bonus succeeded in putting almost $3.5 billion into the hands of veterans and, eventually, into the nation's economy.

Veterans' social welfare policy led to confrontations between Congress and the Roosevelt administration. The bonus marches of 1933 and 1934 were triggered by the Economy Act of March 1933, the same act that had cut congressional salaries and reduced federal expenditures. The act also cut the amount of veteran's benefits and the number of eligible recipients. Especially hard hit were thousands of veterans who needed care for nonservice-connected conditions and who were unemployed because of the Depression. The resulting outcry was such that in 1934, Congress passed new legislation that in effect rescinded the Economy Act. The expansion of veterans' cash, medical, and hospital benefits led President Roosevelt to veto the bill, but it became law when both houses of Congress voted to override the veto. In connection with the provisions for money payments, the new legislation stressed the word *compensation* to define the uniqueness of such payments to veterans.

Veterans were given special attention in the matter of job opportunities, too. From the bonus armies of 1933 and 1934, more than 10,000 veterans— transients stranded in Washington—were enrolled in the CCC and assigned to work camps. Additional camps were established by the FERA for veterans whose physical condition made them ineligible for CCC camps. Still other veterans were assigned to WPA projects. In all, some 17,000 veterans were certified by the Veterans Administration for CCC, FERA, or WPA employment between 1933 and 1935.[77] The bonus payment of 1937 was, of course, of much greater significance because of the number of individuals reached and the dollar amount of benefits received. The bonus concept, joined to the benefit structure of the veterans' legislation of 1934, set a pattern that would influence veterans' legislation during and after World War II.

Older Americans

There was strong political pressure for the federal government to act to provide old age insurance. In California, the Townsend movement, a major lobby for aged pensions under the direction of Francis E. Townsend, gained enormous support with its demand for a $200-a-month pension for all over the age of 60, provided they left the labor market and spent the money. There were many other popular schemes. The Old Folks Picnic Association, End Poverty in California (EPIC), the Ham and Eggs movement, and many others suggested a variety of plans for helping the aging that ranged from free fishing licenses to monthly payments of $400. The proposal of Senator Huey Long of Louisiana to "share our wealth" and provide a minimum income of $5,000 a year for all received enthusiastic support around the nation. Overall, popular pressure pushed the Roosevelt administration to adopt a moderate pension plan for the aged.[78]

> **Watch this video on social movements during the 1930s.**
>
> In what ways did labor, African Americans, and artists exert pressure on the Roosevelt administration?

Labor and Social Welfare

Perhaps the most significant and long-lasting result of the experiment in industrial control was its impact on organized labor and the precedent for social legislation it established. As the United States entered the 1930s and economic depression, labor was largely unorganized. Union gains made during World War I were lost in a postwar environment of generally steady employment, increasing real wages, and political repression. Furthermore, the American Federation of Labor (AFL), representing skilled labor, tended to cooperate with management in a "welfare capitalism" effort. Ignored by that effort was the great mass of unskilled workers in the basic manufacturing industries. Trade union membership declined from 5 million in 1920 to 3.4 million in 1930; membership in the AFL declined from 4.1 million in 1920 to 3 million in 1930.[79] The violent and largely unsuccessful strikes led by the United Mine Workers in 1921 and 1922 and by the United Textile Workers in 1929 further weakened organized labor as the Depression settled in.

The fortunes of labor began to turn in 1932 with the passage of the Norris–LaGuardia Act, which restricted the right of the federal courts to issue injunctions against unions engaged in peaceful strikes and to enforce "yellow dog" contracts. In 1933, the newly formulated codes of the NRA reaffirmed the right of collective bargaining in covered industries, established the 44-hour week, outlawed child labor, and set minimum wages ranging from 30 to 40 cents an hour. The policy rationale for these provisions was to maintain wages at the same time that the elimination of child labor and the reduction in working hours spread jobs among a larger number of adult workers. Falling wages stimulated workers to organize and unions to recruit membership. By 1935, union membership had grown to 3.7 million.[80]

Although the most lasting policy outcome of labor mobilization was the National Labor Relations (Wagner) Act of 1935, much of the most militant union activity took place before the Supreme Court declared the Wagner Act constitutional in 1937. Longshoreman on the West Coast and truck drivers in Minneapolis called general strikes in 1934 that paralyzed American cities. The same year, the autoworkers used the "sit-down strike"—occupying factories to prevent the use of strikebreakers—to wrest concessions from General Motors in Flint, Michigan. Their actions sparked a nationwide wave of sit-down strikes that subsided only when the Wagner Act declared them illegal.

In fact, after the Wagner Act, the expansion of organized labor faltered. Although the largest steel company—U.S. Steel—accepted unionization in 1937, smaller steel companies resisted organizing, which led to the Memorial Day massacre in Chicago and the ultimate defeat of the unions. Only during World War II—during which unions accepted a no-strike pledge in return for government support of organizing—did unions again gain the initiative.

The labor movement was only one of many efforts at social reform during the period that eventually pushed the Roosevelt administration to a more aggressive set of policies. During the early years of the Depression, unemployment councils in many large cities organized protests to demand the expansion of relief. The colorful governor and U.S. senator from Louisiana, Huey Long, promoted a "share our wealth" plan that would have taxed corporate and individual wealth and used the proceeds to reduce poverty. Third parties, like the Farm-Labor Party, also enjoyed significant support, especially in Minnesota, where the party elected three governors and two senators during the 1930s. One of the Farm-Labor senators, Ernest Lundeen, sponsored a more-radical social insurance bill that competed with Roosevelt's Economic Security Act (that eventually became law as the Social Security Act).[81]

Labor's success was not easily attained. Its efforts to organize and to force concessions were matched by management's determination to prevent unionization and to preserve the open shop. In August 1933, President Roosevelt established the National Labor Board to mediate labor disputes. When it failed for lack of authority to enforce decisions, it was replaced by the National Labor Relations Board. The new board, authorized to hold elections to determine the right of unions to conduct collective bargaining, but lacking authority to prevent unfair management practices, was equally unsuccessful in preventing and settling labor disputes. By May 1935, when the NRA was declared unconstitutional, business had generally revolted against the labor provisions of the codes.

The National Labor Relations Act—the Wagner Act—was signed into law on July 5, 1935. The new law contained all that had been foreshadowed in the Norris–LaGuardia Act and NIRA. In addition, it outlawed company-dominated unions and gave the new National Labor Relations Board authority to supervise elections and determine the appropriate bargaining unit, to hear complaints of unfair labor practices, and, when necessary, to petition the courts to enforce its orders. The legal authorization of collective bargaining led to the unionization of large numbers of unskilled workers in basic industries.

The AFL's reliance on craft unions hamstrung its efforts to organize the manufacturing sector. Rather than form an industrial union that would include all autoworkers or steelworkers, the AFL sought to divide workers into a number of distinct crafts and have each craft organized separately. Advocates of industrial unions split with the AFL in 1937 to form the Congress of Industrial Organizations (CIO). Through an aggressive organizing campaign, the CIO and its member unions achieved major victories in the automobile and steel industries.[82]

The CIO also abandoned the AFL's tolerance of racial segregation in unions. Many African Americans were active in union organizing, and A. Phillip Randolph, leader of the Brotherhood of Sleeping Car Porters, emerged as an outspoken leader for both unions and civil rights.

The Roosevelt administration failed to embrace the cause of African Americans. Conservative Southern Democrats demanded that nondiscrimination language be excluded from laws, and they persuaded Roosevelt to refuse support of a federal antilynching bill. Roosevelt sought to use the 1938 election to replace conservative Democrats with those more supportive of New Deal legislation, but this effort failed. As a result, the coalition of conservative Southern Democrats (Dixiecrats) and Republicans blocked liberal legislation after 1939.

▶ Watch this video on Marian Anderson's performance at the Lincoln Memorial in 1939.

Why should we see this performance as an important milestone in the history of social welfare and civil rights?

https://www.youtube.com/watch?v=XF9Quk0QhSE

Although African Americans overwhelmingly supported Roosevelt and the Democratic Party in the 1930s, Roosevelt—fearing a Southern reaction—kept his distance from the civil rights movement.

Although African Americans overwhelmingly supported Roosevelt and the Democratic Party in the 1930s, Roosevelt—fearing a Southern reaction—kept his distance from the civil rights movement. His wife Eleanor, however, became the chief connection between the administration and black leaders. When the famed contralto, Marian Anderson, was denied use of the Daughters of the American Revolution's hall for a concert, Mrs. Roosevelt resigned from the organization and arranged for Anderson to sing at the Lincoln Memorial in April 1939, a venue to which she would return during the March on Washington in 1963.

A report of the La Follette Civil Liberties Committee, the first part of which was made public in December 1937, strengthened the hand of the National Labor Relations Board and ultimately ensured the passage of the Fair Labor Standards Act of June 1938. The report publicized in detail industry's disregard for labor's legal rights. Not the least of its revelations was the fact that a selected list of companies had spent a total of $9.4 million for labor spies, strikebreakers, and munitions between 1933 and 1936.[83] The disclosures were important in moving management toward collective bargaining. As the 1930s ended, organized labor could boast a total membership of 10.6 million. Of the total, 5 million workers belonged to the CIO and 4.6 million belonged to the AFL.[84]

The Fair Labor Standards Act legislatively retrieved those provisions of the NRA that had dealt with work hours, minimum wages, and child labor. The act established a minimum wage of 25 cents an hour (rising to 40 cents an hour in 7 years), a 44-hour week to be reduced to 40 hours in 3 years, and 16 years old as the age below which a child could not work in industries whose products entered interstate commerce. The act's provisions were, for the most part, already a reality for much of organized labor, so those largely affected were nonunionized, unprotected workers—women, minors, and minority group members, the rank and file of the unskilled. As a result, the hourly pay of 300,000 workers was immediately raised, and the workweek was shortened for 2,382,000 people.[85]

The success of the CIO in its efforts to organize the mass industries was enormously significant for unskilled workers. Such workers were frequently members of minority groups, women, and children, and their status was easily exploited in times of labor strife or economic recession. In the strikes of 1921 and 1922, unorganized blacks had been extensively used as strikebreakers. Blacks were often the first to feel the crush of the Depression of the 1930s as social discrimination played its role in decisions to release workers. A National Urban League survey of 106 cities disclosed that 20 to 30 percent of the black population was unemployed in 1931.[86] As the economic situation worsened, many industries replaced men with women at cheaper rates; many replaced men and women with children. In other situations, "desperate heads of families took women's jobs at women's wages, Negro jobs at Negro wages, leaving the minority groups without means of support."[87]

Social workers also experimented with unionization. Many social workers—especially those working for public agencies—demanded more sweeping action to address the Depression that put them to the left of the New Deal and their professional organizations. The Rank-and-File movement and its publication *Social Work Today* became the voice of this concern. At its peak, the Rank-and-File movement claimed 15,000 members. The Rank-and-File movement represented an attempt to redefine social workers *both* as professionals and as workers, workers with the right and need to organize into labor unions. The idea of social workers' unions outlived the demise of the movement in 1942.[88]

Setbacks for Women

The size of the labor force increased between 1930 and 1940. This was true for both male and female workers.[89] As with blacks, the severity of the unemployment situation aggravated long-established patterns of prejudice and discrimination against women. The notion of women's "proper place" was enhanced by the urgency of a drive to "get the men back to work." The country as a whole was convinced that employment for men was the priority, and this was the view of many social workers and social scientists, as well as the official position of unions and government. Congresswoman Florence Kahn said, "Woman's place is not out in the business world competing with men who have families to support."[90] In 1932, Congress established a "married persons' clause" for all federal and service employees, whereby the first employees to be considered redundant when reductions in personnel were necessary were those whose spouses were also federal employees.[91] For the most part, this meant that women were dismissed.

Actually, the get-the-men-back-to-work slogan was aimed at all women, and single women seem to have suffered even greater discrimination than married women. Nevertheless, the percentage of married female workers rose. In 1920, married women comprised 23 percent of female workers; by 1930, one of the earlier years of the Depression, the percentage had risen to 28.9; and in 1940, married women represented 36.7 percent of women in the labor force.[92] During the 1930s, the labor force participation rate of married women increased from 11 to 14 percent. Married or single, the fact was that employers found in women a pool of workers suitable for employment at low wages.

The Eclipse of Reform

The expansion of federal social welfare legislation during the Roosevelt administration was largely confined to the years 1935–1938. In 1937, the administration decided to cut spending on social welfare in an effort to balance the government's budget. Within a few months, the economy had descended into recession, and unemployment, which had never fallen below 10 percent, spiked. Roosevelt's and the Democratic Party's popularity suffered a setback. The 75th Congress that convened in 1939 still boasted a large majority in support of New Deal legislation, although conservative Southern Democrats were able to use their voting strength to tailor legislation to their liking. In particular, they steadfastly blocked policy that would interfere with their states' rights to discriminate against African Americans.[93]

Federal public housing policy as it was defined by the Housing Act of 1937 (Wagner–Steagall Act) demonstrated the political constraints on the New Deal, even when it enjoyed large congressional majorities. Efforts to provide decent housing for poor and working-class families dated from the late 19th century. Typically initiated by charitable organizations, a variety of "social housing" developments advanced the idea that shelter could not be left simply to the laws of supply and demand. During World War I, the federal government had created the United States Housing Corporation and the Emergency Fleet Corporation to help the war effort by building housing in shipbuilding centers; but at the end of the war, these efforts were terminated.[94]

During its early years, the Roosevelt administration initiated a variety of experiments in housing and community development. The Resettlement Administration, under the leadership of Rexford Tugwell, constructed three model towns—including Greenbelt, Maryland; Greendale, Wisconsin; and Greenhills, Ohio—before its efforts were declared unconstitutional by the Supreme Court. A collaboration of the hosiery-workers' union and the PWA led to the construction of a model housing project, the Carl Mackley Houses, in Philadelphia in 1934.[95]

Yet, the path from experimentation to a permanent public housing program was a difficult one. Developers, construction companies, and their allies—the strength of the private housing industry—opposed public intervention in their sector, while conservative politicians railed against the centralization of power in Washington. In the end, the Wagner–Steagall Act included significant limits on the success of public housing. First, public housing projects were initiated by local housing authorities, not by the federal government. As a result, most public housing was limited to central cities; suburban communities often did not even establish housing authorities. Second, stringent limits were placed on the amount that could be spent to construct a unit of public housing. This requirement was included in the legislation to assure that public housing would never compete with the private sector for any but the lowest-quality shelter. Finally, Southern politicians were able to block any attempts to include antidiscrimination language in the bill. As a result, throughout the nation, public housing was constructed on a segregated basis.[96]

Public housing was an early example of how court, private-industry, and Southern opposition could limit the reform impulse of the New Deal. The start of World War II in Europe in 1939 ended the Roosevelt administration's focus on social reform.

? Assess your comprehension of "Mass Movements during the 1930s" by completing this quiz.

CONCLUSION

The Depression of the 1930s left an indelible mark on the United States and on a generation of Americans. Despite the effort expended in the attempt to wrest the country out of the crisis, neither the Franklin Roosevelt nor the New Deal programs achieved success until World War II boosted the economy to full employment. Nevertheless, the president had been able to invest the people with psychological endurance and, in the face of severe challenges from both the political right and the left, to preserve the basic economic system of private property.

The essential conservatism of the New Deal, however, does not negate the fact that the federal government had emerged as the prime promoter of social welfare. Voluntary welfare as well as state and local governments had been tried and found wanting. The extent to which a new realism had taken hold was exhibited in the Supreme Court opinion delivered by Justice Benjamin Cardozo upholding the constitutionality of the Social Security Act:

> The concept of the general welfare is not static. Needs that were narrow or parochial a century ago may be interwoven in our day with the welfare of the nation. What is critical or urgent changes with the times.[97]

The United States emerged from the Depression aware of the hazards of the industrial society and having accomplished a major structural change in its income transfer system. The provision of social insurance—and, for the moment, public assistance, too—represented aggressive federal responsibility for guaranteeing minimum financial security as a matter of right.

Unquestionably, the Social Security Act was the major legislative accomplishment of the New Deal. The act declared the birth of the welfare state and established a direction for its growth and development. As a start, the necessity of opening up jobs for young adults (which required that the elderly be retired from the labor market) and the political clout of older people meant that the welfare measures of the act were geared primarily to persons over age 65. The risks suffered by children and young adults were given short shrift, a situation not really repaired by the minimum wage and hour or child labor provisions of the Fair Labor Standards Act of 1938. For the most part, the Fair Labor Standards Act did little more than give federal sanction to provisions that already existed in many of the states. Nevertheless, precedent for societal protection for all had been established and would serve as a base for substantial expansion of old programs and the creation of new ones.

For social work, the return to prosperity meant a return to a period of further introspection and professionalization. In the early years of the New Deal, many social workers had been active social reformers and community organizers. In 1934, the general sessions and section meetings of the National Conference of Social Work emphasized unemployment, health, and justice as social welfare policy concerns and social legislation as the route to social change. By the end of the decade, professional meetings emphasized social work methodology, social agency administration, and social work education.[98] The Rank-and-File movement, which had fueled radical social work in the early years, attracted less attention and support as the nation came to terms with the approaching world war.

DOCUMENTS

The Depression and the New Deal

The documents used to demonstrate social welfare issues during the Depression of the 1930s are excerpts from the *Monthly Reports of the Federal Emergency Relief Administration* (1933) and from the *Social Security Act* (1935) as originally passed by Congress. The two documents illustrate continuity and change in social policy.

The monthly reports of the FERA set forth the famous *Rules and Regulations*, which not only governed the administration of developing public welfare programs, but also revolutionized the relationship between the public and private sectors of social welfare. The most famous of these regulations, Regulation No. 1, ordered that relief funds be administered by public agencies. This new principle—"public funds in public hands"— removed voluntary agencies from the business of relief. Taking into account the enormous significance of cash relief for social welfare during the Depression, the dominance of the public sector was immediately established.

Nevertheless, the influence of voluntary agency experience and tradition can be detected. Regulation No. 3 requires that need be determined on the basis of individual budgeting and that a variety of individual and family resources be taken into account in establishing the final amount of the relief grant. The requirements for individualized budgeting and resource determination led directly to the investigations of applications and the use of trained investigators at least in supervisory positions.

The Social Security Act was the most important piece of social welfare legislation of the Depression era. It substituted a group of permanent programs for the temporary programs of FERA and, in so doing, acknowledged long-term federal responsibility for social welfare. This new thrust did not, however, make a total break with the past. In fact, a major characteristic of the act is its dual nature, its putting together of old and new orientations.

On the one hand, the Social Security Act establishes a number of social insurance programs to meet the hazards of old age and unemployment. The insurance programs are meant to cover those with former or current workforce connections. They are financed through payroll-tax deductions. Simultaneously, the act provides for a group of categorical non-work-related programs of assistance for the elderly, the blind, and dependent children. These programs are funded through a grant-in-aid formula providing a joint federal–state funding device. They are to be administered by states and provide an income safety net for this population.

The social insurance and public assistance programs differ markedly in their orientation to people in need. The former, perhaps because of the direct taxation involved, makes carefully spelled-out benefits available to claimants as a matter of right. The public assistance categories, because they are based on a "demonstrated need" approach, continue the practice of investigation and individualized budgeting.

The delineation of categories of public assistance recipients indicates the extent to which need per se as a determinant for helping was compromised. Nevertheless, the new public assistance programs were also a break with the past. The Social Security Act requires that each participating state develop a state plan for public assistance and that the plan meet certain requirements. In this regard, the act is standard setting. In addition, the act requires that grants be made in cash and to people living in their own homes, marking the end of institutional almshouse care for the poor. Finally, the act provides for a fair hearing for those applicants who believe they have been unfairly treated. The changes are such that social welfare workers began to talk of a "right to assistance."

MONTHLY REPORT
OF
THE FEDERAL EMERGENCY RELIEF ADMINISTRATION
LETTER OF TRANSMITTAL

JULY 1, 1933

Sir: Pursuant to subsection (d) of section 3 of the Federal Emergency Relief Act of 1933, the Federal Emergency Relief Administration has the honor to submit this report of its activities from May 22, 1933, to June 30, 1933, inclusive. . . .

RULES AND REGULATIONS

Rules and Regulations Nos. 1, 2, and 3 were promulgated by the Federal Emergency Relief Administrator, and were printed and distributed to the governors and State Emergency Relief Administrators. They read as follows:

No. 1

(a) Grants of Federal emergency relief funds are to be administered by public agencies after August 1, 1933.

Just as all State commissions responsible for the distribution of Federal and State funds to local communities are public bodies, so in turn should those local units be public agencies responsible for the expenditure of public funds in the same manner as any other municipal or county department.

This policy obviously must be interpreted on a realistic basis in various parts of the United States. Hundreds of private agencies scattered throughout the land have freely and generously offered their services in the administration of public funds. It would be a serious handicap to relief work if the abilities and interests of these individuals were lost. But these individuals should be made public officials, working under the control of public authority. Thousands of these workers are serving and will continue to serve without pay, but if paid, they should be compensated in the same manner as any other public servant.

It is not the intention of this regulation to instruct the several States to make hasty changes in agreements which the State administration may have made with the private agencies. Adjustment, however, to this policy is to be made no later than August 1, 1933.

This ruling prohibits the turning over of Federal emergency-relief funds to a private agency. The unemployed must apply to a public agency for relief, and this relief must be furnished direct to the applicant by a public agent.

(b) Grants made to the States from Federal funds under the Federal Emergency Relief Act of 1933 may be used for the payment of medical attendance and medical supplies for those families that are receiving relief.

(c) These funds may also be used to pay the cost of shelter for the needy unemployed.

(d) These funds may not be used for the payment of hospital bills or for the boarding out of children, either in institutions or in private homes, or for providing general institutional care. These necessary services to the destitute should be made available through State or local funds.

(e) The personnel employed on work relief projects by the States or their subdivisions are not Federal employees and must not be considered as such; therefore, premiums for accident insurance in connection with work relief programs may not be paid from Federal funds, but should be paid out of State or local moneys.

No. 2

Grants of Federal relief funds cannot be made on the basis of expenditures for rental of buildings used for relief operation; salaries of regularly employed public employees other than those employed full time in connection with emergency unemployment relief and under the supervision of the unemployment relief authority; salaries of relief workers not working directly under the supervision of the unemployment relief authority; and the purchase of automobiles and other equipment used in connection with relief administration.

No. 3

SUPPLEMENT TO RULES AND REGULATIONS NO. 1

Rule No. 1 stated: "Grants of Federal emergency relief funds are to be administered by public agencies after August 1, 1933." The rule further stated, "This ruling prohibits the turning over of Federal Emergency Relief funds to a private agency. The unemployed must apply to a public agency for relief and this relief must be furnished directly to the applicant by a public agent."

Three points need to be clarified:

(a) Public agency.

(b) Public agent or public official.

(c) Use of private agency personnel.

(a) Public agency.—A public welfare department, supported by tax funds and controlled by local government, if approved by the State emergency relief administration to administer unemployment relief, is a "public agency." Where a public welfare department does not exist and a local unemployment relief administration is responsible for unemployment relief this local unemployment relief administration, in order to be recognized as a "public agency" in the meaning of that term as used in Rules and Regulations No. 1, must have the following factors:

(1) It must have the full sanction and recognition of the State emergency relief administration.

(2) It must be vested with full authority and control in the expenditure of State and Federal public funds appropriated for local relief purposes.

(3) It must conform to the rulings of the State emergency relief administration.

(4) It must keep such records and forms as are required by the State emergency relief administration.

NOTE.—This interpretation recognizes as a "public agency," an agency created and sustained by Executive action in the absence of creative local legislation.

(b) Public official or public agent.—"Public official" or "public agent" in the meaning of the term as used in Rules and Regulations No. 1, includes every person who is engaged in carrying out the purposes of the public agency, and so must be:

(1) A member of the official staff of the public agency responsible to the chief executive employed by the public agency to administer the entire organization of unemployment relief. This relationship must be made official by definite appointment and acceptance of such appointment.

(2) The compensation of the "public official" or "public agent" may or may not be paid from public funds. Such official may be loaned by a private agency, but when so loaned must become a member of the official staff of the public agency.

(c) Use of personnel loaned by private agency.—The public agency may make use of personnel of private agencies provided—

(1) Where such personnel is used for the giving of unemployment relief it becomes for the time being an integral part of the public agency. The public agency must assume full responsibility over personnel loaned by the private agency.

(2) That visible evidence of the integration into the public agency is provided as follows:

a. The name of the public agency clearly set out on the office door so that clients may know that they are applying to a public agency for relief.

b. All order forms must be those of the public agency; receipts must be made out to the public agency; identification cards of relief workers must be as staff members of the public agency and relief workers at all times in handling unemployment relief clients must report themselves as public agents or officials.

c. All bills for direct relief, wages for work relief, service or administration costs must be paid directly by the public agency; e.g., when grocery orders are issued by the relief worker the bills must be paid by the public agency directly to the grocer and not through a private agency.

d. It is expected that on other matters than the determination of relief there will be cooperative relationships established between public agencies and private agencies, but the public agency shall not pay for supplemental services so rendered by private agencies.

ADEQUACY OF RELIEF
(Either work relief or direct relief)

Relief shall be given as provided in this act to all needy unemployed persons and/or their dependents. Those whose employment or available resources are inadequate to provide the necessities of life for themselves and/or their dependents are included.

This imposes an obligation on the State emergency relief administration and on all the political subdivisions of the States administering relief, insofar as lies in their power, to see to it that all such needy unemployed persons and/or their dependents shall receive sufficient relief to prevent physical suffering and to maintain minimum living standards.

It also imposes an obligation on the part of the State emergency relief administration and the local relief administration to see that no relief is given to persons unless they are actually in need, and that such relief as is allowed is adjusted to the actual needs of each individual or family.

At the same time the obligation exists to develop maximum efficiency and economy in the furnishing of relief, with a minimum of delay in providing relief to those in distress.

The amount of relief to be given must be based on the following:

(1) An estimate of the weekly needs of the individual or family including an allowance for food sufficient to maintain physical well-being, for shelter, the provision of fuel for cooking and for warmth when necessary, medical care and other necessities. Taxes may be allowed in lieu of allowances for shelter, and not to exceed the normal rent allowance providing such tax allowance is necessary in order to maintain the shelter or home of the relief recipient.

(2) An estimate of the weekly income of the family, including wages or other cash income, produce of farm or garden, and all other resources.

(3) The relief granted should be sufficient to provide the estimated weekly needs to the extent that the family is unable to do so from its own resources.

Any or all of the following types of relief may be allowed under direct relief or under work relief:

(1) Food, and/or food orders or allowance, determined by the number, ages, and needs of the individual members of the family in general accordance with standard food schedules.

(2) Orders or allowances for the provision of shelter, or its equivalent, where necessary.

(3) Orders or allowances for light, gas, fuel, and water for current needs.

(4) Orders or allowances for necessary household supplies.

(5) Clothing or orders or allowances for clothing sufficient for emergency needs.

(6) Orders or allowances for medicine, medical supplies, and/or medical attendance to be furnished in the home.

See further interpretation under *"Direct relief."*

INVESTIGATION AND SERVICE
(Work relief and direct relief)

To carry out the purposes of the Federal Emergency Relief Act of 1933 the investigation of all applications for direct and/or work relief is required. The following rules are hereby established:

(1) Each local relief administration should have at least one trained and experienced investigator on its staff; if additional investigators are to be employed to meet this emergency, the first one employed should have had training and experience. In the larger public welfare districts, where there are a number of investigators, there should be not less than 1 supervisor, trained and experienced in the essential elements of family case work and relief administration, to supervise the work of not more than 20 investigating staff workers.

(2) Registration records of all local applications for relief should be kept at a central office. Where no such central registration index now exists, one should be established by the local relief administration. This is absolutely necessary if duplication is to be avoided where there is more than one agency, either public or private, administering relief.

(3) The minimum investigation shall include a prompt visit to the home; inquiry as to real property, bank accounts, and other financial resources of the family; an interview with at least one recent employer; and determination of the ability and agreement of family, relatives, friends, and churches and other organizations to assist; also the liability under public welfare laws of the several States, of members of a family, or relatives, to assume such support in order to prevent such member becoming a public charge.

(4) Investigation shall be made, not only of persons applying directly to the office but also of those reported to it. In this emergency, it is the duty of those responsible for the administration of unemployment relief to seek out persons in need, and to secure the cooperation of clergymen, school teachers, nurses, and organizations that might assist.

(5) There must be contact with each family through visits at least once a month, or oftener if necessary. The local field worker should be in sufficiently close touch with the family situation to avoid the necessity of applicants reapplying to the office for each individual order.

(6) Investigators should not be overloaded with cases. While no exact standard is being set as to the number of cases per worker, State emergency relief administrators should see to it that a sufficient number of workers are utilized in each local relief district to insure reasonable investigation procedure.

(7) Relief should be given only to persons in need of relief, and on the basis of budgetary deficiency established after careful investigation.

(8) Duplication of relief must be avoided, and every precaution should be taken to prevent overlapping of relief agencies, both public and private.

(9) Frequent and careful reinvestigation should be undertaken at regular intervals in order to establish the continued need of those who are receiving relief in order to determine whether or not some member of the family may have obtained part or full-time work, which would indicate the necessity for cutting down or cutting off on relief. Where adequate staff for investigation is provided, under able direction and supervision, these reinvestigations may be carried out automatically and the relief rolls kept clear of those who do not qualify.

DIRECT RELIEF

Such relief shall be in the form of food, shelter, clothing, light, fuel, necessary household supplies, medicine, medical supplies, and medical attendance, or the cash equivalent of these to the person in his own home.

Direct relief does not include relief—where provision is already made under existing laws—for widows or their dependents, and/or aged persons. There is further disallowed the payment of hospital bills or institutional care, and the costs of the boarding out of children.

Any or all of the following types of relief may be granted:

(1) Food, in the form of food orders, determined by the number, ages, and needs of the individual members of the family in general accordance with standard food schedules.

(2) Orders for the payment of current rent, or its equivalent, where necessary.

(3) Orders for light, gas, fuel, and water for current needs.

(4) Necessary household supplies.

(5) Clothing or orders for clothing sufficient for emergency needs.

(6) Orders for medicine, medical supplies, and/or medical attendance to be furnished in the home.

A broad interpretation of direct relief may be followed by the State relief administration where such is called for in meeting the immediate needs of individuals or families, or in aiding such needy persons in providing the necessities of life for themselves and/or their dependents.

Feed for livestock cannot be allowed as a relief expenditure except feed for domestic livestock may be allowed as a relief expenditure where such allowance makes it possible for the distressed family to produce additional food for the immediate family need.

Seed for gardens under the same reasoning may likewise be allowed as a relief measure.

Tax or mortgage interest payments on real property (home and land) may be allowed in lieu of rent as a relief measure where such allowance is no greater than the normal minimum relief rent allowance and when such payment of tax or mortgage interest is vitally necessary in preventing the loss of the home and the eviction of the owner.

A liberal interpretation of direct relief as above indicated must be controlled by the rule of reason and public policy. Under no circumstances shall an allowance be made which makes provision for other than the emergency needs of the immediate family. State relief administrations are not authorized to make allowances for feed or seed to such an extent that provision is made possible for more than the individual family requirements. Likewise, tax or mortgage interest payments in lieu of rent shall be allowed only on properties occupied and held title to by relief recipients. In no event shall a relief grant be made which directly or indirectly makes possible an increased capital investment in private properties.

WORK RELIEF
(Work relief wages and projects)

Work relief wages in cash or in kind are to be interpreted as follows:

(1) All work relief wages shall be based upon the relief need of the individual and/or his dependents.[1]

(2) The rate of wages should be a fair rate of pay for the work performed. Total compensation should meet the budgetary requirement of the relief recipient.

(3) Payment shall be by check, in cash, or in kind.

(4) Allowance should be on the basis of days' wages, or the equivalent, for the hours worked.

(5) Work relief should be allowed only to those who are employable.

(6) There shall be no discrimination because of race, religion, color, noncitizenship, political affiliation, or because of membership in any special or selected group.

(7) Where skilled personnel is required, skilled wages for skilled work must be paid. Such personnel taken from the work relief lists should be staggered. Where such skilled personnel is required full time, it should be provided otherwise than on a work relief basis.

(8) Work relief projects must be projects undertaken on Federal, State, or local public properties. Work projects for private institutions or agencies, nonprofit or otherwise, are therefore prohibited except as such projects, undertaken by governmental units, may benefit the public health or welfare as, for example, the prosecution of a drainage project which may benefit private interests but is withal of definite benefit to the public health of the community.

It therefore follows that work relief may not be used in the improvement of hospitals, libraries, churches, parks, cemeteries, etc., which are privately owned or incorporated, except that if State or local public moneys are regularly contributed to the support of such institutions, and such public support creates a quasi-public institution which may receive the benefit of work relief.

(9) Work relief projects under this act must be for work undertaken by a State or local relief administration independent of work under a contract or for which an annual appropriation has been made. It must be, in general, apart from normal governmental enterprises and not such as would have been carried out in due course regardless of an emergency.

The construction, as a work relief project, of public buildings, such as schools, firehouses, garages, etc., would in general not be acceptable as a proper work relief project, such construction falling within the usual contract work which would provide labor for those unemployed at large.

(10) Persons employed on work relief projects are not Federal employees and the premiums for their compensation or accident insurance may not be paid from Federal funds. If such insurance is provided, it therefore must be carried by State or local moneys.

---

[1]See further interpretation under "Direct relief" and "Adequacy." Allowances on work relief may be made to cover food, shelter, clothing, light, fuel, necessary household supplies, medicine, supplies, and medical attendance.

Persons employed on work-relief projects by the States and their subdivisions ought to be covered by compensation or accident insurance.

(11) All local work relief projects must be submitted for approval to the State emergency relief administration.

**

THE SOCIAL SECURITY ACT
Approved, August 14, 1935
[PUBLIC—NO. 271—74TH CONGRESS]
[II. R. 7260]
AN ACT

To provide for the general welfare by establishing a system of Federal old-age benefits, and by enabling the several States to make more adequate provision for aged persons, blind persons, dependent and crippled children, maternal and child welfare, public health, and the administration of their unemployment compensation laws; to establish a Social Security Board; to raise revenue; and for other purposes.

Be it enacted by the Senate and House of Representatives of the United States of America in Congress assembled,

TITLE I—GRANTS TO STATES FOR OLD-AGE ASSISTANCE

APPROPRIATION

SECTION 1. For the purpose of enabling each State to furnish financial assistance, as far as practicable under the conditions in such State, to aged needy individuals, there is hereby authorized to be appropriated for the fiscal year ending June 30, 1936, the sum of $49,750,000, and there is hereby authorized to be appropriated for each fiscal year thereafter a sum sufficient to carry out the purposes of this title. The sums made available under this section shall be used for making payments to States which have submitted, and had approved by the Social Security Board established by Title VII (hereinafter referred to as the "Board"), State plans for old-age assistance.

STATE OLD-AGE ASSISTANCE PLANS

SEC. 2 (a) A State plan for old-age assistance must (1) provide that it shall be in effect in all political subdivisions of the State, and, if administered by them, be mandatory upon them; (2) provide for financial participation by the State; (3) either provide for the establishment or designation of a single State agency to administer the plan, or provide for the establishment or designation of a single State agency to supervise the administration of the plan; (4) provide for granting to any individual, whose claim for old-age assistance is denied, an opportunity for a fair hearing before such State agency; (5) provide such methods of administration (other than those relating to selection, tenure of office, and compensation of personnel) as are found by the Board to be necessary for the efficient operation of the plan; (6) provide that the State agency will make such reports, in such form and containing such information, as the Board may from time to time find necessary to assure the correctness and verification of such reports; and (7) provide that, if the State or any of its political subdivisions collects from the estate of any recipient of old-age assistance any amount with respect to old-age assistance furnished him under the plan, one-half of the net amount so collected shall be promptly paid to the United States. Any payment so made shall be deposited in the Treasury to the credit of the appropriation for the purposes of this title.

(b) The Board shall approve any plan which fulfills the conditions specified in subsection (a), except that it shall not approve any plan which imposes, as a condition of eligibility for old-age assistance under the plan—

(1) An age requirement of more than sixty-five years, except that the plan may impose, effective until January 1, 1940, an age requirement of as much as seventy years; or

(2) Any residence requirement which excludes any resident of the State who has resided therein five years during the nine years immediately preceding the application for old-age assistance and has resided therein continuously for one year immediately preceding the application; or

(3) Any citizenship requirement which excludes any citizen of the United States.

PAYMENT TO STATES

Sec. 3. (a) From the sums appropriated therefore, the Secretary of the Treasury shall pay to each State which has an approved plan for old-age assistance, for each quarter, beginning with the quarter commencing July 1, 1935, (1) an amount, which shall be used exclusively as old-age assistance, equal to one-half of the total of the sums expended during such quarter as old-age assistance under the State plan with respect to each individual who at the time of such expenditure is sixty-five years of age or older and is not an inmate of a public institution, not counting so much of such expenditure with respect to any individual for any month as exceeds $30 and (2) 5 per centum of such amount, which shall be used for paying the costs of administering the State plan or for old-age assistance, or both, and for no other purpose: Provided, That the State plan, in order to be approved by the Board, need not provide for financial participation before July 1, 1937 by the State, in the case of any State which the Board, upon application by the State and after reasonable notice and opportunity for hearing to the State, finds is prevented by its constitution from providing such financial participation. . . .

DEFINITIONS

Sec. 6. When used in this title the term "old-age assistance" means money payments to aged individuals.

TITLE II—FEDERAL OLD-AGE BENEFITS

OLD-AGE RESERVE ACCOUNT

Section 201. (a) There is hereby created an account in the Treasury of the United States to be known as the "Old-Age Reserve Account" hereinafter in this title called the "Account." There is hereby authorized to be appropriated to the Account for each fiscal year, beginning with the fiscal year ending June 30, 1937, an amount sufficient as an annual premium to provide for the payments required under this title, such amount to be determined on a reserve basis in accordance with accepted actuarial principles, and based upon such tables of mortality as the Secretary of the Treasury shall from time to time adopt, and upon an interest rate of 3 per centum per annum compounded annually. The Secretary of the Treasury shall submit annually to the Bureau of the Budget an estimate of the appropriations to be made to the Account. . . .

OLD-AGE BENEFIT PAYMENTS

Sec. 202. (a) Every qualified individual (as defined in section 210) shall be entitled to receive, with respect to the period beginning on the date he attains the age of sixty-five, or on January 1, 1942, whichever is the later, and ending on the date of his death, an old-age benefit (payable as nearly as practicable in equal monthly installments) as follows:

(1) If the total wages (as defined in section 210) determined by the Board to have been paid to him, with respect to employment (as defined in section 210) after December 31, 1936, and before he attained the age of sixty-five, were not more than $3,000, the old-age benefit shall be at a monthly rate of one-half of 1 per centum of such total wages;

(2) If such total wages were more than $3,000, the old-age benefit shall be at a monthly rate equal to the sum of the following:

(A) One-half of 1 per centum of $3,000; plus

(B) One-twelfth of 1 per centum of the amount by which such total wages exceeded $3,000 and did not exceed $45,000; plus

(C) One-twenty-fourth of 1 per centum of the amount by which such total wages exceeded $45,000.

(b) In no case shall the monthly rate computed under subsection (a) exceed $85.

(c) If the Board finds at any time that more or less than the correct amount has theretofore been paid to any individual under this section, then, under regulations made by the Board, proper adjustments shall be made in connection with subsequent payments under this section to the same individual.

(d) Whenever the Board finds that any qualified individual has received wages with respect to regular employment after he attained the age of sixty-five, the old-age benefit payable to such individual shall be reduced, for each calendar month in any part of which such regular employment occurred, by an amount equal to one month's benefit. Such reduction shall be made, under regulations prescribed by the Board, by deductions from one or more payments of old-age benefit to such individual.

PAYMENTS UPON DEATH

SEC. 203. (a) If any individual dies before attaining the age of sixty-five, there shall be paid to his estate an amount equal to 3 1/2 per centum of the total wages determined by the Board to have been paid to him, with respect to employment after December 31, 1936.

(b) If the Board finds that the correct amount of the old-age benefit payable to a qualified individual during his life under section 202 was less than 3 1/2 per centum of the total wages by which such old-age benefit was measurable, then there shall be paid to his estate a sum equal to the amount, if any, by which such 3 1/2 per centum exceeds the amount (whether more or less than the correct amount) paid to him during his life as old-age benefit.

(c) If the Board finds that the total amount paid to a qualified individual under an old-age benefit during his life was less than the correct amount to which he was entitled under section 202, and that the correct amount of such old-age benefit was 3 1/2 per centum or more of the total wages by which such old-age benefit was measurable, then there shall be paid to his estate a sum equal to the amount, if any, by which the correct amount of the old-age benefit exceeds the amount which was so paid to him during his life.

PAYMENTS TO AGED INDIVIDUALS NOT QUALIFIED FOR BENEFITS

SEC. 204. (a) There shall be paid in a lump sum to any individual who, upon attaining the age of sixty-five, is not a qualified individual, an amount equal to 3 1/2 per centum of the total wages determined by the Board to have been paid to him, with respect to employment after December 31, 1936, and before he attained the age of sixty-five.

(b) After any individual becomes entitled to any payment under subsection (a), no other payment shall be made under this title in any manner measured by wages paid to him, except that any part of any payment under subsection (a) which is not paid to him before his death shall be paid to his estate. . . .

OVERPAYMENTS DURING LIFE

SEC. 206. If the Board finds that the total amount paid to a qualified individual under an old-age benefit during his life was more than the correct amount to which he was entitled under section 202, and was 3 1/2 per centum or more of the total wages by which such old-age benefit was measurable, then upon his death there shall be repaid to the United States by his estate the amount, if any, by which such total amount paid to him during his life exceeds whichever of the following is the greater: (1) Such 3 1/2 per centum, or (2) the correct amount to which he was entitled under section 202. . . .

DEFINITIONS

SEC. 210. When used in this title—

(a) The term "wages" means all remuneration for employment, including the cash value of all remuneration paid in any medium other than cash; except that such term shall not include that part of the remuneration which, after remuneration equal to $3,000 has been paid to an individual by an employer with respect to employment during any calendar year, is paid to such individual by such employer with respect to employment during such calendar year.

(b) The term "employment" means any service, of whatever nature, performed within the United States by an employee for his employer, except—

(1) Agricultural labor;

(2) Domestic service in a private home;

(3) Casual labor not in the course of the employer's trade or business;

(4) Service performed as an officer or member of the crew of a vessel documented under the laws of the United States or of any foreign country;

(5) Service performed in the employ of the United States Government or of an instrumentality of the United States;

(6) Service performed in the employ of a State, a political subdivision thereof, or an instrumentality of one or more States or political subdivisions;

(7) Services performed in the employ of a corporation, community chest, fund, or foundation, organized and operated exclusively for religious, charitable, scientific, literary, or educational purposes, or for the prevention of cruelty to children or animals, no part of the net earnings of which inures to the benefit of any private shareholder or individual.

(c) The term "qualified individual" means any individual with respect to whom it appears to the satisfaction of the Board that—

(1) He is at least sixty-five years of age; and

(2) The total amount of wages paid to him, with respect to employment after December 31, 1936, and before he attained the age of sixty-five, was not less than $2,000; and

(3) Wages were paid to him, with respect to employment on some five days after December 31, 1936, and before he attained the age of sixty-five, each day being in a different calendar year.

TITLE III—GRANTS TO STATES FOR UNEMPLOYMENT COMPENSATION ADMINISTRATION

APPROPRIATION

SECTION 301. For the purpose of assisting the States in the administration of their unemployment compensation laws, there is hereby authorized to be appropriated, for the fiscal year ending June 30, 1936, the sum of $4,000,000, and for each fiscal year thereafter the sum of $49,000,000, to be used as hereinafter provided.

PAYMENTS TO STATES

SEC. 302. (a) The Board shall from time to time certify to the Secretary of the Treasury for payment to each State which has an unemployment compensation law approved by the Board under Title IX, such amounts as the Board determines to be necessary for the proper administration of such law during the fiscal year in which such payment is to be made. The board's determination shall be based on (1) the population of the State; (2) an estimate of the number of persons covered by the State law and of the cost of proper administration of such law; and (3) such other factors as the Board finds relevant. The Board shall not certify for payment under this section in any fiscal year a total amount in excess of the amount appropriated therefor for such fiscal year.

(b) Out of the sums appropriated therefor, the Secretary of the Treasury shall, upon receiving a certification under subsection (a), pay, through the Division of Disbursement of the Treasury Department and prior to audit or settlement by the General Accounting Office, to the State agency charged with the administration of such law the amount so certified.

PROVISIONS OF STATE LAWS

SEC. 303. (a) The Board shall make no certification for payment to any State unless it finds that the law of such State, approved by the Board under Title IX, includes provisions for—

(1) Such methods of administration (other than those relating to selection, tenure of office, and compensation of personnel) as are found by the Board to be reasonably calculated to insure full payment of unemployment compensation when due; and

(2) Payment of unemployment compensation solely through public employment offices in the State or such other agencies as the Board may approve; and

(3) Opportunity for a fair hearing, before an impartial tribunal, for all individuals whose claims for unemployment compensation are denied; and

(4) The payment of all money received in the unemployment fund of such State, immediately upon such receipt, to the Secretary of the Treasury to the credit of the Unemployment Trust Fund established by section 904; and

(5) Expenditure of all money requisitioned by the State agency from the Unemployment Trust Fund, in the payment of unemployment compensation, exclusive of expenses of administration; and

(6) The making of such reports, in such form and containing such information, as the Board may from time to time require, and compliance with such provisions as the Board may from time to time find necessary to assure the correctness and verification of such reports; and

(7) Making available upon request to any agency of the United States charged with the administration of public works or assistance through public employment, the name, address, ordinary occupation and employment status of each recipient of unemployment compensation, and a statement of such recipient's rights to further compensation under such law.

(b) Whenever the Board, after reasonable notice and opportunity for hearing to the State agency charged with the administration of the State law, finds that in the administration of the law there is—

(1) a denial, in a substantial number of cases, of unemployment compensation to individuals entitled thereto under such law; or

(2) a failure to comply substantially with any provision specified in subsection (a); the Board shall notify such State agency that further payments will not be made to the State until the Board is satisfied that there is no longer any such denial or failure to comply. Until it is so satisfied, it shall make no further certification to the Secretary of the Treasury with respect to such State.

TITLE IV—GRANTS TO STATES FOR AID TO DEPENDENT CHILDREN

APPROPRIATION

SECTION 401. For the purpose of enabling each State to furnish financial assistance, as far as practicable under the conditions in such State, to needy dependent children, there is hereby authorized to be appropriated for the fiscal year ending June 30, 1936, the sum of $24,750,000, and there is hereby authorized to be appropriated for each fiscal year thereafter a sum sufficient to carry out the purposes of this title. The sums made available under this section shall be used for making payments to States which have submitted, and had approved by the Board, State plans for aid to dependent children.

STATE PLANS FOR AID TO DEPENDENT CHILDREN

SEC. 402. (a) A State plan for aid to dependent children must (1) provide that it shall be in effect in all political subdivisions of the State, and, if administered by them, be mandatory upon them; (2) provide for financial participation by the State; (3) either provide for the establishment or designation of a single State agency to administer the plan, or provide for the establishment or designation of a single State agency to supervise the administration of the plan; (4) provide for granting to any individual, whose claim with respect to aid to a dependent child is denied, an opportunity for a fair hearing before such State agency; (5) provide such methods of administration (other than those relating to selection, tenure of office, and compensation of personnel) as are found by the Board to be necessary for the efficient operation of the plan; and (6) provide that the State agency will make such reports, in such form and containing such information, as the Board may from time to time require, and comply with such provisions as the Board may from time to time find necessary to assure the correctness and verification of such reports.

(b) The Board shall approve any plan which fulfills the conditions specified in subsection (a), except that it shall not approve any plan which imposes as a condition of eligibility for aid to dependent children, a residence requirement which denies aid with respect to any child residing in the State (1) who has resided in the State for one year immediately preceding the application for such aid, or (2) who was born within the State within one year immediately preceding the application, if its mother has resided in the State for one year immediately preceding the birth.

PAYMENT TO STATES

SEC. 403. (a) From the sums appropriated therefor, the Secretary of the Treasury shall pay to each State which has an approved plan for aid to dependent children, for each quarter, beginning with the quarter commencing July 1, 1935, an amount, which shall be used exclusively for carrying out the State plan, equal to one-third of the total of the sums expended during such quarter under such plan, not counting so much of such expenditure with respect to any dependent child for any month as exceeds $18, or if there is more than one dependent child in the same home, as exceeds $18 for any month with respect to one such dependent child and $12 for such month with respect to each of the other dependent children. . . .

Sec. 406. When used in this title—

(a) The term "dependent child" means a child under the age of sixteen who has been deprived of parental support or care by reason of the death, continued absence from the home, or physical or mental incapacity of a parent, and who is living with his father, mother, grandfather, grandmother, brother, sister, stepfather, stepmother, stepbrother, stepsister, uncle, or aunt, in a place of residence maintained by one or more of such relatives as his or their own home;

(b) The term "aid to dependent children" means money payments with respect to a dependent child or dependent children.

TITLE V—GRANTS TO STATES FOR MATERNAL AND CHILD WELFARE

Part 1—Maternal and Child Health Services

APPROPRIATION

SECTION 501. For the purpose of enabling each State to extend and improve, as far as practicable under the conditions in such State, services for promoting the health of mothers and children, especially in rural areas and in areas suffering from severe economic distress, there is hereby authorized to be appropriated for each fiscal year, beginning with the fiscal year ending June 30, 1936, the sum of $3,800,000. The sums made available under this section shall be used for making payments to States which have submitted, and had approved by the Chief of the Children's Bureau, State plans for such services.

ALLOTMENTS TO STATES

Sec. 502. (a) Out of the sums appropriated pursuant to section 501 for each fiscal year the Secretary of Labor shall allot to each State $20,000, and such part of $1,800,000 as he finds that the number of live births in such State bore to the total number of live births in the United States, in the latest calendar year for which the Bureau of the Census has available statistics.

(b) Out of the sums appropriated pursuant to section 501 for each fiscal year the Secretary of Labor shall allot to the States $980,000 in addition to the allotments made under subsection (a), according to the financial need of each State for assistance in carrying out its State plan, as determined by him after taking into consideration the number of live births in such State.

(c) The amount of any allotment to a State under subsection (a) for any fiscal year remaining unpaid to such State at the end of such fiscal year shall be available for payment to such State under section 504 until the end of the second succeeding fiscal year. No payment to a State under section 504 shall be made out of its allotment for any fiscal year until its allotment for the preceding fiscal year has been exhausted or has ceased to be available.

APPROVAL OF STATE PLANS

Sec. 503. (a) A State plan for maternal and child-health services must (1) provide for financial participation by the State; (2) provide for the administration of the plan by the State health agency or the supervision of the administration of the plan by the State health agency; (3) provide such methods of administration (other than those relating to selection, tenure of office, and compensation of personnel) as are necessary for the efficient operation of the plan; (4) provide that the State health agency will make such reports, in such form and containing such information, as the Secretary of Labor may from time to time find necessary to assure the correctness and verification of such reports; (5) provide for the extension and improvement of local maternal and child-health services administered by local child-health units; (6) provide for cooperation with medical, nursing, and welfare groups and organization; and (7) provide for the development of demonstration services in needy areas and among groups in special need.

(b) The Chief of the Children's Bureau shall approve any plan which fulfills the conditions specified in subsection (a) and shall thereupon notify the Secretary of Labor and the State health agency of his approval. . . .

Part 2—Services for Crippled Children

APPROPRIATION

Sec. 511. For the purpose of enabling each State to extend and improve (especially in rural areas and in areas suffering from severe economic distress), as far as practicable under the conditions in such State, services for locating crippled children, and for providing medical, surgical, corrective, and other services and care, and facilities for diagnosis, hospitalization, and aftercare, for children who are crippled or who are suffering from conditions which lead to crippling, there is hereby authorized to be appropriated for each fiscal year, beginning with the fiscal year ending June 30, 1936, the sum of $2,850,000. The sums made available under this section shall be used for making payments to States which have submitted, and had approved by the Chief of the Children's Bureau, State plans for such services.

ALLOTMENTS TO STATES

Sec. 512. (a) Out of the sums appropriated pursuant to section 511 for each fiscal year the Secretary of Labor shall allot to each State $20,000, and the remainder to the States according to the need of each State as determined by him after taking into consideration the number of crippled children in such State in need of the services referred to in section 511 and the cost of furnishing such services to them.

(b) The amount of any allotment to a State under subsection (a) for any fiscal year remaining unpaid to such State at the end of such fiscal year shall be available for payment to such State under section 514 until the end of the second succeeding fiscal year. No payment to a State under section 514 shall be made out of its allotment for any fiscal year until its allotment for the preceding fiscal year has been exhausted or has ceased to be available.

APPROVAL OF STATE PLANS

Sec. 513. (a) A State plan for services for crippled children must (1) provide for financial participation by the State; (2) provide for the administration of the plan by a State agency or the supervision of the administration of the plan by a State agency; (3) provide such methods of administration (other than those relating to selection, tenure of office, and compensation of personnel) as are necessary for the efficient operation of the plan; (4) provide that the State agency will make such reports, in such form and containing such information, as the Secretary of Labor may from time to time require, and comply with such provisions as he may from time to time find necessary to assure the correctness and verification of such reports; (5) provide for carrying out the purposes specified in section 511; and (6) provide for cooperation with medical, health, nursing, and welfare groups and organizations and with any agency in such State charged with administering State laws providing for vocational rehabilitation of physically handicapped children.

(b) The Chief of the Children's Bureau shall approve any plan which fulfills the conditions specified in subsection (a) and shall thereupon notify the Secretary of Labor and the State health agency of his approval. . . .

PART 3—CHILD-WELFARE SERVICES

SEC. 521. (a) For the purpose of enabling the United States, through the Children's Bureau, to cooperate with State public-welfare agencies in establishing, extending, and strengthening, especially in predominantly rural areas, public-welfare services (hereinafter in this section referred to as "child-welfare services") for the protection and care of homeless, dependent, and neglected children, and children in danger of becoming delinquent, there is hereby authorized to be appropriated for each fiscal year, beginning with the fiscal year ending June 30, 1936, the sum of $1,500,000. Such amount shall be allotted by the Secretary of Labor for use by cooperating State public-welfare agencies on the basis of plans developed jointly by the State agency and the Children's Bureau, to each State, $10,000, and the remainder to each State on the basis of such plans, not to exceed such part of the remainder as the rural population of such State bears to the total rural population of the United States. The amount so allotted shall be expended for payment of part of the cost of district, county or other local child-welfare services in areas predominantly rural, and for developing State services for the encouragement and assistance of adequate methods of community child-welfare organization in areas predominantly rural and other areas of special need. The amount of any allotment to a State under this section for any fiscal year remaining unpaid to such State at the end of such fiscal year shall be available for payment to such State under this section until the end of the second succeeding fiscal year. No payment to a State under this section shall be made out of its allotment for any fiscal year until its allotment for the preceding fiscal year has been exhausted or has ceased to be available. . . .

PART 4—VOCATIONAL REHABILITATION

SEC. 531. (a) In order to enable the United States to cooperate with the States and Hawaii in extending and strengthening their programs of vocational rehabilitation of the physically disabled, and to continue to carry out the provisions and purposes of the Act entitled "An Act to provide for the promotion of vocational rehabilitation of persons disabled in industry or otherwise and their return to civil employment," approved June 2, 1920, as amended (U.S.C., title 29, ch. 4; U.S.C., Supp. VII, title 29, secs. 31, 32, 34, 35, 37, 39, and 40), there is hereby authorized to be appropriated for the fiscal years ending June 30, 1936, and June 30, 1937, the sum of $841,000 for each fiscal year in addition to the amount of the existing authorization, and for each fiscal year thereafter the sum of $1,938,000. Of the sums appropriated pursuant to such authorization for each fiscal year, $5,000 shall be apportioned to the Territory of Hawaii and the remainder shall be apportioned among the several States in the manner provided in such Act of June 2, 1920, unamended. . . .

PART 5—ADMINISTRATION

SEC. 541. (a) There is hereby authorized to be appropriated for the fiscal year ending June 30, 1936, the sum of $425,000, for all necessary expenses of the Children's Bureau in administering the provisions of this title, except section 531.

(b) The Children's Bureau shall make such studies and investigations as will promote the efficient administration of this title, except section 531.

(c) The Secretary of Labor shall include in his annual report to Congress a full account of the administration of this title, except section 531. . . .

TITLE X—GRANTS TO STATES FOR AID TO THE BLIND

APPROPRIATION

SECTION 1001. For the purpose of enabling each State to furnish financial assistance, as far as practicable under the conditions in such State, to needy individuals who are blind, there is hereby authorized to be appropriated for the fiscal year ending June 30, 1936, the sum of $3,000,000, and there is hereby authorized to be appropriated for each fiscal year thereafter a sum sufficient to carry out the purposes of this title. The sums made available under this section shall be used for making payments to States which have submitted, and had approved by the Social Security Board, State plans for aid to the blind.

STATE PLANS FOR AID TO THE BLIND

SEC. 1002. (a) A State plan for aid to the blind must (1) provide that it shall be in effect in all political subdivisions of the State, and if administered by them, be mandatory upon them; (2) provide for financial participation by the State; (3) either provide for the establishment or designation of a single State agency to administer the plan, or provide for the establishment or designation of a single State agency to supervise the administration of the plan; (4) provide for granting to any individual, whose claim for aid is denied, an opportunity for a fair hearing before such State agency; (5) provide such methods of administration (other than those relating to selection, tenure of office, and compensation of personnel) as are found by the Board to be necessary for the efficient operation of the plan; (6) provide that the State agency will make such reports, in such form and containing such information, as the Board may from time to time require, and comply with such provisions as the Board may from time to time find necessary to assure the correctness and verification of such reports; and (7) provide that no aid will be furnished any individual under the plan with respect to which he is receiving old-age assistance under the State plan approved under section 2 of this Act.

(b) The Board shall approve any plan which fulfills the conditions specified in subsection (a), except that it shall not approve any plan which imposes, as a condition of eligibility for aid to the blind under the plan—

(1) Any residence requirement which excludes any resident of the State who has resided therein five years during the nine years immediately preceding the application for aid and has resided therein continuously for one year immediately preceding the application; or

(2) Any citizenship requirement which excludes any citizen of the United States.

PAYMENT TO STATES

SEC. 1003. (a) From the sums appropriated therefor, the Secretary of the Treasury shall pay to each State which has an approved plan for aid to the blind, for each quarter, beginning with the quarter commencing July 1, 1935, (1) an amount, which shall be used exclusively as aid to the blind, equal to one-half of the total of the sums expended during such quarter as aid to the blind under the State plan with respect to each individual who is blind and is not an inmate of a public institution, not counting so much of such expenditure with respect to any individual for any month as exceeds $30, and (2) 5 per centum of such amount, which shall be used for paying the costs of administering the State plan or for aid to the blind, or both, and for no other purpose. . .

SHORT TITLE

SEC. 1105. This Act may be cited as the "Social Security Act."
Approved, August 14, 1935.

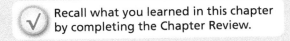

Recall what you learned in this chapter by completing the Chapter Review.

War and Prosperity: 1940–1968

LEARNING OUTCOMES

- Identify the ways in which World War II influenced the development of the American economy and society in the following decades.

- Explain the major social welfare innovations of the postwar period and their relationship to social and economic change.

- Specify the links between the social status of black Americans and women and the origins of the civil rights movements of the period.

CHAPTER OUTLINE

Changing Economic and Demographic Realities 207
 Population Shifts 207
 Technology, Productivity, and
  Economic Insecurity 210
 World War II 212
 Wartime Economic and Social
  Advances 214
 Postwar Optimism 215

Innovations in Social Welfare 218
 Veterans and the GI Bill 218
 The Attack on Public Welfare 219
 Poverty and the Reform of
  Welfare 220
 The War on Poverty 225
 Expanded Benefits for the Aging 230
 Controlling Public Assistance 230

Social Movements and Reform After World War II 232
 Expanding the Civil Rights of
  African Americans 232
 A Renewed Feminist Movement 234
 Civil Rights and Juvenile Justice 235

The period from 1940 to 1968 was one of contradiction—of growth and of conflict, of affluence and of the rediscovery of poverty. The United States fought major wars, first in Europe and the Pacific, and later in Indochina. The military mobilization and wartime production of World War II led initially to economic recovery and subsequently to a "revolution of rising expectations" at home. The 1950s and 1960s—after a century of neglect—refocused the nation on civil rights, as African Americans and women forged a new understanding of the nature of discrimination and exclusion and demanded redress of their grievances.

Supported by military and civilian demands, the years from 1940 to 1968 were prosperous ones that marked a transition from the consumer demand deficiency of the Depression to the threat of inflation of the 1970s, from the problems of mass unemployment to the problems of spiraling inflation. The gross national product (GNP) had managed to climb to almost $100 billion by 1940 as a result of efforts to rearm and to supply future allies. Corrected for inflation, GNP had tripled by 1970.[1] Real disposable personal

CHAPTER OUTLINE *(Continued)*

DOCUMENTS: War and
Prosperity   236

Message on the Public Welfare Program,
  1962   237

Economic Opportunity Act, 1964   243

In re Gault, 1967   246

income—that is, purchasing power available to consumers—more than doubled by 1970, and per capita consumer expenditures and savings rose dramatically.[2] Family income, and therefore, family welfare measured in terms of money, showed significant improvement. All income groups of the population shared in the prosperity, as did most racial and ethnic groups. Median family income grew for whites and nonwhites. Nonwhite families had a median income of $1,614 in 1947, 51 percent of white family median income. In 1950, nonwhite median family income was 54 percent of white median family income; in 1960, 55 percent; and in 1970, 61 percent. This was an improvement in one sense, but the actual dollar gap between white and nonwhite families widened as all incomes grew. The gap went from $1,543 in 1947, to $1,576 in 1950, to $2,602 in 1960, and to $3,957 in 1970.[3]

The same mixed picture of prosperity is demonstrated through the use of the poverty index developed by the Social Security Administration (SSA) to measure the minimum income needed to purchase a subsistence level of goods and services. In 1960, a nonfarm family of four required $3,022 to escape poverty, as defined by the SSA. In that year, almost 40 million individuals were counted as poor, 22.4 percent of the population. In 1970, the poverty index for a nonfarm family of four had risen to $3,968. The number of poor Americans had dropped to 25.4 million, 12.6 percent of the population. But again, there was a difference between the progress of whites and nonwhites. The 17.5 million whites counted poor in 1970 represented 10 percent of all whites in the population; the 8 million nonwhites counted poor represented 32 percent of all nonwhites. The poverty rate for blacks was more than three times that for whites.[4] Conditions were particularly harsh for those in the South and Southwest. Mexican Americans and Native Americans as well as African Americans experienced very high poverty rates and severe discrimination.

The increase in income was in part a result of the expansion of the labor force. The civilian labor force grew from 55.6 million in 1940 to 82.7 million in 1970. The expansion was due to population growth and a long-term increase in labor-force participation rates from 56 percent of the population in 1940 to 61 percent in 1970.[5] The trend was accelerated by World War II, when many women entered the labor force to replace men serving in the armed forces. Although the end of the World War II forced some women out of their wartime jobs, the labor-force participation rate of women never returned to its prewar level. In 1940, 24 percent of all women of working age were in the labor force; by 1970, the figure had risen to more than 43 percent. In 1970, as in 1940, economic necessity made for a higher labor-force participation rate among black women—49 percent as against 42 percent for white women—but the gap had closed appreciably.[6]

The strength of the economy was demonstrated by its ability to resist major recessions at the same time that it absorbed an ever-expanding labor force. In 1940, the unemployment rate stood at 14.6 percent. In 1943, with war production in full swing, the unemployment rate dipped as low as 1.2 percent. Unemployment averaged 4.5 percent during the 1950s, 5.7 percent between 1960 and 1965, and 3.8 percent between 1965 and 1970.

The apparent strength of the economy obscured the extent to which unemployment struck disproportionately at certain groups. In 1960, when white unemployment averaged 4.9 percent, the rate for nonwhites was 10.2 percent. For teenagers, it stood at 14.7 percent. Structural imbalance persisted throughout the era. The unemployment rates for whites and nonwhites in 1970 were 4.5 percent and 8.2 percent, respectively.[7]

▶ **Watch this video about "Rosie the Riveter."**

How would these women's work experience challenge gender stereotype and change the nature of power relations in their families?

Although part of the increased prosperity of the postwar years was a result of economic growth, few people recognized the critical role of social welfare programs in reducing poverty. Besides the growth of wages, income transfers in the form of veterans' benefits, unemployment insurance, Social Security, and, to a lesser extent, public assistance also played a part in the improved well-being of families. The entrance of women into the labor force also played an underappreciated role in reducing poverty in two-adult households. For well over half of the households in which the man was earning a poverty income, the income of the wife became the route out of poverty.[8]

Gender discrimination had been largely condoned during the Depression and World War II. Only the exigencies of war allowed women to hold a "man's job." Increasingly during the 1960s, however, women challenged their economic oppression. By the close of the 1960s, women's wages averaged only 59 percent of wages and salaries received by male workers.[9] Although women's work played a critical role in many family's economic well-being during the 1950s, only in the late 1960s did the modern feminist movement begin to bring attention to its implications for both public and private life. Their growing financial independence had implications for the development of new family forms, for changes in the roles of family members, and for new child-care arrangements.

Although part of the increased prosperity of the postwar years was a result of economic growth, few people recognized the critical role of social welfare programs in reducing poverty.

CHANGING ECONOMIC AND DEMOGRAPHIC REALITIES

Population Shifts

The military and social eruptions of 1940–1970 were accompanied by enormous changes in population size and distribution. Total U.S. population grew from 132.1 million in 1940 to 204.8 million in 1970. Because of the immigration restrictions of the 1920s, the proportion of American residents who were foreign-born declined from 9 percent in 1940 to 5 percent in 1970. However, the changing position of the United States in the world after World War II emerged as a powerful countertrend. First, after turning its back on refugees during the 1930s, the United States accepted displaced persons after World War II. Later, refugees from Communist regimes in Eastern Europe entered as well. Finally, immigration reform in 1965 caused a fundamental shift in U.S. immigration policy, although the immigrant flow before 1970 remained small. Immigration from 1961 to 1970 reached 3,300,000 people.[10]

Immigration policy changed slowly during the postwar years, reflecting the general biases of the American electorate. During the Depression years, immigration was low—in part because of the lack of job opportunities and in part because of the stricter enforcement of the "likely to become a public charge" (LPC) rule, which was used to reinforce defensive and nativist feelings. Emigration was large, primarily for economic reasons. Many returned to their home countries. In particular, many destitute Mexicans and Mexican Americans were forcibly repatriated to Mexico, where they had families and significant support networks.

After the forced deportation of Mexican Americans during the Great Depression, immigration from Mexico increased in response to the labor-force demands of World War II. Increased demand for manual labor, particularly in the fields and on the railroads of the Southwest, meant a growth in the presence of Mexican immigrants. There were 80,000 immigrants in the 1940s, 275,000 in the 1950s, and more than 440,000 in the 1960s—a third of all legal immigrants. There is no agreement about the number of illegal entrants; estimates range widely, varying from 1 million to 8 million at any one time.[11]

When Franklin D. Roosevelt became president, he continued the restrictive immigration policies of the 30 years preceding him. No open door was extended to the refugees from Hitler's Germany. Despite the clear evidence that Roosevelt knew of the events in Germany and the desperate situation of its Jewish population, he neither intervened for their admission nor interfered with the anti-refugee position of the State Department. To the contrary, Jewish refugees were systematically denied admission. The quotas that had been established for Germany and Italy were not increased. In fact, only 48 percent of the existing quota was used in 1941.[12] During the war years, an array of bureaucratic hurdles was used to prevent the admission of Jews into the country.

World War II represented a fundamental pivot in American policy toward Asian immigrants. Since the later 19th century, Asians had been barred from legal entry into the United States and were ineligible for citizenship. The tenuous legitimacy of Asian Americans was clear in the forced relocation of Japanese Americans during World War II. Early in the war, 120,000 Japanese residents—many of whom were American citizens— were removed from their homes on the West Coast to internment camps in the Western deserts and the swampland of Arkansas. Japanese internment left a permanent scar on thousands of internees and the farms and neighborhoods left behind. The federal government accepted responsibility for its mistake only in 1988, when the Civil Liberties Act of that year apologized for the internment and offered reparations to the surviving internees.

Yet, the wall of racial exclusion began to crumble during the war. The wartime alliance of the United States and the Nationalist government of China had domestic implications. Congress repealed the Chinese Exclusion Act of 1882 (and its subsequent additions and amendments), established a small token quota for Chinese immigration, and made Chinese immigrants eligible for naturalization. Even more important to the Chinese community, the War Brides Act of 1946 expedited the entry of Chinese wives and children of members of the armed forces. During 1945–1952, 11,000 Chinese immigrated to the United States, 10,000 of whom were non-quota wives.

The 1946 War Brides Act eased the entry of wives, husbands, and children of servicemen and women. For this group, it waived visa requirements, ignored racial and ethnic restraints, and eliminated prohibitions based on physical and mental handicaps. It was the beginning of a shift in policy from an emphasis on national origins to an emphasis on family affiliation.

Refugee policy changed as well. After World War II, the gates began to open for European refugees. The first Displaced Persons Act, passed in 1948, admitted victims of fascism and also many who were fleeing communist regimes. In 1952, as part of the severe anticommunist spirit of the period, strict anticommunist screening and deportation were introduced. The same act did, however, eliminate all exclusion of entrants on the basis of race or ethnicity. In addition, it laid the basis for emergency, non-quota, admission of those fleeing communism or experiencing emergency hardship. Future legislation allowed for refugees from many parts of the world, including Hungary, Cuba, Tibet, and Vietnam. Not incidentally, the flow of new refugees meant new social welfare needs that, increasingly, were met by voluntary agencies.

The 1965 Immigration Act (Hart–Celler Act) formalized the new criteria for entry into the United States. Race, national origin, and ancestry quotas were replaced by admission standards of family relationship, occupation, and skill. The new preference system exempted spouses and minor children of U.S. citizens from all quotas and gave spouses and children of resident aliens high priority. Married children and siblings also received preferential treatment. Although lawmakers anticipated that the act would stimulate the resumption of European immigration, once immigration was opened to Latin Americans and Asians, their numbers increased rapidly.

Although immigration increased, most of the population expansion from 1940 to 1970 was due to changes in birth and death rates. By the middle of the 1930s, decisions to delay marriage and childbearing had lowered the birthrate to about 17 per 1,000 persons in the population. As the Depression ended at the beginning of World War II and as young people faced the initial prospect of separation, the birthrate briefly increased—and then fell again. Immediately after the war, however, the birthrate soared, reaching a high of 26.6 per 1,000 persons in 1947 and remaining high until the mid-1960s.[13]

The baby boom was accompanied by an increase in life expectancy and a decline in the death rate. In 1940, the estimated average length of life in the United States was 62.9 years. Thirty years later, it stood at 70.8 years. During this period, the estimated average life expectancy among nonwhites rose from 82.7 percent to 90 percent of estimated average life expectancy among whites. Simultaneously, death rates declined for the total population from 10.8 per 1,000 individuals in the population in 1940 to 9.4 in 1970. Most significantly, the death rate among nonwhites declined from 13.8 in 1940 to approximate the national average at 9.5 in 1970.[14] Native Americans also shared in the general decline in mortality rates and rise in life expectancy. But despite improvements in infant and maternal death rates and from some infectious diseases, Native Americans continued to have the lowest life expectancy of any ethnic group in the United States.[15]

The changes in life expectancy reflected better nutrition as incomes rose and sulfa, penicillin, and new medical and surgical procedures became widely available. Poliomyelitis or infantile paralysis—a disease that caused widespread epidemics and even more widespread fear through the first half of the 20th century—was defeated with the development of the first vaccine during the 1950s. The visibility of actual and potential results from improved medical and health care increased demands for broader efforts to improve the nation's health.

Changing birth and death rates produced changing demographic patterns. Over the years, the country's population grew both younger and older. The percentage of those less than 19 years of age grew from 34.2 percent of the total population in 1940 to 37.9 percent of the population in 1970. The percentage of the population over 65 years of age grew from 6.8 percent to 10.2 percent in the same time. Clearly, a declining percentage of "productive" individuals were being called upon to support a growing percentage of the "nonproductive." Added to this was the lack of productivity of those who wanted jobs but could not find them. In this regard, the effect of racial discrimination upon employment opportunities for blacks intensified as the percentage of blacks in the total population grew.[16]

Population growth was accompanied by population shifts and dislocations. World War II accelerated the historical process of industrialization and mechanization. The wartime necessity for spreading industry, shipping, and the training of service personnel across the country to engage in a war being fought on two fronts reinforced the continuous westward movement of the center of population. Defense policy spurred the growth of port cities on the Gulf and Pacific Coasts. Equally important was the movement of the population from rural to urban areas. The pull of jobs in urban centers and the push of technical advances that made small marginal farms obsolete and unprofitable impelled the move of 20 million people from rural to urban areas between 1940 and 1970. Of the total, about 16 million were whites and about 4 million were blacks.[17] By 1950, 64 percent of the country's total population lived in urban areas—64 percent of the white population and 62 percent of the nonwhite population—and the rest lived in rural areas. By 1970, 72 percent of the white population and 81 percent of the nonwhite population lived in urban areas.[18]

The long movement of Americans to metropolitan areas took a decisive turn during the 1940s and 1950s. Many central cities, like Philadelphia and St. Louis, attained their highest population during the early 1950s and began a steady decline. Between World War II and 1970, the United States became a suburban nation.

Yet, the long movement of Americans to metropolitan areas took a decisive turn during the 1940s and 1950s. Many central cities, like Philadelphia and St. Louis, attained their highest population during the early 1950s and began a steady decline. Between World War II and 1970, the United States became a suburban nation. In 1940, two out of three metropolitan residents lived in a central city. By 1960, three out of five lived in a suburb. The growth of suburbs was sharply defined by race. By the 1960s, cities with large black populations surrounded by white suburbs were common throughout the nation.

In the search for factory employment, large numbers of African Americans had left the South. The percentage of the black population residing in the South dropped from 77 percent in 1940 to 52 percent in 1970.

Perhaps of more importance than place of residence was the fact of black urbanization itself, a response to changes in agriculture. For the country as a whole, the relative share of employment in agriculture fell from 15 percent of the civilian labor force in 1940 to 4 percent in 1970.[19] At the same time, mechanization increased the real value of farm output by $6.4 billion between these years. Technological developments—increased mechanization that had led to increased productivity—had necessitated the development of larger farms to ensure adequate monetary returns. Average farm size increased from 167 acres in 1940 to 373 acres in 1970. The size of farms owned by whites more than doubled, but the size of farms owned by blacks grew by only 20 percent.[20] Since average black-owned and black-operated farm holdings had historically been small and only marginally profitable, black families and farm workers suffered disproportionate dislocation. Black migration was inherent in the changed economic situation.

The black migration of the early 1940s was caught up and hidden in the general necessity for wartime mobility. More than 16 million men were transported for military reasons; women, wives, and families followed. An additional 16 million men and women moved for job-related reasons. The general wartime atmosphere was characterized by migration and mobility. Mobility was linked to family disruption. Between 1940 and 1946, the number of divorces increased from 264,000 to 610,000 annually.[21] The divorce rate had shot upward from 2.0 to 4.3 per 1,000 of population. Between 1940 and 1950, the number of births per 1,000 single women, 15 to 44 years, increased from 3.6 to 6.1 for white women and from 35.6 to 71.2 for nonwhite women.[22] Many high school students left school to take jobs. In September 1942, for example, the National Child Labor Committee reported that of the 4 million juveniles who had been employed in industry and agriculture during the preceding summer months, 3 million were still employed as the new school term began. About 75,000 were under age 16. During the midst of the war, J. Edgar Hoover, head of the Federal Bureau of Investigation, reported an alarming increase in juvenile delinquency.[23]

The postwar years aggravated, even institutionalized, the trend toward mobility and its concomitant social risks. Moving was no longer unusual or frightening in a world made familiar by commercial civilian flying and by television. And as automobile ownership mushroomed and discontent with city dwelling surfaced, suburbanization followed upon urbanization. As families moved from their home base, they moved, too, from the support and help of relatives and longtime friends.

Technology, Productivity, and Economic Insecurity

Economic productivity—the increasing output per hour of work—was the key to postwar affluence, consumerism, and leisure. A continuous development of new materials, new products, and new industries stimulated new processes involving greater efficiency in harnessing the uses of energy. The building of specialized, labor-saving machinery, the increasing attention to standardization and use of interchangeable machinery parts, and the extension of mass production techniques further increased productivity. These new processes were enhanced by the development of computer technology, advanced information systems, and systems engineering. World War II had given a big boost to the chemical and airplane industries, to the development and exploitation of synthetics such as nylon and metals such as aluminum, and to the expansion of the importance of electricity. The postwar period saw the continued preeminence of the automobile industry but saw, too, the emergence of major new industries—television, space technology, commercial aviation, and information technology. Industrial and technological advances were reflected in worker productivity and work hours. Between 1950 and 1970, the real GNP per capita rose 50 percent while average annual working hours per worker dropped 8.5 percent.[24]

The impact of industrial and technological change on worker output was reflected not only in a reduction in average work hours but also in the occupational distribution of employees. After 1950, the proportion of employment in manufacturing began to decline, falling to 25 percent by 1970.

At the same time, growing wealth and increasing societal complexity led to rapid expansion in service industries—health, recreation, and so on—and in government. By 1970, employment in services had risen to 17 percent and in government to 18 percent of the total employment picture.[25]

In the wake of depression and war, the American public accepted an expanded role of government in their everyday lives. The Employment Act of 1946 had set "maximum employment, production and purchasing power" as goals of governmental policy. The act's creation of the Council of Economic Advisors led to the conscious use of fiscal and monetary policy and of the federal budget as tools to control employment, production, and price levels—that is, to strive for economic stability. In a related area, there was continued and growing acceptance of the responsibility of government for the income security of those with lifetime attachments to the labor force.

The government's program of Old Age and Survivors Insurance was expanded first to disability and then to health insurance for the aged. The popularity of Social Security showed little sign of abating. With little opposition, payroll taxes were increased from 2 percent of the first $3,000 of income in 1940 to 9.6 percent of $7,800 in 1970.

The public continued to support the expansion of public assistance, especially those titles of the Social Security Act that provided aid for older Americans and people with disabilities. Yet, the increasing number of families that collected Aid to Dependent Children began to attract unfavorable attention. Social Security administrators and Congress had expected income-tested public assistance to "wither away" as more families became eligible for Old Age, Survivors, and Disability Insurance. The increasing number of poor families with children in which the caretaker was not a widow but rather a divorced or unmarried woman, however, fueled ADC's expansion. An additional demographic change—the migration of poor African Americans to the North during these years—exacerbated the issue. Increasingly, many Americans viewed ADC as a "black" program even though the majority of recipients were white.

The Depression had shaken the confidence of Americans in the ability of society to control economic fluctuations. It introduced fears of a permanent mature economy that would stagnate. The events of World War II and the postwar period seemed to most Americans to demonstrate the ability of government to develop control mechanisms to moderate the ups and downs of business cycles and the continued vigor of the economy. A renewed faith in the productive process took hold.

The final reality was that organized labor, as its members became more affluent, was less likely to share political interests with the poor. Beginning with the New Deal, government had legitimated many of labor's demands: the right to organize and bargain collectively, workmen's compensation, minimum wages, old age insurance and unemployment insurance, limitations on hours, and the prohibition of injunctions. Through the process of collective bargaining, labor had not only been able to raise and even control its wage position relative to prices, but it had also been able to have a whole series of fringe benefits instituted comprising a private health and welfare security system. Membership in unions rose to 20 million by 1970.[26] Organized labor increasingly identified itself with the status quo and separated itself from the poor.

World War II

The most dramatic changes of the 30-year period from 1940 to 1970 occurred during World War II. The upheaval of war brought full employment and rising incomes. For oppressed groups, particularly blacks and women, the period offered increased opportunity for economic, educational, and social equality and laid the groundwork for the civil rights and feminist movements of the 1950s and 1960s.

Indicators of change between 1940 and 1945 abound. The GNP, for example, rose from $99.7 billion in 1940 to $211.9 billion in 1945, and although this was a period of rapidly advancing prices, GNP rose 56 percent in "real" terms—that is, corrected for inflation.[27] Furthermore, full employment and progressive taxation brought about basic changes in income distribution—changes that the New Deal had failed to achieve.

In 1940, the total noninstitutional population of the United States was 100.4 million. Of this total, 56 million were in the labor force, including 540,000 in the armed services. Civilian employment stood at 47.5 million. By 1945, the population had risen to 105.5 million. The total labor force had increased to 65.3 million, including the 11 million men and women in the armed forces. This increase in the number of armed forces personnel took these people out of the civilian work force. Nevertheless, total civilian employment rose by 5 million, or 11.1 percent. The increase was made possible by the sharp decline in unemployment and the expansion of the labor force as women, retirees, and children went to work. By 1945, civilian employment had reached 52.8 million. Between 1940 and 1945, unemployment declined from 8 million to 1 million.

Whereas income redistribution during the 1930s had benefited middle-income groups, redistribution during the World War II period favored the lowest income groups. Real income rose for families in all income ranges between 1941 and 1947, but it rose proportionately more for poor families than for rich ones. The average increase in real income of families in the lowest fifth of family income rankings was 41.6 percent; the average increase of families in the highest fifth was 18.3 percent.

In spite of continued economic growth, poverty remained a common feature of American life. A third of Americans still lived on incomes below minimum adequacy in 1949. Even among workers employed full time for the full year, poverty was common. In 1949, more than 20 percent of workers who were fully employed still did not earn enough to pull their families out of poverty.[28] Nevertheless, the expansion of the economy during and after World War II did equalize incomes. Between 1941 and 1947, the share of income that went to the richest 5 percent of households fell from 23 to 17 percent.[29] A combination of factors—decrease in unemployment, an increase in the number of multi-earner families, the opening up of job opportunities for minority groups, and the expansion of government welfare benefits—propelled this shift. The influx of women into the labor force and the shift of blacks from farms to higher-paying factory jobs reinforced the redistribution of income.

Rising incomes combined with restrictions on the availability of civilian goods increased personal savings. During the worst of the Depression in 1933, savings were negative; Americans spent almost $1 billion more than they saved during the Depression. In 1940, personal savings totaled $3.8 billion. It climbed throughout the war, reaching a peak of $37.3 billion in 1944.[30] Thus, during the war years, a huge backlog of savings developed—about 24 percent of annual disposable income, as compared to 3.4 percent of disposable income in prewar years and 6 to 7 percent in postwar years. These savings were really an indicator of deferred consumption. With the end of the war, they fueled the expansion of America's consumer society.

Discrimination and resistance to discrimination in defense employment pushed the Roosevelt administration to create a Fair Employment Practices Committee (FEPC), which was largely ineffective (Figure 7.1).[31] Discrimination in public accommodations and the armed forces also resulted in a series of racial clashes in Newark, New Jersey; Philadelphia, Pennsylvania; Centreville, Mississippi; and Mobile, Alabama. A particularly severe outbreak in Detroit left 35 dead, 700 wounded, and 1,300 under arrest. In Los Angeles, off-duty sailors precipitated the "zoot suit" riots in 1943, in which hundreds of Mexican youths were attacked and arrested.[32]

The growing militancy of minority groups resulted in the creation of a second FEPC in May 1943 with greater enforcement powers. By 1943, black workers held 1 million factory jobs, though largely as unskilled laborers. Black union membership had increased to 500,000. The number of blacks in government rose from 50,000 in 1939 to 200,000 in 1944. Resistance to the induction of blacks under the provisions of the Selective Service Act of 1940 yielded, so that by the end of the war, about 1 million black men and women had served in the armed forces—a remarkable achievement considering that only about 2,000 were drafted during the first year of the act's operation. The war had brought about gains for blacks as a response to economic pressures and to the successful mobilization of protest.[33]

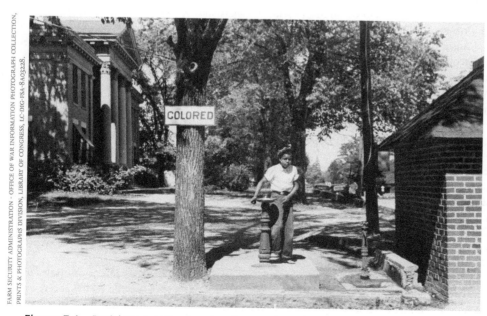

Figure 7.1 Racial segregation in education, and employment—even drinking fountains—was part of everyday life in the South before the 1950s. Halifax, North Carolina.

Other people of color benefited as well. The military draft reduced the supply of workers, while the production needs of the war increased the demand for factory labor. Employment opportunities for minority groups expanded. In addition to women and young adults, African Americans, Native Americans, Mexicans and Mexican Americans, and Puerto Ricans found new opportunities in the busy factories.

During World War II, nearly half a million Native Americans left reservations to work in war industries, and about 25,000 served in the armed forces. When they returned as veterans, they were entitled to job preferences, housing, and the GI Bill for education. Native American veterans became part of the leadership of the Native American protest movement of the 1960s and 1970s.[34]

Wartime Economic and Social Advances

As incomes rose during World War II, the nation's health improved as well. As in other countries, World War II focused the American government on the fitness of its male population and their suitability for military service. Concern about physical and mental health developed as armed services induction procedures revealed serious deficiencies; the inability of large numbers of young people to meet induction standards caused a high rejection rate. To counter this pattern, the military provided routine health care, including dental care, for servicemen and their families. For servicemen themselves, the armed services offered both corrective and preventive care through regular physical and dental examinations and emergency clinic care for minor illnesses. Beyond that, "military medicine" fostered improvements in standards of physical fitness through balanced diets, better clothing, and "more and better hospitals completely staffed."[35]

The federal government demonstrated concern as well for the health of the civilian population. In 1943, Congress appropriated special funds for the Emergency Maternity and Infant Care Program. This program, which was administered by the Children's Bureau through state health departments, provided regular health care for the wives and children of servicemen in the lower pay grades of the armed services. More than 1.2 million women and 230,000 infants were given care during the war years.[36]

Rising incomes made it possible for the civilian population to take advantage of the discovery and development of new drugs and new medical and surgical procedures. Attention to health needs and health care as matters of daily living was demonstrated in new practices such as the stepping up of various inoculation programs. Increased labor participation by women led to improved safety conditions in factories. The National Mental Health Act of 1946 provided new funding for research and training programs, as well as the establishment of community mental health services.

At the same time, the 1940s witnessed the revival of conservatives' political fortunes. Democratic majorities in Congress dwindled during the war, which allowed Republicans and conservative Democrats to kill the Civilian Conservation Corps in 1941 and the WPA in 1943. Expenditures for work relief declined from $1.9 billion in 1940 to less than $5 million by the end of the war.[37] The National Youth Administration (NYA) survived only as a mechanism for administering vocational training for recruits to war industries. In 1948, President Harry Truman proposed a national health insurance scheme, which was killed by the conservatives.

The social legislation of the time was related primarily to the needs of communities disrupted by army camps and war plants and to the needs of families dislocated by the absence of husbands and fathers as they left for the armed forces or for war industries and by the absence of mothers as women took jobs. Housing, day care, education, health, recreation, and transportation needs as they affected "home front" preparations became the focus of concern.

War production, too, created social and cultural challenges. The creation of virtually "instant" cities around massive defense plants, like the Willow Run bomber plant in Michigan, forced government and the private sector to create housing and other essentials for their burgeoning workforces. Throwing so many migrants together with poor housing and little social or cultural infrastructure created social problems as well. Juvenile delinquency and race and ethnic antagonism often accompanied the growth of these establishments.[38]

In November 1940, President Roosevelt named the administrator of the Federal Security Agency coordinator of the Office of Health, Welfare, and Related Defense Activities, with special responsibility for providing service in defense communities and communities near training camps. In May 1941, the Office of Civilian Defense was created in the Office of War Management for the purpose of integrating the provision of health, welfare, and recreation services with other defense activities. The two departments underwent considerable reorganization as experience demonstrated conflicting areas of jurisdiction and the need for clarifying their relationships with a variety of national and local public and voluntary social welfare organizations. By 1943, the government had organized the Office of Community War Services under the Federal Security Agency to take responsibility for coordinating state and local efforts to provide health, welfare, recreation, family, and community services for members of the armed forces and for the civilian population. The Community Facilities Act of 1941 (Lanham Act) provided federal funds for the construction of houses, schools, daycare centers, hospitals, water and sanitation plants, and recreational facilities.

Lanham Act funds helped many communities, but many others suffered upheaval without federal funds to ease the problems of population movement. Local community chests and councils of social agencies took on some of the planning and financing of social services early in the war. Six major voluntary agencies—YMCA, YWCA, National Catholic Community Service, Jewish Welfare Board, Salvation Army, and National Travelers Aid Society—combined efforts through the United Service Organization for National Defense (USO) to provide services for military personnel, war workers, and transients. More than 1,000 USO centers were established.

Fund-raising efforts in the voluntary sector were united by the National War Fund, which combined and regulated the money-raising campaigns of community chest funds with those of the war relief agencies so that traditional social services of local agencies could be financed. Overall control of the whole effort was exercised by the federal government through the War Relief Control Board, which licensed agencies and held authority over all secular wartime charities except for the Red Cross.[39]

Wartime measures for education, like those for health, had implications for future developments. Army examinations had revealed an illiteracy rate of one in five among recruits. At the start of the war, the army asked the WPA to set up programs of adult and worker education and the NYA, a student vocational work program. Their activities were phased out or reduced as the army itself took on some of their tasks and after the U.S. Office of Education was expanded. Perhaps most important in the long run, federal aid was made available for elementary and secondary education in "impacted areas" and for agricultural extension services in rural areas. Education on the college level was also fostered as the federal government let out enormous contracts for research in engineering, science, and civil aeronautics, for education in defense industry management, and for Reserve Officers Training Corps (ROTC).

Postwar Optimism

The widely expected postwar recession never did occur. The liberal monetary and educational provisions of the GI Bill and the beginning contribution of the provisions of the Social Security Act to economic stability were two cushioning factors. Even more important were the combination of increased savings during the full-employment war years and the enormous backlog of demand for major consumer goods that had been unavailable during the war. The postwar spurt in marriages and births added to market demand for goods. Technologies that had been developed during the Depression—television is the great example—finally could generate market demand. The Depression-born fear of a mature, stagnating economy was replaced with a new faith in the vigor of the economic system.

With concern about a return to economic recession and unemployment allayed, the United States entered a period of social complacency. Many in the country seemed pleased with continuing economic growth and intrigued with the promise of automation, of a cybernetic revolution that would provide affluence for all.

The desire for a return to "normalcy" often ran headlong into new realities. The war had given a boost to women's entry into the labor force—a trend that had begun during the Depression. Although many women were forced out of good-paying factory jobs to make room for returning GIs, working wives became a permanent part of the social landscape. Between 1940 and 1950, the share of all households that had a working wife increased from 7 to 13 percent.

However, despite this postwar air of social optimism and political conservatism, some new welfare programs were legislated: the National School Lunch Program in 1946; the Housing Act of 1949; the special Milk Program in 1954; the Indian Health Service in 1955; and finally, in 1960, the Kerr–Mills Act, which provided aid to the medically indigent.

Public welfare had expanded early in the decade through incremental legislative changes that increased the number of potential program recipients and through benefit formula changes that liberalized payments. In 1956, Congress added disability insurance to the Social Security programs. It also legislated health coverage for welfare recipients and added funding for "caretakers" (typically mothers) to the Aid to Dependent Children program. Later in the decade, amendments to the Social Security Act expanded eligibility and funding for states to offer social services to individuals and families likely to become welfare dependent.

For Native Americans, however, the postwar period was very difficult. In 1949, Congress began to shift Native American programs from the federal government to state governments and to back away from the federal protections of the 1934 Reorganization Act. By 1960, several dozen tribes were no longer protected by federal guardianship. While giving Native Americans equal rights with other citizens, the termination of protected status and the return of control to the states meant loss of social programs and aid as well as new taxes and sharp increases in unemployment. For some tribes, it was a disaster. In 1961, President Kennedy ended the termination policy, but not before it became a rallying point for Native American militancy.[40]

During the late 1940s and 1950s, employer-provided fringe benefits became a central element of the American system of social welfare. Three trends converged to produce this shift. First, beginning with the Revenue Act of 1942, the federal government began to encourage corporations to expand pensions and health coverage through the granting of generous tax incentives. Second, in 1948, the Supreme Court ruled (*Inland Steel v. NLRB*) that unions had the right to negotiate over benefits as well as wages. Finally, the significant organizing setbacks for labor unions after the war, especially Operation Dixie—a failed attempt to expand unionization in the South—convinced many unions that it was wiser to expand employer-based systems for health care and pensions than to count on the expansion of the Social Security system.[41]

At the same time, the successes of Social Security had a decisive impact on the politics of social welfare. Historically, many of the "deserving poor" had had to rely on public assistance. By the middle of the 1950s, however, the unemployed, older Americans, people with disabilities, and widows and their children could all count on social insurance programs to protect them against poverty. Although the assistance programs for the elderly and people with disabilities were still important, the public assistance population was increasingly composed of groups that were considered undeserving. Because most widows were eligible for Social Security survivors' benefits, ADC recipients were more likely to live in families headed by a divorced or never-married woman. The departure of the unemployed from assistance programs meant that general assistance recipients were increasingly likely to have spotty work histories. Whereas in the 1930s, the various elements of the Social Security Act were supported by the same constituencies, by the 1950s, its social insurance and assistance programs for the elderly and people with disabilities had remained broadly popular while ADC could count on a much narrower constituency for political support.

Other social policies exacerbated the difference between well-off working families and the poor. The Housing Act of 1949 provided long-term mortgages for new, suburban construction while making it more difficult to gain financing for the purchase of homes in older urban neighborhoods. Rather, the act provided two solutions for declining cities: slum clearance that would eventually displace thousands of families and the expansion of public housing that concentrated the poorest urban residents in a few high-rise projects. During the 1950s, Congress provided new funding for highway construction (but not for mass transit), fueling the abandonment of old urban neighborhoods by better-off workers.[42]

All of these trends—the shift to employer-provided benefits, the split between social insurance and public assistance, and rapid suburbanization—included a racial dimension. Bowing to the demands of Southern conservatives, Congress intentionally excluded farm laborers and domestic workers from Social Security during the 1930s, which left African Americans unprotected. Although this exclusion was eliminated, black workers were more likely than whites to work in jobs without unions or fringe benefits after the war. The plague of chronic joblessness meant that black workers and their families were less likely to qualify for social insurance than public assistance. By the end of the 1950s, politicians and the public increasingly saw black women and children as the primary beneficiaries of ADC. Finally, the move to the suburbs was almost wholly a white phenomenon. Black families—whatever their economic status—were largely confined to deteriorating urban neighborhoods. Even those African Americans who could purchase homes rarely could count on the appreciation of their value to the extent that whites could.

Although often pictured as a quiet decade of affluence and stability, the character of social welfare and its influence on American society had been transformed between 1950 and 1960. By the end of the decade, relatively affluent white suburban workers could count on tax-subsidized, employer-provided fringe benefits and Social Security to provide expanding protection against the risks of an industrial society. Black and Hispanic workers and families increasingly found themselves living in declining urban neighborhoods, threatened by slum clearance or herded into public housing projects and dependent upon public assistance programs. As a result, the late 1950s saw increasingly virulent attacks on public welfare.

> **?** Assess your comprehension of "Changing Economic and Demographic Realities" by taking this quiz.

INNOVATIONS IN SOCIAL WELFARE

Veterans and the GI Bill

Over 16 million Americans participated in the war. Over 400,000 of them died and another 671,000 were wounded. The income needs of the dependents of members of the armed forces were met through a program of family allotments financed jointly by the individual soldier, through a pay deduction, and by the federal government. The allowances were provided for by the Servicemen's Dependents Allowance Act of 1942[43] and were administered by the Office of Dependency Benefits of the War Department. During its first year of operation, ending June 30, 1943, a total of $797 million was disbursed, of which the government had contributed 50 percent. By 1945, allotment payments totaled $3 billion, with the government's contribution rising to $2 billion.[44]

All wives and children of soldiers in the six lowest pay grades of the armed forces qualified for family allotments regardless of income. In addition, soldiers received life and disability insurance as part of the National Life Insurance Act of 1940.

Benefits for veterans of World War II moved beyond those available to veterans of previous wars. In the past, concern had been primarily with income security for dependents of the dead and disabled and with the vocational rehabilitation of the latter. There had long been dissatisfaction with the fact that "veterans without service-connected disabilities were left to their own devices in the matter of their readjustment to civilian life."[45] A first approach to help with readjustment problems was contained in the Selective Training and Service Act of 1940, which provided that inductees "be reemployed at the termination of their period of service in positions of like seniority, status and pay." On November 13, 1942, President Roosevelt appointed the Armed Forces Committee on Postwar Education Opportunities for Service Personnel to study the educational problems that servicemen and servicewomen might encounter after the war. The president's appointment followed upon the urging of the resolution, adopted earlier in 1942, by the American Legion at its annual convention. The Legion was the critical lobbyist for the Servicemen's Readjustment Act of 1944—the famous GI Bill of Rights.

The GI Bill represented the convergence of two key policy rationales—one old and one new. Governments that engage in war require a supply of healthy young bodies to fight. As during previous American wars, the government took an interest in the health and well-being of young men during World War II. In addition, the New Deal had cultivated an expanded view of the role of government in guaranteeing the health and well-being of the population. Although many of the New Deal's programs were blocked during the late 1930s and early 1940s by conservative opposition, tying the "welfare state" to the sacrifice of veterans provided an effective strategy for expanding government programs.

The GI Bill was described by the Senate Finance Committee as "a fundamental bill of rights to facilitate the return of service men and women to civilian life":

> It is a comprehensive statement of the measures presently necessary and . . . represents the very least that should be done at this time in justice to veterans and in enlightened self-interest for the remainder of the country.[46]

The GI Bill represented the triumph of "the idea that the country owes an obligation to the veteran to restore him to the civilian status and opportunities he would have enjoyed had there not been a war."[47] Restoration to civilian status was to be facilitated through provisions for education and training; loans for the purchase of a home, business, or farm; unemployment insurance payments; and veterans' employment services.

A number of factors converged to aid the passage of the GI Bill. There was, of course, very real concern for the welfare of veterans, especially as they returned to an uncertain economy in the midst of reconversion to peacetime operation. The war had also dramatized the poor health and low educational achievement of many potential soldiers.

The GI Bill had a broader economic rationale as well. Many policy commentators feared the resumption of the Depression and economic stagnation at the end of the war. In particular, they feared the return of millions of veterans to a civilian economy with few available jobs. The discharge of millions of veterans into the labor force at a time when war production had ended and thousands of workers were already looking for jobs was seen as a major problem. Thus, the GI Bill was designed to slow the pace at which veterans reentered the labor force.

Actual federal government expenditures for veterans' services and benefits rose to about $3.4 billion for fiscal year 1946. They reached a peak of $9.3 billion, 23 percent of total federal expenditures, in 1950.[48]

The Attack on Public Welfare

At the end of World War II, the elderly were the primary recipients of public assistance in the United States. Then, in 1950, a new public assistance program for the permanently and temporarily disabled was added to the Social Security Act. In addition, Congress added payments for the caretakers of dependent children under the ADC program.

Yet, the steady expansion of public assistance soon provoked a backlash. The increased eligibility of the elderly for old age insurance led to a steady decline in recipients of old age assistance. In addition, recipients of ADC began to shift from the families of widows to those of unmarried mothers.

During the 1950s and early 1960s, welfare reform focused on restricting eligibility. Federal public assistance programs had been designed during the 1930s to give local authority broad discretion, and the Eisenhower administration (1953–1961) was not inclined to expand federal oversight of those programs. In state after state, punitive administrative policies were used to remove recipients from the welfare rolls and to deter new applications. State residency requirements were strictly enforced, so that black migrants who moved from the South to Northern cities, for example, were barred from receiving assistance. Drives to publicize the names of welfare recipients were widespread. As a way of weeding out suspected "fraud," entire caseloads were closed, and all recipients were required to undergo new application investigations. Beyond the overt intention of weeding out ineligible recipients was the covert hope that attrition would result from the unwillingness of many individuals to experience new eligibility investigations set up to deter them.

In a number of states, "suitable home" and "man-in-the-house" policies became bases for determining that the presence of an unrelated man made a home unsuitable for children. The presence of a man, even though unrelated, also was considered evidence that financial need did not exist. In the summer of 1960, the state of Louisiana was found to have used the "suitable home" pretext for closing 6,281 cases, involving 23,549 children. The practice was halted in 1961, when Secretary of Health, Education, and Welfare Arthur Fleming ruled that cases could no longer be closed as a result of unsuitable home findings, unless other suitable living arrangements had been made for the children.[49] Midnight raids to uncover men living with ADC mothers continued well into the 1960s, when they were effectively halted by the March 27, 1967, decision of the Supreme Court of California, which declared that public assistance workers could not be fired for refusing to participate in an unconstitutional invasion of privacy.[50]

The most notorious example of attempts to reduce the welfare rolls occurred in Newburgh, New York. In 1961, the Newburgh city manager promulgated a 13-point code of welfare regulations that included many of the devices being used across the country to control the size of the welfare rolls and to reduce welfare expenditures. For example, applicants new to Newburgh were to give evidence of having come to the city with a concrete offer of employment; assistance was to be denied to applicants who had left a job voluntarily; all new cases were to be reviewed in the city manager's office prior to certification; active cases were to be reviewed monthly by the city's corporation counsel; work was to be mandated for all able-bodied males receiving money payments; and voucher payments were to be substituted for cash. State welfare officials in New York feared that Newburgh officials' behavior could threaten federal funding for the entire state system of welfare benefits. As a result, they pressured the town's welfare administrators to ignore the city manager's directive.[51]

The various attacks on public assistance programs highlighted a slowly changing perception of the adult recipient of public assistance. Thanks to Social Security, the percentage of older Americans and widows receiving public assistance dropped. Increasingly, the public assistance caseload was composed of divorced and single mothers and jobless men. Most significantly, attention was focused on urban ADC mothers who were perceived as women who had children out of wedlock as a way of avoiding work and as predominantly African American, despite the fact that residency requirements had effectively prevented black migrants from swelling the expanding rolls. During the 1950s, at least, increased expenditures for public welfare resulted from normal population growth, expanded programs, and liberalized benefits. Be that as it may, the new image of the welfare recipient undermined public support for public welfare.

Watch this video on the Newburgh welfare controversy.

How did the city policies compare to those implemented as part of "welfare reform" in 1996?

https://www.youtube.com/watch?v=kmjVVAwzKBk

Thanks to Social Security, the percentage of older Americans and widows receiving public assistance dropped. Increasingly, the public assistance caseload was composed of divorced and single mothers and jobless men.

Poverty and the Reform of Welfare

By the 1960s, some of the optimism of the postwar era began to fade. During World War II, high employment and wages combined with the lack of available consumer goods to increase the savings rate. The end of the war and the reconversion to civilian production fueled years of rapid economic growth. A series of recessions started in 1948: 1948–1949, 1953–1954, 1957–1958, and 1961–1963. A renewed and growing concern with unemployment developed when unemployment rates approached 7 percent in 1958 and again in 1961. After each recession, the economy bounced back, but with less than full vigor. Indeed, each period of recovery was less energetic than that which preceded it. While economists defined "full employment" as 2 percent during the war, by the late 1950s, many experts considered 4 percent as unrealistically low.

Despite this, the general view of the 1950s as the era of the affluent society held. What had changed was the view of poverty and of the poor. John Kenneth Galbraith, writing in 1958, implied that poverty was spotty and scattered, not systemic. He identified two types of poverty: insular and case. Insular poverty covered problems that arose from structural unemployment and differential unemployment rates—the special problems of the Appalachian region, for example. Case poverty denoted poverty arising from a personal deficiency, such as ill health, lack of education, or even racial or sexual discrimination. Whether insular or case in nature, the problem was considered one of employability rather than of poverty *per se*.[52]

In fact, the United States rediscovered poverty as a serious social problem only in the early 1960s, when a series of studies and publications made reality unavoidable. The SSA, using 1959 data, established a poverty index and, for the first time, provided an official statistical measure of individuals and groups in poverty. Increased attention came with the publication of Michael Harrington's *The Other America: Poverty in the United States* in 1962 and Dwight MacDonald's "Our Invisible Poor" in 1963.[53] The 1964 *Annual Report of the Council of Economic Advisers* dealt with the situation at length and was transmitted to the Congress along with the *Economic Report of the President*.[54]

Slowly, the response to poverty emerged, shaped by three factors: (1) the identification of depressed geographical areas, (2) the civil rights revolutions, and (3) the shift in the composition of public assistance rolls that began early in the 1960s. Overall, there was a programmatic emphasis on employment: the opening up of employment opportunities and the upgrading of labor market skills of the poor.

The first thrust of legislation was directed at the specialized problems of depressed areas. The Area Redevelopment Act of 1961 focused on problems of regional unemployment. If the poverty in an area was due to a depletion of natural resources and a decline in the demand for the traditional products of the area, then new industry was to be induced to move into the area. If the people of Appalachia suffered from the decrease of jobs in coal mining, then the expansion of factory employment seemed appropriate. In subsequent years, the 1961 legislation was expanded and a broader program, the Economic Development Act, was passed in 1965. Federal grants and loans provided aid to build industry in six depressed regions of the United States: Appalachia, New England, the Coastal Plains, the Ozarks, the Upper Great Lakes, and a poverty-stricken sector of the Southwest.

The statistical count of the poor made the special plight of the minority population clear. The risk of poverty for African Americans was three times as great as that for whites during the 1960s. Discriminatory employment practices were scored as one major factor. The developing civil rights movement of the 1960s was increasingly forceful in pointing out areas of social, political, and economic discrimination and the consequences of this discrimination for unemployment and relief rolls. The Civil Rights Act of 1964 included a title prohibiting racial, sexual, or ethnic discrimination in employment and established an enforcement mechanism, the Equal Employment Opportunity Commission.

The change in the public assistance rolls in the 1960s was the third major force behind the social legislation of the decade. During the previous decade, the number of unemployed had risen faster than the number of relief recipients, but the increases could be related to each other—they went up and down together. But, in 1963, this shifted, and from 1963 to 1970, unemployment rose by less than 300,000 while the number of public assistance recipients increased by more than 6 million.[55] The sharp rise in public assistance recipients was really a jump in ADC recipients, despite the fact that by 1960, the Survivor's Insurance program was covering 1.5 million children and 396,000 widows. Increasingly, a picture of ADC as harboring, and even creating, families broken by illegitimacy, divorce, and desertion developed. This new picture was brought into even sharper focus by the program's continuing emphasis on the unemployable female parent in the home—the worthy-widow halo—at a time when the larger society was increasingly labeling that parent unworthy and employable.

Solutions to case poverty, whatever the cause, were sought in employment training, work incentives, and, above all, counseling services. The addition of federal funding for services to ADC recipients in 1956 was an expression of alarm at the new composition of the ADC rolls and of hope that services might lead to employment and financial independence. In 1962, the Manpower Development and Training Act was intended to provide training or retraining for workers displaced by economic or technological change. This reemphasis on labor market participation—on enhancing occupational potential—was, in part, an extension of the intent of the GI Bill. Regarding welfare recipients, however, it represented a shift from the cash programs of the New Deal to a service approach, which came to full development in the Public Welfare Amendments of 1962.

President Kennedy's inauguration in January 1961 and the appointment of Abraham Ribicoff as secretary of health, education, and welfare provided the opportunity to get public assistance moving toward two new objectives: "Eliminating whatever abuses have crept into these programs and developing more constructive approaches to get people off assistance and back to useful roles in society."[56]

The 1960s marked a high-water mark for the social work profession's influence on welfare policy. In May 1961, the secretary appointed an Ad Hoc Committee on Public Welfare to study "the problems and prospects for public assistance in the next decade." At about the same time, George K. Wyman, an administrator with experience in local, state, and federal welfare and in voluntary social welfare posts, was asked to make a report offering "recommendations and suggestions for administrative and program actions relating to procedures and operations in the Children's Bureau and the Bureau of Public Assistance."[57] The ad hoc committee was composed of 25 public and voluntary social welfare leaders, mostly social workers. Three members of the committee were deans of schools of social work, and a fourth was appointed to be the committee's consultant. Wyman drew on essentially the same group in preparing his report.

The recommendations of the committee were released in September and were "designed to reinforce and support family life through rehabilitation, prevention and protection." Basic to the committee's proposals were adequacy of financial assistance to needy persons and families, efficient administration and organization of public welfare programs, research into the causes of dependency and family breakdown, and, foremost, the provision of rehabilitative services by professionally trained personnel. In a statement reminiscent of Frederic Almy's 1912 warning against the provision of "untrained relief," the committee wrote, "Financial assistance to meet people's basic needs for food, shelter, and clothing is essential, but alone is not enough. Expenditures for assistance not accompanied by rehabilitation services may actually increase dependency and eventual costs to the community."[58] It was convinced that public welfare, through rehabilitation services, could become a "positive wealth-producing force in society" by contributing to an "attack on such problems as dependency, juvenile delinquency, family breakdown, illegitimacy, ill health, and disability."

Of the committee's 10 recommended immediate steps for change in public welfare, 4 were aimed directly at ADC. It was recommended:

1. that "Aid to Dependent Children Families" be strengthened by the initiation of an accelerated, intensive program of rehabilitation services offered by trained personnel;

2. that the temporary (1961) provisions of federal support for unemployed parents and for foster home care for ADC children be extended and a provision to include support for disabled and unemployed fathers living at home be added;

3. that measures for studying and dealing with the problems of illegitimacy be undertaken; and

4. that earnings of youths be exempted as a deduction from the amount of assistance granted to a family.

Other recommendations for immediate action included appropriations for day care, the removal of residence requirements that conflict with "the freedom of movement . . .

essential to economic progress," the limited use of voucher payments for persons with severe problems of money management, and the support of research and demonstration projects concerned with dependency and family breakdown. Although these recommendations applied to all public assistance programs, they, too, held special meaning for change in ADC.

Social work used its influence to push for the expansion of social services and the professionalization of welfare administration. The ad hoc committee strongly recommended that the role of professionally trained social workers in the program be considerably expanded. It urged "that one-third of all persons engaged in social work capacities in public welfare should hold masters' degrees in social work." The significance of professionally trained social workers went beyond the direct provision of service. The committee had interpreted the occurrence of fraud in public welfare as a reflection of a "basic weakness in the standards of moral responsibility in modern society." Committee members thought that well-qualified social workers could offer knowledgeable, well-directed help to build self-respect and reinforce "capacities of persons to meet their problems and to behave responsibly." No wonder, then, that the Public Welfare Amendments of 1962, which were based largely on the committee's recommendations, were familiarly known as the Social Services Amendments.

The Kennedy administration adopted the committee's commitment to social services and professionalization. Secretary Ribicoff addressed a memorandum to the commissioner of Social Security setting forth a series of changes that would be made in public welfare programs. Along with encouraging the locating of deserting fathers and the detection of fraud, the changes were designed "to promote rehabilitation services and develop a family-centered approach." Each state was to be required to have "a statewide staff development plan which would include in-service training and opportunities for professional and technical education." And, in order to emphasize that "our efforts must involve a variety of helpful services, of which giving a money payment is only one, and . . . that the object of our efforts must be the entire family," the name of the Bureau of Public Assistance was to be changed to the Bureau of Family Services.[59]

The reports of the ad hoc committee and of Wyman, the memoranda of Ribicoff to the commissioner of Social Security and to the administrators of state welfare departments, and a combined report of the state welfare administrators were all preludes to President Kennedy's message to Congress on February 1, 1962—the first presidential message entirely on the subject of public welfare. The president expressed concern about poverty that persisted in the midst of abundance and stated that the "reasons are often more social than economic":

> Merely responding with a relief check to complicated social or personal problems . . . is not likely to provide a lasting solution. Such a check must be supplemented, or in some cases made unnecessary, by positive services and solutions, offering the total resources of the community to meet the total needs of the family to help our less fortunate citizens help themselves.[60]

The legislative actions recommended by the president were those previously designated by Ribicoff as necessary to reduce the welfare rolls. He suggested, in addition, the appointment of an Advisory Council on Public Welfare to evaluate public welfare programs in light of "the changing nature of the economic and social problems of the country."

President Kennedy's recommendations had considerable influence upon the substance of the amendments to the Social Security Act, the Public Welfare Amendments of 1962. Their promise of a new approach to the problems of dependency was based upon extensive advice from social welfare experts who implied future savings in public welfare expenditures. Yet, beneath its new rhetoric, the Kennedy administration's approach to public welfare had a long history. It proposed a return to seeking the cause of poverty within the individual—a return to helping individuals change themselves in order to operate successfully in an apparently well-functioning economy. This time, however, the personal counseling was to be buttressed by employment services—job training and job placement.

A significant outcome of this return to tradition was the president's recommendation that federal money be available for services not only for persons who are already dependent, but also for those *likely to become* dependent. The extent to which the prevention of dependency was focused on mothers with children was shown by the suggestion that Congress offer the states the option of combining into a single category of assistance their programs for the aged, blind, and disabled. The drive to simplify and coordinate the administration of public assistance programs did not extend to that category of assistance for families whose members were potentially employable.

Public Law 87-543, the Public Welfare Amendments of 1962, demonstrated the social work profession's success in making rehabilitation services central to welfare policy. The new law, incorporating the recommendations of the president's message, encouraged the states to provide social services leading to self-care and self-support. Encouragement took the form of a change in the grant-in-aid formula, making the federal share of costs 75 percent of expenditures for services to reduce dependency and for training staff to achieve the intent of the law. In line with this intent, the law offered federal money for services not only to current recipients of public assistance but also to former recipients and to persons who were likely to become recipients. The intent was further strengthened by the provision of funding for demonstration projects aimed at experimenting with new methods for offering money payments and social services.

Although the amendments brought about change for all categories of public assistance and for the Child Welfare provisions of Title V of the Social Security Act, the most striking were those dealing directly or indirectly with Title IV, Aid to Dependent Children. The name of the program was changed to Aid and Services to Needy Families with Children, and the program would henceforth be known as AFDC, Aid to Families with Dependent Children. The law reframed the policy rationale for public assistance:

> For the purpose of encouraging the care of dependent children . . . by enabling
> each State to furnish financial assistance and rehabilitation and other services . . .
> to needy dependent children and the parents or relatives with whom they are living
> to help maintain and strengthen family life and to help such parents or relatives to
> attain or retain capability for the maximum self-support and personal independence
> consistent with the maintenance of continuing parental care and protection.[61]

The temporary legislation enacted in 1961 authorizing federal financial participation in aid to children deprived of parental care and support because of the unemployment of a parent was extended, but assistance was denied to an unemployed parent who refused to accept retraining without good cause. In providing for community work and training programs, the amendments attempted to heed President Kennedy's suggestion that work projects "be an opportunity for the individual on welfare, not a penalty." The projects were to be "of a constructive nature, [geared to] the conservation of work skills and the development of new skills." The secretary was to ensure appropriate health, safety, and pay standards for those projects and appropriate arrangements for the care and protection of the child during the parent's absence. An additional work incentive provided that expenses reasonably attributable to work participation be considered in determining the amount of the family's assistance grant. Congress chose to use a carrot, not a stick, to move the unemployed off the welfare rolls.

The 1962 amendments required that states develop a service plan for each child recipient in light of his or her particular home conditions. Such a plan would include the use of protective payments, if the assistance grant were being mismanaged. Funds for day care for children of working parents were authorized, as were funds for the extension of public child welfare services to all political subdivisions of the separate states, in effect paralleling the coverage of AFDC. The services were to be provided, to the extent feasible, by trained personnel.

The Public Welfare Amendments put the social work profession on the spot. Influential members of the profession had asserted not only that increased social service would improve the family life of the poor, but also that this would reduce the number of recipients and the cost of public assistance. However, within a few years, the rolls expanded, leading to embarrassing questions about the effectiveness of social services. The 1962 amendments and their consequences undermined the credibility of the social work profession in public welfare policy.[62] The American Public Welfare Association, a national organization of people concerned with public welfare issues, had predicted such difficulties.[63] Although the social service focus on the 1962 law would carry over to the War on Poverty, social workers and social work services would never again wield such significant influence in welfare policy.

For the moment, however, the enormous expansion in public services gave renewed attention to relationships between public and private agencies and between family and child welfare agencies. It became clear that developments in social welfare were being shaped by public welfare agencies. The development of a professional generalist method of social work helping and the growing need for administrative economy had earlier sparked a series of mergers between voluntary family and children's casework agencies. The enactment of the 1962 amendments to the Social Security Act (moving the public agency into the family and children's counseling services areas) and the voluntary agencies' continuing problem of funding raised questions about the necessity for voluntary agency services at all.[64]

The possibility of a new era of partnership had to await a new technique of funding. The *purchase-of-service* mechanism was embedded in the service amendments. The Social Security Act made federal funds available for contracting for services

> prescribed by the Secretary which in the judgment of the State agency cannot be as economically or as effectively provided by the staff of such State or local agency and are not otherwise reasonably available to individuals in need of them, and which are provided . . . (whether . . . by contract with public . . . or nonprofit private agencies).[65]

In 1962, whatever the problem with relationships between voluntary and public agencies, the future of social work as a profession seemed assured. The social service amendments had reversed Harry Hopkins's 1933 decision that public funding should be distributed through private agencies. The extent of the reversal was indicated by the announcement of prescribed social services to be offered by "State public assistance agencies . . . in order to claim increased Federal funds." The commissioner of Social Security also announced the means by which services were to be made effective: "caseloads of no more than 60 per worker, 1 supervisor for each 5 workers, and home visiting as frequently as necessary."[66]

The War on Poverty

The War on Poverty is one of the most celebrated and maligned episodes in the history of American social welfare policy. The Johnson administration's initiative ultimately deserves neither the praise nor the condemnation it received. Its origins in the new economics" of the 1960s belied any radical intent. Yet, because it took place just as the civil rights movement of the 1960s emerged, it became one of the most visible responses of the federal government to the demands of African Americans for full civil, political, and economic citizenship. Like the civil rights movement, its political popularity among white Americans was short-lived. As the nation distanced itself from the broader movement for African American equality, conservatives were able to cast the War on Poverty as one of the great failures of social policy. Three decades after its end, a conservative generation of welfare reformers saw themselves as undoing its work.

Poverty, which had been nearly invisible during the 1950s, became increasingly prominent in public discussions of the 1960s. The annual reports of the U.S. Department of Commerce were especially effective in identifying poverty groups, those individuals and families particularly vulnerable to the risks of an industrial society. Year after year, the poverty groups were identified as children, the aged, large families, and families headed by women. Rural families and people of color suffered a double risk. Surprisingly, work—even full-time work—was no guarantee against poverty; the "working poor" became identified as one at-risk population group.

The social theories that drove the War on Poverty were often contradictory. On the one hand, they had their origins in the Kennedy administration's economic policy advisors who believed that expanding Americans' capacity to consume was a key to sustained economic growth. The work of scholars like John Kenneth Galbraith had demonstrated that even after a generation of federal income support programs, a significant share of the population did not have even minimally adequate incomes. At the same time, Oscar Lewis's "culture of poverty" theory—and the popularization of the idea of a "vicious cycle" of poverty by Michael Harrington in *The Other America*—focused more on the values and behaviors of the poor as their primary obstacle. Lewis identified more than 50 traits that characterized the culture of poverty, including an inability to delay gratification, fatalism, and sexual promiscuity. As he noted:

> The people in the culture of poverty have a strong feeling of marginality, of helplessness, of dependency, of not belonging. They are like aliens in their own country, convinced that the existing institutions do not serve their interests and needs. Along with this feeling of powerlessness is a widespread feeling of inferiority, of personal unworthiness.[67]

The War on Poverty's efforts to address juvenile delinquency and youth employment, centered in the Justice Department, led to experimenting with a new approach to youth engagement called "community action" as a means of overcoming the apathy and alienation that hampered poor urban residents.

Support for an attack on hunger and poverty was furthered by the growing strength of the civil rights movement. A demonstration climaxed by an historic speech by Reverend Martin Luther King Jr. brought an unprecedented 200,000 people to Washington, D.C., on a march for "jobs and freedom" and an interracial display of solidarity (Figure 7.2). President Lyndon B. Johnson's decision to include the elimination of poverty among his plans for a "Great Society" came at a fortuitous time. A tax cut in 1964 had succeeded in accelerating economic growth, and a renewed faith in an affluent society made a successful War on Poverty seem feasible.

The Kennedy administration had begun planning programs to attack poverty before the president was assassinated in 1963. Upon assuming the presidency, Johnson sought to make poverty policy his own by adopting a war metaphor. In his message urging Congress to "declare war on a domestic enemy which threatens the strength of our Nation and the welfare of our people," President Johnson wrote, "Today, for the first time in our history, we have the power to strike away the barriers to full participation in our society. Having the power, we have the duty."[68]

The Economic Opportunity Act was passed on August 20, 1964. Its declaration of purpose established public policy in relation to the elimination of poverty:

> The United States can achieve its full economic and social potential as a nation only if every individual has the opportunity to contribute to the full extent of his capabilities and to participate in the workings of our society. It is therefore the policy of the United States to eliminate the paradox of poverty in the midst of plenty in this Nation by opening to everyone the opportunity for education and training, the opportunity to work, and the opportunity to live in decency and dignity.[69]

The various titles of the act represented a continuation and intensification of the Kennedy administration's policies—that is, a further continuation of work training, work incentives, social services, and special programs for particular regions.

The Economic Opportunity Act authorized a set of youth programs designed to give young people of low-income and minority group families the education, skills, and experiences deemed necessary for success. The youth programs included federally established Job Corps training centers for out-of-school and unemployed youths requiring general

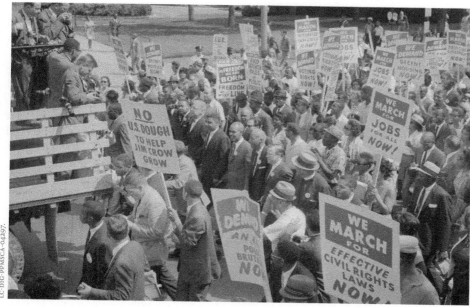

WARREN K. LEFFLER, PRINTS & PHOTOGRAPHS DIVISION, LIBRARY OF CONGRESS, LC-DIG-PPMSCA-04297.

Figure 7.2 The March on Washington in August 1963 is remembered for Martin Luther King's "I Have a Dream" speech. It was supported by a large coalition of social change organizations that demanded jobs and decent housing for all Americans, as well as an end to racial segregation.

and vocational education and help with social and physical difficulties; a work-training program supporting state and local governmental and private nonprofit activities aimed at preventing school dropouts; and a work-study program enabling young people to continue their education in secondary schools, colleges, and universities.

Titles III and IV provided for special programs to combat poverty in rural areas and for programs of employment and investment incentives in poverty areas beyond the reach of the provisions of the Area Redevelopment Act. Grants and loans to farmers and small businesses were the core of these titles. The aim of Title V, described as "Family Unity Through Jobs" by presidential assistant Sargent Shriver, was the development of short-term training and retraining courses leading to the transfer of trainees from relief rolls to jobs. Its central concern was for unemployed parents—fathers and mothers—receiving assistance through the AFDC–UP program. Title V was meant to "demonstrate that public assistance with work and training could be used as a positive instrument to keep families together, to increase employability, and to brighten our communities."[70] Another section of the Economic Opportunity Act created an adult volunteer corps—Volunteers in Service to America (VISTA)—to help with the rehabilitation and improvement of slums and other impoverished areas.

The most controversial—and important—provisions of the Economic Opportunity Act were those included in Title II, Urban and Rural Community Action Programs. Community action programs (CAP) were defined as those that promised progress toward the elimination of poverty; that provided for the "maximum feasible participation" of residents of the geographic areas of group members covered; and that were conducted by public or private, nonprofit community action organizations. The initial popularity of the Office of Economic Opportunity (OEO) stemmed from its ability, through the CAP concept, to fund projects administered by public and voluntary agencies freed from the administrative control of city halls and united funds. Among the more popular programs funded were Head Start (a preparatory education program for preschool, low-income children), Upward Bound (an educational program meant to prevent school dropout and to encourage dropouts to return to school), day-care centers, neighborhood recreation centers, and neighborhood health centers.

The Economic Opportunity Act reinforced the 1962 view that work and jobs were the keys to strengthened family life. The act accelerated the spate of programs designed to remove parents and children from the home and from each other. Job training, job placement, and counseling for a variety of psychological and social ills represented a crash effort to reduce the welfare rolls. Day care, Head Start, and Upward Bound served several purposes at once. For children, they were to be compensation for the failures of parental upbringing and enhancement of potential for adult economic independence. For parents, they were intended to eliminate a barrier to steady employment. The act clearly indicated that employment, as an American value, was at least equal to the value placed on family life and family unity.

At the same time, community action posed a challenge to social work. Efforts to involve the poor in planning new programs implied that professional "experts" were part of the problem, not the solution to the problems of low-income people. Although many social workers were active in efforts to mobilize the poor, other social workers—those who staffed and directed existing welfare bureaucracies—often became the targets of suspicion and protests. The two elements of early 1960s welfare policy—expanding services and professionalization—were split apart during the early years of the War on Poverty.

The OEO soon came under attack. Mayors of cities around the country were politically threatened by the federal funding of projects over which they had no control.

Members of Congress were upset by legal suits brought by government-funded community legal services against federal programs. Communities were shaken by the aggressiveness and hostility of the poor who had found voice in the "maximum feasible participation" concept. Stories of mismanagement, radicalism, and fraud abounded. In time, President Johnson, increasingly enmeshed in the Vietnam War, became disenchanted with community action that not only was costly but also was creating political and social dissensions while seeming to make little direct contribution to its stated goal. The race riots of the summer of 1967—especially those in Newark, New Jersey, as well as Detroit—brought renewed attention to the problems of the ghetto poor, but led more frequently to calls for increased spending on police and prisons than for the expansion of social services.[71]

The Economic Opportunity Act and the War on Poverty did make important contributions to change. The maximum feasible participation concept opened new sources of psychological, financial, and political power as the poor found themselves having a say in, and in some instances even controlling, the programs and institutions that affected their lives. The concept became integral to other legislated social welfare programs, such as the Model Cities legislation of 1966. The poor and other consumers of services became increasingly involved in education and health, as well as welfare, programs. As skills developed, their participation ranged from service to managerial to policy-making positions. CAP opened opportunities for large numbers of minority group members who were educationally prepared for executive and professional jobs but to whom such opportunities had been closed by discrimination. They helped make the "invisible" poor and the members of minority groups more visible and better heard.

An equally significant legacy of community action was the development of community legal services. These services were not specifically mentioned in the Economic Opportunity Act as originally enacted. Once developed as CAP, the importance of legal services for testing and securing the legal rights of the poor through a wide variety of class action suits became obvious, and amendments to the act made specific provision for inclusion. Community legal services, applying pressure for administrative action to implement judicial victories, appeared to be a most important governmental contribution to the welfare of the poor.

An unexpected result of the development of community action was a shift in social workers' views of social welfare, of social agencies, and of their profession. Originally ignored by officials of the OEO, social workers were soon brought into CAP because of their competencies in community organizing, administration, and direct work with clients and client groups. Many social workers viewed the War on Poverty with great enthusiasm and saw it as an opportunity to incorporate social reform into their practice. In contrast to the claims of expertise that the profession had made a few years earlier, many social workers called for community and consumer participation in policy making and decision making, for the input of nonprofessionals into service design and delivery, and for social action to change the system. The National Welfare Rights Organization—a coalition of professionals and welfare clients—played an important role in the policy debates over welfare reform during the late 1960s and early 1970s.[72]

Reform efforts went beyond the issues of community action and welfare reform. The Community Mental Health Act, which provided funds and set up community mental health centers, was passed in 1963. In 1964, Congress passed the Food Stamp Act to help meet the nutritional needs of the poor. Culminating three decades of advocacy, Medicare—health insurance for retirees and people with disabilities—and Medicaid—health insurance for low-income families and individuals—were added to Social Security in 1965. The same year, the Elementary and Secondary Education Act marked the first extension of federal aid for general purposes to local schools. In 1966, the Demonstration (Model) Cities Act sought to address urban decline through a concentration and coordination of housing, health, education, employment, and social services. The Housing and Urban Development Act of 1968 expanded funding for low- and moderate-income housing over the next decade.

Expanded Benefits for the Aging

The aging in particular benefited from the prosperity of the postwar period. Social Security benefits expanded steadily as professionals in the field pushed Congress to increase the number of workers covered and to liberalize payment levels. In 1940, only 58 percent of the workforce was covered; by 1970, more than 90 percent of all workers were included. Coverage was extended to most self-employed, ministers, doctors, farmers, domestic workers, employees of nonprofit organizations, members of the armed forces, and, optionally, state and municipal workers. The number of beneficiaries rose from only 220,000 in 1940 to 3.5 million in 1950 and to well over 25 million in 1970.

In the context of an expanding economy, with increased productivity and output, payment levels were raised throughout the period. In 1950, the program became more redistributive as the replacement rate (the ratio of benefits to a recipient's previous earnings) was increased for low-income workers. Early retirement at age 62 was introduced for women in 1956 and for men in 1961. The program was responsible for a significant decline in the poverty rate for those older Americans. Although benefits still prevented many retirees from escaping poverty, the program's expansion allowed older workers to retire with dignity.[73]

The expansion of Social Security during these years was made simpler by the fiscal structure of the system. Although a large share of the labor force paid into the system through payroll taxes, only a small proportion of the elderly qualified for full benefits. As a result, the Social Security trust funds continued to grow. Congress could expand benefits without worrying about the fiscal health of the system. However, as inflation—the declining value of the dollar—became a public concern in the late 1960s, it created new worries about the future growth of public retirement income.

Older Americans mobilized to make their special needs more visible to the public and to policy makers during the 1950s. Independent organizations and those aligned with organized labor provided crucial support for the passage of Medicare and the expansion of Social Security benefits during the 1960s and after. In 1961, the White House hosted its first Conference on Aging. Congress passed the Older Americans Act in 1965 to help meet the broad social service, legal, nutritional, and economic needs of older people. The act established the Administration on Aging within the federal government and called on the states to create their own agencies on aging. Ultimately, the Older Americans Act led to the creation of a network of local Area Agencies on Aging that provided community services, coordinated and planned activities, sponsored research, established senior centers, and fulfilled other service needs of older Americans. It not only provided money for many activities, but it institutionalized the voice of senior citizen groups in national policy making.[74]

Controlling Public Assistance

Not all groups fared as well as the aged. In particular, recipients of AFDC found themselves subject to increased monitoring. Neither the Public Welfare Amendments of 1962 nor the Economic Opportunity Act of 1964 succeeded in reducing the AFDC rolls. The number of recipients and total expenditures continued a steep climb. More of the poor were being helped, but not in the way Congress had intended. Despite this, the 1966 report of the Advisory Council on Public Welfare urged a continuation of the services approach to change.

But as the American family changed, the nature of public assistance began to change as well. The original purpose of mother's pensions at the beginning of the 20th century was to allow mothers to stay home and care for their children. Yet, by the 1960s, the model "breadwinner" family with a working husband and a stay-at-home mother was in decline. Increasingly, Congress began to demand that welfare mothers, as well, make efforts to achieve self-sufficiency. Nineteen sixty-seven marked the beginning of a trend that would culminate in the abolition of the entitlement to aid in the 1996 welfare law.

The 1962 amendments called on the secretary of health, education, and welfare to appoint an advisory council on public welfare. The council's report, *Having the Power, We Have the Duty,* called on Congress to make public assistance more effective by providing more aid and more services "as a matter of right." The federal government should set nationwide standards for relief grants and assume their full cost above individually stipulated state shares. Discrepancies among state standards would thus be eliminated, and the states, freed of pressures to find new sources of revenues, would be able to concentrate on meeting human needs.[75]

The recommendations of the Advisory Council have been cited as "the last hurrah of the social welfare professionals who had long dominated public assistance policy development."[76] Indeed, those who influenced the shape of the report, despite its fresh declaration of a right to assistance and service, were in many ways out of touch with fellow professionals who were moving in a different direction. Led by James Dumpson, the New York City welfare commissioner, a group of influential professionals began to recommend the separation of cash assistance and services as a means of reducing any possible coercion of welfare recipients by their caseworkers.[77]

Yet, by 1967, the reaction against the War on Poverty had shifted congressional interest from protecting the poor to controlling the expansion of the AFDC. The Social Security Amendments of 1967 legislated both a stick and a carrot attack on the rising AFDC caseload. The law imposed a freeze on children being added to the program because of absence of a parent from the home. By exempting dependency related to the death or unemployment of a parent, the freeze sought to target cases related to divorce or desertion. The law also established the first Work Incentive Program (eventually known as WIN, after having been initially and disastrously labeled "WIP"). WIN disqualified adults and out-of-school older children—female as well as male—from AFDC payments if they refused to accept employment or to participate in training programs without good cause.

To increase the work incentives for recipients, the 1967 amendment also eliminated the 100 percent "tax" on the earnings of recipients. Before 1967, any earnings reported by a recipient led to a dollar-for-dollar cut in his or her benefits. After the passage of the amendments, recipients were allowed to keep the first $30 of their earnings each month; their welfare check would be reduced only by two-thirds of any additional income. "Thirty and a third," as the policy was called, and the expansion of child-care subsidies set a new path for welfare policy. No longer was welfare a "mother's pension" to allow mothers to focus on child-rearing. Now, mothers on welfare would be encouraged, and eventually required, to seek paid labor.

In contrast to the elderly, poor women with children soon faced a backlash. The punitive aspects of the 1967 welfare amendments caused dismay and then outrage among client groups interpreting the freeze as punishment of helpless children, among state administrations facing the prospect of increased and intolerable burdens on state budgets, and among social welfare professionals foreseeing state reductions in relief grants. President Johnson and his successor, President Richard M. Nixon, both delayed implementation of the freeze, which was repealed by congressional action in 1969.

The full effects of the WIN program were temporarily delayed by the administrative discretion permitted state and local departments of welfare in requiring recipient participation. Nevertheless, the intent of Congress and of the secretary of health, education, and welfare was proclaimed in a 1967 announcement of a major administrative restructuring of the department. The Welfare Administration and Bureau of Family Services, established in 1962, were abolished, and a new agency, the Social and Rehabilitation Service (SRS), was created to administer public assistance, rehabilitation, and social services. The secretary's announcement deemphasized family and community services and the substitution of "services aimed at rehabilitation in the broadest sense of the word."[78] The work orientation of SRS was further indicated by the appointment of the former commissioner of the Vocational Rehabilitation Administration as administrator of the new unit.

The separation of social service from cash assistance became standard public assistance policy by 1974. "Separation" was attractive on a number of counts. For those who were determined to infuse AFDC with a work orientation, separation quite literally meant separation of recipients from the requirement of services offered by professional social workers. In line with this, the institution of simple client declaration systems for establishing eligibility for cash benefits eliminated the need for professional skills in all aspects of the money payment process. For clients, separation meant the right to choose service voluntarily, when needed, without fear of losing a grant. For most professionals, separation meant a further delineation of the rights of clients as well as of the poor and of minority group members.

The National Association of Social Workers supported separation and pointed out that:

1. Service, when offered within the context of eligibility investigation, tends to become a condition for obtaining financial assistance. This undermines the concept of assistance as a right and . . . interferes with . . . self-determination in seeking and accepting service.

2. There is no reason to assume that financial need, in itself, necessarily calls for the provision of social services. . . . Separation of assistance from social services will make it possible to organize services so that they reach those who have specific need for them.[79]

Social workers were now free to join other social scientists and social welfare theorists in a search for new forms of income transfers and for new ways of achieving a more equal distribution of income.

> **?** Assess your comprehension of "Innovations in Social Welfare" by taking this quiz.

SOCIAL MOVEMENTS AND REFORM AFTER WORLD WAR II

Expanding the Civil Rights of African Americans

From the end of Reconstruction during the 1870s until World War II, the status of African Americans was largely ignored by the federal government. With the overwhelming proportion of African Americans residing in the rural South, the rights supposed secured after the Civil War were largely ignored by state governments and federal courts.

However, the Great Migration during World War I initiated a massive movement that resulted in black Americans becoming a largely urban and Northern population over the next two generations.

The movement of black Americans to Northern cities sparked a revival of movements to secure their civil rights. While Southern blacks were largely disenfranchised by Jim Crow laws, Northern African Americans became a large and critical voting bloc in a number of Northern cities. At the same time, urban and Northern African Americans were more easily organized and less easily intimidated than their Southern counterparts.

World War II renewed the migration of African Americans to the North, especially to centers of war production. They soon encountered discrimination, which excluded them from better jobs. Even highly skilled African Americans found themselves relegated to low-paying unskilled and dangerous jobs. While the discrimination was not new, the role of the federal government in funding the work and the increasingly organized civil rights community challenged the status quo.

White workers often resisted the employment of blacks in defense industries, and race riots occurred in 1940 and 1941. Faced with widespread exclusion from war industries, black workers mobilized to force the government's hand. A. Philip Randolph, the president of the predominantly black Brotherhood of Sleeping Car Porters, threatened a march on Washington to demand black access to defense jobs. The March on Washington movement spurred grassroots organizing in the black community even though the march itself never took place.

In exchange for cancelling the march, the Roosevelt administration agreed to Executive Order 8802 that established the Committee on Fair Employment Practices (FEPC) and promised "no discrimination in the employment of workers in defense industries or Government because of race, creed, color, or national origin . . . [and] the full and equitable participation of all workers in defense industries, without discrimination."[80] Without strong enforcement powers, the FEPC met with widespread defiance that it was unable to overcome. Yet, the connection between grassroots organizing and pressuring government for action was not wasted. Two decades later, in 1963, Randolph again led a march on Washington that secured landmark civil rights legislation the following year.

The response of the black community to the failure of FEPC was strong and immediate, as several factors came together. First, of course, was the fact that blacks had been migrating to urban industrial centers, where their congregating under conditions of segregation lent strength for joint action. Second, a significant number of African Americans had been educationally prepared and were ready for greater participation in the work opportunities opened up by the war. Experience on Works Progress Administration (WPA) projects, vocational training received by way of the NYA's vocational work program, and defense training financed through programs sponsored by the U.S. Office of Education, all pointed to a source of untapped and underutilized labor. The training was in itself a promise of opportunity that remained unfulfilled, joining other promises to a string of disappointments. The National Defense Advisory Committee's statement against discriminatory hiring practices in defense plants and President Roosevelt's inclusion of a similar statement in a message to Congress, both in 1940, failed to change the situation. The efforts of the Office of Production Management's Negro Employment and Training Branch to facilitate the hiring of blacks in defense industries were unsuccessful. Finally, the ineffectiveness of FEPC was demonstrated when its scheduled public hearings into discrimination on railroads were canceled by the War Manpower Commission despite widespread support by the black press and civil rights leaders.

To white Americans, the civil rights movement seemed to appear from nowhere, but it was based on years of institutional and intellectual effort by blacks and whites who were committed to equality and justice. Within the black community, the commitment to pursuing integration by legal and political means grew out of organizations like the NAACP Legal Defense Fund that systematically attacked the legal foundations of segregation. In addition, African American churches, which for decades had accepted segregation, became central institutions for organizing the black community. Churches and labor unions were among the few places in the United States where black and white Americans could come together as equals. Randolph's Brotherhood of Sleeping Car Porters worked with other unions to put pressure on politicians to support change and to spread methods to mobilize resistance to segregation. In addition, an influential African American press—Baltimore's *Afro-American*, Harlem's *Amsterdam Star News*, the *Chicago Defender*, the *Houston Informer*, and so on—pushed editorially for black rights and simultaneously encouraged blacks to make their own demands.

After the war, the legal foundations of discrimination were systematically undermined by court decisions sparked by the Legal Defense Fund and other advocacy groups. Discrimination in education, public accommodations, and real estate practices—like the *restrictive covenants* that banned owners from selling to Jews or black Americans—were declared unconstitutional. The court battles culminated in 1954 when in *Brown v. Board of Education*, the Supreme Court decided unanimously that in public school education, separate facilities for racial groups were inherently unequal.

The legal strategy was soon joined by direct action. Martin Luther King led the Montgomery bus boycott to integrate public transportation. Students at historically black colleges like Fisk University developed a set of tactics, including the sit-in, to press their demand. During the early 1960s, organizations like the Southern Christian Leadership Council, Congress for Racial Equality, and the Student Nonviolent Coordinating Committee led a series of actions to dramatize the impact of Jim Crow on black lives. Future congressman John Lewis led the Freedom Rides to integrate public transportation in the South. In 1963, the growing civil rights movement organized a new March on Washington to press for jobs and freedom. In contrast to previous efforts, the movement of the early 1960s was successful in pushing the Congress to action—the Civil Rights Act of 1964 and the Voting Rights Act the following year.[81]

By late 1965, the movement entered a new stage. As it turned attention to continuing discrimination in the North, Northern white support for the movement declined. Many poor urban African Americans, caught in a revolution of rising expectations, engaged in riots in Los Angeles in 1965, Newark and Detroit in 1967, and several cities including Washington, D.C., after King's assassination in 1968. A housing act, outlawing discrimination in selling or renting housing, marked the end of legislative efforts during the Johnson administration.

During the early 1960s, organizations like the Southern Christian Leadership Council, Congress for Racial Equality, and the Student Nonviolent Coordinating Committee led a series of actions to dramatize the impact of Jim Crow on black lives.

Watch this video on the role of photography in the civil rights movement.

Assess the relative impact of pictures and words on the audiences' reaction to the articles described.

A Renewed Feminist Movement

The entry of women into the labor force during World War II sparked significant changes in the status of women during the next several decades. Although many women resumed roles as homemakers after the war, feminist writers like Betty Friedan in her 1963 book explained the dissatisfaction that resulted from women's restricted economic, social, and political role.

The Equal Pay Act of 1963 amended the Fair Labor Standards Act to outlaw wage disparities based on gender, although those disparities continued. But the key legislative turning point
for the postwar feminist movement occurred almost by accident. At the end of the debate of
the Civil Rights Act in 1964, Representative Howard Smith of Virginia successfully inserted
"sex" in the list of classes protected by the bill. Practically "below the radar," equal rights for
women became the law of the land. Following the African American movement, feminists
also turned to direct action, including a protest at the Miss America contest in 1968 at which
products associated with traditional women's roles were thrown into a "Freedom Trash Can."
Although women's undergarments were not one of the products, thanks to a New York Post
headline, the protest gave birth to the equation of feminists with "bra burners."[82]

The civil rights movement, with its combination of direct action and legislative and
legal strategies, inspired other groups, including members of other ethnic and racial groups,
people with disabilities, and gay Americans to undertake similar actions. Taken together,
these efforts remade the nature of citizenship and rights over the following decades.

Civil Rights and Juvenile Justice

Social workers saw separation of money payments and services as a part of a new concern for the rights of the poor. Spurred by the civil rights revolution, questions about the
rights of various groups in our society to social well-being were asked and answers were
demanded. Judicial and administrative decisions strengthened the rights of the aged, the
rights of the mentally ill, the rights of the retarded, the rights of tenants, the rights of
prisoners, the rights of minority groups, and the rights of women.

The rights of children, too, were reexamined. The Supreme Court's 1967 decision in
In re Gault challenged the structure of juvenile justice that had existed since the Progressive Era. As originally conceived in 1899, the juvenile court sought to protect children
from the impersonal legal processes of adult courts. Instead of an adversary approach,
the child was to be offered the friendly help of a fatherly judge who would see to individualized treatment and, if necessary, rehabilitation. Seventy years of experience with juvenile courts had demonstrated the reality that services for rehabilitative purposes were a
myth. In practice, the pretext of service was a substitute for justice. Children were incarcerated for indefinite periods. The rhetoric claimed training for a productive adult life;
the actuality most often proved quite the contrary.

In 1967, the Supreme Court decided that children in trouble with the law had many
of the legal rights of adults, including the right to counsel, to confidentiality, and to protection from self-incrimination. Justice Abe Fortas, writing the majority decision, stated:

> While due process requirements will . . . introduce a degree of order and regularity
> to juvenile court proceedings to determine delinquency, and in contested cases will
> introduce some elements of the adversary system, nothing will require that the con-
> ception of the kindly juvenile judge be replaced by its opposite.[83]

The child could have both, justice and service. The juvenile's sudden right to "due process" galvanized the entire judicial and probation systems to a reconsideration of legal
practices. In addition, the fact that there are legal aspects to all child welfare
programs and that workers in these programs have frequent contacts with
courts and lawyers fostered a reawakening of interest in the law on the part of
all social agencies and social welfare personnel engaged in services to children.
The *Gault* decision pointed out the need for a resolution of continuing value
conflicts in all areas of social welfare.

? Assess your comprehension of "Social Movements and Reform After World War II" by taking this quiz.

War and Prosperity

The documents used to support post–World War II occurrences in social welfare are President Kennedy's *Message on the Public Welfare Program* (1962), excerpts from the *Economic Opportunity Act* (1964), and the Supreme Court decision, *In re Gault* (1967). The documents are all products of the 1960s and represent the climax of post–World War II effort to bring economic affluence to bear on the promises of American democracy. The documents represent executive, legislative, and judicial responses to the social welfare issues of the period.

President Kennedy's message to Congress on public welfare programs was historic in its having been the first presidential message entirely devoted to the subject. The message, in effect, reiterates the thrust of Secretary of Health, Education, and Welfare Abraham Ribicoff's memorandum to the commissioner of Social Security. That memorandum bridged the efforts of the late 1950s to contain the growth of the public assistance rolls and the new approach to public welfare legislated by the 1962 Public Welfare Amendments. The secretary's concern was to eliminate fraud, but more than that to infuse public welfare—in reality, AFDC—with a philosophy geared to family stability and family independence. The approach implied a pathological base for poverty and dependence; therefore, the secretary pointed out the need for each state to assess its personnel and training needs to carry out the objectives of a service-oriented program.

President Kennedy's message announces the new orientation to family welfare. It demonstrates administrative discretion at the federal level in shaping and regulating the public assistance programs. It shows, too, the need for congressional action for authorizing and funding new programs. In his leadership capacity, the president recommends congressional support of a new approach to public assistance by providing for the relief of unemployed parents, for community work and training projects, for the expansion and upgrading of social work personnel, and for a consultative Advisory Council on Public Welfare. The president's recommendation of the "rehabilitative road" to change in public welfare is couched in terms that plead for a demonstration of "the compassion of free men . . . in the light of . . . constructive self-interest."

The *Economic Opportunity Act* of 1964 and its heralded War on Poverty were President Johnson's extension of his predecessor's compassion for the poor. The act was also a response to a rediscovery of poverty, this time in the midst of economic plenty. The demand of the poor and particularly of the black minority for participation in the country's economic life, for a share of its wealth, seemed eminently reasonable. In 1964, the country was not yet so embroiled in the Southeast Asia conflicts that decisions about guns or butter had to be made. It seemed possible to have both, and the president, believing that we had the power to eliminate poverty, convinced the Congress that we had the duty to do so.

Ultimately, the *Economic Opportunity Act* was an abortive attempt to eliminate poverty. Nevertheless, it was historically important as an effort to do so. Additionally, the act made significant, perhaps permanent, contributions to social welfare in the United States through the introduction of the maximum feasible participation concept, which, at the least, led to some psychological and political gains in the power of minorities. This new power was demonstrated and furthered by the CAP, among them Head Start and community legal services, funded by the act. It must be pointed out, however, that the overall thrust of the *Economic Opportunity Act* was one of "blaming the victim." The act was meant to change the poor and, in this way, open opportunities for them. Only incidentally did organizations for structural change in "the system" arise.

The War on Poverty was waged in the context of a civil rights revolution. Led by the black community, the United States was swept by demands for increased political, social, and economic equality. Other racial and ethnic groups—Puerto Ricans and Native Americans, for example—added their protests. Many other groups banded together in a fight for social justice. The Supreme Court decision in *In re Gault* represents a judicial response to demand on behalf of the rights of one group of children.

The juvenile court had been formed to provide individualized treatment for children. The erosion and subversion of the intent of the juvenile court is delineated in the opinion written for the Supreme Court by Justice Abe Fortas. In effect, the court's opinion requires attention to due process, to legal rights, as the path to individualized justice for children. The opinion denies that legal justice necessarily eliminates sympathy and compassion or attention to therapeutic and rehabilitative needs of children. In fact, suggests the opinion, "The essentials of due process . . . may be a more impressive and more therapeutic attitude so far as the juvenile is concerned."

The Fortas opinion had sweeping significance for children, for juvenile courts, and for professionals operating in juvenile courts. By extension, the opinion had significance for all of social welfare.

MESSAGE FROM PRESIDENT JOHN F. KENNEDY
PUBLIC WELFARE
February 1, 1962
H. Doc. No. 325

TO THE CONGRESS OF THE UNITED STATES:

Few nations do more than the United States to assist their least fortunate citizens—to make certain that no child, no elderly or handicapped citizen, no family in any circumstances in any State, is left without the essential needs for a decent and healthy existence. In too few nations, I might add, are the people aware of the progressive strides this country has taken in demonstrating the humanitarian side of freedom. Our record is a proud one—and it sharply refutes those who accuse us of thinking only in the materialistic terms of cash registers and calculating machines.

Our basic public welfare programs were enacted more than a quarter century ago. Their contribution to our national strength and well-being in the intervening years has been remarkable.

But the times, the conditions, the problems have changed—and the nature and objectives of our public assistance and child welfare programs must be changed, also, if they are to meet our current needs.

The impact of these changes should not be underestimated.

People move more often—from the farm to the city, from urban centers to the suburbs, from the East to the West, from the South to the North and Mid-west.

Living costs, and especially medical costs, have spiraled.

The pattern of our population has changed. There are more older people, more children, more young marriages, divorces, desertions, and separations.

Our system of social insurance and related programs has grown greatly: In 1940, less than 1 percent of the aged were receiving monthly old-age insurance benefits; today over two-thirds of our aged are receiving these benefits. In 1940, only 21,000 children, in families where the breadwinner had died, were getting survivor insurance benefits; today such monthly benefits are being paid to about 2 million children.

All of these changes affect the problems public welfare was intended to relieve as well as its ability to relieve it. Moreover, even the nature and causes of poverty have changed. At the time the Social Security Act established our present basic framework for public aid, the major cause of poverty was unemployment and economic depression. Today, in a year of relative prosperity and high employment, we are more concerned about the poverty that persists in the midst of abundance.

The reasons are often more social than economic, more often subtle than simple. Some are in need because they are untrained for work—some because they cannot work, because they are too young or too old, blind or crippled. Some are in need because they are discriminated against for reasons they cannot help. Responding to their ills with scorn or suspicion is inconsistent with our moral precepts and inconsistent with their nearly universal preference to be independent. But merely responding with a relief check to complicated social or personal problems—such as ill health, faulty education, domestic discord, racial discrimination, or inadequate skills—is not likely to provide a lasting solution. Such a check must be supplemented, or in some cases made unnecessary, by positive services and solutions, offering the total resources of the community to meet the total needs of the family to help our less fortunate citizens help themselves.

Public welfare, in short, must be more than a salvage operation, picking up the debris from the wreckage of human lives. Its emphasis must be directed increasingly toward prevention and rehabilitation—on reducing not only the long-range cost in budgetary terms but the long-range cost in human terms as well. Poverty weakens individuals and nations. Sounder public welfare policies will benefit the Nation, its economy, its morale, and, most importantly, its people.

Under the various titles of the Social Security Act, funds are available to help the States provide assistance and other social services to the needy, aged and blind, to the needy disabled, and to dependent children. In addition, grants are available to assist the States to expand and strengthen their programs of child welfare services. These programs are essentially State programs. But the Federal Government, by its substantial financial contribution, its leadership, and the standards it sets, bears a major responsibility. To better fulfill this responsibility, the Secretary of Health, Education, and Welfare recently introduced a number of administrative changes designed to get people off assistance and back into useful, productive roles in society.

These changes provided for:

The more effective location of deserting parents;

An effort to reduce that proportion of persons receiving assistance through willful misrepresentation, although that proportion is only a small part of the 1.5 percent of persons on the rolls found to be ineligible;

Allowing dependent children to save money for educational, employment or medical needs without having that amount deducted from their public assistance grants;

Providing special services and safeguards to children in families of unmarried parents, in families where the father has deserted, or in homes in danger of becoming morally or physically unsuitable; and

An improvement in the training of personnel, the development of services and the coordination of agency efforts.

In keeping with this new emphasis, the name of the Bureau of Public Assistance has been changed to the Bureau of Family Services.

But only so much can be done by administrative changes. New legislation is required if our State-operated programs are to be fully able to meet modern needs.

I. PREVENTION AND REHABILITATION

As already mentioned, we must place more stress on services instead of relief.

I recommend that the States be encouraged by the offer of additional Federal funds to strengthen and broaden the rehabilitative and preventive services they offer to persons who are dependent or who would otherwise become dependent. Additional Federal funds would induce and assist the States to establish or augment their rehabilitation services, strengthen their child welfare services, and add to their number of competent public welfare personnel. At the present time, the cost of these essential services is lumped with all administrative costs—routine clerical and office functions—and the Federal Government pays one-half of the total of all such costs incurred by the States. By separating out and identifying the cost of these essential rehabilitation, social work and other service costs, and paying the States three-fourths of such services—a step I earnestly recommend for your consideration—the Federal Government will enable and encourage the States to provide more comprehensive and effective services to rehabilitate those on welfare. The existing law should also be amended to permit the use of Federal funds for utilization by the State welfare agency of specialists from other State agencies who can help mount a concerted attack on the problems of dependency.

There are other steps we can take which will have an important effect on this effort. One of these is to expand and improve the Federal–State program of vocational rehabilitation for disabled people. Among the 92,500 disabled men and women successfully rehabilitated into employment through this program last year were about 15,000 who had formerly been receiving public assistance. Let me repeat this figure: 15,000 people, formerly supported by the taxpayers through welfare, are now back at work as self-supporting taxpayers. Much more of this must be done—until we are restoring to employment every disabled person who can benefit from these rehabilitation services.

The prevention of future adult poverty and dependency must begin with the care of dependent children—those who must receive public welfare by virtue of a parent's death, disability, desertion, or unemployment. Our society not only refuses to leave such children hungry, cold, and devoid of opportunity—we are insistent that such children not be community liabilities throughout their lives. Yet children who grow up in deprivation, without adequate protection, may be poorly equipped to meet adult responsibilities.

The Congress last year approved, on a temporary basis, aid for the dependent children of the unemployed as a part of the permanent aid-to-dependent-children program. This legislation also included temporary provisions for foster care where the child had been removed from his home, and an increase in Federal financial assistance to the aged, blind, and disabled. The need for these temporary improvements has not abated, and their merit is clear. I recommend that these temporary provisions be made permanent.

But children need more than aid when they are destitute. We need to improve our preventive and protective services for children as well as adults. I recommend that the present ceiling of $25 million authorized for annual appropriations for grants to the States for child welfare services be gradually raised, beginning with $30 million for 1963, up to $50 million for the fiscal year ending June 30, 1969, and succeeding years.

Finally, many women now on assistance rolls could obtain jobs and become self-supporting if local day-care programs for their young children were available. The need for such programs for the children, the children of working mothers has been increasing rapidly. Of the 22 million women now working, about 3 million have children under 6, and another 4 1/2 million have school-age children between 6 and 17. Adequate care for these children during their most formative years is essential to their proper growth and training. Therefore, I recommend that the child welfare provisions of the Social Security Act be changed to authorize earmarking up to $5 million of grants to the States in 1963 and $10 million a year thereafter for aid in establishing local programs for the day care of young children of working mothers.

II. PROMOTING NEW SKILLS AND INDEPENDENCE

We must find ways of returning far more of our dependent people to independence. We must find ways of returning them to a participating and productive role in the community.

One sure way is by providing the opportunity every American cherishes to do sound and useful work. For this reason, I am recommending a change in the law to permit States to maintain, with Federal financial help, community work and training projects for unemployed people receiving welfare payments. Under such a program, unemployed people on welfare would be helped to retain their work skills or learn new ones; and the local community would obtain additional manpower on public projects.

But earning one's welfare payments through required participation in a community work or training project must be an opportunity for the individual on welfare, not a penalty. Federal financial participation will be conditioned upon proof that the work will serve a useful community or public purpose, will not displace regular employees, will not impair prevailing wages and working conditions, and will be accompanied by certain basic health and safety protections. Provisions must also be made to assure appropriate arrangements for the care and protection of children during the absence from home of any parent performing work or undergoing training.

Moreover, systematic encouragement would be given all welfare recipients to obtain vocational counseling, testing, and placement services from the U.S. Employment Service and to secure useful training wherever new job skills would be helpful. Close cooperative arrangements would be established with existing training and vocational education programs, and with the vocational and on-the-job training opportunities to be created under the manpower development and training and youth employment opportunities programs previously proposed.

III. MORE SKILLED PERSONNEL

It is essential that State and local welfare agencies be staffed with enough qualified personnel to insure constructive and adequate attention to the problems of needy individuals—to take the time to help them find and hold a job—to prevent public dependency, and to strive, where that is not possible, for rehabilitation—and to ascertain promptly whether any individual is receiving aid for which he does not qualify, so that aid can be promptly withdrawn.

Unfortunately, there is an acute shortage of trained personnel in all our welfare programs. The lack of experienced social workers for programs dealing with children and their families is especially critical.

At the present time, when States expend funds for the training of personnel for the administration of these programs, they receive Federal grants on a dollar-for-dollar basis. This arrangement has failed to produce a sufficient number of trained staff, especially social workers. I recommend, therefore, that Federal assistance to the States for training additional welfare personnel be increased; and that in addition, the Secretary of Health, Education, and Welfare be authorized to make special arrangements for the training of family welfare personnel to work with those children whose parents have deserted, whose parents are unmarried, or who have other serious problems.

IV. FITTING GENERAL CONDITIONS OR SAFEGUARDS TO INDIVIDUAL NEEDS

In order to make certain that welfare funds go only to needy people, the Social Security Act requires the States to take all income and resources of the applicant into consideration in determining need. Although Federal law permits, it does not require States to take into full account the full expenses individuals have in earning income. This is not consistent with equity, common sense, or other Federal laws such as our tax code. It only discourages the will to earn. In order to encourage assistance recipients to find and retain employment, I, therefore, recommend that the act be amended to require the States to take into account the expenses of earning income.

Among relatives caring for dependent children are a few who do not properly handle their assistance payments—some to the extent that the well-being of the child is adversely affected. Where the State determines that a relative's ability to manage money is contrary to the welfare of the child, Federal law presently requires payments to be made to a legal guardian or representative, if Federal funds are to be used. But this general requirement may sometimes block progress in particular situations. In order to recognize the necessity for each State to make exceptions to this rule in a very limited number of cases, I recommend that the law be amended to permit Federal sharing to continue even though protective payments in behalf of children—not to exceed one-half of 1 percent of ADC recipients in each State—are made to other persons concerned with the welfare of the family. The States would be required to reexamine these exceptions at intervals to determine whether a more permanent arrangement such as guardianship is required.

When first enacted, the aid to dependent children program provided for Federal sharing in assistance payments only to the child. Since 1950, there has been Federal sharing in any assistance given to one adult in the household as well as to the child or children. In as much as under current law, there may be two parents in homes covered by this program, one incapacitated or unemployed, I recommend in the interest of equity the extension of Federal sharing in assistance payments both to the needy relative and to his or her spouse when both are living in the home with the child.

V. MORE EFFICIENT ADMINISTRATION

Under present public assistance provisions, States may impose residence requirements up to 5 of the last 9 years for the aged, blind, and disabled. Increased mobility, as previously mentioned, is a hallmark of our times. It should not operate unfairly on either an individual State or an individual family. I recommend that the Social Security Act be amended so as to provide that States receiving Federal funds not exclude any otherwise eligible persons who have been residents of the State for 1 year immediately preceding their application for assistance. I also recommend that the law be amended to provide a small increase in assistance funds to those States which simplify their laws by removing all residence requirements in any of their federally aided programs.

In view of the changing nature of the economic and social problems of the country, the desirability of a periodic review of our public welfare programs is obvious. For that purpose I propose that the Secretary of Health, Education, and Welfare be authorized to appoint an Advisory Council on Public Welfare representing broad community interests and concerns, and such other advisory committees as he deems necessary to advise and consult with him in the administration of the Social Security Act.

No study of the public welfare program can fail to note the difficulty of the problems faced or the need to be imaginative in dealing with them. Accordingly, I recommend that amendments be made to encourage experimental, pilot or demonstration projects that would promote the objectives of the assistance titles and help make our welfare programs more flexible and adaptable to local needs.

The simplification and coordination of administration and operation would greatly improve the adequacy and consistency of assistance and related services. As a step in that direction, I recommend that a new title to the Social Security Act be enacted which would give to States the option of submitting a single, unified State plan combining their assistance programs for aged, blind and disabled, and their medical assistance programs for the aged, granting to such States additional Federal matching for medical payments on behalf of the blind and disabled.

These proposed far-reaching changes—aimed at far-reaching problems—are in the public interest and in keeping with our finest traditions. The goals of our public welfare programs must be positive and constructive—to create economic and social opportunities for the less fortunate—to help them find productive, happy, and independent lives. It must stress the integrity and preservation of the family unit. It must contribute to the attack on dependency, juvenile delinquency, family breakdown, illegitimacy, ill health, and disability. It must reduce the incidence of these problems, prevent their occurrence and recurrence, and strengthen and protect the vulnerable in a highly competitive world.

Unless such problems are dealt with effectively, they fester, and grow, sapping the strength of society as a whole and extending their consequences in troubled families from one generation to the next.

The steps I recommend to you today to alleviate these problems will not come cheaply. They will cost more money when first enacted. But they will restore human dignity; and in the long run, they will save money. I have recommended in the budget submitted for fiscal year 1963 sufficient funds to cover the extension of existing programs and the new legislation here proposed.

Communities which have—for whatever motives—attempted to save money through ruthless and arbitrary cutbacks in their welfare rolls have found their efforts to little avail. The root problems remained.

But communities which have tried the rehabilitative road—the road I have recommended today—have demonstrated what can be done with creative, thoughtfully conceived and properly managed programs of prevention and social rehabilitation. In those communities families have been restored to self-reliance, and relief rolls have been reduced.

To strengthen our human resources—to demonstrate the compassion of free men—and in the light of our own constructive self-interest—we must bring our welfare programs up to date. I urge that the Congress do so without delay.

★★★

THE WAR ON POVERTY

THE ECONOMIC OPPORTUNITY ACT OF 1964

88th Congress
2d Session

Document
No. 86

PUBLIC Law 88-452—Aug. 20, 1964 [78 Stat.]

Public Law 88-452

AN ACT

August 20, 1964
(s 2642)

To mobilize the human and financial resources of the
Nation to combat poverty
in the United States

Be it enacted by the Senate and the House of Representatives of the United States of America in Congress assembled. That this Act may be cited as the "Economic Opportunity Act of 1964."

Economic
Opportunity
Act of 1964

FINDINGS AND DECLARATION OF PURPOSE

SEC. 2. Although the economic well-being and prosperity of the United States have progressed to a level surpassing any achieved in world history, and although these benefits are widely shared throughout the Nation, poverty continues to be the lot of a substantial number of our people. The United States can achieve its full economic and social potential as a nation only if every individual has the opportunity to contribute to the full extent of his capabilities and to participate in the workings of our society. It is, therefore, the policy of the United States to eliminate the paradox of poverty in the midst of plenty in this Nation by opening to everyone the opportunity for education and training, the opportunity to work, and the opportunity to live in decency and dignity. It is the purpose of this Act to strengthen, supplement, and coordinate efforts in furtherance of that policy.

TITLE I—YOUTH PROGRAMS

PART A—JOB CORPS

STATEMENT OF PURPOSE

SEC. 101. The purpose of this part is to prepare for the responsibilities of citizenship and to increase the employability of young men and young women aged sixteen through twenty-one by providing them in rural and urban residential centers with education, vocational training, useful work experience, including work directed toward the conservation of natural resources, and other appropriate activities.

PART B—WORK-TRAINING PROGRAMS

STATEMENT OF PURPOSE

SEC. 111. The purpose of this part is to provide useful work experience opportunities for unemployed young men and young women, through participation in State and community work-training programs, so that their employability may be increased or

Unemployed
youth, work-
experience
opportunities

their education resumed or continued and so that public agencies and private nonprofit organizations (other than political parties) will be enabled to carry out programs which will permit or contribute to an undertaking or service in the public interest that would not otherwise be provided, or will contribute to the conservation and development of natural resources and recreational areas. . . .

Part C—Work-Study Programs

STATEMENT OF PURPOSE

Students, part-time employment

SEC. 121. The purpose of this part is to stimulate and promote the part-time employment of students in institutions of higher education who are from low-income families and are in need of the earnings from such employment to pursue courses of study at such institutions. . . .

TITLE II—URBAN AND RURAL COMMUNITY ACTION PROGRAMS

Part A—General Community Action Programs
STATEMENT OF PURPOSE

SEC. 201. The purpose of this part is to provide stimulation and incentive for urban and rural communities to mobilize their resources to combat poverty through community action programs.

COMMUNITY ACTION PROGRAMS

SEC. 202. (a) The term "community action program" means a program—

(1) which mobilizes and utilizes resources, public or private, of any urban or rural, or combined urban and rural, geographical area (referred to in this part as a "community"), including but not limited to a State, metropolitan area, county, city, town, multicity unit, or multicounty unit in an attack on poverty;

(2) which provides services, assistance, and other activities of sufficient scope and size to give promise of progress toward elimination of poverty or a cause or causes of poverty through developing employment opportunities, improving human performance, motivation, and productivity, or bettering the conditions under which people live, learn, and work;

(3) which is developed, conducted, and administered with the maximum feasible participation of residents of the areas and members of the groups served; and

(4) which is conducted, administered, or coordinated by a public or private nonprofit agency (other than a political party), or a combination thereof. . . .

Part C—Voluntary Assistance Program for Needy Children

STATEMENT OF PURPOSE

SEC. 219. The purpose of this part is to allow individual Americans to participate in a personal way in the war on poverty, by voluntarily assisting in the support of one or more needy children, in a program coordinated with city or county social welfare agencies.

AUTHORITY TO ESTABLISH INFORMATION CENTER

SEC. 220. (a) In order to carry out the purposes of this part, the Director is authorized to establish a section within the Office of Economic Opportunity to act as an information and coordination center to encourage voluntary assistance for deserving and needy children. Such section shall collect the names of persons who voluntarily desire to assist financially such children and shall secure from city or county social welfare agencies such information concerning deserving and needy children as the Director shall deem appropriate.

(b) It is the intent of the Congress that the section established pursuant to this part shall act solely as an information and coordination center and that nothing in this part shall be construed as interfering with the jurisdiction of State and local welfare agencies with respect to programs for needy children. . . .

TITLE III—SPECIAL PROGRAMS TO COMBAT POVERTY IN RURAL AREAS

STATEMENT OF PURPOSE

SEC. 301. It is the purpose of this title to meet some of the special problems of rural poverty and thereby to raise and maintain the income and living standards of low-income rural families and migrant agricultural employees and their families.

PART A—AUTHORITY TO MAKE GRANTS AND LOANS

SEC. 302. (a) The Director is authorized to make—

(1) loans having a maximum maturity of 15 years and in amounts not exceeding $2,500 in the aggregate to any low income rural family where, in the judgment of the Director, such loans have a reasonable possibility of affecting a permanent increase in the income of such families by assisting or permitting them to—

(A) acquire or improve real estate or reduce encumbrances or erect improvements thereon,

(B) operate or improve the operation of farms not larger than family sized, including but not limited to the purchase of feed, seed, fertilizer, livestock, poultry, and equipment, or

(C) participate in cooperative associations; and/or to finance nonagricultural enterprises which will enable such families to supplement their income.

(D) Loans under this section shall be made only if the family is not qualified to obtain such funds by loan under other Federal programs. . . .

TITLE IV—EMPLOYMENT AND INVESTMENT INCENTIVES

STATEMENT OF PURPOSE

SEC. 401. It is the purpose of this title to assist in the establishment, preservation, and strengthening of small business concerns and improve the managerial skills employed in such enterprises; and to mobilize for these objectives private as well as public managerial skills and resources. . . .

Small business concerns, assistance

TITLE V—WORK EXPERIENCE PROGRAMS

STATEMENT OF PURPOSE

SEC. 501. It is the purpose of this title to expand the opportunities for constructive work experience and other needed training available to persons who are unable to support or care for themselves or their families. In carrying out this purpose, the Director shall make maximum use of the programs available under the Manpower Development and Training Act of 1962, as amended, and Vocational Education Act of 1963. . . .

76 Stat. 23, 42
USC2571 note.
77 Stat. 403, 20
USC 35 note

Recruitment and
assignment

VOLUNTEERS IN SERVICE TO AMERICA

SEC. 603. (a) The Director is authorized to recruit, select, train, and—

(1) upon request of State or local agencies or private nonprofit organizations, refer volunteers to perform duties in furtherance of programs combating poverty at a State or local level; and

(2) in cooperation with other Federal, State, or local agencies involved, assign volunteers to work (A) in meeting the health, education, welfare, or related needs of Indians living on reservations, of migratory workers and their families, or of residents of the District of Columbia, the Commonwealth of Puerto Rico, Guam, American Samoa, the Virgin Islands, or the Trust Territory of the Pacific Islands; (B) in the care and rehabilitation of the mentally ill or mentally retarded under treatment at non-profit mental health or mental retardation facilities assisted in their construction or operation by Federal funds; and (C) in furtherance of programs or activities authorized or supported under title I or II of this Act.

***

U.S. SUPREME COURT' DECISION
In re Gault et al. No. 116
Argued December 6, 1966; Decided May 15, 1967

I

On Monday, June 8, 1964, at about 10 A.M., Gerald Francis Gault and a friend, Roland Lewis, were taken into custody by the Sheriff of Gila County. Gerald was then still subject to a six months' probation order which had been entered on Feb. 25, 1964, as a result of his having been in the company of another boy who had stolen a wallet from a lady's purse. The police action on June 8 was taken as a result of a verbal complaint by a neighbor of the boys, Mrs. Cook, about a telephone call made to her in which the caller or callers made lewd or indecent remarks. It will suffice for purposes of this opinion to say that the remarks or questions put to her were of the irritatingly offensive, adolescent, sex variety. . . .

The judge committed Gerald as a juvenile delinquent to the State Industrial School "for the period of his minority [that is, until 21], unless sooner discharged by due process of law." [Gerald was 15.] . . .

II

It is claimed that juveniles obtain benefits from the special procedures applicable to them which more than offset the substance of normal due process. As we shall discuss, the observance of due process standards, intelligently and not ruthlessly administered, will not compel the States to abandon or displace any of the substantive benefits of the juvenile process. But it is important, we think, that the claimed benefits of the juvenile process should be candidly appraised. Neither sentiment nor folklore should cause us to shut our eyes, for example, to such startling findings as that reported in an exceptionally reliable study of repeaters or recidivism conducted by the Stanford Research Institute for the President's Commission on Crime in the District of Columbia. This commission's report states:

"In fiscal 1966 approximately 66 per cent of the 16- and 17-year-old juveniles referred to the court by the Youth Aid Division had been before the court previously. In 1965, 56 per cent of those in the receiving home were repeaters. The S.R.I. study revealed that 61 per cent of the sample juvenile court referrals in 1965 had been previously referred at least once and that 42 per cent had been referred at least twice before."

Certainly, these figures and the high crime rates among juveniles could not lead us to conclude that the absence of constitutional protections reduces crime, or that the juvenile system, functioning free of constitutional inhibitions as it has largely done, is effective to reduce crime or rehabilitate offenders. We do not mean by this to denigrate the juvenile court process. . . .

But the features of the juvenile system which its proponents have asserted are of unique benefit will not be impaired by constitutional domestication. For example, the commendable principles relating to the processing and treatment of juveniles separately from adults are in no way involved or affected by the procedural issues under discussion.

Further, we are told that one of the important benefits of the special juvenile court procedures is that they avoid classifying the juvenile as a "criminal." The juvenile offender is now classed as a "delinquent. . . ." It is disconcerting, however, that this term has come to involve only slightly less stigma than the term "criminal" applied to adults. It is also emphasized that in practically all jurisdictions, statutes provide that an adjudication of the child as a delinquent shall not operate as a civil disability or disqualify him for civil service appointment. There is no reason why the application of due process requirements should interfere with such provisions.

Beyond this, it is frequently said that juveniles are protected by the process from disclosure of their deviational behavior. As the Supreme Court of Arizona phrased it in the present case, the summary procedures of Juvenile Courts are sometimes defended by a statement that it is the law's policy "to hide youthful errors from the full gaze of the public and bury them in the graveyard of the forgotten past."

This claim of secrecy, however, is more rhetoric than reality. Disclosure of court records is discretionary with the judge in most jurisdictions. Statutory restrictions almost invariably apply only to the court records, and even as to those the evidence is that many courts routinely furnish information to the F.B.I. and the military, and on request to government agencies and even to private employers. Of more importance are police records. In most states the police keep a complete file of juvenile "police contacts" and have complete discretion as to disclosure of juvenile records. Police departments receive requests for information from the F.B.I. and other law-enforcement agencies, the Armed Forces, and social service agencies, and most of them generally comply. . . .

In any event, there is no reason why consistently with due process, a State cannot continue, if it deems it appropriate, to provide and to improve provision for the confidentiality of records of police contacts and court action relating to juveniles. It is interesting to note, however, that the Arizona Supreme Court used the confidentiality argument as a justification for the type of notice which is here attacked as inadequate for due process purposes. The parents were given merely general notice that their child was charged with "delinquency." No facts were specified. The Arizona court held, however, that in addition to this general "notice," the child and his parents must be advised "of the facts involved in the case" no later than the initial hearing by the judge. Obviously, this does not "bury" the word about the child's transgressions. It merely defers the time of disclosure to a point when it is of limited use to the child or his parents in preparing his defense or explanation. . . .

The early conception of the juvenile court proceeding was one in which a fatherly judge touched the heart and conscience of the erring youth by talking over his problems, by paternal advice and admonition, and in which, in extreme situations, benevolent and wise institutions of the state provided guidance and help "to save him from a downward career."

Then, as now, goodwill and compassion were admirably prevalent. But recent studies have, with surprising unanimity, entered sharp dissent as to the validity of this gentle conception. They suggest that the appearance as well as the actuality of fairness, impartiality and orderliness—in short, the essentials of due process—may be a more impressive and more therapeutic attitude so far as the juvenile is concerned. . . .

It is not suggested that juvenile court judges should fail appropriately to take account, in their demeanor and conduct, of the emotional and psychological attitude of the juveniles with whom they are confronted. While due process requirements will, in some instances, introduce a degree of order and regularity to Juvenile Court proceedings to determine delinquency, and in contested cases will introduce some elements of the adversary system, nothing will require that the conception of the kindly juvenile judge be replaced by its opposite, nor do we here rule upon the question whether ordinary due process requirements must be observed with respect to hearings to determine the disposition of the delinquent child.

Ultimately, however, we confront the reality of that portion of the Juvenile Court process with which we deal in this case. A boy is charged with misconduct. The boy is committed to an institution where he may be restrained of liberty for years. It is of no constitutional consequence—and of limited practical meaning—that the institution to which he is committed is called an Industrial School. The fact of the matter is that, however euphemistic the title, a "receiving home" or an "industrial school" for juveniles is an institution of confinement. His world becomes "a building with white-washed walls, regimented routine and institutional hours. . . ."

Instead of mother and father and sisters and brothers and friends and classmates, his world is peopled by guards, custodians, state employees, and "delinquents" confined with him for anything from waywardness to rape and homicide.

In view of this, it would be extraordinary if our Constitution did not require the procedural regularity and the exercise of care implied in the phrase "due process." Under our Constitution, the condition of being a boy does not justify a kangaroo court. . . .

If Gerald had been over 18, he would not have been subject to Juvenile Court proceedings. For the particular offense immediately involved, the maximum punishment would have been a fine of $5 to $50, or imprisonment in jail for not more than two months.

Instead, he was committed to custody for a maximum of six years. If he had been over 18 and had committed an offense to which such a sentence might apply, he would have been entitled to substantial rights under the Constitution of the United States as well as under Arizona's laws and constitution. The United States Constitution would guarantee him rights and protections with respect to arrest, search and seizure, and pretrial interrogations. It would assure him of specific notice of the charges and adequate time to decide his course of action and to prepare his defense. He would be entitled to clear advice that he could be represented by counsel, and, at least if a felony were involved, the state would be required to provide counsel if his parents were unable to afford it.

If the court acted on the basis of his confession, careful procedures would be required to assure its voluntariness. If the case went to trial, confrontation and opportunity for cross-examination would be guaranteed. So wide a gulf between the State's treatment of the adult and of the child requires a bridge sturdier than mere verbiage, and reasons more persuasive than cliche can provide. . . .

III

Notice of Charges

Appellants allege that the Arizona juvenile code is unconstitutional or alternatively that the proceedings before the juvenile court were constitutionally defective because of failure to provide adequate notice of the hearings.

No notice was given to Gerald's parents when he was taken into custody, on Monday, June 8. On that night, when Mrs. Gault went to the Detention Home, she was orally informed that there would be a hearing the next afternoon and was told the reason why Gerald was in custody. The only written notice Gerald's parents received at any time was a note on plain paper from Officer Flagg delivered on Thursday or Friday, June 11 or 12, to the effect that the judge had set Monday, June 15, "for further hearings on Gerald's delinquency."

A "petition" was filed with the court on June 9 by Officer Flagg, reciting only that he was informed and believed that "said minor is a delinquent minor and that it is necessary that some order be made by the honorable court for said minor's welfare."

The applicable Arizona statute provides for a petition to be filed in juvenile court, alleging in general terms that the child is "neglected, dependent, or delinquent." The statute explicitly states that such a general allegation is sufficient, "without alleging the facts." . . .

We cannot agree with the court's conclusion that adequate notice was given to this case. Notice, to comply with due process requirements, must be given sufficiently in advance of scheduled court proceedings so that reasonable opportunity to prepare will be afforded, and it must "set forth the alleged misconduct with particularity." . . .

IV

Right to Counsel

Appellants charge that the Juvenile Court proceedings were fatally defective because the court did not advise Gerald or his parents of their right to counsel, and proceeded with the hearing, the adjudication of delinquency and the order of commitment in the absence of counsel for the child and his parents or an express waiver of the right thereto.

The Supreme Court of Arizona pointed out that "[t]here is disagreement [among the various jurisdictions] as to whether the court must advise the infant that he has a right to counsel." . . . It referred to a provision of the juvenile code which it characterized as requiring "that the probation officer shall look after the interests of neglected, delinquent and dependent children," including representing their interests in court. The court argued that "the parents and the probation officer may be relied upon to protect the infant's interests."

Accordingly it rejected the proposition that "due process requires that an infant have a right to counsel." It said that juvenile courts have the discretion, but not the duty, to allow such representation; it referred specifically to the situation in which the juvenile court discerns conflict between the child and his parents as an instance in which this discretion might be exercised.

We do not agree. Probation officers in the Arizona scheme are also arresting officers. They initiate proceedings and file petitions which they verify, as here, alleging the delinquency of the child; and they testify, as here, against the child.

The probation officer cannot act as counsel for the child. His role in the adjudicatory hearing is as arresting officer and witness against the child. Nor can the judge represent the child. There is no material difference in this respect between adult and juvenile proceedings of the sort here involved. In adult proceedings, this contention has been foreclosed by decisions of this court. A proceeding where the issue is whether the child will be found to be "delinquent" and subjected to the loss of his liberty for years is comparable in seriousness to a felony prosecution.

The juvenile needs the assistance of counsel to cope with problems of law, to make skilled inquiry into the facts, to insist upon regularity of the proceedings, and to ascertain whether he has a defense and to prepare and submit it. . . .

We conclude that the Due Process Clause of the Fourteenth Amendment requires that in respect of proceedings to determine delinquency which may result in commitment to an institution in which the juvenile's freedom is curtailed, the child and his parent must be notified of the child's right to be represented by counsel retained by them, or if they are unable to afford counsel, that counsel will be appointed to represent the child.

At the habeas corpus proceeding, Mrs. Gault testified that she knew that she could have appeared with counsel at the juvenile hearing. This knowledge is not a waiver of the right to counsel which she and her juvenile son had, as we have defined it. They had a right expressly to be advised that they might retain counsel. . . .

V

Confrontation, Self-Incrimination, Cross-Examination

Appellants urge that the writ of habeas corpus should have been granted because of the denial of the rights of confrontation and cross-examination in the Juvenile Court hearings, and because the privilege against self-incrimination was not observed. . . .

It would indeed be surprising if the privilege against self-incrimination were available to hardened criminals but not to children. The language of the Fifth Amendment, applicable to the states by operation of the 14th Amendment, is unequivocal and without exception. . . .

With respect to juveniles, both common observation and expert opinion emphasize that the "distrust of confessions made in certain situations" is imperative in the case of children from early age through adolescence.

In New York, for example, the recently enacted Family Court Act provides that the juvenile and his parents must be advised at the start of the hearing of his right to remain silent. The New York statute also provides that the police must attempt to communicate with the juvenile's parents before questioning him, and that a confession may not be obtained from a child prior to notifying his parents or relatives and releasing the child either to them or the Family Court. . . .

It is also urged, as the Supreme Court of Arizona here asserted, that the juvenile and presumably his parents should not be advised of the juvenile's right to silence because confession is good for the child as the commencement of the assumed therapy of the juvenile court process, and he should be encouraged to assume an attitude of trust and confidence toward the officials of the juvenile process.

United States Reports, Vol. 387, Cases Adjudged in the Supreme Court (Washington, DC: U.S. Government Printing Office, 1967), pp. 1–81.

 Recall what you learned in this chapter by completing the Chapter Review.

8

Conservative Resurgence and Social Change: 1968–1992

PEARSON EDUCATION, INC.

LEARNING OUTCOMES

- Describe the major economic and social trends that influenced social welfare between 1968 and 1992.

- Summarize the major changes in the social welfare system during these years.

- Explain how social movements influenced social welfare policy between 1968 and 1992.

CHAPTER OUTLINE

Economic and Social Trends   252
A Struggling Economy   252
Changing Employment
    Patterns   253
The Changing Family   254
Poverty and Income
    Distribution   256

Innovations in Social Welfare   258
Expenditures for Social Welfare   258
Challenging the Welfare State:
    Welfare Reform   260
Child Welfare and the Aging   263
The Unemployed   266
Veterans   268
Personal Social Services   268

Social Movements   269
The New Right   269
The Expansion of Civil Rights   270
Women   274

Conclusion   275

**DOCUMENTS: Conservative
Resurgence and Social Change   276**
*Message on Reform in Welfare,
    1969   277*
*Standard of Review for Termination of
    Disability Benefits, 1984   283*

In 1971, President Richard Nixon vetoed the amendments to the Economic Opportunity Act. The veto was not that surprising. After all, this legislation carried on many War on Poverty programs that Nixon and his party had opposed. What was startling was the tone of his objections. Nixon abandoned traditional mainstream conservative objections to the cost and potential waste associated with social welfare programs and instead focused on its potential for undermining the American family. In his veto message, Nixon asserted that "for the Federal Government to plunge headlong financially into supporting child development would commit the vast moral authority of the National Government to the side of communal approaches to child-rearing over [and] against the family-centered approach."[1] Within a year, the battle over the family widened with the Supreme Court's decision in *Roe v. Wade* that American women had a constitutional right to abortion services. Congressional passage of the Equal Rights Amendment to the U.S. Constitution in 1972 set off another symbolic battle over the nature of gender and the relationship of the public and private spheres.

Two major forces framed the history of social welfare between 1968 and 1992. First, in contrast to the previous two decades, the economy grew at a much slower pace. The transition to a postindustrial, information economy combined with a deliberate effort to control inflation to keep economic growth slow and unemployment high. As a result, public welfare faced a host of new demands for services and benefits at a time when there was little economic growth to pay for them.

Second, the 1971 veto message marked the beginning of a sustained ideological attack on social welfare programs. The conservative New Right was deeply suspicious of all government programs and saw social welfare as connected to the declining competitiveness of the American economy, the weakening of its family structure, and the general decline of American moral character.

For a time, the economic conservatism of the battle against inflation and the social conservatism of the battle over the family combined to form a powerful social movement that sought to reduce fundamentally the public commitment to social welfare. President Ronald Reagan used the early years of his presidency to lay out a new departure for social welfare, one that would shift power from the federal government to the states, from the public sector to voluntary associations, from open-ended "entitlements" to federal aid to limited block grants.

For the most part, "Reaganism" did not accomplish its goals. The structure of social welfare in 1992 looked more or less the way it had a decade earlier. However, the large tax cuts implemented by Congress and the president in 1981 combined with slow economic growth to limit the reach and effectiveness of existing programs. Rather than marking a new departure in social welfare, the 1980s were a period of declining effectiveness and the neglect of new, pressing social problems such as homelessness and the AIDS epidemic.

> The United States was not unique. The welfare state came under attack throughout the Western world.

The United States was not unique. The welfare state came under attack throughout the Western world. One response to the poor performance of the economy was the abandonment of social welfare programs and efforts to mitigate the inequalities of the marketplace. In constant dollars, per capita expenditures for social welfare had increased at an annual rate of 6.5 percent in 1970. It continued to increase during the 1970s, but at a slower rate. By the late 1980s, the rate of increase had fallen to 1 percent. The impact of conservatism was not the elimination of programs, but incremental declines in funding for them.[2]

ECONOMIC AND SOCIAL TRENDS

A Struggling Economy

Unemployment during the 1970s averaged 5.4 percent in the first half of the decade and jumped to 8.3 percent in the recession of 1975, before falling to 5.8 percent in 1979. Consumer prices, driven by the sharp rise in oil prices, went up throughout the decade. Inflation remained out of control until the recession of 1982–1983. The recession slowed the inflation rate, but at a heavy price for American workers. Unemployment rose to 9.5 percent and declined only slowly in the years following. At the end of the 1980s, another recession increased unemployment again.

Nowhere were the slowdown of economic growth and the shortfall in its distribution to American families from 1970 to 1990 clearer than in the data on gross national product (GNP) and on family income. GNP and median family income grew during the period, but at a disappointing pace. After adjusting for inflation, the rise in GNP between 1970 and 1990 was just over 40 percent. Household median income in constant dollars rose and fell during the period in response to changes in levels of unemployment and to price increases. But in 1990, it was roughly what it had been in 1979 and only slightly higher than it was in 1970.[3] While median income remained level, the gap between the very rich and the very poor grew markedly. The number of billionaires quadrupled during the 1980s; the number of people below the poverty line increased by 35 percent.[4]

During the 1970s, the Organization of Petroleum Exporting Countries (OPEC) twice restricted output to increase the price of oil. As millions of Americans waited in line at gas stations, it became clear that the United States was one part of a global economy. Domestic inflation had disturbing implications for those who lived on fixed incomes especially, as well as for those who worked and found their ability to purchase goods and services declining. Rising prices combined with rising unemployment hit most heavily those least able to withstand wage and job loss.

Economic security had grown more elusive for many Americans. From World War II until the 1970s, Americans had assumed that economic growth, consumerism, and affluence were the answers to the nation's social and economic problems. During the 1970s and 1980s, however, a new set of concerns—the environment, urban decline, and globalization—framed unregulated economic growth as part of the problem, not the solution. Where the War on Poverty had assumed that economic growth could increase the incomes of the poor without harming the rest of society, a "zero sum" economy increasingly pitted social groups against one another. Unions demanded wage and benefits increases to offset the erosions of inflation. Employers sought a more flexible labor market and lower taxes to stimulate investments.

Changing Employment Patterns

The transition to an information economy was complicated by government monetary policy and its implication for unemployment. Since 1946, the federal government had committed itself to pursuing maximum employment policies, a pledge it had reiterated with the passage of the Humphrey–Hawkins Full Employment and Balanced Growth Act of 1978. Yet, the same year, the Federal Reserve Board began using high interest rates as a means of slowing inflation. As a result, unemployment began a steady rise, reaching 11 percent in 1982, the highest level since the Great Depression. How could government commit itself both to "full employment" and to using unemployment to fight inflation? Economists had provided an answer with one acronym: NAIRU. The "nonaccelerating-inflation rate of unemployment" was defined as the lowest unemployment rate that was consistent with low inflation. This rate—estimated at around 6 percent during the 1980s—was redefined as the "natural" rate of full employment. Thus, for more than a decade, government policy defined a stagnant economy with more than 6 million unemployed workers as full employment.

The fight against inflation during the 1970s and 1980s harmed not only those who were unemployed; the loss of production because of slow economic growth harmed all Americans. Indeed, a conservative estimate of the lost production between 1974 and 1995 was equal to $1.6 trillion— nearly three months of the gross domestic product (GDP) in 1995.[5] The years between 1968 and 1992 were characterized by a shift from an industrial economic base to a service economy. From 1970 to 1990, employment

 Watch this video on NAIRU.

Notice that the video assumes a very sharp relationship between unemployment and inflation. If the curve had a different shape, we could reach very different conclusions about the "natural" rate of unemployment

https://www.youtube.com/
watch?v=zajMQzFTCNA

increased by 47 percent, but manufacturing employment increased by only 2 percent, while the number of jobs in service industries rose by 92 percent. Of the 18 million new jobs created between 1980 and 1990, 88 percent were in services, finance, and sales. Factory employment declined during this period, although manufacturing productivity and output increased.[6]

For displaced workers of the industrial labor force, the result was unemployment and increased economic uncertainty. The expanding service sector had historically been a major source of employment for women and ethnic minorities, albeit one with generally low wages and poor working conditions. In 1990, 45 percent of the workforce was female, but 61 percent of those employed in services were women; 10 percent of those in the workforce were African Americans, 12 percent of those in services. In the lowest-paying sector of the service industry, personal services and hospitals, about 75 percent of the employees were female and 15 percent black; less than 10 percent were white men. The new service jobs were likely to carry lower wages and be subject to involuntary temporary, part-time, and part-year employment. These workers were less likely to receive pensions or health care through their employer. As a result, the proportion of workers who did not receive employer-provided health care, but could not afford individual policies, increased.

The Changing Family

Conservatives were right that family life was changing in important ways during the 1970s and 1980s, although they erred in seeing all of the trends as negative.[7] At the start of the 1990s, family life was very different from the typical domestic unit for which our social programs had been designed 55 years earlier. In 1935, at the time of the passage of the Social Security Act, a majority of families consisted of a mother who was a homemaker, a father who went to work, and perhaps three children. In contrast, the average household in 1990 was no longer a two-parent home with several children. This description applied to less than 30 percent of American households and 38 percent of families. Only 13 percent of families included two parents, one wage earner, one homemaker, and one or more children. The median age of first marriage rose during the 1980s, and single-person households increased as young adults were likely to spend a number of years living on their own before they married. The continuing popularity of marriage was countered by rising divorce rates.

The number of female-headed households rose sharply, with the fastest increase during the 1970s. In the 1980s, the increase in families headed by a single woman or by a grandmother continued, but at a slower pace. By 1990, 51 percent of all black children under age 18, 27 percent of Hispanic children, and 16 percent of white children were living with just one parent. In 20 years, the proportion of families that were headed by women had doubled. The number of such families increased by 75 percent among African Americans and by 106 percent among whites. Because absent parents rarely provided sufficient child support, the children in these households were being supported largely by their mothers.

The average size of the U.S. household decreased about 21 percent from 1970 to 1990. However, this drop was not distributed equally throughout the population. There were more people who never married, more families that had no children, and more families that had just one child. In 1990, half of all American families had no current child-rearing responsibilities. There were also families that continued to have three, four, or five children. The result was that 80 percent of children were supported by only 30 percent of the adult population. This unequal distribution of the task of supporting children had a racial dimension. The birthrate was significantly higher in the black community than in the white community.

The distribution of children had political implications. The sentimental view of mothers and children that had fueled *maternalism* earlier in the century was in decline. Single mothers were no longer the objects of pity. Rather, they were often seen as at fault and expected to both work and rear their children. As a result, it became harder to obtain money for programs for the support of women and children that were seen as a less universal need than it was in the past. Some indications of this effect were seen in the increasing reluctance to support public education in some parts of the country.

The battle over the government's role in helping families was seen in the effort to guarantee family leave for new parents. The Democratic-controlled Congress passed the Family and Medical Leave Act in 1990, but George H. W. Bush vetoed the bill and Congress upheld his veto. That bill would have required employers with 50 or more employees to provide unpaid leave to new parents as well as to workers who needed to care for a sick family member. At the time, about 15 states had legislation protecting jobs for workers when they needed extended time away for family or medical reasons, but for most American families, there was no parental leave. Finally, the Family and Medical Leave Act became the first legislation signed into law by President Clinton in 1993.[8]

Many Americans had fond memories of the "traditional" breadwinner family of the 1950s. Even though American families were better off because of women's earnings, and men and women shared the responsibilities of parenthood more equally, nostalgia prompted many Americans to decry the changes in family life. As a result, efforts by the Carter administration to reach a consensus on "family policy" foundered. Debates over abortion, equal rights, and the proper role of the federal government found no middle ground during these years.

In 1935, when the Social Security Act was passed, persons 65 years of age and over represented 6 percent of the total population. Between 1970 and 1990, this percentage increased from 9.7 to more than 12. The proportion of the working population—persons between 18 and 64 years of age—declined. Falling birthrates, combined with increased life expectancy, led to a new population pattern and a new set of social welfare needs. They also led to many concerns about the dependency ratio—the ratio between workers and nonworkers in society. Although increasing productivity more than compensated for the increasing dependency ratios, many academic and political leaders called for radical changes in retirement and Social Security policies to respond to the new demographic realities.

With increased numbers, the aging became more politically effective. They needed and demanded new programs and expanded benefits, as the working population may have felt less able to provide them.[9] This was offset in part by the increase of women in the labor force. The proportion of women working rose sharply in the 20th century. In 1900, 20 percent of adult women worked. The proportion of adult women who were in the labor force increased from 49 percent in 1970 to 69 percent in 1990.[10] The reality of women in the workforce and the increased expectation that women hold jobs outside the home had an impact not only on family social and economic status, but also on many social welfare programs. The social insurance system came under scrutiny for its treatment of working women. Issues of child care moved to the fore of public attention, while programs for poor women "not expected to work" became more suspect than in the past.

The decade of the 1970s brought a current of economic, social, and political malaise to American life. As in other eras leading to periods of reform, old values and old beliefs were scrutinized. But the frustrations and disappointments of the 1970s made "traditional" values more attractive to many Americans. Indeed, as distrust of government and of political leaders deepened, and the economic situation worsened, the general citizenry seemed to lose hope that positive change would occur for the country as a whole; individuals and self-interest groups began to look even more to their own. As faith in collective action faded, the traditional American confidence in the efficacy of individual effort prevailed. Ronald Reagan won the presidential election of 1980 on the promise of a return to conservative values that would restore the country's greatness.

The cost of high unemployment during the late 1970s and early 1980s fell disproportionately on low-income families. Their situation was further undermined by the budget policies of the Reagan administration. Although President Reagan failed to secure the large cuts in domestic programs he sought early in his administration, he did succeed in reducing federal income taxes, especially for those in high-income brackets. As a result, throughout the 1980s, there was great pressure on the federal government to reduce spending. The resulting scramble to protect existing programs meant that new social needs—such as the increased visibility of the homeless and the emergence of the AIDS epidemic—had a hard time securing the funding they needed. Increasingly, government returned to a "residual" approach to the problems of the poor. Public programs acted only as a tattered safety net for those who could not fend for themselves.

Poverty and Income Distribution

The American economy had hit the equivalent of the *trifecta* between World War II and 1970. Rapid economic growth and the expansion of social welfare programs had reduced both the poverty rate and overall income inequality across the nation. During the early 1970s, a number of commentators suggested that "the goal of eliminating income poverty as stated by President Johnson in 1964 had been virtually achieved before the onset of the 1974–75 recession."[11] If Americans felt like they had hit the jackpot during the early postwar years, the 1970s and 1980s made many Americans feel snakebitten. Suddenly, in the late 1970s, economic inequality began to increase, a trend that would persist for most of the next four decades.

The War on Poverty had led to a dramatic decrease in poverty in the late 1960s. During the 1970s, the poverty rate remained stable at about 11 to 12 percent, but rose to 15.2 percent during the Reagan recession of 1982–1983. Indeed, by 1990, 33.6 million people were counted poor—32 percent more than in 1970.

Second, the distribution of poverty was far from random. On the contrary, it was structured by race, ethnicity, sex, family situation, age, and employment status. For whites, the official poverty rate was about 11 percent in 1990; for Hispanics, 25 percent; for African Americans, 30 percent; and for Native Americans, 31 percent. The rate for households where the head worked full time was 4 percent; the rate for nonworking households, 25 percent.

Poverty among two-parent families decreased sharply while that of single-parent families rose. By the end of the period, 34 percent of one-parent, female-headed households were poor. During much of the 1970s, increased job opportunities and wage hikes helped. But much of the financial success was dependent upon the higher labor-force participation of women, of working wives and mothers. Obviously, two-parent (and possibly two-earner) families were in better financial shape, but the implications of having both parents working and out of the home remained unexplored. Major questions about marriage, family life, and child care remained unanswered.

The biggest decline in poverty was among the aging. Although Social Security had constructed a floor under retirement income, that floor still left nearly a quarter of older

Americans living in poverty. While the national poverty rate remained stable during the 1970s and 1980s, the rate for older Americans was cut in half, reaching 12 percent in 1990. This dramatic decline in poverty was due largely to the expansion of Social Security and other programs for the aging during the early 1970s. Old Age, Survivors, and Disability Insurance (OASDI) benefits had increased by only 27 percent between 1959 and 1968; but in the next three years, they increased by 52 percent. Starting in 1975, increases in program benefits were *indexed*, so they kept pace with increases in prices and average wages. In 1974, Congress passed legislation that combined Old Age Insurance (OAI), Aid to the Blind, and Aid to the Temporarily and Permanently Disabled to create Supplemental Security Income (SSI). Where benefits and eligibility had been left to the states in the old programs, SSI was *federalized* with a uniform level of benefits and eligibility criteria across the nation, although some states decided to add a supplement to federal benefits. Additionally, the passage of the Supplemental Security Act, which began operation in January 1974, provided a means-tested income transfer program guaranteeing a minimum income for the elderly and disabled. Furthermore, SSI benefits, like social insurance, were indexed to keep pace with inflation. Automatic increases in transfer payments continued to help this group when food, heat, and housing costs did not outstrip gains. Nevertheless, the aging continued to be vulnerable to poverty. Many, if not "in poverty," lived *close* to poverty. More than 20 percent of the aged lived below 125 percent of the poverty line.

At the same time, changes in family structure placed more children at risk of poverty. In 1959, the poverty rate for children under the age of 18 was 26 percent, about one-quarter higher than that for the population as a whole. During the 1960s, the poverty rate for children fell faster than that for the entire population, to 15 percent in 1970. However, over the next 20 years, much of this improvement was lost. By 1990, the child poverty rate stood at 20 percent, nearly 1½ times the total population figure of 13.5 percent.

A number of social realities increased the risk of poverty for American children. Changes in fertility rates meant that poorer groups in the population were having a larger share of all children. In addition, increased rates of divorce and single parenthood meant that a larger proportion of children relied on the income of one parent. Finally, beginning in the middle of the 1970s, states began a concerted effort to restrict Aid to Families with Dependent Children (AFDC). States used a variety of administrative barriers to restrict the growth of the welfare rolls and failed to adjust benefits for inflation, leading to a decline of more than a third in the value of benefits, when corrected for inflation. African American and Hispanic children suffered the most from all of these changes. By 1990, nearly 40 percent of them were living in poverty.

For Native Americans, the years of Presidents Nixon, Ford, and Carter were a mix of progress and retreat. There were improvements in health services and education. There was even some political representation in Western states. But the loss of land was still in progress, with only minimal repayments.

Reagan administration policies hit Native Americans very hard. Unemployment on the reservations reached 80 percent during the early 1980s. Partly in response to the leasing of tribal reservation land to white families, partly in response to the high unemployment rates and lack of opportunities on the reservations, many Native Americans migrated to urban areas. They still fared very poorly. High unemployment rates and very low incomes were typical. Native Americans were not eligible for state social services or support. They had to rely on federal programs for job training, housing assistance, and child welfare services. Thus, the social service cutbacks of the Reagan years affected this population with particular force. Poverty rates reached as high as 57 percent in some parts of the West.[12]

Frustration in regard to the eradication of poverty was aggravated by failure to agree on how to define it. Measuring poverty as an absolute dollar amount, as with the annually computed poverty index, was increasingly questioned. In 1959, the poverty line for a family of four was about one-half the median family income ($2,793 versus $5,417). As the growth of family incomes outstripped inflation, the gap between the two increased. In 1990, the median family income of $35,353 was nearly three times the poverty line for a family of four ($12,293). The deprivation of the poor resulted both from their lack of income and from the fact that they were falling behind the experience of average families.

Since the end of World War II, income distribution in the United States became less equal. As shown in Table 8.1, most of this change occurred after 1980. This happened despite economic growth, a War on Poverty, an increase in the labor-force participation of women, and an expansion of social insurance benefits and social services. Control of income and of wealth in the United States became more concentrated at the top. The growth of wealth of the top-income quintile, increased inequality of wages, rising regressive Social Security taxes and state and local sales taxes, and a decrease in the progressivity of federal income taxes all played their part. A combination of market factors and government policy led to a situation in which the rich became richer and the poor, poorer.[13]

Property and other assets were even less equally distributed than income. Whereas the top 1 percent of families controlled 4 percent of all income in 1988, they controlled 20 percent of all net financial assets, a larger share of the nation's wealth than the bottom 80 percent of the population. The economic gap between the races was more dramatic for wealth than income. African American married couples had a family income in 1988 that was about 80 percent that of white couples, but the net worth of the average black couple ($17,437) was just 27 percent that of white couples ($65,024).[14]

> **?** Assess your comprehension of "Economic and Social Trends" by completing this quiz.

INNOVATIONS IN SOCIAL WELFARE

Expenditures for Social Welfare

Total federal expenditures for social welfare continued to expand during the 1970s and 1980s, but the increase was not steady across the period. Government expenditures for health, education, and welfare rose from $3.9 billion in the pre-Depression year of 1929 to

Table 8.1   Distribution of Income

Income Class	Percentage of National Income		
	1947	1980	1990
Lowest quintile	5.1	5.1	3.9
Second quintile	11.8	11.6	9.6
Third quintile	16.7	17.5	16.0
Fourth quintile	23.2	24.3	24.1
Highest quintile	43.2	41.5	46.4

Source: Author's calculation from Current Population Survey, various years.

$145.6 billion in 1970, and then almost doubled to $290 billion by 1975. By 1978, expenditures stood at $394 billion. The difference between 1970 and 1978 was almost $250 billion. Some of the increase was due to inflation and some due to population growth. But, in 1987 prices, per capita welfare expenditures rose from $698 in 1950 to $1,952 in 1970 to $3,364 in 1978. In 1990, as in 1975, social welfare expenditures were 19.1 percent of GDP and 56.6 percent of total government outlays. The early 1970s represented a high point in the expansion of federal spending on social welfare, as Social Security, public assistance, food, and community development programs all gained widespread support in Congress. After the middle of the 1970s, however, public support for welfare expansion declined. Only programs that included automatic cost-of-living increases were able to keep pace with the high inflation of the period.

The dualism of the American social welfare system—the split between generous programs for the worthy and punitive ones for the undeserving—expanded during these years. About half the $1,045 billion spent for social welfare purposes went for non–means-tested social insurances and government retirement programs and 25 percent went for education. Non–means-tested programs are programs for all income groups, not programs only for the poor. Less than 16 percent went to programs particularly targeted to the poor: public assistance, Medicaid, food stamps, and some service and employment training programs.

The conservative resurgence did reverse the trend toward the federal government accounting for a larger and larger share of public expenditures. In 1929, the federal government contributed 21 percent of total governmental outlays for social welfare. By 1970, the federal share had risen to more than 50 percent. It peaked at 63 percent in 1984 and, by 1990, had dropped to just under 60 percent. With expenditures for education excluded, the federal government's share of the cost of public social welfare in 1990 was 76 percent.

The pressure to limit the federal budget highlighted the difference between *entitlement* programs—for which the government committed itself to providing funding for all those eligible for a program—and *discretionary* programs—for which there were no such guarantees. In large measure, the increases in federal expenditures for social welfare were due to outlays that were not subject to administrative discretion. The bases of outlays for the social insurances, other governmental health and retirement programs, public assistance programs, and others are mandated by law.

The persistent effort to limit social welfare expenditure also meant that government was less ready to meet new social problems as they emerged. Homelessness, although not an entirely new problem, became more common and visible during the 1970s and 1980s as a result of cuts in general assistance, the increasing cost of housing, and deinstitutionalization all increased the numbers of persons without a fixed residence. Efforts to address the problem typically involved voluntary agencies and local government until the passage of the McKinney–Vento Homeless Assistance Act of 1987, which provided funding for a variety of services. The halting commitments of the 1980s focused on providing temporary shelter for homeless individuals and families, and shelters remained the dominant response to homelessness for the next three decades.[15]

The health emergency associated with the human immunodeficiency virus (HIV), too, suffered from the budget pressures during this period. First identified among intravenous drug-users and gay men in the early 1980s, HIV/AIDS, without any known treatment or cure, quickly spread to other groups in the population. Still, its association with "undeserving" populations combined with the antigovernment rhetoric of the 1980s served to slow governments' response to the epidemic.[16]

The dualism of the American social welfare system—the split between generous programs for the worthy and punitive ones for the undeserving—expanded during these years.

Although "cutting welfare" remained a popular goal, identifying who and where to cut remained a challenge. The efforts of Richard Nixon in the budgets of 1974 and 1975 to eliminate social welfare programs that he deemed unsuccessful and wasteful met with limited success.[17] The campaign to abolish the Office of Economic Opportunity (OEO) was instructive. OEO itself was abolished, but its major programs—the community action programs, community legal services, and Head Start—were assigned to other agencies and continued with budgets essentially uncut. In the case of Head Start, the budget was even increased. Gerald Ford also discovered that efforts to cut programs often failed. Notwithstanding the president's opposition, Congress refused to postpone salary increments for federal employees and resisted limiting the increase in veterans' benefits to the levels suggested by the Ford administration, even when these measures were touted as anti-inflationary. President Carter found it necessary to yield to congressional pressures against withholding funds for a variety of local public works and to respond to the demands of black organizations and their leaders that funds for the employment of black youth be restored. The Reagan administration efforts to restructure and cut back some Social Security benefits were unsuccessful, as were his protracted efforts to eliminate community legal services. President Bush continued the effort to reduce health, education, and welfare benefits, but constituencies for social welfare measures were organized and acted effectively.

Food stamps were one program that did not suffer from efforts to limit its growth. Starting with a relatively small appropriation of $550 million in 1970, it reached $17.7 billion in 1990.[18] The program is funded totally by the federal government. The program's focus on reducing hunger, its administrative home in the Department of Agriculture, and the continued support of agribusiness and farm state legislators assured the program's popularity. As a fully federally funded program, Food Stamps—in contrast to AFDC—did not provoke opposition from governors and state legislatures.

Challenging the Welfare State: Welfare Reform

In 1935, when provision was made in the Social Security Act for aid to dependent children, the conviction held that mothers, despite their poverty, should remain at home with their children. The 1967 amendments to the Social Security Act officially reversed this historic policy, reflecting the extent to which mothers of young children had moved, in public thinking, from unemployable to employable. Congress increased appropriations for day-care programs and instituted the Work Incentive Program (WIN). WIN required that an assessment be made of the employability not only of unemployed fathers and out-of-school older children, but also of mothers. The transfer of administrative responsibility for OEO "work experience" programs from the Department of Health, Education, and Welfare to the Department of Labor further clarified the new congressional direction. In 1971, Congress moved again to increase the work incentives for welfare recipients. Ideological support for this new approach came in 1971, when the House Ways and Means Committee extolled as a primary virtue of day care its ability to free mothers for work:

> Your committee is convinced that . . . the child in a family eligible under these programs will benefit from the combination of quality child care and the example of an adult in the family taking financial responsibility for him.[19]

Efforts to reform welfare during the 1970s and 1980s were caught in social and policy crosscurrents. For a time, the concept of a negative income tax (NIT)—in which low-income families would be guaranteed a minimum annual income—commanded broad support across the political spectrum. Yet, arguments about how high to set the minimum effectively blocked legislation from moving forward. Although both liberals and conservatives supported expanding the work opportunities of welfare recipients, conservatives were more interested in using "workfare" as a disincentive to keep people off the rolls, whereas liberals favored the expansion of job training and education as a means of making recipients more employable.[20]

The best opportunity for a shift toward a national, NIT system occurred during the early 1970s after President Nixon's address to the nation about his welfare reform plan in August 1969.[21] For those "American families who cannot care for themselves in whichever state they live," a new program, the Family Assistance Plan (FAP), was proposed as a substitute for AFDC. "Workfare" would replace welfare. An NIT mechanism was designed to set a floor on income while still encouraging people to work. The FAP included a national minimum income, although it was set so low that only states with extremely low AFDC payments would benefit. Where working adults were involved, the subsidy was to be reduced as earned income went up, until a "breakeven point" in total income was reached. The program would, therefore, be available to the working as well as the nonworking poor. Mothers with very young children would be permitted to remain at home. In immediately employable families, however—that is, in two-parent families or in single-parent families with school-age children—financial aid would be conditioned upon the willingness of at least one adult to accept training or employment. In the president's words, FAP coupled "basic benefits to low-income families with children with incentives for employment and training to improve the capacity for employment of members of such families." In essence, workfare became the ideological base for different levels and plans of support for different groups of recipients. For poor families judged employable, inadequate grants were to be the incentive for work.

The Commission on Income Maintenance Programs, appointed by President Johnson, released its report in November 1969, four months after President Nixon's message on reform in welfare. Like the Nixon plan, the commission's recommendations involved an NIT, although benefits were more generous. Although its policy recommendations were similar to Nixon's, the commission relied on a more structural explanation of poverty to justify them. The commission wrote:

> ▶ **Watch this video on the Family Assistance Plan.**
> Forty years after the battle over the FAP, former administration officials discuss the failure of the FAP. Notice how far the welfare reform debate drifted from 1970 until the 1990s.
>
> https://www.youtube.com/watch?v=IjWN-gy81wU

> It is often argued that the poor are to blame for their own circumstances and should be expected to lift themselves from poverty. The Commission has concluded that these are incorrect. Our economic and social structure virtually guarantees poverty for millions of Americans. Unemployment and underemployment are basic facts of American life. The risks of poverty are common to millions more who depend on earnings for their income. . . . The simple fact is that most of the poor remain poor because access to income through work is currently beyond their reach.[22]

The legislative battles over Nixon's Family Assistance Plan marked either a missed opportunity or a critical turning point in the history of welfare policy. FAP was debated throughout 1970, 1971, and much of 1972. Although both parties were dissatisfied with the existing AFDC program, they could not agree on the nature of its problems or the contours of a solution. Ultimately, while moderate Democrats and Republicans sought to create a compromise that would become law, conservatives and liberals refused to support the package. Conservatives like Russell Long, senator from Louisiana and chair of the Senate Finance Committee, pushed for tighter work requirements and lower benefits while liberals sought more generous payments. The National Welfare Rights

Organization—a grassroots organization of welfare mothers and social workers—pushed liberals to resist a compromise that would attract moderate support. Eventually, Nixon himself abandoned welfare reform. In its place, a number of piecemeal measures became law, the most important of which was the creation of Supplemental Security Income (SSI) to replace categorical programs for the aged, blind, and disabled. The new federal program became law in 1973.

SSI marked a major policy success in addressing continuing poverty among older Americans and people with disability. In place of a patchwork of state programs with different benefit levels and eligibility requirements that combined state and federal funding, SSI provided a uniform program that was federally funded. The program was designed to *supplement* old age and disability insurance. Indeed, beneficiaries who were eligible for both Social Security and SSI typically escaped poverty, although many SSI recipients—including children and those who immigrated as older adults—did not qualify for the social insurance program.[23]

However, public interest in poor families receded once the most favored of the poor had been cared for. Pressures from the states for reform in welfare lessened as the elimination of the Old Age Assistance, Aid to the Blind, and Aid to the Disabled categories of public assistance lowered demands on state treasuries. Pressures from the elderly and disabled diminished with SSI's guarantee of income. Additionally, the introduction of "income disregards" as work incentive, and expansions of AFDC–UP and of in-kind programs that reduced inequalities between the working and nonworking poor, lowered the push for change. In the absence of comprehensive reform, smaller changes like these reshaped the policy landscape.

President Carter introduced a more elaborate NIT plan in 1978. The Better Jobs and Income Program, as it was named, was similar to that proposed earlier by Nixon. A federal guarantee of minimum income was provided; benefit scales provided work incentives; job training and child care were planned. The Carter proposal moved beyond the Nixon FAP in that its coverage would have included individuals as well as families, and in its provision of jobs. But, like the Nixon proposal, Carter's plan failed to receive congressional approval.

The failure to reach consensus on welfare reform during the 1970s had been attributed to several factors. Arguments had ensued as to whether to pursue an incremental or comprehensive strategy. Incrementalism was meant to improve the current system without changing its categorical nature and its divided administrative structure. Proponents of incrementalism pointed not only to the reality of a system in place but also to the more likely chance that piecemeal change could be achieved. Proponents of comprehensive reform held the many criticisms of public welfare to mean that a new package of programs, integrated toward common purposes, had to be devised.[24]

The Carter proposal had hoped to achieve reform at no increase in costs beyond those of current public welfare programs. This goal had to be abandoned almost immediately. The job proposal became a source of difficulty, too. Some criticized the plan for establishing the federal government as a true "employer of the last resort." And as with the Nixon plan, there was sharp disagreement about the level of grants. Political agreement among interest groups was impossible to come by.[25]

The historical opportunity for creating an NIT system had passed by the end of the 1970s. Welfare had become caught in the vortex of the battle over the "traditional family." Public support of single mothers through AFDC became a convenient target for conservatives who objected to the new values around gender equality and sexuality that were spreading through American society. At the same time, the findings from income maintenance experiments in New Jersey, Denver, and Seattle failed to put to rest concerns over the impact of higher welfare payments on family stability and work effort. Finally, the new reality of married women's involvement in the workplace undermined a welfare system based on the assumption that women's place was in the home.[26]

Still, the Family Support Act of 1988—passed after arduous negotiations between Congress and the Reagan administration—should have laid the basis for a new approach to welfare. Senator Daniel Patrick Moynihan of New York, who earlier in his career had sounded alarm over the problems of African American families as part of the Johnson administration and had designed the FAP when he served as a domestic policy advisor to Nixon, championed the Family Support Act. For social conservatives, the 1988 law included increased requirements for paternity establishment and child support enforcement. All welfare recipients except those with very young children were required to either find employment or make efforts to increase their self-sufficiency through education or training. To back up the work requirements of the Family Support Act, Congress made new funding available for training and education through the Jobs Opportunities and Basic Skills (JOBS) program. In addition, states were required to provide transitional child care, transportation, and health care benefits to women who had moved from welfare to work.[27]

Yet, historical timing was not on the side of the Family Support Act. Within a year of its passage, the United States had fallen into recession. As unemployment increased, the number of welfare recipients began to rise for the first time since the early 1980s. The states found themselves having to contend with a 40 percent increase in welfare recipients as the total number of individuals on AFDC and general assistance increased from 10.4 million in 1987 to 14.9 million in 1992. Faced with the increased welfare rolls, the states largely failed to comply with mandates around transitional transportation and child care and refused to commit the matching funds that were necessary to make use of the JOBS funding. By the early 1990s, the rise in recipients set off a backlash at the state level—tied to reducing the cost of the program—that shifted the welfare reform debate in a new, more conservative direction.

Changes in family life and in the labor-force participation of women raised questions about the social insurance program, just as they had about the AFDC program. The social insurance program—old age insurance—was designed for a nuclear family with two parents and one (male) wage earner. For non-employed women, in an era of widespread marital instability, problems arise in a system where benefits derive from the income of the employed spouse and are not portable. Employed women, too, appear dissatisfied with the way in which benefits were calculated, feeling that there were often inequities.[28]

Yet, there was no way to improve the treatment of women without increasing the cost of the program. A full recognition of women's earning through a system of "earnings sharing" that gave women credit for both their and their spouse's contributions would benefit many working wives; but to keep the system revenue neutral, the benefits of stay-at-home spouses would have to be cut. With most of the attention during the 1980s focused on the fiscal soundness of the Social Security funds, increasing the system's gender equity went unaddressed.[29]

Child Welfare and the Aging

The rejection of welfare reform set federal policies for children and older Americans on divergent policy trajectories. In place of a system of income support that would reduce child poverty, Congress showed increased interest in the treatment of abused and neglected children. At the same time, the elderly benefited from increased funding on income support programs—even in the face of public concern about their cost—and expanded services.

The perceived success of Head Start during the War on Poverty provided momentum for the expansion of federal involvement in early childhood education. The Comprehensive Child Development Act of 1971, which was passed by both houses of Congress, would have provided significant funding for child care and set national standards of child-care workers. Although the bill would have made it easier for poor mothers to seek employment, the bill became a lightning rod for conservative concerns about an overreaching federal government. When President Nixon vetoed the bill, he suggested that it would cause the "Sovietization" of child-rearing in the United States.[30]

Still, the years between 1968 and 1992 were a period of increased federal involvement in child welfare. The identification of the "battered child syndrome" by Henry Kempe in 1962 has sparked an interest in possible child abuse and the passage of mandatory reporting legislation in all 50 states by 1968. In 1974, Congress passed the Child Abuse Prevention and Treatment Act (CAPTA), which provided the first federal funding for child protective services. These efforts were expanded by the Adoption Assistance and Child Welfare Act of 1980, which took a more active role in shaping the nature of child protective services and efforts to prevent "foster care drift," in which children found themselves without a plan for either a return to their parents or another permanent home.[31]

The increases in Social Security benefits legislated in the late 1960s and early 1970s transformed old age insurance into a true "retirement wage" that rapidly reduced poverty among older Americans. Yet, the combination of higher benefits indexed to prices, high inflation, and slow wage growth (which reduced the flow of taxes into the system) generated an incipient fiscal crisis for Social Security.

The 1979 Advisory Council on Social Security concluded that our social insurances were basically sound.

> The Council is unanimous in finding that the social security system is the government's most successful social program. It provides basic retirement, disability and survivorship protection, which American workers can supplement with their own savings and private pensions, and it will continue to provide this protection for as far ahead as anyone can see.
>
> After reviewing the evidence, the Council is unanimously convinced that all current and future social security beneficiaries can count on receiving all the benefits to which they are entitled.[32]

Yet, the fiscal problems of the system continued to mount. Despite some alteration in benefit calculations during the Carter administration, inflation and rising unemployment led to deficits in the OASDI funds in 1978, 1979, and 1980. In June 1980, the trustees recommended that the retirement trust fund be permitted to borrow from the other trust funds. For the longer run, there was widespread concern about the distribution of the payroll tax receipts among the health funds, the disability fund, and the retirement system, and a potential need to finance in part from general revenues if benefits were not to be cut below planned levels. The Advisory Council recommended that health insurance be financed from general revenues, thus preserving for OAI the image of "contributions" and "earned entitlements" to retirement income. Conservatives proposed cuts in benefits and increases in the retirement age as ways of "saving" the Social Security system.

President Reagan's initial reaction was to recommend major cuts in Social Security, including reductions in benefit payments for early retirement, elimination of the minimum benefit, and a postponement of the annual cost-of-living adjustment. In contrast to its acceptance of other Reagan welfare cuts, Congress almost unanimously rejected his Social Security proposals. To defuse the controversy, Reagan appointed a bipartisan National Commission on Social Security Reform in 1981 to examine the entire social insurance system and make recommendations that would lead to "long-term solvency" and ensure both "financial integrity" and "the provision of appropriate benefits."[33]

The commission considered a variety of approaches to the system's problems, but it ultimately recommended a set of incremental proposals that did not alter the basic elements of the retirement program. It recommended, first of all, that "Congress . . . not alter the fundamental structure of the . . . program or undermine its fundamental principles." It was to remain a compulsory, non–means-tested, contributory program, which gave low-income workers a better return on their contributions than those who were higher up on the wage scale. To meet fiscal need, it proposed a partial taxation of higher-income retirees' benefits, a gradual increase in the retirement age (to 67), and increases in the contribution rate.[34]

The 1983 Social Security reform law sought to eliminate the short-term financial problems with the system and to shift tax policy to build up the trust funds with an eye toward the retirement of the baby-boom generation early in the 21st century. The balance went up immediately and the assets of the Old Age and Survivors Insurance (OASI) trust fund grew rapidly. At the time, projections were that the trust fund would rise to $12 trillion by 2030, the height of the impact of the retirement of baby boomers.

The Social Security Act, as originally legislated, provided work-related benefits much in the way such benefits would have been provided through private insurance. The notion of equity was the tie among wages, tax contributions, and benefits. Amendments to the act have steadily altered this approach to reflect need and adequacy as well as equity. The passage of the SSI program in 1972 provided a means-tested income transfer program that guaranteed a minimum income for the elderly and disabled. Furthermore, SSI benefits, like OAI benefits, were indexed to keep pace with inflation. This change made it possible to rethink the extent to which the insurance programs should be used to redress inequities in wage and employment patterns. Increasingly, policy focused more on the "health" of the plan's finances and less to the income adequacy of the program.

While Social Security was attracting widespread attention from policy makers and the public, a quieter revolution was expanding the public costs of so-called "private" pensions. Economic slowdowns sent many companies into bankruptcy, often taking their employees' pension plan with them. These "defined-benefit" plans were generally funded and controlled by companies. Although they received generous tax benefits for creating the programs, there was little government oversight of the plans' financial security.

While Social Security was attracting widespread attention from policy makers and the public, a quieter revolution was expanding the public costs of so-called "private" pensions.

In response to several well-publicized company bankruptcies, including the Studebaker automobile company, Congress in 1974 passed the Employee Retirement Income Security Act (ERISA) that set out new regulations for pension plans and established a quasi-governmental insurance system—the Pension Benefit Guaranty Corporation—to cover losses associated with the termination of defined-benefit plans. However, the real impact of the events of the early 1970s was to reorient pensions from *defined-benefit*—in which employers promised specific pensions for workers based on their years of service—to defined-contribution plans—in which workers contributed to individual plans, sometimes with employer matches. Subsequent revenue acts developed a variety of special accounts—of which Individual Retirement Accounts and 401(k) accounts were the most popular—to facilitate this shift toward private pension accounts. Although these plans were attractive to workers, they required workers to assume most of the risk associated with retirement planning. Furthermore, except for the highest-paid workers, these plans rarely assured adequate retirement income.

The implication of these changes during the 1970s was not immediately apparent. In contrast to the very public debate over the future of Social Security, these "private" accounts typically passed "below the radar." Although they involved trillions of dollars in tax breaks, public policy analysts found it nearly impossible to assess their full implications. Over time, however, it became clear that the mass of the tax breaks associated with these plans flowed to the richest Americans and bypassed those with greater need. Over time, even without efforts to "privatize" Social Security, American retirement security began to tilt strongly toward private plans and increased income inequality among older Americans.[35]

The issues were joined in the discussions about the provision of health benefits and long-term care. Medicare was designed to provide the aged with prepaid hospital insurance financed by payroll taxes and a medical insurance program to pay doctors' bills, outpatient hospital care, and some additional health services, financed by a combination of recipient payments and general tax revenues. It was intended to be a non–means-tested program.

In order to pass Medicare and Medicaid in the 1960s, Congress had set rules that gave hospitals and health providers few incentives to contain cost. Between 1965 and 1990, health care expenses as percent of gross domestic product (GDP) more than doubled, reaching 12 percent in 1990. With the rise in health care costs, efforts to contain expenses increased. In 1983, Congress placed a lid on Medicare reimbursements for hospital stays with the introduction of the diagnosis-related groups (DRGs) billing system. Patients were being discharged from hospitals "quicker but sicker." The concept of approved reimbursement rates was extended to physicians' services. In 1988, 37 percent of all Medicare-approved physicians were accepting Medicare-approved rates for fees. Unfortunately, there was evidence that patients might be experiencing cost shifting and restricted access to medical care. Premium increases and benefit cuts combined to increase older Americans' out-of-pocket health care costs. In 1980, the aged used 13 percent of their income for health care; that figure rose to 18.5 percent by 1990.[36]

In addition to cutting services, the effort to control public payment for health care for the aging meant placing a larger share of the cost on middle- and upper-income workers and beneficiaries. Thus, in 1990, while the maximum wages to be taxed for retirement, survivors, and disability income was set at $51,300 annually, workers with incomes up to $125,000 paid a Medicare tax of 1.45 percent. In 1988, Congress passed legislation, the Medicare Catastrophic Health Care Act, that extended hospital care for all under Medicare, to be paid for by a surtax on the incomes of middle- and upper-income aged. The bill was repealed just one year later when older Americans realized that the catastrophic health care bill did not cover long-term custodial care and was a substantial tax on a small part of the population.

The increased number of Americans over the age of 80 made long-term care a pressing issue. Yet, in the absence of public insurance for nursing home care, the federal government backed into its policy. Increasingly, Medicaid—the health care program for low-income Americans—became the chief funder of nursing home care. However, to qualify for Medicaid, the elderly were required to "spend down" their assets. Often, senior citizens would see their life savings quickly evaporate before they became poor enough to receive Medicaid. In reality, we had a policy for the public funding of nursing home care, but it required some wrenching economic choices for older Americans and their families.

The Unemployed

Although the debate over welfare and the fiscal crisis of Social Security attracted the greatest headlines, some of the sharpest policy changes of the 1970s and 1980s involved provisions for the unemployed. Unemployment remained a problem throughout the period, largely because of the deliberate use of unemployment as a means of fighting inflation. Yet, even though government policy increased the number of unemployed Americans, the government took less responsibility for their economic security during the 1970s and 1980s than it had in earlier decades.

Changes in the workplace contributed to the decreasing effectiveness of unemployment insurance. The economic transition underway during the 1970s and 1980s meant that fewer of the unemployed experienced temporary layoffs, and more were displaced from their jobs. In addition, a greater share of Americans were working part-time or temporary jobs. Many who held these jobs failed to qualify for unemployment insurance when they lost their jobs.

The sharpest changes in the unemployment system occurred in the early years of the Reagan administration. Before 1981, when the national unemployment rate went above a certain level, all of the eligible unemployed were entitled to collect unemployment for an additional 13 weeks after their 26 weeks of basic coverage expired. As part of his "economic recovery" plan in 1981, President Reagan proposed and Congress enacted limits on the availability of extended benefits except in individual states that were experiencing high unemployment.

The combination of a changing labor market and deliberate government policy took its toll on the unemployed. In 1980, 44 percent of the unemployed had received unemployment compensation. By 1985, the percentage had fallen to 32 percent. When the economy again fell into recession in 1989, less than a third of the unemployed were eligible for unemployment compensation.[37]

At the same time, public employment—another means of reducing unemployment—was shrinking. During the early 1970s, Congress passed the Comprehensive Employment and Training Act (CETA), which, in addition to providing funding for job training, funded public service employment for city governments. During the recessions of 1974–1975 and 1980, CETA public service employment provided many jobs and helped to cushion the impact of the recessions in many metropolitan areas. Yet, the program was widely unpopular in Congress and was terminated in 1981. Cuts in federal funding for public service employment combined with the shrinking tax base of many American cities to severely reduce the availability of public employment. Because public employment was a significant source of white-collar jobs for African Americans in American cities, the cuts to public employment fell disproportionately on the black community.

The last line of defense for the unemployed—general assistance—was also in eclipse during these years. States eliminated or severely limited their programs. For example, in the early 1980s, Pennsylvania restricted general assistance benefits to a few months out of the year, a reform that many commentators tied to the increase in homelessness in the commonwealth. In 1990, 22 states had statewide programs; 17 more had programs in some counties; and in 6 states, there was a program of small emergency grants in some counties. In 7 states, there was no program at all. General assistance was concentrated in large cities and provided financial and medical assistance to low-income individuals and families who were not eligible for federally funded assistance programs. Maximum cash benefits ranged from a low of 5 percent of the poverty line in Charleston County, South Carolina, to a high of only 77 percent of the poverty line in Portland, Maine.[38] Most of the programs emphasized the necessity to work for clients deemed employable, but the meaning of employability was not clear. Were those classified as employable truly capable of sustaining employment? Second, even if they were employable, were they getting realistic help in a job search? For those who were not immediately employable, what kinds of training programs were to be provided and who would be admitted?

Veterans

It was hoped that the coming together of women, black and white, rich and poor, on problems of discrimination might result in common demand for change—change reflected in the welfare of poor families. Thirty-five years earlier, some observers thought veterans would play such a catalytic role. The 1956 report of the President's Commission on Veterans' Pensions analyzed the meaning of the special status accorded veterans:

> Veterans and their families will eventually be a majority of the population of the United States. Veterans in modern times are better off economically than nonveterans in similar age groups.[39]

The 1956 commission pointed to the extent to which basic needs of "all citizens, veterans and non-veterans alike, for economic security are being increasingly met through federal, state and private programs." In summary, the commission concluded, "Military service in time of war or peace is the obligation of citizenship and should not be considered inherently a basis for future Government benefits," and "all veterans' benefits should be meshed with the nation's general security system."

The commission's report of 1956 wielded little influence. But the benefits awarded in 1966 to veterans of the Korean War (retroactively) and the Vietnam War suggested some policy shifts. Certainly, the educational benefits for these groups did not compare favorably with those provided for veterans in 1944. Veterans of Vietnam in particular paid the price of our unhappiness with that war.

Personal Social Services

The history of social services was a harbinger of the pressure to cut social welfare spending. Although social services had been included in Social Security since the 1950s, it had remained a small part of welfare spending through the 1960s. During the War on Poverty, however, a combination of looser federal regulation and states' interest in shifting costs to the federal government led to an explosion in federal spending on social services. Between 1965 and 1972, for example, total outlays for social services increased from $159 million to $4 billion—a 19-fold increase when controlled for inflation. Much of this increase resulted from a broader interpretation of regulations that allowed spending on those "likely to become" dependent on welfare. In response to this increase, Congress added a new title to the Social Security Act in 1974—Title XX—that imposed a cap on federal spending on social services.[40]

The Reagan administration used its first budget in 1981 to change Title XX from a "capped entitlement" to a block grant (Social Service Block Grant) subject to the congressional appropriation process. By 2016, the appropriation for Title XX had fallen to $1.58 billion. When corrected for inflation, the federal government's spending on social services had fallen by 93 percent between 1972 and 2016.[41] The block grant mechanism became a means of limiting public spending on a variety of functions by making the federal commitment subject to the vagaries of budget debate.

? Assess your comprehension of "Innovations in Social Welfare" by completing this quiz.

SOCIAL MOVEMENTS

The New Right

Conservative movements drew little support during the early postwar years, but the social and political changes of the 1960s and 1970s mobilized new constituencies and organizations. The success of the civil rights movement provoked a *white backlash* in both the North and South. The changing status of women and the challenge to traditional sexual mores and gender roles provoked a powerful antifeminist movement. Underlying these social and cultural reactions was an insistent economic conservatism that argued that the welfare state and "excessive regulation" were responsible for the stagnation of the economy. Meanwhile, antitax revolts mobilized property owners in a movement against rising property taxes and government expenditures. Poor urban residents—who had been the focus of policy innovations during the 1970s—now were recast as an "urban underclass" that would require "tough love" to rejoin the mainstream.

 Watch this video on the Equal Rights Amendment, which began with broad political support but was eventually defeated by conservative attacks.

https://www.youtube.com/watch?v=YWyv5Fw0JSk

Just as the drive to expand the civil rights of black Americans had become the model for other civil rights movements, the rearguard efforts of segregationists provided a vocabulary for newer conservative causes. Segregationists had objected to the trampling of "states' rights" and the "imposition" of new requirements at odds with the Southern status quo. In the wake of the Supreme Court's guaranteeing a women's right to an abortion and the success of feminists in gaining passage of the Equal Rights Amendment by Congress in 1972, antifeminists saw a plot to undermine women's traditional role. Although their claims that the ERA would require same-sex bathrooms and women's role as combat soldiers were specious, the charge that women's purity would be compromised by equality proved powerful (Figure 8.1).

Conservatives had long been suspicious of government action, but by the early 1970s, they had been joined by many traditionally liberal constituencies. The war in Vietnam, government surveillance of protesters, and the Watergate affair had led many Americans to view the government in a less favorable light. Ronald Reagan, in his inaugural address in 1981, seemed to capture many Americans' cynicism when he concluded:

> In this present crisis, government is not the solution to our problem; government is the problem.[42]

From the start of the 1980 presidential campaign, the Republican candidate Reagan argued that the Democratic Party had been unable to meet new and serious economic and social conditions. As president, Reagan acted to reduce government expenditures and taxes. Arguing for "supply-side" economics, deregulation of business, and tax cuts as a means of stimulating economic growth, President Reagan attacked domestic social welfare programs. President George H. W. Bush (1989–1993), while couching his arguments in a "kinder and gentler" manner, continued to allow his concern for interest rates and budget stability to take precedence over considerations of individual well-being. Changes in the economy, political structure, family organization, and the age structure of the U.S. population combined to make large social welfare changes necessary. However, necessary social interventions took a back seat to tax cuts and budget restraint.

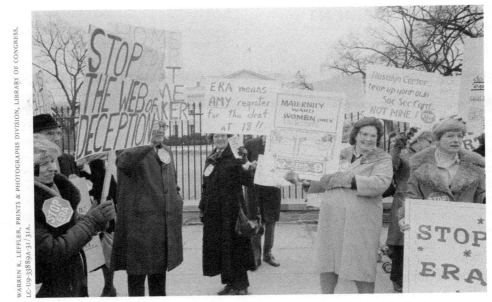

Figure 8.1   Anti-ERA demonstration in front of White House, 1977. Efforts to put a ban on gender discrimination in the U.S. Constitution provoked a strong reaction of women and men who claimed that the Equal Rights Amendment would require unisex bathrooms, the abolition of Social Security survivors' benefits, and women to register for the draft and become combat soldiers.

The Expansion of Civil Rights

The state of the economy was only one factor shaping social welfare. The concern of the 1960s with the rights of oppressed groups, paced by the militancy of the black community, led to advances in rights to privacy, due process, and equal protection. The emergence of many groups—women, students, children, the aging, Native Americans, prisoners, homosexuals, and others—demanding change resulted in their gaining at least some basic recognition. The historical value of individualism broadened to a demand for group-determined rights.

The American Indian Movement organized for militant defense of the rights of Native Americans. The 1970s saw the formation of a new Council of Energy Resources, which took to the courts to fight for rights to the development of the coal, oil, and other resources needed to promote industries on the reservations. There were setbacks, but there were also victories. Some land claims were won, some land was put in trust for development for the benefit of Native Americans, and additional sums of money were appropriated to the Bureau of Indian Affairs for education. Nonetheless, Native Americans remained the poorest of the poor in the United States.

The period from 1970 to 1990 included conflicting trends in civil rights. In the 1970s, successes in extending civil liberties were scored in affirmative action programs and in efforts to replace institutionalization with community-based programs. Judicial decisions required the payment of reparations to groups who had been shown to suffer from discriminatory pay and promotion differentials. In July 1980, the Supreme Court, in *Fullilove v. Klutznick*, upheld the use of quotas for minority contractors when it decided that Congress could award federal funds on the basis of race to redress past racial discrimination.[43] The courts seesawed on the issue of affirmative action throughout the decade. In 1984, the Supreme Court decided in a 6–3 decision that seniority overrules affirmative action concerns with regard to layoffs.[44] A May 1986 decision confirmed that position, but found that the adoption of hiring goals favoring minorities would be a permissible way for a government employer to redress its past discrimination.[45] In July 1986, in two cases, one involving New York City sheet metal workers and one involving firefighters in Cleveland, the use of affirmative action in the workplace to address past discrimination was endorsed when less drastic approaches would not work. In February 1987, in a 5–4 decision, the court endorsed "catch-up quotas" to counter severe past discrimination against blacks, and the following month, it extended preferential hiring to women.[46]

By 1989, however, as its composition changed and conservatives achieved a majority, the Supreme Court began to back away from its support of affirmative action. In January, the court invalidated a Richmond law that set aside 30 percent of public works funds to minority-owned construction companies.[47] This was followed by a series of decisions against the use of racial or sex preferences to remedy past discrimination and making it increasingly difficult for plaintiffs to prove employment discrimination. In 1990, Congress passed a bill to reverse the Supreme Court's decisions and shift the burden of proof back to employers on discrimination issues. Employees did not have to demonstrate discrimination; employers would have to show that a practice that hurts women or minorities was necessary to the success of the business. The bill facilitated opportunities for employees to challenge court orders, granted victims of intentional discrimination the right to recover compensatory and punitive damages, and reaffirmed that any intentional job bias was illegal. President Bush vetoed the bill on October 22, 1990, on the grounds that it would force employers to adopt hiring and promotion quotas to avoid discrimination suits. The Senate failed by one vote to override the veto, but the following year, Congress passed and the president signed into law the Civil Rights Act of 1991.

The same pattern of expansion and then a retrenchment applied to immigration policy. In 1965, the tie between the admission of immigrants and their ethnic origin was broken, and for over a decade, it appeared that the U.S. fear of alien cultures was fading. Concerns about the economic success of a more open policy began arising during the early 1980s. By 1980, there were political, medical, and economic doubts about the entry of immigrants, who were seen by American labor as competitors for jobs, and about the participation of "foreigners" in education, health, and welfare services.

Refugees became a significant share of the increase in the foreign-born population during the 1970s and 1980s. Refugees from Indochina, refugees from Haiti, and, in 1980, a new Cuban refugee population arrived in large numbers. Indeed, the anticipated ceilings on immigration of about 290,000 people annually were only a small part of the picture. Many more immigrants came into the country as close relatives of U.S. citizens or as refugees than were entering under the hemispheric quotas. Of the 1.5 million legal immigrants in 1990, fewer than 300,000 came under the immigration quotas; the remainder, 1.2 million, were exempt from numerical limitations.[48] Added to this were large numbers of illegal entrants, many from Mexico.

Both the refugees from Cuba and those from Haiti were greeted with less than open arms. It was rumored that President Fidel Castro of Cuba had been releasing prisoners and mental patients to come to the United States. The presence of the AIDS virus in both the Cuban and Haitian refugees was seen as another barrier to their admission. In the end, the Cuban refugees were admitted and the Haitians rejected. After much bureaucratic maneuvering, the political arguments in favor of embarrassing the communist regime overcame other objections, and the Cuban refugees were admitted and given generous support by the U.S. government. The Haitian refugees were sent back to Haiti or placed in long-term detention because they were seeking refuge only from poverty, not from political persecution.[49]

Immigration policy became dominated by two economic concerns. One was the fear for jobs. Advocates of immigration reform in 1965 imagined that European immigration would resume after Congress passed the law and that highly skilled workers would dominate the new immigrant wave. As it turned out, Latin America and Asia were the sources of most new immigrants, and they were more likely to compete for less-skilled jobs. Further, it was feared that immigrants would avail themselves too extensively of education services and public aid—cash welfare programs, food stamps, and Medicaid. In 1982, the Supreme Court ruled that all children regardless of immigration status had the right to attend public schools. Local and state officials continued to raise the issue of immigrant eligibility, often noting that while the federal government controlled immigration, local governments often absorbed the cost of newcomers. Earlier in our history, immigrants were suspect for their religious and political ideas because they were feared as anarchists or communists or because of their possible allegiance to an enemy country. By 1990, however, economic issues had replaced political ones as the center of concern.

For children, too, there was a retreat from rights during the 1980s. The promise of the *Gault* decision of 1967, protecting the rights of children in trouble with the law, was compromised. There was visible return to giving priority to rehabilitation over justice in juvenile proceedings despite the paucity of resources that undermined the quality of services.

On a state level, the intent of laws such as Pennsylvania's Act 148, designed to support deinstitutionalization and community/own-home planning for children, was countered by a lack of supportive community services and by active efforts to legally cut the tie between dependent children and their mothers. The Office of Child Development's thrust toward "permanency planning," though overtly intended to protect children from the uncertainties of longtime foster care placements, unnecessarily risked the permanent separation of some children from their natural parents. The notion of going "beyond the best interest of the child"[50] to forge new permanent ties could, in the 1990s, prove an updated version of "binding out."

People suffering from mental illness and mental retardation also saw their rights expand during the 1970s, but then fail to be fully realized. Since the early 19th century, institutions—first called "insane asylums" and later called "state hospitals"—had been the major policy response for this population. By the 1960s, innovations in therapy and research had led to the beginning of a community mental health system that would treat people with mental illnesses in their own communities.

But the institutions persisted, typically filled with individuals without resources or support to explore alternatives. In 1972, however, the Supreme Court (*Wyatt v. Stickney*) ruled that states could not continue to "warehouse" the mentally ill and mentally retarded. The court recognized a "right to treatment" that placed the burden on states to create noninstitutional alternatives to institutionalization that would reintegrate these populations into the community.

During the 1970s, lawsuits and public policy emptied many institutions. In 1955, more than 500,000 Americans lived in state psychiatric hospitals; by the 1990s, fewer than 60,000 did. In some states, massive efforts were made to provide services to reintegrate the mentally ill and mentally retarded, while in other localities, "dumping" was a more accurate description of the policy implementation. Concerns about cost, the hostility of current residents to the creation of community-based group homes (the acronym

NIMBY—not in my backyard—came into common usage), and the largely untested strategies for community integration hampered efforts and led to mixed results.

During the 1980s, even successful programs found themselves scrambling for funding. On the one hand, as with many voluntary social welfare efforts stretching back more than a century, advocates of community action were shown to be overly optimistic about the ability of voluntary efforts to reintegrate these populations. On the other hand, government found itself quite adept at first limiting and then cutting funding available for programs. Eventually, many mentally ill individuals found themselves re-institutionalized, this time in prisons and jails instead of state hospitals.

The retreat on civil rights hit welfare families most severely. During the 1960s, the Supreme Court had strengthened the rights of welfare recipients by supporting their claims to due process, privacy, and the right to migrate. Between 1970 and 1990, a combination of legislation, court decisions, and administrative actions weakened these new, insecure rights. The federal government weakened its prohibitions on house searches while the New York state legislature used the failure to find standard housing as a means of denying welfare payments to new migrants.

Congress and the general public expanded their support for work requirements for welfare recipients during these years. With the passage of the Family Support Act in 1988, in every state, AFDC recipients with children age six or older were required to work or attend a job training program or school. A state could require participation in work or education programs even for recipients with children as young as three years. If a recipient did not meet the state's behavioral rules, he or she might be "sanctioned"—that is, his or her grant might be reduced or even eliminated.[51]

Perhaps the most visible civil rights battle of the period was in the area of access to abortion. In two 1973 cases (*Roe v. Wade* and *Doe v. Bolton*), the Supreme Court established women's control over their own bodies by supporting their right to abortion during the first trimester of pregnancy. Since then, there have been repeated attempts by "pro-life" groups to argue the viability and rights of the fetus over the rights of the mother. While abortion was legal in the United States, proponents of abortion, the "pro-choice" groups, feared the implications for women of the changing composition of the Supreme Court.

For poor women, the battle had already been lost, since the court ruled that the states were not required to make Medicaid funds available for abortions except in pregnancies resulting from rape or directly threatening their health.[52] By 1990, an uneasy balance had been reached on abortion. The public overwhelmingly supported abortion as part of the right to privacy, but was unwilling to pay the cost of this right for women who could not afford it. In reality, an increasing proportion of women were denied this reproductive right, either because they could not afford it or because services were not accessible.

One group—people with physical or mental disabilities—fared better in Congress and the courts. The Americans with Disabilities Act of 1990 established comprehensive civil rights and aimed to reverse the stigmatization of people with disabilities. The law prohibited discrimination against people with physical or mental impairments in employment, transportation, and public accommodations. The regulations implementing the legislation required that new construction for public accommodations—schools, libraries, restaurants, and hospital and nursing home rooms, for example—be accessible. Existing businesses were required to make alterations to buildings to accommodate special needs unless they could show that expenses would be too great. The intent was to integrate those who have disabilities into all aspects of life.

The Americans with Disabilities Act of 1990 established comprehensive civil rights and aimed to reverse the stigmatization of people with disabilities.

Unfortunately, concern for the welfare of disabled people did not extend to their pension and public welfare rights. Despite repeated court rulings that disability insurance benefits could not be arbitrarily cut off, the Social Security Administration was slow to revise its eligibility procedures. Government used a variety of administrative procedures to limit the number of people receiving Disability Insurance (DI) or SSI. For adults, the General Accounting Office (GAO) reported that over one-half of the applicants who had been denied benefits between 1984 and 1987 reported not working, and many reported they did not anticipate ever working again. Over two-thirds of those denied DI and not able to work reported serious income inadequacy, as did those denied benefits but working at least part time.[53]

The right of children with disabilities to income support received a boost in 1990 when the Supreme Court ruled that the adult standard for establishing a disability applied to young people as well. As a result, eligibility for SSI for children began to expand after 1990. Yet, the results were mixed. No sooner did the court decision take effect than budget-cutters in Congress looked to the incomes of children with disabilities as a source of "savings." The 1996 welfare reform law repealed this new entitlement.

Women

A staff report of the U.S. Commission on Civil Rights charged that federal and state welfare programs, federal job training programs, and social insurance and private pension plans all discriminated against women. AFDC and its work programs were subject to special attack. Not only were low AFDC benefits keeping women and their families in poverty, but WIN, when it did succeed in placing women in jobs, had done so at discriminatory, low-entry wage levels in jobs that offered little chance for advancement. Significantly, a staff member of the U.S. Commission on Civil Rights had this to say about the commission's first hearings on women's rights:

> The value of having low-income women in these hearings is that they educate us and tell us problems. They also find . . . there are laws that cover them. . . . And these hearings get action . . . because they draw attention.[54]

That hearing took place in 1974. A Department of Justice Task Force on Sex Discrimination issued a report in 1979 with a broad overview of sexual discrimination in our pension system.[55]

Many studies and reports on the changing position of women were issued in the late 1970s. The Department of Labor held a major conference analyzing "Women's Changing Roles at Home and on the Job" in 1977.[56] That same year, the Social Security amendments legislated that the secretary of health, education, and welfare, in consultation with the Task Force on Sex Discrimination in the Department of Justice, make a detailed study of unequal treatment of men and women under the Social Security Act, and started an exploration of ways of eliminating dependency as a factor in the determination of spouse's benefits.[57] The Task Force on the Treatment of Women was appointed, and its report was issued early in 1978.[58] Secretary Joseph A. Califano Jr. also requested that the Advisory Council on Social Security "consider the criticism that the present benefit structure does not recognize the changing role of women in our society." Reactions to the 1978 Task Force report and letters sent to the Advisory Council became basic data for the 1979 HEW report, *Social Security and the Changing Roles of Men and Women*. Although the 1979 report analyzed options for change and did not make definite recommendations, it did serve a basic purpose: "to focus public debate on concerns about the way social security relates to the present complex and diversified structure of American society." Later in 1979, the Advisory Council stated the issue as follows:

> Two new objectives [for Social Security] are commanding increasing attention. First, from the recognition that women are important contributors to the economic well being of the family, whether they work inside or outside the home, comes the desire that women be entitled to benefits in their own right, not simply or primarily as economic dependents of their spouses. Second, in addition to individual equity, equity is now also tested by whether couples with the same total earnings receive the same protection, regardless of which partner earned what share.[59]

Issues of women's rights were raised on many fronts: the courts, Congress, the administration, the women's movement, and the public generally. But change for women generally and for poor women in particular did not occur with the predicted swiftness. Ambivalence about ways to help poor women combined with a broader ambivalence about the proper role of all women in our society. The failure to achieve ratification of the Equal Rights Amendment by the required approval of three-fourths of the states and the rescinding of approval by several states indicate the indecision of the period.

> **?** Assess your comprehension of "Social Movements" by completing this quiz.

CONCLUSION

In 1970, social welfare seemed open to new endeavors, new efforts to help those in need. But by 1990, the attention to federal budget deficits dampened the interest not only in social services but also in any expansion of programs for retirees, for women, or for the unemployed. Welfare reform, too, was put on hold. President Carter had urged Congress to consider the establishment of a national minimum benefit level pegged at 65 percent of the poverty threshold, as well as additional allocations for job development,[60] but President Reagan moved toward social welfare cutbacks.

Combined with budget restraints was the desire to narrow the role of the federal government. Revenue sharing, block grants, and the proposed return to the states of responsibility for many job training, education, community development, justice, and health programs were a retreat from the longtime trend toward centralized—that is, federal—responsibility for social welfare. Behind the Reagan drive to return responsibility for many programs to the states was a desire to cut total expenditures for social welfare. Funding for social programs was contained by the device of expanding block grants so that they had to cover more programs. Expansion of any one program then comes at the expense of a reduction in another. President Bush was inclined to further President Reagan's move toward block grants, with the states making the allocation decisions.

Conservative Resurgence and Social Change

President Richard M. Nixon's *Message on Reform in Welfare* (1969) is one of two documents used to illustrate social welfare events during the 1970s and 1980s. Although the message was written in 1969, it was considered as H.R. 1 in 1970. The debate that swirled around the message and the bill highlighted the major issues in public welfare.

The FAP proposed in the message was the center of controversy. In the initial debate, attacks came from both liberals and conservatives. The merits of the NIT approach to helping poor families, the sufficiency of the guaranteed basic allowance, the work-incentive features, and the inclusion of benefits for the working poor were all subject to scrutiny by proponents and opponents. Liberals generally approved the plan to federalize aid for poor families. They were dismayed, however, by the seemingly punitive "workfare" aspects of the message and by the low guaranteed basic allowance of $1,600 a year for a family of four. Conservatives were frightened by the possibility that an income transfer program guaranteeing benefits for the working poor would attract people to the welfare rolls and weaken their attachment to the labor force.

What comes through forcefully in the message is the switch from a service approach to welfare to an income-workfare approach. Moreover, the message makes clear that mothers are now to be considered employable—or potentially employable. The implication was a reversal of the "own home" philosophy of child care proclaimed by President Theodore Roosevelt at the first National Conference on Children and Youth in 1909.

As criticisms of H.R. 1 became more volatile, the Nixon administration and Congress responded with changes in the original proposal. The basic guaranteed allowance was raised, but supplementation through food stamps was eliminated. Even more serious from the point of view of welfare recipients in the more generous North was the threat of a cutback in their grants. The plan, as originally devised, offered protection against such a loss by requiring the states to supplement the guaranteed allowance. This was also eliminated. Work requirements became more stringent, specifying that mothers with children over three years old be available for work. Three-quarters of the minimum wage was stipulated as acceptable pay.

On the one side were those who worried about the inadequacies and injustices of the program. On the other side was a group concerned with mounting costs. Analyses of multiple program benefits and their overlap increased the anxiety of those who feared the erosion of work incentives. Stalemate ensued, and the proposal was quietly abandoned.

President Jimmy Carter's Better Jobs and Income Program was, in its essential thrust, similar to the FAP. The two plans differed in two major aspects: (1) the Carter plan provided universal coverage, whereas the Nixon proposal was for families only; and (2) the Carter proposal included job creation. Despite the differences, the Carter plan also failed to achieve approval.

The increased interest in workforce participation and a desire to reduce the number of people receiving government income transfer payments led, by the late 1970s, to renewed vigor in removing people from the disability rolls. The administration pursued a disability review process that required claimants to show that there had not been sufficient improvement to stop their disability payments. Claimants sued, holding that although they had the burden of coming forward with some evidence of disability initially, in review the administration had the burden of showing that they were no longer disabled.

The administration lost many individual cases on this issue. They announced a policy of non-acquiescence: They would obey the court in a particular case but would not generalize the principle to apply it to other claimants. They chose not to seek review of these cases in the Supreme Court.

Congress moved to resolve the matter when it passed new regulations for termination of disability benefits based on medical improvement. The standard established by Congress in 42 U.S.C.S. § 423f requires that, in order to cease paying disability benefits, substantial evidence demonstrates sufficient medical improvement that the individual is now well enough to "engage in substantial gainful activity."[61]

The text of this statute applied to Title II benefits (DI). A similar statute with identical language covered SSI. The law also provides for continuation of disability benefits during an administrative appeal in a termination case.[62] Slowly, benefits were restored to some people with disabilities.

REFORM IN WELFARE
MESSAGE FROM PRESIDENT RICHARD M. NIXON
August 11, 1969

TO THE CONGRESS OF THE UNITED STATES:

A measure of the greatness of a powerful nation is the character of the life it creates for those who are powerless to make ends meet.

If we do not find the way to become a working nation that properly cares for the dependent, we shall become a Welfare State that undermines the incentive of the working man.

The present welfare system has failed us—it has fostered family breakup, has provided very little help in many States and has even deepened dependency by all too often making it more attractive to go on welfare than to go to work.

I propose a new approach that will make it more attractive to go to work than to go on welfare, and will establish a nationwide minimum payment to dependent families with children.

I propose that the Federal government pay a basic income to those American families who cannot care for themselves in whichever State they live.

I propose that dependent families receiving such income be given good reason to go to work by making the first sixty dollars a month they earn completely their own, with no deductions from their benefits.

I propose that we *make available an addition to the incomes of the "working poor,"* to encourage them to go on working and to eliminate the possibility of making more from welfare than from wages.

I propose that these payments be made upon certification of income, with demeaning and costly investigations replaced by simplified reviews and spot checks and with *no eligibility requirements that the household be without a father*. That present requirement in many States has the effect of breaking up families and contributes to delinquency and violence.

I propose that all employable persons who choose to accept these payments be required to register for work or job training and *be required to accept that work or training*, provided suitable jobs are available either locally or if transportation is provided. Adequate and convenient day care would be provided children wherever necessary to enable a parent to train or work. The only exception to this work requirement would be mothers of pre-school children.

I propose *a major expansion of job training and day care facilities*, so that current welfare recipients able to work can be set on the road to self-reliance.

I propose that we also provide uniform Federal payment minimums for the present three categories of welfare aid to adults—the aged, the blind and the disabled.

This would be total welfare reform—the transformation of a system frozen in failure and frustration into a system that would work and would encourage people to work.

Accordingly, we have stopped considering human welfare in isolation. The new plan is part of an overall approach which includes a comprehensive new Manpower Training Act, and a plan for a system of revenue sharing with the State to help provide all of them with necessary budget relief. Messages on manpower training and revenue sharing will follow this message tomorrow and the next day, and the three should be considered as parts of a whole approach to what is clearly a national problem.

Need for New Departures

A welfare system is a success when it takes care of people who cannot take care of themselves and when it helps employable people climb toward independence.

A welfare system is a failure when it takes care of those who *can* take care of themselves, when it drastically varies payments in different areas, when it breaks up families, when it perpetuates a vicious cycle of dependency, when it strips human beings of their dignity.

America's welfare system is a failure that grows worse every day.

First, it fails the recipient: In many areas, benefits are so low that we have hardly begun to take care of the dependent. And there has been no light at the end of poverty's tunnel. After four years of inflation, the poor have generally become poorer.

Second, it fails the taxpayer: Since 1960, welfare costs have doubled and the number on the rolls has risen from 5.8 million to over 9 million, all in a time when unemployment was low. The taxpayer is entitled to expect government to devise a system that will help people lift themselves out of poverty.

Finally, it fails American society: By breaking up homes, the present welfare system has added to social unrest and robbed millions of children of the joy of childhood; by widely varying payments among regions, it has helped to draw millions into the slums of our cities.

The situation has become intolerable. Let us examine the alternatives available:

—We could permit the welfare momentum to continue to gather speed by our inertia; by 1975 this would result in 4 million more Americans on welfare rolls at a cost of close to $11 billion a year, with both recipients and taxpayers shortchanged.

—We could tinker with the system as it is, adding to the patchwork of modifications and exceptions. That has been the approach of the past, and it has failed.

—We could adopt a "guaranteed minimum income for everyone," which would appear to wipe out poverty overnight. It would also wipe out the basic economic motivation for work, and place an enormous strain on the industrious to pay for the leisure of the lazy.

—Or, we could adopt a totally new approach to welfare, designed to assist those left far behind the national norm, and provide all with the motivation to work and a fair share of the opportunity to train.

This administration, after a careful analysis of all the alternatives, is committed to a new departure that will find a solution for the welfare problem. The time for denouncing the old is over; the time for devising the new is now.

Recognizing the Practicalities

People usually follow their self-interest.

This stark fact is distressing to many social planners who like to look at problems from the top down. Let us abandon the ivory towers and consider the real world in all we do.

In most States, welfare is provided only when there is no father at home to provide support. If a man's children would be better off on welfare than with the low wage he is able to bring home, wouldn't he be tempted to leave home?

If a person spent a great deal of time and effort to get on the welfare rolls, wouldn't he think twice about risking his eligibility by taking a job that might not last long?

In each case, welfare policy was intended to limit the spread of dependency; in practice, however, the effect has been to increase dependency and remove the incentive to work.

We fully expect people to follow their self-interest in their business dealings; why should we be surprised when people follow their self-interest in their welfare dealings? That is why we propose a plan in which it is in the interest of every employable person to do his fair share of work.

The Operation of the New Approach

1. We would assure an income foundation throughout every section of America for all parents who cannot adequately support themselves and their children. For a family of four with less than $1,000 income, this payment would be $1,600 a year; for a family of four with $2,000 income, this payment would supplement that income by $960 a year.

Under the present welfare system, each State provides "Aid to Families with Dependent Children," a program we propose to replace. The Federal government shares the cost, but each State establishes key eligibility rules and determines how much income support will be provided to poor families. The result has been an uneven and unequal system. The 1969 benefits average for a family of four is $171 a month across the nation, but individual State averages range from $263 down to $39 a month.

A new Federal minimum of $1,600 a year cannot claim to provide comfort to a family of four, but the present low of $468 a year cannot claim to provide even the basic necessities.

The new system would do away with the inequity of very low benefits levels in some States, and of State-by-State variations in eligibility tests, by establishing a Federally-financed income floor with a national definition of basic eligibility.

States will continue to carry an important responsibility. In 30 States, the Federal basic payment will be less than the present levels of combined Federal and State payments. These States will be required to maintain the current level of benefits, but in no case will a State be required to spend more than 90% of its present welfare cost. The Federal government will not only provide the "floor," but it will assume 10% of the benefits now being paid by the States as their part of welfare costs.

In 20 States, the new payment would exceed the present average benefit payments, in some cases by a wide margin. In these States, where benefits are lowest and poverty often the most severe, the payments will raise benefit levels substantially. For 5 years, every State will be required to continue to spend at least half of what they are now spending on welfare, to supplement the Federal base.

For the *typical "welfare family"*—a mother with dependent children and no outside income—the new system would provide a basic national minimum payment. A mother with three small children would be assured an annual income of at least $1,600.

For the family headed by an employed father or working mother, the same basic benefits would be received, but $60 per month of earnings would be "disregarded" in order to make up the costs of working and provide a strong advantage in holding a job. The wage earner could also keep 50% of his benefits as his earnings rise above that $60 per month. A family of four, in which the father earns $2,000 in a year, would receive payments of $960, for a total income of $2,960.

For *the aged*, *the blind* and *the disabled*, the present system varies benefit levels from $40 per month for an aged person in one State to $145 per month for the blind in another. The new system would establish a minimum payment of $65 per month for all three of these adult categories, with the Federal government contributing the first $50 and sharing in payments above the amount. This will raise the share of the financial burden borne by the Federal government for payments to these adults who cannot support themselves, and should pave the way for benefit increases in many States.

For the *single adult* who is not handicapped or aged, or for the *married couple without children*, the new system would not apply. Food stamps would continue to be available up to $300 per year per person, according to the plan I outlined last May in my message to the Congress on the food and nutrition needs of the population in poverty. For dependent families there will be an orderly substitution of food stamps by the new direct monetary payments.

2. *The new approach would end the blatant unfairness of the welfare system.* In over half the States, families headed by unemployed men do not qualify for public assistance. In no State does a family headed by a father working full-time receive help in the current welfare system, no matter how little he earns. As we have seen, this approach to dependency has itself been a cause of dependency. It results in a policy that tends to force the father out of the home.

The new plan rejects a policy that undermines family life. It would end the substantial financial incentives to desertion. It would extend eligibility to *all* dependent families with children, without regard to whether the family is headed by a man or woman. The effects of these changes upon human behavior would be an increased will to work, the survival of more marriages, the greater stability of families. We are determined to stop passing the cycle of dependency from generation to generation.

The most glaring inequity in the old welfare system is the exclusion of families who are working to pull themselves out of poverty. Families headed by a non-worker often receive more from welfare than families headed by a husband working full-time at very low wages. This has been rightly resented by the working poor, for the rewards are just the opposite of what they should be.

3. *The new plan would create a much stronger incentive to work.* For people now on the welfare rolls, the present system discourages the move from welfare to work by cutting benefits too fast and too much as earnings begin. *The new system would encourage work by allowing the new worker to retain the first $720 of his yearly earnings without any benefit reduction.*

For people already working, but at poverty wages, the present system often encourages nothing but resentment and an incentive to quit and go on relief where that would pay more than work. The new plan, on the contrary, would provide a supplement that will help a low-wage worker—struggling to make ends meet—achieve a higher standard of living.

For an employable person who just chooses not to work, neither the present system nor the one we propose would support him, though both would continue to support other dependent members in his family.

However, a welfare mother with pre-school children should not face benefit reductions if she decides to stay home. It is not our intent that mothers of pre-school children must accept work. Those who can work and desire to do so, however, should have the opportunity for jobs and job training and access to day care centers for their children: this will enable them to support themselves after their children are grown.

A family with a member who gets a job would be permitted to retain all of the *first $60 monthly income*, amounting to $720 per year for a regular worker, *with no reduction of Federal payments*. The incentive to work in this provision is obvious. But there is another practical reason: Going to work costs money. Expenses such as clothes, transportation, personal care, Social Security taxes and loss of income from odd jobs amount to substantial costs for the average family. Since a family does not begin to *add* to its net income until it surpasses the cost of working, in fairness this amount should not be subtracted from the new payment.

After the first $720 of income, the *rest* of the earnings will result in a systematic reduction in payments.

I believe the vast majority of poor people in the United States prefer to work rather than have the government support their families. In 1968, 600,000 families left the welfare rolls out of an average caseload of 1,400,000 during the year, showing a considerable turnover, much of it voluntary.

However, there may be some who fail to seek or accept work, even with the strong incentives and training opportunities that will be provided. It would not be fair to those who willingly work, or to all taxpayers, to allow others to choose idleness when opportunity is available. Thus, they must accept training opportunities and jobs when offered, or give up their right to the new payments for themselves. No able-bodied person will have a "free ride" in a nation that provides opportunity for training and work.

4. *The bridge from welfare to work should be buttressed by training and child care programs.* For many, the incentives to work in this plan would be all that is necessary. However, there are other situations where these incentives need to be supported by measures that will overcome other barriers to employment.

I propose that *funds be provided for expanded training and job development programs* so that an additional 150,000 welfare recipients can become job worthy during the first year.

Manpower training is a basic bridge to work for poor people, especially people with limited education, low skills and limited job experience. Manpower training programs can provide this bridge for many of our poor. In the new Manpower Training proposal to be sent to the Congress this week, the interrelationship with this new approach to welfare will be apparent.

I am also requesting authority, as a part of the new system, to provide child care for the 450,000 children of the 150,000 current welfare recipients to be trained.

The child care I propose is more than custodial. This Administration is committed to a new emphasis on child development in the first five years of life. The day care that would be part of this plan would be of a quality that will help in the development of the child and provide for its health and safety, and would break the poverty cycle for this new generation.

The expanded child care program would bring new opportunities along several lines: opportunities for the further involvement of private enterprise in providing high quality child care service; opportunities for volunteers; and opportunity for *training and employment in child care centers of many of the welfare mothers themselves.* I am requesting a total of $600 million additional to fund these expanded training programs and child care centers.

5. *The new system will lessen welfare red tape and provide administrative cost savings.* To cut out the costly investigations so bitterly resented as "welfare snooping," the Federal payment will be based upon a certification of income, with spot checks sufficient to prevent abuses. The program will be administered on an automated basis, using the information and technical experience of the Social Security Administration, but, of course, will be entirely separate from the administration of the Social Security trust fund.

The States would be given the option of having the Federal government handle the payment of the State supplemental benefits on a reimbursable basis, so that they would be spared their present administrative burdens and so a single check could be sent to the recipient. These simplifications will save money and eliminate indignities; at the same time, welfare fraud will be detected and lawbreakers prosecuted.

6. *This new department would require a substantial initial investment, but will yield future returns to the Nation.* This transformation of the welfare system will set in motion forces that will lessen dependency rather than perpetuate and enlarge it. A more productive population adds to real economic growth without inflation. The initial investment is needed now to stop the momentum of work-to-welfare, and to start a new momentum in the opposite direction.

The costs of welfare benefits for families with dependent children have been rising alarmingly the past several years, increasing from $1 billion in 1960 to an estimated $3.3 billion in 1969, of which $1.8 billion is paid by the Federal government, and $1.5 billion is paid by the States. Based on current population and income data, the proposals I am making today will increase Federal costs during the first year by an estimated $4 billion, which includes $600 million for job training and child care centers.

The "start-up costs" of lifting many people out of dependency will ultimately cost the taxpayers far less than the chronic costs—in dollars and in national values—of creating a permanent underclass in America.

From Welfare to Work

Since this Administration took office, members of the Urban Affairs Council, including officials of the Department of Health, Education and Welfare, the Department of Labor, the Office of Economic Opportunity, the Bureau of the Budget, and other key advisers, have been working to develop a coherent, fresh approach to welfare, manpower training and revenue sharing.

I have outlined our conclusions about an important component of this approach in this message; the Secretary of HEW will transmit to the Congress the proposed legislation after the summer recess.

I urge the Congress to begin its study of these proposals promptly so that laws can be enacted and funds authorized to begin the new system as soon as possible. Sound budgetary policy must be maintained in order to put this plan into effect—especially the portion supplementing the wages of the working poor.

With the establishment of the new approach, the Office of Economic Opportunity will concentrate on the important task of finding new ways of opening economic opportunity for those who are able to work. Rather than focusing on income support activities, it must find means of providing opportunities for individuals to contribute to the full extent of their capabilities, and of developing and improving those capabilities.

This would be the effect of the transformation of welfare into "workfare," a new work-rewarding system:

For the first time, all dependent families with children in America, regardless of where they live, would be assured of minimum standard payments based upon uniform and single eligibility standards.

For the first time, the more than two million families who make up the "working poor" would be helped toward self-sufficiency and away from future welfare dependency.

For the first time, training and work opportunity with effective incentives would be given millions of families who would otherwise be locked into a welfare system for generations.

For the first time, the Federal government would make a strong contribution toward relieving the financial burden of welfare payments from State governments.

For the first time, every dependent family in America would be encouraged to stay together, free from economic pressure to split apart.

These are far-reaching effects. They cannot be purchased cheaply, or by piecemeal efforts. This total reform looks in a new direction; it requires new thinking, a new spirit and a fresh dedication to reverse the downhill course of welfare. In its first year, more than half the families participating in the program will have one member working or training.

We have it in our power to raise the standard of living and the realizable hopes of millions of our fellow citizens. By providing an equal chance at the starting line, we can reinforce the traditional American spirit of self-reliance and self-respect.

***

STANDARD OF REVIEW FOR TERMINATION
OF DISABILITY BENEFITS

A recipient of benefits under this subchapter or subchapter XVIII of this chapter based on the disability of any individual may be determined not to be entitled to such benefits on the basis of a finding that the physical or mental impairment on the basis of which such benefits are provided has ceased, does not exist, or is not disabling only if such finding is supported by—

(1)   substantial evidence which demonstrates that—

   (A)   there has been any medical improvement in the individual's impairment or combination of impairments (other than medical improvement which is not related to the individual's ability to work), and

   (B)   (i)   the individual is now able to engage in substantial gainful activity, or

      (ii)   if the individual is a widow or surviving divorced wife under section 402(e) of this title or a widower or surviving divorced husband under section 402(f) of this title, the severity of his or her impairment or impairments is no longer deemed, under regulations prescribed by the Secretary, sufficient to preclude the individual from engaging in gainful activity; or

(2)   substantial evidence which—

   (A)   consists of new medical evidence and (in a case to which clause (ii)(II) does not apply) a new assessment of the individual's residual functional capacity, and demonstrates that—

      (i)   although the individual has not improved medically, he or she is nonetheless a beneficiary of advances in medical or vocational therapy or technology (related to the individual's ability to work), and

      (ii)   (I)   the individual is now able to engage in substantial gainful activity, or

         (II)   if the individual is a widow or surviving divorced wife under section 402(e) of this title or a widower or surviving divorced husband under section 402(f) of this title, the severity of his or her impairment or impairments is no longer deemed under regulations prescribed by the Secretary sufficient to preclude the individual from engaging in gainful activity, or

(B)   demonstrates that—

(i)   although the individual has not improved medically, he or she has undergone vocational therapy (related to the individual's ability to work), and

(ii)   the requirements of subclause (I) or (II) of subparagraph (A)(ii) are met; or

(3)   substantial evidence which demonstrates that, as determined on the basis of new or improved diagnostic techniques or evaluations, the individual's impairment or combination of impairments is not as disabling as it was considered to be at the time of the most recent prior decision that he or she was under a disability or continued to be under a disability, and that therefore—

(A)   the individual is able to engage in substantial gainful activity, or

(B)   if the individual is a widow or surviving divorced wife under section 402(e) of this title or a widower or surviving divorced husband under section 402(f) of this title, the severity of his or her impairment or impairments is not deemed under regulations prescribed by the Secretary sufficient to preclude the individual from engaging in gainful activity; or

(4)   substantial evidence (which may be evidence on the record at the time any prior determination of the entitlement to benefits based on disability was made, or newly obtained evidence which relates to that determination) which demonstrates that a prior determination was in error.

Nothing in this subsection shall be construed to require a determination that a recipient of benefits under this subchapter or subchapter XVIII of this chapter based on an individual's disability is entitled to such benefits if the prior determination was fraudulently obtained or if the individual is engaged in substantial gainful activity (or gainful activity in the case of a widow, surviving divorced wife, widower, or surviving divorced husband), cannot be located, or fails, without good cause, to cooperate in a review of the entitlement to such benefits or to follow prescribed treatment which would be expected to restore his or her ability to engage in substantial gainful activity (or gainful activity in the case of a widow, surviving divorced wife, widower, or surviving divorced husband). Any determination under this section shall be made on the basis of all the evidence available in the individual's case file, including new evidence concerning the individual's prior or current condition which is presented by the individual or secured by the Secretary. Any determination made under this section shall be made on the basis of the weight of the evidence and on a neutral basis with regard to the individual's condition, without any initial inference as to the presence or absence of disability being drawn from the fact that the individual has previously been determined to be disabled. For purposes of this subsection, a benefit under this subchapter is based on an individual's disability if it is a disability insurance benefit, a child's, widow's, or widower's insurance benefit based on disability, or a mother's or father's insurance benefit based on the disability of the mother's or father's child who has attained age 16.

Public Law 98–460, 98th Congress, September 15, 1984

 Recall what you learned in this chapter by completing the Chapter Review.

9

Social Welfare and the Information Society: 1992–2016

DEVELOPMENTAL, 2013 (MURAL, FAITH IN CHRIST MINISTRIES, LOS ANGELES, CA), CLAIRFOSTER J. BROWNE/PHOTOGRAPH BY CAMILO J. VERGARA

LEARNING OUTCOMES

- Examine the impact of changes in domestic life and demography on social welfare policies since the 1990s.

- Assess the impact of welfare reform and health care reform on the well-being of Americans.

- Summarize the role of social movements in contemporary American social controversies.

CHAPTER OUTLINE

Social and Economic Change   287
   The Economy: Productivity, Growth, and Employment   287
   Poverty   290
   Changes in Family Composition   292
   America's Changing Demography   293

Innovations in Social Welfare   293
   The Fall and Rise of Health Care Reform   293
   Addressing Poverty and Dependency: The Scope of Welfare Reform   298

Social Movements and Grassroots Change   302
   Welfare Reform and "Immigration Control"   302
   The Return to Voluntarism and the Rise of Privatization   303
   The Continuing Battle for Social Justice   306
   Abortion and the Right to Privacy   308
   The Great Lockup   310

Conclusion   311

The 1990s and 2000s were a period of wild swings for the economic and social well-being of Americans. The nation endured two recessions, the second of which caused economic dislocation comparable only to that of the Great Depression, but it also included a period of rapid economic growth that lifted the incomes of low-wage workers for the first time in a generation. Politically, too, the breakdown of reliable coalitions led to erratic outcomes. One of the most conservative administrations in generations—that of George W. Bush—was sandwiched between those of two Democrats—Bill Clinton and Barack Obama—while Congress went from overwhelmingly Democratic in 1992 to strongly Republican in 1994 to strongly Democratic in 2006 and 2008. After the 2014 elections, both houses of Congress again were controlled by Republicans.

    The erratic character of economic and political life had an impact on social welfare policy. The conservative rise of the mid-1990s led to a fundamental restructuring of public assistance in 1996, ending families' entitlement to aid from states and the federal government. The Democrats return to power after 2006 allowed

CHAPTER OUTLINE *(Continued)*

DOCUMENTS: Social Welfare and the Information Society 313

Personal Responsibility and Work Opportunity Reconciliation Act, 1996 314

State of California, Proposition 187, Illegal Aliens—Public Services, Verification, and Reporting, 1994 317

U.S. Supreme Court, Lawrence v. Texas, *2003* 321

liberals to achieve a goal they had sought for two generations—a national health insurance plan that would go a long way toward reducing the number of uninsured in the population. Although the Supreme Court would confirm the Affordable Care Act's constitutionality in 2012, many states took advantage of the court's limiting of Medicaid reform to restrict the laws effectiveness.

The 1990s began in the shadow of a recession. After falling to 5.3 percent of the labor force in 1989, the unemployment rate rose to 7.5 percent in 1992. Yet, the economic gloom of the early 1990s rapidly dissolved. By 1996, the unemployment rate had fallen to under 5.5 percent, the figure that many economists had claimed was the lowest unemployment could go without sparking inflation. In the years that followed, it fell even lower, reaching just over 4 percent by the end of the 1990s, even though inflation remained relatively low.

In spite of the remarkable economic growth of the 1990s, however, the business cycle still existed. Beginning in 2000, the American economy began to falter. Within three years, unemployment had increased to over 6.4 percent of the civilian labor force; the federal government—which had experienced its first years of budget surpluses in two generations—was forecasting record deficits; and the economy could do no better than anemic growth.

Yet, the recession of the early 2000s was simply a prelude to a much more significant recession between 2007 and 2009. Sparked by the near crash of the world financial system brought about by speculation in the American mortgage industry and international sovereign debt, that recession pushed unemployment over 10 percent for the first time since the 1980s. What is more, in contrast to the 1980s, unemployment remained at above 9 percent for more than two years, causing millions of families to face downward mobility as they lost their jobs and homes. Although unemployment insurance provided some protection for families, cutbacks in that program since the 1980s made it less effective than it had been formerly.

The American public's confidence was shaken by other events. In 2001, the worst terrorist attack on American soil destroyed the World Trade Center in New York and heavily damaged the Pentagon. In the next several years, America launched wars in Afghanistan and Iraq that the Bush administration viewed as battles in the "war against terrorism." At home, a set of unpopular tax cuts was enacted by Congress, raising the prospect that the old Reagan gambit—using high deficits as a way of cutting social programs—would again be used by a conservative president.

After two decades of sluggish economic growth, the robust economy of the 1990s puzzled policy makers and scholars. Although many reasons for the turnaround were suggested, the most compelling explanation linked economic growth to the transition of the United States (and much of the world) to an information-based economy. By the middle of the 1990s, technological discoveries in biotechnology, communications, and computers had pushed the world economy in a new direction. New products, new markets, and higher efficiency led to increases in productivity and the standard of living that had not been seen since the early 1970s.

The new economic and social realities of the 1990s undermined some of the old ways of addressing social problems.

Yet, social policy ideas failed to keep pace with economic growth. The new economic and social realities of the 1990s undermined some of the old ways of addressing social problems. Social welfare programs between the 1930s and 1980s had sought to promote stability in the workplace and in family life. Although workers and families still found stability attractive, American business and domestic life failed to deliver. Increasingly, the American workplace was organized along flexible lines; there were more turnover, more part-time workers, and more temporary employees. At the same time, the decline of the traditional family—spurred by increases in divorce rates, single motherhood, and the increased visibility of gay and lesbian populations—made many assumptions of 20th-century social welfare programs obsolete.

Powerful interests blocked many attempts to address the new realities at work and at home. Attempts to reform the health care system foundered because of opposition from the insurance and pharmaceutical industries. Although a Family and Medical Leave Act was passed and signed into law in 1993, more ambitious plans to provide support to families failed. In their everyday lives, more and more Americans were living new realities without much support from innovative social policies.

Americans did unite, however, around one "reform," a restructuring of the federal public assistance program that ended the entitlement to aid, required recipients to seek work, and set a five-year time limit on the receipt of aid. Although the real impact of welfare reform on the lives of poor people remained controversial, it marked a major change in the way the federal government articulated its responsibility for addressing poverty and dependency.

SOCIAL AND ECONOMIC CHANGE

The Economy: Productivity, Growth, and Employment

Since 1970, the federal government had struggled to use monetary and fiscal policy to ensure sustained economic growth. During the 1970s, the economy swung between periods of rapid growth and recession. After the economic slowdown of 1981–1982, the economy grew, but unemployment remained stubbornly high.

During the 1990s, it appeared that the economy finally got it right. After the recession of 1991, the economy expanded for the remainder of the decade. Gross domestic product grew every quarter between 1992 and 2000, increasingly by 31 percent in real terms between 1993 and 2000. Productivity moved ahead as well. Although output per hour for all persons had increased only by 1 percent between 1992 and 1995, productivity accelerated during the last half of the decade. Output per hour in the business sector rose by 17 percent between 1993 and 2000.[1]

Much of the robust economic expansion could be linked to the technological revolutions of the 1980s and 1990s. After many years of investment, the application of computers and communications innovations began to make the economy more efficient and productive. In manufacturing, computers assumed a greater role in production and the management of inventories. In the burgeoning service sector, the expansion of the Internet created new industries and made existing services more efficient. Even as unemployment declined as low as 4 percent at the end of the decade, the threat that inflation would short-circuit the expansion seemed distant. Yet, at the same time, a digital divide opened, as low-income groups were unable to gain the computer literacy, Internet access, and computers that would allow them to link to these new resources.

The new economy carried new costs. The success of the restructuring of the American economy was based on a newly "flexible" labor force. More workers found themselves working without fringe benefits. The risks of displacement were higher. More workers found themselves permanently working in "temporary" jobs. Thus, even as incomes went up and unemployment declined, workers faced a new world of insecurity that neither the private sector nor the government was prepared to address.

An "informal econ-
omy" composed of
businesses and workers
who operated in a twi-
light zone between the
established economy
and the world of crime
became a more import-
ant part of all pro-
ductive activities. The
informal economy was
particularly important
for low-income work-
ers. Many jobs in the
personal and domestic
service sec-tor—such
as house and office
cleaners, and child-care
workers—operated in
the informal economy,
avoiding Social Security
and other taxes.

At the bottom of the economic ladder, an old phenomenon gained greater prominence. An "informal economy" composed of businesses and workers who operated
in a twilight zone between the established economy and the world of crime became a
more important part of all productive activities. The informal economy was particularly
important for low-income workers. Many jobs in the personal and domestic service sector—such as house and office cleaners, and child-care workers—operated in the informal
economy, avoiding Social Security and other taxes. Even in the most advanced sectors of
the economy—like the skyscrapers that housed investment banks and stockbrokers—
informal workers often comprised a large share of the labor force.[2]

Welfare provided one motivation for workers to enter the informal economy.
Because a large share of earnings was subtracted from one's benefits under Aid to Families with Dependent Children (AFDC) and other public assistance programs, welfare
mothers often constructed survival strategies that included "off the books" work. At
the same time, the growth of the informal economy provided a safety valve for welfare
reform. Poor women on welfare often had more sources of income than official statistics suggested. As states moved to restrict welfare payments, poor women were likely to
expand their efforts in other areas.[3]

Unemployment fell, but it remained unequally distributed. Among whites, unemployment fell from 4.8 to 3.6 percent between 1990 and 1999, but the unemployment rate of African Americans fell from 11.4 to 8.3 percent over the same period.
Teenagers who were in the labor force in 1999 still had an unemployment rate of
15 percent.

In the previous two decades, government policy makers had used unemployment
to keep inflation down. As a result, even as the economy improved, low-wage workers hardly benefited. Finally, in the late 1990s, a sustained period of low unemployment
improved the economic position of low-wage workers. Low-wage workers—whose
incomes had hardly increased at all during the 1980s—enjoyed the first real increase in
their wages as the century came to a close. Only in 1997 did the upper limit for the bottom 20 percent of the income distribution reach its 1990 level.[4]

The idea of neoliberalism captured many of the economic reforms of the period. Its
advocates contended that the political and economic changes of the 1970s—particularly
the expansion of social benefits and increased regulation of industry—were hamstring-
ing the national economy. Only by cutting social welfare programs and liberating industry from burdensome regulations could it flourish.[5]

One strategy of neoliberalism was expanding the globalization of the economy. The
declining economic competitiveness of some sectors of the U.S. economy were held up
as examples of why the nation could no longer afford higher standards of living, a safer
workplace, or clean air or water.

Yet, to its critics, neoliberalism had a hidden agenda: shifting the relative social power
of social elites. For critics, the expansion of social policies during the early postwar years
had boosted the ability of workers to demand a larger share of an expanding economy's
benefits. The new policies rarely produced the economic benefits they promised, but
they did make the lives of workers more precarious.

The performance of the U.S. economy between 1993 and 2016 seemed to support
neoliberalism's critics. The supposedly "job killing" policies of the Clinton and Obama
administrations—increased taxes for high-income households, expanding the Earned
Income Tax Credit, new regulations of the financial industries and polluters—were
accompanied by healthy economic growth, while the tax-cutting and deregulation of the
Bush administration between 2001 and 2009 produced halting growth followed by devastating economic collapse.

Indeed, the Great Recession was largely the result of neoliberal policies. The immediate cause of the recession was the near collapse of large parts of the home mortgage market. After the savings-and-loan crisis of the 1980s, mortgages were typically securitized—combined and sold on the global financial markets. These changes accelerated during the 1990s when Clinton and the Republican leadership in Congress collaborated on the deregulation of the securities industry and the elimination of the barrier between commercial and investment banking that had been constructed during the New Deal. When home prices stopped rising in 2006, it became clear that many of the mortgages and the securities that were backed by those mortgages were not as secure or valuable as investors had believed. A crisis of confidence and liquidity spread through the world economy in September 2008. After one major investment bank, Lehman Brothers, was allowed to fail, world credit markets ground to a halt. The Federal Reserve system and the federal government quickly changed course and sponsored a major bailout of other financial institutions that were judged to be "too big to fail."[6]

Although the bailout was judged a success in rescuing the financial sector, the longer-term effects of the crisis proved to be more difficult to address. The unemployment rate rose from 4.6 percent in 2006 to 10.1 percent in October 2009 and did not fall below 9.5 percent through the fall of 2010. Finally, the pace of decline accelerated in 2012, eventually leading to unemployment falling to 5 percent by the end of 2015.

Yet, the labor force problems were hardly solved. Although the working-age population grew by nearly 20 million between 2007 and 2015, the number of employed workers in 2015 was less than 3 million above its pre-recession figure. Instead, 15 million more adults had withdrawn from the labor force. Although overall unemployment had fallen, teenage workers and African Americans still experienced unemployment rates over 10 percent.

The impact of the credit crisis and the decline in home prices led to an explosion in home foreclosures as millions of families could no longer afford their mortgages. The first wave of foreclosures in 2007 and 2008 affected many homeowners who bought homes that they never could have afforded, but by 2009 and 2010, the bulk of foreclosures were the result of families facing unemployment and declining economic fortunes.[7]

 Watch this video on the eviction resulting from foreclosure.

Notice the contrast between how polite everyone is and the impact on the person who is evicted. What alternatives to eviction might have been considered in this case?

https://www.youtube.com/watch?v=UXep2SsJIHw

Income inequality, which had begun to increase during the 1970s and 1980s, accelerated in the first decade of the 21st century. Although families with the lowest wages saw some improvement during the 1990s, these gains were lost during the recession of the early 2000s, and the 2007–2009 recession left average families' income at the same level it had been 30 years earlier. Meanwhile, the large share of the expanding economic pie continued to go to the most affluent. In 1990, the income cutoff for the top 5 percent of the population ($118,163) was just over 7.5 times as large as the cutoff for the bottom 20 percent ($15,589). This ratio increased sharply during the decade, reaching a peak of 8.22 in 1997 before declining slightly. Only the top 5 percent showed substantial gains (see Figure 9.1). Whereas in 1947, the poorest 20 percent of households had received 5.1 percent of the income, by 1998 they had only 3.6 percent. In contrast, the top 20 percent in 1998 received 49.1 percent; almost half of that, 21.2 percent, went to the top 5 percent of households.

During the first decade of the 21st century, the distribution of economic gains became even less equal. In 2001, the top 1 percent of tax units received 17 percent of national income. In six short years, this proportion increased to 23 percent. Cumulatively, since the late 1970s, the bottom fifth of the income distribution had seen their after-tax income rise by 11 percent, while the average of those between the 80th and 98th percentile had

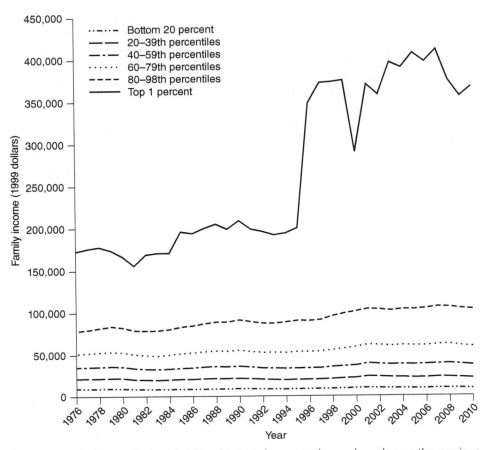

Figure 9.1 For most American families, incomes have not changed much over the previous 35 years. However, for the wealthiest 1 percent of the population, it was a different story.
Source: Author's calculation using Integrated Public Use Microdata Series, U.S. Census Bureau, Current Population Survey, 1976–2010

increased by 55 percent. But even the rich did poorly compared to the very rich. The top 1 percent of householders' after-tax income increased by 256 percent between 1979 and 2006. Looked at another way, between 2002 and 2007, the income of the bottom 99 percent increased by 1.3 percent per year, while that of the top 1 percent rose by 65 percent. Perhaps the most outrageous pattern, however, occurred during the recession. While most Americans' income fell by nearly 7 percent a year between 2007 and 2008, that of the top 1 percent grew by 47 percent.[8]

Poverty

The good economic conditions of the 1990s reduced poverty, but it still remained higher than it had been 20 years earlier. Then the recession of 2007–2009 pushed the largest number of Americans into poverty—43.6 million in 2009—since the official poverty rate was first calculated in the 1960s. Although the national income grew rapidly during the

1990s, the proportion of the population below the poverty line declined slowly. After rising from 12.8 to 15.1 percent between 1989 and 1993, poverty fell steadily, reaching 11.3 percent in 2000, its lowest level since 1979. However, the recession of 2007–2009 led poverty to rise rapidly, reaching 14.8 percent in 2014. Children, African Americans, Hispanics, and female-headed households continued to have significantly greater risks of poverty than the population as a whole.

After rising from 12.8 to 15.1 percent between 1989 and 1993, poverty fell steadily, reaching 11.3 percent in 2000, its lowest level since 1979. However, the recession of 2007–2009 led poverty to rise rapidly, reaching 14.3 percent in 2009.

African Americans enjoyed a rapid decline in poverty between 1990 and 2001, the rate falling from 32 to 23 percent; by 2009, it had risen to 26 percent. Although the white poverty rate in 1998—10.5 percent—was significantly lower than the black rate, white poverty was far more common than it had been in the early 1970s. Hispanic poverty rates also dropped at the end of the 1990s, but stood at 26 percent in 2014.[9]

The official poverty measure had been largely unchanged since the 1960s, in spite of the creation of many new programs—like Food Stamps and the Earned Income Tax Credit—which were not counted as income. Early in the Obama administration, the Census Bureau released a Supplemental Poverty Measure (SPM), which significantly changed the calculation of poverty. First, rather than simply adjusting the old measure, the SPM used the actual behavior of consumers to estimate the income necessary to sustain a minimally adequate level of consumption. Second, the new measure included both the impact of taxes (including refundable tax credits like the EITC) and noncash benefits, like Supplementary Nutritional Assistance Program (SNAP, or Food Stamps).[10]

The SPM gave a different perspective on the history and incidence of poverty. Where the official poverty rate showed little improvement in poverty rates since the 1970s, using the SPM methods, researchers found that there had been steady declines in the share of the population falling below the SPM thresholds. In the late 1960s, 25 percent of Americans lived in poverty using the SPM, but just before the 2007–2009 recession, only 15 percent had. The SPM resulted in higher poverty rates for older Americans, because of out-of-pocket medical costs, and lower poverty rates for children, because of the role of the EITC, other tax credits, and SNAP.

The SPM incorporated variations in the cost of housing across cities and metropolitan areas. When the poverty measure was first developed in the 1960s, food was the largest expense for low-income families, often accounting for a third of a household's budget. By the early 21st century, however, the cost of food had dropped and the availability of SNAP reduced its share of the household's budget. Instead, housing became the largest challenge for low-income families. Several administrations—both Democratic and Republican—sought to boost the homeownership rate, but in the face of stagnant incomes, these increases were often the result of risky mortgages that ultimately led to higher foreclosure rates. Meanwhile, low-income renters were faced with a declining affordable housing stock, declines in housing subsidies, and exploding rents that frequently absorbed more than half a family's income.

Although President Clinton had been elected on a promise to "make work pay," the number of Americans whose work did not pay enough to get them out of poverty increased during his administration. The expansion of low-wage employment and the informal economy combined with welfare reform to increase the importance of the working poor. In 1990, 2 million persons worked full-time for the full year, but remained in poverty. By 1998, 2.8 million Americans were in this unenviable condition.

Children, however, continued to bear the real cost of social change and public neglect.

Children, however, continued to bear the real cost of social change and public neglect. Although their poverty rate fell from 20.6 to 16.3 percent between 1990 and 2001, they still remained more likely to be poor than either the working-age population or the aged. The expansion of female-headed households was one contributor to children's difficulties. In 2001, 24 percent of female-headed households still lived in poverty. Although the risk of child poverty remained high for black children, it fell from 44.8 to 30.2 percent between 1990 and 2001. The two recessions of the 2000s reversed any improvement in the poverty status of children. By 2014, the child poverty rate stood at 21.1 percent, roughly where it had been 25 years earlier.

Changes in Family Composition

After the rapid changes of the previous two decades, the structure of family life was relatively stable during the 1990s. As the baby-boom generation entered middle age, the number of two-parent households with children increased by 700,000 from 1990 to 1995. This came after a 20-year decline. The divorce rate decreased from 23 divorces per 1,000 married women in 1980 to 20.5 in 1995. But the median age of marriage continued to rise, as did the number of people who never marry. Births to unmarried mothers were still going up, albeit at a slower rate.[11]

Women's labor-force participation—irrespective of race, ethnicity, marital status, or the presence of children—continued to rise. In 2014, 65 percent of all never-married women and 67 percent of all married women were in the labor force. Two-earner families as well as single-parent working households were typical.[12]

Rising life expectancy and falling fertility rates meant that the U.S. population continued to age. Median age went from 32.8 years in 1990 to 35.8 years in 2000. As the population aged, more two-earner families were finding themselves caught in a time bind. By 1996, some 10 to 12 percent of the workforce had responsibility for the care of an aging parent. Demographers estimated that by 2020, 33 percent of working-age adults would have this responsibility.

One of the first pieces of legislation signed by President Clinton was the Family and Medical Leave Act of 1993. The act requires employers to grant workers up to 12 weeks of unpaid leave annually for the birth or adoption of a child, to care for an ill family member, or to recover from serious illness. Although the leave is unpaid, health benefits remain intact throughout the period. When workers return to their jobs, they are guaranteed an equivalent position with seniority maintained. The legislation applies to private and public employers with 50 or more workers.

Regulations issued in early 1995 defined family members for whose care a worker might take leave as a spouse, a child, or a parent. Leave is not granted to care for the parent of a spouse, nor it is to be applicable for the care of a partner. The definition of covered illness has been extended so that it is clear that problems connected with pregnancy are included and that the leave need not be for consecutive days. Substance abuse and stress were covered if they constitute mental illness.[13]

That the leave was unpaid clearly limited its usefulness in meeting the needs of most workers. In general, women with higher incomes have received more family benefits. A 1990 national child-care survey found, for example, that 39 percent of women in professional occupations but only 15 percent of women in production, 11 percent of women in services, and none in agriculture were offered at least one child-care benefit by their employers. Two-career families were most likely to make use of the offered benefit, while single parents were the least likely. The Family Leave Act was a small step forward in meeting the needs of working families.

America's Changing Demography

Immigration led to a marked shift in the ethnic composition of the American population during the 1990s and 2000s. In the middle of the 20th century, the United States was typically defined as black or white. By the first decade of the new century, the influx of Asian Americans and Latin Americans created a more complex mosaic. In 1980, 80 percent of Americans were non-Hispanic whites; in 2014, only 63 percent were. Overall, changing immigration patterns as well as differential birthrates created one of the largest racial and ethnic shifts in the U.S. history.[14]

The Census Bureau estimates that the proportion of people of color would continue to rise. In 2000, the American population was 12 percent African American, 3.6 percent Asian, and 0.9 percent Native American. That year, Hispanics for the first time outnumbered African Americans; by 2010, Hispanics numbered over 50 million (16 percent of the entire population), while 39 million (13 percent) Americans identified themselves as black. The 2000 census, for the first time, allowed individuals to identify themselves as multiracial. In 2000, 2.4 percent of the population identified themselves with more than one race, a figure that increased to 2.9 percent 10 years later. By 2050, the estimates indicated that the proportion of African Americans will increase from 13 to 15 percent of the population. Those of Asian extraction would increase from 5 to 8 percent of the population, and Hispanics would increase from 16 to 24 percent of the population. By 2050, non-Hispanic whites share of the population would fall to 50 percent. These dramatic shifts have had major implications for social welfare in the United States. Immigration policy, affirmative action, public welfare, social services, education, health care, and social security are just some of the areas affected by the new demographic realities.

> **?** Assess your comprehension of "Social and Economic Change" by completing this quiz.

INNOVATIONS IN SOCIAL WELFARE

The Fall and Rise of Health Care Reform

At least since the Truman administration, presidents had proposed schemes to achieve comprehensive health care coverage for all Americans. During the 1970s, both political parties had advanced proposals to achieve the goal, but could not agree on a final plan. As the Republican Party drifted to the right during the 1970s and 1980s, it was inclined to trust market-based solutions rather than support comprehensive reform. As health care became a partisan, rather than a national goal, it became more difficult to achieve the right political environment in which it could be achieved. The Clinton administration missed an opportunity to achieve health care reform in the early 1990s. The Democratic victories in the 2006 and 2008 elections finally led to its enactment, although the virulence of Republican opposition during 2010 left the ultimate fate of the plan uncertain six years after its passage.

For more than four decades, increases in health care costs had absorbed an increasing share of national income. The steady stream of new technologies has made health care more expensive as well as more effective. Additionally, demand for health care has risen as the population has aged and as public and private insurance provide a ready market for health and medical services. In 1965, before Medicare and Medicaid, health expenditures absorbed just under 6 percent of our gross national product; in 2013, they absorbed 17 percent.[15]

The number of individuals without any health insurance had risen as well. In 1987, about 31 million people were uninsured throughout the year; by 1994, this was up to 40 million people. The 2007–2009 recession boosted the number of uninsured to 50 million persons, 17 percent of the population. This increase in the health insurance gap occurred despite the large expansion of Medicaid coverage and the increasing proportion of the population eligible for and covered by Medicare. In 1987, 76 percent of the population had employment-related coverage for health; in 1994, only 70 percent were so insured. Changes in the labor market—the downsizing of large manufacturing and the expansion of temporary and part-time work—were largely responsible.[16] Even Americans with health insurance had to worry about gaps in their coverage and the risk that they would be dropped by their plan if they got too sick.

The government safety net constructed during the 1960s—Medicare, Medicaid, and the Veterans' Administration health system—met many of the health care needs of the aging, the poor, and veterans with service-connected problems. Medicaid covered long-term care for the poor, who make up about half of all people in nursing homes. But less than half of poor people received it, and for those it did cover, availability of care was a major problem. Hospital emergency rooms often substituted for doctors' offices. Remarkably, President George W. Bush suggested at one point that access to care was not really a national problem because the uninsured could always go to the emergency room.[17]

Overall, the United States has lagged behind other developed countries in the provision of health care to all residents. We spent more per capita and had less satisfactory results. Infant mortality was higher, and life expectancy was lower. This was particularly true for people of color—African Americans, nonwhite Hispanics, and Native Americans—whose poverty is accompanied by poor health and shorter lives. Public health, environmental programs, and medical research take up a small percentage of health care expenditures as compared to personal health care expenses.

The Failure of Comprehensive Reform in the 1990s

Debates about our health care system—or, more precisely, about the financing and the availability of health care—occupied center stage during the early years of Clinton's presidency. The 35 working groups that made up the Hillary Rodham Clinton Task Force on Health Care Reform produced a detailed health plan more than 1,300 pages long. The bill, the Health Security Act (S1757), was introduced in Congress in the fall of 1993. It provided for universal access to a comprehensive package of benefits, using managed care to control utilization and costs. The plan involved many regional health alliances, each of which would have three different plans to offer consumers. It was a highly complex bill with an enormous amount of detail on eligibility, coverage, premiums, and benefits. During much of 1993 and 1994, it was explained, debated, ridiculed, defended, and finally defeated. President Clinton had hoped that the prospect of containing health care costs would build business support for his plan, but the strong opposition of the lobbyists for small businesses—many of which did not offer health care to any employees—and the fear of increased government regulation eventually convinced larger businesses to oppose it, as well. Without business support, the plan never came to a vote in Congress.[18]

A piecemeal approach, in the Congress and at the state level, replaced the effort to achieve a major overhaul of health care financing in the United States. Congress began to consider a number of proposals for smaller expansions of Medicare and Medicaid, and for the regulation of private health insurance plans to keep insurance companies from dropping people.[19]

In the face of congressional inaction, the private sector undertook its own form of "health care reform." Although opponents of government reform had raised the specter of bureaucratic controls of the patient–doctor relationship to defeat the Health Security Act, the rise of managed care did just that, but without the protections that the Clinton bill had included. Exclusion of preexisting conditions, routine denial of expensive treatment, and the frantic effort to get people out of hospitals faster and faster reignited the demands for reform as the decade came to a close.

Health care for the poor followed a similar pattern. Although Republican proposals to turn Medicaid funding into a block grant failed, more Medicaid recipients found themselves unwillingly pushed into managed care plans. Because poor people often lacked the knowledge and skill to negotiate the complex regulations that governed these plans, they were likely to find themselves denied needed services and frustrated when they were sick. The costs and benefits of managed care remained difficult to assess. Did managed care encourage companies to offer preventative care to keep the cost of treating more serious illnesses down, or did they simply use administrative hurdles to make it more difficult for recipients to receive the care they needed?

The decline in the welfare rolls after welfare reform reduced the number of working-age Americans on Medicaid. Those who left the welfare rolls were supposed to have access to transitional medical coverage, but many states failed to inform former recipients of this right. In Pennsylvania, for example, the state was forced to sign a consent decree in 1999 in which it promised to preserve the medical coverage of all welfare recipients who had left the rolls, a reversal of the routine cutoff that had been implemented in 1997. The passage of a national children's health insurance program (CHIP) in 1997 compensated for the many children losing Medicaid coverage as a result of welfare reform.[20]

The elderly are vulnerable to changes in health policy. Older Americans already pay much more for their own health care than they did prior to the passage of Medicare. Further increasing costs and reducing coverage would be a serious drain on the incomes of many. The elderly are worried, too, about the availability and ease of access to doctors and health care providers, and they felt threatened by health maintenance organizations (HMOs) and managed care. A more extreme proposal would offer a privatization alternative. Recipients could elect to have the government set up individual medical savings accounts and have private health insurance with high deductibles.

Even when Congress appeared to make progress on health care, the results were often confusing. In 1997, a bill was signed into law to require insurers to provide parity between coverage for physical and behavioral health. Although the intent of the bill was to expand the coverage of individuals and families for behavioral health services, insurers were able to use managed care as a means of restricting patients' access to these services.[21]

The failure of the Clinton health care plan set the stage for Republicans to capture both houses of Congress in 1994. Although they would lose the Senate briefly in 2001 and 2002, Republicans retained control of at least one house until the 2006 elections. At the behest of President Bush, in 2003, Congress passed legislation to add prescription drug coverage to Medicare (Part D). Consistent with the ideological foundation of the Republican Congress, the legislation gave a major role to private insurance companies in offering coverage to older Americans and people with disabilities. While the legislation offered choice to recipients, it was less clear that Medicare Part D provided the optimal protection. Most notably, the structure of the program required recipients to make substantial out-of-pocket copayments when their annual drug cost exceeded $2,250. Only when their annual costs exceed $6,000, did Part D again pay most of the cost. In addition, the legislation explicitly forbade Medicare from attempting to negotiate cheaper prices for drugs, again adding to the cost of the plan. Although the president heralded prescription drug coverage as this administration's major domestic legislative achievement, it raised as many doubts as it addressed about the Republicans' market-based approach to health care.[22]

The Medicare Modernization Act of 2003 also established the Medicare Advantage program that provided subsidies to private insurance companies to offer an alternative to the standard Medicare coverage. Medicare Advantage was widely seen as providing overly generous subsidies for the insurance companies and undermining political support for standard Medicare. Indeed, curtailing these subsidies became a significant element of Barack Obama's health care plan, and opponents of these changes portrayed the proposals as attacks on Medicare itself. A significant decline in older Americans' support of Democrats in the 2010 election may have been a result of this confusion.

Achieving Comprehensive Reform in 2010

With the exception of Medicare Part D, the two parties remained far apart in their approach to health care reform through the 1990s and 2000s. Republicans argued that individual health savings accounts were the best answer to the soaring costs of health care, although there was little evidence to support that position. Democrats, meanwhile, groped toward a strategy that would address the uninsured and soaring costs but that would avoid the label of government-run health care that had doomed the Clinton plan.

Democratic successes in the 2006 and 2008 elections provided them with the window to move forward with a new effort at comprehensive reform. The basic outlines of reform were set in place early in 2009. Individuals would be required to have health insurance. If they were not covered by an employer or existing government plan, Americans would be able to purchase insurance through health care exchanges organized at the state level or by the federal government if a state failed to act. These exchanges would negotiate with private insurance companies to provide similar coverage and rates to those received through employer-based plans. A system of subsidies would assure that low-income households could afford insurance. Employers who did not offer coverage for their employees would be required to pay taxes that partially covered the cost of those subsidies and to eliminate their "free ride" for not insuring their workers.[23]

The major bone of contention among those considering reform was the so-called public option. This proposal would require the government to offer plans through the exchanges that would compete with the private insurance plan. The goal of the public option was to provide leverage that the government could use to impose cost containment of private plans. Yet, although it would have covered only a small percentage of the population, the public option raised the specter of "government-run" health care again. Ultimately, because of resistance by more conservative Democrats—and in what was ultimately a vain effort to attract any Republican support—the public option was dropped from the final legislation.

Legislative strategy also played a role in the passage of reform. During the fall and early winter of 2009, both houses of Congress passed versions of health care reform. In the Senate, however, the bill had to be weakened to attract all 60 Democrats and avoid a Republican filibuster. The Democrats' strategy, however, was thrown into disarray by a special election. Ted Kennedy, who had been a senator since 1963 and had been the foremost advocate of health care reform for more than four decades, died in August 2009. The election to replace him in January 2010 led to a Republican victory, which destroyed the Democrats' "veto-proof" majority. After several months of uncertainty, Congress and the president moved forward using the budget reconciliation process (which could not be filibustered) to enact the final bill. Because of this change of strategy, the final bill, passed in March 2010, was somewhat more liberal than that passed by the Senate the previous year.

The signing of the health care reform law by President Obama, however, was hardly the end of the process, and the prospects for fully implementing the law remained cloudy. Almost immediately, the law was challenged in federal court. The suit brought by a number of Republican state attorneys general argued that the requirement that individuals purchase insurance violated the interstate commerce clause of the Constitution. Although dominant legal opinion belittled this argument, a federal district judge ruled in favor of the law's opponents. Ultimately, the litigation would find its way to the Supreme Court, which in 2012 upheld the core of the law. However, the court ruled that the federal government could not require states to implement the law's expansion of Medicaid. As a result, many Republican-controlled states refused to expand Medicaid, thereby denying coverage for some of their poorest residents.[24]

At a more basic level, the law required states to proceed with a variety of reforms. Many states—usually those dominated by Republicans—resisted these requirements. Most threatening to the law, however, was the long period of time it would take to implement it fully. Republican victories in the 2010 elections gave support to the party's efforts to repeal the law. Even after the law was fully implemented, however, the possibility that Republicans would win the presidency and control of Congress in 2016 posed the possibility that health care reform could be undone.

The Affordable Care Act was subjected to intense partisan attacks, many of which sought to confuse people who would actually benefit from the law. Still, during its first full year of implementation, the number of uninsured Americans dropped by 9 million. This still left 33 million Americans without coverage, including many immigrants, poor people living in states that failed to expand Medicaid, and young adults who chose not to get insurance.[25]

The final reconciliation bill also allowed Congress to enact reform to student loan programs. Since the 1960s, the majority of loans to college students had flowed through private banks that received subsidies and guarantees for handling the business. Yet, during the 1990s and early 2000s, two problems gained visibility. First, a number of scandals surfaced in which SLM Corporation (better known as Sallie Mae)—the major servicer of student loans—and a number of banks used kickbacks and other shady business practices to gain student loan business. In the face of lax federal oversight, New York State took the lead in forcing lenders and universities to change their practices to reduce students' debt. Second, proprietary or for-profit educational institutions used government-guaranteed student loans and grants for low-income students to enroll students in programs without concern for whether the program benefited the student financially or if they were able to repay their loans. It was not unusual for programs in car mechanics or culinary arts to leave students with tens of thousand dollars of debt, but without increased earning power.[26]

In response to these problems, the Obama administration proposed and Congress passed legislation to substitute direct government loans for the subsidies to private lenders. This allowed the government to reduce the incentive for corruption and increased its regulatory authority over proprietary schools. As with health care, the passage of legislation was hardly the end of the battle. Private universities and trade schools mounted a giant lobbying effort, accusing the government of a "takeover" of student loans. The effort succeeded in delaying implementation of parts of the reform law.

The signing of the health care reform law by President Obama, however, was hardly the end of the process, and the prospects for fully implementing the law remained cloudy. Almost immediately, the law was challenged in federal court.

 Watch this video that explains the Affordable Care Act.

Should we consider it a success because of what it accomplished, or a failure because of the problems that remain?

https://www.youtube.com/watch?v=wMuXcuudvCc

Addressing Poverty and Dependency: The Scope of Welfare Reform

The most lasting change in American social welfare during the 1990s was the reform of programs for low-income Americans. As in previous decades, middle-class Americans had a distorted view of the size of the welfare population, how long recipients stayed on the rolls, and the cost of public programs. The massive entry of women into the labor force in the previous three decades had undermined a major assumption of public assistance: that mothers should stay home with their children. Finally, new research results suggested that long-term dependency was a much more significant problem than had previously been believed.

The welfare population of the 1990s was sharply divided into two strata. The vast majority of women who ever collected welfare did so for less than two years. Yet, a significant minority stayed on welfare for more than eight years. Thus, depending on how one phrased it, welfare could be seen as a temporary program or a permanent trap. During the early 1990s, the second image of the welfare population—that it was dominated by a permanent dependent population—drove the welfare debate.

The new alarm with long-term dependency was supported as well with a healthy dose of self-interest and ideology. The driving force behind welfare reform during the early 1990s was cost, not so much for the federal government, but for the states. In reality, the federal government spent $20 billion on AFDC in its peak year, less than 2 percent of the federal budget of over $1 trillion in the early 1990s.[27]

For the states, however, the rise in welfare rolls had a more severe fiscal impact. In 1992, more than 20 percent of expenditures by the states went to public welfare—including AFDC and Medicaid. Increased welfare rolls, declining state revenues (because of a recession), and the requirement that states balance their budgets combined to focus attention on reducing the cost of the program.

The first indicator of the fiscal problem was the fate of the Family Support Act (FSA), which had been enacted in 1988. Although the FSA refocused AFDC on the goal of self-sufficiency, much of the federal financing for the job-training program (Jobs Opportunities and Basic Skills [JOBS]) went unused because it required state matching funds. In the stringent budget years of the early 1990s, state legislatures were unwilling to spend their own dollars to promote self-sufficiency, even if the federal government offered to match their effort.

The Changing Dynamics of the Welfare Debate

Concerns about cost combined with worries about morality. During the late 1980s and early 1990s, the proportion of children born out of wedlock rose. Part of this rise was a statistical artifact—the fall of the marital fertility rate meant that a larger share of births occurred out of wedlock. Although the out-of-wedlock birthrate rose by 37 percent between 1985 and 1992, the percent of all births that occurred outside of marriage increased from 22 to 30. Moreover, out-of-wedlock births became more visible in the white community. As late as 1980, African Americans had accounted for more out-of-wedlock births than whites. By 1992, however, 59 percent of out-of-wedlock births were to whites and only 38 percent were to blacks.[28]

The increased strength of the New Right within the Republican Party put pressure on legislators to focus on the problem of illegitimacy. Yet, instead of asking complex questions about the opportunity structure for poor teenagers, the availability of sex education, and the adequacy of reproductive services, conservatives dwelt on the supposed incentive that AFDC provided for young women to have children out of wedlock. Whatever the merits of their arguments, the battle against illegitimacy had a major impact on the politics of welfare.

As conservatives focused on the role of costs and morality in welfare reform, many liberals and moderates—many of whom called themselves New Democrats—were rethinking their position on public assistance. Mainstream academic thought had become more skeptical about the effects of welfare on the poor. First, David Ellwood and Mary Jo Bane concluded that previous research had understated the importance of long-term dependency. The 19th-century belief that welfare was a trap that fostered dependency and undermined efforts at self-sufficiency took on a new shine in light of their findings.[29] Ellwood and Bane also suggested that welfare bureaucracies at the state and local levels had become a barrier to the reduction of dependency. Second, William J. Wilson, the eminent African American sociologist, gave new credence to the belief that poor neighborhoods had become seedbeds for dependency and other "pathologies." Again, a 19th-century image—that the poor lived in a different social and moral universe than the mainstream—found intellectual support.[30]

This line of academic research found a responsive chord among many liberal politicians. For three decades, liberals had been pilloried by conservatives because of their "permissiveness," their unwillingness to stand up for traditional moral positions on family, work, and gender. A new position on welfare—one that stressed responsibility, work, and self-sufficiency—provided a way for liberals and moderates to defend themselves against charges of permissiveness.

Ellwood again provided the crucial synthesis. In his book, *Poor Support*, Ellwood was able to articulate an analysis of poverty that merged traditional liberalism with the New Democratic concern with responsibility. Ellwood argued that changes in welfare had to be teamed with efforts to improve the status of low-wage workers. By "making work pay," through the expansion of tax credits and increases in the minimum wage, Ellwood's plan would increase the incentives of welfare recipients to enter the workforce. Time limits and work requirements would give them additional incentives to get off welfare.[31]

Ellwood's proposals became the core of Bill Clinton's welfare reform agenda during the 1992 presidential election. During the first year of his presidency, Clinton was able to get Congress to agree to a critical part of his plan, the expansion of the Earned Income Tax Credit (EITC) as part of the Omnibus Budget Reconciliation Act of 1993. The EITC had first been enacted in the 1970s to provide a small wage subsidy for low-income workers with children. The 1993 legislation increased both the size of the tax credit and the number of families who were eligible for it.

The Clinton administration moved more slowly on the reform of public assistance. In the meantime, many states had received waivers from the federal government to adopt experimental schemes for welfare. A few of these actually expanded cash assistance. For example, a number of states increased the earnings disregard, so that welfare recipients could earn more without having their welfare benefits reduced. For the most part, however, the waiver programs tested a set of initiatives to reduce benefits. These included more aggressive efforts to require welfare recipients to work or face sanctions, and a set of behavioral reforms focusing on the supposed immoral behavior of welfare recipients. Welfare recipients in some states faced cuts in their benefits if their children missed school too often, if they failed to document their children's vaccination records, or if they missed a rent payment.

The most widely debated of these behavioral reforms was the "family cap." Until 1996, welfare benefits were tied to family size. If a welfare recipient had an additional child while on welfare, her check would rise to reflect the increase in family size. The family cap froze the family's payment at its level before the new baby was born. To many Americans, the image of a welfare recipient having additional children brought together all of the negative stereotypes of the poor—irresponsibility, promiscuity, dependency, and rising costs. The family cap became the shorthand for an increased focus on "personal responsibility" in the welfare debate.

By the time President Clinton released his plan for welfare reform in the summer of 1994, events had largely overtaken the administration. Clinton's efforts to reform health care were in the last stage of their slow death. Efforts at the state level had moved the welfare debate in a more conservative and harsh direction. Finally, that fall, the Republicans achieved a resounding electoral victory in congressional elections, capturing majorities in both the Senate and the House of Representatives for the first time in four decades. If welfare reform were to occur during the 1990s, it would take the ideas of congressional Republicans as its starting point.

Welfare reform was a key tenet of the "Contract with America," which many Republicans credited with their electoral victory in 1994. The Personal Responsibility Act (H.R. 4) introduced in 1995 outlined a radical shift in welfare policy.[32] The entitlement to welfare would be ended and a host of welfare programs, including AFDC, food stamps, federal child welfare spending, and Medicaid, would be transformed into a block grant to the states. Welfare recipients would be required to work, and limits would be set on the time one could collect welfare. In addition, a number of groups of mothers and children would be defined as undeserving and ineligible of aid: teen mothers, those who refused to work, immigrants, and convicted drug felons.

The New Consensus over Welfare Reform

Although the debate over welfare reform during 1995 and 1996 was acrimonious, there was much that the two sides held in common. Both the Clinton administration and Congress wanted stronger work requirements and supported the idea of time limits. In addition, although they squabbled over the nature of federal–state cooperation, both sides anticipated that welfare reform would give the states more discretion in charting welfare policy. In addition, adopting time limits implied that the "entitlement" to cash assistance would be weakened.

The Clinton administration and Congress used the popularity of welfare reform as a cover for policy changes that could not be enacted on their own. For example, the Supreme Court decision of 1990 had extended Supplemental Security Income (SSI) to children who suffered from a set of behavioral disabilities. Both the administration and Congress were willing to include a reversal of this decision in the welfare reform legislation.

The battle over welfare waxed and waned during 1995 and 1996 as the president and congressional Republicans played an elaborate game of chicken. The public backlash over the budget deadlock of 1995–1996 and the resulting shutdown of the federal government gave the president and congressional Democrats the upper hand through most of 1996. As a result, they were able to make significant changes in the Republicans' original plan. Food stamps, Medicaid, and child welfare services were removed from the block grant and remained entitlements. The amount of money available for child care increased substantially. Many of the behavioral reforms—such as the family cap—changed from a national mandate to a state option. In addition, Congress agreed to "maintenance of effort" stipulations that required states to continue their welfare spending.

Yet, as the 1996 elections approached, it was clear that President Clinton and many Democrats feared that they would be blamed if no welfare reform was enacted. As a result, after President Clinton vetoed several versions of the bill, the Personal Responsibility and Work Opportunity Reconciliation Act (PRWORA) of 1996 was passed and signed into law in August.

The welfare reform debate ended where it had started: with a preoccupation with reducing the cost of welfare. The new legislation ended the entitlement to cash assistance. Temporary Assistance for Needy Families (TANF) was substituted for AFDC.

Combined with the adoption of time limits and work requirements, the states were able to use their new authority to discourage families from applying for welfare and to raise barriers to their receiving benefits. The major "liberal" element in the law was a dramatic expansion in the size of the child-care and development block grant that provided a large increase in subsidized child care for low-income families.[33]

The most glaring omission of the welfare reform law was its failure to require states to offer educational and training opportunities to welfare recipients. Pennsylvania was representative of many states in its adoption of a "rapid attachment" strategy, which put an incentive on getting welfare recipients into low-wage jobs and off welfare as quickly as possible. Although congressional supporters might claim that they wished to break the cycle of dependency, the lack of substantial job training opportunities ensured the cycle of poverty would continue.

In 2005, Congress reauthorized TANF. The new legislation included two major changes. First, in line with the Bush administration's efforts to politicize the debate over family life, the new bill included funding for "marriage promotion" efforts. Second, the bill tightened the work requirements governing state plans to compel states to place more welfare recipients into work programs.

The Impact of Welfare Reform

If the purpose of welfare reform was primarily to reduce the cost of public assistance, it was a stunning success in its first several years. When PRWORA was signed in 1996, the average AFDC caseload nationally was about 12.5 million individuals. By March 1999, the TANF caseload had fallen to 7.3 million recipients. By 2004, fewer than 5 million Americans were served by TANF. Yet, the wide variations of declines from state to state suggested that these data were not the result of the overall improvement in the economic status of the poor, but rather testimony to the states' increased ability to use welfare rules to push poor families off the rolls or to discourage them from entering. Thus, while Minnesota recorded a 13 percent decline between January 1997 and March 1999, Wisconsin—with the most publicized efforts to reduce their rolls—recorded a 78 percent decline.[34]

In some states, like general assistance before it, public assistance for needy families began to disappear, in spite of "maintenance of efforts" requirements. Idaho, which had provided aid to 24,000 individuals in 1996, had only 2,461 on its TANF rolls in March 2002. In the South, Florida and Georgia had a million people on welfare in 1996, but only a quarter of that number in 2002.

In spite of the devastating recession of the late 2000s, TANF caseloads remained fairly stagnant. While the number of Americans receiving food stamps (which had been renamed the Supplemental Nutritional Assistance Program [SNAP]) increased to more than 36 million during the recession, the number of individuals receiving TANF benefits actually fell from 4.4 million in October 2005 to 4.3 million in March 2010.[35]

The evidence on the well-being of former recipients, however, hardly provided a cause for celebration. Most of those who left welfare, although earning more than they would have collected from welfare, continued to live in poverty. The failure of welfare reform to provide much incentive to the state to train and educate recipients meant that as recipients left the rolls, they found themselves in low-wage and irregular jobs that could not lift them out of poverty.

Female heads of household and their children were especially hard hit. Between 1993 and 1995, they had benefited as a group by the improving economic conditions, their average earning rising from $14,668 to just under $17,000. But as welfare reform pushed millions of poorly educated women into the labor force, it exerted a downward pressure on their wages. Between 1995 and 1997, as the economy soared and unemployment dropped below 5 percent, the wages of female heads of household stalled, increasing by only a few hundred dollars per year. After 1998, even these gains ceased.[36]

Careful analyses of evidence on low-wage, female-headed families suggested that as public assistance became a smaller share of family income, women scrambled to make ends meet. Old survival strategies—accepting "off the books" employment, obtaining resources from friends and families, doubling up to reduce housing costs—had again become permanent parts of the family economy of the poor. During the 1960s, it had been said that welfare policy should provide "floors and doors"—a safety net and opportunities to escape poverty. By 2011, the welfare system, serving an ever-smaller share of families in need, seemed to offer neither.

The new welfare regime required public assistance workers to use considerable discretion in the use of sanctions. The new behavioral and work requirements incorporated into state TANF programs meant that clients who did not meet these standards could have their benefits either partially or fully cut off. In some states, policy worked to differentiate clients to provide greater latitude in the imposition of sanctions, while in other places, all clients faced welfare cutoffs regardless of their mental or physical ability.[37]

The long-term impact of welfare reform on children's well-being is hard to assess. Although the welfare reform law had expanded funding for child care, the Department of Health and Human Services estimated that the child care and development block grant provided funding for only 1.25 million children out of the 10 million who were income eligible for child care subsidies. The experience of states that made a real effort to provide adequate child care provides one indication of the gap between the demand for child care and the available resources. In Illinois, for example, the use of subsidized child care expanded by 80 percent between 1997 and 1999.[38]

> **?** Assess your comprehension of "Innovations in Social Welfare" by completing this quiz.

SOCIAL MOVEMENTS AND GRASSROOTS CHANGE

Welfare Reform and "Immigration Control"

The welfare reform law targeted the cutoff of aid to immigrants as a major policy focus. Despite voluminous data demonstrating that the availability of public assistance and social services had little to do with the dynamics of migration, lawmakers viewed welfare reform as an easy way to promote a popular cause. In 1994, California Proposition 187 demonstrated the popular appeal of limiting the availability of educational and social services for immigrants and undocumented migrants. The initiative barred undocumented migrants from using schools, hospitals, and public assistance and sought to give teachers, social workers, and hospital personnel responsibility for identifying ineligible individuals. Although the major provisions of the initiative were blocked by the courts, "Prop 187" became a model for congressional action. Some of the harshest changes in the welfare law were directed at preventing noncitizens from receiving means-tested programs. In 1996, Congress also passed legislation that raised the income threshold required to sponsor new immigrants, enacted new penalties against those who overstayed temporary visas, limited the due process rights of migrants who could not demonstrate they were in the United States legally, and put new money into the militarization of the border between the United States and Mexico.[39]

By 1997, congressional Republicans—many chastened by their electoral defeats in the 1996 election—moved to restore some of the benefits denied to immigrants. Yet, the true irony of the immigrant bashing of the 1990s was that it accelerated the pace at which immigrants attained citizenship. With even legal immigrants finding themselves denied benefits and at risk for harassment, many Americans who had been born in other countries decided that their futures were more secure as citizens.

The punitive approach to immigration provoked a backlash. During 2006, the Republican-controlled Congress debated legislation to criminalize undocumented workers and build 700 miles of walls along the Rio Grande to keep Latin American, undocumented workers out, a proposal opposed even by the president. In the heat of the 2006 midterm elections, the president abandoned the search for a more comprehensive approach to immigration reform and ultimately signed a bill authorizing the construction of the wall. In the face of Republican hostility, Latin American voters, many of whom supported George W. Bush for reelection, voted in greater numbers for Democrats in 2006, a major reason why they retook both houses of Congress.

Still, immigration remained a contested issue during the Obama administration. Efforts to reach a comprehensive approach that would increase border security and provide a path toward citizenship for the estimated 14 million undocumented people living in the United States failed. Instead, many cities, towns, and states experimented with their own form of immigration reform. For example, in 2010, Arizona passed a law that required local law enforcement officials to check the immigration status of persons they deemed suspicious, a policy that many saw as racial profiling. Although this and similar approaches were judged to be unconstitutional by federal courts, politicians continued to be rewarded for supporting these efforts. Yet, other localities took the opposite approach. They passed legislation to provide undocumented immigrants with access to identification and to limit local police departments' participation in immigration enforcement.[40]

> *Yet, other localities took the opposite approach. They passed legislation to provide undocumented immigrants with access to identification and to limit local police departments' participation in immigration enforcement.*

The Return to Voluntarism and the Rise of Privatization

Since the 1980s, many conservatives had argued that one consequence of the expansion of social welfare programs had been to discourage voluntarism. Thus, as the federal government began to limit social programs, advocates tried to demonstrate the vitality of the voluntary sector and its capacity to take up the slack created by a shrinking government role. During the 1980s, these efforts had often appeared as little more than window dressing designed to deflect criticism of program cuts.

Certainly, the fate of homelessness policy during the 1980s and 1990s suggested that the claims of voluntarists rarely were consistent with realities. As the homeless became a more visible part of the social landscape during the 1980s, public attention focused on the role of voluntary organizations, including churches and other religious organizations, in responding to the needs of this population. Yet, it was only with the passage of federal legislation that adequate funding for homeless programs became available.

Inconvenient realities did not weaken the enthusiasm of budget-cutters for the possibilities of voluntary activity. The welfare reform law provided new opportunities for voluntary organizations to become involved in the routine provision of services to the poor. In addition, PRWORA opened up the opportunities for religious congregations to become eligible for welfare funding. Supported by a body of research on the importance of churches in aiding the poor, federal and state policies encouraged religious congregations to take a more active role in poverty policy.[41] The expanding role of religion in public policy affected educational policy as well. In contrast to the 1960s, when Congress took special care in defining a role for religious schools in funding for elementary and secondary education, by the 1990s, many federal and state policy makers were willing to move aggressively to make public funding available for church schools. A number of states and localities adopted "voucher" plans that made certificates available to low-income parents that they could use for either public or private education.

The cause of faith-based social welfare received a big boost from the inauguration of George W. Bush in 2001. The president claimed that his "compassionate conservatism" could be implemented by expanding the role of religious institutions in providing social services. Although Congress resisted his proposals, the Bush administration used a number of executive orders to expand religion's role in public social welfare in spite of the constitutional concerns raised by these policies.

The September 11 tragedy highlighted both the strengths and weaknesses of voluntary social welfare. There was a huge outpouring of concern for the victims of terrorism, with more than $2.4 billion being donated to private charities. Yet, the coordination of aid was poor, with help not always reaching those most in need. The Red Cross drew particular criticism because it was slow to distribute aid and used September 11 funds for purposes not directly connected to the disaster. As a result, an August 2002 poll reported that 42 percent of respondents had lost confidence in private charities as a result of September 11, while only 19 percent had gained confidence.[42]

The efficacy of voluntary charity was dealt a blow in August 2005 when Hurricane Katrina blasted through the Gulf Coast and New Orleans, leaving that city almost entirely submerged for three days.

The efficacy of voluntary charity was dealt a blow in August 2005 when Hurricane Katrina blasted through the Gulf Coast and New Orleans, leaving that city almost entirely submerged for three days. The Bush administration's approach to social welfare was cast in dramatic relief as actually helping victims of the tragedy took a back seat to a public-relations effort to show that the president "cared" about what had happened. Yet, as government failed in its most basic responsibilities—providing food and water, searching for survivors, caring for the sick, and burying the dead—the administration's claims ran headlong into a monstrous reality. The fact that a large number of the victims of the hurricane were poor and black only served to underline the limits of voluntarism and the failure of conservative governance.

Yet, Hurricane Katrina did benefit many. In an age of privatization and outsourcing, private contractors who provided the food, housing, social services, and transportation for the hurricane's victims often were handsomely rewarded for their work, even when it was shoddy or failed to reach victims. Although personal responsibility was the hallmark of conservative social policy, this principle did not extend to private contractors, or for that matter, to the president.

Private, for-profit businesses had a larger role in social welfare by the late 1990s. The availability of third-party reimbursements under private health insurance, Medicare, and Medicaid had greatly expanded the role of for-profit enterprises in some fields of social welfare during the 1970s and 1980s. Child care, nursing homes, hospitals, and residential treatment facilities all expanded. Between 1977 and 1987, the for-profit share of establishments increased by 80 percent in child care, 22 percent in individual and family services, and 45 percent in residential care.[43]

This trend accelerated during the next 20 years. The 1996 welfare reform law, for example, enabled for-profits to enter the child welfare field in greater numbers. In addition, businesses discovered a new set of "profit centers" in certain areas of social welfare, for example, in data processing and research and evaluation.

The entry of for-profit enterprises into child welfare took on particular urgency because of other changes in policy. After a decade of supporting family preservation as the chief approach to child welfare, Congress in 1997 passed the Adoption and Safe

Families Act (ASFA), which placed additional pressure on child welfare agencies to find permanent homes for children removed from homes because of abuse or neglect. After three decades of increased effort to preserve the link between children and their parents, ASFA was a shift back to an older tradition of child rescue, harking back to the approach of 19th-century "child savers."[44]

Welfare reform meant more than changes in a handful of means-tested programs. It symbolized a whole set of changes affecting social welfare during the 1990s. From the New Deal until the 1970s, government had moved steadily to expand the right of ordinary citizens to protection against the risks of poverty and discrimination. Yet, the cost of providing these rights set off a strong backlash. As the public sector sought to reduce taxes and the programs supported by them, policy was increasingly farmed out to non-public institutions. The expanded role of nonprofits, religious institutions, and for-profit businesses was as much a part of welfare reform as the death of AFDC and the birth of TANF.

Although welfare reform offered new opportunities to for-profit business, Old Age, Survivors, and Disability Insurance (OASDI), the core of the Social Security program, offered the most lucrative target. The trust funds for the program ran persistent deficits during the 1970s and early 1980s. After the Social Security reform of 1983, however, the program had been put on a path toward surpluses for the remainder of the 20th century and into the first decades of the next.

Yet, the specter of a "Social Security crisis" remained. In many respects, the politics of Social Security policy were the reverse of the health care reform experience. In health care reform, a popular reform proposal was sidetracked because it would threaten the power and profits of insurance companies, hospitals, and other health care providers. With Social Security, the potential profits of privatization kept "reform" alive even though the public embraced the existing system.

During the 1990s, however, Social Security faced a new challenge: the interests of the financial services industry. The major conservative proposal for privatizing Social Security was to allow individuals to create their own retirement account in lieu of paying Social Security taxes. If such a proposal were enacted, literally billions of dollars that are currently collected in payroll taxes would instead filter through banks, stockbrokers, and other financial institutions. The financial services industry spent much of the decade spreading a message that workers could not count on Social Security when they retired. Over time, these coordinated attacks increased public concern about the system.[45]

In spite of these efforts, however, support of the existing system continued to frustrate those who wished to undermine it. President Clinton's proposal to commit a large share of future budget surpluses to Social Security was warmly received by the public. The future of Social Security, however, was put in jeopardy by the actions of the George W. Bush administration and Congress between 2001 and 2003. With the support of the president, Congress passed a series of tax cuts heavily tilted toward the richest Americans. As a result, the federal budget—excluding Social Security taxes—went from a surplus of $236 billion in 2000 to a projected deficit of $455 billion in 2003, before the impact of the 2003 tax cuts had been felt.

Where the Clinton administration had proposed that the budget surplus of his administration be used to insure Social Security's economic well-being, President Bush chose the exact opposite strategy; he planned to use ballooning deficits in the budget to force a restructuring of the system in the coming years.

President Bush again miscalculated. His 2005 proposal to shift Social Security to private accounts met with such a chilly reception from the public and Congress that it never came for a vote. Yet, the first decade of the 21st century continued the pattern of the previous 30 years with tax-subsidized private pensions accounting for a larger share of retirement income.

In some ways, those backing private pensions had already won the battle. Since the resolution of the Social Security crisis in 1983, most public policy around the income security of the aged had been directed to private plans. The expansion of individual retirement accounts (IRAs), 401(k) accounts, and other "defined-contribution" plans had far exceeded increases in public pensions.[46]

During the 1990s, the proportion of the population that depended on these private plans increased dramatically, reaching more than half of the elderly by 2000. Yet, this growth was spread unequally across the population; two-thirds of the richest fifth of the population had pensions, but less than 20 percent of the bottom fifth did. As a result, of the $88 billion of pensions distributed in 1990, 57 percent went to the richest fifth of the population.

The rise of publicly subsidized private pensions had both economic and political implications. Thanks to the Social Security system, the distribution of income among the elderly had become more equal between 1960 and 1990. During the 1990s and 2000s, however, inequality among the elderly increased because of the rapid rise in pensions.

More significantly, the increased role of private pensions puts the political support for Social Security in jeopardy. Still, one of the reasons for the Bush administration's push for Social Security privatization in 2005 was that it posed one of the last chances to enact reform before the bulk of the baby boom generation reached retirement age. The first baby-boomers reached retirement age in 2012, and demographers estimate that more than 3 million Americans will become eligible for benefits each year for the next two decades. Ironically, many of the "tea party" supporters who vehemently opposed the Affordable Care Act were Social Security and Medicare recipients who approved of those programs.

The Continuing Battle for Social Justice

Americans continued to struggle with the definition of rights and responsibilities during the first decades of the 21st century. Welfare reform had been justified as a means of righting this balance by requiring poor people to be more responsible; at the same time, many of them lost any right to assistance from the federal government. Although policies that were meant to correct social inequality were under attack, those tied to the right of privacy gained more support from the political and legal systems.

Education

Educational programs have been the target for the backlash against people of color and of different ethnic groups. The drive to require all teaching to be done in English targeted Hispanic-speaking children, a growing group in the United States. For immigrants, legal and illegal, there are now many challenges to their right to public education.

The elimination of remedial courses, in the name of economy, at colleges and universities hurt black, Hispanic, and Native American students particularly hard. In the 1992–1993 school year, 11 percent of white but 15 percent of Native American and 19 percent of black, Hispanic, and Asian American undergraduates took remedial courses. Changing college admission standards and cutting the number of remedial courses, or offering them only at junior colleges, blocked the efforts of students to correct inadequate education at the elementary and secondary school levels.[47]

The Supreme Court ruled against a school desegregation program in Kansas City where magnet city schools were used to bring white students from the suburbs into the inner city, one of many court decisions limiting the responsibilities of schools to promote desegregation. The black community appeared split on the issue. Some saw the retreat from integrated schooling as a retreat from equality, while others urged a return to neighborhood schools with an equalization of facilities and opportunities.

At the same time, the same suspicion of the federal government that fueled other conservative movements took aim at the seemingly innocuous topic of educational standards. The Common Core Initiative was founded by the National Governors Association as part of the educational standards movement. Its initial standards for mathematics and English language arts gained the support of many influential education funders, including the William and Melinda Gates Foundation, and were quickly adopted by a number of states in 2010. However, after Common Core was embraced by the Obama administration, it became a symbol of federal intrusion into local educational policy. A number of states rescinded their adoption of the standards, and in 2015, the legislation that renewed federal aid to education—the Every Student Succeeds Act—explicitly prohibited the U.S. Department of Education from influencing states' adoption of Common Core. Opponents of Common Core used language of "interference" and "pollution" that has been common in conservative rhetoric since the battles over equal rights since the 1970s. For example, Senator Mike Lee noted: "Common Core has become polluted with federal guidelines and mandates that interfere with the ability of parents, teachers and principals to deliver the education our children deserve."[48]

Large cuts in the budget for the Bureau of Indian Affairs have led to what the Office of Indian Education Programs called "a major, major problem," putting children in physical danger in buildings with inadequate ventilation, plumbing, and fire-escape routes. The quality of education provided is reflected in the level of spending. Although the Bureau of Indian Affairs is required to finance tribal schools at the per student average for their state, the rule was ignored because insufficient funding was provided by Congress. Congress had, in effect, opted to continue separate and unequal education for Native Americans.[49]

In U.S. colleges and universities, consideration of race, ethnicity, and gender as part of admission decisions has been attacked vigorously. Objections have been particularly vociferous in California and in Texas. In California, Governor Pete Wilson urged that there be no preferential admission. Shortly thereafter, a suit was filed against the medical and law schools of the University of California attacking preferential consideration. The University of California banned admissions that used race or gender as a criterion. Other state legislatures, governors, and university boards were considering and acting to eliminate preferential admissions on the basis of race or ethnicity. A major decision banning preferential admissions came in a 1996 University of Texas case in the Fifth Circuit Court of Appeals that clearly banned race-based admissions. In 2003, however, the Supreme Court—in *Gratz v. Bollinger* and *Grutter v. Bollinger*—ruled that promoting racial diversity in education settings was a legitimate criterion for college admissions. Although the decisions restricted the practices that could be used to promote diversity and called for a time limit on the use of affirmative action, proponents of affirmative action saw these decisions as significant victories.

Affirmative Action in the Labor Market

The courts, which in the past had supported the drive of vulnerable groups, particularly blacks and women, to seek a redress of the opportunity structure they faced in the market, have now moved against preferential hiring and contracting.

Almost any set of data that is examined shows the subordinate position of women and of people of color in our economy. Wages, incomes, promotion rates, middle management, top management, number of contractors, number of independent manufacturing firms—the numbers all tell the same story. Women and minorities suffer severely because of their gender and their race. Yet, there is a growing series of objections from white men who claim to have suffered because of affirmative action programs. A National Opinion Research Center survey in 1990 found that only 7 percent of white Americans had personally experienced reverse discrimination, and 16 percent knew of someone who had. On the other hand, 70 percent thought that whites were being hurt by affirmative action programs.[50]

Efforts to eliminate affirmative action programs gained ground at the state and the federal levels. In California, an initiative to outlaw affirmative action received strong support in the fall of 1996. Other states were attempting similar actions, with varying results. The Supreme Court ruled in 1995 in a 5–4 decision that the federal government was highly restricted in its use of affirmative action programs applied to contractors with the federal government. Federal "set-aside" provisions were not ruled out completely, but they were ordered to meet the more stringent requirements already set for the states. The Pentagon, rather than providing a set-aside provision for minority contractors in long-distance telephone services, gave them a pricing advantage in their bids. The program appeared to be successful, but officials later began backing away from it.

President Clinton ordered a review of the federal government's affirmative action programs. A report, released in May 1995, concluded that race or sex could be acceptable as one of several factors in such programs, and that programs involving "goals" rather than quotas should be used.[51] The president supported reform, but not abolition, of affirmative action programs.

Abortion and the Right to Privacy

In the early 1990s, the right to abortion that the Supreme Court had established in 1973 seemed to be at risk. The appointment of conservative justices to the Supreme Court during the 1980s and early 1990s had decisively changed its ideological complexion. In spite of strong support for abortion rights in public opinion polls, state legislators became increasingly willing to enact restrictions on reproductive services.

The *Webster* decision, announced by the Supreme Court in 1989, provided an equivocal reassertion of *Roe v. Wade*. The court agreed that the right to abortion was constitutionally guaranteed, but the decision expanded the ability of states to limit that right through notification procedures, waiting periods, and the regulation of providers. Although abortion rights advocates were relieved that the court did not overturn *Roe*, the decision made that "right" seem less real. In fact, it became increasingly difficult for a majority of women to gain access to abortion services, as clinics closed their doors and few hospitals offered abortions. In addition, an underground network of terrorists targeted abortion clinics and physicians for violence at the same time that civil disobedience campaigns like "Operation Rescue" impeded women's ability to exercise reproductive choice safely and peaceably.[52]

At the same time, the foundation of *Roe v. Wade* in the "right to privacy" first articulated in the Supreme Court's *Griswold* decision in 1965 made steady progress. In 2003, to the surprise of many, the Supreme Court took the unusual step of claiming that an earlier court decision on the rights of adults to engage in consensual sex—whatever their gender—had been incorrect. The decision in *Lawrence v. Texas* was notable because it used evolving thought in Europe and recent scholarship in gay and lesbian history to support the decision. (See the end of this chapter for excerpts from this decision.)

The *Lawrence* decision was notable as well because the rights of sexual minorities had become a major flashpoint in the culture wars. By the early 21st century, virtually no Americans defended the morality of racial and gender discrimination; the struggles were primarily about how much needed to be done to remedy them. In contrast, a significant minority of Americans continued to view gay, lesbian, bisexual, and transgender people as sinful. The legitimacy of discrimination against sexual minorities affected many social policies from the debate over civil unions or gay marriage to the rights of domestic partners to work-related benefits to the funding of HIV/AIDS drugs and services. As the 21st century began, activists were developing new strategies for mobilizing public sentiment about these issues (Figure 9.2).

In 2004, the debate over gay civil rights took a public turn when the supreme court of Massachusetts found that the commonwealth's constitution provided the legal basis for same-sex marriage. Congress had already acted in the 1990s to "defend marriage" against the progress of civil unions. Now, conservatives demanded a constitutional amendment to prevent same-sex marriage (and perhaps recognized civil unions as well).

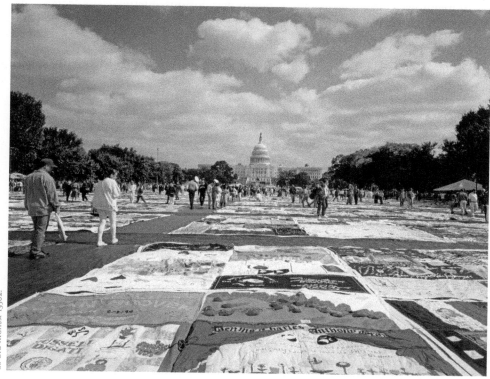

HIGHSMITH (CAROL M.) ARCHIVE, PRINTS & PHOTOGRAPHS DIVISION, LIBRARY OF CONGRESS, LC-DIG-HIGHSM-13502.

Figure 9.2   As the 20th century drew to a close, new pressing social issues—such as the AIDS epidemic—stimulated new social movements. Although many of these movements borrowed methods from past social movements, including the civil rights movement, they also created new ways of dramatizing their concerns and influencing public policy.
Source: AP/World Wide Photo.

Although many states passed bans on same-sex marriage, over time, it was hard for most Americans to reconcile their dislike of discrimination with the advocacy of a same-sex marriage ban. Even the political benefits of opposition to gay marriage declined over time. Where in 1996, 68 percent of Americans opposed gay marriage, by 2010, the proportion had declined to 53 percent.[53]

As public opposition weakened, marriage equality advocates were successful at casting the issue as one of discrimination and equal rights. Although the movement faltered in 2008 when Californians supported Proposition 8, which reversed the legislature's passage of marriage equality, it made steady progress in courts and state legislature. Finally, in 2015, the Supreme Court held that the 14th Amendment—equal protection under the law—required states to recognize same-sex marriages.[54]

The Great Lockup

The biggest retreat on human rights occurred largely out of the public's view. During the 1990s, a larger share of Americans found themselves under the control of the criminal justice system. As prison construction boomed, imprisonment became the most common American response to behavior that was out of the mainstream. By the end of the century, the United States had locked up a larger share of its population than any democracy ever had.

In many ways, the imprisonment boom was curious. Victimization rates—the number of Americans who had actually suffered from a criminal act—declined steadily during the 1990s. In 1993, 5.2 percent of Americans over the age of 12 had experienced some personal crime, and 31 percent had experienced a crime against property. By 2003, both of these rates had declined significantly, to 2.3 percent for personal crimes and to 16.1 percent for property crimes.[55]

While actual crime plummeted and arrests remained stable, the number of Americans under correctional supervision—in prison, on probation, or on parole—exploded.

Yet, this decline in real criminal behavior had little impact on the number of arrests. In 1990, there were 12 arrests for every 1,000 Americans. By 1997, this rate had only declined to 10.4. The disparity between victimization and arrests was even greater for personal crimes. Although the victimization rate for violent crimes had declined from 4.9 to 3.7 percent between 1993 and 1998, the number of arrests for violent crimes fell only from 2.9 to 2.7 per 1,000 during the 1990s.

While actual crime plummeted and arrests remained stable, the number of Americans under correctional supervision—in prison, on probation, or on parole—exploded. In 1990, 4.3 million adults were under correctional supervision. In 2006, the number had reached 7.2 million.

The real focus of the great lockup, however, was racial minorities. By 1996, 2 percent of all whites in the United States were under correctional supervision, but 9 percent of African Americans were. At every stage of the criminal justice system, African Americans found themselves likely to suffer harsher punishments than whites.

By the second decade of the 21st century, many states were looking for ways to reverse the great lockup. Still, it carried huge implications for the future of social welfare in the United States. As the amount of prison construction expanded, the amount of school construction languished. The cost of incarcerating such a large share of the population restricted funding for programs that might reduce crime further. Truly frightening was the fact that the costs paled in comparison to what would happen in the future. The popularity of "three strikes" laws, which required life sentences without parole for repeat offenders, made it likely that the prison system of the 21st century would be home to a large, aging population.

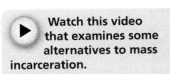

Watch this video that examines some alternatives to mass incarceration.

What barriers can you anticipate that might prevent these policies from gaining wider acceptance?

https://www.youtube.com/watch?v=h6g9L2VqPNk

But the implications of criminal justice policy went beyond prison walls. A criminal record made it more difficult for former inmates to reintegrate in American society. As a result, the great lockup added incentives for former inmates to enter the informal economy, in either criminal or quasi-criminal activities. At the same time, the lockup of so many men meant that the chances of poor women to find stable partners declined. Even as conservatives called for reinforcing the traditional family, their advocacy of harsh criminal justice policy worked to remove men from poor neighborhoods.

The disparate treatment of African Americans in the criminal justice system came to a head during 2014–2015 in Missouri and Maryland, in cases where unarmed black males were killed while in police custody, sparking demonstrations and civil disorder. The movement coalesced around the slogan "Black Lives Matter," which overnight became a rallying cry for a variety of constituencies that saw these deaths as only one symptom of a larger systemic racism that continued to disadvantage people of color.

Notably, "#Black Lives Matter" used the hashtag to spread its message through the various forms of social media that had proliferated in global society over the previous decade. In 2011, Occupy Wall Street began as a conventional demonstration and sit-in in lower Manhattan, but then spread nationally and internationally thanks to social media. Largely focused on the increasing inequality of income and wealth and the disproportionate influence of the "one percent," the Occupy movement popularized new forms of organizing and collective decision-making. Although it fell short of its goals and was eventually evicted from Zuccotti Park, the movement remained influential. In 2016, the first socialist presidential candidate to generate widespread support in nearly a century—Bernie Sanders—incorporated the rhetoric of the "one percent" and the political mobilization of young adults as the foundation of his campaign.[56]

> **?** Assess your comprehension of "Social Movements and Grassroots Change" by completing this quiz.

CONCLUSION

American society between 1993 and 2016 was buffeted by crosscurrents. As revolutions in technology and economic restructuring pushed individuals and families into a brave new world of computers, genetic engineering, and instantaneous global communications, the fear of change provided a large audience for those who appealed to tradition. The solutions that Americans had developed earlier in the century for the problems of industrial society were less effective at addressing the problems of an information society. As a result, Americans experimented with new ideas at the same time that they hoped the old ones could get them through.

Most important, the implications of the new social and economic realities had yet to penetrate government and the political system. Much like the late 19th century, public policy could not keep up with the rapid changes that Americans were experiencing. The public looked to government for solutions to the new realities it faced: less stable jobs, more frequent need for retraining, the challenges of dual-earner families, and acceptance that "life without father" was now the common experience for many children. Yet, the political system seemed intent on rehashing a set of ideological disputes from the previous 20 years. At a time when business seemed interested in managing the realities of a new, diverse workforce, the political system used affirmative action as a wedge issue to divide the public. Where most Americans had come to accept new sexual mores and wanted policy that would prevent these behaviors from leading to illness and death, politicians wanted to discuss the need for "abstinence" and to block the distribution of condoms and family planning information.

The first years of the new century posed a great challenge to American democracy. Buffeted by many new problems—globalization, international terrorism, the wars in Iraq and Afghanistan, a new wave of immigration, and Hurricane Katrina—many asked if the American people could disenthrall themselves from the comfortable, simplistic view of the world marketed by conservative politicians and develop new answers for a new century. With the close 2016 presidential election in which Donald Trump lost the popular vote but triumphed in the Electoral College, the answer to that question remained very much up in the air. Americans seemed torn between a pessimistic, defensive posture toward change and an optimistic openness to its new possibilities. Only time would tell which side of their character would prevail.

DOCUMENTS

Social Welfare and the Information Society

The single most important policy innovation of the 1990s was the reform of the public assistance system brought about by PRWORA of 1996. This act changed federal funding for cash assistance to poor families from an open-ended entitlement to a block grant. The act focused the new cash assistance program—TANF—on the short-term relief of need; assistance was limited to five years and states were allowed to impose stricter time limits if they wished. In addition to pushing the states to require welfare recipients to work, the act identified a set of groups—unmarried teen mothers, drug felons, and immigrants—for even greater restrictions on their ability to qualify for assistance.

In order to justify this new departure, the 104th Congress began the act with a set of "Findings" that sought to connect welfare dependency, illegitimacy, and the "crisis" of the American family. As often occurs, advocates of welfare reform drew selectively on a large and complex body of data to support their position. The findings reproduced here are as notable for what they leave out as for what they include. For example, no mention is made of the increasingly unequal distribution of income, worker displacement, or high unemployment that sparked the increase in the welfare rolls during the early 1990s.

Undocumented foreign workers, or "illegal aliens" as many conservatives chose to call them, were also a focus of the supporters of California Proposition 187. This citizen initiative was proposed by Governor Pete Wilson in August 1995 and passed into law on November 4 of that year. The proposal was a response to the fear of Californians that a large number of immigrants—legal and illegal—would threaten wage rates, increase the costs of public welfare, and lead to overcrowding in the schools. The legislation barred all undocumented workers and their families from using public social services, publicly funded health care services, public elementary or secondary schools, or public postsecondary educational institutions. The institutions involved were required to notify the attorney general of California and the U.S. Immigration and Naturalization Service of the presence of any "illegal alien."

Emergency health care, the Supplemental Food Program for Women, Infants, and Children (WIC), school lunches and breakfasts, and public education are the only federally mandated benefits available to undocumented workers. Thus, this act effectively would have removed any safety net. In response to a suit brought by the American Civil Liberties Union, the Mexican American Legal Defense and Education Fund, and other immigrant rights groups, most of Proposition 187 was declared unconstitutional in California just one year after it was enacted. It will be years before the case reaches the Supreme Court. Meanwhile, however, the intent to discourage Mexican immigration is clear.

Changes in Americans' ideas about gender and sexuality were at the heart of social transformations of the 1990s and early 21st century. The Supreme Court entered this debate in its 2003 decision overruling Texas's anti-sodomy law. The court had to reverse its 1986 decision that upheld a similar law in Georgia. Justice Kennedy did so by drawing on recent work by scholars who found that legal discrimination against gays and lesbians is a relatively recent development. He also cited the findings of European courts to rebut the belief that "Western civilization" had a long-standing antipathy to gays and lesbians.

The legal strategy used by the court majority, however, could come to haunt pro-choice forces in the future. Justice Scalia, in a characteristically forceful dissent, noted that the Court had chosen not to overrule *Roe v. Wade* in 1992 because of its respect for precedents, *stare decisis*. If the court were willing to overturn precedents in this case, Scalia suggested, it might eventually revisit whether *stare decisis* needed to be respected in the case of abortion.

UNITED STATES PUBLIC LAWS
104TH CONGRESS—SECOND SESSION

PUBLIC LAW 104-193 [H.R. 3734]
AUGUST 21, 1996

PERSONAL RESPONSIBILITY AND WORK
OPPORTUNITY RECONCILIATION ACT
OF 1996

104 P.L. 193; 110 STAT. 2105;
1996 ENACTED H.R. 3734;
104 ENACTED H.R. 3734

An Act

To provide for reconciliation pursuant to section 201(A)(1) of the concurrent resolution on the budget for fiscal year 1997.

Be it enacted by the Senate and House of Representatives of the United States of America in Congress assembled,

SECTION 1. SHORT TITLE

This Act may be cited as the "Personal Responsibility and Work Opportunity Reconciliation Act of 1996."

TITLE I—BLOCK GRANTS FOR TEMPORARY
ASSISTANCE FOR NEEDY FAMILIES

Sec. 101. FINDINGS.
The Congress makes the following findings:

(1) Marriage is the foundation of a successful society.

(2) Marriage is an essential institution of a successful society, which promotes the interests of children.

(3) Promotion of responsible fatherhood and motherhood is integral to successful child rearing and the well-being of children.

(4) In 1992, only 54 percent of single-parent families with children had a child support order established and, of that 54 percent, only about one-half received the full amount due. Of the cases enforced through the public child support enforcement system, only 18 percent of the caseload has a collection.

(5) The number of individuals receiving aid to families with dependent children (in this section referred to as "AFDC") has more than tripled since 1965. More than two-thirds of these recipients are children. Eighty-nine percent

of children receiving AFDC benefits now live in homes in which no father is present.

    (A) (i) The average monthly number of children receiving AFDC benefits—
        (I) was 3,300,000 in 1965;
        (II) was 6,200,000 in 1970;
        (III) was 7,400,000 in 1980; and
        (IV) was 9,300,000 in 1992.

    (ii) While the number of children receiving AFDC benefits increased nearly threefold between 1965 and 1992, the total number of children in the United States aged 0 to 18 has declined by 5.5 percent.

    (B) The Department of Health and Human Services has estimated that 12,000,000 children will receive AFDC benefits within 10 years.

    (C) The increase in the number of children receiving public assistance is closely related to the increase in births to unmarried women. Between 1970 and 1991, the percentage of live births to unmarried women increased nearly threefold, from 10.7 percent to 29.5 percent.

(6) The increase of out-of-wedlock pregnancies and births is well documented as follows:

    (A) It is estimated that the rate of nonmarital teen pregnancy rose 23 percent from 54 pregnancies per 1,000 unmarried teenagers in 1976 to 66.7 pregnancies in 1991. The overall rate of nonmarital pregnancy rose 14 percent from 90.8 pregnancies per 1,000 unmarried women in 1980 to 103 in both 1991 and 1992. In contrast, the overall pregnancy rate for married couples decreased 7.3 percent between 1980 and 1991, from 126.9 pregnancies per 1,000 married women in 1980 to 117.6 pregnancies in 1991.

    (B) The total of all out-of-wedlock births between 1970 and 1991 has risen from 10.7 percent to 29.5 percent and if the current trend continues, 50 percent of all births by the year 2015 will be out-of-wedlock.

(7) An effective strategy to combat teenage pregnancy must address the issue of male responsibility, including statutory rape culpability and prevention. The increase of teenage pregnancies among the youngest girls is particularly severe and is linked to predatory sexual practices by men who are significantly older.

    (A) It is estimated that in the late 1980's, the rate for girls age 14 and under giving birth increased 26 percent.

    (B) Data indicates that at least half of the children born to teenage mothers are fathered by adult men. Available data suggests that almost 70 percent of births to teenage girls are fathered by men over age 20.

    (C) Surveys of teen mothers have revealed that a majority of such mothers have histories of sexual and physical abuse, primarily with older adult men.

(8) The negative consequences of an out-of-wedlock birth on the mother, the child, the family, and society are well documented as follows:

    (A) Young women 17 and under who give birth outside of marriage are more likely to go on public assistance and to spend more years on welfare once enrolled. These combined effects of "younger and longer" increase total AFDC costs per household by 25 percent to 30 percent for 17-year-olds.

    (B) Children born out-of-wedlock have a substantially higher risk of being born at a very low or moderately low birth weight.

(C) Children born out-of-wedlock are more likely to experience low verbal cognitive attainment, as well as more child abuse, and neglect.

(D) Children born out-of-wedlock were more likely to have lower cognitive scores, lower educational aspirations, and a greater likelihood of becoming teen-age parents themselves.

(E) Being born out-of-wedlock significantly reduces the chances of the child growing up to have an intact marriage.

(F) Children born out-of-wedlock are 3 times more likely to be on welfare when they grow up.

(9) Currently 35 percent of children in single-parent homes were born out-of-wedlock, nearly the same percentage as that of children in single-parent homes whose parents are divorced (37 percent). While many parents find them-selves, through divorce or tragic circumstances beyond their control, facing the difficult task of raising children alone, nevertheless, the negative consequences of raising children in single-parent homes are well documented as follows:

(A) Only 9 percent of married-couple families with children under 18 years of age have income below the national poverty level. In contrast, 46 percent of female-headed households with children under 18 years of age are below the national poverty level.

(B) Among single-parent families, nearly 1/2 of the mothers who never married received AFDC while only 1/5 of divorced mothers received AFDC.

(C) Children born into families receiving welfare assistance are 3 times more likely to be on welfare when they reach adulthood than children not born into families receiving welfare.

(D) Mothers under 20 years of age are at the greatest risk of bearing low birth weight babies.

(E) The younger the single-parent mother, the less likely she is to finish high school.

(F) Young women who have children before finishing high school are more likely to receive welfare assistance for a longer period of time.

(G) Between 1985 and 1990, the public cost of births to teenage mothers under the aid to families with dependent children program, the food stamp pro-gram, and the medicaid program has been estimated at $120,000,000,000.

(H) The absence of a father in the life a child has a negative effect on school performance and peer adjustment.

(I) Children of teenage single parents have lower cognitive scores, lower educational aspirations, and a greater likelihood of becoming teenage parents themselves.

(J) Children of single-parent homes are 3 times more likely to fail and repeat a year in grade school than are children from intact 2-parent families.

(K) Children from single-parent homes are almost 4 times more likely to be expelled or suspended from school.

(L) Neighborhoods with larger percentages of youth aged 12 through 20 and areas with higher percentages of single-parent households have higher rates of violent crime.

(M) Of those youth held for criminal offenses within the State juvenile justice system, only 29.8 percent lived primarily in a home with both parents. In con-trast to these incarcerated youth, 73.9 percent of the 62,800,000 children in the Nation's resident population were living with both parents.

(10) Therefore, in light of this demonstration of the crisis in our Nation, it is the sense of the Congress that prevention of out-of-wedlock pregnancy and reduction in out-of-wedlock birth are very important Government interests and the policy contained in part A of title IV of the Social Security Act (as amended by section 103(a) of this Act) is intended to address the crisis. . . .

PART A—BLOCK GRANTS TO STATES
FOR TEMPORARY ASSISTANCE FOR NEEDY FAMILIES

401 Sec. 401. Purpose.

(a) In General.—The purpose of this part is to increase the flexibility of States in operating a program designed to—

(1) provide assistance to needy families so that children may be cared for in their own homes or in the homes of relatives;

(2) end the dependence of needy parents on government benefits by promoting job preparation, work, and marriage;

(3) prevent and reduce the incidence of out-of-wedlock pregnancies and establish annual numerical goals for preventing and reducing the incidence of these pregnancies; and

(4) encourage the formation and maintenance of two-parent families.

(b) No Individual Entitlement.—This part shall not be interpreted to entitle any individual or family to assistance under any State program funded under this part. . . .

***

Prop. 187   NOVEMBER ELECTION PROPOSITIONS

INITIATIVE STATUTE—ILLEGAL ALIENS—PUBLIC
SERVICES, VERIFICATION, AND REPORTING

PROPOSITION 187

PROPOSED LAW

The People of California find and declare as follows:

SECTION 1. Findings and Declaration.

That they have suffered and are suffering economic hardship caused by the presence of illegal aliens in this state.

That they have suffered and are suffering personal injury and damage caused by the criminal conduct of illegal aliens in this state.

That they have a right to the protection of their government from any person or persons entering this country unlawfully.

Therefore, the People of California declare their intention to provide for cooperation between their agencies of state and local government with the federal government, and to establish a system of required notification by and between such agencies to prevent illegal aliens in the United States from receiving benefits or public services in the State of California.

SECTION 2. Manufacture, Distribution or Sale of False Citizenship or Resident Alien Documents: Crime and Punishment.

Section 113 is added to the Penal Code, to read:

113. Any person who manufactures, distributes or sells false documents to conceal the true citizenship or resident alien status of another person is guilty of a felony, and shall be punished by imprisonment in the state prison for five years or by a fine of seventy-five thousand dollars ($75,000).

SECTION 3. Use of False Citizenship or Resident Alien Documents: Crime and Punishment.

Section 114 is added to the Penal Code, to read:

114. Any person who uses false documents to conceal his or her true citizenship or resident alien status is guilty of a felony, and shall be punished by imprisonment in the state prison for five years or by a fine of twenty-five thousand dollars ($25,000).

SECTION 4. Law Enforcement Cooperation with INS.

Section 834b is added to the Penal Code, to read:

834b. (a) Every law enforcement agency in California shall fully cooperate with the United States Immigration and Naturalization Service regarding any person who is arrested if he or she is suspected of being present in the United States in violation of federal immigration laws.

(b) With respect to any such person who is arrested, and suspected of being present in the United States in violation of federal immigration laws, every law enforcement agency shall do the following:

(1) Attempt to verify the legal status of such person as a citizen of the United States, an alien lawfully admitted as a permanent resident, an alien lawfully admitted for a temporary period of time or as an alien who is present in the United States in violation of immigration laws. The verification process may include, but shall not be limited to, questioning the person regarding his or her date and place of birth, and entry into the United States, and demanding documentation to indicate his or her legal status.

(2) Notify the person of his or her apparent status as an alien who is present in the United States in violation of federal immigration laws and inform him or her that, apart from any criminal justice proceedings, he or she must either obtain legal status or leave the United States.

(3) Notify the Attorney General of California and the United States Immigration and Naturalization Service of the apparent illegal status and provide any additional information that may be requested by any other public entity.

(c) Any legislative, administrative, or other action by a city, county, or other legally authorized local governmental entity with jurisdictional boundaries, or by a law enforcement agency, to prevent or limit the cooperation required by subdivision (a) is expressly prohibited.

SECTION 5. Exclusion of Illegal Aliens from Public Social Services.

Section 10001.5 is added to the Welfare and Institutions Code, to read:

10001.5. (a) In order to carry out the intention of the People of California that only citizens of the United States and aliens lawfully admitted to the United States may receive the benefits of public social services and to ensure that all persons employed in the providing of those services shall diligently protect public funds from misuse, the provisions of this section are adopted.

(b) A person shall not receive any public social services to which he or she may be otherwise entitled until the legal status of that person has been verified as one of the following:

(1) A citizen of the United States.
(2) An alien lawfully admitted as a permanent resident.
(3) An alien lawfully admitted for a temporary period of time.

(c) If any public entity in this state to whom a person has applied for public social services determines or reasonably suspects, based upon the information provided to it, that the person is an alien in the United States in violation of federal law, the following procedures shall be followed by the public entity:

(1) The entity shall not provide the person with benefits or services.

(2) The entity shall, in writing, notify the person of his or her apparent illegal immigration status, and that the person must either obtain legal status or leave the United States.

(3) The entity shall also notify the State Director of Social Services, the Attorney General of California, and the United States Immigration and Naturalization Service of the apparent illegal status, and shall provide any additional information that may be requested by any other public entity.

SECTION 6. Exclusion of Illegal Aliens from Publicly Funded Health Care.

Chapter 1.3 (commencing with Section 130) is added to Part 1 of Division 1 of the Health and Safety Code, to read:

CHAPTER 1.3. PUBLICLY-FUNDED HEALTH CARE SERVICES

130. (a) In order to carry out the intention of the People of California that, excepting emergency medical care as required by federal law, only citizens of the United States and aliens lawfully admitted to the United States may receive the benefits of publicly-funded health care, and to ensure that all persons employed in the providing of those services shall diligently protect public funds from misuse, the provisions of this section are adopted.

(b) A person shall not receive any health care services from a publicly-funded health care facility, to which he or she is otherwise entitled until the legal status of that person has been verified as one of the following:

(1) A citizen of the United States.

(2) An alien lawfully admitted as a permanent resident.

(3) An alien lawfully admitted for a temporary period of time.

(c) If any publicly-funded health care facility in this state from whom a person seeks health care services, other than emergency medical care as required by federal law, determines or reasonably suspects, based upon the information provided to it, that the person is an alien in the United States in violation of federal law, the following procedures shall be followed by the facility:

(1) The facility shall not provide the person with services.

(2) The facility shall, in writing, notify the person of his or her apparent illegal immigration status, and that the person must either obtain legal status or leave the United States.

(3) The facility shall also notify the State Director of Health Services, the Attorney General of California, and the United States Immigration and Naturalization Service of the apparent illegal status, and shall provide any additional information that may be requested by any other public entity.

(d) For purposes of this section "publicly-funded health care facility" shall be defined as specified in Sections 1200 and 1250 of this code as of January 1, 1993.

SECTION 7. Exclusion of Illegal Aliens from Public Elementary and Secondary Schools.

Section 48215 is added to the Education Code, to read:

48215. (a) No public elementary or secondary school shall admit, or permit the attendance of, any child who is not a citizen of the United States, an alien lawfully admitted as a permanent resident, or a person who is otherwise authorized under federal law to be present in the United States.

(b) Commencing January 1, 1995, each school district shall verify the legal status of each child enrolling in the school district for the first time in order to ensure the enrollment or attendance only of citizens, aliens lawfully admitted as permanent residents, or persons who are otherwise authorized to be present in the United States.

(c) By January 1, 1996, each school district shall have verified the legal status of each child already enrolled and in attendance in the school district in order to ensure the enrollment or attendance only of citizens, aliens lawfully admitted as permanent residents, or persons who are otherwise authorized under federal law to be present in the United States.

(d) By January 1, 1996, each school district shall also have verified the legal status of each parent or guardian of each child referred to in subdivisions (b) and (c), to determine whether such parent or guardian is one of the following:

(1) A citizen of the United States.

(2) An alien lawfully admitted as a permanent resident.

(3) An alien admitted lawfully for a temporary period of time.

(e) Each school district shall provide information to the State Superintendent of Public Instruction, the Attorney General of California, and the United States Immigration and Naturalization Service regarding any enrollee or pupil, or parent or guardian, attending a public elementary or secondary school in the school district determined or reasonably suspected to be in violation of federal immigration laws within forty-five days after becoming aware of an apparent violation. The notice shall also be provided to the parent or legal guardian of the enrollee or pupil, and shall state that an existing pupil may not continue to attend the school after ninety calendar days from the date of the notice, unless legal status is established.

(f) For each child who cannot establish legal status in the United States, each school district shall continue to provide education for a period of ninety days from the date of the notice. Such ninety day period shall be utilized to accomplish an orderly transition to a school in the child's country of origin. Each school district shall fully cooperate in this transition effort to ensure that the educational needs of the child are best served for that period of time.

SECTION 8. Exclusion of Illegal Aliens from Public Postsecondary Educational Institutions.

Section 66010.8 is added to the Education Code, to read:

66010.8 (a) No public institution of postsecondary education shall admit, enroll, or permit the attendance of any person who is not a citizen of the United States, an alien lawfully admitted as a permanent resident in the United States, or a person who is otherwise authorized under federal law to be present in the United States.

(b) Commencing with the first term or semester that begins after January 1, 1995, and at the commencement of each term or semester thereafter, each public postsecondary educational institution shall verify the status of each person enrolled or in attendance at that institution in order to ensure the enrollment or attendance only of United States citizens, aliens lawfully admitted as permanent residents in the United States, and persons who are otherwise authorized under federal law to be present in the United States.

(c) No later than 45 days after the admissions officer of a public postsecondary educational institution becomes aware of the application, enrollment, or attendance of a person determined to be, or who is under reasonable suspicion of being, in the United States in violation of federal immigration laws, that officer shall provide that information to the State Superintendent of Public Instruction, the Attorney General of California, and the United States Immigration and Naturalization Service. The information shall also be provided to the applicant, enrollee, or person admitted.

SECTION 9. Attorney General Cooperation with the INS.

Section 53069.65 is added to the Government Code, to read:

53069.65. Whenever the state or a city, or a county, or any other legally authorized local governmental entity with jurisdictional boundaries reports the presence of a person who is suspected of being present in the United States in violation of federal immigration laws to the Attorney General of California, that report shall be transmitted to the United States Immigration and Naturalization Service. The Attorney General shall be responsible for maintaining on-going and accurate records of such reports, and shall provide any additional information that may be requested by any other government entity.

SECTION 10. Amendment and Severability.

The statutory provisions contained in this measure may not be amended by the Legislature except to further its purposes by statute passed in each house by rollcall vote entered in the journal, two-thirds of the membership concurring, or by a statute that becomes effective only when approved by the voters.

In the event that any portion of this act or the application thereof to any person or circumstance is held invalid, that invalidity shall not affect any other provision or application of the act, which can be given effect without the invalid provision or application, and to that end the provisions of this act are severable.

★★★

SUPREME COURT OF THE UNITED STATES

No. 02-102

JOHN GEDDES LAWRENCE AND TYRON GARNER, PETITIONERS

v.

TEXAS

ON WRIT OF CERTIORARI TO THE COURT OF APPEALS OF TEXAS,

FOURTEENTH DISTRICT
[June 26, 2003]

JUSTICE KENNEDY delivered the opinion of the Court.

Liberty protects the person from unwarranted government intrusions into a dwelling or other private places. In our tradition the State is not omnipresent in the home. And there are other spheres of our lives and existence, outside the home, where the State should not be a dominant presence. Freedom extends beyond spatial bounds. Liberty presumes an autonomy of self that includes freedom of thought, belief, expression, and certain intimate conduct. The instant case involves liberty of the person both in its spatial and more transcendent dimensions.

I

The question before the Court is the validity of a Texas statute making it a crime for two persons of the same sex to engage in certain intimate sexual conduct. In Houston, Texas, officers of the Harris County Police Department were dispatched to a private residence in response to a reported weapons disturbance. They entered an apartment where one of the petitioners, John Geddes Lawrence, resided. The right of the police to enter does not seem to have been questioned. The officers observed Lawrence and another man, Tyron Garner, engaging in a sexual act. The two petitioners were arrested, held in custody over night, and charged and convicted before a Justice of the Peace.

The complaints described their crime as "deviate sexual intercourse, namely anal sex, with a member of the same sex (man)." App. to Pet. for Cert. 127a, 139a. The applicable state law is Tex. Penal Code Ann. §21.06(a) (2003). It provides: "A person commits an offense if he engages in deviate sexual intercourse with another individual of the same sex." . . .

The petitioners exercised their right to a trial *de novo* in Harris County Criminal Court. They challenged the statute as a violation of the Equal Protection Clause of the Fourteenth Amendment and of a like provision of the Texas Constitution. Tex. Const., Art. 1, § 3a. Those contentions were rejected. The petitioners, having entered a plea of *nolo contendere*, were each fined $200 and assessed court costs of $141.25. App. to Pet. for Cert. 107a-110a.

The Court of Appeals for the Texas Fourteenth District considered the petitioners' federal constitutional arguments under both the Equal Protection and Due Process Clauses of the Fourteenth Amendment. After hearing the case en banc the court, in a divided opinion, rejected the constitutional arguments and affirmed the convictions. 41 S. W. 3d 349 (Tex. App. 2001). The majority opinion indicates that the Court of Appeals considered our decision in *Bowers v. Hardwick*, 478 U. S. 186 (1986), to be controlling on the federal due process aspect of the case. *Bowers* then being authoritative, this was proper.

We granted certiorari, 537 U. S. 1044 (2002), to consider three questions:

(1) Whether Petitioners' criminal convictions under the Texas "Homosexual Conduct" law—which criminalizes sexual intimacy by same-sex couples, but not identical behavior by different-sex couples—violate the Fourteenth Amendment guarantee of equal protection of laws?

(2) Whether Petitioners' criminal convictions for adult consensual sexual intimacy in the home violate their vital interests in liberty and privacy protected by the Due Process Clause of the Fourteenth Amendment?

(3) Whether *Bowers v. Hardwick*, 478 U. S. 186 (1986), should be overruled? Pet. for Cert. i.

The petitioners were adults at the time of the alleged offense. Their conduct was in private and consensual.

II

We conclude the case should be resolved by determining whether the petitioners were free as adults to engage in the private conduct in the exercise of their liberty under the Due Process Clause of the Fourteenth Amendment to the Constitution. For this inquiry we deem it necessary to reconsider the Court's holding in *Bowers*.

There are broad statements of the substantive reach of liberty under the Due Process Clause in earlier cases, including *Pierce v. Society of Sisters*, 268 U. S. 510 (1925), and *Meyer v. Nebraska*, 262 U. S. 390 (1923); but the most pertinent beginning point is our decision in *Griswold v. Connecticut*, 381 U. S. 479 (1965).

In *Griswold* the Court invalidated a state law prohibiting the use of drugs or devices of contraception and counseling or aiding and abetting the use of contraceptives. The Court described the protected interest as a right to privacy and placed emphasis on the marriage relation and the protected space of the marital bedroom. *Id.*, at 485.

After *Griswold* it was established that the right to make certain decisions regarding sexual conduct extends beyond the marital relationship. In *Eisenstadt v. Baird*, 405 U. S. 438 (1972), the Court invalidated a law prohibiting the distribution of contraceptives to unmarried persons. The case was decided under the Equal Protection Clause, *id.*, at 454; but with respect to unmarried persons, the Court went on to state the fundamental proposition that the law impaired the exercise of their personal rights, *ibid.* It quoted from the statement of the Court of Appeals finding the law to be in conflict with fundamental human rights, and it followed with this statement of its own:

> "It is true that in *Griswold* the right of privacy in question inhered in the marital relationship. . . . If the right of privacy means anything, it is the right of the *individual*, married or single, to be free from unwarranted governmental intrusion into matters so fundamentally affecting a person as the decision whether to bear or beget a child. Id., at 453.

The opinions in *Griswold* and *Eisenstadt* were part of the background for the decision in *Roe v. Wade*, 410 U. S. 113 (1973). As is well known, the case involved a challenge to the Texas law prohibiting abortions, but the laws of other States were affected as well. Although the Court held the woman's rights were not absolute, her right to elect an abortion did have real and substantial protection as an exercise of her liberty under the Due Process Clause. The Court cited cases that protect spatial freedom and cases that go well beyond it. Roe recognized the right of a woman to make certain fundamental decisions affecting her destiny and confirmed once more that the protection of liberty under the Due Process Clause has a substantive dimension of fundamental significance in defining the rights of the person.

In *Carey v. Population Services Int'l*, 431 U. S. 678 (1977), the Court confronted a New York law forbidding sale or distribution of contraceptive devices to persons under 16 years of age. Although there was no single opinion for the Court, the law was invalidated. Both *Eisenstadt* and *Carey*, as well as the holding and rationale in *Roe*, confirmed that the reasoning of *Griswold* could not be confined to the protection of rights of married adults. This was the state of the law with respect to some of the most relevant cases when the Court considered *Bowers v. Hardwick*.

The facts in *Bowers* had some similarities to the instant case. A police officer, whose right to enter seems not to have been in question, observed Hardwick, in his own bedroom, engaging in intimate sexual conduct with another adult male. The conduct was in violation of a Georgia statute making it a criminal offense to engage in sodomy. One difference between the two cases is that the Georgia statute prohibited the conduct whether or not the participants were of the same sex, while the Texas statute, as we have seen, applies only to participants of the same sex. Hardwick was not prosecuted, but he brought an action in federal court to declare the state statute invalid. He alleged he was a practicing homosexual and that the criminal prohibition violated rights guaranteed to him by the Constitution. The Court, in an opinion by Justice White, sustained the Georgia law. Chief Justice Burger and Justice Powell joined the opinion of the Court and filed separate, concurring opinions. Four Justices dissented.

. . .

In academic writings, and in many of the scholarly *amicus* briefs filed to assist the Court in this case, there are fundamental criticisms of the historical premises relied upon by the majority and concurring opinions in *Bowers*. . . . We need not enter this debate in the attempt to reach a definitive historical judgment, but the following considerations counsel against adopting the definitive conclusions upon which *Bowers* placed such reliance.

At the outset it should be noted that there is no longstanding history in this country of laws directed at homosexual conduct as a distinct matter. Beginning in colonial times there were prohibitions of sodomy derived from the English criminal laws passed in the first instance by the Reformation Parliament of 1533. The English prohibition was understood to include relations between men and women as well as relations between men and men. See, *e.g.*, *King v. Wiseman*, 92 Eng. Rep. 774, 775 (K. B. 1718) (interpreting "mankind" in Act of 1533 as including women and girls). Nineteenth-century commentators similarly read American sodomy, buggery, and crime-against-nature statutes as criminalizing certain relations between men and women and between men and men. . . . The absence of legal prohibitions focusing on homosexual conduct may be explained in part by noting that according to some scholars the concept of the homosexual as a distinct category of person did not emerge until the late 19th century. See, *e.g.*, J. Katz, The Invention of Heterosexuality 10 (1995); J. D'Emilio & E. Freedman, Intimate Matters: A History of Sexuality in America 121 (2d ed. 1997) ("The modern terms *homosexuality* and *heterosexuality* do not apply to an era that had not yet articulated these distinctions"). Thus early American sodomy laws were not directed at homosexuals as such but instead sought to prohibit nonprocreative sexual activity more generally. This does not suggest approval of homosexual conduct. It does tend to show that this particular form of conduct was not thought of as a separate category from like conduct between heterosexual persons.

Laws prohibiting sodomy do not seem to have been enforced against consenting adults acting in private. A substantial number of sodomy prosecutions and convictions for which there are surviving records were for predatory acts against those who could not or did not consent, as in the case of a minor or the victim of an assault. As to these, one purpose for the prohibitions was to ensure there would be no lack of coverage if a predator committed a sexual assault that did not constitute rape as defined by the criminal law.

. . .

In summary, the historical grounds relied upon in *Bowers* are more complex than the majority opinion and the concurring opinion by Chief Justice Burger indicate. Their historical premises are not without doubt and, at the very least, are overstated.

. . .

Of even more importance, almost five years before *Bowers* was decided the European Court of Human Rights considered a case with parallels to *Bowers* and to today's case. An adult male resident in Northern Ireland alleged he was a practicing homosexual who desired to engage in consensual homosexual conduct. The laws of Northern Ireland forbade him that right. He alleged that he had been questioned, his home had been searched, and he feared criminal prosecution. The court held that the laws proscribing the conduct were invalid under the European Convention on Human Rights. *Dudgeon v. United Kingdom*, 45 Eur. Ct. H. R. (1981) ¶52.

Authoritative in all countries that are members of the Council of Europe (21 nations then, 45 nations now), the decision is at odds with the premise in *Bowers* that the claim put forward was insubstantial in our Western civilization.

In our own constitutional system the deficiencies in *Bowers* became even more apparent in the years following its announcement. The 25 States with laws prohibiting the relevant conduct referenced in the *Bowers* decision are reduced now to 13, of which 4 enforce their laws only against homosexual conduct. In those States where sodomy is still proscribed, whether for same-sex or heterosexual conduct, there is a pattern of nonenforcement with respect to consenting adults acting in private. The State of Texas admitted in 1994 that as of that date it had not prosecuted anyone under those circumstances.

. . .

In explaining the respect the Constitution demands for the autonomy of the person in making these choices, we stated as follows: "These matters, involving the most intimate and personal choices a person may make in a lifetime, choices central to personal dignity and autonomy, are central to the liberty protected by the Fourteenth Amendment. At the heart of liberty is the right to define one's own concept of existence, of meaning, of the universe, and of the mystery of human life. Beliefs about these matters could not define the attributes of personhood were they formed under compulsion of the State." Persons in a homosexual relationship may seek autonomy for these purposes, just as heterosexual persons do. The decision in *Bowers* would deny them this right.

. . .

To the extent *Bowers* relied on values we share with a wider civilization, it should be noted that the reasoning and holding in *Bowers* have been rejected elsewhere. The European Court of Human Rights has followed not *Bowers* but its own decision in *Dudgeon v. United Kingdom*. See *P. G. & J. H. v. United Kingdom*, App. No. 00044787/98, ¶56 (Eur. Ct. H. R., Sept. 25, 2001); *Modinos v. Cyprus*, 259 Eur. Ct. H. R. (1993); *Norris v. Ireland*, 142 Eur. Ct. H. R. (1988). Other nations, too, have taken action consistent with an affirmation of the protected right of homosexual adults to engage in intimate, consensual conduct. See Brief for Mary Robinson et al. as *Amici Curiae* 11-12. The right the petitioners seek in this case has been accepted as an integral part of human freedom in many other countries. There has been no showing that in this country the governmental interest in circumscribing personal choice is somehow more legitimate or urgent.

. . .

Bowers was not correct when it was decided, and it is not correct today. It ought not to remain binding precedent. *Bowers v. Hardwick* should be and now is overruled.

The present case does not involve minors. It does not involve persons who might be injured or coerced or who are situated in relationships where consent might not easily be refused. It does not involve public conduct or prostitution. It does not involve whether the government must give formal recognition to any relationship that homosexual persons seek to enter. The case does involve two adults who, with full and mutual consent from each other, engaged in sexual practices common to a homosexual lifestyle. The petitioners are entitled to respect for their private lives. The State cannot demean their existence or control their destiny by making their private sexual conduct a crime. Their right to liberty under the Due Process Clause gives them the full right to engage in their conduct without intervention of the government. "It is a promise of the Constitution that there is a realm of personal liberty which the government may not enter." *Casey*, supra, at 847. The Texas statute furthers no legitimate state interest which can justify its intrusion into the personal and private life of the individual.

Had those who drew and ratified the Due Process Clauses of the Fifth Amendment or the Fourteenth Amendment known the components of liberty in its manifold possibilities, they might have been more specific. They did not presume to have this insight. They knew times can blind us to certain truths and later generations can see that laws once thought necessary and proper in fact serve only to oppress. As the Constitution endures, persons in every generation can invoke its principles in their own search for greater freedom.

The judgment of the Court of Appeals for the Texas Fourteenth District is reversed, and the case is remanded for further proceedings not inconsistent with this opinion. It is so ordered.

. . .

JUSTICE SCALIA, with whom THE CHIEF JUSTICE and JUSTICE THOMAS join, dissenting.

"Liberty finds no refuge in a jurisprudence of doubt." *Planned Parenthood of Southeastern Pa. v. Casey*, 505 U. S. 833, 844 (1992). That was the Court's sententious response, barely more than a decade ago, to those seeking to overrule *Roe v. Wade*, 410 U. S. 113 (1973). The Court's response today, to those who have engaged in a 17-year crusade to overrule *Bowers v. Hardwick*, 478 U. S. 186 (1986), is very different. The need for stability and certainty presents no barrier.

Most of the rest of today's opinion has no relevance to its actual holding—that the Texas statute "furthers no legitimate state interest which can justify" its application to petitioners under rational-basis review. *Ante*, at 18 (overruling *Bowers* to the extent it sustained Georgia's anti-sodomy statute under the rational-basis test). Though there is discussion of "fundamental proposition[s]," *ante*, at 4, and "fundamental decisions," *ibid.* nowhere does the Court's opinion declare that homosexual sodomy is a "fundamental right" under the Due Process Clause; nor does it subject the Texas law to the standard of review that would be appropriate (strict scrutiny) if homosexual sodomy *were* a "fundamental right." Thus, while overruling the *outcome* of *Bowers*, the Court leaves strangely untouched its central legal conclusion: "[R]espondent would have us announce . . . a fundamental right to engage in homosexual sodomy. This we are quite unwilling to do." 478 U. S., at 191. Instead the Court simply describes petitioners' conduct as "an exercise of their liberty"—which it undoubtedly is—and proceeds to apply an unheard-of form of rational-basis review that will have far-reaching implications beyond this case. *Ante*, at 3.

I

I begin with the Court's surprising readiness to reconsider a decision rendered a mere 17 years ago in *Bowers v. Hardwick*. I do not myself believe in rigid adherence to *stare decisis* in constitutional cases; but I do believe that we should be consistent rather than manipulative in invoking the doctrine. Today's opinions in support of reversal do not bother to distinguish—or indeed, even bother to mention—the paean to *stare decisis* coauthored by three Members of today's majority in *Planned Parenthood v. Casey*. There, when *stare decisis* meant preservation of judicially invented abortion rights, the widespread criticism of *Roe* was strong reason to *reaffirm* it:

> "Where, in the performance of its judicial duties, the Court decides a case in such a way as to resolve the sort of intensely divisive controversy reflected in *Roe*[,] . . . its decision has a dimension that the resolution of the normal case does not carry. . . . [T]o overrule under fire in the absence of the most compelling reason . . . would subvert the Court's legitimacy beyond any serious question." 505 U. S., at 866–867.

Today, however, the widespread opposition to *Bowers*, a decision resolving an issue as "intensely divisive" as the issue in *Roe*, is offered as a reason in favor of *overruling* it. See *ante*, at 15–16. Gone, too, is any "enquiry" (of the sort conducted in *Casey*) into whether the decision sought to be overruled has "proven 'unworkable,'" *Casey, supra*, at 855.

Today's approach to *stare decisis* invites us to overrule an erroneously decided precedent (including an "intensely divisive" decision) *if*: (1) its foundations have been "eroded" by subsequent decisions, *ante*, at 15; (2) it has been subject to "substantial and continuing" criticism, *ibid.*; and (3) it has not induced "individual or societal reliance" that counsels against overturning, *ante*, at 16. The problem is that *Roe* itself—which today's majority surely has no disposition to overrule—satisfies these conditions to at least the same degree as *Bowers*.

. . .

It seems to me that the "societal reliance" on the principles confirmed in *Bowers* and discarded today has been overwhelming. Countless judicial decisions and legislative enactments have relied on the ancient proposition that a governing majority's belief that certain sexual behavior is "immoral and unacceptable" constitutes a rational basis for regulation. See, e.g., *Williams v. Pryor*, 240 F. 3d 944, 949 (CA11 2001) (citing *Bowers* in upholding Alabama's prohibition on the sale of sex toys on the ground that "[t]he crafting and safeguarding of public morality . . . indisputably is a legitimate government interest under rational basis scrutiny"); *Milner v. Apfel*, 148 F. 3d 812, 814 (CA7 1998) (citing *Bowers* for the proposition that "[l]egislatures are permitted to legislate with regard to morality . . . rather than confined to preventing demonstrable harms"); *Holmes v. California Army National Guard* 124 F. 3d 1126, 1136 (CA9 1997) (relying on *Bowers* in upholding the federal statute and regulations banning from military service those who engage in homosexual conduct); *Owens v. State*, 352 Md. 663, 683, 724 A. 2d 43, 53 (1999) (relying on *Bowers* in holding that "a person has no constitutional right to engage in sexual intercourse, at least outside of marriage"); *Sherman v. Henry*, 928 S. W. 2d 464, 469–473 (Tex. 1996) (relying on *Bowers* in rejecting a claimed constitutional right to commit adultery). We ourselves relied extensively on *Bowers* when we concluded, in *Barnes v. Glen Theatre, Inc.*, 501 U. S. 560, 569 (1991), that Indiana's public indecency statute furthered "a substantial government interest in protecting order and morality," *ibid.*, (plurality opinion);

. . .

State laws against bigamy, same-sex marriage, adult incest, prostitution, masturbation, adultery, fornication, bestiality, and obscenity are likewise sustainable only in light of *Bowers'* validation of laws based on moral choices. Every single one of these laws is called into question by today's decision; the Court makes no effort to cabin the scope of its decision to exclude them from its holding. . . . The impossibility of distinguishing homosexuality from other traditional "morals" offenses is precisely why *Bowers* rejected the rational-basis challenge. "The law," it said, "is constantly based on notions of morality, and if all laws representing essentially moral choices are to be invalidated under the Due Process Clause, the courts will be very busy indeed."

JUSTICE THOMAS dissenting. I join JUSTICE SCALIA'S dissenting opinion.

I write separately to note that the law before the Court today "is . . . uncommonly silly." *Griswold v. Connecticut*, 381 U. S. 479, 527 (1965) (Stewart, J., dissenting). If I were a member of the Texas Legislature, I would vote to repeal it. Punishing someone for expressing his sexual preference through noncommercial consensual conduct with another adult does not appear to be a worthy way to expend valuable law enforcement resources.

Notwithstanding this, I recognize that as a member of this Court I am not empowered to help petitioners and others similarly situated. My duty, rather, is to "decide cases 'agreeably to the Constitution and laws of the United States.'" *Id.*, at 530. And, just like Justice Stewart, I "can find [neither in the Bill of Rights nor any other part of the Constitution a] general right of privacy," *ibid.*, or as the Court terms it today, the "liberty of the person both in its spatial and more transcendent dimensions," *ante*, at 1.

 Recall what you learned in this chapter by completing the Chapter Review.

Notes

Chapter 1

1. Aileen S. Kraditor, *Means and Ends in American Abolitionism: Garrison and His Critics on Strategy and Tactics, 1834–1850* (New York: Pantheon Books, 1969).

2. John Higham, *Strangers in the Land: Patterns of American Nativism 1860–1925*, second edition (New Brunswick, NJ: Rutgers University Press, 2002).

Chapter 2

1. Daniel K. Richter, *Before the Revolution: America's Ancient Past* (Cambridge, MA: Belknap Press of Harvard University Press, 2011).

2. Rhode Island, *Records of the Colony of Rhode Island and Providence Plantations in New England*, Vol. 1, 1636–1663 (Providence, RI: A. Crawford Greene and Brother, 1856), 184–185.

3. Danby Pickering, ed., *The Statutes at Large from the Thirty-Ninth Year of Q. Elizabeth to the Twelfth Year of K. Charles II, Inclusive*, Vol. 7 (Cambridge: Bentham & Bathurst, 1763), 30–37.

4. William Quigley, "Work or Starve: Regulation of the Poor in Colonial America," *University of San Francisco Law Review* 31 (Fall 1996): 41.

5. Katherine D. Hardwick, *As Long as Charity Shall Be a Virtue: Boston Private Charities from 1657 to 1800* (Boston: Massachusetts Charitable Society, 1964), 5.

6. Thomas J. Scharf and Westcott Thompson, *History of Philadelphia, 1609–1884* (Philadelphia: L. H. Everts, 1884), 1452–1453.

7. Raymond A. Mohl, "Poverty in Early America, a Reappraisal," *New York History* 50, no. 1 (January 1969): 19.

8. David Hackett Fischer, "Growing Old in America," *Aging, the Individual and Society: Readings in Social Gerontology*, ed. Jill Quadagno (New York: St. Martin's Press, 1980), 34–45.

9. Carl N. Degler, *At Odds: Women and the Family in America from the Revolution to the Present* (Oxford: Oxford University Press, 1980), 194.

10. Edith Abbott, *Women in Industry: A Study in American Economic History* (New York: D. Appleton, 1909), 21.

11. Massachusetts, *Acts and Laws, passed by the Great and General Court or Assembly of His Majesty's Province of the Massachusetts-Bay in New-England* (Boston: Kneeland and Glenn, 1754).

12. Quoted in Abbott, *Women in Industry*, 33.

13. Milton T. Rolla, *Household Manufacturers in the United States, 1640–1860* (Chicago: University of Chicago Press, 1919), 6.

14. Virginia, *The Statutes at Large: Being a Collection of All the Laws of Virginia from the First Session of the Legislature in the Year 1619*, Vol. 1 Act 27 (New York: Piser and Russell, Printer, 1846), 336.

15. Massachusetts, *Records of the Governor and Company of the Massachusetts Bay in New England*, Vol. 2 (Boston: William White, 1853–1854), 6.

16. Massachusetts, *Acts and Resolves, Public and Private, of the Province of the Massachusetts Bay*, Vol. 1 (1703) (Boston: Wright and Potter, 1869), 538–539.

17. Quoted in Marcus Wilson Jernegan, *Laboring and Dependent Classes in Colonial America, 1607–1783* (Chicago: University of Chicago Press, 1931), 98–99.

18. Ibid., 102, 233–234.

19. Robert E. Cray Jr., *Paupers and Poor Relief in New York City and Its Rural Environs, 1790–1830* (Philadelphia: Temple University Press, 1988), 42–43.

20. Ibid., 79–81.

21. Massachusetts, *Acts and Resolves*, Chapter 28, section 7 (1692–1693). Quoted in John Cummings, "Poor Laws of Massachusetts and New York: With Appendices Containing the United States Immigration and Contract-Labor Laws," *Publications of the American Economic Association* 10, no. 4 (July 1895): 27.

22. Jill S. Quadagno, "Policies toward the Elderly," *Old Age in a Bureaucratic Society*, ed. David Van Tassel and Peter N. Stearns (Westport, CT: Greenwood Press, 1986), 129–136.

23. Scharf and Thompson, *History of Philadelphia*, 1450.

24. Gary B. Nash, "Poverty and Poor Relief in Pre-Revolutionary Philadelphia," *William and Mary Quarterly*, third series, 33 (January 1976), 12–13.

25. Raymond A. Mohl, *Poverty in New York: 1783–1825* (New York: Oxford University Press, 1971), 57.

26. Ibid., 42.

27. Pennsylvania, "An Act for the Relief of the Poor," *Statutes at Large of Pennsylvania*, Vol. 2, chap. 154 (1705–1706): 251.

28. Mohl, *Poverty in New York*, 57.

29. Ibid., 42.

30. David J. Rothman, *The Discovery of the Asylum* (Boston: Little, Brown, 1971).

31. Richter, *Before the Revolution*. See also Francis Jennings, *The Invasion of America: Indians, Colonialism, and the Cant of Conquest* (New York: W. W. Norton, 1976).

32. Cotton Mather, "A Letter [An Horrid Snow]," in *American Poetry and Prose*, ed. Norman Foerster (New York: Houghton Mifflin, 1934), 79–80.

33. Jeannette Nichols and Roy F. Nichols, *The Growth of American Democracy* (New York: Appleton-Century, 1939), 16.

34. U.S. Department of Commerce, Bureau of the Census, *Historical Statistics of the United States: Colonial Times to 1957* (Washington, DC: Government Printing Office, 1960), 756.

35. Merrill Jensen, ed., *English Historical Documents: American Colonial Documents to 1776* (London: Eyre and Spottiswoode, 1955), 480.

36. David Schneider, *The History of Public Welfare in New York State, 1609–1866* (Chicago: University of Chicago Press, 1938), 87.

37. William Byrd, "The History of the Dividing Line [Life in North Carolina] [March 25, 1728]," in Foerster, *American Poetry and Prose*, 87–92.

38. Letter to Richard Jackson, May 5, 1753, in *The Writings of Benjamin Franklin*, Vol. 3, *1750–1759*, ed. Albert Henry Smith (New York: Macmillan, 1907), 134–135, 137.

39. "Essay on the Labouring Poor," in *The Writings of Benjamin Franklin*, Vol. 5, 124–125.

40. Joseph Townsend, "A Dissertation on the Poor Laws by a Well-Wisher to Mankind," in *A Select Collection of Scarce and Valuable Economic Tracts*, ed. J. R. McCulloch (London: Lord Overstone, 1859), 397–449.

41. U.S. Congress, *Medical Care of Veterans*, 90th Cong., 1st sess. (April 17, 1967), 21.

42. Ibid., 28.

Chapter 3

1. James Madison, "Vices of the Political System of the United States," *The Papers of James Madison*, Vol. 9 (Chicago: University of Chicago Press, 1975), 351.

2. Page S. Smith, *The Shaping of America: A People's History of the Young Republic*, Vol. 3 (New York: McGraw-Hill, 1980), 50–94; Charles A. Beard and Mary R. Beard, *A Basic History of the United States* (New York: The New Home Library, 1944), 209–214; Roger Daniels, *Coming to America: A History of Immigration and Ethnicity in American Life* (New York: HarperCollins, 1990), 114.

3. U.S. Department of Commerce, Bureau of the Census, *Historical Statistics of the United States: Colonial Times to 1957* (Washington, DC: Government Printing Office, 1960; hereafter cited as *Historical Statistics*).

4. David Hackett Fischer, "Growing Old in America," *Aging, the Individual and Society: Readings in Social Gerontology*, ed. Jill Quadagno (New York: St. Martin's Press, 1980), 34–45.

5. Daniels, *Coming to America*, 112–118, 268–270.

6. Edward C. Kirkland, *A History of American Economic Life* (New York: F. S. Crofts, 1941), 144.

7. *Historical Statistics*, 302.

8. Walter W. Jennings, *A History of Economic Progress in the United States* (New York: Thomas Y. Crowell, 1926), 759.

9. Vernon Louis Parrington, *Main Currents in American Thought, Vol. 2, The Romantic Revolution in America* (New York: Harcourt, Brace, 1930), 104.

10. Jennings, *History of Economic Progress*, 153.

11. Ibid., 166.

12. For a detailed description of the boarding house system, see Vera Shlakman, *Economic History of a Factory Town*, (Northampton, MA: Smith College, Department of History, 1935).

13. Jennings, *History of Economic Progress*, 303.

14. For an interesting discussion of this point, see Thomas Dublin, *Women at Work* (New York: Columbia University Press, 1979).

15. *Historical Statistics*, 14.

16. S. E. Forman, *The Rise of American Commerce and Industry* (New York: The Century, 1927), 195, 471.

17. Jennings, *History of Economic Progress*, 295–310. See also Philip S. Foner, *History of the Labor Movement in the United States* (New York: International Publishers, 1947), 143–166.

18. Nick Salvatore, *Eugene V. Debs: Citizen and Socialist* (Urbana: University of Illinois Press, 1982), 23–24.

19. Mary Ryan, *Cradle of the Middle Class: The Family in Oneida County, New York, 1790-1865* (Cambridge and New York: Cambridge University Press, 1981).

20. Horace Mann, *Education and Prosperity*, Old South Leaflet No. 144 (Boston: Directors of Old South Work, Old South Meeting House, 1848), 6.

21. Smith, *Shaping of America*, 197.

22. Jeannette Nichols and Roy F. Nichols, *The Growth of American Democracy* (New York: Appleton-Century, 1939), 182.

23. "Pastoral Letter of the General Association of Massachusetts to the Congregational Churches under Their Care," reprinted in *The Liberator*, August 11, 1837.

24. For an in-depth study of drinking in the United States during the early decades of the 19th century, see W. J. Rorabaugh, *The Alcoholic Republic* (New York: Oxford University Press, 1979).

25. Ibid., 8–9.

26. Judith Papachristou, *Women Together: A History in Documents of the Women's Movement in the United States* (New York: Knopf, 1976), 19.

27. Ibid., 20. On the history of the temperance movement, see Joseph R. Gusfield, *Symbolic Crusade: Status Politics and the American Temperance Movement* (Urbana: University of Illinois Press, 1963).

28. Dorothea L. Dix, *Memorial, Praying a Grant of Land for the Relief and Support of the Indigent Curable and Incurable Insane*

in the United States." In Dorothea L. Dix, *Poverty, U.S.A., On Behalf of the Insane Poor* (New York: Arno Press, 1971), 213.

29. Ibid., 25.

30. President Franklin Pierce, "Veto Message—An Act Making a Grant of Public Lands to the Several States for the Benefit of Indigent Insane Persons," May 3, 1854, http://www.presidency.ucsb.edu/ws/?pid=67850.

31. John V. N. Yates, *Report of the Secretary of State on the Relief and Settlement of the Poor*. Reprinted in *Poverty, U.S.A., the Almshouse Experience* (New York: Arno Press, 1971), 942.

32. B. J. Klebaner, "Public Poor Relief in America 1790–1860" (PhD diss., Columbia University, 1952), 329.

33. Thomas Paine, *The Rights of Man*, in *Basic Writings of Thomas Paine* (New York: Wiley, 1942), 253. Italics in original.

34. Mathew Carey, *Appeal to the Wealthy of the Land, Ladies as Well as Gentlemen, on Character, Conduct, Situation and Prospects of Those Whose Sole Dependence for Subsistence Is on the Labour of Their Hands* (Philadelphia: Stereotyped by L. Johnson, 1833), 3–34.

35. Ibid.

36. Josiah Quincy, *Report of the Committee to Whom Was Referred the Consideration of the Pauper Laws of This Commonwealth*. Reprinted in *Poverty, U.S.A., the Almshouse Experience*, 7.

37. The Society for the Prevention of Pauperism in the City of New York, *The First Annual Report, to Which Is Added a Report on the Subject of Pauperism* (New York: J. Seymour, 1818), 3.

38. Ibid., 16.

39. Ibid., 18.

40. Ibid., 12.

41. Ibid., 5.

42. Quincy, *Report of the Committee*, 9.

43. Ibid., 10.

44. Yates, *Report*, 941–942.

45. Ibid., 955.

46. Sophonisba Breckinridge, ed., *Public Welfare Administration in the United States* (Chicago: University of Chicago Press, 1927), 149.

47. Klebaner, "Public Poor Relief in America," 73–74, 86, 89; David J. Rothman, *The Discovery of the Asylum* (Boston: Little, Brown, 1971), 180–205.

48. Grace Abbott, *The Child and the State*, Vol. 2 (Chicago: University of Chicago Press, 1938), 29.

49. Homer Folks, *The Care of Destitute, Neglected and Delinquent Children* (New York: Macmillan, 1911), 52–55.

50. Rothman, *Discovery of the Asylum*, 215.

51. Rothman, *Discovery of the Asylum*, 214.

52. Abbott, *Child and the State*, 357–361.

53. Robert A. Bremner, *From the Depths: The Discovery of Poverty in the United States* (New York: New York University Press, 1956), 39.

54. Folks, *Care of Destitute*, 41.

55. Edith Abbott, *Some American Pioneers in Social Welfare: Select Documents with Editorial Notes* (Chicago: University of Chicago Press, 1937), 132.

56. Charles Loring Brace, *The Dangerous Classes in New York* (New York: Wynkoop and Hallenbeck, 1880), 224–266.

57. Ibid.

58. Henry W. Thurston, *The Dependent Child* (New York: Columbia University Press, 1930), 121.

59. Breckinridge, *Public Welfare Administration*, 149.

60. Ibid., 150.

61. Ibid., 154.

62. Ibid., 153–154.

63. Ibid., 152.

64. Ibid, 142.

65. Michael B. Katz, *In the Shadow of the Poorhouse* (New York: Basic Books, 1986), 16–19.

66. Klebaner, "Public Poor Relief in America," 73–74; Rothman, *Discovery of the Asylum*, 287–295.

Chapter 4

1. U.S. Department of Commerce, Bureau of the Census, *Historical Statistics of the United States: Colonial Times to 1957* (Washington, DC: Government Printing Office, 1960), 7, 143 (hereafter cited as *Historical Statistics*).

2. S. E. Forman, *The Rise of American Commerce and Industry* (New York: Century, 1927), 317.

3. *Historical Statistics*, 7.

4. An excellent overview of this process is presented in the video production series *500 Nations* by Jack Leustig, *The Attack on Culture*, Vol. 8 (Burbank, CA: TIG Productions, 1994).

5. Quoted in John Rhea Dulles, *The United States Since 1865* (Ann Arbor: University of Michigan Press, 1971), 41.

6. *Historical Statistics*, 56–57.

7. Roger Daniels, *Coming to America: A History of Immigration and Ethnicity in American Life* (New York: HarperCollins, 1990), 265–284.

8. Richard Hofstadter, *Social Darwinism in American Thought* (Boston: Beacon Press, 1955).

9. Walter W. Jennings, *A History of Economic Progress in the United States* (New York: Thomas Y. Crowell, 1926), 380; Lawrence Goodwyn, *Democratic Promise: The Populist Moment in America* (New York and Oxford: Oxford University Press, 1976).

10. Forman, *Rise of American Commerce*, 471.

11. *Historical Statistics*, 14.

12. Alexander Keyssar, *Out of Work: The First Century of Unemployment in Massachusetts* (New York: Cambridge University Press, 1986).

13. Jennings, *History of Economic Progress*, 409.

14. *Historical Statistics*, 302.

15. Ibid., 297.

16. Ibid., 546.

17. Ibid., 139.

18. Forman, *Rise of American Commerce*, 481.

19. *Historical Statistics*, 139.

20. Jennings, *History of Economic Progress*, 447.

21. Brian Gratton, "The New History of the Aged: A Critique," *Old Age in a Bureaucratic Society*, ed. David van Tassel and Peter N. Stearns (Westport, CT: Greenwood Press, 1986), 17.

22. Michael B. Katz, *Poverty and Policy in American History* (New York: Academic Press, 1983), 76; Seamus Metress, "The History of Irish-American Care of the Aged," *Social Service Review* 59, no. 1 (March 1985): 24.

23. Michael B. Katz, *In the Shadow of the Poorhouse* (New York: Basic Books, 1986), 87.

24. Robinson E. Adkins, 90th Congress, 1st session. House Committee Print. no. 4. *Medical Care of Veterans* (Washington, DC: Government Printing Office, 1967), 49.

25. Ibid., 52.

26. U.S. Sanitary Commission, *Documents of the U.S. Sanitary Commission* (New York: US Sanitary Commission, 1862). Document No. 49.

27. Charles J. Stille, *History of the United States Sanitary Commission* (Philadelphia: Lippincott, 1866), 524.

28. U.S. Sanitary Commission, *The Sanitary Commission of the United States Army: A Succinct Narrative of the Works and Purposes* (New York: Sanitary Commission, 1864).

29. Stille, *History of the United States Sanitary Commission*, 82.

30. U.S. Sanitary Commission, *Documents of the U.S. Sanitary Commission*, Document No. 4042.

31. U.S. Congress, H. R. Report No. 45, 41st Cong., 3rd sess. (1871).

32. Knowlton Durham, *Billions for Veterans* (New York: Brewer, Warren and Putnam, 1932), 25–26.

33. The President's Commission on Veterans' Pensions, *The Historical Development of Veterans' Benefits in the United States*, H.R. Report on Veterans' Benefits in the United States, 84th Cong., 2nd sess., No. 244, (May 9, 1956), 17–18.

34. State of New York, "An Act to Provide for the Relief of Indigent Soldiers, Sailors and Marines, and the Families of Those Deceased," *General Statutes of the State of New York* (Albany: Weed, Parsons and Company, 1888), 58–59.

35. Theda Skocpol, *Protecting Soldiers and Mothers: The Political Origins of Social Policy in the United States* (Cambridge, MA: Belknap Press of Harvard University Press, 1992), 102–152.

36. William Miller, *A New History of the United States* (New York: Braziller, 1958), 219.

37. Elizabeth Wisner, *Social Welfare in the South* (Baton Rouge: Louisiana State University Press, 1970), 107.

38. George R. Bentley, *A History of the Freedmen's Bureau* (New York: Octagon, 1970); Leon F. Litwack, *Been in the Storm So Long: The Aftermath of Slavery* (New York: Knopf, 1979).

39. President Andrew Johnson, "Veto Message, the Freedmen's Bureau," *Andrew Johnson, His Life and Speeches*, ed.

Lillian Foster (New York: Richardson and Company, 1866), http://teachingamericanhistory.org/library/document/veto-of-the-freedmens-bureau-bill/.

40. Eric Foner, *Reconstruction: America's Unfinished Revolution, 1863–1877* (New York: Harper and Row, 1988).

41. New York Association for Improving the Condition of the Poor, *Thirty-Second Annual Report 1875* (New York, 1875), 367.

42. Jeannette Nichols and Roy F. Nichols, *The Growth of American Democracy* (New York: Appleton-Century, 1939), 450.

43. Russell H. Conwell, *Acres of Diamonds* (Philadelphia: Temple University Press, 1959), 18–19.

44. American Association of Social Sciences, Department of Social Economy, "Pauperism in the City of New York," *Journal of Social Sciences* 6 (1874), 74–85.

45. Mrs. Charles Russell (Josephine Shaw) Lowell, "The Economic and Moral Effects of Public Outdoor Relief," *Proceedings of the National Conference of Charities and Corrections* (1890), 81–91.

46. Community Service Society of New York, *Frontiers in Human Welfare: The Story of a Hundred Years of Service to the Community of New York, 1848–1948* (New York: Community Service Society of New York, 1948), 35.

47. Katz, *In the Shadow of the Poorhouse*, 184–186.

48. The Reverend Oscar C. McCulloch, "The Tribe of Ishmael, a Study in Social Degradation," *Proceedings of the National Conference of Charities and Corrections* (1888), 154–159.

49. Amos Griswold Warner, *American Charities* (New York: Thomas Y. Crowell, 1894), 36–63.

50. Katz, *In the Shadow of the Poorhouse*, 49–50.

51. Fred H. Wines, "Causes of Pauperism and Crime," *Proceedings of the National Conference of Charities and Corrections* (1886), 207–214.

52. Franklin B. Sanborn, "Indoor and Outdoor Relief," *Proceedings of the National Conference of Charities and Corrections* (1890), 73–80.

53. Charles D. Kellogg, "Charity Organization in the United States: A Report of the Committee on History of Charity Organization," *Proceedings of the National Conference of Charities and Corrections* (1893), 72.

54. Ibid., 82.

55. Ibid., 93.

56. Jane Addams et al., *Philanthropy and Social Progress* (New York: T.Y. Crowell, 1893), 135.

57. Frank D. Watson, *The Charity Organization Movement in the United States* (New York: Macmillan, 1922), 215, 225–226.

58. Judith Papachristou, *Women Together: A History in Documents of the Women's Movement in the United States* (New York: Knopf, 1976), 143–144.

59. Zilpha D. Smith, "Report of the Committee on the Organization of Charity," *Proceedings of the National Conference of Charities and Corrections* (1888), 120–130.

60. Kellogg, *Charity Organization in the United States*, 52–93.

61. Allen F. Davis, *Spearheads for Reform: The Social Settlements and the Progressive Movement, 1890–1914* (New York: Oxford University Press, 1967).

62. Humphreys S. Gurteen, *A Handbook of Charity Organization* (Buffalo, NY: Courier, 1882), 120–123.

63. Jane Addams, "Social Settlements," *Proceedings of the National Conference of Charities and Corrections* (1897), 339.

64. State of Illinois, "*An Act to Regulate the Treatment and Control of Dependent, Neglected, and Delinquent Children,*" *Laws of the State of Illinois* 131 (1899), http://homicide.northwestern.edu/docs_fk/homicide/laws/ill_juvenile_court_act_1899.pdf.

65. New York, State Board of Charities, *Eighth Annual Report* (Albany, NY: Weed, Parsons, and Company, 1875).

66. New York, "An Act to Provide Better Care of Pauper and Destitute Children," Laws of the State of New York (Albany, NY: Charles Van Benthuysen and Sons, 1875).

67. Anne B. Richardson, "Massachusetts Institutions: Supplementary Work in the Care of Dependent and Delinquent Children," *Proceedings of the National Conference of Charities and Corrections* (1886), 131–138.

68. Warner, *American Charities*, 99.

69. Commonwealth of Pennsylvania, *Report of the Commissioners of Public Charities for the Year 1882*, Legislative Document No. 5 (Harrisburg, PA: Edwin K. Myers, 1882).

70. Michael Barga, "Children's Aid Society of Pennsylvania (1882–present)," *The Social Welfare History Project*, http://www.socialwelfarehistory.com/programs/child-welfarechild-labor/childrens-aid-society-of-pennsylvania/.

71. Charles S. Hoyt, "The Causes of Pauperism," *Extract from the Tenth Annual Report of the State Board of Charities of the State of New York* (Albany, NY: J. B. Parmenter, 1877).

72. Board of Commissioners of Public Charities of the State of Pennsylvania, *Fourteenth Annual Report*, 1883, 2.

73. Henry W. Thurston, *The Dependent Child* (New York: Columbia University Press, 1930).

74. Ibid., 191–192.

75. Homer Folks, *The Care of Destitute, Neglected and Delinquent Children* (New York: Macmillan, 1911), 80.

76. Andrew Sinclair, *The Better Half: The Emancipation of the American Woman* (New York: Harper & Row, 1965), 194.

77. *Historical Statistics*, 49.

78. Ibid., 22. See also Ernest R. Groves, *The American Woman: The Feminine Side of a Masculine Civilization* (New York: Arno Press, 1972), 112.

79. Papachristou, *Women Together*, 90.

80. Frances E. Willard, *Woman and Temperance, or Work of the Woman's Christian Temperance Union* (Hartford, CT: Park, 1884), 457–459.

81. Ibid.

82. Sheila M. Rothman, *Woman's Proper Place: A History of Changing Ideals and Practices* (New York: Basic Books, 1978), 26–42, 97–132.

83. Papachristou, *Women Together*, 88–97.

84. Sharlene J. Hesse, *Working Women and Families* (Beverly Hills, CA: Sage, 1979), 42.

85. Joan D. Mandle, *Women and Social Change in America* (Princeton, NJ: Princeton Book Company, 1979), 23.

86. U.S. Department of Labor, Women's Bureau, *1969 Handbook on Women Workers*, Bulletin No. 294 (Washington, DC: Government Printing Office, 1969); *Historical Statistics*, 132–133.

87. Edith Abbott, *Women in Industry: A Study in American Economic History* (New York: D. Appleton, 1909), 123.

88. "Discussion on Charity Organization," *Proceedings of the National Conference of Charities and Corrections 1888*, 420.

89. Forman, *Rise of American Commerce*, 337.

90. Terence V. Powderly, *Proceedings of the General Assembly, 1882*, 278. Quoted in Philip S. Foner, *History of the Labor Movement in the United States*, Vol. 1 (New York: International Publishers, 1947), 508.

91. Nick Salvatore, *Eugene V. Debs: Citizen and Socialist* (Urbana: University of Illinois, 1982).

92. Ewan Clague, *The Bureau of Labor Statistics* (New York: Praeger, 1968), 8.

93. Forman, *Rise of American Commerce*, 292.

94. Goodwyn, *Democratic Promise*.

Chapter 5

1. Herbert Hoover, *The New Day* (Stanford, CA: Stanford University Press, 1928), 16.

2. S. E. Forman, *The Rise of American Commerce and Industry* (New York: Century, 1927), 369.

3. U.S. Department of Commerce, Bureau of the Census, *Historical Statistics of the United States: Colonial Times to 1957* (Washington, DC: Government Printing Office, 1960), 414 (hereafter cited as *Historical Statistics*); Robert J. Gordon, *The Rise and Fall of American Growth: The U.S. Standard of Living Since the Civil War* (Princeton, NJ: Princeton University Press, 2016).

4. Forman, *Rise of American Commerce*, 442.

5. *Historical Statistics*, 139.

6. Ibid., 14.

7. U.S. Bureau of the Census, *Fourteenth Census of the United States: 1920*, Vol. 3, 15; *Fifteenth Census of the United States: 1930*, Vol. 2, 27.

8. *Historical Statistics*, 14.

9. Alfred D. Chandler, *The Visible Hand: The Managerial Revolution in American Business* (Cambridge, MA: Belknap Press of Harvard University Press, 2002); Arthur R. Burns, *The Decline of Competition* (New York: McGraw-Hill, 1936).

10. U.S. Commission on Industrial Relations, *Final Report* (Washington, DC: Government Printing Office, 1915), 8.

11. U.S. Bureau of the Census, *Sixteenth Census of the United States: 1940*, *Comparative Occupation Statistics for the United States, 1870 to 1940*, 93.

12. Robert Hunter, *Poverty* (New York: Grosset & Dunlap, 1904), 2–7, 56–65, 76–88, 96–97, 350–351, reprinted in *Poverty and Social Welfare in the United States*, ed. Roy Lubove (New York: Holt, Rinehart & Winston, 1972), 7–18; John A. Ryan, *A Living Wage: Its Ethical and Economic Aspects* (New York: Macmillan, 1910), 123–177. Ryan estimated the minimum "living wage" at more than $900 for the large Eastern cities.

13. *Historical Statistics 73*, 409.

14. Ibid., 278.

15. Slaughterhouse Cases, 16 Wallace 36, 1873, Opinion of Justice Samuel Miller, U.S. Supreme Court; Steven Hahn, *A Nation Under Our Feet: Black Political Struggles in the Rural South from Slavery to the Great Migration* (Cambridge, MA: Belknap Press of Harvard University Press, 2003).

16. C. Vann Woodward, *The Strange Career of Jim Crow* (New York: Oxford University Press, 1957).

17. *Plessy v. Ferguson*, 163 U.S. 537 (1896).

18. William Miller, *A New History of the United States* (New York: Braziller, 1958), 355–356.

19. Louis R. Harlan, ed., *The Booker T. Washington Papers*, Vol. 1 (Urbana: University of Illinois Press, 1972), 333.

20. Woodward, *Strange Career of Jim Crow*.

21. Lillian Brandt, "The Make-up of Negro City Groups," *Charities and the Commons* 15 (October 7, 1905): 7.

22. *Historical Statistics*, 46. New York, Pennsylvania, Ohio, Illinois, and Michigan accounted for 78 percent of this.

23. Thomas L. Philpott, *The Slum and the Ghetto: Immigrants, Blacks, and Reformers in Chicago, 1880–1930* (Belmont, CA: Wadsworth Publishing, 1991).

24. Phyllis J. Day, *A New History of Social Welfare* (Englewood Cliffs, NJ: Prentice Hall, 1989), 247.

25. Roger Daniels, *Coming to America: A History of Immigration and Ethnicity in American Life* (New York: HarperCollins, 1990), 114.

26. U.S. Department of Homeland Security, *Yearbook of Immigration Statistics*. https://www.dhs.gov/yearbook-immigration-statistics (accessed May 9, 2016).

27. Daniel J. Tichenor, *Dividing Lines: The Politics of Immigration Control in America* (Princeton, NJ: Princeton University Press, 2002).

28. Daniels, *Coming to America*.

29. Theda Skocpol, *Protecting Soldiers and Mothers: The Political Origins of Social Policy in the United States* (Cambridge, MA: Harvard University Press, 1992).

30. Arthur Miles, *An Introduction to Public Welfare* (Washington, DC: Heath, 1947), 124.

31. Theodore Roosevelt, "Reform Through Social Work," *McClure's Magazine*, Vol. 26 (March 1901): 448–454.

32. Arthur S. Link, *American Epoch: A History of the United States Since the 1890's* (New York: Knopf, 1955), 68.

33. Sidney Lens, *Poverty: America's Enduring Paradox* (New York: Thomas Y. Crowell, 1969), 212.

34. Charles Faulkner, "Twentieth Century Alignments for the Promotion of Social Order," *Proceedings of the National Conference of Charities and Corrections 1900*, 2–6.

35. Mary E. Richmond, "The Family and the Social Worker," *Proceedings of the National Conference of Charities and Corrections: 1908*, 76–79.

36. U.S. Bureau of the Census, *Sixteenth Census of the United States: 1940 Population* (Washington, DC: Government Printing Office, 1943), 93, 100.

37. National Child Labor Committee, *The Child Labor Bulletin 3*, No. 1, (May 1914).

38. Owen R. Lovejoy, "Report of the Committee on Standards of Living and Labor," *Proceedings of the National Conference of Charities and Corrections: 1912*, 386.

39. U.S. 37 stat. 79, approved April 7, 1912.

40. *Hammer v. Dagenhart*, 247 U.S. Reports 251, 268 (June 1918), to be found in Grace Abbott, *The Child and the State* (Chicago: University of Chicago Press, 1938), 495–506.

41. "State Child-Labor Standards, January 1, 1930," a chart prepared by the U.S. Department of Labor, Children's Bureau, and reprinted by permission of the Federal Board for Vocational Education (Washington, DC: Government Printing Office, 1930), chart no. 2.

42. United States Bureau of the Census, *Fifteenth Census of the United States: 1930*, Vol. 2, 1180–1196.

43. Lovejoy, "Report of the Committee on Standards of Living and Labor," 383.

44. Edward C. Kirkland, *A History of American Economic Life* (New York: Appleton-Century-Crofts, 1969), 409.

45. Paul H. Douglas, *Real Wages in the United States, 1890–1926* (Boston: Houghton Mifflin, 1930), 208.

46. George Soule, *American Economic History* (New York: Dryden Press, 1957), 277.

47. Douglas, *Real Wages in the United States*, 112–114.

48. Ibid., 384.

49. An excellent review of this history may be found in Clarke A. Chambers, *Seedtime of Reform* (Minneapolis: University of Minnesota Press, 1963), 151–182.

50. Roy Lubove, *The Struggle for Social Security 1900–1935* (Pittsburgh, PA: University of Pittsburgh Press, 1986).

51. Clarke A. Chambers, *Paul U. Kellogg and the Survey* (Minneapolis: University of Minnesota Press, 1971), 36.

52. Special message by the President of the United States to the Senate and House of Representatives, "Conclusions of the White House Conference Meeting of 1909," reprinted in Committee on Socially Handicapped—Dependency and Neglect, *Dependent and Neglected Children* (New York: Appleton-Century, 1933), 56.

53. Abbott, *The Child and the State*, Vol. 2, 332, 395.

54. Sheila M. Rothman, *Woman's Proper Place: A History of Changing Ideals and Practices* (New York: Basic Books, 1978).

55. Alice Higgins, "Helping Widows to Bring Up Citizens," *Proceedings, NCCC: 1910*, 140.

56. Skocpol, *Protecting Soldiers and Mothers*, 424–479; Gwendolyn Mink, *The Wage of Motherhood: Inequality in the Welfare State, 1917–1942* (Ithaca, NY: Cornell University Press, 1995).

57. Mary E. Richmond, "Public Pensions to Widows—Discussion," *Proceedings, NCCC: 1912*, 492–493.

58. Ibid.

59. Frederic Almy, "Public Pensions to Widows: Experiences and Observations Which Lead Me to Oppose Such a Law," *Proceedings, NCCC: 1912*, 482.

60. Abbott, *The Child and the State*, Vol. 2, 229.

61. U.S. Department of Labor, Children's Bureau, *Administration of Mother's Aid in Ten Localities*, Children's Bureau Publication No. 184 (Washington, DC: Government Printing Office, 1928), 4, 25–26.

62. C. C. Carstens, "Discussion" of Emma O. Lundberg's "The Present Status of Mother's Pension Administration," *Proceedings, National Conference of Social Work: 1921*, 230–240.

63. Mary F. Bogue, *Administration of Mother's Aid in Ten Localities: With Special Reference to Health, Housing, Education and Recreation*, Children's Bureau Publication No. 184 (Washington, DC: Government Printing Office, 1928), 5.

64. J. S. Parker, *Social Security Reserves* (Washington, DC: American Council on Public Affairs, 1942).

65. *Historical Statistics*, 139, 723.

66. "The Negroes in the Cities of the North," *Charities and the Commons* 15 (October 7, 1905).

67. W. E. Burghardt Du Bois, "National Committee on the Negro," *The Survey* 22 (June 12, 1909): 407–408; and Du Bois, "National Negro Conference," *The Survey* 24 (April 23, 1910): 124.

68. George Burman Foster, "The Status and Vocation of Our Colored People"; George Edmund Haynes, "The Basis of Race Adjustment"; W. E. B. DuBois, "Social Effects of Emancipation"; Ida B. Wells-Barnett, "Our Country's Lynching Record"; Sophonisba Breckinridge, "The Color Line in the Housing Problem"; and George Packard, "A Civic Problem and a Social Duty," all in *The Survey* 29 (February 1, 1913): 567–581.

69. Franz Boas, "The Negro and the Demands of Modern Life: Ethnic and Anatomical Considerations," *Charities and the Commons* 15 (October 7, 1905): 2.

70. Steven Diner, "Chicago Social Workers and Blacks in the Progressive Era," *Social Service Review*, 44 (December 1970): 393–410.

71. All material dealing with the expansion of benefits to veterans in the Progressive and pre-Depression eras is based on information to be found in U.S. Congress, House Committee Print No. 4, *Medical Care of Veterans*, 90th Cong., 1st sess. (April 17, 1967).

72. U.S. Congress, Congressional Research Service, *Veterans Affairs: Presumptive Service Connection and Disability Compensation* (Washington, DC: Congressional Research Service, 2010), 4.

73. Roy Lubove, *The Professional Altruist: The Emergence of Social Work as a Career, 1880–1930* (New York: Atheneum, 1969).

74. Alexander Johnson, *A Guide to the Study of Charities and Correction by Means of the Proceedings of the National Conference of Charities and Corrections: Using Thirty-four Volumes, 1874–1907* (Indianapolis, IN: National Conference of Charities and Corrections, 1908), http://hdl.handle.net/2027/mdp.39015050938961.

75. George A. Bellamy, "The Culture of the Family from the Standpoint of Recreation," *Proceedings, National Conference of Charities and Corrections, 1914* (Fort Wayne, IN: Fort Wayne Printing Company, 1914), 104–105.

76. Arthur Kennedy, ed., *Settlement Goals for the Next Third of a Century: A Symposium* (Boston: National Federation of Settlements, 1926), 45.

77. Porter R. Lee, "Social Work: Cause and Function," *Proceedings, National Conference of Social Work: 1929*, 20.

78. An interesting analysis of the development of social work may be found in Stanley Wenocur and Michael Reisch, *From Charity to Enterprise: The Development of American Social Work in a Market Economy* (Urbana and Chicago: University of Illinois Press, 1989).

79. Mink, *The Wage of Motherhood*.

80. George J. Sanchez, *Becoming Mexican American: Ethnicity, Culture, and Identity in Chicano Los Angeles, 1900–1945* (Oxford and New York: Oxford University Press, 1993).

81. Lens, *Poverty: America's Enduring Paradox*, 209–210; Nick Salvatore, *Eugene V. Debs: Citizen and Socialist* (Urbana: University of Illinois, 1982).

82. Lincoln Steffens, *The Shame of the Cities* (New York: McClure, Phillips, 1904); David Graham Phillips, "The Treason of the Senate," *Cosmopolitan* 40 (March 1906): 603–610.

83. Alice Stone Blackwell, "Editorial," *The Woman's Journal* (April 11, 1911).

84. U.S. Department of Labor, Women's Bureau, *Handbook on Women Workers*, Bulletin No. 294 (Washington, DC: Government Printing Office, 1969); *Historical Statistics*, 132–133.

85. Annie Marion MacLean, *Wage-Earning Women* (New York: Macmillan, 1919), 178.

86. Hoover, *The New Day*.

87. Jane Addams, *The Second Twenty Years at Hull House* (New York: Macmillan, 1930), 10–48.

88. Robert Fisher, *Let the People Decide: Neighborhood Organizing in America* (New York: Twayne Publishing, 1994), 1–31.

89. Emil Frankel, *Poor Relief in Pennsylvania: A State-Wide Survey of Pennsylvania* (Commonwealth of Pennsylvania: By the Public Board of Welfare, 1925), 65–66.

90. Margaret E. Rich, *A Belief in People: A History of Family Social Work* (New York: Family Service Association of America, 1956), 74.

Chapter 6

1. Maurice Leven, Harold G. Moulton, and Clark Warburton, *America's Capacity to Consume* (Washington, DC: Brookings Institution, 1934).

2. Frederick Lewis Allen, *Only Yesterday* (New York: Bantam, 1959), 241.

3. U.S. Department of Commerce, Office of Business Economics, *The National Income and Product Accounts of the United States, 1929–1965—Statistical Tables* (Washington, DC: Government Printing Office, 1966).

4. U.S. Department of Commerce, Bureau of the Census, *Historical Statistics of the United States: Colonial Times to 1957* (Washington, DC: Government Printing Office, 1960), 73 (hereafter cited as *Historical Statistics*).

5. William H. Matthews, "Breaking the Poverty Circle," *The Survey 52* (April 15, 1924): 96–98.

6. Lucille Eaves, "Studies of Breakdowns in Family Income," *The Family 10* (December 1929): 228.

7. Ibid., 227.

8. Marion Elderton, ed., *Case Studies of Unemployment* (Philadelphia: University of Pennsylvania Press, 1931), xxiv.

9. Ibid.

10. *Historical Statistics*, 141.

11. Ibid., 283.

12. U.S. Department of Agriculture, Economic Research Service, *The Farm Income Situation* (July 1958).

13. *Historical Statistics*, 7, 47.

14. Dayton Duncan, *The Dust Bowl: An Illustrated History* (San Francisco: Chronicle Books, 2012).

15. *Historical Statistics*, 278.

16. Ibid.

17. U.S. Department of Commerce, Bureau of the Census, *Statistical Abstract of the United States* (Washington, DC: Government Printing Office, 1969), Table 892, 590.

18. *Historical Statistics*, 283, 286.

19. Ibid., 278.

20. Phyllis J. Day, *A New History of Social Welfare* (Englewood Cliffs, NJ: Prentice Hall, 1989), 300.

21. Committee on Economic Security, Social Security in America, *The Factual Background of the Social Act as Summarized from Staff Reports for the Committee* (Washington, DC: Government Printing Office, 1937), 229.

22. E. Wright Bakke, *The Unemployed Man: A Social Study* (New York: E. P. Dutton and Company, 1934), xxiii–xxiv.

23. S. Breckinridge, "The Activities of Women Outside the Home," in *Recent Social Trends in the United States: Report of the President's Research Committee on Social Trends*, Vol. 1 (New York: McGraw-Hill, 1933), 711–717.

24. *Historical Statistics*, 23.

25. Ibid., 30.

26. Caroline Bird, *The Invisible Scar* (New York: David McKay, 1966), 41–70.

27. Joan Hoff Wilson, *Herbert Hoover: Forgotten Progressive* (Boston: Little Brown, 1975).

28. U.S. 72nd Cong., 1st sess., Public Law No. 72-2 (1932).

29. 47 Stat. 1932, 709.

30. Elderton, *Case Studies of Unemployment*, xlix.

31. U.S. Congress, House, *Platforms of the Two Great Political Parties, 1932* (Washington, DC: Government Printing Office, 1945), 335, 340, 343.

32. William Leuchtenberg, *Franklin D. Roosevelt and the New Deal* (New York: Harper & Row, 1963), 11.

33. President Franklin D. Roosevelt, "Acceptance of the Nomination for the Presidency," Chicago, Illinois, July 2, 1932, in *The Pubic Papers and Addresses of Franklin D. Roosevelt*, Vol. 2, ed. S. I. Rosenan (New York: Russell and Russell, 1969), 647–659.

34. Anne O'Hare McCormick, "Vast Tides That Stir the Capital," *New York Times Magazine*, May 7, 1933. Also found in Frank Freidel, ed., *The New Deal and the American People* (Englewood Cliffs, NJ: Prentice Hall, 1964), 5.

35. *Historical Statistics*, 409, 473.

36. Gordon Hamilton, "Refocusing Family Casework," *Proceedings: National Conference of Social Work: 1931*, 176.

37. Joanna C. Colcord, "Unemployment Relief, 1929–32," *The Family 13* (December 1932): 270–274.

38. U.S. Federal Emergency Relief Administration, *Monthly Report*, May 22–June 30, 1933, 1–2.

39. U.S. Federal Emergency Relief Administration, *Final Statistical Report* (Washington, DC: Government Printing Office, 1942).

40. A. F. Kifer, "The Negro Under the New Deal: 1933–1941" (PhD diss., University of Wisconsin, 1961).

41. Harry L. Hopkins, "The Developing National Program of Relief," *Proceedings: NCSW*, 1933, 65–67, 71.

42. President Franklin D. Roosevelt, "Annual Message to Congress," January 4, 1935, in *Public Papers and Addresses of Franklin D. Roosevelt*, Vol. 4 (New York: Random House, 1938), 15–25.

43. Ibid., 43–46.

44. Ibid., 15–25.

45. Ibid.

46. William Hodson, "Unemployment Relief," in *Social Work Year Book: 1937* (New York: Russell Sage Foundation, 1937), 522.

47. Helen Seymour, *When Clients Organize* (Chicago: American Public Welfare Association, 1937), 16–17.

48. U.S. Federal Emergency Relief Administration, *Monthly Report*, 7.

49. Ibid., 10.

50. Hopkins, "Developing National Program," 68.

51. Ibid., 69.

52. United States, Committee on Economic Security, *Report of the Committee on Economic Security* (Washington, DC: Government Printing Office, 1935), 3.

53. Ibid., 25.

54. Ibid., 44.

55. United States, President, *Message of the President Recommending Legislation on Economic Security* (Washington, DC: Government Printing Office, 1935), 43–46.

56. U.S. 74th Cong., 1st sess., Public Law No. 271.

57. Michael K. Brown, *Race, Money, and the American Welfare State* (New York: Cornell University Press, 1999).

58. James T. Patterson, *America's Struggle Against Poverty in the Twentieth Century* (Cambridge, MA: Harvard University Press, 2000).

59. *Report of the Committee on Economic Security*, 36.

60. U.S. Congress, Senate, Committee on Finance, *Statement of Miss Katherine F. Lenroot, Hearings on S. 1130, The Economic Security Act*, January 22 to February 20, 1935, revised, 337–341.

61. U.S. Congress, Senate, Committee on Finance, *Statement of Mr. Jacob Kepecs, Hearings on H.R. 4120, The Economic Security Act*, January 1935, 500–503.

62. *Statement of Miss Katherine F. Lenroot*, 337–341; *Statement of Mr. Jacob Kepecs*, 500–503.

63. Edwin Witte, *The Development of the Social Security Act, a Memorandum on the History of the Committee on Economic Security and Drafting and Legislative History of the Social Security Act* (Madison: University of Wisconsin Press, 1962), 164.

64. Mary S. Labaree, "Unmarried Parenthood under the Social Security Act," *Journal of Progressive Human Services* 6 no. 2 (November 2, 1995): 73–76.

65. Ibid., 78.

66. American Association of Social Workers, "This Business of Relief," in *Proceedings of the Delegate Conference, Washington, D.C.*, (New York: AASW, 1936).

67. Aubrey Williams, "The Works Progress Administration," *AASW Proceedings* (1936). 128, 137.

68. Ewan Clague, "The Social Security Act as a Relief Measure," *AASW Proceedings* (1936), 78–82.

69. Dorothy C. Kahn, "The Use of Cash, Orders for Goods, or Relief in Kind, in a Mass Program," *Proceedings: NCSW* (1933), 273.

70. Harry L. Hopkins, *Spending to Save* (New York: W. W. Norton, 1936), 81.

71. *Report of the Committee on Economic Security*, 30.

72. Ibid., 239.

73. Family Welfare Association of America, "The Crisis in Community Programs" (March 1936), unpublished manuscript.

74. Ibid.

75. Family Welfare Association of America, Committee on Relationship between Family and Children's Work, "Preliminary Report" (November 1937), unpublished manuscript.

76. Frank J. Hertel, "Family Social Work," *Social Work Year Book, 1951* (New York: American Association of Social Workers, 1951), 187.

77. U.S. Congress, House Committee Print No. 4, Medical Care of Veterans, 90th Cong., 1st sess. (April 17, 1967), 154–155.

78. D. H. Fischer, *Growing Old in America* (New York: Oxford University Press, 1978).

79. Arthur S. Link, *American Epoch: A History of the United States Since the 1890's* (New York: Knopf, 1955), 347; David Brody, *Workers in Industrial America: Essays on the Twentieth Century Struggle* (New York: Oxford University Press, 1980), 48–81.

80. Link, *American Epoch*, 395.

81. Frances Fox Piven and Richard A. Cloward, *Poor People's Movements: Why They Succeed, How They Fail* (New York: Random House, 1977), 41–95.

82. Piven and Cloward, *Poor People's Movements*, 96–180; David Montgomery, *Workers' Control in America: Studies in the History of Work, Technology, and Labor Struggles* (Cambridge and New York: Cambridge University Press, 1980), 153–180.

83. U.S. Congress, Senate, Committee on Education and Labor, 74th Cong., 1st sess., *Hearings on Senate Resolution 266*; and 75th Cong., 1st sess., *Hearings on Senate Resolution 60*.

84. Link, *American Epoch*, 431–432.

85. Dixon Wecter, *The Age of the Great Depression: 1929–1941* (New York: Macmillan, 1948), 119–120.

86. National Urban League, "The Negro in the Industrial Depression: Negroes Out of Work," *Nation* (April 22, 1931), 441–442.

87. Bruce Minton and John Stuart, *Men Who Lead Labor* (New York: Modern Age, 1937), 167.

88. Stanley Wenocur and Michael Reisch, *From Charity to Enterprise: The Development of American Social Work in a Market Economy* (Urbana: University of Illinois Press, 1989), 182–207.

89. *Historical Statistics*, 71.

90. Quoted in William H. Chafe, *The American Woman* (New York: Oxford University Press, 1972), 107.

91. Ibid., 283.

92. *Historical Statistics*, 72.

93. Ira Katznelson, *When Affirmative Action Was White: An Untold Story of Racial Inequality in Twentieth-Century America* (New York: W. W. Norton, 2005).

94. Gail Radford, *Modern Housing for America: Policy Struggles in the New Deal Era* (Chicago: University of Chicago Press, 1996), 7–28.

95. Ibid.

96. Katznelson, *When Affirmative Action Was White*.

97. *Helvering v. Davis*, 301 U.S. 619 (1937).

98. National Conference on Social Welfare, *Proceedings, 1934*, and *Proceedings, 1936* (Chicago: University of Chicago Press, 1934 and 1936).

Chapter 7

1. United States, President, *Economic Report of the President: 1974, Together with the Annual Report of the Council of Economic Advisers* (Washington, DC: Government Printing Office, 1974), 249, 259.

2. Ibid.

3. U.S. Bureau of the Census, *Statistical Abstract of the United States: 1973*, 94th ed. (Washington, DC: Government Printing Office, 1973), 328.

4. U.S. Bureau of the Census, *Current Population Reports*, Series P-60, no. 77 (Washington, DC: Government Printing Office, 1971).

5. *Economic Report of the President: 1974*, 276.

6. For a good discussion, see *Economic Report of the President: 1973* (Washington, DC: Government Printing Office, 1973), 89–112.

7. U.S. Bureau of the Census, *Statistical Abstract of the United States 2012*, Table 588, https://www.census.gov/prod/2011pubs/12statab/labor.pdf.

8. Authors' calculation using Steven Ruggles, J. Trent Alexander, Katie Genadek, Ronald Goeken, Matthew B. Schroeder, and Matthew Sobek, *Integrated Public Use Microdata Series: Version 5.0* [machine-readable database] (Minneapolis: University of Minnesota, 2010).

9. *Economic Report of the President: 1974*, 219.

10. Roger Daniels, *Coming to America: A History of Immigration and Ethnicity in American Life* (New York: HarperCollins, 1990), 288; U.S. Bureau of the Census, *Statistical Abstract 1992*, 113th ed. (Washington, DC: Government Printing Office, 1992), 10.

11. Daniels, *Coming to America*, 311.

12. David S. Wyman, *Abandonment of the Jews: America and the Holocaust: 1941–1945* (New York: Pantheon Books, 1984), 136.

13. *Statistical Abstract: 1973*, 51; U.S. Department of Commerce, Bureau of the Census, *Historical Statistics of the United States: Colonial Times to 1957* (Washington, DC: Government Printing Office, 1960), 23 (hereafter cited as *Historical Statistics*).

14. *Statistical Abstract: 1973*, 58–59.

15. Phyllis J. Day, *A New History of Social Welfare* (Englewood Cliffs, NJ: Prentice Hall, 1989), 367.

16. *Statistical Abstract: 1973*, 30, 31.

17. U.S. Bureau of the Census, *Current Population Reports*, Series P 23, no. 29 (February 1970).

18. Ibid.

19. U.S. Bureau of Economic Analysis, *Long Term Economic Growth, 1860–1970* (Washington, DC: Government Printing Office, 1973), 76.

20. *Statistical Abstract: 1973*, 585.

21. *Vital Statistics of the United States*, 1942, 1947.

22. *Statistical Abstract: 1973*, 54.

23. Nathan E. Cohen, *Social Work in the American Tradition* (New York: Dryden Press, 1958), 226.

24. National Commission on Productivity, *Second Annual Report* (Washington, DC: Government Printing Office, 1973), 8.

25. U.S. Bureau of Economic Analysis, *Long Term Economic Growth*, 76.

26. *Statistical Abstract: 1973*, 250.

27. Ibid.

28. Mark J. Stern, "Poverty and Family Composition," in *The "Underclass" Debate: Views from History*, ed. Michael B. Katz (Princeton, NJ: Princeton University Press, 1993), 220–253.

29. *Historical Statistics*, 167.

30. *Economic Report of the President: 1974*, 272.

31. Executive Order 8802 of June 25, 1941, Vol. 6, *Federal Register*, 3109.

32. George J. Sanchez, *Becoming Mexican American: Ethnicity, Culture, and Identity in Chicano Los Angeles, 1900–1945* (New York: Oxford University Press, 1993), 261–267.

33. John Hope Franklin, *From Slavery to Freedom* (New York: Vintage, 1969), 573–607; Geoffrey Perrett, *Days of Sadness, Years of Triumph: The American People, 1939–1945* (New York: Coward, McCann, and Geoghegan, 1973), 143–154, 310–324.

34. Day, *New History*, 360.

35. U.S. Congress, House Committee Print No. 4, *Medical Care of Veterans*, 90th Cong., 1st sess., April 17, 1967, 168.

36. National Association of Social Workers, *Encyclopedia of Social Work* (New York: NASW, 1971), 554.

37. U.S. Bureau of the Census, *Statistical Abstract of the United States 1948* (Washington, DC: Government Printing Office, 1948), 246–247.

38. Lowell J. Carr, *Willow Run: A Study of Industrialization and Cultural Inadequacy* (New York: Harper, 1952).

39. Russell H. Kurtz, ed., *Social Work Yearbook: 1945* (New York: Russell Sage Foundation, 1945), pp. 84–92, 163, 479–485, 502, 505.

40. Day, *New History*, 322–323.

41. Nelson Lichtenstein, "From Corporatism to Collective Bargaining: Organized Labor and the Eclipse of Social Democracy in the Postwar Era," in *The Rise and Fall of the New Deal Order, 1930–1980*, ed. Steve Fraser and Gary Gerstle (Princeton, NJ: Princeton University Press, 1989), 140–144.

42. Thomas J. Sugrue, "The Structures of Urban Poverty: The Reorganization of Space and Work in Three Periods of American History," in Katz, *The "Underclass" Debate*, 85–117.

43. U.S. Congress, Public Law No. 625, 77th Cong., 2nd sess., June 23, 1942.

44. Russell H. Kurtz, ed., *Social Work Yearbook: 1947* (New York: Russell Sage Foundation, 1947), 414.

45. United States, President's Commission on Veterans' Pensions, *The Historical Development of Veterans' Benefits in the United States, a Report on Veterans' Benefits in the United States*, 84th Cong., 2nd sess., House Committee Print No. 244 (May 9, 1956), 57.

46. U.S. President's Commission on Veterans' Pensions, *Historical Development*, 53.

47. Ibid., 55.

48. *Historical Statistics*, 740.

49. Winifred Bell, *Aid to Dependent Children* (New York: Columbia University Press, 1965).

50. Man-in-the-house rules and durational residence requirements were finally eliminated by *King v. King*, 392 U.S. 309

(1968), and by *Shapiro v. Thompson*, 364 U.S. 618 (1969), respectively.

51. "New York: The Welfare City," *Time*, July 28, 1961. http://www.time.com/time/magazine/article/0,9171,938174,00.html.

52. John Kenneth Galbraith, *The Affluent Society* (Boston: Houghton Mifflin, 1958).

53. Michael Harrington, *The Other America: Poverty in the United States* (New York: Macmillan, 1962); Dwight MacDonald, "Our Invisible Poor," *New Yorker* (January 19, 1963): 37.

54. United States, President, *Economic Report of the President: 1964, Together with the Annual Report of the Council of Economic Advisers* (Washington, DC: Government Printing Office, 1964), 55–83.

55. U.S. Bureau of the Census, *Statistical Abstract of the United States: 1964* (Washington, DC: Government Printing Office, 1964); U.S. Bureau of the Census, *Statistical Abstract of the United States: 1971* (Washington, DC: Government Printing Office, 1971).

56. Office memorandum, Abraham Ribicoff to W. L. Mitchell, commissioner of Social Security, December 6, 1961, in U.S. Congress, House Committee on Ways and Means, *Hearings on H.R. 10032, Public Welfare Amendments of 1962*, 87th Cong., 2nd sess. (February 7, 9, and 13, 1962), 158–162.

57. George K. Wyman, "A Report for the Secretary of Health, Education, and Welfare," August 1961, in *Hearings on H.R. 10032, Public Welfare Amendments*, 108.

58. United States, Department of Health, Education, and Welfare, *Report of the Ad Hoc Committee on Public Welfare to the Secretary of Health, Education, and Welfare* (Washington, DC: Government Printing Office, 1961).

59. Office memorandum, Abraham Ribicoff to W. L. Mitchell, commissioner of Social Security, December 6, 1961, reprinted in J. B. Hames and Yvonne Ekern, *Legal Research, Analysis, and Writing*, fifth edition (New York: Pearson, 2014).

60. United States, Congress, House Committee on Ways and Means, *Message from the President of the United States Relative to a Public Assistance and Welfare Program* (1962). 12459 H. doc. 325.

61. U.S. Congress, House of Representatives, *Compilation of the Social Security Laws, including the Social Security Act, as Amended, and Related Enactments through December 31, 1962*, House Document No. 616, 87th Cong., 2nd sess., 132.

62. Gilbert Steiner, *Social Insecurity* (Chicago: Rand McNally, 1966), 142–147.

63. American Public Welfare Association, "Statement Submitted to the Advisory Council on Public Welfare," (August 12, 1965), 6.

64. Herman Levin, "The Essential Voluntary Agency," *Social Work* 11, no. 1 (January 1966): 98–106.

65. U.S. Congress, *Compilation of the Social Security Laws*, Title IV, Sec. 403, 136.

66. U.S. Department of Health, Education, and Welfare, Social Security Administration, Bureau of Family Services, press release (January 6, 1963).

67. Oscar Lewis, "The Culture of Poverty," *Society* 35, no. 2 (January–February 1998): 7.

68. United States, President Lyndon B. Johnson, "Message on Poverty," March 16, 1964.

69. U.S. 88th Cong., 2nd sess., Public Law 88-452, Sec. 2.

70. U.S. Senate Committee on Labor and Public Welfare, *The War on Poverty: The Economic Act of 1964, a Compilation of Materials Relevant to S. 2642, prepared for the Select Subcommittee on Poverty of the U.S. Senate Committee on Labor and Public Welfare*, 88th Cong., 2nd sess., Document No. 86, (July 23, 1964), 65.

71. Thomas F. Jackson, "The State, the Movement, and the Urban Poor: The War on Poverty and Political Mobilization in the 1960s," in Katz, *The "Underclass" Debate*, 403–439.

72. Frances Fox Piven and Richard Cloward, *Poor People's Movement: How They Succeed, Why They Fail* (New York: Random House, 1977), 264–362.

73. June Axinn, "Social Security: History and Prospects," *Current History* 65, no. 384 (August 1973): 52–56.

74. John B. Williamson, Linda Evans, and Lawrence A. Powell, *The Politics of Aging* (Springfield, IL: Charles B. Thomas, 1982), 89–101; Robert H. Binstock, "The Politics of Aging Interest Groups," in *The Aging in Politics*, ed. Robert D. Hudson (Springfield, IL: Charles B. Thomas, 1981), 52–71.

75. U.S. Department of Health, Education, and Welfare, Welfare Administration, *Having the Power, We Have the Duty*, report of the Advisory Council on Public Welfare to the Secretary of HEW (Washington, DC: Government Printing Office, 1976).

76. Gilbert Steiner, *The State of Welfare* (Washington, DC: Brookings Institution, 1971), 109.

77. U.S. Department of Health, Education, and Welfare, "Report of the Task Force in Social Services," September 1, 1966.

78. National Association of Social Workers, *Washington Memorandum*, No. 90-1-9, August 30, 1967.

79. National Association of Social Workers, *Policy Statement on Separation of Social Services and Income Security Programs*, June 29, 1967.

80. David Lucander, *Winning the War for Democracy: The March on Washington Movement, 1941–46* (Urbana: University of Illinois Press, 2014).

81. Joni Hersch and Jennifer Bennett Shinall, "Fifty Years Later: The Legacy of the Civil Rights Act of 1964," *Journal of Policy Analysis and Management* 34, no. 2 (Spring 2015): 424–456;

82. Lindsy Van Gelder, "The Truth About Bra-burners," *Ms* 3:2 (September 1992): 80.

83. *In re Gault*. 387 U.S. 1 (1967).

Chapter 8

1. Gilbert Y. Steiner, *The Children's Cause* (Washington, DC: Brookings Institution, 1976), 113.

2. All data on social welfare expenditures in this chapter are from U.S. Social Security Administration, *Social Security*

Bulletin 52, no. 11 (1989), and *Social Security Bulletin* 53, no. 12 (1990), unless otherwise indicated. Poverty data are from U.S. Bureau of the Census, *Current Population Reports*, Series P-60, *Characteristics of the Population Below the Poverty Level*, selected years. Data on the income of households, families, and persons are from U.S. Bureau of the Census, *Current Population Reports*, Series P-60, *Money Income of Households, Families and Persons in the U.S.*, selected years.

3. U.S. Bureau of Economic Analysis, *The National Income and Product Accounts of the United States: 1929–1982*.

4. For an analysis of the changes in the distribution of income and wealth during this period, see Kevin Phillips, *The Politics of Rich and Poor* (New York: Random House, 1990).

5. William Baumol and Alan S. Binder, *Macroeconomics: Principles and Policy*, 7th ed. (New York: The Dryden Press, 1998), 118.

6. U.S. Department of Labor, Bureau of Labor Statistics, *Employment and Earnings*, January issues.

7. All demographic data in this chapter are derived from U.S. Bureau of the Census, *Current Population Reports*, Series P-20, *Population Characteristics*, selected years, unless otherwise indicated.

8. *New York Times*, July 26, 1990, A16.

9. June Axinn and Mark J. Stern, *Dependency and Poverty: Old Problems in a New World* (Lexington, MA: Lexington Books, 1988), 31–49.

10. U.S. Department of Labor, Bureau of Labor Statistics, *Employment in Perspective: Working Women*, monthly; and *Historical Statistics of the United States: Colonial Times to 1970*.

11. Robert J. Lampman, "Changing Patterns of Income, 1960–1974," in *Toward New Human Rights: The Social Policies of the Kennedy and Johnson Administrations*, ed. David Warner (Austin: University of Texas Press, 1977), 122.

12. Phyllis J. Day, *A New History of Social Welfare* (Englewood Cliffs, NJ: Prentice Hall, 1989), 366–370.

13. U.S. Bureau of the Census, "Household Wealth and Asset Ownership: 1988," *Current Population Reports*, Series P-70, No. 22 (Washington, DC: Government Printing Office, 1990).

14. Melvin L. Oliver and Thomas M. Shapiro, *Black Wealth, White Wealth: A New Perspective on Racial Inequality* (New York and London: Routledge, 1995), 69.

15. Dennis Culhane, Stephen Metraux, and Thomas Byrne, "A Prevention-Centered Approach to Homelessness Assistance: A Paradigm Shift?" *Housing Policy Debate* 21, no. 2 (2011): 295–315; Mark J. Stern, "The Emergence of Homelessness as a Public Problem," *Social Service Review* 58, no. 2 (June 1984): 291–301.

16. Cindy Patton, *Sex and Germs: The Politics of AIDS* (Boston: South End Press, 1985).

17. Edward R. Fried et al., *Setting National Priorities: The 1974 Budget* (Washington, DC: Brookings Institution, 1973), 170–232; Barry M. Blechman et al., *Setting National Priorities: The 1975 Budget* (Washington, DC: Brookings Institution, 1974), 18–42, 166–206.

18. United States, Congressional Research Service, "Cash and Noncash Benefits for Persons with Limited Income: Eligibility Rules, Recipient and Expenditure Data, FY 1988–90."

19. *Report on H.R. 1*, U.S. Congress, House Committee on Ways and Means, 92nd Cong., 1st sess., 1971, 163.

20. Christopher Leman, *The Collapse of Welfare Reform: Political Institutions, Policy, and the Poor in Canada and the United States* (Cambridge, MA: MIT Press, 1980).

21. President Richard M. Nixon, "Message on Reform in Welfare," August 11, 1969.

22. U.S. Department of Health, Education, and Welfare, *Poverty amid Plenty: The American Paradox*, report of the President's Commission on Income Maintenance Programs, November 1969.

23. Vincent J. Burke and Vee Burke, *Nixon's Good Deed: Welfare Reform* (New York: Columbia University Press, 1974).

24. Leman, *Collapse of Welfare Reform*.

25. For a detailed description of discussions of welfare reform, see Gordon L. Weil, *The Welfare Debate of 1978* (White Plains, NY: Institute for Socioeconomic Studies, 1978); Irving Garfinkel, "Welfare Reform: Two Views," *Journal/The Institute for Socioeconomic Studies* 4, no. 4 (1979): 58–72.

26. Alicia H. Munnell, ed., *Lessons from the Income Maintenance Experiments: Proceedings of a Conference Held at Melvin Village, New Hampshire* (Boston: Federal Reserve Bank of Boston, 1986).

27. Michael B. Katz, *The Price of Citizenship: Redefining the American Welfare State* (New York: Metropolitan Books, 2001), 57–75.

28. U.S. Department of Health, Education, and Welfare, *Social Security and the Changing Roles of Men and Women*, (February 1979).

29. United States, Advisory Council on Social Security, *Reports of the 1979 Advisory Council on Social Security*, 1.

30. Gilbert Y. Steiner with Pauline H. Milius, *The Children's Cause* (Washington, DC: Brookings Institution, 1976).

31. Jane Waldfogel, *The Future of Child Protection* (Cambridge, MA: Harvard University Press, 1998), 64–93.

32. United States, Advisory Council on Social Security, *1979 Report*, 91.

33. Executive Order 12335, December 16, 1981, published in *Weekly Compilation of Presidential Documents* 17 (December 21, 1981), 137–194.

34. Axinn and Stern, *Dependency and Poverty*, 121–151.

35. Jacob S. Hacker, *The Divided Welfare State: The Battle over Public and Private Social Benefits in the United States* (Cambridge and New York: Cambridge University Press, 2002), 124–178.

36. U.S. House of Representatives, Select Committee on Aging, *The President's 1986 Budget: An Assault on America's Aged and Poor*, Comm. Pub. No. 99-481 (Washington, DC: Government Printing Office, 1985).

37. John O'Connor, "US Social Welfare Policy: The Reagan Record and Legacy," *Journal of Social Policy* 27, no. 1 (January 1998): 37–61; U.S. Employment and Training Administration, *Unemployment Insurance Statistics* (Washington, DC: Government Printing Office, monthly); U.S. Department of

Labor, *Annual Report of the Secretary of Labor* (Washington, DC: Government Printing Office, annual).

38. Steven G. Anderson, Anthony P. Halter, and Brian M. Gryzlak, "Changing Safety Net of Last Resort: Downsizing General Assistance for Employable Adults," *Social Work* 47, no. 3 (July 2002): 249–258.

39. Quoted in U.S. Congress, House Committee Print No. 4, *Medical Care of Veterans*, 90th Cong., 1st sess., April 17, 1967, 255. Prepared for the use of the Committee on Veterans' Affairs.

40. Sheila B. Kamerman and Alfred J. Kahn, *Social Services in the United States: Policies and Programs* (Philadelphia: Temple University Press, 1976); Martha Derthick, *Uncontrollable Spending for Social Service Grants* (Washington, DC: Brookings Institution, 1975).

41. United States, Congressional Research Service, *Social Service Block Grant: Background and Funding* (Washington, DC: Congressional Research Service, 2016), https://www.fas.org/sgp/crs/misc/94-953.pdf.

42. Ronald Reagan, "First Inaugural Address" in *Speaking My Mind: Selected Speeches* (New York: Simon and Schuster, 1989), 59–66.

43. *Fullilove v. Klutznick*, 448 U.S. 448 (1980).

44. *Firefighters' Local Union #1784 v. Stotts*, 467 U.S. 561 (1984).

45. *Wygant v. Jackson Board of Education*, 476 U.S. 267 (1986).

46. Local Number 28, *Sheet Metal Workers' International Association v. Equal Employment Opportunity Commission*, 478 U.S. 421 (1986); Local Number 93, *International Association of Firefighters v. City of Cleveland and Cleveland Vanguards*, 478 U.S. 501 (1986). *United States v. Paradise*, 480 U.S. 149 (February 25, 1987); *Johnson v. Transportation Agency of Santa Clara County*, 480 U.S. 616 (1987).

47. *City of Richmond v. J.A. Croson Co.*, 488 U.S. 469 (1989)

48. U.S. Immigration and Naturalization Service, *Statistical Yearbook*, 1991.

49. Pastora San Juan Cafferty, Barry R. Chiswick, Andrew M. Greeley, and Teresa A. Sullivan, *The Dilemma of American Immigration Policy: Beyond the Golden Door* (New Brunswick, N.J.: Transaction Books, 1983), 3–37; Roger Daniels, *Coming to America: A History of Immigration and Ethnicity in American Life* (New York: HarperCollins, 1990), 328–349, 378–380.

50. Joseph Goldstein, Anna Freud, and Albert J. Solnit, *Beyond the Best Interest of the Child* (New York: Free Press, 1979).

51. Frances Piven and Richard Cloward, "Eroding Welfare Rights," *Civil Liberties Review* 2 (Winter–Spring 1974): 41–51; Laurie Udesky, "Welfare Reform and Its Victims," *The Nation* 251, no. 9 (September 24, 1990): 302–306.

52. *Harris v. McRae*, 448 U.S. 297 (1980).

53. U.S. General Accounting Office, *Social Security Disability* (Washington, DC: Government Printing Office, November 1989).

54. "Rights Panel Charges Programs to Help Women Actually Hurt Them; Below Poverty Level No Better Off," *New York Times*, June 20, 1974, 44, http://nyti.ms/1shIyZW.

55. U.S. Department of Justice, Task Force on Sex Discrimination, *The Pension Game: American Pension System from the Viewpoint of the American Woman* (Washington, DC: Government Printing Office, 1979).

56. U.S. Department of Labor, National Commission for Manpower Policy, *Women's Changing Roles at Home and on the Job*, Special Report No. 26 (September 1978).

57. U.S. Congress, "Social Security Financing Amendments," Public Law 95-216, Sec. 341.

58. U.S. Department of Health, Education, and Welfare, *Social Security and the Changing Roles of Men and Women* (February 1979), 4–7.

59. Advisory Council on Social Security, *1979 Report*, 91.

60. Weil, *Welfare Debate of 1978*, 98.

61. "Supplemental Security Income for the Aged, Blind, and Disabled," 42 U.S.C.S. § 1382.

62. "Social Security Disability Benefits Reform Act of 1984," Public Law 98-460, § 2(a).

Chapter 9

1. "Economic Indicators," June 2003. Prepared for the Joint Economic Committee by the Council of Economic Advisors (Washington, DC: Government Printing Office, 1999).

2. Saskia Sassen, "The Informal Economy," in *Dual City: Restructuring New York*, ed. John H. Mollenkopf and Manuel Castells (New York: Russell Sage Foundation, 1991), 79–102.

3. Kathryn Edin and Laura Lein, *Making Ends Meet: How Single Mothers Survive Welfare and Low-Wage Work* (New York: Russell Sage Foundation, 1997).

4. U.S. Census Bureau, "Money Income in the United States, 2001," *Current Population Report* 60–206 (Washington, DC: Government Printing Office, 2002).

5. David Harvey, *A Brief History of Neoliberalism* (New York: Oxford University Press, 2005); Mark Blyth, *Austerity: The History of a Dangerous Idea* (New York: Oxford University Press, 2013).

6. *New York Times*, "Credit Crisis—The Essentials," updated July 12, 2010, http://topics.nytimes.com/top/reference/timestopics/subjects/c/credit_crisis/index.html.

7. Dan Immergluck, "Too Little, Too Late, and Too Timid: The Federal Response to the Foreclosure Crisis at the Five-Year Mark," *Housing Policy Debate* 23, no. 1 (January 2013): 199–232.

8. Emmanuel Saez, "Striking It Richer: The Evolution of Top Incomes in the United States," http://elsa.berkeley.edu/~saez/saez-UStopincomes-2008.pdf.

9. U.S. Census Bureau, *Income, Poverty, and Health Insurance Coverage in the United States: 2009* (Washington, DC: Government Printing Office, 2010). http://www.census.gov/prod/2010pubs/p60-238.pdf.

10. Karen Short, "The Supplemental Poverty Measure 2014," P60-254 (September 2015), http://www.census.gov/content/dam/Census/library/publications/2015/demo/p60-254.pdf.

11. Carol J. De Vita, *The United States at Mid-Decade* (Washington, DC: Population Reference Bureau, Inc., 1996).

12. Bureau of Labor Statistics, "Labor Force Statistics Derived from the Population Survey, 1948–1987," Bulletin 2307 (August 1988).

13. Mary Rowland, "A Clearer Picture of Unpaid Leave," *New York Times*, January 29, 1995, 13.

14. U.S. Census Bureau, "U.S. Interim Projections by Age, Sex, Race, and Hispanic Origin," http://www.census.gov/ipc/www/usinterimproj/.

15. Unless otherwise specified, data on health care are from U.S. Centers for Medicare and Medicaid Statistics, http://www.cms.gov.

16. Center on Budget and Policy Priorities, "Number Without Health Insurance Remains at Record Level," October 6, 1995, 1–2.

17. Dan Froomkin, "Mock the Press," *Washington Post*, July 11, 2007, http://www.washingtonpost.com/wp-dyn/content/blog/2007/07/11/BL2007071101146_pf.html.

18. Paul Starr, *The Social Transformation of American Medicine* (New York: Basic Books, 1982).

19. Abigail Trafford and Spencer Rich, "Health Care Reform in Congress?" *Washington Post*, September 20, 1994, 12–14.

20. Families USA, "One Step Forward, One Step Back: Children's Health Coverage After CHIP and Welfare Reform," (October 1999).

21. U.S. Congress, "Mental Health Parity Act of 1996," Public Law 105-34, 111 Stat. 788 (1997).

22. "Medicare Prescription Drug, Improvement, and Modernization Act of 2003," Public Law 108-173.

23. "Health Care Reform." http://topics.nytimes.com/top/news/health/diseasesconditionsandhealthtopics/health_insurance_and_managed_care/health_care_reform/index.html (accessed November 9, 2010).

24. Mark A. Hall and Fritz Allhoff, eds. *The Affordable Care Act Decision: Philosophical and Legal Implications* (New York: Routledge, 2014).

25. Jessica C. Smith and Carla Medalia, *Health Insurance Coverage in the United States, 2014* (Washington, DC: Government Printing Office, 2015), http://census.gov/content/dam/Census/library/publications/2015/demo/p60-253.pdf.

26. Peter S. Goodman, "The New Poor: In Hard Times, Lured into Trade School and Debt," *New York Times*, March 14, 2010.

27. U.S. Census Bureau, *Statistical Abstract of the United States 1998* (Washington, DC: Government Printing Office, 1998), 312.

28. Ibid., 76.

29. Mary Jo Bane and David T. Ellwood, *Welfare Realities: From Rhetoric to Reform* (Cambridge, MA: Harvard University Press, 1994), 28–66.

30. William J. Wilson, *The Truly Disadvantaged: The Inner City, the Underclass, and Public Policy* (Chicago: University of Chicago Press, 1987), 20–62.

31. David T. Ellwood, *Poor Support: Poverty in the American Family* (New York: Basic Books, 1988), 231–244.

32. U.S. Congress, 104th Congress, "Personal Responsibility Act of 1995," H.R. 4.

33. U.S. Congress, 104th Congress, "The Personal Responsibility and Work Opportunity Reconciliation Act of 1996," Public Law 104–193.

34. U.S. Department of Health and Human Services, Temporary Assistance for Needy Families (TANF) Program, *Fifth Annual Report to Congress*, (August 2002), 20–21.

35. U.S. Department of Health and Human Services, Administration for Children and Families, "TANF—Data and Reports," http://www.acf.hhs.gov/ofa/programs/tanf/data-reports (accessed November 9, 2010).

36. U.S. Department of Health and Human Services, *Fifth Annual Report to Congress*, 132–133.

37. Richard C. Fording, Joe Soss, and Sanford F. Schram, "Devolution, Discretion, and the Effect of Local Political Values on TANF Sanctioning," *Social Service Review* 81, no. 2 (June 2007): 285–316.

38. U.S. Department of Health and Human Services, *Fifth Annual Report to Congress*, 132–133.

39. Douglas S. Massey, "March of Folly: U.S. Immigration Policy after NAFTA," *The American Prospect* 37 (March–April 1998): 22–33.

40. Randal C. Archibold, "Arizona Enacts Stringent Law on Immigration," *New York Times*, April 23, 2010.

41. Ram Cnaan, "Our Hidden Safety Net," *Brookings Review* 17, no. 2 (Spring 1999): 50.

42. Paul C. Light, "Rebuilding Trust in Charity," https://www.brookings.edu/opinions/rebuilding-trust-in-charity/ (accessed November 22, 2010).

43. Lester M. Salamon, "The Marketization of Welfare: Changing Nonprofit and For-Profit Roles in the American Welfare State," *Social Service Review* 67 (March 1993): 32.

44. Amy D'Andrade and Jill Duerr Berrick, "When Policy Meets Practice: The Untested Effects of Permanency Reforms in Child Welfare," *Journal of Sociology and Social Welfare* 33, no. 1 (March 2006): 31–52; Jane Waldfogel, *The Future of Child Protection: How to Break the Cycle of Abuse and Neglect* (Cambridge, MA: Harvard University Press, 1998), 65–93.

45. Robert J. Shiller, *The New Financial Order: Risk in the 21st Century* (Princeton, NJ: Princeton University Press, 2003).

46. Jacob S. Hacker, *The Divided Welfare State: The Battle over Public and Private Social Benefits in the United States* (Cambridge and New York: Cambridge University Press, 2002).

47. "Report Warns Against Reducing Remedial Classes in Colleges," *New York Times*, February 13, 1996.

48. Fred Lucas, "GOP Senators Blast Obama 'Coercion' of Schools Through Common Core," *The Blaze*, February 5, 2014, http://www.theblaze.com/stories/2014/02/05/gop-sens-blast-obama-coercion-of-schools-through-common-core/.

49. "Schools on Reservation Crumbling for Lack of Repair Money," *New York Times*, September 3, 1995.

50. Orlando Patterson, "Affirmative Action on the Merit System," *New York Times*, August 9, 1995.

51. Robert Pear, "Report to Clinton Has a Mixed View on Minority Plans," *New York Times*, May 31 , 1995.

52. "Abortion: The Rate vs. the Debate," *New York Times*, February 25, 1996.

53. Jeffrey M. Jones, "Americans' Opposition to Gay Marriage Eases Slightly," http://www.gallup.com/poll/128291/Americans-Opposition-Gay-Marriage-Eases-Slightly.aspx (accessed November 9, 2010).

54. John Schwartz, "Highlights from the Supreme Court Decision on Same-Sex Marriage," *New York Times*, July 20, 2015, http://www.nytimes.com/interactive/2015/us/2014-term-supreme-court-decision-same-sex-marriage.html.

55. U.S. Department of Justice, Bureau of Justice Statistics, "Federal Justice Statistics, 2008—Statistical Tables," http://bjs.ojp.usdoj.gov/index.cfm?ty=pbdetail&iid=1745 (accessed November 9, 2010).

56. Craig Calhoun, "Occupy Wall Street in Perspective," *British Journal of Sociology* 64, no. 1 (March 2013): 26–38; Francis Shor, "'Black Lives Matter': Constructing a New Civil Rights and Black Freedom Movement," *New Politics* 15, no. 3 (Summer 2015): 28–32.

Credits

Photo Credits

Chapter 1

p. 1: Detroit Publishing Company Photograph Collection, Prints & Photographs Division, Library of Congress, [LC-D401-13645].
p. 5: Prints & Photographs Division, Library of Congress, [LC-USZC2-3731].

Chapter 2

p. 15: Detroit Publishing Company Photograph Collection, Prints & Photographs Division, Library of Congress, [LC-D4-13954].
p. 27: Prints & Photographs Division, Library of Congress, [LC-USZ62-50489].

Chapter 3

p. 34: 1946- Carol M. Highsmith Archive, Prints & Photographs Division, Library of Congress, [LC-DIG-highsm-13502].
p. 39: American cartoon print filing series, Prints & Photographs Division, Library of Congress, [LC-USZ62-9646].

Chapter 4

p. 77: National Archives and Records Administration.
p. 93: Charles F. Bretzman Collection, Prints & Photographs Division, Library of Congress, [LC-USZ62-83407].
p. 104: Rogers, W. A. (William Allen), Prints & Photographs Division, Library of Congress, [LC-USZ62-106101].

Chapter 5

p. 115: Lewis Wickes Hine, Prints & Photographs Division, Library of Congress, [LC-DIG-nclc-01131].
p. 137: Lewis Wickes Hine , Prints & Photographs Division, Library of Congress, [LC-DIG-nclc-05087].

Chapter 6

p. 156: National Archives and Records Administration.
p. 160: Prints & Photographs Division, Library of Congress, [LC-DIG-ppmsca-19155].
p. 161: Prints & Photographs Division, Library of Congress, [LC-DIG-ppmsca-19156].

Chapter 7

p. 205: Farm Security Administration - Office of War Information Photograph Collection, Prints & Photographs Division, Library of Congress, [LC-DIG-fsa-8e09022].

p. 213: Farm Security Administration - Office of War Information Photograph Collection, Prints & Photographs Division, Library of Congress, [LC-DIG-fsa-8a03228].
p. 227: Warren K. Leffler, Prints & Photographs Division, Library of Congress, [LC-DIG-ppmsca-04297].

Chapter 8

p. 251: Pearson Education, Inc.
p. 270: Warren K. Leffler, Prints & Photographs Division, Library of Congress, [LC-U9-33889A-31/31A].

Chapter 9

p. 285: *Developmental*, 2013 (mural, Faith in Christ Ministries, Los Angeles, CA), Clairfoster J. Browne/Photograph by Camilo J. Vergara.
p. 309: Highsmith (Carol M.) Archive, Prints & Photographs Division, Library of Congress, [LC-DIG-highsm-13502].

Text Credits

Chapter 1

p. 1: Quote by George Santayana; p. 1: Quote by Henry Ford; pp. 11–14: "From the Thirty-Ninth Year of Q. Elizabeth, to the Twelfth year of K. Charles II. Inclusive" in the Statutes at Large by Danby Pickering. Published by Cambridge University Press.

Chapter 2

p. 16: From "Records of the Colony of Rhode Island and Providence Plantations, in New England, Vol. 01" 1636–1663 edited by John Russell Bartlett. Providence: A. C. Greene and Brothers, State Printers, 1856; p. 17: From "'The Statutes at Large from the First Year of King James the First to the Tenth Year of the Reign of King William the Third, Vol. 03" by Owen Ruffhead. Published by Basket Woodfall and Strahan Publishers, 1763; p. 18: From "Women in Industry: A Study in American Economic History." Published by D. Appleton & Company, 1909; p. 18: From "An Act For Granting The Sum of Fifteen Hundred Pounds To Encourage The Manufact[ory][ure] of Linen in Province Laws 1753-1754." Published by Secretary of the Commonwealth, 1753; p. 19: From "Women in Industry: A Study in American Economic History by Edith Abbott." Published by D. Appleton & Company, 1909; p. 19: From "Household Manufactures in the United States, 1640–1860" by Rolla Milton Tryon. Published by University of Chicago Press Books, 1917; p. 19: From "'The Statutes at Large: Being a Collection of All the Laws of Virginia from the First Session of the Legislature in the Year 1619, Vol. 01" by William Waller Hening, 1823; p. 19: "From "Records of the Governor and Company of the Massachusetts Bay in New England, 1642–1649, Vol 02." Published by

Boston White Publishers, 1853; p. 20: From "An Act of Supplement To The Acts Referring To The Poor, &c in Province Law 1703–1704." Published by Secretary of the Commonwealth, 1703; p. 20: From "Laboring and Dependent Classes in Colonial America, 1607-1783: Studies of the Economic, Educational, and Social Significance of Slaves, Servants, Apprentices and Poor Folk by Marcus Wilson Jernegan." Published by University of Chicago Press Books, © 1931; p. 20: From "An Act For Regulating of Townships, Choice of Town Officers, And Setting Forth Their Power in Province Law 1692-1693." Published by Secretary of the Commonwealth, 1692; p. 21: From "Poverty in New York, 1783–1825 by Raymond A Mohl." Published by Oxford Publishing Limited, © 1971; pp. 21–22: From "An Act for the Relief of the Poor in The Statutes at Large of Pennsylvania from 1682–1801, Vol. 02, 1700 to 1712," 1896; p. 24: From "The Growth of American Democracy: Social: Economic: Political by Jeannette Paddock Nichols and Roy Franklin Nichols." Published by D. Appleton & Company, © 1939; p. 26: From "Histories of the Dividing Line Betwixt Virginia and North Carolina by William Byrd." Published by Houghton Mifflin Harcourt, © 1929; p. 28: From "On The Labouring Poor in The Writing of Benjamin Franklin, Vol. III, 1750–1759" by Benjamin Franklin. Published by Macmillan Publishers Ltd., 1905; pp. 28–29: From "On The Labouring Poor in The Writing of Benjamin Franklin, Vol. V, 1767–1772" by Benjamin Franklin. Published by Macmillan Publishers Ltd., 1906; p. 29: From "A Dissertation on the Poor Laws by a Well-Wisher to Mankind" by John Ramsay McCulloch in A Select Collection of Scarce and Valuable Economical Tracts. Published by Lord Overstone, 1859; p. 29: From "Medical Care of Veterans by Robinson E Adkins." Published by U.S. Government Printing Office, 1967; pp. 31–32: From "An Act of Supplement To The Acts Referring To The Poor, &c in Province Law 1703-1704." Published by Secretary of the Commonwealth, 1703.

Chapter 3

p. 35: From "Vices of the Political System of the United States, April 1787 by James Madison in the Papers of James Madison, Vol. 09." Published by University of Chicago Press, © 1975; p. 40: From "The Hireling and the Slave" by William John Grayson. Published by John Russell, 1855; p. 41: From "Society in America, Vol. 02 by Harriet Martineau." Published by Saunders and Otley, 1837; p. 44: From "Old South Leaflets No 144 Education and Prosperity by Old South Leaflet No. 144." Published by Old South Meeting House, 1848; p. 44: From "The Growth of American Democracy: Social: Economic: Political by Jeannette Paddock Nichols and Roy Franklin Nichols." Published by D. Appleton & Company, © 1939; p. 45: From "Pastoral Letter of the General Association of Massachusetts" by Sarah Grimke. Published by The Liberator, 1837; p. 45: From "Women Together: A History in Documents of the Women's Movement in the United States by Judith Papachristou." Published by Knopf Doubleday Publishing Group (Alfred A. Knopf), © 1976; p. 46: From "The Lily" 1848; p. 47–48: From "Memorial of D. L. Dix, Praying a Grant of Land for the Relief and Support of the Indigent Curable and Incurable Insane in the United States, 30th Congress 1st Session, Miscellaneous No. 150" by Dorothea Lynde Dix. Published by U.S. Government Printing Office, 1848; p. 48: From "XIV President of the United States: 1853–1857, Vento Message" by Franklin Pierce. Published by Franklin Pierce, 1854; p. 49: From "Report of the Secretary of State on the Relief and Settlement of the Poor" by John V N Yates. Published by U.S. Government Printing Office, 1971; p. 49: From "Rights of Man, Part 02 by Thomas Paine." Published by J.S. Jordan, 1792; p. 50: From "Appeal to the Wealthy of the Land, Ladies as Well as Gentlemen, on the Character, Conduct, Situation, and Prospects of Those Whose Sole Dependence for Subsistence Is on the Labour of Their Hands" by Mathew Carey. Published by L Johnson, 1833; p. 50: From "Report of the Committee to Whom Was

Referred, The Consideration of the Pauper Laws of This Commonwealth." Published by The Commonwealth of Massachusetts, 1821; p. 50: From" The First Annual Report of the Managers the Society for the Prevention of Pauperism in the City of New York, to Which Is Added a Report on the Subject of Pauperism" by Matthew Clarkson. Published by J. Seymour, 1818; p. 51: From "The First Annual Report of the Managers the Society for the Prevention of Pauperism in the City of New York, to Which Is Added a Report on the Subject of Pauperism" by Matthew Clarkson. Published by J. Seymour, 1818; p. 51: From "Report of a Committee on the Subject of Pauperism" Published by J. Seymour 1818; p. 52: From "Report [of] the Committee to Whom Was Referred, The Consideration of the Pauper Laws of This Commonwealth." Published by The Commonwealth of Massachusetts, 1821; p. 52: From "Report of the Secretary of State on the Relief and Settlement of the Poor" by John V N Yates. Published by U.S. Government Printing Office, 1971; p. 53: From "Report of the Secretary of State on the Relief and Settlement of the Poor" by John V N Yates. Published by U.S. Government Printing Office, 1971; p. 54: From "The Child and the State, Vol. 02 by Grace Abbott." Published by University of Chicago Press Books, © 1938; p. 55: From "The Care of Destitute, Neglected, and Delinquent Children" by Homer Folks. Published by Macmillan Publishers Ltd., 1911; p. 55: From "Register of Pennsylvania, Devoted to the Preservation of Facts and Documents and Every Kind of Useful Information Respecting the State of Pennsylvania, Vol. 15 from January 1835 to July 1835" by Samuel Hazard. Published by Samuel Hazard, 1835; p. 55: From "New York House of Refuge, Second Annual Report." Published by Hachette Book Group USA, © 1971; p. 55: From "The Depths: The Discovery of Poverty in the United States by Robert A Bremner." Published by New York University Press, © 1956; p. 56: From "The Dangerous Classes of New York and Twenty Years Work Among Them by Charles Loring Brace." Published by Wynkoop & Hallenbeck, 1872; p. 56: From "Some American Pioneers in Social Welfare by Edith Abbott." Published by University of Chicago Press, © 1937; p. 57: From "Report of Select Committee Appointed to Visit Charitable Institutions Supported by the State and all City and County Poor and Work Houses and Jails of the State of New York: Transmitted to the Legislature" by C. Van Benthuysen, 1857; pp. 60–63: From "Report of a Committee on the Subject of Pauperism." Published by J. Seymour 1818; pp. 63–67: From "Report of a Committee on the Subject of Pauperism." Published by J. Seymour, 1818; pp. 67–73: From "Constitution By-Laws." Published by U.S. Constitution, 1828; pp. 73–76: From "XIV President of the United States: 1853–1857 Vento Message" by Franklin Pierce. Published by Franklin Pierce, 1854.

Chapter 4

p. 79: From "The Rise of American Commerce and Industry" by Samuel Eagle Forman. Published by Century, © 1927; p. 80: From "The United States Since 1865 by Foster Rhea Dulles." Published by University of Michigan Press, © 1971; p. 84: From "U.S. Sanitary Commission, Document No. 49." Published by U.S. Sanitary Commission, 1862; p. 85: From "U.S. Sanitary Commission, Document No. 4042." Published by U.S. Sanitary Commission, 1865; p. 85: From "History of the United States Sanitary Commission, Being the General Report of its Work During the War of the Rebellion" by Charles J Stille. Published by Wolters Kluwer, 1866; p. 85: From "History of the United States Sanitary Commission, Being the General Report of its Work During the War of the Rebellion" by Charles J Stille. Published by Wolters Kluwer, 1866; p. 85: From "Congress of the United States, 3rd Session 41st Congress." Published by U.S. Government Printing Office, 1870; p. 86: From "Laws of the State of New York, An Act to Provide for the Relief of Indigent Soldiers, Sailors and Marines, and the Families of Those Deceased." Published by New York State, 1887; p. 87: From "A New History of The United States by William Miller." Published by George Braziller, Inc, © 1958; p. 88: From "The Congressional Globe: Containing the Debates and Proceedings of the First Session of the Thirty-Ninth Congress." Published by U.S. Government Printing Office, 1866; p. 90: From "New York Association for Improving the Condition of the Poor, Thirty-Second Annual Report." Published by New York State, 1875; p. 91: From "Acres of Diamonds by Russell H Conwell." Published by Temple University Press; p. 92: From "American Charities; a Study in Philanthropy and Economics" by Amos Griswold Warner. Published by Harper Collins Publishers, 1894; pp. 94–95: From "Indoor And Outdoor Relief by Franklin B Sanborn in Proceedings of the National Conference of Charities and Correction at the Seventeenth Annual Session Held In Baltimore." Published by National Conference of Charities And Corrections(NCCC), 1890; p. 95: From "Charity Organization in the United States: A Report of the Committee on History of Charity Organization by Charles D Kellogg in Proceedings of the National Conference of Charities and Correction at the Twelth Annual Session Held In Chicago." Published by National Conference Of Charities And Corrections(NCCC), 1893; p. 95: From "In Bohemia by John Boyle O'Reilly in Philanthropy and Social Progress." Published by John Boyle O'Reilly, 1886; p. 95: From "The Charity Organization Movement in the United States: A Study in American Philanthropy, Vol. 19" by Frank Dekker Watson. Published by Macmillan Publishers Ltd, 1922; p. 95: From "To the Editor of the Times-Democrat." Published by The Times and Democrat, 1903; p. 96: From "A Handbook of Charity Organization" by Humphreys S Gurteen. Published by Courier Publishing, 1882; p. 97: From "Social Settlements by Jane Addams in Proceedings of the National Conference of Charities and Correction at the Twenty-Fourth Annual Session Held In Toronto, Ontario." Published by National Conference Of Charities And Corrections (NCCC), 1897; p. 98: From "An Act to Provide Better Care of Pauper and Destitute Children." Published by The New York State, 1875; p. 98: From "American Charities; a Study in Philanthropy and Economics by Amos Griswold Warner." Published by Harper Collins Publishers, 1894; p. 98: From "Thirteenth Annual Report of The Board of Commissioners of Public Charities of The State of Pennsylvania for 1882, Legislative Document No. 05." Published by Commonwealth of Pennsylvania, 1882; p. 99: From "The Causes of Pauperism, Tenth Annual Report of the New York State Board of Charities by Charles S Hoyt." Published by New York State Board of Charities, 1877; p. 99: From "Twenty-Eighth and Twenty-Ninth Annual Report Boston Children Aid Society." Published by Boston Children's Aid Society, 1893; p. 99: From "Twenty Fourth Annual Report of the Boston Children Aid Society." Published by Boston Children's Aid Society, 1888; p. 102: From "Discussion on Charity Organization in Proceedings of the National Conference of Charities and Correction at the Fifteenth Annual Session Held In Buffalo, N.Y, July 05–11, 1888." Published by National Conference Of Charities And Corrections (NCCC), 1888; p. 102: From "Women & Social Change in America" by Joan D Mandle. Published by Princeton Book Company, © 1979; p. 102: From "Proceedings of the General Assembly." Published by U.S. Government Printing Office, 1882; p. 103: From "The Bureau of Labor Statistics" by Ewan Clague. Published by ABC-CLIO LLC, © 1968; pp. 107–108: From "Laws of The State of New York in An Act to Provide for the Relief of Indigent Soldiers, Sailors and Marines, and the Families of Those Deceased." Published by New York State, 1887; pp. 108–110: From "The Economic and Moral Effects of Public Outdoor Relief by Charles Russell Lowell in Proceedings of the National Conference of Charities and Correction at the Seventeenth Annual Session Held In Baltimore." Published by National Conference Of Charities And Corrections(NCCC), 1890;

pp. 111–114: From "An Act to Prohibit the Coming of Chinese Laborers to the United States from The Statutes At Large of The United States of America from December 1887 to March 1889 and Recent Treaties, Postal Conventions, and Executive Proclamations, Vol. XXV." Published by U.S. Constitution, 1889.

Chapter 5

p. 118: From "Final Report of the Commission on Industrial Relations." Published by U.S Government Printing Office, 1915; p. 119: From "The Klan of Tomorrow by Hiram W. Evans in A New History of the United States" by William Miller. Published by George Braziller Inc, © 1958; p. 119: From "Booker T. Washington Papers Volume 1: Volumes 1–14" by Booker T. Washington, Louis R. Harlan and Raymond Smock. Published by University of Illinois Press, © 1972; June Axinn, Mark J. Stern, Social Welfare: A History of the American Response to Need, 9e, © 2018 by Pearson Education, Inc., New York, NY; p. 123: From "An Introduction to Public Welfare" by Arthur Parker Miles. Published by D.C. Heath, © 1947; p. 123: From "American Epoch: A History of the United States Since the 1890's" by Arthur Stanley Link. Published by Knopf Doubleday Publishing Group (Alfred A. Knopf), © 1955; p. 123: June Axinn, Mark J. Stern, Social Welfare: A History of the American Response to Need, 9e, 9780134303734, © 2018 by Pearson Education, Inc., New York, NY; pp. 123–124: From "Twentieth Century Alignments for the Promotion of Social Order, Proceedings, NCCC: 1900" by Charles Faulkner. Published by National Conference of Charities and Corrections, 1900; p. 124: From "37 U.S. statute 79, 1912, United States Children's Bureau." Published by Department of Health and Human Services, 1912; p. 124: From "Twentieth Century Alignments for the Family and the Social Worker Proceedings, NCCC: 1908" by Mary E. Richmond. Published by National Conference of Charities and Corrections, 1908; p. 124: From "Twentieth Century Alignments for the Report of the Committee on Standards of Living and Labor, Proceedings, NCCC: 1912" by Owen R. Lovejoy. Published by National Conference of Charities and Corrections, 1912; p. 125: From "The Child and the State" by Grace Abbott. Published by University of Chicago Press Books, © 1938; p. 125: From "Twentieth Century Alignments for the Report of the Committee on Standards of Living and Labor, Proceedings, NCCC: 1912" by Owen R. Lovejoy. Published by National Conference of Charities and Corrections, 1912; p. 127: From "Real Wages in the United States, 1890–1926" by Paul Howard Douglas. Published by Houghton Mifflin Harcourty, © 1930; p. 128: From "Paul U. Kellogg and the Survey: Voices for Social Welfare and Social Justice" by Clarke A. Chambers. Published by University Of Minnesota Press, © December 22, 1972; p. 129: From "Dependent and Neglected Children: Report of the Committee on Socially Handicapped - Dependency and Neglect" by Homer Folks and John Prentice. Published by D. Appleton & Company, © 1933; p. 129: From "The Child and the State" by Grace Abbott. Published by University of Chicago Press Books, © 1938; p. 130: From "Helping Widows to Bring Up Citizens, NCCC: 1910" by Alice Higgins. Published by National Conference of Charities and Corrections (NCCC), 1910; p. 130: From "Public Pensions to Widows - Discussion, Proceedings, NCCC: 1912" by Mary E. Richmond. Published by National Conference of Charities and Corrections (NCCC), 1912; pp. 130–131: From "Public Pensions to Widows: Experiences and Observations Which Lead Me to Oppose Such a Law by Frederic Almy." Published by National Conference of Charities and Corrections (NCCC), 1912; p. 131: From "Discussion by C.C Carstens in The Present Status of Mother's Pension Administration Proceedings." Published by NCSW, 1921; p. 131: From "Children's Bureau Publication No. 184." Published by U.S Government Printing Office, 1928; p. 132: From "The Negro and the Demands of Modern Life: Ethnic and Anatomical Considerations by Franz Boas in

Charities and the Commons: A Weekly Journal of Philanthropy and Social Advance, Vol. 15." Published by New York Charity Organization Society, 1905; p. 135: From "The Culture of the Family from the Standpoint of Recreation, Proceedings, NCCC: 1914." Published by National Conference Of Charities And Corrections(NCCC), 1914; p. 136: From "Social Work: Cause and Function by Porter R. Lee, Proceedings, NCCC: 1929." Published by NCSW, 1929; p. 139: From "Editorial by Alice Stone Blackwell in The Woman's Journal." Published by Woman's Journal, 1911; p. 140: From "Wage-Earning Women by Annie Marion MacLean." Published by Woman's Journal, 1919; p. 141: From "Social Security Reserves by J S Parker and Edwin E Witte." Published by American Council on Public Affairs, © 1942; p. 141: From "The New Day: Campaign Speeches of Herbert Hoover by Herbert Hoover." Published by Stanford University Press, © 1928; p. 142: From "A Belief in People: A History of Family Social Work by Margaret Elden Rich." Published by Family Service Association of America, © 1956; p. 142: From "Poor Relief in Pennsylvania: A State-Wide Survey of Pennsylvania by Emil Frankel." Published by Commonwealth of Pennsylvania: By the Public Board of Welfare, 1925; pp. 144–146: From "The Family and the Woman's Wage, Proceedings of the National Conference of Charities and Corrections." Published by National Conference Of Charities And Corrections (NCCC)/90157, 1909; pp. 144–146: From "Public Pensions To Widows Experiences And Observations Which Lead Me To Oppose Such A Law in Proceedings Of The National Conference Of Charities And Corrections." Published by Buffalo Charity Organization Society, 1912; pp. 146–147: From "Law of the State of the Illinois Enacted By the Forty-Seventh General Assembly at the Regular Biennial Session." Published by U.S. Constitution, 1911.

Chapter 6

p. 157: From "Only yesterday by Frederick Lewis Allen." Published by Penguin Random House, © 1959; p. 158: From "The Unemployed Man: A Social Study by Edward Wight Bakke." Published by E.P. Dutton & Company, © 1934; p. 158: From "Studies of Breakdowns in Family Income" by Lucille Eaves in The Family, Vol. 10. Published by The Family, © 1929; p. 158: From "Case studies of unemployment by Marion Elderton." Published by University of Pennsylvania Press, © 1931; p. 162: From "Social security in America: the Factual Background of the Social Security Act as Summarized from Staff reports to the Committee on Economic Security." Published by U.S. Government Printing Office, 1937; p. 163: From "U.S. 72nd Congress, 1st session, Public Law No. 2." Published by U.S. Government Printing Office, 1932; p. 163: From "U.S. 72nd Congress, 1st session, Public Law No. 2." Published by U.S. Government Printing Office, 1932; p. 164: From "Case studies of unemployment" by Marion Elderton. Published by University of Pennsylvania Press, © 1931; p. 164: From "Platforms of the two great political parties, 1932" by William D Graf and South Trimble. Published by U.S. Government Printing Office, 1945; p. 164: From "Acceptance of the Nomination for the Presidency" by Franklin Delano Roosevelt in The Public Papers and Addresses of Franklin Delano Roosevelt, Vol. 02." Published by Russell Publishing Limited, © 1969; p. 167: From "Proceedings of the National Conference of Social Work." Published by The Conference, © 1931; p. 168: From "Proceedings of the National Conference of Social Work." Published by The Conference, © 1931; p. 169: From "Annual Message to Congress" by Franklin Delano Roosevelt in The Public Papers and Addresses of Franklin D. Roosevelt: The Continuing Struggle for Liberalism, 1938. Published by Penguin Random House, © 1938; p. 170: From "Unemployment Relief" by William Hodson in Social Work Year Book, Volume 4. Published by Russell Sage Foundation, © 1937; p. 170: From "The Developing National Program of Relief" by Harry L Hopkins in Proceedings of the National Conference of Social Work, Volume 60. Published by the Conference, © 1933; p. 170: From "Rules and Regulations in Monthly Report of the Federal Emergency Relief Administration, May 22–June 30, 1933." Published by U.S. Government Printing Office, 1933; p. 171: From "Report to the President of the Committee on Economic Security." Published by U.S. Government Printing Office, 1935; p. 171: From "Report to the President of the Committee on Economic Security." Published by U.S. Government Printing Office, 1935; pp. 171–172: From "Message of the President Recommending Legislation on Economic Security: Message from the President of the United States Transmitting a Recommendation for Legislation on the Subject of Economic Security." Published by U.S. Government Printing Office, 1935; p. 172: From "U.S. 74th Congress, 1st session, Public Law No. 271." Published by U.S. Government Printing Office, 1936; p. 174: From "Report to the President of the Committee on Economic Security." Published by U.S. Government Printing Office, 1935; pp. 175–176: From "Unmarried Parenthood under the Social Security Act" by Mary S. Labaree in Proceedings of the National Conference of Social Work, Selected Papers ... Annual Conference, Volume 66. Published by the Conference, © 1939; pp. 176–177: Aubrey Williams; p. 177: From "Spending to Save: The Complete Story of Relief." Published by W W Norton & Company, © 1936; p. 178: From "Report to the President of the Committee on Economic Security." Published by U.S. Government Printing Office, 1935; p. 178: From "Family Welfare Association of America (FWAA)." Published by The Social Welfare History Project, © 2014; pp. 179–180: From "Family Welfare Association of America (FWAA)." Published by The Social Welfare History Project, © 1933; p. 180: From "Family Social Work" by Frank J. Hertel in Social Work Year Book 1951: A Description of Organized Activities in Social Work and in Related Fields: Eleventh Issue by Margaret B. Hodges. Published by National Association of Social Workers, © 1951; p. 184: From "Men who Lead Labor" by Richard Bransten, Bruce Minton and John Stuart. Published by Modern Age Books, © 1937; p. 185: From "The American Woman: Her Changing Social, Economic, and Political Roles, 1920-1970" by William Henry Chafe. Published by Oxford Publishing Limited, © 1937; p. 186: Helvering v. Davis 301 U.S. 619, 1937, U S Supreme Court. pp. 189–195: The United States House of Representatives, Monthly Report of The Federal Emergency Relief Administration Letter of Transmittal, 1933; pp. 195–204: The Social Security Act, Approved, August 14, 1935, [Public—NO. 271—74th Congress] [II. R. 7260], U.S. Constitution.

Chapter 7

p. 218: From "A report on veterans' benefits in the United States. Published by U.S. Government Publishing Office; p. 218: From "Selective Training and Service Act of 1940." Published by U.S. National Archives and Records Administration; p. 218: From "U.S. Senate, 78th Congress, Finance Committee, Report 755" by The United States Senate Committee on Finance; p. 222: From "Public Welfare Amendments of 1962, H.R. 10606, 87th Congress, 2nd session, Public Law 87-543." Published by United States Department of Health & Human Services; p. 222: From a Report for the Secretary of Health, Education, and Welfare by George K. Wyma. Published © 1961; p. 222: From "Report of the Ad Hoc Committee on Public Welfare to the Secretary of Health, Education, and Welfare." Published by United States Department of Health & Human Services; p. 223: From "Message to Congress on Public Welfare" by John F. Kennedy; p. 224: From "The United States Social Security Administration." Published by the United States Social Security Administration; p. 225: From "Bureau of Family Services, press release, January 6, 1963." Published by United States Department of Health & Human Services; p. 226: From "The Culture of Poverty" by Oscar Lewis in Society, Vol 35, Issue 02, pp. 07-09. Published by Springer, © 1998; p. 227: From "Message on Poverty" by Lyndon B. Johnson; p. 227: From "Public Law 88-452, Secession 02." Published by U.S. Government Publishing Office; p. 228: From "The war on poverty, the Economic opportunity act of 1964. A compilation of materials relevant to S. 2642, prepared for the Select Subcommittee on Poverty of the Committee on Labor and Public Welfare, United States Senate." Published by U.S. Government Publishing Office; p. 231: From "The State of Welfare" by Gilbert Yale Steiner. Published by Brookings Institution Press, © 1971; p. 232: From "Washington Memorandum, No. 90-1-9." Published by National Association of Social Workers, © 1967; p. 232: From "National Association of Social Workers, Policy Statement on Separation of Social Services and Income Security Programs." Approved by the Board of Directors, June 29, 1967. Published by National Association of Social Workers (NASW) © June 29, 1967; p. 233: From "Executive Order 8802." Published by The White House; p. 235: From "U.S. Supreme Court's Decision In re Gault et al. No. 116, Argued December 6, 1966 in United States Reports, Vol. 387, Cases Adjudged in the Supreme Court." Published by U.S. Supreme Court; pp. 242–246: From "Act of August 20, 1964 (Economic Opportunity Act of 1964), Public Law 88-452, 78 STAT 508, which mobilized the human and financial resources of the Nation to combat poverty in the United States." Published by National Archives and Records Administration; pp. 246–250: U.S. Supreme Court's Decision In re Gault et al. No. 116, Argued December 6, 1966 from United States Reports, Vol. 387, Cases Adjudged in the Supreme Court. Published by U.S. Supreme Court.

Chapter 8

p. 251: From "The Children's Cause" by Gilbert Yale Steiner and Pauline H. Milius. Published by Brookings Institution, © 1976; p. 256: From "Changing Patterns of Income, 1960–1974" by Robert J. Lampman in Toward New Human Rights: The Social Policies of the Kennedy and Johnson Administrations edited by David C. Warner. Published by University of Texas at Austin, © 1977; p. 258: June Axinn, Mark J. Stern, Social Welfare: A History of the American Response to Need, 9e, 9780134303734, © 2018 by Pearson Education, Inc., New York, NY;

p. 260: H.R. 1, The Social Security Amendments of 1971, as Amended and Ordered Reported to the House of Representatives, 92nd Congress, 1st session, U.S. Government Publishing Office, 1971; p. 261: Poverty Amid Plenty: The American Paradox: The Report of the President's Commission on Income Maintenance Programs, U.S. Government Publishing Office, 1969; p. 264: From "Reports of the 1979 Advisory Council on Social Security." by Social Security Administration, 1980; p. 268: House Committee Print No. 4, Medical Care of Veterans, 90th Congress, 1st Session, U.S. Government Publishing Office, 1967; p. 268: Report of the President's Commission on Veterans' Pensions, U.S. Government Publishing Office, 1956; p. 269: Proceedings of a Conference on the National Longitudinal Surveys of Mature Women, U.S. Department of Labor, 1978; p. 274: The Pension Game: The American Pension System from the Viewpoint of the Average Woman, U.S. Government Publishing Office, 1979; p. 274: US Commission on Civil Rights USCCR, New York Times, 1974; pp. 274–275: Social Security and the Changing Roles of Men and Women, U.S. Department of Health, Education, and Welfare, 1979; p. 275: From "Reports of the 1979 Advisory Council on Social Security." by Social Security Administration, 1980; pp. 277–283: From "327 - Special Message to the Congress on Reform of the Nation's Welfare System." The White House, 1969; pp. 283–284: Public Law 98-460, 98th Congress, An Act, U.S. Government Publishing Office, 1984.

Chapter 9

p. 290: Integrated Public Use Microdata Series, Current Population Survey, 1976–2010; p. 307: Common Core Polluted by Federal Guidelines and Mandates, Mike Lee, 2013; pp. 314–317: Public Law 104–193, 104th Congress, An Act, U.S. Government Publishing Office; pp. 317–321: Official California Legislative Information, http://www.wwnorton.com/college/history/archive/resources/documents/ch37_03.htm, 1994; pp. 321–328: Lawrence v. Texas 539 U.S. 558, U.S. Supreme Court, 2003.

Index

A

Abbott, Edith, 102, 129
Abbott, Grace, 129
abolitionism, 46
abortions, 273
    access to, 273
    and right to privacy, 308–310
Act of Settlement (1662), 16
Act to Prohibit the Coming of Chinese Laborers to the United States (1888), 106, 111–114
Act to Provide for the Better Care of Pauper and Destitute Children, 98
Act to Provide for the Relief of Indigent Soldiers, Sailors and Marines, and the Families of Those Deceased (1887), 106–108
Act to Regulate the Treatment and Control of Dependent, Neglected, and Delinquent Children, 97, 129
Addams, Jane, 96, 97, 128, 133
Ad Hoc Committee on Public Welfare (1961), 222
Adler, Felix, 128
Adoption and Safe Families Act (ASFA) (1997), 304
Adoption Assistance and Child Welfare Act (1980), 264
Advisory Council on Public Welfare, 231, 236, 241
Advisory Council on Social Security (1979), 264
Affirmative action programs, 270, 307–308
African Americans
    churches, 234
    civil rights movement, 226
    criminal justice system, 311
    eviction from farms during Great Depression, 159
    female-headed households, 254
    immigration, 293
    integration for, 234
    marginalization of, 5
    during postwar period, 215–217
    poverty, 221, 290–292
    in pre-Civil War period, 36
    press, 234
    during Progressive Era, 119–122
    rate of employment, 210, 288
    slavery, 24
    social welfare for, 5
    unions and, 103
    workforce, 254
    work opportunities, 233
aging, the
    child welfare and, 263–266
    condition during post-Civil War period, 83
    conservative resurgence and social change, 263–266
    expanded benefits for, 230
    income support programs, 264
Agrarian movement, 103–105
Agricultural Adjustment Act, 164
Agricultural Adjustment Act (AAA), 159
agricultural crisis, 158–162
agriculture sector, changes, 210
Aid and Services to Needy Families with Children, 224
AIDS epidemic, 256
Aid to Dependent Children (ADC), 143, 172, 174, 200–201, 211, 219–220, 222, 224, 241
Aid to Families with Dependent Children (AFDC), 224, 230, 257, 260, 261, 262, 263, 273, 274, 279, 288, 298, 305
Aid to the Blind, 257, 262
Aid to the Disabled, 262
Aid to the Temporarily and Permanently Disabled, 257
Alien and Sedition Acts, 37
almhouses
    retreat from, 56–58
almshouses, 21, 83
Almy, Frederic, 130, 131, 143–144, 147, 151, 153, 155, 222
American Association for Labor Legislation, 127
American Association for Old Age Security, 127
American Charities (Warner), 92, 166
American Civil Liberties Union, 313
American colonies
    class differences in, 25
    Poor Law principles in, 17–22
        centrality of women's work and colonial economy, 18
        settlement and family responsibility, 18
    population growth in, 23–24
    treatment of veterans in, 29–30
American Equal Rights Association, 100
American Federation of Labor (AFL), 103, 118, 182
American Indian Movement, 270
American Legion, 218
American plan, 126
American Public Welfare Association, 225
American Revolution, 25, 43
American Society for the Promotion of Temperance, 45
American Sociological Conference (1902), 127
Americans with Disabilities Act (1990), 273
American Woman Suffrage Association, 100

An Act for the Relief of the Poor 1601 (43 Elizabeth), 11–14
An Act of Supplement to the Acts Referring to the Poor (Massachusetts Bay, 1692), 31–32
Annual Report of the Council of Economic Advisers (1964), 221
antebellum period. *See* pre-Civil War period
Anthony, Susan B., 100
anti-Chinese agitation, 6
anti-immigrant sentiments, 5, 81
antitax revolts, 269
apprenticeship, 19, 55
Area Agencies on Aging, 230
Area Redevelopment Act (1961), 221
Armed Forces Committee on Postwar Education Opportunities for Service Personnel, 218
Articles of Confederation, 35
Asian Americans
    education, 306
    immigration, 293
Associations for Improving the Condition of the Poor, 51

B

Bakke, E. Wright, 166
Banking Bill, 165
Barnett, Canon Samuel, 95–96
battered child syndrome, 264
Bellamy, George, 135
benevolent societies, 49–50
Bethesda House for Boys, 54
Better Jobs and Income Program, 262, 276
The Binding of Moses Love (1747), 31, 33
The Birth of a Nation (film), 119
Birtwell, Charles W., 99
Black Codes, 87
blacks. *See* African Americans
Bloomer, Amelia, 46
Boas, Franz, 132
bonus marches, 181
Boston Episcopal Society, 18
Boston House of Reformation, 54
Boston's Children's Aid Society, 99
Bowen, Louise de Koven, 132
Brace, Charles Loring, 56–58, 99
Brandeis, Louis, 125
Breckenridge, Sophonisba, 132
Brotherhood of Sleeping Car Porters, 233, 234
Brown v. Board of Education, 234
Bryan, William Jennings, 104
Buffalo Charity Organization Society, 130

Bureau of Indian Affairs, 270, 307
Bureau of Labor Statistics, 103
Bureau of Public Assistance, 222
Bureau of Refugees, 88
Bush, George H.W., 255, 260, 269, 271, 275, 285, 294, 303, 304
Byrd, William, 26

C

Califano, Joseph A., 274
California Proposition (187), 302, 313
Cardozo, Benjamin, 186
Carey, Mathew, 49, 50
Carnegie, Andrew, 91, 118
Carstens, C. C., 131
Carter, Jimmy, 260, 262, 275, 276
case poverty, 220, 221
Case Studies of Unemployment, 166
cash assistance program, 313
cash welfare programs, 272
Castro, Fidel, 271
Catt, Carrie Chapman, 140
Century of the Child (twentieth century), 3
character reform, 142
Charities and the Commons, 128, 132
Charity Organization and Social Settlements (COS), 97
Charity Organization Movement, 90–95, 130
Charity Organization Societies, 84, 96, 135
Charity Organization Society leaders, 7
Charleston Orphan House, 54
Chase, Stuart, 138
Chief Joseph, of Nez Perce, 79
Child Abuse Prevention and Treatment Act (CAPTA, 1974), 264
childbearing, 18
child-care benefit, 292
child protective services, 264
children
      civil rights of, 235
      during civil war period and after, 97–99
      conservative resurgence and social change, 263–266
      indenture and apprenticeship for, 20
      during information society era, 292
      New Deal economic policy, 175
      pre–civil war period, 53–56
Children's Aid Society, New York, 55–56
Children's Bureau, 222
children's health insurance program (CHIP), 295
children's institution, 54
Child Welfare League (CWL) of America, 174
Chinese Exclusion Act (1882), 81, 106, 208
Chinese immigration, during Civil War period and after, 81
civil disobedience campaigns, 308
Civilian Conservation Corps (CCC), 161
civil rights
      abortion and right to privacy, 308–310
      affirmative action programs in labor market, 307–308
      of children, 235
      educational programs, 306–307

expansion of, 270–274
of sexual minorities, 308–309, 321–328
Civil Rights Act (1964), 221
Civil Rights Act (1991), 271
civil rights movement, 221, 226
Civil War, 34, 35, 53
Civil War pensions, 83
Civil War period and after (1860-1900)
      Act to Prohibit the Coming of Chinese Laborers to the United States, 107–110
      aging and, 83
      Agrarian Movement, 103–105
      agriculture production, 82
      Asian population, 80–81
      changing economic and demographic realities, 77–83
      Charity Organization Movement, 90–95
      child welfare, 97–99
      Chinese immigration during, 81
      cities, growth of, 81–82
      cotton production, 82
      depression of 1890s, 103
      dominance of East in manufacturing, 83
      expansion of government's role, 84
      gross national product, 78
      industrial development, 78
      innovations in social welfare services, 83–99
      issue of immigration and migration, 80
      naturalization and citizenship, 79–81
      North during, 78
      older population, 83
      population growth, 78–79
      progress on science and invention, 77–78
      Settlement House Movement, 95–97
      situation of Southern states, 86–89
      social welfare and urban expansion, 89–90
      social welfare needs of soldiers and their families, 84–86
      structure of rural life, 81–82
      urban issues rise, 90–95
Civil Works Administration (CWA), 167
Clague, Ewan, 177
Clayton Antitrust Act (1914), 138
Cleveland, Grover, 81
Clinton, Bill, 255, 285, 292, 294, 299, 300, 305, 308
Coit, Stanton, 96
College Settlement, New York, 96
Collier's Weekly, 128
Colonial welfare legislation, 21
Commission on Industrial Relations report, 118
Committee on Disabled Soldiers and Sailors, 29
Commons, John R., 128
community action programs (CAP), 228, 236
community chest funds, 215
Community Facilities Act (1941), 215
community legal services, 260
Community Mental Health Act (1963), 229
community mental health services, 214
Comprehensive Child Development Act (1971), 264
Comprehensive Employment and Training Act (CETA), 267
Conference on Aging (1961), 230
Congressional Reconstruction, 87
Congress of Industrial Organizations (CIO), 183

Conservative Era (1968–1992)
      child welfare and the aging, 263–266
      civil rights, 270–274
      conservative resurgence and social change, 276–284
      employment patterns, 253–254
      family patterns during, 254–256
      immigration policies during, 271
      poverty and income distribution during, 256–258
      renewal, and social changes, 251–252
      social movements, 269–275
      social welfare programs, 258–260
      unemployment, provisions for, 266–268
      veterans, provisions for, 268
      welfare reform, 260–263
Constitution of the Female Orphan Asylum, 68–73
Constitution of the United States
      amendments, 138, 140
      Eighteenth Amendment, 140
      Fifteenth Amendment, 100
      Fourteenth Amendment, 81, 87, 100
      Nineteenth Amendment, 122, 140
      preamble of, 35
      Seventeenth Amendment, 122
      Sixteenth Amendment, 138
      Twenty-First Amendment, 136, 141
Continental Congress, 36
Contract with America, 300
Conwell, Russell, 91
Coolidge, Calvin, 181
cotton gin, 39
cotton production, 39–41, 82
Council of Economic Advisors, 211
Council of Energy Resources, 270
Coxey, Jacob, 136
criminal justice system, 310
Crow, Jim, 119
cultural bias, 8

D

Dawes Act (1887), 79, 162
Dawes Commission, 134
Debs, Eugene, 138
Declaration of Independence, 35
Declaration of Sentiments, 44
defined-benefit, pension plans, 265
DeForest, Robert W., 129
Deinstitutionalization, 272
Demonstration (Model) Cities Act (1966), 230
Dependent Pension Act (1890), 86
Dependent Pension Act of 1890, 86
Devine, Edward T., 129, 150
Dewey, John, 138
diagnosis-related groups (DRGs) billing system, 266
Disability Insurance (DI), 274, 284
discretionary programs, 259
Displaced Persons Act (1948), 208
Dix, Dorothea L., 47
Dixie, Operation, 216
Doe v. Bolton, 273
Dorothea Dix's Memorial, 48
Douglas, Paul, 138
Du Bois, W. E. B., 132

Due Process Clause of Fourteenth Amendment, 249, 322, 323, 325, 326
Dumpson, James, 231

E

The Economic and Moral Effects of Public Outdoor Relief (1890), 106, 107–110
Economic Development Act (1965), 221
Economic Opportunity Act (1964), 227, 228, 229, 230, 236, 251
Economic Opportunity Act (1964), 236, 242
economic recession, 216
Economic Report of the President, 221
Economy Act of March 11 (1933), 165
educational programs, 306–307
Eighteenth Amendment to the Constitution, 140
eight hour movement, 126
elderly. *See* aging, the
Elementary and Secondary Education Act (1965), 230
Elizabethan Poor Law principles, 11–14
   family responsibility, principle of, 16
   local responsibility, principle of, 16
   residency requirement of legal settlement, 16
Ellwood, David, 299
Emancipation Proclamation, 132
Emergency Appropriation Act, 169
Emergency Maternity and Infant Care Program, 214
Employee Retirement Income Security Act (ERISA) (1974), 265
employment
   in agriculture sector, 210
   changing patterns, 253–254
   and investment incentives, 245
   low-wage, 291
   in manufacturing industry, 211
   Native Americans, 271
   in service sector, 211
Employment Act (1946), 211
End Poverty in California (EPIC), 182
English "Acte for Reliefes of Souldiours" (1593), 29
English Poor Laws, 3
Enrollment Act of 1863, 84
entitlement programs, 259
epidemics, 209
Epstein, Abraham, 127
Equal Employment Opportunity Commission, 221
Equal Rights Amendment (1972), 251, 269
European Court of Human Rights, 324, 325
Executive Order 8802, 233
expansion of public education, 44

F

Fair Employment Practices Committee (FEPC), 213
Fair Labor Standards Act (1938), 184
faith-based social welfare, 304
family
   agencies, 166, 170, 178, 179
   changes in composition, during information society era, 292

changing views during Progressive Era, 124, 126
   Charity Organizations and, 130
   during Conservative Era, 254–256
   income, during war and prosperity, 206
   during postwar period, 210
   responsibility, principle of, 16, 19, 21
      family governance, 18
Family and Medical Leave Act (1990), 255, 287
Family and Medical Leave Act (1993), 292
The Family and the Woman's Wage (1909), 143–146
Family Assistance Plan (FAP), 261, 276
family cap, 299
Family Court Act, 250
Family life, 162–163
Family Support Act (FSA) (1988), 263, 273, 298
Family Welfare Association of America (FWAA), 158, 166
Farm Credit Administration, 159
Farm Security Administration, 159
Faulkner, Charles, 123
Federal Emergency Relief Act, 168
   Hopkins's administration of, 167–168
   rules and regulations, 170
Federal Emergency Relief Administration (FERA), 157, 167–168, 189–195
Federal Employee's Act (1906), 127
federal income tax, establishment, 138
Federal public housing policy, 185
Federal Reserve Board, 253
Federal Reserve system, 138
Federal Security Agency, 215
Federal Surplus Commodities Corporation, 167
Federal Trade Commission Act, 139
Female Orphan Asylum of Portland, Maine, 59, 67, 68
Fifteenth Amendment to the Constitution, 100
Fifteenth Annual Conference of Charities and Corrections, 92
First Annual Report of the Managers of the Society for the Prevention of Pauperism in the City of New York (1818), 59–67
First Conference of Charities and Corrections, 91
Fleming, Arthur, 219
Folks, Homer, 143, 150
Food and Drug Act (1906), 138
Food Stamp Act (1964), 229
Force Bill, 39
Ford, Gerald, 260
Ford, Henry, 117, 257
Ford Motor Company, 126
Fortas, Abe, 235, 237
401(k) accounts, 265, 306
Fourteenth Amendment to the Constitution, 81, 87, 100
Frankel, Emil, 142
Franklin, Benjamin, 6, 28
   views on welfare, 28–29
Fraternal Order of Eagles, 127
Freedmen's Bureau, 86–89
"free" labor system, 21
Freud, Sigmund, 135, 142

Friends Almshouse, 17
Full Employment and Balanced Growth Act (1978), 253
Fullilove v. Klutznick, 270
Funds to Parents Act (1911), 131, 143

G

Gadsden Purchase, 38
Galbraith, Kenneth, 220, 226
gay civil rights, 309
General Accounting Office (GAO), 274
General Federation of Women's Club, 101
get-the-men-back-to-work slogan, 185
GI Bill of Rights, 218–219
Glass–Steagall Act, 165
Grand Army of the Republic (GAR), 85
Grant, Ulysses S., 84
The Grapes of Wrath, 159
Gratz v. Bollinger, 307
Great Awakening of 1820s, 42
Great Depression, 4, 6, 207, 209, 211, 253, 285
   banking crisis, 165
   economic collapse, 156–158
   economic indicators, 165
   establishment of FERA, 167–168
   family life during, 162–163
   and farmers, 158–162
   funds for relief, 166–167
   gross national product (GNP), 165
   Hoover's response, 163–164
   housing crisis, 165
   human crisis, 159
   income and savings of families, 165
   labor movement and social reforms, 182–184
   new concept of poor, 158
   Roosevelt's New Deal policy, 164–168
   Social Security Act, 170–172
   social welfare programs, 178–180
   unemployment, 165
   unionization of workers, 184
   and veterans, 181
Great depression
   mass movements during 1930s, 180–186
Griffith, D. W., 119
gross domestic product (GDP), 253
gross national product (GNP), 205, 252–253
Grutter v. Bollinger, 307

H

Ham and Eggs movement, 182
Hamilton, Gordon, 167
Hamilton's Report of Manufacture, 40
Hampton Institute, 88
Harding, Warren G., 134
Harriman, E. H., 138
Harrington, Michael, 221
Hart–Celler Act (1965), 208
Harvard University, 25
Hayes, Rutherford B., 80, 89
Haymarket riot, 90
Haymarket Square riot, 125
Head Start program, 228, 260, 264

health care reform, 293–297
    achievement in 2010, 296–297
    failure of comprehensive reform in
        1990s, 294–296
    health insurance, 127
    history of, 2–3
health care services, publicly-funded, 319–321
health insurance, 294
    for aged, 211
    for retirees, 229
health maintenance organizations (HMOs), 295
Health Security Act, 294
Hepburn Act (1906), 138
Hertel, Frank J., 180
Hillary Rodham Clinton Task Force, on Health
    Care Reform, 294–295
Hispanics
    education, 306
    poverty, 290–292
Homestead Act (1862), 79, 82
Hoover, Herbert, 141, 163–164
Hopkins, Harry, 167–168, 225
Horatio Alger myth, 92
House of Refuge for Delinquent Boys
    (Massachusetts, 1847), 55
House Ways and Means Committee, 260
Housing Act (1937), 165
Housing Act (1949), 216, 217
Housing and Urban Development Act (1968), 230
Howard, Atlanta, and Fisk universities, 88
Howard, Oliver O., 88, 89
Howe, Samuel Gridley, 54
Hoyt, Charles S., 99
Hull, Cordell, 138
Hull House, Chicago, 96
human nature views, 7
human rights, 310
Hunter, Robert, 20, 118
Hurricane Katrina, 304, 312

I

Ickes, Harold, 166
Illinois Funds to Parents Act, 131
immigration, and immigrants
    in America, 5
    during Civil War period and after, 80
    in colonial America, 24
    during postwar years, 207–210
    during progressive era, 118
    welfare reform and, 302–302
Immigration Act (1965), 208
immigration policy, 207, 271
imprisonment, 310–311
income
    distribution of, 258
    inequality, 289
    transfer program, 257, 265
Income Maintenance Programs, 261
indenture contracts, 20, 24
indenturing, 20
Indian Health Service (1955), 216
Indian Reorganization Act (1934), 162
Indian Wars, 42
individual adjustment profession, 3

Individual Retirement Accounts, 265, 306
indoor relief, 21
industrialization, 41–42
industrial labor force, 254
infant mortality, 294
information society era (1992–2007)
    America's changing demography, 293
    changes in family composition during, 292
    economy during, 287–290
    education programs during, 306–307
    Family and Medical Leave Act, 287, 292
    health care reforms, 293–297
    immigration control, 302–303
    increase in imprisonment during, 310–311
    poverty, 290–292
    right to abortion and, 308–310
    right to privacy and, 308–310
    rise of privatization, 303–306
    social justice and, 306–311
    social welfare and, 313–314
    welfare reforms during, 298–302
Inland Steel v. NLRB, 216
In re Gault decision (1967), U.S. Supreme
    Court, 235, 236, 237, 246–248, 272
    confrontation, self-incrimination, and
        cross-examination, 250
    notice of charges, 248–249
    right to counsel, 249–250
insane asylums, 272
institutional child care, 54
insular poverty, 220
International Labor Union (ILU), 102
Interstate Commerce Act (1887), 90
Interstate Commerce Commission (ICC), 138

J

Jackson, Andrew, 39, 43
Jacksonian political democracy, 43
Jim Crow laws, 119
Job Corps training centers, 227
Jobs Opportunities and Basic Skills (JOBS)
    program, 263, 298
Johnson, Andrew, 87, 88
Johnson, Lyndon B., 226, 227, 229, 232, 236, 261
Jungle, The (Sinclair), 138
juvenile court movement, 129
Juvenile justice, and civil rights, 235

K

Kahn, Dorothy, 177
Kahn, Florence, 185
Keating–Owen bill, 125
Kelley, Florence, 125, 128, 143
Kellogg, Charles D., 95
Kellogg, Paul, 128
Kempe, Henry, 264
Kennedy, John F., 216, 222, 224, 226, 237
Kennedy, Ted, 296, 313
Kepecs, Jacob, 174
Kerr–Mills Act (1960), 216
Keynesian theory of effective demand, 165
King, Martin Luther, Jr., 226
Klan, Ku Klux, 89

Knights of Labor, 102, 125
Know-Nothing party, 37

L

Labaree, Mary S., 175
labor force
    affirmative action programs, 307–308
    participation rate of women in, 206, 292
    social welfare policy, 288
labor movement, during Civil War, 89–90,
    102–103
La Follette Civil Liberties Committee, 184
Lanham Act. See Community Facilities Act (1941)
Lathrop, Julia, 129
Latin Americans, immigration, 293
Lawrence v. Texas, 308
Laws of the State of New York One Hundred and
    Tenth Session, 107–108
Lee, Porter R., 136, 145
legal settlement, residency requirement of, 16
Lehman Brothers, 289
Lenroot, Katherine, 174
Letchworth, William F., 98
Lewis, Oscar, 226
life expectancy, 209
"likely to become a public charge" (LPC) rule, 207
Lily, The (newspaper), 46
Lincoln, Abraham, 85
Lindsey, Ben, 130
Lippmann, Walter, 138
local governments, reforms during Progressive
    Era, 139
local responsibility, principle, 16
lockup, 310–311
London, Jack, 138
Long, Huey, 182
Lowell, Josephine Shaw, 91, 95, 102, 106, 142
Lundberg, Emma O., 131
Lundeen, Ernest, 183
Luther, Martin. See King, Martin Luther, Jr.

M

MacDonald, Dwight, 221
Mackay, Thomas, 148
Madison, James, 35
"man-in-the-house" policy, 219
Mann, Horace, 44
Manpower Development and Training Act
    (1962), 221, 245
March on Washington Movement, 233
Marital counseling, and marriage clinic, 180
Martineau, Harriet, 41
Maryland's Workmen's Compensation Act, 127
Massachusetts Province Laws (1753–1754), 18
maternalism, 122
Mather, Cotton, 24
Matthews, William H., 128
McCulloch, Oscar C., 92
McLean, Francis, 142
Mechanics' Union Trade Association,
    Philadelphia, 42
Medicaid, 229, 259, 266, 272, 273, 294,
    298, 304

Medicare, 229, 294–296, 304
    Advantage program, 296
    Part D, 296
Meikeljohn, Alexander, 138
mental illness, 292
Message on Reform in Welfare (1969), 276
Message on the Public Welfare Program (1962), 236
Mexican American Legal Defense and Education Fund, 313
Mexican Americans, forced deportation during Great Depression, 207–208
Mexican War (1846–1848), 42, 48
Middle Atlantic States. *See also* New England
    growth of manufacturing, 83
    pre-civil war period (1777-1860), 40
military medicine, 214
Milk Program (1954), 216
minimum wage legislation, 184
minority majority nation, 5
Model Cities legislation (1966), 229
mortgage, 289
Mothers' Aid Program, 175
Mother's Assistance programs, 131
Mother's Pension law, 142
mother's pensions, 122, 126, 130–131
Murphy, Edgar Gardner, 128

N

NAACP Legal Defense Fund, 234
National American Women's Suffrage Association (NAWSA), 139–140
National Association for the Advancement of Colored People, 132
National Association of Social Workers, 232
National Child Labor Committee, 128, 210
National Commission on Social Security Reform (1981), 265
National Conference of Charities and Corrections, 91, 95, 106, 123–125, 127, 130
National Conference on Children and Youth (1909), 276
National Conference on Workmen's Compensation, 127
National Consumer's League, 127
National Defense Advisory Committee, 233
national health insurance scheme, 214
National Homes for Disabled Volunteer Soldiers, 134
National Industrial Recovery Act, 164
National Industrial Recovery Act (NIRA), 159, 164
    Title II of, 166
National Labor Congress (1866), 89
National Labor Relations Act, 183
National Labor Relations Board, 183
National Life Insurance Act (1940), 218
National Mental Health Act (1946), 214
National Recovery Administration (NRA), 166
National School Lunch Program (1946), 216
National War Fund, 215
National Welfare Rights Organization, 229
National Woman Suffrage Association, 100
National Women's Christian Temperance Union (WCTU), 101
National Youth Administration's (NYA) vocational work program, 214

Native Americans
    American Indian Movement, 270
    and apprenticeship, 20
    civil rights, 271
    during Civil War period and after, 79–80
    consequence of colonization, 23–26
    education programs for, 306
    immigration, 293
    New Deal policies for, 161–162
    population growth during pre-civil war period, 36–38
    postwar period and, 216
    programs, 216
    during Progressive Era, 136
    Reagan administration policies impact, 257
    unemployment rates, 257
    during World War II, 214
nativism, 6
Naturalization Act (1795), 37
negative income tax (NIT), 260, 262
Neighborhood Guild of New York City, 96
New Deal economic policy, 164–168
    1939 amendments, 172–173
    agricultural and land policy, 158–162
    banking crisis, 165
    cash programs, 222
    child welfare, 175
    Congress of Industrial Organizations (CIO), 183
    early responses of, 165
    experimental monetary policy measures, 165
    Hopkin's relief measures, 167–168
    housing policy, 165
    labor movement, 182–184
    monetary policies, 165
    package for farmers, 159
    permanent programs of income maintenance, 172
    private property, 165
    public assistance, 173–176
    reduction in farm tenancy, 161
    relief expenditures, 167
    remedial legislation for relief programs, 166–167
    social insurance benefits, 173
    Social Security Act (1935), 170–172
    state-administered assistance programs, 173–176
    strategies, 165
    Title I of the NIRA established a set of industry codes, 166
    and women, 185
New Deal programs. *See* New Deal economic policy
New England
    emigration of Puritans, 24
    European population growth, 24
    expansion of indenture and apprenticeship, 20
    growth of manufacturing, 83
    immigration in, 24
    industrialization and urbanization, 42
    practice of apprenticeship, 20
    production of finished cotton goods, 40
    Puritan work ethics, 19
    seventeenth-century, 17
    and territorial expansion, 39

New York association, 85
New York Association for Improving the Conditions of the Poor, 157
New York City, 49, 51
New York House of Refuge, 54
New York (City) House of Refuge, 54
New York Society for the Prevention of Pauperism, 50, 51, 54, 63
New York State Board of Charities, 98, 99
New York welfare system, 52
Nightingale, Florence, 85
NIMBY (not in my backyard), 273
Nineteenth Amendment to the Constitution, 122, 140
Nixon, Richard M., 232, 251, 260, 261, 264, 276, 292–298
nonaccelerating-inflation rate of unemployment (NAIRU), 253
non–means-tested programs, 259
Norris–LaGuardia Act (1932), 182, 183
Northern reform movement, 46

O

Obama, Barack, 285, 296, 297
occasional poor, 52
Office of Civilian Defense, 215
Office of Community War Services, 215
Office of Dependency Benefits of the War Department, 218
Office of Economic Opportunity (OEO), 228, 244, 260, 282
Office of Health, Welfare, and Related Defense Activities, 215
Office of Indian Education Programs, 307
Office of Production Management's Negro Employment and Training Branch, 233
Office of War Management, 215
Old Age, Survivors, and Disability Insurance (OASDI), 257, 264, 305
Old Age and Survivors Insurance, 211
Old Age Assistance, 262
Old Age Insurance (OAI), 172, 264, 265
Older Americans Act (1965), 230
old folks homes, 83
Old Folks Picnic Association, 182
Omnibus Budget Reconciliation Act, 299
Organization of Petroleum Exporting Countries (OPEC), 253
Orphan Asylum of New York, 54
The Other America: Poverty in the United States (Michael Harrington), 221

P

Paine, Thomas, 49, 50
Palmer, Mitchell, 141
passport system, 17
patriotism, 23
Patrons of Husbandry (the Grange), 101
pauperism, 20, 50–51, 53
    report, 60–68
Pauper Laws, 52
Pennsylvania, statute of, 21, 22

Pennsylvania Board of Commissioners of Public Charities, 99
Pennsylvania's Act (148), 272
Pension Benefit Guaranty Corporation, 265
peoples of color, social welfare for, 4. *See also* African Americans
permanency planning, 272
permanent poor, 52
personal responsibilities, 6
Personal Responsibility Act (H.R. 4) (1995), 300
Personal Responsibility and Work Opportunity Reconciliation Act (PRWORA, 1996), 300, 301, 303, 313–317
Philadelphia House of Refuge, 54, 55
Pierce, Franklin, 48, 59, 60, 73, 88
Pinckney, Merritt W., 130, 143, 149, 152, 153
Pittsburgh Survey (1907–1908), 128
Poor Law principles, 3, 8, 10, 50
    in American colonies, 17–22
    challenges, 26–29
    coercive work features, 21
    protection against strangers, 22
    for public aid, 19
    social change and, 26–29
Poor Relief in Pennsylvania, 142
Poor Support (David Ellwood), 299
population shifts, 207–210
Populist movement, 103
Populist revolt (1890s), 119
Port Royal Experiment (1862), 87
post-war period (1940-1968)
    benefits for aging during, 230
    economic insecurity during, 210–212
    economic/social advances during, 214–215
    families during, 207–208
    optimism during, 215–217
    overview, 205–207
    population shifts during, 207–210
    poverty during, 220–225
    technology and production during, 210–212
    War on poverty during, 225–230
    welfare reform during, 220–225
poverty, 21
    Carey's argument, 49–50
    children at risk of, 257
    during Conservative Era, 256–258
    during information society era, 290–292
    Paine's views, 49
    during post-war period, 220–225
    during Progressive Era, 118–119
    and reform of welfare programs, 220–225
    social welfare policy for reduction of, 290–292
    special programs in rural areas for elimination, 245
    types of, 220
    "vicious cycle" of, 226
    War on Poverty initiatives, 225–230
poverty index (Social Security Administration), 206, 221, 258
pre-civil war period (1777-1860)
    child welfare, 53–56
    corporate factory-establishment, 41
    cotton production, 39–41
    destitution in the North, 40–41
    distilling industry, 45
    documents, 59–76

economic depressions, 42
establishment of formal institutions for social welfare, 47–58
ethnicity, 36
factory system of employment, 41
immigrants during the 1840s, 37
industrialization and urbanization, 42
life expectancy, 36
Middle Atlantic states, 40
migration, 36–38
Native American population during, 38
population growth, 36–38
public education, expansion of, 44
reform and social change, 42–46
retreat from almshouse, 56–58
slave population, 37–38
slavery and freelabor, 39–42
social welfare programs and services, 47–58
technological revolution, 45
territorial expansion, 38, 39
textile factories, 39
urban center population, 41–42
women status, 44–46
pregnancies, 273
President Calvin Coolidge's veto, 181
presidential preference laws, 122
President's Commission on Veterans' Pensions, 268
private pensions, 264, 265
privatization, social security, 305
Proceedings of the National Conference of Charities and Corrections (1880–1929), 107–110, 135
professionalism, in social welfare, 2
Progressive Era (1900–1930)
    advocacy of child and women's labor legislation, 144–146
    African Americans family welfare of, 132–133
    agriculture revolutions, 117
    changes in organization of industry, 117–118
    corporations dominance, 118
    economic and regulatory reforms, 138
    economic progress and social mobility, 121
    end of reforms, 141–142
    increase in GDP, 117
    juvenile court movement, 129
    labor productivity, 120
    Laws of the State of Illinois, 146–147
    life in Northern and Southern cities, 120–121
    Native Americans life during, 136
    old age security, 127
    political reforms, 139
    population shifts, 117
    poverty and, 118–119
    professionalization of social work, 134–136
    protecting vulnerable families, 128–132
    public pensions to widows, 147–155
    reform activities, 136–142
    reformation of local politics, 139
    revolutions in technology and communication, 116
    rise of public welfare, 123
    telephone, impact on communications., 116
    unionization, 140
    urban migration, 117
    veterans, welfare of, 133–134

white–black relations, 120
    women, status of, 139–141
    women's suffrage movement, 139–141
    working class, 118–119
    workmen's compensation, 121
"Prop 187." *See* California Proposition (187)
Proposition 187, 302, 313, 317–321
Protestantism, 42
public assistance programs, New Deal, 173–176
public education, 255
    expansion of, 44
Public Law 87-543, 224
publicly-funded health care services, 319–321
Public Pensions to Widows (1912), 143, 147–151
public relief, 142
    funds for relief, 166–167
public welfare
    attack on, 219–220
    expanding, 126–128
    during post-war period (1940-1968), 215–217
Public Welfare Amendments (1962), 222–224, 236, 245
public welfare and workmen's compensation, 126–128
public welfare programs, 219–220, 222, 236–238, 241
Public Works Administration (PWA), 166
public works funds, 271
purchasing power of consumer, 206
Puritan Calvinism, 19
Puritan Commonwealth, 24
Puritanism, in colonial America, 24
Puritan work ethics, 19

Q

Quincy, Josiah, 50, 52

R

race riots, 229, 233
racial profiling, 303
racial segregation, in education and employment, 213
Randolph, A. Philip, 233
Rank-and-File movement, 179
Reagan, Ronald, 252, 256, 257, 260
Reaganism, and unaccomplished goals, 252
real disposable personal income, 205–206
Reconstruction Finance Corporation (RFC), 163
Red Cross, 215, 304
redemptioners, 25
reform activities, of the Progressive Era, 136–142
refugee policy
    for Europeans, 208
    for reducing immigration, 207
refugees admissions, 271
Removal Act of 1830, 38
Reorganization Act (1934), 216
Report of the Commissioners of Public Charities for the Year 1882, 98
Rescue, Operation, 308
Reserve Officers Training Corps (ROTC), 215
residency requirements, 16–17, 22, 37
Revenue Act (1942), 216

Reverend Oscar C. McCulloch's Report to the Fifteenth Annual Conference of Charities and Corrections, 92
Ribicoff, Abraham, 222, 223, 236
Richardson, Anne B., 98
Richmond, Mary, 97, 124, 130, 135, 143, 154
Richmond law, 271
Roe v. Wade, 251, 273, 308, 314
Roosevelt, Franklin D., 164–167, 169, 170, 171, 181, 182
    first new deal and, 164–168
    New Deal programs of, 164–168
    second new deal and, 168–176
Roosevelt, Theodore, 127, 129, 133, 138, 276
Rules and Regulations (by FERA), 170, 188–191
Russell Sage Foundation, 167

S

same-sex marriages, 310
Sanborn, Franklin B., 94, 95
school desegregation program, 306
School for Idiots (Massachusetts), 54
schooling expansion, in American colonies, 25
scientific philanthropy, 135
Scots Charitable Society, 17
Scudder, Vida, 96
second Great Awakening, 42
Selective Training and Service Act (1940), 218
Select Senate Committee to Visit Charitable and Penal Institutions, 53
Seminole Indian Wars, 48
Senate Finance Committee, 218, 261
separate but equal doctrine, 119
Servicemen's Dependents Allowance Act (1942), 218
Servicemen's Readjustment Act (1944), 218
Settlement, 16
Settlement House Movement, 84, 95–97, 123, 132
Seventeenth Amendment to the Constitution, 122
The Shame of the Cities, 139
Sheppard–Towner Act, 129, 172
Sheridan, Philip, 79
Sherman Antitrust Act, 90, 138
Simkhovitch, Mary K., 135
Sixteenth Amendment to the Constitution, 138
slave population
    pre-civil war period (1777-1860), 37–38
    and territorial expansion, 39
slavery, 24, 36
SLM Corporation (Sallie Mae), 297
Smith, John, 24
Social and Rehabilitation Service (SRS), 232
social change, 3
social Darwinism, 91, 94
Social Diagnosis, 97
Social Diagnosis (Richmond), 124, 135
social insurance, 126
social insurance system, 255, 265
Socialist Party, 138
social movements during conservative era, 269–275
social reforms
    for African Americans, 132–133
    end, during Progressive Era, 141–142

for juvenile courts, 128
for public welfare, 126–128
Public Welfare Amendments (1962), 220–225
social research as tool, 128
for vulnerable families, 128–132
for womens, 139
social research, 128
Social Security, 216, 229–230
    crisis, 305
    taxes, 305
    trust funds, 230
Social Security Act, 211, 219, 223, 225, 238–241, 254, 255, 260, 265
Social Security Act (1935), 129, 170
    child welfare, 175
    evolution, 171
    Ewan Clague's description of the potentialities of, 177
    as a family welfare measure, 176
    for old age assistance, 175
    recommendations for federal involvement in a program, 172
    state-administered assistance programs, 173–176
    Titles (I-X), 195–204
Social Security Administration (SSA), 206, 274
Social Security Amendments (1967), 231
Social Security Amendments (1983), 274
Social Security beneficiaries, 2
Social Security system, 8
Social Service Amendments (1974), 225
social services, personal, 268
Social Unit Plan (Cincinnati), 142
social welfare programs, 2, 207, 229, 251, 255, 288. *See also* Civil War period and after (1860–1900)
    for addressing poverty and dependency, 298–302
        changing dynamics of welfare debate, 298–300
        impact of welfare reform, 301–302
        new consensus over welfare reform, 300–301
    America's changing demography and, 293
    and changes in family composition, 292
    civil rights and responsibilities
        abortion and right to privacy, 308–310
        affirmative action in labor market, 307–308
    education, 306–307
    expenditures for, 258–260
    faith-based, 304
    goals of, 2
    and government financial capacity, 4
    during Great Depression Era, 178–180
    great lockup, 310–311
    growth in expenditures for, 6
    health care reform, 293–297
        achievement in 2010, 296–297
        budget reconciliation process, 296
        failure of comprehensive reform in 1990s, 294–296

impact of social security on politics, 216
innovations in, 122–136
new alignments in, 178–180
for productivity, growth, and employment, 287–290
during Progressive Era, 122–136
Reaganism and, 252
for reduction of poverty, 290–292
and social institution's effectiveness, 6
and status of women, 4
for veterans, 29–30, 133–134
voluntarism and rise of privatization, impact of, 303–306
for welfare reform and "immigration control," 302–303
workmen's compensation, 126
social work, professionalization, 134–136
social workers, family life and, 3
social works, role of, 176–178
Society for Encouraging Industry and Employing the Poor (1751), 18
Society for the Prevention of Pauperism, (1818), 50, 51, 54, 59
Society of House Carpenters, 18
soldiers. *See* veterans
Spencer, Herbert, 80, 90
Stanton, Elizabeth Cady, 100
state hospitals, 272
Steinbeck, John, 159
Stover, Charles B., 96
substance abuse, 292
suffrage movement, 100, 139
suitable home policy, 219
Supplemental Nutritional Assistance Program (SNAP), 301
Supplemental Security Act (1974), 257
Supplemental Security Income (SSI), 257, 274, 300

T

Talladega College, 88
Task Force on Sex Discrimination, 274
Task Force on the Treatment of Women, 274
"tax-and-spend" policies, 4
tax system, 21
Temperance Movement, 45, 46, 101
Temporary Assistance for Needy Families (TANF), 300, 301, 313
Temporary Relief Administration, New York, 167
Texas Annexation (1845), 38
"The Causes of Pauperism" (1877), 99
The Constitution and By-Laws of the Female Orphan Asylum of Portland, Maine (1828), 67–69
Townsend, Francis E., 182
Trail of Tears, 38
The Treason of the Senate, 139
Triangle Shirt-Waist Company fire (1911), 139
Truman, Harry, 214
Tugwell, Rexford, 185
Tuskegee Institute, 119
Twenty-First Amendment to the Constitution, 136, 141

U

unemployment system, 266–268
unions, 234, 253
    African Americans and, 103
    Great Depression and, 182
    women role in, 140
    working hours legislation, 125–126
United Service Organization for National Defense
    (USO), 215
United States Immigration and Naturalization
    Service, 320, 321
University of Brown, 25
University of Dartmouth, 25
University of Pennsylvania, 25
University of Princeton, 25
University of Rutgers, 25
Upward Bound program, 228
Urban and Rural Community Action
    Programs, 228
urbanization, 42
urban poverty, 21
Ursuline Sisters, 54
U.S. Office of Education, 215, 233
U.S. Sanitary Commission, 84

V

veterans
    during Conservative Era, 268
    GI Bill and, 218–219
    during Great Depression, 181
    social welfare for, 4, 133–134
    treatment in American colonies, 29–30
    of Vietnam, 268
    welfare programs for, 29–30
        Civil War period and after, 84–86
        Great Depression Era, 181
        for Progressive Era, 133–134
Veterans' Administration health system, 294
Veterans' Bureau, 134
Veto of the Ten-Million Acre Bill (Pierce), 73–76
Virginia settlers, 24
Vocational Education Act (1963), 245
Vocational Rehabilitation Administration, 232
vocational rehabilitation for disabled people, 239
voluntarism, 303–306
voluntary assistance program for needy
    children, 244
voluntary retirement, 83
Volunteers in Service to America (VISTA), 228

W

Wagner Act, 182
Wagner–Steagall Act, 185

Wald, Lillian, 129
war against terrorism, 286
war and prosperity (1940–1968)
    civil rights and juvenile justice, 235
    population shifts, 207–210
    postwar optimism, 215–217
    poverty and reform of welfare, 220–225
    pubic welfare, 219–220
    public assistance, 230–232
    social security benefits, 230
    technology, productivity, and economic
        insecurity, 210–212
    veterans and GI Bill, 218–219
    war on poverty, 225–230, 236, 237
    wartime economic and social advances,
        214–215
    World War II, 212–214
War Brides Act (1946), 208
War Manpower Commission, 233
Warner, Amos G., 91, 92, 94, 98, 158
War of 1812, 42, 48
War on Poverty, 225–230, 236, 237, 253, 256,
    258, 264
War Relief Control Board, 215
War Risk Insurance Act, 133
wartime economic and social advances, 214–215
Washington, Booker T., 119, 132
Watergate affair, 269
welfare capitalism, 126
welfare programs, scope of, 298–302
welfare reforms, 220–263
    changing dynamics of, 298–300
    and "immigration control," 302–303
    impact of, 301–302
    new consensus over, 300–301
    Personal Responsibility and Work
        Opportunity Reconciliation Act
        (PRWORA), 300, 301, 303
    Temporary Assistance for Needy Families
        (TANF), 300, 301, 305
What Is Social Casework? (Richmond), 135
white-collar employment, 267
White House Conference on Aging (1961), 230
White House Conference on Child Dependency
    (1909), 129
White House Conference on Children (1909),
    3, 143
white male suffrage, 44–45
widow's pensions. *See* mother's pensions
Willard, Frances E., 101
Williams, Aubrey, 176–177
Wilson, Pete, 313
Wilson, William J., 299
Wilson, Woodrow, 133
Wines, Fred H., 94
Winkle, Rip Van, 105

women
    centrality of women's work and colonial
        economy, 18
    civil rights, during Conservative Era, 274–275
    during Civil War period and after, 100–102
    colleges for, 101
    in Colonial period, 18
    employment during Great Depression, 185
    influence, during Progressive Era, 122–123
    New Deal economic policy, 185
    of postwar period and work, 102
    during pre-Civil War period, 44–46
    social reform for, 139
    social welfare needs of, 100–102
    and unionization, 140
    working, in postwar period, 102
    working hours legislation, 125–126
Women's Bureau, Department of Labor, 140
Women's Central Association of Relief for the Sick
    and Wounded of the Army, 84
women's colleges, foundation, 101–102
women's movement, 100
Women's Rights Convention, 44
Woods, Robert A., 128
work experience programs, 245
workhouses, 21
Work Incentive Program (WIP), 231, 260
working conditions, social reforms for, 124–126
workmen's compensation, 126
Works Progress Administration (WPA) projects,
    169, 215, 233
work-study programs, 243
work-training programs, 243
World Trade Center, 286
World War II, 205, 206, 209, 212–214, 253
Wyatt v. *Stickney*, 272
Wyman, George K., 222–223

X

xenophobia, 37

Y

Yates, John V. N., 49, 52, 53, 94
Yates report, 52, 157
Youth Aid Division, 246
youth programs
    general community action
        programs, 244
    job corps, 243
    voluntary assistance program for needy
        children, 244
    work-study programs, 243
    work-training programs, 243